James E. Cowell
722 Embarcadero del Norte
Goleta, Calif.

PREFACE

The United States Army is an honored institution. It has a fascinating history, interesting customs and traditions, and a way of life necessarily distinct from that of the civilian population. The best testimonial to the accomplishments of those who have filled its ranks is our great nation: their sweat and blood made it possible and sustained it against all enemies. This text is but a résumé of its record and, at the same time, a challenge to the Army man of today. By equalling the achievements of the past, those who now man the ramparts can transmit the record to the soldiers of the future, unbroken, enriched, and enlarged.

The purposes of this text are to show, in a general way, the origin and growth of the United States Army and its great accomplishments in both peace and war; to teach the principles of war and illustrate their application by examples drawn from American military history; and to bring out the attributes and contributions of American military leaders. Woven into the text is a record of the coordination or lack of coordination of the foreign and military policies of the United States and the basic causes that have led to the various wars in which the Army has participated.

This manual presents the elementary facts of American military history which, it is hoped, will interest the student in an ever-expanding study of the past, from which he will acquire knowledge and wisdom from the experiences of others. No profession can benefit more directly from the study of history than the military, for as Marshal Foch has said, ". . . no study is possible on the battlefield; one does there simply what *one can* in order to apply what *one knows*."

The space allotted to each chapter accords in general with the length of instruction time allowed to cover the various periods of American military history in the ROTC course. Each chapter was designed to stand by itself. The chapters dealing with military operations that occurred in the United States or its territories are of special value and are therefore treated in more detail because it is frequently possible for ROTC students to visit the scenes of some of the events described. This is not possible for the great wars of the 20th century. In addition, operations in World Wars I and II were so stupendous as to almost defy study on the ground. For the same reasons the map coverage emphasizes the battlefields of wars fought on American soil, particularly those of the Revolutionary and Civil Wars. For more detailed map studies of World Wars I and II the student should consult material included in the two series: U. S. ARMY IN THE WORLD WAR, 1917–1919, and U. S. ARMY IN WORLD WAR II.

ROTC Manual

No. 145–20

HEADQUARTERS,
DEPARTMENT OF THE ARMY
Washington 25, D.C., *17 July, 1959*

AMERICAN MILITARY HISTORY

1607—1958

---

* This manual supersedes ROTCM 145–20, 17 July 1956.

MAPS

ILLUSTRATIONS

Credit—

    Wisconsin Historical Society—p. 25.

    The National Archives—pp. 33, 93 (right photo), 113, 140, 170 (left photo), 212, 217, 223, 241, 245, 262, 289, 328, 338.

    Library of Congress—pp. 35, 145, 257, 270.

    National Park Service—pp. 37, 93 (left photo).

    The Smithsonian Institute—p. 351.

    All others from the files of the Department of Defense

INTRODUCTION

The Nature of War. In the broadest sense, modern war is the application of political, psychological, economic, and physical pressure by a state or a group of states against another state or group of states or by a segment of the population of a state against the established government of the state. In a narrow sense, war is the use of force or violence by a state or group of states against another state or group of states or by a segment of a people against the established government.

The object of a use of force or war is to impose the will of the state, group of states, or segment of the people upon the enemy. Aggressive states or fanatical segments of a state enter war deliberately by a means and at a time of their own choosing. Peaceful states or segments of a people are forced into war to protect their legitimate interests.

Modern war has become increasingly total. It includes political warfare to isolate the enemy country from neutral or friendly countries; psychological attacks to weaken and disorganize the enemy country from within and to create opposition to it in other countries; economic pressure to harm the enemy's economy; and application of force against the enemy country and its armed forces.

Until the latter part of the 18th century wars were relatively simple. As technology has developed warfare has grown in complexity. Since the beginning of the industrial revolution warfare has had an ever-increasing impact on society. The existence of the United States as a political force in the world spans the period marked by the rapid technological development. The American Revolution was the prelude to an era of modern wars, the desperate struggles that have grown in intensity and destructiveness down to the present time. Today, warfare embraces so many facets and the armed forces are capable of dealing such devastating blows at such great distances that all mankind is to some extent in the zone of combat. Even small wars have a certain impact upon all the people of the world. Developments in warfare continue at an accelerated rate and American survival as a great power depends upon the military posture of the nation. Preparedness for war is, therefore, an important consideration, for each individual of the United States must be prepared to perform effectively in an essential role or become a weak link in the chain of national security.

1

Development of Warfare. From the crude organizational, tactical, and technical beginnings that existed at the dawn of history mankind has evolved the strategical and tactical ideas and the complicated organizations and technologies of the armed forces now maintained by the great powers. The process of development was very slow for many centuries. Primitive weapons were of limited range and wielded by individuals who were organized into units according to the prevailing tactical theories of the countries concerned. In time, the horse was integrated into military organization and played a highly important role in warfare down to World War II and a significant one on certain fronts of that war as well. Animal-drawn transportation was introduced in the remote past and greatly altered the logistics of land warfare.

The introduction of gunpowder led to more radical changes in warfare on land and sea. These changes were slow in developing because technical and industrial advances had to be made before the invention could be exploited fully. The invention of the steam engine and the industrial revolution accelerated technological changes in warfare. Warfare at sea was soon completely altered, and the railway profoundly changed the logistical situation of land forces. The number, power, and range of both individual and crew-served weapons grew rapidly, and the latter steadily gained in importance. The development of communications kept pace. The telegraph made it possible for commanders to employ much greater forces in pursuit of tactical and strategical objectives than before.

The advent of the internal combustion engine led to still greater technological changes, particularly in land warfare, and made aerial warfare possible. The track-laying vehicle made possible the application of mechanization to mobile land warfare with profound effect upon military organization and operations. Finally, radio and radar made possible the coordination of mechanized, three-dimensional warfare.

The development of rocket propulsion, atomic power plants and atomic bombs and artillery, and the hydrogen bomb have started a new cycle that challenges the general staffs of all nations at this time. The future history of the United States may well depend upon the solutions of the many problems posed by these developments.

While all these tremendous changes have been taking place in warfare on the grand scale, guerilla warfare has steadily gained in importance. This type of warfare was never more extensively employed than in World War II. After the great mechanized forces of the invaders had passed partisans became active. Like sand in a delicate mechanism they handicapped the Axis aggressors on all fronts.

But weapons and machines do not make war. It is man, the wielder of weapons and the master of machines, who makes war. Whether the war he wages is on the grand scale or in the form of guerilla activity, therefore, the quality of the fighting man and his leaders will determine the effectiveness of any military force. When disciplined soldiers, skilled in the use of superior weapons, are organized into units and trained together, they become an effective military tool under the control of their commander.

The Principles of War. Thucydides, a general in the Athenian Army, wrote the first great military history about 400 B. C. Since his time many other military men or scholars, such as Caesar, Machiavelli, Frederick the Great, Napoleon, Von Moltke, Von Schlieffen, and others, have recorded their experiences or observations on war. Military students of all nations have studied these works and have analyzed the campaigns of the great captains with a view to determining the fundamental principles underlying the conduct of war. Jomini, Clausewitz, Ardant duPicq, Mahan, Foch, Douhet, and Fuller have been foremost in this analytical work. They have shown conclusively that weapons, organization, transportation, and tactics change, but the fundamental principles of war never change.

Today, all great nations recognize the principles of war and incorporate them in Army doctrine. The number of principles enumerated by the various powers varies, depending upon the interpretation. The United States Army recognizes nine and includes them in the *Field Service Regulations*. Their proper application, it holds, is essential to the exercise of effective command and to the successful conduct of military operations. The military student must make these principles a part of himself by analyzing their use in past campaigns and by applying them in the solution of current problems. If he does this in training, he will be better prepared to apply the principles in actual battle.

The principles of war are interrelated. They are not absolute and have been successfully violated at times, but only for very special reasons that had been carefully considered beforehand. The principles do not operate with equal force under all circumstances. They are applied in combination to specific situations. The combinations will vary according to the factors that influence operations, such as the nature of the terrain, the relative strength of the opposing forces—in terms not only of their numbers but also of their composition, their armament, their state of training, their morale, their supply—the effect of weather, and the mission of the command. The art of generalship is to be found in the application of the principles.

When determined for the conduct of a war or a lengthy campaign, the combination of principles selected is called *strategy;* when adopted for a single battle, the combination of principles is called *tactics*. There are further refinements. The broad policy decisions governing the over-all conduct of war are known as *grand strategy*, the prerogative of the chief of state and his principal advisers. At the opposite end of the scale are *minor tactics*, the term used to describe the maneuver of small units. The important thing to remember is that the principles apply to decisions at all echelons of command from the squad to the Chief of Staff of the Army and the President or Commander in Chief.

The nine principles or *fundamental truths governing the prosecution of war* are concisely stated as objective, offensive, simplicity, unity of command, mass, economy of force, maneuver, surprise, and security.

Objective. Every military operation must be directed toward a decisive, obtainable objective. The destruction of the enemy's armed forces and his will to fight is the ultimate military objective of war. The objective of each operation must contribute to this ultimate objective. Each intermediate objective must be such that its attainment will most directly, quickly, and economically contribute to the purpose of the operation. It must permit the application of the maximum means available. Its selection must be based upon consideration of means available, the enemy, and the area of operations. Secondary objectives of any operation must contribute to the attainment of the principal objective.

Offensive. Only offensive action achieves decisive results. Offensive action permits the commander to exploit the initiative and impose his will on the enemy. The defensive may be forced on the commander, but he should adopt it deliberately only as a temporary expedient while awaiting an opportunity for offensive action or for the purpose of economizing forces on a front where a decision is not sought. Even on the defensive the commander seeks every opportunity to seize the initiative and achieve decisive results by offensive action.

Simplicity. Simplicity must be the keynote of military operations. Uncomplicated plans, clearly expressed in orders, promote common understanding and intelligent execution. Even the most simple plan is usually difficult to execute in combat. *Simplicity must be applied to organization, methods, and means in order to produce orderliness on the battlefield.*

Unity of command. The decisive application of full combat power requires unity of command. Unity of command obtains unity of effort by the coordinated action of all forces toward a common goal. Coordination may be achieved by direction or by cooperation. It is best achieved by vesting a single commander with requisite authority. Unity of effort is furthered by willing and intelligent cooperation among all elements of the forces involved.

Mass. Maximum available combat power must be applied at the point of decision. Mass is the concentration of means at the critical

4

time and place to the maximum degree permitted by the situation. Proper application of the principle of mass, in conjunction with the other principles of war, may permit numerically inferior forces to achieve decisive combat superiority. Mass is essentially a combination of manpower and fire power and is not dependent upon numbers alone; the effectiveness of mass may be increased by superior weapons, tactics, and morale.

Economy of force. Minimum essential means must be employed at points other than that of decision. To devote means to unnecessary secondary efforts or to employ excessive means on required secondary efforts is to violate the principle of both mass and the objective. Limited attacks, the defensive, deception, or even retrograde action are used in noncritical areas to achieve mass in the critical area.

Maneuver. Maneuver must be used to alter the relative combat power of military forces. Maneuver is the positioning of forces to place the enemy at a relative disadvantage. Proper positioning of forces in relation to the enemy frequently can achieve results which otherwise could be achieved only at heavy cost in men and material. In many situations maneuver is made possible only by the effective employment of fire power.

Surprise. Surprise may decisively shift the balance of combat power in favor of the commander who achieves it. It consists of striking the enemy when, where, or in a manner for which he is unprepared. It is not essential that the enemy be taken unaware but only that he become aware too late to react effectively. Surprise can be achieved by speed, secrecy, and deception, by variation in means and methods, and by the use of seemingly impossible terrain. Mass is essential to the optimum exploitation of the principle of surprise.

Security. Security is essential to the application of the other principles of war. It consists of those measures necessary to prevent surprise, avoid annoyance, preserve freedom of action, and deny to the enemy information of our forces. Security denies to the enemy and retains for the commander the ability to employ his forces most effectively.

At first glance the principles of war seem to be mere platitudes. It is only by illustration of their employment in historical examples that they can be understood as living truths rather than as mere abstractions.

Leadership. At a time when the Army was scattered about the country in small garrisons and when company commanders were mighty men, it was said that "A company is as good as its captain who is responsible for all it does or fails to do." This old saying is still a fair guide to the value of any command from the squad to the very largest, because effective leadership is essential to the efficiency of any unit. The qualities of the leader who exerts such an influence upon a unit are, therefore, of far-reaching importance to anyone who aspires to command.

Military leadership includes professional and technical competence, but it also includes much more; it is a matter of integrity, personality, and character—character above everything else. Reduced to their simplest terms the principles of leadership are *Duty*, *Honor*, *Country*, as emblazoned on the coat of arms of the United States Military Academy. These principles are the fundamentals upon which leadership in the Army has been based.

The identification of a commander with his men and his regard for their welfare, the accuracy of a commander's analysis of his problem, the correctness of his decision, and the effectiveness of his actions to put that decision into effect—together with the vigor of his supervision of the execution of that decision—combine to constitute one of the most vital elements in the achievement of military success.

For many years the Army has required periodic reports on the leadership performance of its officers. These reports are used to determine which officers are best qualified for important assignments and for advancement. The form and content of the reports have varied greatly, for the qualities of leadership are intangible and no suitable measuring stick has been devised by which to gauge them accurately.

The Army has given a great deal of thought to the art of leadership, and much literature on the subject has evolved from this thinking. By making himself familiar with this literature and other basic works dealing with leadership, the student can gain a theoretical understanding of the qualities of the successful military leader and the fundamental principles that guide him.

With this preparation, the student can read more intelligently the biographies and memoirs of earlier military leaders and better evaluate the reasons for their successes or failures. Theoretical leadership problems or exercises on the sandtable or map and tactical walks or rides also serve a useful purpose in leadership training. But in the last analysis, military leadership can be learned only from actual experience in the command of men.

National Military Systems. In modern times the various nations have adopted different military systems. Every country adopts a system that it believes will most effectively support its particular national policy. For many years the military system of Great Britain was based upon maintaining naval supremacy and the balance of power in Europe as the best support for an expanding world-wide empire. Accordingly, it supported a large navy and a small, disciplined army ready for use either alone or with allies as required. Lately, however, Great Britain has maintained important air and somewhat augmented land forces to compensate for the imbalance existing in Europe. The Russian military system has been adjusted to the expansionist program of a land power for a very long time. It has therefore consistently maintained immense armies, but lately, with new horizons in view, it has also expanded vastly the air and naval arms while maintaining large, mobile land forces and thus has great aggressive capabilities.

Initially the United States, taking advantage of a favorable geographical position behind the ocean barriers and the balance of power existing in Europe, based its military system on a small standing army bulwarked by citizen soldiers and the possibility of acquiring greater strength by temporary alliances in extraordinary emergencies. Later a modern navy was included in the system. But since World War II the intransigence and military might of Soviet Russia and the destruction of the balance of power in Europe and the Far East have caused a complete change in the American military system. Accordingly, the United States now maintains large air, sea, and land forces ready for immediate action and has strengthened these forces by those of allies.

The military system of the United States has developed as a result of national experience and national necessity. The form of government, the traditions of the people, and the nature of the country and its geographical position in relation to other powers have had a profound influence upon American military institutions, which in turn have faithfully reflected the American philosophy and way of life. The American system has been developed so as to place the minimum burden upon the people and to give the Nation a reasonable defense without sacrificing any fundamental values. The ROTC, as the primary source of Reserve officers, is an important element of the system.

The Value of History in the Military Profession. The value of history in military education has always been recognized in the United States Army, as in most armies. It has been at the base of military instruction in the service academy, colleges, and schools, since their inception. In this emphasis on the value of history in military instruction, the United States Army has followed the advice of the great captains of the past as well as of others who have more recently made their mark on the pages of history.

An understanding of military history, especially American military history, is vital to a comprehension of the principles of war and the influence of tactics and techniques on operations, to the development of *esprit de corps* and morale among the troops without which no body of troops can achieve any great results, to the training of troops, to the development of leadership, and to military planning. Those officers charged with planning future national security must study the past to understand the present in order to project themselves into the future. In a broader sense the study of American military history is important for all officers, because each official act of every officer in the Army contributes good or bad history to add to the lengthening record of our country.

Summary. The object of this course in military history is to provide the ROTC student with a sound foundation in the principles of war, as exemplified in American military history. The course is also designed to show the development of the military art in the United States Army. In addition, an understanding of the great accomplishments and sacrifices of the officers and men who have served in the Army during the past should enable the ROTC student to understand better the role he must play eventually, if the United States is to continue virile and strong.

The course in military history constitutes the framework upon which other ROTC courses are oriented and developed. The limited time available to cover the subject makes it necessary to restrict the text to important activities and actions of the United States Army, except where the other armed forces are so involved as to make their inclusion mandatory. Battle experience is emphasized because, in the last analysis, the real mission of the Army is to be prepared to fight to insure the safety of the Nation.

For more detailed accounts of the Army's activities and operations, the student is referred to other historical works.

QUESTIONS

1. Explain how technological developments have affected the security of the United States.
2. Enumerate the principles of war recognized by the United States Army and explain how these principles were developed. How can a military student learn to apply the principles?
3. Discuss briefly the basic qualities demanded of leaders in the United States Army.
4. Explain briefly some of the factors that have influenced the military system of the United States.
5. Explain briefly the value of history in the military profession.

Reading List

(NB: All of these references have general application to the whole book)
General
Beard, Charles A. *The Republic*. New York, 1943.
Bemis, S. F. *A Diplomatic History of the United States*. New York, 1950.
Burr, John G. *The Framework of Battle*. New York, 1943.
The Constitution of the United States of America and The Declaration of Independence.

Fuller, J. F. C. *Armament and History*. New York, 1945.

---------. *The Foundation of the Science of War*. London, 1925.

Hittle, J. D. *The Military Staff*. Harrisburg, 1949.

Montross, Lynn. *War Through the Ages*. New York, 1944.

Phillips, Thomas R. (ed.). *Roots of Strategy*. Harrisburg, 1941.

Spaulding, Oliver L. *The United States Army in War and Peace*. New York, 1937.

Spaulding, Oliver L., Hoffman Nickerson, and John W. Wright. *Warfare: A Study of Military Methods from the Earliest Times*. New York, 1925.

United States Army, Office, Chief of Military History:

    Kreidberg, M. A. and Merton G. Henry. *History of Military Mobilization in the United States Army*. Washington, 1956. (DA Pam 20-212.)

    Lerwill, Leonard L. *The Personnel Replacement System in the United States Army*. Washington, 1954. (DA Pam 20-211.)

    Robinett, Paul M. (ed.). *The Writing of American Military History: A Guide*. Washington, 1956. (DA Pam 20-200.)

    Sparrow, John C. *History of Personnel Demobilization in the United States Army*. Washington, 1952. (DA Pam 20-210.)

The Fighting Man

Ardant DuPicq. *Battle Studies*. Translated by John N. Greely and Robert C. Cotton. New York, 1921.

Department of the Army. *Medal of Honor of the United States Army*. Washington, 1948.

Mathews, William and Dixon Wecter. *Our Soldiers Speak, 1775-1918*. Boston, 1943.

Leadership

Freytag-Loringhoven, Hugo von. *Power of Personality in War*. Translated by Oliver L. Spaulding. Harrisburg, 1955.

Robinett, Paul M. (ed.). *Preparation for Leadership in America*. Washington, 1950.

United States Army.

    Leadership. Washington, 1951. (FM 22-10.)

    Command and Leadership for the Small Unit Leader. Washington, 1953. (FM 22-100.)

Operations

Fuller, J. F. C. *Decisive Battles of the U. S. A.* New York, 1942.

Steele, Matthew F. *American Campaigns*. Washington, 1909. 2 vols.

Swinton, E. D. *Defence of Duffer's Drift* (Fiction). Washington, 1916.

CHAPTER 1
THE BACKGROUND

Introduction. *General.* The first American national army did not come into being until 1775 when thirteen English colonies in North America banded together to throw off British rule. The influences that went into the shaping of this army were many and varied deriving from American experience since the first settlement at Jamestown in 1607 and from European experience that went back many centuries further.

Out of the chaos and division that marked the centuries following the downfall of the Western Roman Empire, new national states began to emerge in Europe at the end of the 15th century and warfare took on new patterns. The evolution of warfare from the 14th through the 17th centuries saw the gradual replacement of loosely knit aggregations of feudal nobles and their retainers by professional armies that served the new national states. Simultaneously, new weapons employing gunpowder gradually replaced earlier ones such as the sword, lance, crossbow, longbow, catapult, and pike. Medieval castles toppled before the power of crude artillery, and armored knights on horseback proved unable to stand before disciplined infantry. The changes were generally complete by the early years of the 17th century, and a period of relative stability ensued in the development of both weapons and tactics.

Eighteenth century society. A military organization normally reflects the society from which it springs, and in this respect the armies of 18th century Europe were no exception. Though Europe's feudal nobles no longer exercised political power independent of their kings, they remained the dominant privileged class, proprietors of the great estates and leaders of the national armies of the time. The great masses of the people remained for the most part without property and without voice in the government, either tilling the soil on the nobles' estates or working in the shops and handicraft industries of the merchants in the towns. Absolute monarchy was the prevailing form of government in every European country save England and certain smaller states on the continent. In England, where the constitutional power of Parliament had been successfully established over the King, Parliament was by no means a democratic institution but one controlled by the landed gentry and the wealthy merchants.

Eighteenth Century Warfare. *Organization of the armies.* The military distinction nobles had formerly found in leading their own knights in battle they now sought as officers in the armies of their respective kings. Princes, counts, earls, marquises, and barons, men who held their positions by hereditary right, royal favor, or purchase, filled the higher commands, while "gentlemen" of lesser rank usually served as captains and lieutenants of companies. Advancement to higher ranks depended more upon wealth and influence at court than on genuine ability. The 18th century produced its share of able commanders such as the Duke of Marlborough in England, Marshal Saxe in France, Prince Eugene of Savoy and Frederick the Great in Prussia, but it also had its share of inept ones. Officers commanding regiments and companies were responsible for recruiting men to fill the ranks. The common soldier was normally bound to the service for long periods and had little prospect of ever advancing to commissioned rank. Pay was poor and discipline harsh, making recruiting no easy task. It is not surprising that the ranks were often filled with the dregs of society with some leavening perhaps of the truly adventurous among the poor.

Discipline was the main reliance for making such an army fight. Penalties for even minor offenses ran as high as a thousand lashes, and executions by hanging or firing squad were frequent. The habit of obedience inculcated on the drill ground carried over into battle where it has often been said the men advanced preferring the uncertainties of combat to the certainty of death if orders were disobeyed. Professional and organizational pride, allegiance to popular commanders and the usual desire for the rewards of victory reinforced the pressure of discipline. Yet the necessity for strict discipline goes far to explain the manner in which 18th century armies fought. Discipline and control by officers could best be exercised by employment of close and regular formations learned through long practice on the drill ground. Little could be left to the individual initiative of the men in the ranks.

Character of the warfare. In contrast to modern warfare, 18th century warfare had a sort of formal character and was conducted by a set of rules, almost like a game. It was considerably less destructive than warfare today, although individual battles were actually more bloody than modern ones. The objectives of war were normally limited to territorial gains, not the subjugation of whole peoples or nations. A wise commander was sparing of the blood of his soldiers, since it took time to recruit, organize, and train professional replacements. Except in areas where military operations took place, the masses in the warring nations carried on their everyday life as usual. Supplies were usually obtained by systematic and regular procedures, not by indiscriminate plundering.

Most of the significant European wars of the period were fought over terrain that was open, relatively flat, and thickly populated.

Normally, fighting took place only during favorable weather and during daylight hours; rain or darkness quickly called a halt to a battle; by December opposing armies usually retired to winter quarters to await the coming of spring to resume hostilities. Road and river transportation systems were, for the time, highly developed, making for facility of movement of men and supplies. Food for men and forage for horses were usually available in the areas of military operations. Each nation normally had a series of fortresses or magazines along the line of march of its army in which replacement supplies and foodstuffs could be stored. All these factors contributed toward making the use of parade ground tactics most practicable on the battlefield or in the war of maneuver.

The combat arms and their weapons. The combat branches of the 18th century armies corresponded closely in their functions to their modern counterparts. The basic arm was infantry, whose mission then as now was to close with the enemy and destroy him. The two supporting elements were cavalry (whose modern equivalent is armor) and artillery. Because of the open nature of the country, cavalry could be employed to full advantage. As for artillery it was used in both attack and defense, either in campaigns of maneuver or in siege warfare. Again the characteristically open terrain, affording good fields of fire, and the existence of road nets adequate for the type of vehicles used, permitted full employment of artillery within its technical limitations. Some 18th century commanders used the three arms skillfully in combination. Yet it was the clash of infantry that usually decided the issue; in the 18th century the infantry can truly be called the "Queen of Battles."

The standard infantry weapon of the time was the flintlock musket with bayonet. Probably the most famous model was "Brown Bess," the one used in the British Army. "Brown Bess" had a smooth bore barrel 3 feet 8 inches long with a 14-inch bayonet, and fired a round lead ball about three-quarters of an inch in diameter.

The flintlock was highly inaccurate since the barrel had no rifling and the charge necessarily fitted loosely. It misfired frequently and was useless when the powder in the priming pan got wet. The musket was slow to load and fire, the normal rate being one to two rounds a minute with a wooden ramrod, perhaps double that with an iron one. When the ball hit within its effective range, 150 to 200 yards, its impact was terrific. But its inefficiency as a firearm made its attached bayonet as important as its fire-power. In battle infantry normally relied on the bayonet to give the final blow to an enemy softened by musketry fire. Smokeless powder was then unknown, and after a volley or two the battlefield was blanketed with smoke. This phenomenon explains the use of brightly colored uniforms to distinguish friend from foe.

Cavalrymen were variously armed with pistol and lance, carbine and sword, depending on the country and the time. Pistol and carbine were discharged at close range against the ranks of opposing infantry or cavalry while lance and sword were used for close-in shock action.

There were many different kinds of artillery in use. The larger pieces were mainly for siege warfare and were relatively immobile. Artillery used in the field was lighter and mounted on wheeled carriages pulled by horses. Whether siege or field, these artillery pieces were, like the muskets, smooth bore muzzle-loaders, very limited in range and highly inaccurate. Loading and firing were even slower than in the case of the musket for the cannon barrel had to be swabbed out after each round to prevent any residue of burning powder from causing a premature explosion. There was no traverse and the whole carriage had to be moved to change the direction of fire. Cannon fired mainly solid iron balls, grapeshot, and canister. Grapeshot was a cluster of small iron balls attached to a central system (thus resembling a bunch of grapes) and dispersed by the explosion of a propellant charge; canister consisted of loose pellets placed in a can, and when fired had even greater dispersion than grape. Both grape and canister were reserved for use at close range. Explosive shells were known and sometimes used at longer ranges, but the problems involved in preventing premature explosions were still too great to permit their general employment.

Linear tactics. The tactics in vogue in the 18th century are usually designated linear tactics to distinguish them from earlier mass formations such as the Spanish Square and the column formations employed later by Napoleon. In the employment of linear tactics troops marched onto the battlefield in columns and then deployed into line. A line consisted of a number of battalions or regiments—the terms were then practically synonymous—formed three ranks deep. There normally were two or three such lines with 300- to 600-yard intervals separating them. In the ranks the men stood shoulder to shoulder and delivered their fire. Loading, firing, and bayonet charge were all performed at command in a drill involving many separate motions. Firing was by volley, the purpose being to achieve the greatest mass of firepower over a given area. Little or no training was given in individual aimed fire, which was not thought to be warranted either by the accuracy of the flintlock musket or by the character of the soldiery.

As a prelude to battle, both armies would undertake a series of maneuvers, each commander seeking both to protect strategic objectives within his own territory and to bring the enemy to battle under the most favorable circumstances of terrain. Surprise was sought but not often achieved in the open country of Europe. The battle normally came when both sides had decided to commit their forces to a test of strength or when one maneuvered the other into a position from which he could not retreat without giving battle.

If a battle was decided upon, both forces would be drawn up in a similar formation, the infantry in the center, cavalry on the flanks or in the rear, artillery in line with the infantry, and a reserve force in the rear. The battle would be opened by artillery fire from both sides. In the midst of this fire, the attacking infantry would move forward maintaining the rigid linear formation in which it was trained. At a range of 50 to 100 yards, the attacking line would halt on the command of its officers. At a second command, a volley was fired and would be answered by the opposing line. The exchange of volleys would continue until one side determined to try to carry the field with the bayonet or a cavalry charge. At some critical moment the reserve might be brought up by either commander and committed in order to turn the tide of battle.

If either side was able to carry the field, and particularly if large numbers of officers were casualties, the enemy ranks would break up, with individuals fleeing, all discipline gone, their only thought survival. It was then that the victorious commander was granted the opportunity for his greatest success and the defeated commander faced his most serious test. A successful pursuit might well mean the attainment of the final objective—destruction of the enemy's army. On the other hand, if the defeated commander could withdraw his force in some semblance of order, he might fall back to a fortress or other defensible position to re-form and carry on the fight. What happened at this stage of the battle depended largely on the state of reserves on each side, the availability of cavalry for pursuit or on the defender's side for rear guard action, the state of disorganization of the victor's forces, the time of day, and the availability of a good line of retreat. If the vanquished were completely broken the pursuit was largely a job for the cavalry who mercilessly rode down the fleeing enemy.

Eighteenth century battles were not, however, limited to frontal assaults. Feints were used to achieve surprise and extensive maneuvers undertaken in an effort to achieve superiority at the point of contact. The successful tactics of good 18th century commanders and of those who followed, finally produced the principles of war as we know them today.

Siege warfare. Not all 18th century battles were fought in the open. Fortresses played a vital role in the defense system of all European nations, normally being constructed along the frontiers to impede the advance of an invading army. By 1700 the arts of both fortification and siegecraft had been reduced to formal principles by a distinguished soldier and engineer in the service of Louis XIV of France, Marshal Vauban.

The system devised by Vauban was known as an approach by parallel lines. The first parallel was constructed about 600 yards from the fortress walls. Zig-zag approach trenches were then dug forward about 200 yards to points from which a second parallel was constructed. By the same process a third parallel was dug. Infantry and siege artillery were moved forward as each parallel was completed until, in the third, they were beneath the outer wall of the fortress. From this vantage point the artillery could breach the main wall and the infantry could take the fortress by storm. At this juncture the fortress commander usually surrendered. If he did not, the infantry would attempt to carry the fortress by storm. Under Vauban's system the capture of a fortress by a superior besieging force was usually only a matter of time.

Colonial America. *General.* In Colonial America neither formal battles in the open nor formal sieges were the normal modes of making war. America was a new continent, heavily forested and sparsely populated. The main enemy that the English colonists had to contend with during the first century after settlement was the primitive and savage Indian, who neither knew the rules of formal warfare nor cared to learn them. Colonial society from its very beginning developed along more democratic and individualistic lines than society in England or continental Europe. These factors combined to produce different forms of military organization from those of Europe and different methods of employing them on the battlefield.

Society and government. It would be a mistake to call the society that took form in the thirteen English colonies in North America a new society, for in most respects it followed the English pattern of social, economic, and political organization. But England itself had stronger democratic traditions than existed on the Continent, and important differences in the environment gave these English traditions much stronger force in America. Here there was no titled nobility exercising a monopoly on governmental office or holding a vested title to most of the land. While an aristocracy of wealth soon appeared, it was never able to exercise the same prerogatives as a titled nobility. Besides it was far easier to move from the poorer to the wealthier class, since acquisition of landed wealth was easier in a country where land was plentiful and labor scarce to work it. If older settled areas tended to develop something approaching the pattern of European class distinction, new frontiers were constantly opening up where dissatisfied individuals could move and find new opportunities. Each successive frontier exercised its leavening influence on the older society, for on the frontier a man's worth was largely determined by his ability to work and fight in the struggle to carve a new home out of the wilderness. Life under these conditions bred a spirit of fierce individualism and self-reliance very different from that of the European peasant or laborer.

In political life, this spirit found expression in the popular assemblies that played an increasingly important part in the government of each of the colonies. Each colony had a government modeled generally on England's. Though there were variations in the pattern, the normal form consisted of a royal governor appointed by the British Crown, a council appointed by the governor from the ranks of a colonial aristocracy, and a popular assembly elected by the landholders. Modeled on the British House of Commons, these popular assemblies in the colonies rested on a much broader democratic base, since property ownership—the main qualification for voting in Britain and America in this age—was far more widespread in the colonies.

Indian warfare. The Indian method of warfare in the forest, perforce adopted by the white man also, was the most significant influence in developing and preserving the spirit of individualism and self-reliance in the military sphere. When the white man came, the Indian relied on bow and spear, tomahawk and knife, but he soon learned the value of the white man's musket and was not long in obtaining quantities of them in trade for his valuable furs. With bow or musket, his method of fighting was the same. Indian tribes had no organized system of war; warriors simply formed voluntary bands under war chiefs and took off on the warpath. In battle each Indian fought a separate opponent without regard for his fellows, seeking to acquire as many scalps as he could. Indians avoided pitched battle whenever possible, seeking victory instead by surprise and careful utilization of cover and concealment. Only when they had the advantage did they close in for hand-to-hand combat. In such combat the Indian brave lacked neither skill nor courage. But knowing little and caring less about the rules of civilized warfare he slaughtered men, women, and children indiscriminately. The favorite Indian tactic was a surprise raid on an isolated settlement. When the settlers organized a pursuit, the Indians lay in wait and ambushed them.

The white man soon adapted his tactics to the Indian's, quickly learning the value of surprise and stealth himself. To avoid ambush he sent out scouts as the Indian did; instead of fighting in the closed formations of Europe, he too adopted the open formation and fought from behind trees, rocks, and fences. In such fighting more depended on individual initiative and courage than on strict discipline and control.

The white settler learned to benefit from some of the enemy's weaknesses. For all their cunning, the Indians never learned the lesson of proper security and did not post guards at night. Nor did they like to fight in winter. Expeditions into the Indian country used as their favorite technique an attack on an Indian village at dawn and in the winter season. This attack almost invariably came as a surprise and the white men, imitating the savagery of their opponents, burned the Indian's villages and sometimes slaughtered braves, squaws, and papooses.

Frontier forts. The settlers also tried to provide some permanent protection for their frontiers by erecting forts along the westernmost line of settlement in each colony, moving them forward as the line of settlement moved. These forts were not the elaborate earth and masonry structures of Europe, but simple rectangular inclosures, their walls constructed of upright pointed logs. Normally there were wooden blockhouses on each corner. These rude frontier forts served as points to which settlers and their families could retreat for protection in time of Indian troubles. Having no artillery the Indians found them hard to take and could rely only on burning arrows to set them afire, on surprise attack, or on direct frontal assault. From the last alternative they almost invariably flinched. Their war chiefs possessed no power to order any group of braves to undertake an assault in which they would suffer heavy casualties for the sake of gaining an objective.

Militia. For this sort of fighting, colonial governments relied not on professional soldiers but on the body of citizens. Each colony had its Militia organization, normally based on the principle that every able-bodied male from 16 to 60 should render military service. The Militia was an ancient British institution, but since Britain's wars after 1660 were fought on the sea or in foreign lands the Militia there came to exist largely on paper while professional soldiers and seamen fought Britain's battles. In the colonies, the old institution survived and took on new strength. Each member of the Militia was obligated to appear for training at his county or town seat a certain number of days each year and to hold himself in readiness for call in case of an Indian attack or other emergency.

Militia—selection for active combat. A general call for the whole Militia of a colony almost never occurred. Instead the Militia served as a training and mobilization base from which individuals or units could be selected for active operations. When a particular area of a colony was threatened, the colonial government would direct the Militia commander in that area to call out his men. For expeditions into the Indian country, individuals from many local units were usually selected and formed into an organized force for the occasion. Selection was generally by volunteering, but local commanders could draft both men and property if necessary. As a rule, the selected men were obligated to serve for a stipulated length of time, normally the estimated length of the campaign. In Indian expeditions this was seldom more than 6 months.

Militia—choice of officers. For a military organization, the Militia was a most democratic institution. Though general officers and

18

regimental colonels were appointed by royal governors or the colonial
assembly, company officers were elected by the men. This did not
necessarily mean that any man might become an officer though it
clearly put a premium on popularity as well as ability. The expenses of providing distinctive uniforms and arms and the tradition
of leadership in certain families normally kept the officers' commissions in the hands of the well to do.

Militia—supply. Each individual Militiaman was expected to provide his own weapons and clothing and food for a short expedition.
The weapon in almost universal use in the colonies until about 1750
was the musket, generally the same type as that used by the European soldier. There were few if any bayonets; the colonial Militiaman might well use a hatchet or hunting knife as a substitute in
hand-to-hand combat.

Supply was not altogether an individual responsibility. Local authorities maintained reserve supplies of muskets to arm those too
poor to buy them; they also collected stores of ammunition and sometimes small cannon that could be dragged along through the wilderness. For really long campaigns the colonial government had to take
charge, the assembly appropriating the money to buy supplies and
designating supply officers or contractors to handle purchasing and
distribution. In this case there might be more cannon, but the use
of anything but the smaller pieces of artillery was impractical because
of the lack of roads and clear fields of fire in the forest. Cannon
were more frequently used for defense of forts or towns.

Militia—control. Within each colony, the popular assembly exercised close control over all matters relating to the organization and
use of Militia, largely through its control of the purse. It must be
kept in mind that there were 13 Militias, not one, and that each
of the 13 was organized and administered under a separate set of
laws. Each colonial government concentrated on the defense of
its own frontiers and cooperation among the Militias of the various
colonies was normally confined to specific Indian expeditions in
which two or more colonies had a definite interest. Thus there appeared very early in our history a tradition of separatism among
the various colonies that was to have lasting effects. The individual
Militiaman and his immediate commanders were apt to be bound
by even narrower local ties and to show little enthusiasm in fighting
for anything that did not affect their own community.

Militia—military capabilities. As a part-time citizen army the
Militia was naturally not the well-disciplined cohesive force that was
the professional army of the age. Its efficiency also varied from colony to colony and even from locality to locality within the same colony
depending on the ability and determination of commanders and the
presence or absence of an enemy threat. When engaged in eliminating

an Indian threat to their own community, Militiamen might be counted on to make up in enthusiasm what they lacked in discipline and formal training, but when the Indian threat was pushed westward there was a general tendency for people along the seaboard to relax. Training days, one a week in the early days of settlement, fell to one a month or even one a year. Festivities rather than military training increasingly became the main purpose of these gatherings, and the efficiency of the Militia in these regions declined accordingly. In some towns and counties, the military tradition of the earlier period was kept alive only by volunteers who formed units of their own within the Militia such as the Ancient and Honorable Company of Artillery in Boston. On the frontier the situation was different, for Indian raids were still a constant threat and the Militia had to be constantly ready for instant action. There training days were more frequent and the Militia's efficiency in frontier warfare was the main guarantee of the settlers' survival.

The Colonies in the World Conflict, 1689–1763. Warfare with the Indians was not the only military problem of the colonial period. Between 1689 and 1763, in four great wars fought in Europe between various coalitions of states, France and England were invariably on opposite sides, and their respective colonies in North America inevitably followed suit. In fact one of the major issues, if not the major one, involved in all the fighting was control of the North American continent (map 1).

Americans and Europeans called these wars by different names. The war of the League of Augsburg (1689–97) was known in America as King William's War, the War of Spanish Succession (1701–13) as Queen Anne's War, the War of Austrian Succession (1744–48) as King George's War, and the final and decisive conflict, the Seven Years War (1756–63), as the French and Indian War.

While Britain was colonizing the eastern seaboard from Maine to Georgia, France was extending its power over Canada and Louisiana and asserting its claim to the Great Lakes region and the Mississippi Valley. The main center of French military strength was in Canada. The strategic line along which most of the fighting took place in the colonies was that between New York and Quebec either on the lake and river chain that connects the Hudson and the St. Lawrence in the interior or along the seaways leading from the Atlantic up the St. Lawrence. In the French and Indian War another front was opened in the Ohio Valley.

Character of French effort. The character of much of the fighting in the colonial wars with the French was much the same as that in the Indian wars. For although the French maintained garrisons of Regulars in Canada, they were never sufficient to bear the brunt of the fighting. Instead they relied heavily on Indian allies whom they

20

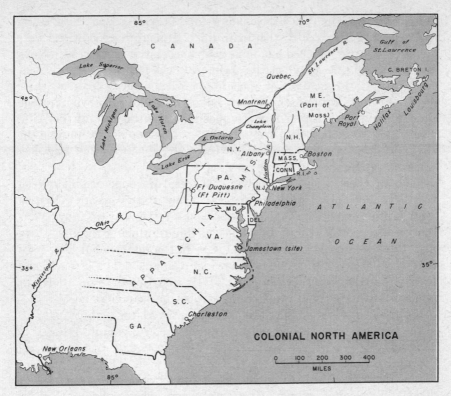

Map 1. Colonial North America.

equipped with firearms. The French constructed forts at strategic points and garrisoned them with small numbers of Regulars, a few of whom were normally sent along with Indian raiding parties to supervise operations. The French were far more successful than were the English in promoting good relations with the Indians and learned the lessons of forest warfare very quickly. Using these methods, the French gained many local successes and indeed kept the frontiers of the English colonies in a continual state of alarm; but they were never able to achieve decisive results.

Character of British effort. It was the British and their colonists who usually took the offensive and sought to strike by land and sea at the very citadels of French power. The British Navy's control of the sea played a very important role, for it made possible the mounting of sea expeditions and at the same time rendered it difficult for the French to reinforce their small regular garrisons. In 1710 a combined British and colonial expedition captured the French fort at Port Royal on Nova Scotia, and by the treaty of peace in 1713 Nova Scotia became an English possession. In 1745 an all-colonial expedition captured Louisbourg on Cape Breton Island only to have it bargained away in 1748 in exchange for Madras, a post the French had captured from the British in India. Numerous expeditions were mounted against Quebec but none was successful until 1759. Nova Scotia was thus the only positive gain from the first three wars. And meantime the French threat was intensified as they expanded their system of forts around the Great Lakes and moved down into the Ohio Valley, establishing Fort Duquesne at the junction of the Allegheny and Monongahela Rivers in 1753. This move precipitated the final and decisive conflict the following year, a conflict that began in America rather than in Europe.

Each of these wars saw varying degrees of cooperation between British and colonial military forces. One of the greatest British contributions made throughout was that of the Royal Navy. The British also sent Regulars to America, though during the first three wars they did not participate in the war in the interior but were used only in the expeditions by sea against Canada. The French and Indian War, however, saw the use of British Regulars on all fronts in approximately equal proportions with American colonials.

Volunteer forces. While the Militia played an important part in the colonial wars, it had to be supplemented by volunteer forces of varying degrees of professionalism. For the expeditions against Canada, for instance, volunteer forces were necessarily the primary reliance. Unlike the Militia, volunteer forces were built from the top down. The commanding officers were first chosen by one of the colonial governors or assemblies and the men were enlisted by them. The choice of a commander was made with due regard for his popularity in the colony and hence his ability to persuade officers and men to serve under him. The Militia was the base from whence the volunteers were recruited. The officers were invariably men whose ranks derived from the Militia and whose total experience was in it. Volunteer forces were enlisted in the service and pay of one of the colonies and therefore were dependent upon appropriations of money made by that colony's assembly. Assemblies were usually parsimonious, and neither officers nor men were anxious to commit themselves for longer than a year or so. Volunteers were therefore enlisted usually only for a single campaign, not for long periods as in European armies. At the end of the campaign, they reverted to the Militia, thus providing it with a leavening of experienced personnel.

Lack of colonial unity. The colonial effort in these wars was never a united one. There was no over-all colonial organization to compel cooperation in an effort for the good of all, and no colony was usually willing to make any significant contribution to the common effort unless it appeared to be, in its own interest. At a colonial congress held in Albany in 1754, Benjamin Franklin urged on the various colonies a plan of union, but it was not accepted. The British

Government intervened and from time to time set quotas of troops, supplies, and money, but these quotas were seldom met. With short enlistments, poorly trained officers, and poor discipline by European standards, even the best of the colonial units were often held in contempt, before the French and Indian War, by British officers, who tended to ignore their peculiar virtues in the type of guerilla warfare waged in the American interior.

Colonials in British service. The difficulties in securing a sustained and cooperative colonial effort forced the British to assume an ever-increasing part of the burden of the wars in North America. Individual colonies were reimbursed for part of the expenses incurred in prosecuting the war. Increasing numbers of British Regulars were sent to North America. Finally certain colonial units were made part of the British Regular Establishment or officers were appointed by the British Government and sent out to recruit Colonials in their regiments. These colonial units in the British Establishment were the nearest thing to a Regular force the Americans had before the Revolution.

The French and Indian War. All these methods of raising forces reached their culmination in the French and Indian War, the first truly large-scale conflict on the North American continent. The war began in America two years before it did in Europe when in 1754 a force of Virginia Militia under Lt. Col. George Washington was driven back from Fort Duquesne by the French and forced to surrender. After a series of such early reverses the British Government under the inspired leadership of William Pitt was able to achieve a combination of British and colonial arms that succeeded in overcoming the last French resistance in Canada and in finally removing the French threat from North America. This war was a training ground for leaders on both sides in the American Revolution.

Braddock's defeat. Before the British could go on to win North America, they first had to learn a lesson in the methods of waging war in the interior. In 1755 the British sent to America two regiments of Regular troops under Maj. Gen. Edward Braddock, a soldier of some 45 years' experience on continental battlefields. Braddock's mission was to accomplish the task in which the Virginia Militia had failed, that is, to drive the French from Fort Duquesne. Accustomed to the parade ground tactics and the open terrain of Europe, all Braddock's faith was in disciplined Regulars and close order formations. He had even more than the usual contempt of a regular British officer for Militia and Indians. Early in June 1755, Braddock set out on the long march through the wilderness to Fort Duquesne with a total force of 2,200 including a body of Virginia Militia (map 2). He was accompanied by Washington as an aide-de-camp. His force proceeded through the wilderness in traditional column formation with 300 axe-

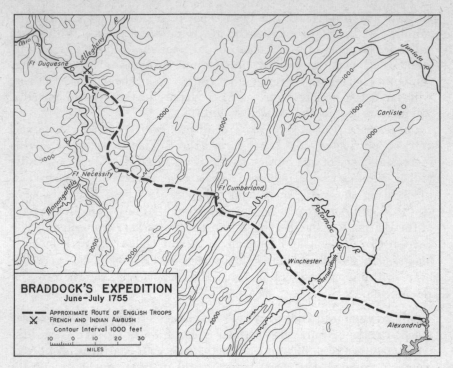

Map 2.   Braddock's expedition, June–July 1755.

men in front to clear the road and a heavy baggage train of wagons in
the rear.   The heavy wagon train so slowed his progress that about
half-way he decided to let it follow as best it could and proceeded ahead
with about 1,300 selected men, 10 cannon, and a convoy of 30 wagons
and several packhorses.   In a ravine just past the Monongahela River
on 9 July 1755, Braddock's advance guard under Lt. Col. Thomas
Gage came under the fire of about 70 French Regulars, 150 Canadians,
and 650 Indians concealed in the forest.   Instead of deploying his men
in open formation and taking cover, Braddock advanced his force in
mass formation to Gage's assistance, attempting to answer the concealed fire with volleys in traditional European fashion.   The Virginians alone took to the woods and tried to answer Indian fire in
Indian style.   The volleys of the Regulars were wasted on the air
while the French and Indians poured in their fire with telling effect,
decimating Braddock's troops and killing or wounding two-thirds of
his officers.   Mortally wounded himself, Braddock finally attempted
to withdraw his force, but the belated order to retreat simply produced
the panic that so frequently fell on Regulars when their officers were
killed and their formations broken.   The retreat became a wild flight
that did not stop even when the terrified troops reached the baggage
trains many miles to the rear.   Despite the completeness of their victory, the French and Indian force was incapable of an effective pur-

Braddock's defeat, 9 July 1755.

suit, for the few French Regulars present had little control over the Indians who preferred to loot the battlefield and scalp the wounded.

Braddock's defeat—lessons learned. Although Braddock was aware of the possibilities of ambush and had sent out scouts, he violated the principles of security and maneuver. He had such faith in regular methods that he believed an ambush could be repelled simply by standing and fighting in regular formation. It was in this he proved so badly mistaken. The lessons of Braddock's defeat were not that Regular forces or European methods were useless in America or that undisciplined American Militia were superior to British Regular troops. They were rather that tactics and formations would have to be adapted to terrain and the nature of the enemy and that Regulars, where employed in the forest, would have to learn to travel faster and lighter and take advantage of all the devices of cover, concealment, and surprise. Or better still they would have to employ colonial troops and Indian allies versed in this sort of warfare as the French had long since learned to do.

The British employed both methods in the ensuing years of the French and Indian War. Light infantry, trained as scouts and skirmishers, became a permanent part of the British Army organization. These troops were, when engaged in operations in the forest, clad in green or brown clothes instead of the traditional redcoat of the British soldier, their heads shaved, their skins sometimes painted like the Indians'. The most proficient of the light infantry troops were special ranger companies recruited in the colonies and placed in the Regular British Establishment.

FALL OF WOLFE. *During the fighting at Quebec in 1759, Gen. James Wolfe, in command of the British forces opposing the French under Montcalm, fell in action.*

The importance of Regulars. The French and Indian War was not entirely a war of forest engagements. Where British Regulars had the opportunity to fight in the open, they showed the same superiority the woodsmen did in their native element. The final and decisive battle of the war was fought in the open field on the Plains of Abraham before the French citadel at Quebec in 1759. In this battle the training and discipline of the Regulars and the initiative, determination, and courage of their commander, Maj. Gen. James Wolfe, carried the day. In a daring move, Wolfe's men scaled the cliffs leading to the plains one night and appeared in traditional line of battle before the city the next morning. Maj. Gen. the Marquis de Montcalm, the able French commander, accepted the challenge, but his troops proved unable to withstand the withering fire of Wolfe's exceptionally well-disciplined regiments.

The ultimate lesson of the colonial wars then was that European and American tactics each had their place, and either could be decisive where conditions were best suited to their use. But they also proved that only troops possessing the organization and discipline of Regulars, whatever their tactics, could actually move in, seize and hold objectives, and thus achieve decisive results.

Logistics. Difficulties of supply and transport in a vast undeveloped and sparsely populated country limited both the size and variety of forces employed. The settled portions of the colonies produced enough food, but few manufactured goods. Muskets, cannon, powder, ball, tents, camp kettles, salt, and a variety of other articles necessary even for the simple military operations of the period had to come from Europe. Roads, even in the settled areas, were poor and inadequate; forces penetrating into the interior had to cut their roads as they went, as Braddock did. These logistical difficulties go far to explain why the fate of America was settled in battles involving hardly one-tenth the size of forces engaged in Europe in the Seven Years War.

While there were organized cavalry units among the Colonial Militia, particularly in the south, it does not appear that cavalry was ever extensively employed either in the Indian wars or in those with the French. The terrain over which the wars were fought was not suitable for cavalry. Forage was difficult to obtain outside the settled regions and transporting it placed too heavy a burden on the line of supply. Horsemen were difficult to conceal in operations where surprise was often the prime element of success. The reconnaissance role of cavalry was performed by the colonial scout or the friendly Indian on foot.

Similarly, difficulties of transport kept down both the size and number of cannon. For such expeditions by sea as those against Port Royal, Louisbourg, and Quebec, either naval guns could be used or cannon transported by sea. But trained gunners were scarce, and it was difficult to maneuver the pieces once ashore. Wolfe was able to take only two small cannon up the cliffs to the Plains of Abraham. To transport cannon along the difficult inland routes to Fort Duquesne and in northern New York involved more effort than could usually be justified by the results.

The American Rifle. By the end of the French and Indian War, a new weapon had appeared on the frontier in Pennsylvania and to the southward, far better suited to use in guerilla warfare than the musket. This weapon was later to gain fame as the Kentucky Rifle. The effects of rifling a gun barrel, that is, of making spiral grooves that imparted a spinning effect to the bullet giving it greater range and accuracy, had been known for some centuries in Germany and Switzerland. But the early rifles made there were too heavy and slow to load to be of military use. The Germans who settled in Pennsylvania developed, around 1750, a much lighter model far easier and faster to load. They used a bullet smaller than the bore and a greased patch to keep the fit tight. This early American rifle could, in proper hands, hit a target the size of a man's head at 200 yards.

Despite its superior range and accuracy, it was to take almost a hundred years of development before the rifle would supplant the musket as the standard infantry weapon. At first each of these rifles was hand made and each required a separate bullet mould. The standard bayonet would fit none of them. The rifle was effective only in the hands of an expert trained in its use. The rate of fire was only about one-third that of the musket, and therefore, without bayonet, the rifle could hardly be used by troops in the line. For the guerilla tactics of the frontier, in which men did not fight in line, but from behind trees, bushes, and rocks, it was obviously a superior weapon. Thus, like the tactics of the American forest, it would have its place in any future war fought in America.

The Colonial Heritage. In this very brief sketch of weapons, tactics, and military organization in 18th century Europe and America, enough has been said to give a general idea of the setting in which the United States Army came into being. In the Indian wars and the colonial wars with France, Americans had gained considerable military experience, albeit much of it in guerilla warfare along the frontiers that did not require the same degree of organized effort and professional competence as European style warfare. It must be kept in mind that the major effort against the French in Canada had been organized and directed by the British Government. Many colonial officers later to become famous in the Revolution—among them George Washington, Israel Putnam, Horatio Gates, Philip Schuyler, and John Stark—had served their military apprenticeship in the French and Indian War, but none had held high positions of command.

Certain traditions had been established that were to influence American military policy and practices right down to the two great world wars of our time. One of these was the tradition of the Militia as the main reliance for defense and volunteer forces for special emergencies. The fear of a standing army of professionals had already appeared. The colonial experience also established a strong tradition of separatism among the colonies themselves for each had for a long period of years run its own military establishment. Within each colony too the civilian authority represented in the popular assembly had always kept a strict rein of control over the military, another tradition that was to have marked effect on American military development.

Certain characteristics of the American soldier that were to be fairly constant throughout all future wars had also made their appearance. He was inclined to be highly individualistic and to resent discipline and the inevitable restrictions of military life; he sought to know why he should do things before he would put his heart into doing them; and if in the end he accepted discipline and order as a stern necessity he did so with the idea of winning victory as quickly as possible so that he could get back to his normal civilian pursuits.

These traditions and these characteristics were the product of a society developing along democratic lines. The military strengths and weaknesses they engendered were to be amply demonstrated when the American soldier took up arms against his erstwhile comrade, the British Regular, in the American Revolution.

QUESTIONS

1. Discuss the relationship between tactics and weapons in 18th century Europe.

2. Name the principal combat arms in the 18th century European army and describe the role of each in battle.

3. Show how the differences in European and American social and political organization affected the forms of military organization in each place.

4. Contrast Indian warfare with the formal warfare of 18th century Europe.

5. What principle or principles of war do you think Braddock violated?

6. How did the British remedy the defects in their style of fighting that were revealed by Braddock's defeat?

7. What were the respective virtues and defects of European Regulars and Colonial Militia?

8. What practices of the colonial period had lasting effects on American military development?

Reading List

Fortescue, J. W. *History of the British Army.* Vol. II. London, 1897– . 14 vols.

Osgood, Herbert L. *The American Colonies in the Eighteenth Century.* New York, 1924. 4 vols.

Wade, Herbert T. *A Brief History of the Colonial Wars in America from 1607 to 1775.* New York, 1948.

CHAPTER 2

BEGINNINGS OF THE AMERICAN REVOLUTION—
THE FIRST YEAR

The Causes. The roots of the American Revolution lie deep in colonial history. For a century and a half before 1763 the colonies had been developing their own society, economic life, and government with only a minimum of interference from London. After 1763 the government of George III and his ministers changed the old policy of "salutary neglect," tightening up the existing restrictive laws on colonial trade and attempting to levy direct taxes on the colonists. The new policy was not without its justification, for the taxes were levied to defray expenses incurred in the late war and to help meet the cost of stationing British garrisons in the colonies to keep the Indians in check. But the colonists saw little further need for such British protection now that the French threat was removed. They protested that only their own assemblies had the right to tax them and viewed the British soldiers sent to America not as protectors but as instruments of British oppression. British laws requiring colonial governments to provide quarters, supplies, and transportation for these troops increased colonial resentment. The occasional quartering of British redcoats on private property heightened it.

The Revolution as Civil War. The colonial leaders moved toward separation gradually; their initial objective was to secure recognition of their rights and liberties within the British Empire. It was only the dogged determination of George III and his ministers to use military force to coerce the colonists that led to the ultimate decision for independence. This decision was far from a unanimous one: perhaps one-fourth of the colonists remained loyal to Britain. Within the mother country also there was considerable opposition to the policy of military coercion pursued by the ministry. The Revolution thus took on some of the aspects of a civil war fought within the British Empire.

The Immediate Background. The immediate chain of events leading to armed conflict began in December 1773, when a group of Boston patriots dumped the tea aboard a British vessel into the harbor in violent protest against a British import duty on that commodity. In reprisal, the British Government in America closed the port of Boston, placed the whole colony of Massachusetts under the military rule of Maj. Gen. Thomas Gage, and passed other repressive measures, collectively known as the "Intolerable Acts." These acts were interpreted by patriots throughout the colonies as evidence of British intent to reduce them all to complete subservience. Steps were taken to form revolutionary governments in each colony, and the First Continental Congress gathered at Philadelphia on 5 September 1774 to discuss concerted measures to protect American rights.

Military Preparations. Simultaneously preparations for military resistance began. They consisted, for the most part, of establishing the control of the revolutionary governments over the Militia in each colony and of shaping from it an effective military force. What happened in Massachusetts is of greatest significance. The revolutionary government there, fairly typical of that in the other colonies, consisted of a Provincial Congress that took over from the old popular assembly, a central Committee of Safety, and various local conventions and committees in each township. The local committees forced the resignation of Militia officers with Loyalist sympathies and reorganized the Militia under patriot commanders. The Provincial Congress then, following the old colonial tradition of selection, directed officers in each township to enlist a third of their men into Minutemen organizations to be ready to act at a moment's warning. Into the Minutemen companies went the younger and more active members of the Militia. The rest were organized into alarm companies as a reserve.

The Provincial Congress and the local organizations also began to accumulate ammunition and other military stores. The major depot for these stores was established at Concord.

Lexington and Concord. Information of these preparations leaked to General Gage in Boston, and on the night of 18–19 April 1775 he sent out an expedition of about 700 picked men under Lt. Col. Francis Smith to seize and destroy the military stores at Concord (map 3). Despite Gage's efforts to preserve secrecy, preparations for the movement caught the eye of patriots in Boston, and two messengers—Paul Revere and William Dawes—rode out a few hours ahead of the British to give the alarm. When the British reached Lexington at dawn on 19 April, they found themselves confronted by a small force of local Minutemen, drawn up in a line on the village green. Just who fired the first shot, the one "heard round the world," remains an intriguing mystery. Whoever did, it led the impatient and nervous British Regulars, without orders from their commanders, to fire into the Minutemen, killing 8 and wounding 10. The rest quickly dispersed and the British column proceeded to Concord, where the redcoats destroyed such of the military stores as they could find.

It was when the British began their return march to Boston that they first ran into serious difficulties. The alarm had been going out to farm and village, and both Minutemen and alarm companies had

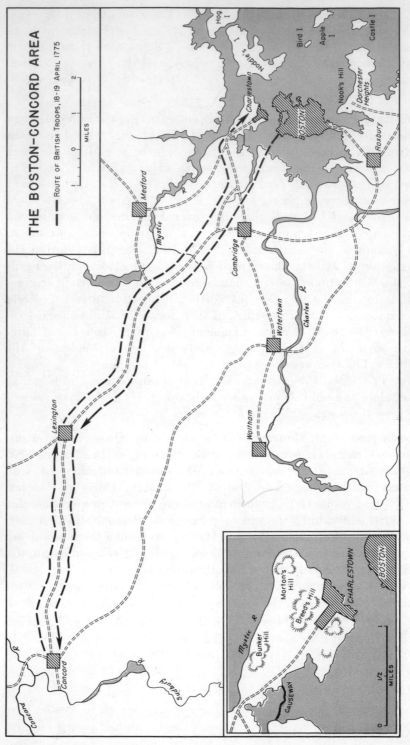

Map 3. The Boston-Concord area.

32

The Day of Lexington and Concord.

been gathering. From behind trees and fences and from vacant houses along the road they poured their fire into the British column. Gage in Boston received word of what was happening and sent a relief force with several pieces of artillery to join Smith at Lexington. The relief saved Smith's force from annihilation, but still from Lexington to Charlestown the fire continued and the British had no surcease until they were safely under the protective guns of their fleet. The British lost about 273 men out of a total force of 1,500 to 1,800. The fact that the force was not wiped out was testimony to the poor marksmanship of farmers armed with muskets.

Lexington and Concord had tremendous psychological effect in arousing the colonies to determined resistance. Regardless of who fired the first shot, the British got the blame, and news of the events of 19 April was carried by messengers through the colonies to the southward. Military preparations in all the colonies were quickened and royal governors were forced to flee to British warships. In the immediate area around Boston, Militia and volunteer forces from the other New England colonies rallied to join the Massachusetts men in a siege of Boston.

Ticonderoga and Crown Point. In early May 1775, other New England forces, led by Col. Ethan Allen of Vermont and Col. Benedict Arnold of Connecticut, seized the British fort at Ticonderoga, the strong point between Lakes George and Champlain on the water route between New York and Canada. The superannuated British commander, with a garrison of only about 40 men, surrendered without a fight. From there Arnold and Allen proceeded further north to Crown Point, a fort the British demolished and evacuated before their arrival. These successes gave the Americans both strategic bases and valuable artillery pieces and other military supplies sorely needed for the siege of Boston, but it would take much time and effort to get the cannon there.

Bunker Hill. In late May, Gage's force in Boston was reinforced from England, bringing it to a total of about 6,500 men. With the British reinforcements came three major generals of considerable military experience and reputation who were to play leading roles in the Revolution—William Howe, Henry Clinton, and John Burgoyne. All were anxious to take the offensive and get what Burgoyne referred to as "elbow room." However, it was the Colonials who first took the initiative and, on the night of 16 June 1775, threw up entrenchments on Breed's Hill on the Charlestown isthmus overlooking Boston from the north (map 3). The original intent had been to fortify Bunker Hill, nearer the narrow neck of the isthmus, but for reasons not clear even today they decided to move in closer. Nevertheless, Bunker Hill was to give its name to the battle that ensued.

In moving onto Breed's Hill the Americans placed themselves in a position where they could easily have been cut off had the British landed in their rear at the neck of the isthmus. But other councils prevailed in Boston. Gage, with the approval of Howe, to whom tactical control was entrusted, decided on the morning of 17 June that the rebels must be dislodged before they could complete their works. Scorning elaborate maneuver, he evidently calculated that the ill-trained American Militia would disintegrate when faced with disciplined Regulars and that such a defeat administered in a direct attack on the hill would show the rebels the futility of resisting British power. Howe's force of around 2,200 men was ferried from Boston to Charlestown and in midafternoon on 17 June began the attack on the American front and flanks. The Americans behind their entrenchments held their fire while the British Regulars sweated up the hill under their heavy packs. When the redcoats came within 50 yards, they opened a devastating fire. Twice the well-formed British lines broke and retreated, leaving large numbers killed and wounded on the field. By this time the Americans were nearly out of powder, and a third British attack with the bayonet carried the hill. The Militia, without bayonets or other means of close-in defense, withdrew across the neck of the isthmus to the mainland. But Howe's victory had cost him more than 1,000 casualties to the Americans' 400, and his forces were too disorganized to undertake a pursuit. His experience at Bunker Hill made Howe thereafter wary of attacking Americans in fortified positions, even under the most favorable circumstances. The British again retired to Boston and the siege was resumed.

Bunker Hill was more notable for the failure of both sides to observe the principles of war than for intelligent military leadership.

34

Battle of Bunker Hill, 17 June 1775.

In moving onto Breed's Hill the Americans exposed an important part of their force to destruction in an indefensible position, violating the principles of concentration of force and maneuver. They also violated the principle of unity of command, for to this day no one can say what their command structure was. The British, for their part, sacrificed all the advantages the American blunders gave them by violating the principles of maneuver and surprise, undertaking a suicidal attack on a fortified position rather than cutting it off from the rear. On the other hand, the untrained Militia showed surprising steadfastness in the face of attack by Regulars, and the rapidity with which the entrenchments were dug on Breed's Hill evidenced a proficiency in the use of the spade unknown and unencouraged in European armies. On another score, Bunker Hill created a dangerous myth that untrained and hastily raised Militia were the equal of trained troops under any circumstances, a myth to which the future course of the Revolution and of our national history was many times to give the lie.

The New England Army. The New England army that fought the Battle of Bunker Hill was hardly an army at all in the true sense of the word, but rather a conglomeration of Militia and volunteers under the loose control of several military commanders. The general scheme adopted by the New England colonies after Lexington and Concord was gradually to replace the Militia and Minutemen by volunteer forces organized in the traditional colonial manner, the officers appointed and the men enlisted under them. None were enlisted, nevertheless, beyond the end of the year 1775, and the Connecticut men only until 10 December 1775. Each of the separate colonies appointed its own commanders and there was no over-all commander for the whole force. Militia and Minutemen units were the recruiting ground for the volunteer forces. While the enlistment of the volunteer force went on, Militia units of various sorts continued to come and go.

Adoption of the Army by Congress. The Massachusetts Provincial Congress, conscious of the necessity for enlisting the support of all the colonies in resistance to Britain, appealed to the Second Continental Congress then sitting at Philadelphia to adopt the new army. Congress did so on 14 June 1775—an anniversary date still remembered in the Army of today. In view of the difficulty of transport and supply, no effort was made to raise proportionate forces from the other colonies to make the army at Boston a genuinely national one. However, 10 companies of riflemen were authorized to be raised in Pennsylvania, Virginia, and Maryland and enlisted until the end of the year. The choice of riflemen attested to the belief that specialists in the use of this new weapon would be a valuable adjunct to the musketry of New England. In recognition of the need for specialists of a different kind, Congress voted on 27 July 1775 to incorporate Col. Thomas Gridley's Regiment of Massachusetts Artillery into the army.

Choice of Washington as Commander in Chief. The day after it voted to adopt the New England army, Congress chose George Washington to be its Commander in Chief. The choice was dictated as much by political and geographic considerations as by military ones. The New Englanders felt there was no better means of obtaining southern support than by choosing a southerner as continental commander. Washington's military experience was perhaps greater than that of any other southerner. His impressive appearance and his work in the military committees of Congress inspired the confidence of his fellow members. Of others who had greater military experience, none gave evidence of the same well-rounded personality, steadfast character, and political sagacity.

Washington himself recognized, when he accepted the command, that he lacked the military training, experience, and knowledge that it required. His whole military experience had been in frontier warfare during the French and Indian War. In that experience he had exhibited ample evidence of those qualities that make a natural leader of men—courage, initiative, perseverance, and resourcefulness—but he had never participated in operations on the scale of those he was now called upon to direct. Since 1758 he had been largely absorbed in the affairs of his large plantation at Mount Vernon and in the political life of his native colony of Virginia. Nevertheless, he brought to his task traits of character and abilities as a leader that in the end more than compensated for his military deficiencies.

Gen. George Washington.

Among these were a determination and steadfastness of purpose rooted in an unshakable conviction of the righteousness of the American cause, a scrupulous sense of honor and duty, and a dignity that inspired the respect and confidence of those around him. Washington so respected the good opinion of his contemporaries and posterity that he exerted himself always to discharge to the best of his ability any responsibility assigned him. Conscious of his own defects, he was always willing to profit by experience. From the trials and tribulations of eight years he was to learn the essentials of strategy, tactics, and military organization.

The other generals. Congress also provided Washington with a group of assistants, four major generals and eight brigadiers. The same mixture of geographical, political, and military considerations was evident in their choice. Two-thirds of the generals came from New England since most of the troops under arms also came from there. Of the major generals the most notable was Charles Lee, an ex-British officer of considerable experience and reputation, and of the brigadiers, Horatio Gates, Richard Montgomery, and Nathanael Greene, the first two also ex-members of the British Army.

Deficiencies of the Army. Washington described the Army of which he formally took command on 3 July 1775 as "a mixed multitude of people . . . under very little discipline, order or government." The various colonial contingents were under different forms of organization and had different supply and pay systems. The size of regiments varied from 500 to 1,000 men. There were more than a dozen different kinds of muskets, almost all the property of the individual soldiers. Discipline was lax throughout, with men coming and going between their homes and camp without much regard for the normal rules of military life. The respect ordinarily paid by soldiers to their officers was unknown. In the Militia privates selected their officers and in the volunteer forces soldiers chose under whom they would serve. The officers had only the most elementary preparation for their positions and were, therefore, inefficient. The men, like all untrained soldiers, neglected field sanitation and did not take proper care of their persons or their camps. Shelters in which the men lived varied from tents to rude huts constructed of boards, brush, sailcloth, and turf. The arrival of the 10 rifle companies from southward, after a remarkable march, added to the strength of the army but at the same time introduced a new element of discord. These men were primarily individualists and rejected all discipline. Finding few targets to engage their attention, they tended to waste ammunition and to become restless and troublesome. In sum, although the human material was good it was untrained and there was no skilled cadre or doctrine to assist General Washington in the training. Both officers and men had to learn their jobs in the hard school of active operations and combat.

Attempts to inculcate discipline. Washington was well aware that, although the enthusiasm of a day might sustain the soldiery for a Bunker Hill, the task of driving the British from Boston would require discipline, organization, and technical military competence. He therefore set out to create out of the volunteers a force that could fight in the manner of European Regulars. Various punishments were instituted as a means of enforcing discipline—lash, pillory, wooden horse, and drumming out of camp. Elementary rules of sanitation were instituted. A strenuous effort was made to halt the random comings and goings of officers and men and to institute regular roll calls and returns of strength. Courts-martial sat almost constantly and many officers were dismissed.

Building the Army. The inculcation of discipline had to go on under extremely difficult circumstances. At the same time the siege of Boston had to be maintained and the army reenlisted in the Continental service rather than in that of the various individual colonies. Washington asked Congress for advice concerning the new establishment, and a committee of Congress visited camp in September 1775. Out of conferences emerged a plan for an army of 26 regiments of infantry of 728 men each, plus 1 regiment of riflemen and 1 of artillery, 20,372 men in all, to be uniformly paid, supplied, and administered by the Continental Congress and to be enlisted to the end of the year 1776. In each of the 26 Regular infantry regiments there were to be 8 companies, each of 86 men and 4 officers, plus an 8-man regimental staff.

The plan meant reducing 38 regiments of irregular size to 28 of uniform size and a corresponding reduction of officers of all grades. Few officers were willing to accept a reduction in rank. The men also saw their first obligation to their families and were reluctant to remain in the ranks. Few would take service under any but officers of their own choosing, or in regiments from any locality but their own. The reenlistment proceeded but slowly, and 10 December was fast approaching. This was the day when the Connecticut men were to go home, and no satisfactory force was available to replace them. Pressure was brought to bear to persuade the men to enlist or even to remain until the end of the month, but most went home anyway. Militia from Massachusetts and New Hampshire had to be hastily called in to fill their places.

The Continental Army. On 1 January 1776, the change-over from the old to the new army formally took place. Enlistments were still far from sufficient to fill the 28 regiments and men continued to come in slowly. Early in March 1776, when Washington set out to force the British out of Boston, his returns showed only 9,170 Continentals on the rolls. This failure to secure even for one year an army adequate to the task forced Washington to rely continually on short-term Militia to supplement his Regular force.

The great mistake. In retrospect, it is very clear that a great mistake was made in 1775 in enlisting an army for only one year. As events proved, Washington needed an army enlisted for the duration of the war, one that could be held together long enough to gain real proficiency. The obstacles to such a course in 1775, however, were almost insuperable. The long colonial tradition was one of short-term service for a single campaign. Almost everyone viewed the struggle with England as likely to be short. Washington himself had that conception when he first arrived in Boston, writing his wife that he expected to be back at Mount Vernon the following spring. Congress, directing a revolution that depended entirely on popular support for sustenance, could hardly be blamed for its failure to use more drastic measures to force men to undertake military service. And the trials encountered in enlisting only half an army for one year indicate how difficult it would have been to persuade even fewer to sign up for an indefinite period. Many patriots thought that to raise a long-term standing army, even among Americans, would be but to exchange an old tyranny for a new one.

The shortage of supplies. Just as serious as the manpower problem was the shortage of supplies. The colonies had long relied on England for their manufactured goods and had no ready substitute for this source in 1775. Shortages in the Army before Boston ran the whole catalogue of contemporary military supply—powder, muskets, cannon, cloth for uniforms, bayonets, camp kettles and other utensils, cartridge boxes, and salt. There was no shortage of provisions for the time being, though transportation problems and lack of salt to preserve meat threatened such shortages for the future. The Americans lost at Bunker Hill principally because they ran out of powder and had no bayonets. During the siege of Boston, Washington was reluctant to attack Gage not only because of the disorganized state of his army but also because of critical shortages of powder, cannon, and even muskets. Most of the departing Militia and volunteers took their muskets with them since they were, for the most part, their private property. To halt this practice, Washington tried to purchase these muskets for incoming recruits, but on inspection he found many of them to be in such bad shape as to be useless. Spears were constructed as a substitute for bayonets and indeed some men, for lack of muskets, were armed only with these spears.

The supply situation gradually improved during the long period of inaction before Boston that lasted from June 1775 to March 1776. Congress and the individual colonies sponsored voyages to the West Indies, whence the French and Dutch had conveniently exported quantities of war materials. Washington put some of his troops on board ship and this improvised Navy succeeded in capturing numerous British supply ships. He also sent Col. Henry Knox, later to become his Chief of Artillery, to Ticonderoga from whence in the winter of 1775–76 Knox brought some fifty pieces of captured cannon to Cambridge over poor or nonexistent roads in ice-bound New York and New England.

The Siege of Boston. With the arrival of the artillery and with his supply position generally much improved, Washington was finally ready in early March 1776 to attempt to drive the British from Bos-

OX-DRAWN SLEDS guided by soldiers of the Continental Army leave Ticonderoga with artillery for the siege of Boston.

ton.   With the Militia his army now numbered about 14,000.   On 4 March American infantry and artillery occupied Dorchester Heights, from which position their guns could dominate Boston from the south (map 3).   Gage had meantime been succeeded by Maj. Gen. William Howe, who had long had serious doubts of the feasibility of using Boston as the main base for the prosecution of the war.   While he at first thought of launching an assault against Dorchester Heights, for several days the weather was too bad to permit sending boats across the harbor and the American dispositions were such as to prevent any approach to the heights by land.   The Americans took advantage of this enforced delay to fortify Nook's Hill, standing still closer and in a more threatening position to the city.   Howe recognized the difficulty of his position and finally decided to evacuate the city, sailing to Halifax in Nova Scotia on 17 March.   The British left behind in Boston large stores of military supplies, including 250 cannon.

The Invasion of Canada.   While Washington was organizing his army and gaining his bloodless victory at Boston, other American forces took the offensive in an effort to secure Canada as a fourteenth American colony hoping to prevent its use as a British base in an invasion of the other thirteen.   The American plan called for a two-pronged attack on Quebec—one column under General Montgomery to proceed from Ticonderoga up Lake Champlain and the Richelieu River to the St. Lawrence, the other under Col. Benedict

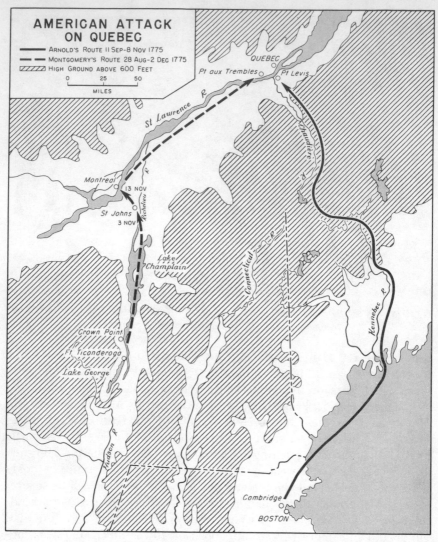

Map 4. *American attack on Quebec.*

Arnold to follow a more difficult and less known route up the Kennebec River in Maine, across the Height of Land, and down the Chaudiere (map 4). The concept was a bold one in the light of existing shortages of manpower and supplies and the wild and difficult country through which the expedition must pass. Time was of the essence since the men on these expeditions were, like those before Boston, initially enlisted only until the end of the year. Yet there was a bare chance of success, for the British Governor-General of Canada, Maj. Gen. Sir Guy Carleton, had hardly 1,000 Regulars at his disposal and there were high hopes that the inhabitants of Canada, mainly French, would rally to the American cause.

Montgomery started early in September from Ticonderoga but was delayed in capturing the British fort at St. Johns until 3 November. From thence he moved swiftly and on 13 November captured Montreal; by 22 November he had secured his position along the lower reaches of the St. Lawrence and was ready to move against Quebec. Yet this was too late for him to join Arnold in a surprise attack on the Canadian citadel. The latter had emerged at the mouth of the Chaudiere opposite the city on 8 November after a march through the wilderness that is one of the epics of American military history. Boats furnished by a contractor proved leaky, supplies of food ran short, and the portage between the Kennebec and the Chaudiere was far more difficult than had been anticipated. One group of 400 men turned back at the halfway point. The rest went on, half-starved, sick, and exhausted. About 650 of them reached Point Levis, slipped across the St. Lawrence in canoes at night, and clambered the steep banks to the Plains of Abraham on 12 November. This force proved inadequate for the capture of Quebec and Arnold moved back to Point Aux Trembles to await Montgomery.

Montgomery's force meanwhile had been seriously reduced by disease and desertion. The much hoped-for aid from the Canadians did not materialize. Men whose enlistments expired at the end of the year had little stomach for further campaigning and many left for home. After leaving garrisons at St. Johns and Montreal, Montgomery had only 300 men with which to join Arnold. By the time he arrived, Carleton in Quebec had rallied a sizable force from among the English settlers in Canada.

The attack on Quebec. Despite all the discouraging circumstances, Arnold and Montgomery refused to give up, and on the first snowy night, 30–31 December 1775, launched a desperate attack on Quebec, timed in large measure because of the expiration of the men's enlistments the next day. The attack was a failure, Montgomery was killed, and Arnold badly wounded in the leg. Arnold still refused to give up and continued to direct a siege from his hospital bed. He was later forced to relinquish command on 1 April 1776 after his leg was re-injured in a fall from a horse. During the siege, when the British in Quebec actually outnumbered their besiegers, smallpox broke out in the American Army, further depleting its ranks. Reinforcements arrived early in April, but they were over-matched by new arrivals of British Regulars from England. Finally Carleton sallied forth in early June and drove the Americans back across the St. Lawrence at all points where they had penetrated into Canada. With an army ill-supplied and decimated by disease, Maj. Gen. John Sullivan, the new commander, gave up the effort and fell back to the head of Lake Champlain.

Analysis of failure. The American failure before Quebec can hardly be attributed to any lack of leadership on the part of Montgomery and Arnold, both of whom exhibited daring, courage, and tenacity in the face of almost insuperable obstacles. Few campaigns in our history have required equal physical endurance from both officers and men. It was mainly deficiencies in organization, training, discipline, and particularly in the system of short enlistments, combined with almost insuperable logistical obstacles, that defeated the Americans. And the defeat left the road open for a British invasion of New York from the Canadian base.

The War in the South. While the major theater of war during the first year was in the North, events were also transpiring in the South that were to have major influence on the future course of the conflict. Shortly after Lexington and Concord, patriot Militia drove British royal governors to seek refuge aboard warships off the coast and seized British military installations ashore with their stores. There was considerable Tory strength in the southern colonies, and the fleeing royal governors of Virginia and North Carolina urged the British Government to send an expedition to cooperate with these Tories in reestablishing British rule in the southern provinces. In response, the British Government organized a combined naval and military force under the joint command of General Clinton and Adm. Peter Parker to go south in early 1776.

Unfortunately for the British, the expedition was delayed, and by the time it arrived off the coast of North Carolina and Virginia, Militia had dispersed the Tory forces organized in those colonies. Clinton therefore decided the British force must try to regain a base of operations at Charleston in South Carolina, the largest port in the southern colonies. But before Clinton and Parker could get to Charleston, the patriots had vastly strengthened the defenses of that city. Congress authorized the raising of 14 Continental battalions in the South and detached Maj. Gen. Charles Lee from Washington's army to direct the defense of Charleston. In addition, South Carolina Militia rallied in large numbers under Col. William Moultrie. By the time Parker's fleet arrived off Charleston on 1 June 1776, fortifications in the harbor had been strengthened and were manned by nearly 6,000 men. Moultrie, contrary to the advice of Lee, who thought the post might well become a trap, concentrated his men in a fort on Sullivan's Island later named Fort Moultrie. Parker's ships would have to pass this fort in order to enter the harbor. Parker landed Clinton's force on an adjacent island from which it was anticipated the British soldiers could wade the passage and join in the naval attack on Fort Moultrie. But on 28 June, when Parker signaled the attack, the water was too deep and Clinton's army had to stand idly by while artillery in the fort wreaked havoc with Parker's fleet. Parker even had his breeches blown off. He had to reembark Clinton's troops and return north with his battered fleet to join Howe, who by then was concentrating both army and fleet for an attack on New York. The British were not to turn their attention southward again for almost three years.

Results of the First Year. The results of the first year were in no sense decisive on any front. The British had withdrawn from Boston to re-form and await reinforcements that would give them an army equal to the task of subduing the rebellious colonies. The American offensive against Canada had failed, as had the British effort to reestablish control of the southern colonies. The greatest American achievement of the year had not been a tactical one at all, but the creation of an army. Seriously imperfect as it might yet be, this army was nevertheless in being, a barrier to the concentrated effort the British would make the following year to subdue the Colonies.

QUESTIONS

1. What part did British military policy play in leading to the American Revolution?

2. Trace the steps by which the Continental Army was formed beginning with the first preparations for war in Massachusetts.

3. What is the significance in American military history of the date 19 April 1775?

4. Analyze the conduct of both sides in the Battle of Bunker Hill, showing how each did or did not observe each of the nine principles of war.

5. What were the principal weaknesses of the New England army before Boston and how did Washington try to correct them?

6. Which side do you think gained the most from the first year of hostilities? Give reasons for your answer.

Reading List

Books applying to the Revolution as a whole

Adams, Charles F. *Studies Military and Diplomatic*. New York, 1911.

Alden, John R. *The American Revolution, 1775–83*. New York, 1954.

Bolton, Charles K. *The Private Soldier under Washington*. New York, 1902.

Miller, John C. *The Triumph of Freedom, 1775–83*. Boston, 1948.

Montross, Lynn. *Rag, Tag and Bobtail, The Story of the Continental Army, 1775–83*. New York, 1952.

Wallace, Willard M. *Appeal to Arms—A Military History of the Revolution*. New York, 1951.

Ward, Christopher. *The American Revolution*. New York, 1952. 2 vols.

Wrong, G. M. *Washington and His Comrades in Arms*. New Haven, 1921.

Specifically on the first year

Freeman, Douglas S. *George Washington*. Vol. III: *Planter and Patriot*. New York, 1951.

French, Allen. *The First Year of the American Revolution*. Boston, 1934.

Smith, Justin H. *Our Struggle for the Fourteenth Colony—Canada and the American Revolution*. New York, 1907. 2 vols.

CHAPTER 3

THE AMERICAN REVOLUTION—LONG ISLAND TO PRINCETON

The Declaration of Independence. During the first year, the Americans fought ostensibly only to preserve their rights within the British Empire. The second year saw the adoption of the Declaration of Independence on 4 July 1776, proclaiming that the thirteen colonies "are and of Right ought to be Free and Independent States." This ringing declaration announced to the world the birth of a new nation and sharply defined the issues in the developing conflict, leaving little question that it would be a long and difficult one.

The American Military Potential. The thirteen states proclaiming their independence in 1776 possessed a total population of approximately two and a half million people. Though this population was hardly a third of that of Great Britain, it was sufficient to provide a far larger potential of military manpower than the British could possibly put into the field given the difficulty of transporting troops and supplies across the Atlantic. But a considerable proportion were Loyalists, usually called Tories, who might be expected to serve the British rather than the American cause. Others were indifferent and could be swayed in accordance with the way the tides of war affected their individual fortunes. The American economy was not one that could support a large military force continually in the field. The shortage of arms and ammunition and the facilities for producing them placed a limit on the number of men who could be kept under arms. If large numbers of men were drained off into the military service, even the production of foodstuffs could not be maintained at the level necessary to support the population. In addition, the spirit of the people and their way of life militated against the establishment of a large standing army. Most of the men of military age were farmers who married young and immediately started large families. Few of them, regardless of their patriotic sentiments, were ready to undertake long terms of military service, fearing that if they did their farms and families would suffer unduly.

Weakness of Governmental Machinery. Even more serious was the fact that the Americans lacked adequate governmental machinery for harnessing the resources, human and material, they did possess. The constitutions adopted in each of the thirteen new states generally vested most of the powers of government in state legislatures, successors to the popular assemblies of the colonial period. Powers of governors were carefully restricted in accordance with the prevailing attitude of suspicion of all strong executive authority. Similarly, in the approach to the problem of union among the states, there was the same general spirit of distrust of centralized authority. The existing Continental Congress, simply a gathering of delegates chosen by the various state legislatures and without express powers of its own or an executive to carry out its enactments, was continued as the only central governing body.

The Articles of Confederation. Articles of Confederation stipulating the terms of union and granting Congress specific powers were drawn up shortly after the Declaration of Independence, but jealousies among the states prevented their ratification until 1781. In the interim Congress did exercise most of the powers granted it under the Articles, but these were insufficient to enable it efficiently to direct the war effort. Congress had no power under the Articles either to levy taxes or to raise military forces directly under its own auspices. It could only determine the Confederation's need for troops and money and set quotas for the states to meet in proportion to their population and wealth.

Finance. The states seldom filled their quotas of men, never those of money. Finance was the weakest spot in a generally weak governmental structure. If Congress had no power to tax, the state legislatures were reluctant to exercise the power they did possess. In this they only reflected a general popular opposition to taxation. Lacking other resources, both Congress and the states resorted to issues of paper currency in ever-increasing quantities. While a useful expedient in the early part of the war, this method inevitably led to first gradual and then uncontrolled inflation of the paper currency's value. This process of depreciation gradually robbed both states and Congress of the power to pay the troops, buy supplies, and otherwise meet the expenses of war.

Summary. In the lack of a central government and of an adequate financial structure lay the roots of a failure to harness the resources of the country in support of the war effort and to provide Washington with an Army adequate to meet the British on equal terms. In the end these weaknesses made French aid an essential ingredient of American success.

Congress and the Army. Lacking an executive, Congress had to rely on various boards and committees to perform its executive functions. For handling affairs relating to the Army, Congress set up in June 1776 the Board of War and Ordnance chosen from its membership. This gave way in 1777 to a board composed of members from outside Congress. Neither of these arrangements worked well, and Congress was continually regulating purely administrative matters by action of the entire membership or appointing special committees to go to camp. Inspired by fear of seizure of political control by military leaders, Congress kept a suspiciously watchful eye on the military force and its commanders. Washington countered these suspicions very effectively by constantly deferring to congressional wishes. And he was rewarded by the assiduity with which Congress usually adopted his recommendations. The faults in military policy during the Revolution were due less to congressional failure to enact wise laws than to the lack of adequate governmental machinery to carry out the laws that were enacted.

Channels of administration and supply were confused and divided between Congress and the states. By the military provisions of the Articles, the states were responsible for raising troops for the Continental Army, for initially organizing and equipping them, and for appointing officers through the rank of colonel. Congress issued commissions for the officers selected by the states and itself appointed all general officers. Once the Continental Army was in the field, Congress was also mainly responsible for administering and supplying it. Over the Militia, which had to be so frequently called out to supplement the Continentals, Congress had no express control at all, though it frequently had to arrange for the supply and administration of Militia forces operating with the Army.

Organization of the Army. The Continental Army was organized generally on the British model. It was mainly composed of infantry and artillery, with very little cavalry. The basic unit of organization was the regiment or battalion composed of 8 companies, instead of 10 as in the British Army. Organization above this level was highly flexible. A brigade was usually formed of several regiments and was commanded by a brigadier general; a division, by a similar grouping of several brigades commanded by a major general. Artillery was organized into a brigade of four regiments under a chief of Artillery, Brig. Gen. Henry Knox, but the various companies were usually distributed among the infantry battalions. There was a small corps of engineers and an even smaller contingent of artificers, who handled the servicing and repair of ordnance. Supply and transport were under the supervision of The Quartermaster General, but civilians rather than service troops were usually employed to do the actual work.

The staff. On the advice of Washington, Congress provided him with a staff generally corresponding to that in the British Army. The most important staff officer was The Quartermaster General, responsible not only for transportation and delivery of supplies but also for arranging the camp, regulating marches, and establishing the order of battle of the Army. In addition, the staff included an Adjutant General charged with issuing orders in the name of the commander and handling other administrative details; a Judge Advocate

General responsible for legal affairs; a Paymaster General and Commissary General of Musters responsible for personnel administration; a Commissary General of Provisions responsible for procurement of food; a Clothier General responsible for procurement of clothing; a Chief Surgeon as head of the hospital service; and a Chief Engineer in charge of bridges and fortifications.

With the exception of The Quartermaster General, all these staff officers had primarily administrative and supply functions. The modern concept of a general staff that acts as a sort of collective brain for the commander had no real counterpart in the 18th century. For advice on matters of strategy and operations, Washington relied on a Council of War made up of his principal subordinate commanders. Aides-de-camp took care of routine headquarters work, such as the writing and delivery of orders, messages, and reports.

Weaknesses. Both organization and staff work suffered from the confusion in the governmental levels at the top and from the other manifold troubles that plagued the Continental Army in general. Regiments organized by the various States inevitably had different forms of organization, different methods of drill, and different standards of discipline and training. Militia organizations usually provided additional variety to the pattern. Owing to the failure of the States to meet their quotas, regiments were constantly understrength. There were few Americans with knowledge or experience in staff work, and the direction of administrative and supply functions under conditions of divided authority and inadequate means was a task requiring a perseverance that even fewer possessed. Staff officers, like the men of the Continental Army, often found their private affairs more pressing than military service. Others resigned because they were simply overwhelmed by the immense difficulty of supplying and administering an army for which Congress was unable to provide the necessary means. As a result, both supply and administration were poorly handled and the proper functions of the administrative staff often devolved on an overworked commander and his aides.

Britain's Problem. Despite the weakness in American organization, the British Government faced no easy task in subduing the revolt. While England had the central administration and well-organized Army and Navy the Americans so sorely lacked, the whole establishment was ill-prepared for a long struggle in the Colonies. A large burden of debt incurred in the wars of the preceding century had forced economies in both Army and Navy that had deprived them of much of their strength. Administrative and supply systems, though far superior to anything the Americans could improvise, were also characterized by division and confusion of authority. The ministers serving George III were mostly mediocre men, and many of them were both corrupt and incompetent. The Army had to be considerably expanded to provide the force of 40 to 50 thousand men Maj. Gen. Sir William Howe said would be necessary in America and at the same time to maintain garrisons in other parts of the world. Unable to persuade enough citizens to enlist, Britain had to resort to hiring mercenaries from small German states, particularly Hesse-Cassel (hence Hessians). Once having raised the force, Britain had to transport it across three thousand miles of the Atlantic— a voyage of two to four months—and support it in America.

While Britain's control of the sea enabled her to land troops almost at will on the long American coastline, logistical problems multiplied rapidly once British forces moved inland. There were no strategic centers by whose capture the British could have put an end to the revolt. Instead, they had to establish their rule over a vast geographic area for which they could not possibly have furnished adequate occupation troops. To achieve a victory that would have had any meaning, they had to persuade the majority of the people to accept British rule again. It was with this in mind that General Howe undertook his campaign in 1776 with sword in one hand and olive branch in the other.

American Grass Roots Strength. To reconcile the people to British rule was an almost impossible task. The organization the patriots lacked at the top they did have in the grass roots, that is, in most of the local communities throughout America. If Tories were numerous, their influence was seldom proportionate to their numbers. Except in certain areas where Tories were heavily concentrated, the patriots were usually able to seize the machinery of local government, to hold it until the British Army appeared, and then to regain it when it went away.

The Militia. Farmers, though unwilling to enlist in the Army, were willing to take up arms in the Militia when called by local authority. The Militia system was undoubtedly a most expensive and inefficient method of mobilizing manpower, but it had the strength of long tradition behind it and it enabled men to devote part of their time to military service while still remaining part of the agricultural labor force. Inherently weak in organization and discipline, Militia could not stand against the British in the open field but could conduct effective guerilla warfare. Granted the lack of governmental machinery for mobilizing and maintaining a Regular Army adequate to meet the British on equal terms, the Militia system at least enabled the Americans to keep an army in the field usually numerically equal to the British, even if inferior in discipline and training.

The Campaign in New York. With the evacuation of Boston the attention of both Washington and Howe shifted to New York. Both recognized that it was a position offering the British the greatest strategic advantage. It held a central position between New England and the colonies to the southward. Its sea approaches were well suited to amphibious landing. If there was any strategic approach by which the British could gain victory, it would be by driving from New York up the Hudson River and joining forces with British troops advancing down the lake and river chain from Canada, thus dividing New England from the rest of the country. New York also could provide a good jumping off point for an advance on the seat of the Continental Congress at Philadelphia.

Washington moves to New York. With these considerations in mind, in April and May 1776 Washington brought most of his army down from Boston to New York. His force on arrival numbered about 10,000 Continentals and Militia. By dint of the efforts of Congress and the neighboring States, this force was raised by 26 August, the day the battle for New York began, to something over 20,000, the largest number Washington had under his personal command at any time during the Revolution. Most of the men were either Militia or recently enlisted Continentals who had not been exposed to the discipline and training given the previous year before Boston. Only a few southern regiments that Congress had authorized in the interim were enlisted beyond the end of the year 1776.

Howe's advantage. Against Washington's heterogeneous force, General Howe brought from Halifax and England a body of 32,000 well-trained British and Hessian Regulars, supported by a powerful British Fleet under his brother, Adm. Lord Richard Howe. In early July 1776 the first part of the force arrived from Halifax and debarked on undefended Staten Island. There General Howe waited for a month and a half while the rest of the British land and naval forces sent from England gathered.

The geography of the area gave the Howe brothers an advantage that General Washington was all too slow in recognizing. The city of New York stood on Manhattan Island separated from the mainland by the Hudson River on the New Jersey side and the Harlem River on the New York side (map 5). There was only one connecting link, Kingsbridge, over the Harlem River at the northern tip of Manhattan. Across the East River on Long Island, Brooklyn Heights stood in a position dominating the southern tip of Manhattan. With the naval forces at their disposal, the Howes could land troops on either Long Island or Manhattan proper and send their warships up the Hudson and East Rivers a considerable distance.

Command of the sea thus gave the British the initiative and rendered any position Washington's army might take on the two islands virtually untenable from the start. The American commander might better have withdrawn to the highlands along the Hudson north of the city, an easily defensible position well suited to American capabilities.

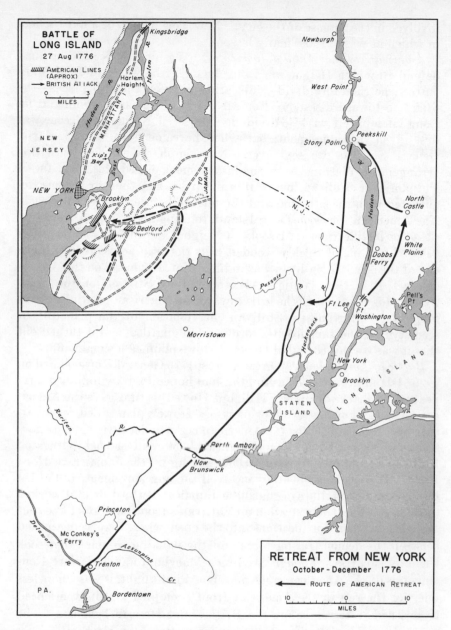

Map 5. *Retreat from New York, Oct–Dec 1776. Inset, Battle of Long Island, 27, Aug 1776.*

There he could prevent General Howe from moving up the Hudson or, in case the British chose Philadelphia as their objective, shift his forces quickly to New Jersey to counter a move in that direction. But Washington feared the loss of New York without a fight would be a serious psychological blow to the American cause. Furthermore, it does not appear that at the time he realized the military difficulties

53

involved in the defense of the city. New York was to be a hard school in which he was to learn many lessons.

American command and dispositions. Washington decided he must defend Brooklyn Heights on Long Island if he was to defend Manhattan; he therefore divided his army between the two places—the first step toward disaster. For all practical purposes, command on Long Island itself was also divided. Maj. Gen. Nathanael Greene was first given the assignment, but when he came down with malaria, General Sullivan was sent over. Not completely satisfied with this arrangement, Washington at the last moment placed Maj. Gen. Israel Putnam over Sullivan, but Putnam hardly had time to become acquainted with the situation and the terrain before the British struck. The American forces on Long Island, totaling about 10,000, were disposed in fortifications on Brooklyn Heights and in forward positions back of the line of thickly wooded hills that ran across the southern end of the island. Sullivan was in immediate command on the American left, Brig. Gen. William Alexander, Lord Stirling, on the right. Four roads ran through the hills toward the American positions (inset map 5). Unfortunately Sullivan, in violation of the principle of security, left the Jamaica-Bedford road unguarded, and it turned out that it was via this road that General Howe planned his main effort.

Battle of Long Island. On 22 August 1776 General Howe landed on Long Island in force. Washington had hoped to draw him into a repeat performance of Bunker Hill, but Howe this time gave the Americans lessons in maneuver and surprise. Howe's plan called for an attack by a force of 5,000 on the American right under Stirling, a demonstration by a similar force on Sullivan's front, and the main attack on Sullivan's flank by a force of 10,000 moving up the Jamaica-Bedford Road. It was an excellently conceived turning movement, and aided by the American failure to guard the Jamaica-Bedford Road it worked perfectly. The demonstration on Sullivan's front lured his forces out from behind their fortifications into the open, where they were crushed between the demonstrating force and the flanking columns that took them by surprise. Though Stirling's Maryland and Delaware Continentals on the American right put up a valiant fight, it was a hopeless one, for the rest of the American front crumpled and inexperienced troops fled in terror before the British and Hessian bayonets. The remnants fell back to the entrenchments on Brooklyn Heights.

One of the great mysteries of the Revolution is why General Howe failed to follow up his success and launch a direct attack on the disorganized and panicky Americans on the heights. Perhaps it was because he had bitter memories of Bunker Hill, or perhaps because he looked on the destruction of Washington's army as of lesser import than the reconciliation of the country to British rule. In any case, he decided to take the fortifications on the heights by regular

Retreat from Long Island, 1776.

approaches in the traditional style of Vauban, a process that would require several days.

American evacuation of Long Island. This delay enabled the Americans to escape, for Washington now realized that the position on Long Island was untenable and that at any moment the British Fleet might sail up the East River and cut off his entire force. Luckily wind and weather held up British warships. Boats were collected from all available sources around New York City, and skilled fishermen from Col. John Glover's Marblehead Regiment were put to operating them. Despite several incidents that threatened disaster, the evacuation was successfully completed under the cover of darkness on the night of 29–30 August, and the British awoke the next morning to find their quarry gone.

Kip's Bay. Having reconcentrated his forces in Manhattan, General Washington deployed them at the danger points stretching from the city to Harlem Heights on the north end. Garrisons in Fort Washington and Fort Lee guarded the Hudson on the New York and New Jersey sides respectively. But morale was now at a low ebb; militia began to take off by companies, and there was a high rate of desertion among the Continentals. Beyond this, the position of the whole army was still precarious, for the British clearly had the capability of landing on the New York mainland in Washington's rear and isolating his force on Manhattan Island.

General Howe's next move, on 15 September, was not onto the mainland but in the center of Manhattan Island at Kip's Bay—the site of present 34th Street and East River but then well above the city.

Connecticut Militia posted at this point broke and ran without making any effective resistance to the British landing. Washington, seized by one of his rare fits of temper, raged at the troops and beat them with the flat of his sword but to no avail. All Howe had to do now was to move rapidly across the island in order to cut off American troops in lower Manhattan. But again he delayed, awaiting the landing and assembly of his whole force, and Putnam was able to bring the troops from the city up the west side of the island to join the rest of the American forces in new fortifications on Harlem Heights.

Harlem Heights. The day after Kip's Bay, a small battle occurred that gave evidence for the first time in the New York campaign that Americans, if well led, were capable of defeating regulars in the open field. Lt. Col. Thomas Knowlton led a picked body of 120 men out to reconnoiter the enemy lines and engaged in a spirited exchange of fire with British pickets. When Knowlton retired in an orderly manner, the British sent a detachment of 400 light infantry to follow him. Learning that the British detachment was unsupported, Washington laid a trap by having a small force demonstrate on the British front while a much larger one hid in the woods. At the same time Knowlton, reinforced by Virginia riflemen, slipped around to take the British in the rear. The British discovered the hidden force early enough and retired, but in their withdrawal they ran into Knowlton's command. A sharp action followed into which both sides threw reinforcements. The British were thrown back, but Washington decided to break off the battle when he saw that Howe was going to move up in force. The little victory on Harlem Heights did much to restore the morale of a defeated army. Knowlton, killed in action, left a fine example of courage and heroism for the American Army.

White Plains. After a month of delay in front of Harlem Heights, in mid-October General Howe finally took the obvious course and landed at Pell's Point on the New York mainland in Washington's rear. Washington now quickly got out of the Manhattan trap, crossing the Harlem River at Kingsbridge and moving his army into position at White Plains. He left about 6,000 men behind in Fort Washington and Fort Lee under the command of General Greene. After a costly assault to gain one hill, Howe delayed an attack on Washington's main position, and Washington again moved away to the north toward the highlands. Howe now quickly seized the opportunity to interpose his army between Washington and the Hudson River forts, moving to Dobbs Ferry on the Hudson.

Fall of Fort Washington and Fort Lee. General Washington should have evacuated the forts and reconcentrated his army on the New Jersey side of the Hudson. But on the advice of Greene, he decided to hold on, and again divided his army into three main portions. One part, about 8,000 men, he left with Maj. Gens. Charles Lee and William Heath at Peekskill and North Castle respectively to guard the passes through the highlands, and moved with a second part, about 5,000 men, across the Hudson into New Jersey. General Howe then moved quickly against the third part, the troops defending Forts Washington and Lee. The attack against Fort Washington was supported by British warships on the Hudson, and the fort's garrison surrendered on 16 November after only spotty resistance. In this disaster the Americans lost nearly 3,000 men, mostly as prisoners of war, and large quantities of munitions. Three days later Maj. Gen. Lord Charles Cornwallis landed with 4,500 men on the Jersey shore eight miles above Fort Lee, and Greene decided on a hasty evacuation. He got out with most of his men but was forced to leave almost all his supplies behind.

The Retreat Across New Jersey. General Washington gathered the remnants of his army behind the Hackensack River and began a rapid retreat across New Jersey with Howe's advance forces under General Cornwallis in rapid pursuit. With each step in the withdrawal the Army dwindled in strength, and few companies of New Jersey Militia rallied to the cause. In early December the remaining force, only about 3,000 men, got across the Delaware into Pennsylvania just as Cornwallis was arriving in Trenton. But winter was approaching and General Howe decided that the time for active campaigning was at an end. Instead of collecting boats and continuing the pursuit of Washington, as Cornwallis urged, Howe ordered his men into winter quarters, confident that he could shatter the small remaining rebel force with one blow the following spring. Howe placed garrisons at Perth Amboy, New Brunswick, Princeton, Trenton, and Bordentown, and sent a detachment to Rhode Island that captured Newport and remained as a garrison there. The rest of the British Army retired to winter among the delights of New York City.

The Northern Front. Meanwhile, on the old familiar battleground around Lake Champlain, the campaign of 1776 was ending more favorably for the Americans (map 9). With reinforcements that brought his total force to about 10,000 British, Hessians, Canadians, and Indian auxiliaries, Brig. Gen. Sir Guy Carleton sought to follow up his victories won in Canada in June and pursued the retreating American forces down to the head of Lake Champlain with the obvious intention of driving through to form a junction with Howe in New York. To oppose him, Maj. Gen. Philip Schuyler managed to raise a force of about 9,000 Regulars and Militia. It was not Schuyler, however, but Brig. Gen. Benedict Arnold, his subordinate, who seized the initiative. Arnold built a "fleet" of small boats on Lake Champlain and manned them with soldiers. This improvised navy was able to so delay Carleton's advance that mid-October found him only so far as Crown Point with the strong defenses of Ticonderoga still before him. To take Ticonderoga would require an orthodox siege operation and with winter approaching Carleton prudently decided it was too late in the season. So he retired to Canada, leaving the British with no forward base from which to launch the next year's campaign, a fact that was to have immense strategic significance.

American Cause at Low Ebb. This successful defensive was at the time far overshadowed by the disastrous defeats Washington had suffered. The approach of the end of 1776 found the American cause at a low ebb. Three different forces remained in the field—Washington's army in Pennsylvania, Heath's and Lee's forces guarding the Highlands along the Hudson, and Schuyler's army in New York. All were being rapidly depleted by desertion, disease, and the departure of Militia units. Most appalling of all was the fact that the terms of enlistment of the major portion of the troops remaining expired at the end of the year 1776. In December 1776 Washington was faced with the same task that had proven so difficult under far better conditions a year earlier, the reconstitution of the Continental Army.

The New Establishment. Even before the defeats in New York, Washington had been urging on Congress the necessity of long-term enlistments and of offering sufficient inducement to keep experienced men in the service. After his bitter disappointments with Militia and untrained Continentals, who ran away on Long Island and at Kip's Bay, his importunities became more urgent. On 2 October 1776 Congress finally responded by voting a new military establishment that on paper at least had the appearance of adequacy. Eighty-eight battalions of troops, about 60,000 men, were to be raised by the states and placed on the Continental Establishment enlisted to "serve during the present war." Unfortunately this latter provision was weakened by another law permitting an alternative term of enlistment for three years.

Troops in the new establishment were not to be recruited directly into the Continental service but in various state lines. States would control the appointment of officers through the rank of colonel. It was to be a truly Continental army raised from all the states in proportion to population. Quotas varied from 15 battalions respectively for Virginia and Massachusetts to 1 for Delaware and 1 for Georgia. A continental bounty of $20, 100 acres of land, and a new suit of clothes was authorized for each private or noncommissioned officer who enlisted.

In short, the new army was to be raised in accordance with the provisions of the unratified Articles of Confederation, and it promised to have all the weaknesses inherent in the military provisions of that document. The congressional legislation left many questions unanswered as to the extent of Washington's control or influence on appointments, promotions, and dismissals of the officers of the various state lines. There was soon ample evidence that political favoritism would play a more important part in state appointments than military ability and that the old experienced officers already with the Army would be slighted in favor of new and inexperienced men. To regulate these questions, most of the state governors promised to send commissions to Washington's camp.

Neither new regiments nor state commissions put in their appearance during the dark days of December 1776. And Washington soon learned that few of the men of his existing army could be tempted even by the bounty to remain in the service. Schuyler, Heath, and Lee had much the same experience. It was evident that Congress had acted too late to provide an army to tide over the winter, that few new troops would come in before spring 1777. Washington asked Congress for an increase from 88 to 110 battalions, less with any genuine conviction that the men could be raised to fill the entire quota than on the hope that "the officers of a hundred and ten battalions will recruit many more men than those of eighty-eight." The members of Congress, who had fled from Philadelphia to Baltimore, this time quickly acceded to Washington's wishes, voting on 26 December 1776 not only to grant him the right to raise the additional forces but also dictatorial powers for a period of six months to appoint and remove officers, to apply to the states for Militia levies, and to seize private property and enforce martial law.

The Decision to Attack. The vote of dictatorial powers was not the end that Washington was seeking, and indeed he used them very sparingly. He perceived that only by reawakening the spirit of the Army and of the people by some spectacular stroke could he hope to check the tide of despair and confusion that was sweeping the American states. Appraising the possibilities, he decided to concentrate all the troops available from the old Army of 1776 and strike a blow at the British before the end of December. Washington had been pressing General Lee to join him with the troops from Peekskill since he had begun the retreat across New Jersey, but Lee was dilatory, evidently placing his own military judgment above that of Washington. Finally Lee did move and—one might even say fortunately—he himself was captured by the British en route. His troops, their numbers dwindled from 5,000 to 2,000, came on to join Washington. Eight decimated regiments were also drawn from Schuyler's troops in New York. The arrival of about 2,000 Pennsylvania Militia brought Washington's total force to something like 7,000 men by Christmas 1776.

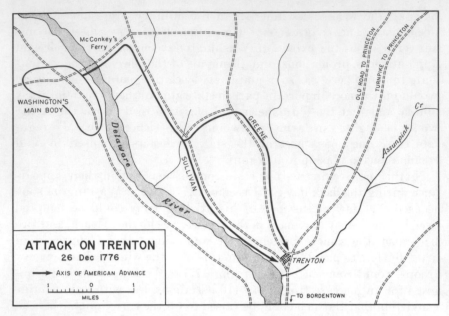

Map 6. Attack on Trenton, 26 Dec. 1776.

The Battle of Trenton.   The scattered British dispositions in New Jersey invited surprise attack.   From a patriot butcher who passed as a Tory, Washington learned that the Hessian garrison at Trenton numbered 1,400 men and that its commander, Col. Johannes Rall, was given to heavy drinking and neglect of security.   Trenton therefore was chosen as the objective of a surprise attack to be delivered one hour before dawn on 26 December.   Washington's plan called for the main force of 2,400 men to cross the Delaware at McConkey's Ferry and then proceed in two divisions by separate roads running into the main street of Trenton from opposite ends (map 6).   A supporting force, mainly Militia, under Col. John Cadwalader was to cross below near Bordentown and engage the Hessians at that point.   A smaller force of Militia under Brig. Gen. James Ewing was to cross directly opposite Trenton to block the route of escape across Assunpink Creek.

The main force was safely ferried across the Delaware by Colonel Glover's Marblehead men, despite the large cakes of ice in the river. It was 0300, 26 December, before they were all assembled and the silent march to Trenton began.   Shoeless men left a trail of blood in the new fallen snow.   Meanwhile, Cadwalader was able to get only part of his force across and Ewing none.   Disappointing though this was, it did not prevent the success of the main attack.   The two columns, under Greene and Sullivan, converged on the town at 0800, later than scheduled but still in time to achieve complete surprise.   Hessian sentries gave the alarm too late, for before the rest of the soldiery could be roused and formed in line of battle the two columns closed in on

ARTILLERY AT TRENTON. Alexander Hamilton's company of New York Artillery opened the fight at dawn, blasting the bewildered Hessians as they tried to form ranks in the street. The most significant artillery piece used by the Continental forces is the 6-pounder brass field gun, seen in the center of the photograph.

them from both ends of the town. Rall's efforts to rally his men failed and he himself was killed. Within an hour and a half after the attack began, the Hessians surrendered. Only 400 were able to escape to Bordentown. About 30 were killed and the prisoner count was 918. The Americans lost only 4 killed—2 from freezing—and 4 wounded.

Washington had hoped to continue to Bordentown, but learning that Cadwalader and Ewing had failed to cross in force, seeing that his men were exhausted, and desiring to get the captured Hessians and supplies to safety, he decided to return across the Delaware. But once across and the men rested, he determined to strike another blow. By an impassioned appeal to their patriotism coupled with a bounty of $10, he was able to persuade most of the men enlisted to the end of the year to volunteer to remain for six weeks longer. General Heath was ordered to join him with the remaining force left guarding the highland passes on the Hudson. Encouraged by the victory at Trenton, Pennsylvania and New Jersey Militia began to come in in greater numbers. By these expedients Washington was able to gather a sufficient force to put 5,200 men, about half Militia, across the Delaware again on the night of 30–31 December 1776.

The Battle of Princeton. Meanwhile the British had not been idle. Cornwallis, their commander in New Jersey, also gathered most of his scattered forces and on 2 January 1777 moved into Trenton with

6,000 men, taking a position confronting Washington along Assunpink Creek (map 6). Washington's back was to the Delaware and Cornwallis was confident that he had no safe line of retreat. His men being exhausted from a long march, the British commander thought he could safely delay his attack until the following morning, 3 January. But Washington, learning of a road by which he could escape around the British rear, slipped away in the night leaving campfires brightly burning to deceive the British. His objective was to seize British supplies at Princeton and New Brunswick.

By sunrise, when Cornwallis awoke to find no enemy in front of him, the American Army was within two miles of Princeton. There they ran into two British regiments just leaving Princeton to join Cornwallis. In the ensuing engagement the Americans inflicted heavy losses on these British Regulars and drove them in disorderly retreat toward Trenton and New Brunswick. Washington had difficulty in restraining himself from following to New Brunswick but desisted, knowing that his men were exhausted and that Cornwallis would soon be behind him. Prudently he moved north to Morristown, where woods and hills afforded natural protection against British attack, and went into winter quarters there. From Morristown he could move quickly to counter any British effort to advance up the Hudson or overland against Philadelphia. But Howe had had enough of winter war. He withdrew all his troops from New Jersey save those along the Raritan River between New Brunswick and Perth Amboy. For six months the whole front was quiet.

Significance of the Victories. In large measure, the victories at Trenton and Princeton accomplished what Washington had set out to do. They infused new life into the American cause, new confidence in the Army and its commander. Recruiting of the new Army was thus facilitated, and the Militia encouraged to come in to hold the line while the new Army was being formed. Valuable military supplies had been taken from the British. In terms of territory, the greater part of New Jersey had been freed from British occupation, giving the patriot elements there an opportunity to deal with the numerous Tories who abounded in certain sections. All in all, Trenton and Princeton proved that the results of the New York campaign had not been so disastrous as it at first appeared. True the British had New York and some of the surrounding country, but only there and at Newport, R. I., did they have footholds at the end of 1776. Americans could well afford to trade a little space for a great deal of time.

Washington's Growing Generalship. Not the least important thing about Trenton and Princeton was the fact that they showed Washington to be a far abler general than his professional critics had thought after the defeats in New York. He had concentrated the remnants of an army dispirited by defeat and continued withdrawals, and with it he had executed a brilliant offensive, striking the enemy by surprise with superior numbers at critical points. In truth it can be said that in the execution of the two strokes east of the Delaware, Washington applied all nine of the principles of war successfully. Only the weakness of his army prevented him from following through to gain more decisive results, for he clearly had the inclination to do so after both Trenton and Princeton. Though not yet completely master of the techniques and tactics of European-style warfare, Washington was learning what was more important—to adapt both his strategy and his tactics to the terrain on which he had to fight and to the capabilities of his own army and his opponent's.

QUESTIONS

1. Why were the Americans unable to put an army into the field in 1776 larger than that of the British?

2. How did the division of authority between Congress and the states work against the development of an efficient military establishment?

3. Contrast the strategic situation of the Americans with that of the British at the opening of the campaign of 1776.

4. Analyze the conduct of the commanders on both sides in the New York campaign, showing in what ways each did or did not observe the principles of war and the results of their actions.

5. Why did the decisive British victory in New York not end the war? If the Americans had won such a decisive victory would it have ended it?

6. Show how Washington's conduct of the Trenton and Princeton campaigns illustrates all nine of the principles of war. What principles did the British violate?

Reading List

See reading list at the end of chapter 3 for books pertaining to the Revolution generally.

Andersen, Troyer S. *The Command of the Howe Brothers during the American Revolution.* New York, 1936.

Bill, Alfred H. *The Campaign of Princeton, 1776–1777.* Princeton, 1948.

Freeman, Douglas S. *George Washington,* Vol. IV: *Leader of the Revolution.* New York, 1951.

Johnston, Henry P. *The Battle of Harlem Heights, September 16, 1776.* New York, 1897.

CHAPTER 4

THE AMERICAN REVOLUTION—BRANDYWINE TO NEWPORT

The Army of 1777. Washington's hopes in 1777 for an army even approximating the size Congress had voted were doomed to disappointment. Of the 76,000 men authorized in 1776, only 8,000 had enlisted in the Continental service when Washington took the field in May 1777. The total enlistment for the year was 34,820, but nothing like this number was ever under arms at any given time. Battle casualties, sickness, and desertion kept the Continentals under Washington below 10,000 at all times, and the number in the northern army under Schuyler and Gates never exceeded 3,000. Those who did enlist for three years or for the duration gave the Continental Army a hard core of veterans, but since they were so few the old practice of supplementing the Continentals with Militia had to continue.

The problem of securing and keeping good officers was also acute. Many were disappointed by appointments and promotions made by Congress and the states; practically all found their pay and the provision for retirement inadequate in view of the mounting cost of living. Some able men, like Col. John Stark of New Hampshire, resigned. Others, like Benedict Arnold, whose promotion to major general was delayed while men with less brilliant records were advanced ahead of him, nursed grudges.

Foreign Aid. A brighter spot in the picture was the arrival of military supplies from France. The French court had been carefully watching the American revolt, seeking an opportunity to redress the balance of power in Europe so heavily tipped in England's favor by her victory in the Seven Years' War. In 1776 Congress sent a mission to France to seek supplies and financial aid and to sound out the French Government on the possibilities of entering the war on the American side. The French ministers preferred to move with caution, awaiting some proof of the American states' ability and determination to resist, but did agree to the secret dispatch of military supplies under the guise of a commercial transaction. The supplies arriving in early 1777 were the beginning of what was to be a continuous flow. The French Charleville musket, an improved flintlock superior in some respects to "Brown Bess," eventually became almost the standard arm of the Continental infantry.

Foreign volunteers. The supplies were accompanied by an influx of foreign officer volunteers, men of professional experience in European armies. While the Continental Army was sadly in need of professional guidance, most of these men were ill-adapted to give it. Many were impecunious fortune seekers, who neither spoke English nor understood how to handle American citizen-soldiers. The American mission in Paris, anxious to secure good will abroad, at first issued commissions wholesale, much to the embarrassment of Congress and of Washington. On Washington's advice, Congress finally repudiated most of these commissions. Some of the foreign volunteers, however, were given positions of importance in the Continental Army and rendered invaluable service. To name only a few, Louis DuPortail, a Frenchman, and Thaddeus Kosciuszko, a Pole, did much to advance the art of engineering in the Continental Army; Casimir Pulaski organized its first genuine cavalry contingent; and Baron Friedrich W. A. von Steuben provided effective instruction in organization and drill. The Marquis de Lafayette, an influential French nobleman who financed his own way, stood in a separate category and, at the age of 21, was given a command as a major general under Washington.

British Strategy in 1777. The operations of the British Army in 1777 provided one of the most striking examples in military history of the dangers of divided command. At the beginning of the campaign the British had two forces based respectively on New York and Canada. Logically the situation called for a combined effort of the two to secure the Hudson River line by forming a junction in the vicinity of Albany. But the two forces were under separate commanders—General Howe in New York and Lt. Gen. John Burgoyne, who had replaced Carleton, in Canada. Burgoyne started an advance south from Canada in June on the assumption that Howe would move north to meet him. But Howe decided that his objective should be Philadelphia. The ultimate blame for the events that followed probably rests with Lord George Germain, head of the British Colonial Office in London, who blithely approved both plans and issued no instructions to insure coordination between the two commanders. Yet neither Howe nor Burgoyne can be absolved, for each persisted in going his own way without regard for the other's actions. Howe did leave a small force in New York under General Clinton but it was only enough for a "starved offensive," and Clinton did not even attempt to create a diversion to aid Burgoyne until it was too late.

The campaign of 1777 thus falls into two parts: the first, a conflict between Washington's and Howe's armies in Pennsylvania; the second, a struggle along the northern reaches of the Hudson. Washington perceived the connection between the two much more clearly than did Howe. His dispositions show a clear appreciation of the importance of the principles of mass and economy of force. The major portion of his army he kept with him in front of Howe, while he detached a small part to the northward to aid in defeating Burgoyne, including therein a contingent of riflemen well suited to operations in the wooded terrain of the north. A third force, reduced to an absolute minimum, he kept under General Putnam in the New York Highlands to oppose any advance north by Clinton.

Howe's Drive to Philadelphia. Both Washington and Howe spent the entire spring and most of the summer in fruitless maneuver in New Jersey. Uncertain as to Howe's intentions, the American commander constantly sought to keep in position to block a move either up the Hudson or against Philadelphia. Strong forts were built along the Delaware River to block any approach by sea to the Continental capital. Finally in mid-August Howe retired to New York, placed most of his army aboard ship, sailed down the coast and up Chesapeake Bay to Head of Elk in Maryland (map 7). Howe's intention to take Philadelphia was now abundantly clear, and Washington rapidly moved southward to meet him. On 11 September 1777 he took up a defensive position near Chad's Ford on Brandywine Creek, athwart the main road to Philadelphia, with a force of about 11,000 men.

Battle of Brandywine. Washington disposed his army in two main parts, one directly opposite Chad's Ford under his personal command and the other under General Sullivan guarding the right flank upstream where the creek was easily fordable at many points. Howe again, as on Long Island, conceived a turning movement that almost succeeded in trapping the American Army. While Lt. Gen. Wilhelm von Knyphausen's Hessian troops demonstrated opposite Chad's Ford, a larger force under Lord Cornwallis marched upstream, crossed the Brandywine, and moved around to take Sullivan in the rear. American intelligence was faulty, and Washington was led to believe the main attack would develop on his front. Only at the eleventh hour did he get positive information of Cornwallis' movement. Sullivan was in process of changing front when the British struck him at 1600 and his men retreated in confusion. Meanwhile, Washington had hastily dispatched General Greene with two brigades to support Sullivan, and, in a valiant rear-guard action, Greene's troops saved the rest of the army from envelopment. The detachment of Greene weakened the front opposite the ford, and Washington had also to retreat before Knyphausen. Nevertheless, the trap was averted and the army retired in good order to Chester.

Fall of Philadelphia. Washington's army still lay between Howe and Philadelphia and was in good condition to fight. At Warren's Tavern on 16 September Washington almost took the British by surprise, but rain intervened, wetting the powder and ball of the American troops, who had few cartridge boxes. Washington then withdrew across the Schuylkill, leaving Brig. Gen. Anthony Wayne with a rear

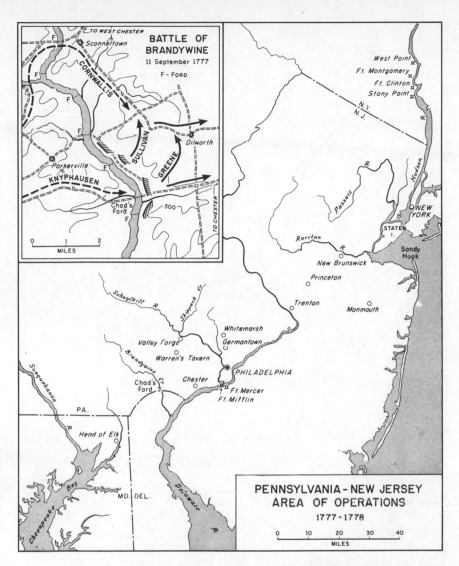

Map 7. Pennsylvania-New Jersey area of operations, 1777–1778.

guard on the other side of the river. A British contingent took Wayne's force by surprise and in a silent bayonet attack (the British Regulars had even removed the flints from their guns) almost annihilated it. Howe followed with a feint at Washington's right, forcing the latter to move further up the Schuylkill; whereupon he quickly recrossed the river and interposed his army between Washington and Philadelphia. On 26 September he moved into the city unopposed.

Battle of Germantown. Once in Philadelphia, Howe dispersed his forces, stationing 9,000 men at Germantown north of the city,

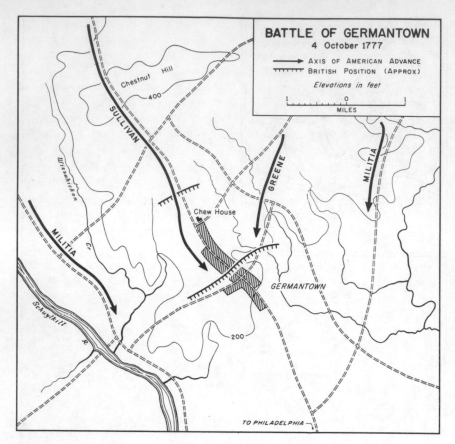

Map 8. Battle of Germantown, 4 October 1777.

3,000 in New Jersey, and the remainder in Philadelphia itself. Washington now sought to repeat his victory at Trenton by a surprise attack on the British contingent at Germantown. The plan was much like that used at Trenton but involved far more complicated movements of much larger bodies of troops. Four columns marching over separate roads were to converge on Germantown simultaneously. Sullivan and Greene with Continental divisions were to attack the British front and right respectively, while Militia in two separate columns undertook the envelopment of both British flanks (map 8). All four columns were to arrive within two miles of the enemy's pickets at 0200, halt there until 0400, and make simultaneous attacks at 0500.

The columns started on the night of 3 October from a camp on Skippack Creek, about 16 miles north of Germantown, but failed to arrive in time to coordinate their attacks; the two Militia columns never really got into the battle at all. A heavy fog hanging over the area at dawn made it difficult to distinguish friend from foe. Sullivan's column arrived first, a half hour before Greene's, and

68

drove the British back in hard fighting until finally held up by British fire from the Chew House, a stone mansion, at the entrance to Germantown. At this moment Greene's men arrived and launched an attack on the British right, also with considerable success at first. But one of Greene's units departed without orders in the direction of the firing at the Chew House and in the dense fog exchanged fire with some of Sullivan's men. The British, with better discipline and cohesion, were able to re-form in the fog and send fresh troops into the fray. Some of the Americans ran out of ammunition; they had come into battle with but 40 rounds apiece. Whatever the cause, the seeming victory was suddenly turned into defeat. About 0900, the Americans began to retreat in disorder and left the British in command of the field. Howe followed cautiously for a few miles but was unable to exploit his victory.

Germantown was a confused battle. Washington's conception of the attack was bold, but his plans violated the principle of simplicity. The American troops were unfamiliar with the roads over which they had to move and the directions given their commanders were complicated. The timely convergence of four columns would have been a difficult maneuver for even the best-trained troops, and the Continentals were still very inexpert in organized troop movements, the Militia even worse.

End of the 1777 Campaign. Following Germantown, Washington took up a position at Whitemarsh. General Howe, anxious to secure his line of supply, moved against the forts on the Delaware in cooperation with his brother, Admiral Howe, and reduced them in a series of engagements in October 1777. Afterward, in early December, Howe marshalled his whole army and moved up as if to attack Washington at Whitemarsh, but he finally withdrew to winter quarters in Philadelphia without giving battle. Washington then moved into winter quarters 20 miles northwest of the city at Valley Forge, an easily defensible site with wooded hills on either side where he could block any British effort to penetrate further west into Pennsylvania.

Analysis of the Pennsylvania Campaign. Howe's capture of Philadelphia was an empty victory as long as Washington's army remained intact and Burgoyne was left to fight his battles alone in the north. Howe was an able tactician who never lost a battle to Washington when in personal command on the field. But his strategy was never as sound as his tactics. By making the capture of cities and not the destruction of the Continental Army his objective, he always failed to achieve decisive results. Once he had gained a city, he relaxed, giving himself over to the pleasures of life. While he won battles, he came close to losing a war.

On the other hand, Brandywine, Germantown, and all the intermediate maneuvers of 1777 revealed that, while both officers and men of the Continental Army were rapidly improving, they still had much to learn. Advances had been made by the artillery and engineers, but there was still a glaring lack of cavalry. Even a small cavalry force should have been able to discover Cornwallis' movement at Brandywine, but Washington had none. Whether he appreciated the value of cavalry or understood its use is a debatable point. Other factors may explain his failure to organize the cavalry contingent authorized by Congress. Good cavalry horses were scarce north of Virginia; forage was difficult to obtain and when obtained placed a heavy burden on an already overloaded transport system. Shortly after Brandywine, Maj. Gen. Casimir Pulaski organized a small corps of cavalry, but even the efforts of this Polish cavalry expert were never crowned with outstanding success.

There were other deficiencies of even greater moment. The green Continental Army still lacked the discipline and organization necessary to enable it to move rapidly and efficiently and strike coordinated blows against the enemy, and the men still understood but poorly the use of the bayonet, the weapon with which the British soldier fought most effectively. These deficiencies were to receive primary attention in the training given during the bitter winter at Valley Forge.

Burgoyne's Advance From Canada. While Howe was moving on Philadelphia, Burgoyne was advancing south from Canada, confidently expecting to reach Albany by fall and thus forge a chain separating New England from the rest of the American states (Map 9). He started down Lake Champlain in June with 7,200 British and Hessian Regulars, 250 Canadians and Tories, and about 400 Indians. Another force of 700 Regulars and Tories and about 1,000 Indians was detached under Col. Barry St. Leger to overrun American defenses in the Mohawk Valley and join Burgoyne before Albany. While St. Leger's men were equipped lightly for rapid movement, Burgoyne's force was encumbered with excessive personal baggage and an enormous wagon train, including 138 pieces of artillery, much more than he was likely to be able to use.

The American force gathered to oppose Burgoyne's army was initially a very weak one. There were 2,500 Continentals and Militia under Maj. Gen. Arthur St. Clair at Ticonderoga, the main defense work on Lake Champlain, and 450 Continentals at old Fort Stanwix, the center of American defenses in the Mohawk Valley. Dissension over command further weakened the American opposition. Maj. Gen. Philip Schuyler, the New Yorker in command of the northern army, was unpopular with the New Englanders, who wanted to replace him with Maj. Gen. Horatio Gates.

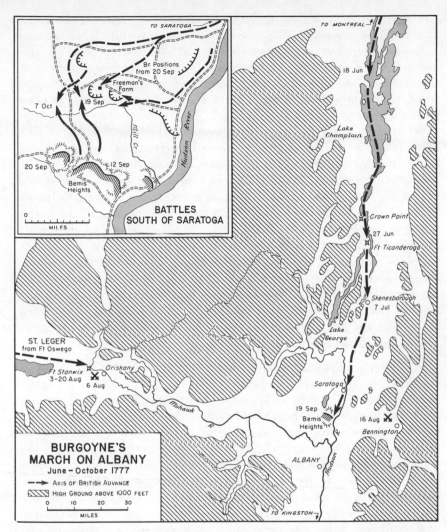

Map 9. *Burgoyne's march on Albany, June-October 1777.*

Fall of Ticonderoga. Transporting his army in boats on Lake Champlain, Burgoyne appeared before Fort Ticonderoga on 27 June 1777. Ticonderoga's defenses had been tremendously strengthened by Kosciuszko, the Polish engineer, but St. Clair did not have enough men to fortify and man two prominent hills overlooking the fort. The British placed artillery on these heights and forced St. Clair to evacuate; whereupon the whole American defense around Lake Champlain collapsed.

Schuyler's retreat. The way was open for the advance southward, but Burgoyne's troubles were just beginning. When his main army reached Skenesborough on 7 July 1777 in pursuit of the Americans he decided to push on overland instead of returning to Ticonderoga and proceeding by water on Lake George. Yet he designated the lake route for most of his baggage and supplies unduly complicating a supply and transport problem that would have been difficult enough under any circumstances. The route he chose ran through wooded ravines and over deep streams; the only existing roads were wagon trails. The supply route from Lake George to the army was even more difficult.

Schuyler fell back before Burgoyne to the mouth of the Mohawk delaying the British advance by felling trees, destroying bridges, and scattering boulders along the route. The British army, still with 58 pieces of artillery in its train, was slowed to a pace of about a mile a day. Supplies of food, forage, horses, oxen, and carts began to run short. Yet Schuyler's position was weak. His army gathered strength but slowly as he fell back. Washington detached troops from the main army and from Putnam's command in the Highlands to join him, but the New England Militia, reluctant to serve under Schuyler, rallied only in small numbers. By early August he had 4,500 men, but morale was low and desertion rife. Despite his troubles, Schuyler made the courageous decision to detach a force under General Arnold to go to the Mohawk Valley, to relieve Fort Stanwix, besieged by St. Leger.

St. Leger's Defeat. Moving down Lake Ontario to Oswego and on east to Fort Stanwix, St. Leger arrived there on 2 August parading his force of Regulars, Tories, and Indians before the garrison in an effort to persuade them to surrender. But seeing the Indians, the men in the garrison could have little doubt of their fate if they laid down their arms and determined to hold out at all costs. On 4 August a force of 800 Militia commanded by Brig. Gen. Nicholas Herkimer set out to relieve the fort. St. Leger sent a group of Indians and Tories to ambush Herkimer in a ravine near Oriskany village, six miles from Stanwix. The Militia, violating the principle of security, carelessly moved through the ravine in double file with no scouts on the flanks. The Indians suddenly opened fire from all sides. The surprise was far greater than that achieved against Braddock in 1755. But Herkimer was no Braddock. Mortally wounded in the leg, he had himself propped up against a great tree, whence he directed the Militia in a bloody afternoon battle interrupted by a violent summer thunderstorm. Forming a great irregular circle behind the trees and fighting with tomahawk, pistol, musket, and knife, the Militia finally beat off the Indian attack. They suffered so heavily themselves that they abandoned the effort to relieve Stanwix, but Oriskany had a telling psychological effect on the Indians, who had little love for such pitched battles.

Two weeks later, Arnold arrived in the Mohawk Valley with 950 Continentals just as St. Leger was completing approach trenches to

Stanwix. Hoping to avoid a costly battle, Arnold devised a clever ruse to disperse St. Leger's Indians. Employing a half-wit Tory and a friendly Oneida Indian as his messengers, he spread the rumor that the Continentals were approaching "as numerous as the leaves on the trees." The Indians, who had special respect for any madman and wanted no repetition of Oriskany, fled from St. Leger's camp in panic, and the British leader was forced to abandon the siege. He would be of no aid to Burgoyne. Arnold, leaving a small garrison at Stanwix, returned to rejoin the American forces below Saratoga the first week in September.

Bennington. Before Arnold returned, other events had given a new complexion to the whole situation on the northern front. Along the Hudson, as along the Mohawk, Burgoyne's employment of Indians stirred old memories of scalping, fire, and pillage. Burgoyne's efforts to restrain his savage allies were never very successful. The murder and scalping of a beautiful white woman, Jane McCrea, in late July 1777 dramatized the Indian threat as nothing else probably could have and furnished the finest sort of propaganda for the patriots. In late July there began a rising of New England and New York Militia that rapidly swelled the numbers opposing Burgoyne.

John Stark, the ex-Continental colonel, was commissioned a brigadier general by the state of New Hampshire and placed in charge of that state's Militia. Refusing to obey Schuyler's order to join the main army, Stark took up a position at Bennington guarding an important American supply depot and by 15 August gathered a force of around 2,000 men.

Events proved that Stark was in exactly the right place. On 11 August Burgoyne detached a force of 650 men under the Hessian Colonel Baum to forage for cattle, horses, and transport in southern Vermont. Baum headed toward Bennington, and there on 16 August he was attacked on the front and flanks by Stark's Militia and his command virtually annihilated. Reinforcements sent by Burgoyne arrived on the field just as the battle was ending and were in turn soundly defeated. Burgoyne not only failed to secure supplies but lost about one-tenth of his command.

Burgoyne's Defeat. By the first of September Burgoyne knew positively that Howe was on his way to Philadelphia and that he could expect little help from that quarter. The British commander was faced with a difficult decision—he could either attack, gain a decisive victory, and reach Albany before winter or retire to Ticonderoga. A gambler by nature, Burgoyne rashly decided to winter in Albany or lose his army. After some time spent awaiting the arrival of supplies, on 13–14 September 1777 he crossed the Hudson to the west side at Saratoga and prepared to advance against the American positions. About these positions or the terrain in front of him he knew little, for most of his Indians had deserted and his intelligence was as bad as his supply line.

The American force opposing him had undergone marked changes. On 19 August it had gotten a new commander, General Gates, Congress having finally decided to defer to New England sentiment. Gates inherited a vastly improved situation. Militia from New England and New York rallied to the army, Arnold returned, and Washington sent a veteran regiment of riflemen under Col. Daniel Morgan, an invaluable asset in subsequent forest fighting. By the time Burgoyne moved up to attack, the Americans outnumbered him 7,000 to 6,000 and their army was still growing.

Freeman's Farm. Gates moved his army on 12 September into a strong position on Bemis Heights below Saratoga directly athwart Burgoyne's route of advance. The Hudson was on the right, bluffs and woods on the left. Its only weakness lay in the fact that there was a greater height to the west, dominating the position, which Gates failed to fortify (inset, map 9).

Burgoyne approached within four miles of the American position before he learned of its existence, but he subsequently obtained general information of American dispositions and learned of the unfortified height, which he made the principal objective of his attack on 19 September. Burgoyne sent Brig. Gen. Simon Fraser with 2,000 infantry and a brigade of artillery to seize the height on the American left, Brig. Gen. Hamilton with 1,100 against the American center, and Maj. Gen. Friedrich A. von Riedesel with 1,100 Germans along the Hudson River. The attack had to be made through forests where neither British superiority in artillery nor the bayonet could have telling effect. Each British column had to advance up a separate ravine out of contact with the others. Nevertheless, if Fraser could gain control of the height overlooking the American position, the plan had some chance of success.

Gates wanted to await the British attack within his lines on Bemis Heights, but Arnold persuaded him to send two regiments forward on the left to block any British effort to flank the American position. One of these, Morgan's riflemen, met Fraser's advance guard at a point south of Freeman's Farm, brushed it aside, and pushed forward only to be repulsed by Fraser's main body. The battle then developed around this point. Gates sent several regiments to support Arnold, who expanded his attack against Hamilton in the center. Thinking he had found a weak spot between Fraser and Hamilton, Arnold called for still more reinforcements but Gates refused to send them. Then Riedesel moved into the battle, forcing Arnold's men back. The British held the field when night fell, but their losses were double those of the Americans, accurate rifle fire having taken a devastating toll. The American position on Bemis Heights was still secure.

Clinton's offensive. After the fight at Freeman's Farm, Burgoyne remained inactive for three weeks, having received word that General Clinton in New York had finally started to move northward to relieve him. On 6 October Clinton successfully stormed Forts Clinton and Montgomery below West Point, and it did not appear that General Putnam's remaining forces could prevent him from reaching Albany. Gates refused to take Clinton's threat very seriously. He did send the garrison from Fort Stanwix to reinforce Putnam but maintained his force on Bemis Heights intact. Gates estimated the situation correctly, for after capturing the forts Clinton merely sent an advance guard on to Kingston and he himself returned to New York for reinforcements.

Bemis Heights. Gates strengthened his entrenchments, fortified the height on his left, and awaited the attack he was sure Burgoyne would have to make. Militia reinforcements increased his force to more than 10,000 men by 7 October. Meanwhile, Burgoyne's position grew daily more desperate. Food was running out; the meadows were grazed bare by the animals; and every day more men slipped off into the forest, deserting the lost cause. American riflemen kept the British outposts under continual harassing fire. Burgoyne could gain little intelligence of American movements and dispositions. On 7 October he decided to make a reconnaissance in force to feel out the weak points in the American position. Learning of the British approach, Gates sent out a force, including Morgan's riflemen, to meet them. The British were repulsed and the Americans took the offensive. Arnold, who had been ordered to stay in his tent following an argument with Gates, rushed into the fray and, according to some accounts, assumed direction of the offensive. In any event, the British were driven back to their fortified positions and suffered casualties five times those of the Americans. Two days later Burgoyne withdrew to a position in the vicinity of Saratoga.

The Surrender. Militia soon worked around to the rear of this position and cut Burgoyne's routes of escape. Having no news from Clinton and despairing of relief from that quarter, Burgoyne surrendered his army, now reduced to 5,000, on 17 October. Clinton's troops at Kingston then hastily retreated to New York. Unfortunately the large Militia force that had gathered under Gates also dissolved. Only the Continental contingents sent north by Washington returned to strengthen the main army.

The importance of Saratoga. Saratoga eliminated an important part of the British Army and delivered into the hands of the Americans large quantities of valuable military stores. It removed the danger of a British advance southward from Canada to split the American states in twain. Most important of all, it convinced the French Court that the time had come to enter the war on the side of

*Surrender of Lt. Gen. John Burgoyne to Maj. Gen. Horatio Gates at Saratoga,
17 October 1777.*

the Americans. In February 1778 France negotiated a treaty of
alliance with the American states tantamount to a declaration of war
against England. French participation was to be the factor that
finally and decisively tipped the scales in favor of the Americans. It
is for this reason that Saratoga ranks as one of the decisive battles of
history.

Valley Forge. The news of Saratoga heartened Washington
greatly as he moved into winter quarters at Valley Forge, but his
own problems became too great to permit unrestrained rejoicing. The
army at Valley Forge was soon in desperate condition, its men suffering almost unbelievable hardships. About one-half had no shoes or
stockings, others no pants or blankets. Weeks passed during which
there was no meat, and a thin soup constituted the main course three
times a day. Men who did have shoes were sometimes reduced to
boiling and eating them. The construction of fortifications to guard
the valley had to come first, and it was not until well into January that
the shivering army could get out of its tattered tents and into log huts.
Fortunately, it was a relatively mild winter.

Valley Forge is mainly remembered today for the patriotism, perseverance, and devotion to duty of the small body of officers and men,
less than 6,000 in all, that stayed with the Army during this winter of

suffering in 1777–78. Less well known are the reasons why the Army suffered. There was no real shortage of food or clothing in the country. The governmental and military agencies charged with procuring and delivering supplies simply failed to function efficiently.

The reasons for this logistical failure were many and varied. Wagons for transport were scarce as was salt for preserving meat. Valley Forge was in a relatively inaccessible area. Yet these physical factors did not play so important a part as lack of adequate finance, organization, or effort to meet the challenge they presented. Depreciation of the Continental currency joined with uncontrolled mercantile speculation to force prices the government had to pay ever higher. Congress, which had fled to York, Pa., after the fall of Philadelphia, was divided into bitter factions. Factionalism exhibited itself, among other ways, in an unsuccessful attempt by one clique, including members of the new Board of War, to replace Washington with Gates, the hero of Saratoga. The victory at Saratoga, generally ascribed to the Militia, tended to weaken support for a long-term Continental Army. The confusion and dissension in Congress was reflected in disorganization and inefficiency in the Quartermaster and Commissary Departments, the most vital supply agencies of the Army. Heads of both departments resigned during the Valley Forge crisis. Lack of leadership at the top and the lure of private trade slackened the efforts of subordinates to meet their responsibilities. So while the army at Valley Forge shivered and went hungry, food rotted and clothing lay unused in depots throughout the country. Even in the vicinity of Valley Forge, some farmers sold their produce for British gold and refused the depreciated Continental currency.

Rebirth of the Army. It is perhaps a measure of the extent to which mankind profits from adversity that the Continental Army emerged from Valley Forge a stronger, more effective force than before. Having successfully quashed the scheme to replace him with Gates, Washington was able to get Congress to accept his recommendations for reorganization of the Army in early 1778. Maj. Gen. Nathanael Greene, Washington's ablest lieutenant, was made Quartermaster and Jeremiah Wadsworth, Commissary. These men introduced new efficiency in their departments that endured at least for a time. Despairing now of filling his battalions with men enlisted for the duration or three years, Washington got Congress to recommend to the states that the ranks be filled with men drafted from the Militia for one year's service. Men enlisted for the duration or three years would count against state quotas as the equivalent of three one-year draftees.

The work of Von Steuben. Most important of all, the Continental Army, during its last months at Valley Forge, profited from professional instruction. Washington had long perceived the need for standardizing organization and training but had found no one qualified to carry out the task until Baron von Steuben appeared at Valley Forge in February 1778.

Steuben had seen service as a captain on Frederick the Great's staff during the Seven Years' War and had mastered the elements of the Prussian military system, considered the best in Europe at the time. By 1778 he was seeking employment, and the French War Minister, aware of the American need for professional guidance, persuaded him to offer his services to the Americans.

Accepting Steuben at first only as a volunteer without rank, Washington sent him to inspect the camp at Valley Forge. The baron was appalled at what he saw. Different drill manuals and methods, British, French, and Prussian, and different forms of organization were in use in the various state lines. All units were understrength and some regiments were stronger than brigades, some companies stronger than regiments. There was general neglect of weapons and insufficient knowledge of their use in battle. Yet the discerning eye of the Prussian recognized in the men who had endured the rigors of Valley Forge the best of soldier material. Indeed, he thought, no European army could have held together under such hardships.

Impressed with the baron's judgment, Washington made him temporary Inspector General, a new staff office, and instructed him to work out a standard training program for the Continental Army. Steuben began to write out his drill lessons in French, having them translated into English by his own and Washington's aides. He then organized a model company and personally undertook to drill these men in the movements he was introducing. When he had progressed far enough with the model company, he extended the drill to the entire army, keeping the model company about six lessons ahead. Subordinate inspectors general were appointed for each brigade. To meet the problem of understrength, Steuben formed provisional battalions at full strength and rotated surplus officers and noncommissioned officers in the work of drilling, thus forming a cadre able to train the new recruits with whom it was hoped the ranks would be filled in the spring.

In this manner, Steuben taught the army to march in regular columns of twos and fours in uniform step, to fire volleys at regular command, to change from column into line and line into column with precision, and to use the bayonet effectively. Though he used the Prussian model, he adapted it to the characteristics of the American soldier, eliminating all but the most essential maneuvers and motions. Form and ceremony he subordinated to the interests of practicality. Recognizing the importance of skirmishers in America, he took the lead in organizing elite companies of light infantry as a part of every American regiment. He was also a pioneer in impressing on officers their obligations to the men they commanded. American officers, following British traditions, tended to regard their responsibility as only that of leading their men in battle. Steuben, by drilling the men himself

Valley Forge, 1778. Maj. Gen. Friedrich Wilhelm von Steuben training American forces at Valley Forge, Pa.

and by attention to their sufferings and wants at Valley Forge, taught by example that the officer's responsibility extended to every phase of army activity. Steuben was quick to recognize that the American soldier had to be told why he should do things before he would do them well, and he applied this philosophy in his training program. His trenchant good humor and his outbursts of profanity, the only English he knew, delighted the soldiers of the Revolution and made the rigorous drill and discipline he instituted more palatable. Thus, ironically, a Prussian, whose traditions would seem to have been most alien to the American scene, first adapted the discipline and method of Europe to the ingrained individualism of the American soldier.

The Blue Book. Pleased with Steuben's work, Washington secured his formal appointment as Inspector General, and in this post Steuben extended his work to other parts of the Army. The standard drill regulations developed at Valley Forge were formally codified in *Regulations for the Order and Discipline of the Troops of the United States*, the so-called Blue Book. For many years to come this was to be the official training manual of the American Army, and its influence is still alive in the United States Army of the present day.

The British Position, 1778. While Washington's army underwent the trials of Valley Forge, Howe remained inactive in Philadelphia. Howe refrained from attacking not only because he disliked winter war, but also because Valley Forge was a well-nigh impregnable position. Moreover, he was sick of his role in the war and had already submitted his resignation. In the winter of 1777–78 he was merely holding his army together until his successor, Gen. Sir Henry Clinton, could take over.

The British position was much altered by French entry into the war. Britain would now have to defend its farflung possessions in the West Indies, the Mediterranean, and India and not fight solely in North America. The French Fleet, much improved since the Seven Years' War, posed a definite threat at sea. The British Government decided that under these circumstances Philadelphia would be untenable and ordered Clinton, as soon as he assumed command, to evacuate the city and take his forces back to New York by sea. When he arrived in New York, parts of his army were to be detached to Florida, the West Indies, and Canada to protect these areas against French attack.

The Monmouth Campaign. Clinton decided to evacuate the major portion of his army from Philadelphia by land rather than by sea, fearing the approach of a French fleet under Admiral D'Estaing (map 7). He began his march with about 10,000 men on 18 June 1778. Washington reoccupied Philadelphia immediately and then followed Clinton, undecided at first whether he should attack the British column while it was strung out on the road or merely try to harass its progress. The army he brought from Valley Forge was not only better trained but also larger than that of the previous year, new enlistments and Militia draftees having brought its total strength to around 13,500 men. Additional troops of the New Jersey Militia were in the field in a position to harass Clinton's movement.

On 26 June Clinton arrived at Monmouth Court House with Washington's army close behind and the Militia hovering about his flanks. All Washington's generals save Wayne and Lafayette advised against a direct attack. Maj. Gen. Charles Lee, who had been exchanged and restored to a position as virtually second in command, was most vehemently opposed. Lee had little appreciation of the training undertaken under Steuben and evidently looked on Washington's army as the same unreliable force he had left after the defeats in New York. Despite all this adverse advice, Washington finally decided to attack the first grand British division as it moved out from Monmouth. One part of the Army under a subordinate was to launch the attack, and Washington with the rest would move in to support it.

Lee at first declined command of the attacking force but, on learning it would include almost half the army, changed his mind. Yet he had little confidence in the success of the endeavor, and this probably explains his subsequent conduct. Lee moved forward on the morning of 27 June—a hot, sultry day—and made contact with the British near Monmouth. But he gave no clear orders to his subordinates and apparently had no definite objectives so that the ensuing battle degenerated into a series of separate skirmishes. Finally Lee gave the order to retreat and his force started back, no one apparently knowing what had gone wrong. Washington, moving up with the main force, met Lee, exchanged harsh words with him, and assumed direction of what now had to be a defense against a British counterattack. The general engagement that followed lasted until 1800, the tide flowing one way and then the other. Casualties from sunstroke and heat prostration were almost as heavy on both sides as those from enemy fire. For the first time the Americans fought well with the bayonet, as well as with musket and rifle, and their battlefield behavior generally reflected the effects of the training at Valley Forge.

Both sides still held the field when night fell. In the night Clinton slipped away, as Washington had at Princeton, and in a few days successfully completed his retreat to New York.

Cooperation With the French. Despite the check at Monmouth, Washington still had high hopes that the war against Britain could be won by a combined Franco-American attack in the year 1778. Having learned the importance of naval power in his three years' experience conducting campaigns along the American coastline, he sought the cooperation of the French Navy in an attack on one or the other of the two remaining British positions along the American coast, New York and Newport. Admiral D'Estaing's squadron, carrying 4,000 French Regulars and superior to Admiral Howe's British fleet at New York, appeared off the coast on 8 July. Washington and D'Estaing at first agreed on a combined land and sea attack against New York, but D'Estaing was unable to get his deep-draft ships across the bar that extended from Staten Island to Sandy Hook to get at Howe's smaller fleet; after 11 days of waiting, the two commanders agreed to transfer the attack to the other and weaker British stronghold at Newport, R. I.

Newport. The British garrison at Newport consisted of only about 3,000 men, but the city stood on an island and its approaches were very difficult. Washington hastily reinforced General Sullivan's small command in Rhode Island, and a call for Militia eventually swelled his force to around 10,000. A plan was agreed upon whereby the French fleet would land troops on the west side of the island and Sullivan would cross over and mount the assault from the east. D'Estaing arrived off Newport on 29 July; it was another week before Sullivan's army was collected and ready. However, arrangements for cooperation were poor and relations between the American and French commanders were strained from the start. The French landing was interrupted by a reinforced British fleet from New York, and D'Estaing had to halt the disembarkation of troops to put out to sea to meet it. On 12 August a great gale scattered both fleets and the British returned to New York to refit. But D'Estaing's squadron was also damaged and the admiral was piqued by Sullivan's failure to inform him of his movements. He consequently sailed away to tasks he considered more pressing in the West Indies, and Sullivan was left to extricate his force from an untenable position as best he could. The only result was embittered relations between American and French commanders that Washington had great difficulty in smoothing over.

Strategic Picture, End of 1778. Newport was the last important action of 1778. While the fiasco there was being played out to its disappointing end, Washington had moved his army back to White Plains in fundamentally the same position he had held in 1776 before the retreat across New Jersey. In this general area he was to spend the next three years awaiting an opportunity to strike a decisive blow in cooperation with the French fleet.

QUESTIONS

1. What were the virtues and defects of General Howe as a military leader? Illustrate from the campaign of 1777.
2. Compare the American Army of 1777 with that of 1776.
3. What were the principal mistakes made by Burgoyne that led to his defeat? What generals on the American side do you think took best advantage of them?
4. What principles of war are illustrated, either by omission or observance, in the Saratoga campaign?
5. What was the significance of the victory at Saratoga?
6. How did the U. S. Army profit from the winter of adversity at Valley Forge?

Reading List

See also reading list at end of chapter 2.

Alden, John R. *General Charles Lee: Traitor or Patriot.* Baton Rouge, 1951.

Bill, Alfred H. *Valley Forge: The Making of an Army.* New York, 1952.

Gottschalk, Louis R. *Lafayette Joins the American Army.* Chicago, 1937.

Nickerson, Hoffman. *The Turning Point of the Revolution.* Boston, 1928.

Palmer, John M. *General Von Steuben.* New Haven, 1937.

CHAPTER 5

THE AMERICAN REVOLUTION—THE LAST YEARS

Expansion of the War. After France entered the war in 1778, it rapidly became a major European as well as an American conflict. In 1779 Spain declared war against England, and in the following year Holland followed suit. Britain's concern with maintaining its position vis-a-vis its European enemies weakened the effort against the American rebels. Yet the Americans were unable to take full advantage of Britain's embarrassments, for their effort came to suffer more and more from lack of strong direction and adequate finance as the war dragged on. In addition, the interests of European states fighting Britain did not necessarily coincide with American interests. Spain and Holland did not ally themselves with the American states at all, and even France found it more expedient to devote its major effort to the West Indies. Lastly, the spread of the war to include old traditional enemies intensified the British war effort and produced some, if not enough, of that characteristic British tenacity that has produced victory for England in so many wars. Despite many new commitments, Britain was able to maintain in America an army usually superior in numbers to the dwindling Continental Army. Transferring their main effort from north to south, the British turned to more ruthless and destructive measures to subdue the revolt and made far more extensive and efficient employment of Tories than earlier.

Stalemate in the North. Monmouth was the last general engagement in the north between Washington's and Clinton's armies. In 1779 the situation there became a stalemate and remained one until the end of the war. Washington set up a defense system around New York, its center at West Point on the Hudson. In late spring 1779 Clinton made his last serious effort to draw Washington out of his fortifications and into battle in the open field, descending in force on unfinished American installations forward of West Point at Verplanck's and Stony Points. But Washington refused to take the bait, and Clinton withdrew to New York leaving small garrisons at the captured positions. Washington then launched a small counteroffensive, more notable because it gave testimony to the improved skill of his soldiers than for its strategic consequences. General Wayne with an elite corps of light infantry moved swiftly down the Hudson in boats on the night of 15 July 1779 and took the British by surprise in a daring bayonet attack on Stony Point. The British garrison surrendered after only a brief struggle. Stony Point demonstrated the value of the new light infantry organization formed at Valley Forge and, even more than Monmouth, showed that trained American soldiers could now wield the bayonet as effectively as the British. But Wayne proved unable to take Verplanck's Point and Washington finally ordered him to withdraw with his prisoners and captured supplies. Neither side made any further moves.

Arnold's treason. The only other serious threat to Washington's defenses came in 1780, not as the result of a British military movement but rather the treason of Benedict Arnold. Arnold had proved himself one of the most capable of American field commanders in the early stages of the war, but he lacked character and stability. Disgruntled by what he considered to be the failure of Congress to give proper recognition to his abilities and tempted by the lucrative financial rewards offered by the British, Arnold finagled an appointment as commander at West Point and then entered into a plot to deliver this key post to the British. Washington discovered the plot just in time to foil it, but Arnold escaped to become a British brigadier.

The Indian Frontier. Though Burgoyne's defeat ended any further danger of a full-scale British attack based on Canada, the British from their northern bases continued to incite the Indians along the frontier to bloody raids on American settlements. From Fort Niagara and Detroit they sent out their bands, usually led by Tories, to pillage, scalp, and burn in the Mohawk Valley of New York, the Wyoming Valley of Pennsylvania, and the new American settlements in Kentucky. In August 1779 Washington profited from Clinton's inaction to detach General Sullivan with a Continental force to move against the Indian tribes of the six Nations in Pennsylvania and New York, destroy their villages and capture hostages as a means of stopping their depredations against border settlements. Although Sullivan laid waste the Indians' villages, and defeated a force of warriors and Tories at Newton on 29 August, he failed to destroy or cripple the enemy and their depredations were renewed the following year.

George Rogers Clark. The blow against the British and the Indians harrying the settlements in Kentucky was struck not by the Continental forces but by an expedition sponsored by the state of Virginia. In the fall and winter of 1778-79, young Lt. Col. George Rogers Clark with a force of 175 men, ostensibly recruited for the defense of Kentucky, overran all the British posts in what is today Illinois and Indiana and struck fear in the hearts of the Indians of the Old Northwest. However, Clark, like Sullivan, was unable to strike at the ultimate source of the trouble, in this case Detroit, and, though the Indians were given a severe setback by these two expeditions, they continued to cause trouble along the frontiers. After 1779 the task of fighting them devolved mainly on local Militia.

British Invasion of the South. Unable to accomplish anything decisive in the North, the British in late 1778 began to transfer their main effort to the South. Tory strength was greater in the South and the area was closer to the West Indies, where the major portion of the British Fleet had to stand guard against the French. The King's ministers hoped to bring the southern states back into the British fold one by one and from bases there and in New York, to strangle the recalcitrant north. Yet General Clinton, British Commander in Chief in North America, never seemed to have considered such an ambitious project feasible unless his home government sent many more reinforcements to America than it was ever able to provide. His own approach was cautious and based on the sound theory that the British Army could never operate safely very far from the coast where the British Navy could nurture it. In his view, the most important thing was to seize and hold the coastal bases. He believed the Chesapeake Bay area of as great or greater strategic importance than the lower south in this regard, and he sought both to secure a base there and to paralyze the populous state of Virginia as an American supply base for armies in both north and south.

The conquest of Georgia. Georgia, a weak and thinly populated state, was chosen as the first objective; it was quickly overrun in the winter of 1778–79 by two British forces, one sent from New York and the other moving north from Florida. Alarmed at the course of events, Congress sent Maj. Gen. Benjamin Lincoln of Massachusetts south to Charleston in December 1778 to organize the southern effort. Lincoln gathered 3,500 Continentals and Militia but failed in an effort to recover Georgia. In May 1779, while Lincoln was maneuvering along the Georgia border, the British commander, Maj. Gen. Augustine Prevost, slipped away to besiege Charleston, and the city only barely managed to hold out until Lincoln returned to its relief (map 10).

The siege of Savannah. In the fall of 1779 the arrival off the coast of Georgia of D'Estaing's fleet with 6,000 French troops gave the Americans a temporary superiority in the southern theater. D'Estaing landed 3,500 of his Regulars along the north bank of the Savannah River on 12 September, and Lincoln hurried south with 1,350 Americans to join him in a siege of the main British base at Savannah. Instead of attacking immediately while the British were still unprepared, D'Estaing called on Prevost to surrender. He delayed while the latter was supposedly considering his terms, but Prevost took advantage of the time to strengthen his entrenchments and call in reinforcements from outlying posts. The French and Americans then resorted to an approach by regular parallels, but before they could be completed D'Estaing decided he could not leave his fleet any longer in a position dangerously exposed to autumn storms. Consequently, on

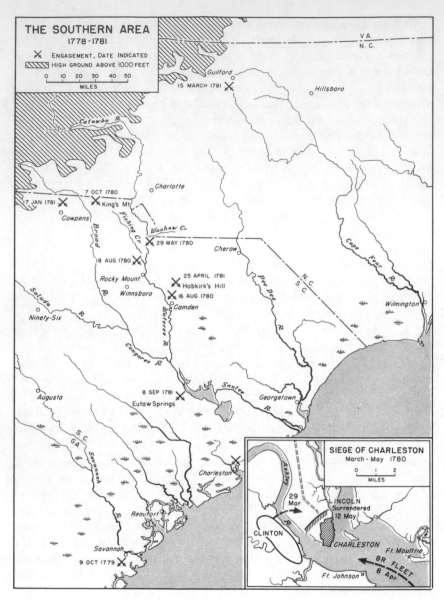

Map 10. The Southern Area, 1778–1781.

9 October a direct assault was undertaken, which the British from their strongly entrenched positions repulsed in an action strongly reminiscent of Bunker Hill, the French and Americans this time suffering the heavy losses. Lincoln, unable to persuade D'Estaing to remain longer, returned to Charleston, and the second attempt at Franco-American cooperation ended in much the same atmosphere of bitterness and disillusion as the first.

Disaster in the South. Meanwhile Clinton, urged on by the British Government, had determined to push the campaign in the South in earnest. In late spring 1779 he sent a naval raiding force under Adm. George Collier into the port area inside Hampton Roads in Virginia, and Collier was successful in destroying such large quantities of supplies, ships, and installations that Virginia's ability to serve as a base for supply and reinforcement of the lower south was seriously affected. In October 1779 Clinton withdrew the British garrison at Newport and pulled in his troops from outposts around New York. By the end of the year he was ready to move south against Charleston with a large part of his force. With D'Estaing's withdrawal, the British regained control of the sea along the American coast, giving Clinton a mobility that Washington was unable to match. Nor did Washington, by this time, have either the numbers or the supplies to enable him to divert more than small piecemeal reinforcements southward.

Surrender at Charleston. Having learned from his experience in 1776, Clinton determined this time to aproach Charleston from the land side. Landing first on John's Island to the south, he then moved up to James Island and thence to the south bank of the Ashley River. There in March 1780 he was joined by part of the garrison from Savannah and reinforcements from New York, bringing his total force to around 14,000, including sailors and marines ashore. Against him Lincoln could muster hardly 6,000 men, including two understrength brigades of Continentals Washington had managed to send south. Clinton had achieved a decisive concentration of force at a critical spot. Lincoln undoubtedly should have evacuated the city and retired to the hinterlands where he could maneuver, but, under strong pressures from the South Carolina authorities, he determined on a citadel defense. He concentrated virtually his entire force on the neck of land between the Ashley and Cooper Rivers above the city, and left Fort Moultrie in the harbor lightly defended. On 29 March Clinton crossed the Ashley and began to construct parallels within 1,800 yards of Lincoln's defenses. On 8 April British warships successfully forced the passage past Moultrie, and the city was invested from both land and sea. The siege then proceeded in traditional 18th century fashion to its inevitable end. On 12 May 1780, with Clinton's approach trenches within 250 yards of the American positions, Lincoln surrendered his entire force of 5,466 men, the greatest disaster to the American cause during the entire Revolution.

Tarleton at the Waxhaws. At the time Charleston surrendered, Col. Abraham Buford with 350 Virginians, the last remaining organized American force in the South, was moving south to reinforce the garrison. Buford's force was overtaken at the Waxhaws, a district near the North Carolina border, on 29 May and virtually annihilated by British cavalry under Lt. Col. Banastre Tarleton, an able, daring, and ruthless officer, whose name was to become anathema to patriots throughout the South. Tarleton surprised Buford with a sudden cavalry charge and slaughtered most of his men, refusing to honor the white flag Buford displayed.

Civil War in the South. After the capture of Charleston, Clinton returned to New York with a third of his force, leaving General Cornwallis with 8,000 men to follow up the victory. Cornwallis established seaboard bases at Savannah, Beaufort, Charleston, and Georgetown, and in the interior extended his line of control along the Savannah River, westward to Ninety-six, and northward to Camden and Rocky Mount. Cornwallis' force was too small to police so large an area, even with the aid of the numerous Tories who, encouraged by British successes, took to the field. American guerillas, principally led by Brig. Gens. Thomas Sumter and Andrew Pickens and Lt. Col. Francis Marion, harried British posts and lines of communication and battled the bands of Tories. A bloody, ruthless, and confused civil war ensued in the South, its character determined in no small degree by Tarleton's action at the Waxhaws.

Defeat at Camden. On 22 June 1780 two more understrength Continental brigades from Washington's army arrived at Hillsboro, N. C., and these became the nerve center of guerilla resistance. Congress in July, without consulting Washington, named General Gates, the hero of Saratoga, commander of the Southern Department. Gates soon lost his northern laurels by adopting an aggressive plan hardly suited to his capabilities. Determining to attack the British post at Camden, he marched his army in great haste toward that point through Tory country where the men had to subsist on green corn. By the time he approached Camden, Militia reinforcements had brought his force to 4,100 men, but stomach upsets left only 3,000 fit for duty and of these but 900 were trained and disciplined Continentals. Gates made the additional mistake of detaching 400 men, including 100 Continentals, to go with General Sumter to raid a British wagon train.

Cornwallis learned of Gates' approach and hurried north from Charleston with reinforcements. With an army of 2,200, nearly all Regulars, he contacted Gates' force outside Camden on the night of 15–16 August, but both commanders cautiously decided to await morning before giving battle. In the morning, Gates deployed his force with the Militia on the left and the Continentals under Maj. Gen. Johann De Kalb on the right. The Militia were still forming in the hazy dawn when Cornwallis struck, and they fled in panic before the British bayonets. De Kalb's Continentals put up a valiant fight but were so outnumbered once the Militia fled that it was a hopeless one. Tarleton's cavalry pursued the fleeing Americans for 30 miles, killing or making prisoners of those who lagged in their flight. Gates himself fled too fast for Tarleton, reaching Hillsboro, 160 miles away, in three days. There he was able to gather only about 800 survivors of the southern Army. To add to the extent of the disaster, Tarleton caught up with Sumter and virtually destroyed his force in a surprise attack at Fishing Creek on 18 August.

Nadir of the American Cause. Defeat in the South was not the only discouraging aspect of the situation in 1780. In the North, the high patriotic enthusiasm of the early years waned as the war dragged on, and a creeping paralysis in the war effort set in. By 1780 the Continental currency had practically depreciated out of existence, rendering Congress impotent to pay the soldiers or purchase supplies. At Morristown, N. J., in the winter of 1779–80 the Army suffered worse hardships than it had at Valley Forge. Congress could do little more than shift its responsibilities to the states, giving each the task of providing clothing for its own troops and furnishing certain quotas of specific supplies for the entire Army. Such a system proved entirely inadequate. Not only were the states laggard in furnishing the specific supplies, but when they did it was seldom at the time and place at which they could be most profitably used. This breakdown in the supply system was more than even General Greene as Quartermaster General could cope with, and in early 1780, under heavy criticism in Congress, he resigned his position.

Under such supply and financial difficulties, Washington was hard put to it to hold even a small army together. Recruiting of Continentals, difficult to begin with, became practically impossible when the troops could be neither adequately paid nor supplied and had to suffer such winters as that at Morristown. Both Congress and the states increased the bounties for enlistment again and again with little result except to create a large group of bounty jumpers who enlisted in one state only to desert and enlist in another and to cause resentment among the veterans who had enlisted earlier for much smaller inducements. The other expedient for securing men, the conscription of Militia for one year's service, also failed to produce the numbers expected. The states adopted conscription reluctantly and applied it only sporadically.

While recruiting lagged, morale among the troops that did remain, ill-supplied and ill-paid, naturally fell. Mutinies in 1780 and 1781 were suppressed only by measures of great severity. That Washington did manage to maintain a force in being is a tribute both to his great leadership and to the devotion to duty of the great majority of his veteran officers and men.

Efforts at reorganization. Congress made some efforts to remedy the situation toward the end of 1780. Col. Timothy Pickering, an able administrator, was made Quartermaster General, and Robert Morris, a wealthy Philadelphia merchant, was induced to accept a position as Superintendent of Finance. Morris, working closely with Pickering, introduced a new policy of supplying the Army by private contracts, using his own personal credit as guarantee for eventual payment in gold or silver. Moreover, in 1781, the old cumbersome Board of War was abolished and a single full-time Secretary of War assigned its functions. General Lincoln, exchanged after Charleston, was appointed to this position. To conform to reality, the authorized size of the Army was reduced from the 110 battalions voted in 1776 to 59 in 1781—50 of infantry, 4 each of cavalry and artillery, and 1 of artificers. If filled, these units would still have provided an Army of around 40,000, but the regiments remained far below strength. Nevertheless, the net effect of the reforms was sufficient to make possible one great and decisive burst of energy in 1781.

New leadership in the South. Congress also provided new leadership in the South, this time accepting Washington's recommendations. General Greene replaced Gates in command; Brig. Gen. Daniel Morgan was assigned to command the light infantry under Greene; and Lt. Col. Henry Lee was sent south with his legion, a mixed organization of cavalry and infantry, to provide a mobile force capable of cooperation with guerilla units. Greene, Morgan, and Lee were to give the southern army the leadership it had long lacked, leadership that was to compensate, in some measure, for what that army lacked in numbers and material means.

King's Mountain. The blow that turned the tide in the South, however, had already been struck before Greene assumed command. In late 1780 Cornwallis, with Clinton's reluctant consent, set out on an invasion of North Carolina. He ordered Maj. Patrick Ferguson, who had successfully organized the Tories in the upcountry of South Carolina, to move north simultaneously with his "American Volunteers," spread the Tory gospel in the North Carolina backcountry, and join the main army at Charlotte with a maximum number of recruits. Ferguson was the leading rifleman of the British army, a man almost as feared and hated by the patriots as Tarleton. Ferguson's Tory detachment was armed with rifles and muskets. But the rifles, unlike American ones, had been adapted to carry a bayonet.

Ferguson's advance northward alarmed the frontiersmen in what is now Tennessee, in the mountains of southwest Virginia, and in western North Carolina. A picked force of mounted Militia riflemen, under the command of such great natural leaders as Cols. John Sevier, Isaac Shelby, William Campbell, and Benjamin Cleveland, assembled on the Catawba River in western North Carolina and set out to find Ferguson. Ferguson started to retreat south but was brought to bay at King's Mountain on 7 October (map 10). The frontier Militia numbered 1,400, the Tories about 1,000. Dismounting and tying their horses, the frontiersmen aligned their units in a horseshoe formation around the base of the mountain and advanced against Ferguson's position. It was rifle against rifle and American patriot against American Tory, for Ferguson was the only Regular British soldier in the battle. The hardihood and marksmanship of the American frontiersmen was too much for the Tories, and Ferguson's bayonets were unable to stem the tide of advance as the Americans closed. "Tarleton's Quarter" was the cry at the finish as many a patriot avenged the death of his friends at the hands of British soldiers or Tory bands. Practically none of Ferguson's men escaped death or capture.

King's Mountain was as fatal to Cornwallis' plans as Bennington had been to those of Burgoyne. The North Carolina Tories, cowed by the fate of their compatriots, would render him little support. The British commander abandoned his campaign to subjugate North Carolina and on 14 October began a wretched retreat in the rain back to Winnsboro, S. C., with Militia harassing his progress. Sickness and lack of supplies had their inevitable effect on British strength and morale. King's Mountain also upset temporarily Clinton's plan to establish a base in Virginia. An expedition of 2,500 men under Maj. Gen. Alexander Leslie, sent for that purpose, had to be diverted to reinforce Cornwallis.

Greene's Southern Campaign, 1780–81. The frontier Militia had turned the tide but, having done so, returned to their homes. To keep it flowing against the British was the task of Nathanael Greene. At Charlotte, N. C., where he took over from Gates early in December 1780, Greene found an army that, although numbering on paper 3,400, had only 1,500 present and fit for duty, and of these only 949 were Continentals. The army lacked clothing and provisions and it had little systematic means of procuring them. Greene faced his problem realistically. He decided he must not, like Gates, rush into battle with a superior British force but would instead, with the cooperation of Marion, Sumter, and Pickens, conduct essentially guerilla operations, harrying Cornwallis' lines of supply and wearing down the strength of his army. He hoped for a gradual accretion of his own strength to the point where it would enable him eventually to defeat a weakened British army in the field. As a first step he had his engineers explore and map the surrounding country so that no move would have to be made without some knowledge of the terrain. Next he determined to get out of the devastated area around Charlotte and into richer country, where he could live off the land. The best position, he found, would be at Cheraw Hill in South Carolina, but, since it was further away from Cornwallis' camp than Charlotte, to move there with his entire army would give the inhabitants the impression he was retreating. He therefore decided to move only part of his army to Cheraw and sent the rest under Morgan west across the Catawba into an area closer to Cornwallis' camp. This seeming violation of the principle of mass, was amply justified in view of the type of operation

Greene intended to conduct. Divided forces could live off the land much easier than could one large force. Furthermore, it virtually forced Cornwallis to divide his army also, for the British commander soon perceived that if he moved against Morgan with his entire army Greene could advance against Charleston, and that if he moved against Greene, Morgan could take the British posts in the west at Ninety-Six and Augusta.

Cornwallis' plans. Greene's plan was particularly effective in view of the character of the general opposing him. Unlike Clinton, Cornwallis was extremely aggressive, rashly so it proved, and willing to cut loose from his supply depots on the coast to wage war in the interior. Disregarding Clinton's admonitions that he should push his designs against North Carolina only if it involved no risk to the British posts in South Carolina and Georgia, Cornwallis in 1781 decided to risk everything on a successful invasion, practically burning his bridges behind him by depleting his Charleston base and bringing almost all his supplies forward. Clinton's wisdom was greater than his forcefulness, and he allowed the headstrong Cornwallis to go his way. He was aware that his subordinate enjoyed greater support in London than he did and had established almost separate channels of communication with the King's ministers. Divided command was once again to pave the road to British disaster.

Cowpens. Puzzled by Greene's dispositions, Cornwallis divided his army not into two but three parts. He sent a holding force to Camden to contain Greene, and directed Tarleton with a fast-moving contingent of 1,100 infantry and cavalry to find and crush Morgan. With his main army he moved cautiously up toward North Carolina, confidently expecting to cut off the remainder of Morgan's force after its defeat by Tarleton. On 17 January 1781 Tarleton finally caught up with Morgan west of King's Mountain at a place called the Cowpens (map 11). There Morgan had determined to make his stand, with his back parallel to the Broad River a few miles in his rear and an open sparsely forested area on his front and right. Morgan's force was numerically almost equal to that of Tarleton, but it was three-quarters Militia and his cavalry was much inferior.

Morgan fully understood the limitations of his Militia and adopted a plan whereby its capabilities could be used to full advantage. He selected a hill as the center of his position and formed his main line of Continental infantry on it, deliberately leaving his flanks open, ordinarily a dangerous thing to do. Well out to the front of the main line he posted Pickens' Militia riflemen in two lines, instructing the first line to fire two volleys and then fall back to the second, the combined line to fire until the British pressed them, then to fall back to the rear of the Continentals and re-form as a reserve. Behind the

Brig. Gen. Daniel Morgan.　　　　*Maj. Gen. Nathanael Greene.*

hill he placed Lt. Col. William Washington's cavalry detachment, ready to charge the attacking enemy at the critical moment. Every man in the ranks was informed of the plan of battle and the part he was expected to play in it.

On finding Morgan, Tarleton ordered an immediate attack. His men moved forward in regular formation, were checked by the Militia rifles but took the retreat of the first two lines to be the beginning of a rout and rushed headlong into the steady fire of the Continentals on the hill. When the British were well advanced, the cavalry struck them on the right flank, and Pickens' Militia, having re-formed, drove out from behind the hill to hit the British left. Caught in a clever double envelopment, reminiscent of the great Carthaginian victory at Cannae in 216 B. C., the British surrendered after suffering heavy losses. Tarleton managed to escape with only a small force of cavalry that he had held in reserve.

Greene's maneuvers. Cornwallis was still near at hand with the main British army, and Morgan had far too few men to risk a fight. He therefore swiftly marched to rejoin Greene, covering 100 miles and crossing two rivers in five days. Cornwallis moved much too slowly to trap him. With Greene's army again consolidated, Cornwallis was in much the same position he had been after King's Mountain. But this time he was too heavily committed to the campaign in North Carolina to withdraw. Hoping to match the rapid movement of the Americans, he destroyed all his superfluous supplies, baggage, and wagons. This action inspired Greene's next moves. Ignoring Morgan's advice to retreat west to the mountains where Cornwallis could not follow, Greene determined instead to move north toward Virginia, tempting Cornwallis to follow but keeping just far

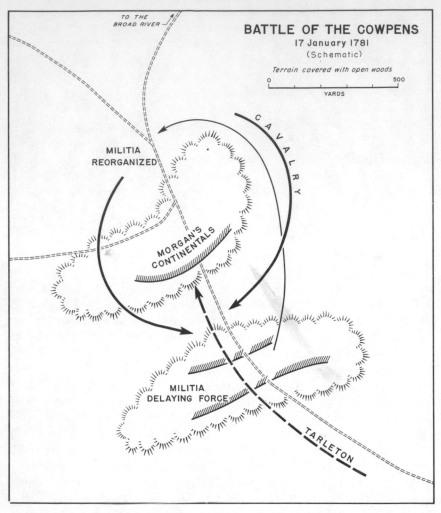

Map 11.   Battle of the Cowpens, 17 January 1781.

enough in front of him to avoid battle with his superior force.   In
this way he expected to gradully wear down Cornwallis' strength and
exhaust his remaining supplies while he himself would gather strength.
So Greene retreated, through North Carolina, up into southern Virginia, then back into North Carolina again, with Cornwallis always
in hot pursuit.

  Guilford Court House.   Finally on 15 March 1781, at Guilford
Court House in North Carolina, ground he had himself chosen, Greene
halted and prepared to meet Cornwallis' attack.   By this time he had
1,500 Continentals and 3,000 Militia to the 1,900 British Regulars
Cornwallis could muster.   Greene disposed his Militia much as Morgan had at Cowpens.   But this time, once the men had fired their

volleys, they fled the field completely. The British finally won the battle, mainly because of the superiority of their artillery, but suffered casualties of about one-fourth of the force engaged. Greene withdrew his army to a point 10 miles away in much better shape than it had been at Charlotte six months earlier. Cornwallis, on the other hand, now had a decimated force and almost no supplies. It was impossible for him to maintain his position in the interior any longer. He withdrew to Wilmington along the coast where he could be supplied by sea, and from there decided to move northward to join the British forces General Clinton had sent to Virginia.

Completion of Greene's campaign. Cornwallis thus abandoned the lower south, and Greene pushed quickly into South Carolina to reduce the British posts in the interior. His tactics continued to be much the same as they had been in the campaign against Cornwallis. He fought two battles—at Hobkirk's Hill on 25 April, and at Eutaw Springs on 8 September—and lost both but with approximately the same results as at Guilford Court House. One by one the British posts in the interior of South Carolina and Georgia fell to Greene's army, to Militia and partisans, or to Lee's legion. By October the British had been forced to withdraw to their port strongholds along the coast—Charleston and Savannah. If Greene had lost battles, he had won a campaign. In doing so, he had paved the way for the greater victory to follow at Yorktown.

The War in Virginia. Meanwhile Clinton had been devoting increased attention to Virginia (map 12). He had no desire to make a major effort there, but he did hope to disrupt the state by raids, to arouse the Tories, and to establish a naval base on Chesapeake Bay. Eventually he thought such a base might be used as the starting point for one arm of a pincers movement against Pennsylvania, for which his own idle force in New York would provide the other.

Arnold's invasion. After dispatching General Leslie's force to reinforce Cornwallis, Clinton sent a smaller expedition of 1,600 men to Virginia under the American traitor, Benedict Arnold. Arnold met only feeble opposition and conducted a destructive raid up the James River all the way to Richmond. General Washington, seeing a small British force in such an isolated position, made an effort to trap Arnold. The French, during the summer of 1780, had moved into the vacated British base at Newport. General Washington persuaded the French naval commander there, Admiral Destouches, to send a squadron into the Chesapeake and dispatched Lafayette with 1,200 Continentals overland to Virginia to cooperate with him. Unfortunately for Washington's plan, a British fleet drove the French back to Newport, and Clinton, in response to the threat, sent sizable reinforcements to Virginia under Maj. Gen. William Phillips. Lafayette was left to face this vastly superior force alone. Phillips,

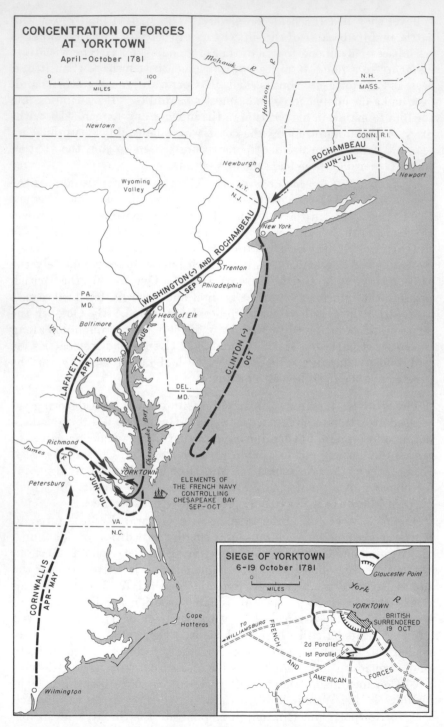

CONCENTRATION OF FORCES AT YORKTOWN
April–October 1781

0   100
MILES

Mohawk R
Hudson R
N.H.
MASS.
CONN. R.I.
Newtown
Newburgh
ROCHAMBEAU
JUN–JUL
Newport
Wyoming Valley
N.Y.
N.J.
New York
WASHINGTON (–) AND ROCHAMBEAU
Trenton
SEP
PA.
MD.
Philadelphia
Baltimore
AUG
Head of Elk
CLINTON (–)
OCT
LAFAYETTE
APR
Annapolis
VA.
DEL.
MD.
Chesapeake Bay
Richmond
James
R
YORKTOWN
JUN–JUL
Petersburg
ELEMENTS OF THE FRENCH NAVY CONTROLLING CHESAPEAKE BAY SEP–OCT
VA.
N.C.
CORNWALLIS
APR–MAY
Cape Hatteras
Wilmington

SIEGE OF YORKTOWN
6–19 October 1781

0   1
MILES

York R
Gloucester Point
YORKTOWN
BRITISH SURRENDERED 19 OCT
TO WILLIAMSBURG
FRENCH AND AMERICAN FORCES
2d Parallel
1st Parallel

Map 12. Concentration of forces at Yorktown.

who assumed the British command, continued Arnold's raiding tactics along the James, and Lafayette was unable to impose any effective opposition.

Cornwallis and Clinton.   In late May 1781 Cornwallis arrived from Wilmington with the remnants of his army and took command of all the British forces in Virginia, now numbering 7,000 men, nearly a third of the total British strength in America.   Cornwallis had abandoned the lower south without even informing Clinton of his intention.   He now proposed to carry out major operations in the interior of Virginia, but Clinton saw as little practical value in such a move as Cornwallis did in Clinton's plan to establish a base in Virginia and carry out a pincers movement against Pennsylvania.   The two commanders were soon working at cross purposes.   Cornwallis at first turned to the interior as if to pursue his own designs and engaged in a fruitless pursuit of Lafayette north of Richmond.   Then, on receiving Clinton's positive orders to return to the coast, establish a base, and return part of his force to New York, Cornwallis moved back down the Virginia peninsula and took up his station at Yorktown. At this small tobacco port on the York River, just off Chesapeake Bay, he proposed to establish the base that Clinton desired.   In the face of Cornwallis' insistence that he must keep all his troops with him, Clinton vacillated, reversing his own orders several times and in the end granting Cornwallis' request.   Meanwhile, Lafayette followed Cornwallis cautiously down the peninsula, lost a skirmish with him at Green Spring near Williamsburg on 6 July, and when the British moved into Yorktown took up a position of watchful waiting nearby. The stage was set for the final act of the Revolution.

The Yorktown Campaign.   Cornwallis' move to Yorktown gave Washington the opportunity to strike the decisive blow in cooperation with the French fleet that he had long awaited.   During the spring and summer of 1781 he toyed with the idea of attempting such a blow against New York.   He learned that Adm. Francois de Grasse with a powerful French fleet intended to come to the American coast in late summer, and he persuaded the French commander at Newport, Lt. Gen. the Comte de Rochambeau, to bring his 4,000 French troops to join him in New York.   Rochambeau placed his army under Washington's command.   The total combined Franco-American force numbered less than 10,000, and both Washington and Rochambeau soon decided they could make little progress against Clinton's 17,000 men in well-fortified positions.   Then on 14 August Rochambeau received word from De Grasse in the West Indies that he intended to come to the Chesapeake later that month and that he could remain only until 15 October.   De Grasse's proposed movement shaped Washington's plans.   He saw immediately that if he could achieve a superior concentration of force on the land side while De Grasse held the bay he could destroy the British army at Yorktown before Clinton had a chance to relieve it. In the movements that followed, the excellent cooperation between French and Americans contrasted sharply with the divided counsels of the British. A French squadron of eight ships of the line under Admiral Barras immediately put out to sea from Newport to join De Grasse. Washington sent orders to Lafayette to contain Cornwallis at Yorktown, and then, after making a feint in the direction of New York to deceive Clinton, on 21 August started the major portion of his own and Rochambeau's troops on a rapid secret movement south to Virginia, leaving only 2,000 Americans behind to watch Clinton. The route lay overland through New Jersey, Pennsylvania, and Maryland to Head of Elk, Annapolis, and Baltimore, where an improvised flotilla of boats was readied to take the men down the Chesapeake and up the James River to a landing near Williamsburg.

Battle of the Virginia Capes. On 30 August, while Washington was on the move southward, De Grasse arrived in the Chesapeake with his entire fleet of 24 ships of the line and a few days later debarked 3,000 French troops to join Lafayette. De Grasse had wisely refused to heed the instructions of the French Government to divert 10 of his ships for convoy duty. In contrast, the British naval commander in the West Indies, Adm. Sir George Rodney, had divided his fleet, taking 3 ships of the line to England, leaving 3 in the West Indies, and sending only 14 north to join Adm. Thomas Graves' squadron at New York. Graves put out to sea in late August with 19 ships of the line hoping either to intercept Barras' squadron or to block De Grasse's entry into the Chesapeake. He failed to find Barras, and when he arrived off Hampton Roads on 5 September he found De Grasse already in the bay. The French admiral sallied forth to meet Graves and the two fleets fought an indecisive action off the Virginia capes. Yet the victory for all practical purposes lay with the French, for, while the fleet maneuvered at sea for days following the battle, Barras' squadron slipped into Chesapeake and the French and American troops got past into the James River. Also at the end of the maneuvering, De Grasse got back into the bay and joined Barras, confronting Graves with such a decidedly superior naval force that he decided to return to New York to refit.

The siege. When Washington's army arrived on 26 September, the French fleet was in firm control of the bay, blocking Cornwallis' sea route of escape. Virginia Militia poured in and when the siege operation was begun on 6 October the army numbered about 15,500— 8,845 Americans and 7,800 French Regulars—to Cornwallis' 6,000 men. The decisive concentration of force had been achieved; it remained only to reap its benefits. Washington's main concern was to keep De Grasse in the bay long enough to complete the siege, and with Rochambeau and Lafayette's cooperation he got the French admiral to agree to extend his stay beyond 15 October if necessary.

The siege, carried on in traditional 18th century fashion, was the type of operation in which the French were masters. Cornwallis obligingly abandoned his forward position on 30 September, and on 6 October the first parallel was begun 600 yards from his main position. Artillery was placed in position along the trench and began its destructive work on 9 October. By 11 October the zig-zag connecting trench had been dug 200 yards forward, and work on the second parallel had begun. Two British redoubts had to be reduced by French and American light infantry in order to extend the line to the York River. This accomplished, Cornwallis' only hope was escape. On the night of 16 October he attempted to get his troops across the York to Gloucester Point, where the American line was thinly held, but a storm upset his plans. After this failure there was no other hope but relief from New York.

Clinton's delay. Clinton had been considering such a relief for some time, but there was doubt whether Graves' fleet, even when reinforced by three more ships from England, was equal to the task. There were also delays in refitting. Yet the greatest delay sprang from Clinton's indecision and failure to appreciate Cornwallis' plight until too late. Graves set sail on 17 October with 7,000 troops aboard. On that very day Cornwallis had begun negotiations on terms of surrender.

The surrender. After a destructive artillery barrage on the preceding day, a British drummer on 17 October mounted the parapet before Cornwallis' defenses and beat a parley. Firing ceased and the next day commissioners from both sides met to agree on terms of surrender. On 19 October 1781 Cornwallis' entire army of 6,000 marched out to lay down their arms while the British band played an old tune called "The World Turned Upside Down." This climactic campaign of the Revolution illustrates the successful application of the principles of the offensive, objective, mass, maneuver, and cooperation by the French and American allies.

The End of Active Hostilities. So far as active campaigning was concerned, Yorktown ended the war. Both Greene and Washington maintained their armies in position near New York and Charleston for nearly two years more, but the only fighting was some minor skirmishing in the South. Cornwallis' defeat resulted in the overthrow of the British cabinet and the formation of a new government in England that decided the war in America was lost. With some success, Britain devoted her energies to trying to salvage what she could in the West Indies and India. The independence for which Americans had fought thus virtually became a reality when Cornwallis' command marched out of its breeched defenses at Yorktown.

Surrender of Cornwallis at Yorktown, 19 October 1781.

Ingredients of American Success. The American victory in the War of the Revolution was the product of interaction of many complicated factors. The British were at a disadvantage from the start since they had to transport and maintain an army across 3,000 miles of ocean and reestablish military control over a vast geographic area with poor interior lines of communication. Yet given British control of the sea, the better organization of the British Military Establishment, the greater experience, training, and discipline of British officers and men, and the greater material resources Britain possessed, the outcome of the war was no foregone conclusion. The British Government and British military leaders forfeited many of their advantages by failing to develop the principle of unity of command and a coherent and consistent strategy for winning the war.

These British faults would hardly have been decisive, nevertheless, had Americans not been able to take advantage of them. The Americans created a government and an army while engaged in a major war, and while the army never grew to impressive size it did eventually achieve proficiency equal to that of the professional armies of the age. One of the principal ingredients of American success lay in the development of a group of capable and dedicated military leaders in this army who grew in stature as they gained in experience. Among these Washington stands preeminent with Nathanael Greene in undisputed second place. But other Americans like Daniel Morgan, Anthony Wayne, and Henry Knox, and the foreign volunteers like Von Steuben and Lafayette should not be forgotten.

Another ingredient of American success was the enthusiasm of the American soldier for his cause. It is no disparagement of the British and Hessian professionals to say that they never showed the same spirit as the Americans and that their principal virtues were revealed only in those situations where discipline and training counted most. Only men with some dedication to a cause could have endured the hardships of the march on Quebec, the crossing of the Delaware, Valley Forge, Morristown, and Greene's forced marches in the southern campaign of 1781. The rising of the Militia on numerous occasions gave evidence of the same spirit. The fault of the Militia was seldom lack of enthusiasm, but rather lack of discipline and training to make efficient use of that enthusiasm in open field battle. If Militia ran away on Long Island, at Kip's Bay, Camden, and Guilford Court House, they also gave impressive performances under different conditions at Lexington and Concord, Bennington, King's Mountain, the Cowpens, and in dozens of minor guerilla actions. The Continental Army gave the American cause that continued sustenance that only a permanent force in being could, but it was the Militia that more than once provided the essential margin of superiority without which the Americans could never have won.

Another essential ingredient was French aid—money, supplies, and in the last phase military force. Without French aid the patriots might have fought the British indefinitely in the interior of the country, but it seems unlikely they could have won a complete and decisive victory. The bulk of the muskets, bayonets, and cannon used by the Continental Army came from France. It was the predominance of French naval power and the presence of a French army that made the final stroke of the Revolution at Yorktown possible.

Military Lessons of the Revolution. The lessons that might have been learned from the Revolution were many, for, although the Americans finally won, it was in spite of, rather than because of, their system of military mobilization and administration. The experience of the Revolution demonstrated first and foremost the need for strong, central direction in war and the subordination of state to national interests. If anything was made clear, it was that no efficient and uniform national army could ever be formed on the scale necessary for a major war as long as the individual states had primary responsibility for recruiting and organizing the regiments. The Revolution also showed that the task of creating an army was a long and arduous one, that men must be enlisted for the duration of the war, that they must be subjected to a long period of training and discipline, and that there must be a sound and well-regulated system for the procurement and distribution of supplies. It also indicated that conscription, honestly, fairly, and uniformly administered, would be the most efficient and equitable system of raising such an army and that volunteers, even when encouraged by generous bounties, could not be persuaded to enlist in sufficient number. It did not prove that the Militia system as such was a failure, only that Militia or any other force on short-term enlistments and subject only to state control could never provide an effective and continuous force for a major war.

The men who drew up the Federal Constitution in 1787 profited from the experience of the Revolution and provided a Central Government with power to tax and raise military forces and a strong executive to carry out the decisions of Congress. The strictly military lessons of the Revolution were not so clearly appreciated or applied. The legend grew in America that an army could spring to arms overnight when the country was threatened. The legend took for its historical examples Lexington and Concord, Bunker Hill, Bennington, and King's Mountain and conveniently neglected the lessons of Long Island, Kip's Bay, Trenton, Germantown, Valley Forge, Stony Point, and Camden. The Militia was credited with having won the Revolution, and the long arduous process by which the Continental Army was forged into an effective fighting instrument forgotten. Much of the valuable contribution of von Steuben was consequently lost, and military policy was too frequently shaped in terms of the legend.

QUESTIONS

1. Why did the British transfer their main effort from north to south?

2. How did the conflict of views between Cornwallis and Clinton affect the British conduct of the war in 1780 and 1781? On which one do you think the greatest blame lies for the surrender at Yorktown?

3. Compare the performance of the Militia at Camden, King's Mountain, Cowpens, and Guilford Court House. What conclusions can you draw as to its virtues and defects as opposed to those of the Continental line?

4. Describe Greene's strategy in the southern campaign and show why it was successful.

5. What principles of war did Lincoln violate at Charleston? The British at Yorktown?

6. How does the Yorktown campaign illustrate the importance of the principle of mass?

7. What were the military lessons of the American Revolution?

Reading List

See list at end of chapter 3 for books applying to the whole Revolution.

Bolton, Charles K. *The Private Soldier Under Washington.* New York, 1902.

Dean, Sydney W. *Fighting Dan of the Long Rifles.* Philadelphia, 1942.

Draper, Lyman C. *King's Mountain and Its Heroes.* New York, 1929.

Freeman, Douglas S. *George Washington*, Vol. V, *Victory With the Aid of France.* New York, 1952.

Landers, Howard E. L. *The Virginia Campaign and Blockade and Siege of Yorktown.* Washington, 1931.

Lee, Henry. *Memoirs of the War in the Southern Department of the United States.* New York, 1869.

CHAPTER 6
1783–1812

The Question of a Peacetime Army. After Cornwallis was taken, the War of the Revolution gradually came to an end. On 30 November 1782, a year after the fighting had stopped, an armistice was agreed upon. It came into effect formally in late January 1783, when France signed preliminary articles of peace with Britain, and it was officially proclaimed by Congress on 11 April 1783. The definitive treaty of peace was signed on 3 September 1783. By this time the Continental Army had all but disappeared. While the peace negotiations were in progress, Congress had been wrestling with the question of demobilization, only to find itself becoming inextricably involved in a tangled web of postwar problems. Among the foremost of these were the matter of the Army's pay and the size of the peacetime establishment. Settlement of the pay accounts, which were months in arrears, and a decision whether officers were to receive half-pay for life, as they had been promised, hinged not only upon the ability of Congress to obtain funds for the purpose, but also upon the outcome of the political struggle in Congress between those who wanted a strong national government and those who preferred the existing loose federation of sovereign states. During the winter of 1782–83 the Army grew impatient. Having failed to obtain full redress from the state governments in the matter of pay and pensions, the officers were persuaded to look to Congress and to make common cause with the nationalists. Rumors that the Army would take matters into its own hands gained strength when several anonymous addresses were circulated among the officers at Newburgh urging them not to fight if the war continued or not to lay down their arms if peace were declared unless their pay accounts were settled. Congress finally gave in to the arguments of the nationalists, agreed to pay the men their back pay, and decided to give the officers full pay for five years in lieu of half-pay for life. Still the Government hesitated to disband the Army as long as the definitive treaty of peace was not ratified. With discontent mounting among the rank and file, Congress in May 1783 at last instructed Robert Morris to give the men three months' pay and directed Washington on 26 May to furlough the "war men"—the soldiers who had enlisted for the duration of the war. By mid-June most of the common soldiers and many of the officers had started for their homes. On 3 November 1783 Washington, in his last general order, directed the Army to turn in its arms and disband. Congress had not, however, provided for a permanent establishment. Until it should do so, a few Continentals would have to remain under arms to guard the military supplies at West Point and take over the ports and posts to be evacuated by the British. For these purposes Washington thought it necessary to retain in service one infantry regiment and a battalion of artillery totaling about 600 men.

In the spring of 1783 Congress had appointed a committee, with Alexander Hamilton as chairman, to study and recommend a plan for a permanent military establishment. General Washington, to whom the committee turned for advice, pointed out that a large standing army in time of peace had always been considered "dangerous to the liberties of a country" and that the Nation was "too poor to maintain a standing army adequate to our defense." The question might also be considered, he continued, whether any surplus funds that became available should not better be applied to "building and equipping a Navy, without which, in case of War we could neither protect our Commerce, nor yield that assistance to each other which, on such an extent of seacoast, our mutual safety would require." Nevertheless, it was his opinion, Washington wrote, that a small Regular army was indispensable in order to "awe the Indians, protect our Trade, prevent the encroachment of our Neighbors of Canada and the Floridas, and guard us at least from surprises; also for security of our magazines." He therefore recommended a force of four regiments of infantry and one of artillery, totaling 2,630 officers and men. Each infantry regiment was to have eight companies, of 50 rank and file (corporals and privates) and 3 sergeants each. This was a slight departure from the regimental structure of the Continental Army at the end of the Revolution. The smaller regiments proposed by Washington would, he pointed out, be more suited for detached garrison service and could easily be increased in strength in case of need. For the infantry he recommended the following disposition: one regiment along the northeastern frontier, with headquarters and four companies at the northern end of Lake Champlain; a second regiment in the forts along the Great Lakes, with headquarters and three companies at Niagara, another three companies at Detroit, and smaller detachments at three other posts; a third regiment in six posts from Fort Pitt to the mouth of the Ohio River; and the fourth regiment along the frontiers of Georgia and the Carolinas.

Hamilton's committee submitted its report to Congress on 18 June 1783. It had heard the views of General von Steuben, of Maj. Gen. L. L. DuPortail, Chief Engineer of the Army, and of General Lincoln, Secretary at War, in addition to those of Washington; but the committee, although drawing upon these various proposals, submitted its own plan, which Congress rejected. Sectional rivalries, opposition on the ground of unconstitutionality, and, above all, objections to the expense of maintaining the proposed army were too strong to be overcome. During the next two months members of the committee conferred with General Washington and made minor changes in the report. The committee finally recommended a peacetime army of 3,223 officers and men, more than 20 percent larger than that proposed by Washington. The report provided for four infantry regiments, each consisting of eight companies organized into two battalions, totaling 2,404 officers and men. In addition, there was to be a corps of artillerists and engineers, consisting of two battalions of artillery plus sappers, miners, and artificers (the engineers and service troops of that time), totaling 819 officers and men. A regiment of dragoons, originally included in the report, was eliminated in the final version. The difference in strength between the force proposed by the committee and that recommended by Washington was accounted for chiefly by the larger infantry companies. By decreasing the pay of the regimental staff officers and of the subalterns, the committee hoped to provide a larger force at less expense. Although he agreed that detached service along the frontiers and coasts would probably require more men than he had taken into account, Washington differed with the committee's opinion that a larger establishment could be provided more economically than the one he had recommended. A considerable number of the delegates to Congress had similar misgivings, for when the committee once more presented its report, on 23 October, Congress again refused to accept it. During the winter of 1783–84 the matter rested. Under the Articles of Confederation an affirmative vote of the representatives of nine states was required for the exercise of certain important powers, including military matters, and on few occasions during this winter were enough states represented for Congress to renew the debate.

In the spring of 1784 the question of a permanent peacetime army became mixed up with the politics of state claims to western lands. The majority of men in the infantry regiment and artillery battalion that constituted the "Regular" Army were from Massachusetts and New Hampshire, and, because the rest of the Continental Army had been discharged those states wanted to be rid of the financial burden of paying the extra pay that the legislatures had promised the men on enlistment. Congress refused to take over the responsibility unless the New England states would vote for a permanent military establishment. The New England representatives, led by Elbridge Gerry of Massachusetts, insisted that Congress had no authority to maintain a standing army, but at the same time they wanted the existing troops to occupy the western forts, which were situated in land claimed by the New England states. New York vigorously contested the New England claims to western lands, particularly in the region around Oswego and Niagara, and the delegates from New York refused to vote for any Regular military establishment unless Congress gave the state permission to garrison the forts with its own state forces. The

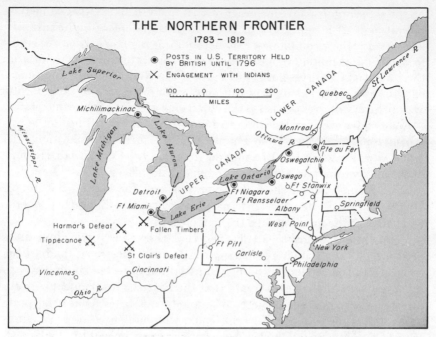

Map 13.   The northern frontier (1783–1812).

result was that attempts to establish a permanent national army failed.

The Frontier Posts.   The posts that had been the object of concern and discussion dominated the Great Lakes and the St. Lawrence River (Map 13).   Located on American territory south of the United States-Canadian boundary established by the peace treaty of 1783, they were in the hands of British troops when the war ended; but by the terms of the treaty they were to be turned over to the United States as speedily as possible.   Congress was agreed on the necessity of maintaining a force in readiness to occupy the posts as soon as the British troops left.   The problem was how and by whom the troops were to be raised.   A decision was even more urgent because the Government was in the midst of negotiating a treaty with the Indians in the Northwest, and it was thought that a sizable force "to awe the Indians" would facilitate the negotiations.   But the deadlock between the New England states and New York continued until early June 1784.

Finally, on the last two days of the session, Congress rushed through a compromise.   To placate the New Yorkers and satisfy the economy-minded New Englanders, the existing infantry regiment and battalion of artillery were ordered to be disbanded, except for an artillery company of 58 officers and men at West Point and a detachment of 29 officers and men at Fort Pitt.   The support of delegates who favored retaining a Federal army was obtained by tying the discharge of the existing force to a measure that provided for the immediate recruitment of a new force of 700 men, a regiment of eight infantry and two artillery companies. By not making *requisitions* on the states for troops, but merely *recommending* that the states provide them from their Militia, Congress got rid of most of the New England opposition on this score; by not assigning a quota for Massachusetts and New Hampshire, Congress satisfied the objections of most of the other states.

Four states were called upon to furnish troops according to the following quota: 260 men from Pennsylvania, 165 from Connecticut, 165 from New York, and 110 from New Jersey. Lt. Col. Josiah Harmar of Pennsylvania was appointed commanding officer. Only New Jersey and Pennsylvania showed any enthusiasm for raising the troops. By the end of September 1784 these two states had filled their quotas and had sent the men forward to the frontiers.

Meanwhile, Congress had learned that there was little immediate prospect of the British evacuating the frontier posts. Canadian fur traders and the settlers in Upper Canada had objected so violently to this provision of the peace treaty that the British Government secretly directed the Governor-General of Canada not to evacuate the posts without further orders. General Knox, who had succeeded Washington as Commander in Chief of the Army, was informed by the British commander in Canada that he had received no instructions about the posts and that without instructions the British troops would remain. Then, the failure of the United States to comply with a stipulation in the treaty regarding the recovery of debts owed to Loyalists provided the British with an excuse to postpone the evacuation of the posts for 12 more years. Therefore the New Jersey contingent of Colonel Harmar's force was sent to Fort Stanwix, in upstate New York, to assist in persuading the Iroquois to part with their lands. The remainder of the force moved to Fort MacIntosh, 30 miles down the Ohio River from Fort Pitt, where similar negotiations were carried out with the Indians of the upper Ohio.

Toward a More Perfect Union. The postwar problems had revealed a number of serious defects in the Articles of Confederation. The Federal Government lacked a separate executive branch and a judiciary. Congress, which exercised a certain amount of executive power as well as legislative, lacked an independent income. To some of the delegates, the conflicts and dissension between the states over the western lands seemed to carry the seeds of civil war. The opposition of New England delegates to a Federal army appeared to others as having been expressly designed to prevent Congress from acting in such circumstances.

Rioting and disturbances in Massachusetts throughout the fall and winter of 1786–87 supported the pessimism of those who feared the collapse of the new nation. A severe commercial depression following on the heels of the immediate postwar boom was causing particular distress among the back-country farmers. Angry mobs gathered in the Massachusetts hills, broke up the meetings of the courts, harried lawyers and magistrates out of the villages, and began moving toward the Government arsenal in Springfield. On 20 October 1786 Congress called on several of the states to raise a force of 1,340 officers and men to serve for three years. This time the New England States did not object to Congress taking action, but none of the troops voted by Congress reached the scene before the embattled farmers were dispersed by Massachusetts Militia. In late January 1787 an attack on the Springfield Arsenal led by Daniel Shays was thrown back by a force of local Militiamen with a "whiff of grapeshot." A few days later a large reinforcement of Militia from the eastern part of the state arrived at Springfield and put an end to the disorders. Recruiting for the force authorized by Congress continued until the following April. By then about 550 men had been enlisted and the question of expense was becoming bothersome. Congress therefore directed the states to stop recruiting and to discharge the troops already raised, except two artillery companies which were retained as a guard for the West Point and Springfield Arsenals. Shays' "rebellion" was thus responsible for the first augmentation of the Federal Army. More important was its effect in helping to persuade Americans that a stronger government was needed.

Rising concern over the ineffectiveness of the Federal Government, particularly in matters of finance and commercial regulation, finally led to the convening of a Constitutional Convention in the spring of 1787. To strengthen the military powers of the Government was one of the principal tasks of the Convention, a task no less important than establishing its financial and commercial authority. The general problem facing the Convention, that of power and the control of power, came into sharp focus in the debates on military matters, since the widespread suspicion of a strong central government and the equally widespread fear of a standing army were merged in the issue of the Government's military powers. Those who mistrusted a powerful government argued against a broad grant of authority not only in the fields of taxation and commercial regulation, but, and with especial force, in the matter of military affairs as well. Men like Alexander Hamilton, who on the other hand sought to give the Central Government wide latitude in handling both purse and sword, were also somewhat wary of standing armies. They, too, were concerned over the possible usurpation of political power by the military or its use by officeholders as an instrument for perpetuating their personal power. The Hamiltonians nevertheless were willing to have the country run the risk of being less free in order to be more safe. These differences of opinion were adjusted and the problem solved by the same excellent system of checks and balances that characterized the other features of the new framework built into the Constitution.

The new Constitution clothed the Central Government with adequate authority to raise and maintain an army without calling upon the states. By giving Congress the power to levy taxes, the Constitution provided the Central Government with the necessary financial means; by creating a separate executive branch, the Constitution made it possible for the daily business of the Government to be conducted without constant reference to the states. In the division of powers within the Federal Government, that of declaring war and of raising armies and providing for a navy was assigned exclusively to Congress, although in time of emergency Congress has often vested the President with more or less discretion in the matter of raising and maintaining armed forces. An important innovation was the assignment of all executive power to the President. Thus the Secretary of War became directly responsible to the President, and not to Congress. The Constitution specifically provided that the President should be Commander in Chief of the Army and Navy. As such his powers are exclusive, limited in their extent only "by their nature and by the principles of our institutions." The President therefore has the right to assume personal command of forces in the field, but for reasons of expediency he customarily delegates it. As Commander in Chief he is responsible for the employment and disposition of the armed forces in time of peace and for the general direction, when Congress has declared war and provided the means for carrying it on, of military and naval operations in war.

Washington, who had presided over the Constitutional Convention, became the first President under the new Constitution in March 1789, and on 7 August Congress created the Department of War. There was no change, however, in either the policy or the personnel of the Department. General Knox, who had been handling military affairs under the old form of government, remained in charge. Since there was no navy, a separate Department of the Navy was unnecessary, and naval affairs were included at first under the jurisdiction of the War Department. Harmar, who had been given the rank of brigadier general in 1787, was confirmed in his appointment, as were his officers, and the existing establishment was taken over intact into the service of the United States.

The Army in the Northwest. In August 1789 the authorized strength of the Army amounted to 960 officers and men; actual strength was about 750 or 800. All the troops, except the two artillery companies retained after Shays' Rebellion, were stationed along the Ohio River in a series of forts built after 1785. For a few years the troops had been chiefly occupied in driving squatters out of the public domain, a type of duty that neither endeared Harmar to the settlers nor trained his men for Indian fighting. After the enactment of the Northwest Ordinance in 1787, settlers began pouring into the Ohio country and trouble with the Indians immediately developed.

Washington, as early as 1783, had expressed himself in favor of enlarging the Army. Furthermore, during Washington's two terms as President, the strategic position of the United States changed as a result of the outbreak of war in Europe. There was consequently a progressive increase in the authorized strength of the Regular peacetime establishment from 1,283 officers and men in 1790 to 3,324 in 1796. In addition, Congress in March 1792 authorized the raising of three regiments to meet the temporary emergency caused by the Indians in the northwest, so that from 1792 to 1796 the total authorized strength of the Army including the emergency forces ranged from about 5,300 to 6,100 officers and men.

To General Harmar fell the honor of leading the first Regular troops that saw action after the Revolution, and with this honor he had to be content, for he derived no other from his campaign. Having decided to chastise the Indians in Ohio, Secretary Knox in June 1790 ordered Harmar to consult with Arthur St. Clair, Governor of the Northwest Territory, as to the best means of doing so. Under an authorization given to him the preceding fall, St. Clair called on Pennsylvania and Kentucky to send 1,500 Militiamen to Harmar at Cincinnati. By the end of September Harmar had assembled a motley collection of 1,453 men, including 320 Regulars, with which he set out for the Indian country. After struggling through the wilderness for more than two weeks his force reached the neighborhood of the principal Indian villages near what is now Fort Wayne, Ind. Instead of pushing on with his entire strength, Harmar on three successive occasions violated the principle of mass by sending forward small unsupported detachments of about 200 to 500 Militia plus 50 or 60 Regulars. The undisciplined Militia could not be restrained from scattering in search of Indians and plunder, and, after two of the detachments suffered heavily in brushes with the Indians, Harmar took the rest of his army back to Cincinnati (map 13). His conduct was severely criticized, but a court of inquiry, noting the untrained troops with which Harmar had been provided and the lateness of the season, exonerated him of blame.

The next year, in the spring of 1791, Congress resolved to take stern measures against the Indians. A second infantry regiment was added to the Regular Army and the President was authorized to raise a corps of 2,000 men for a term of six months, either by calling for Militia or by enlisting volunteers into the service of the United States. Governor St. Clair was commissioned a major general and placed in command of the expedition. So slow did recruiting and the procuring of supplies proceed that St. Clair was unable to set out before 17 September, more than two months after the date originally planned, and only by calling on the neighboring states for Militia was he able to bring his force up to strength. When it finally marched out of Fort Washington (the army post at Cincinnati), St. Clair's force consisted of about 600 Regulars, which was almost all the actual infantry strength of the U. S. Army, plus about 800 enlisted "levies" and 600 Militiamen.

The general was determined not to repeat Harmar's tactical mistakes and he carried his determination to the point of not sending out scouts on local reconnaissance. By 3 November St. Clair had advanced about 100 miles northward from Cincinnati and was encamped for the night near the headwaters of the Wabash River. The next morning, just before dawn, a horde of about 1,000 savages, which had surrounded the camp during the night, fell upon the unsuspecting troops. Untrained, low in morale as a result of inadequate supplies, and led by a general who was suffering from rheumatism, asthma, and "colic," the Army was thrown into confusion by the sudden assault. St. Clair and less than half his force survived unscathed. Out of approximately 1,400 men engaged in the action, about 637 were killed and 263 wounded. The rest fled back to Cincinnati in disorder. It was an excellent example of what could happen through failure to adhere to the principle of security.

Alarmed and outraged over the defeat of St. Clair, Congress doubled the authorized strength of the Army by providing for three additional regiments, two of which were to be infantry and the other a composite regiment of infantry and light dragoons. Although these new regiments were to be added to the Regular Army, they were intended as a temporary augmentation to be "discharged as soon as the United States shall be at peace with the Indian tribes." The bad effects of short-term enlistments were to be avoided.

Anthony Wayne, the dashing commander of the Pennsylvania Line during the Revolution, was appointed major general to succeed St. Clair. Recruiting began in midsummer, and in November 1792 Wayne moved his growing force from Fort Pitt to a camp about 30 miles down the Ohio River, where he spent the winter training and drilling his men. Correcting previous mistakes, General Wayne insisted on rigid discipline and strict training. Conscious of the welfare of his men, he saw to it that supplies were adequate and equipment satisfactory. At the same time the Army was reorganized into a "Legion," a term widely used during the 18th century and which had come to mean a composite organization of all combat arms under one command. In the reorganization of 1792 the Army, instead of being composed of regiments, was made up of four "sub-legions," each commanded by a brigadier general and each consisting of two infantry battalions, one battalion of riflemen, one troop of dragoons, and one company of artillery. To develop an *esprit de corps*, he had each sub-legion wear

Maj. Gen. Anthony Wayne

distinctive insignia. In honor of the reorganization, Wayne gave the
name of "Legionville" to his camp on the Ohio.

In the spring of 1793 General Wayne took the Legion down the
river to Cincinnati. While attempting to persuade the Indians to
submit peacefully he continued to drill his men. By early October
the negotiations with the Indians had broken down, and the Legion
set out over the route that Harmar and St. Clair had taken with most
unfortunate results. Wayne was in even poorer health than St. Clair
but of stronger will. Like St. Clair, he moved slowly and methodically, building a series of forts and blockhouses along his line of
march. In spite of his efforts to improve morale, he found desertion
as serious a problem as it had been for Harmar and St. Clair.

After spending the winter at one of the forts, the Legion continued
its march northward, and on the site of St. Clair's defeat Wayne
built Fort Recovery. Here, at the end of June 1794, the Indians

Battle of Fallen Timbers, 20 August 1794.

attempted to repeat their earlier success by making a full-scale assault against the fort. In a day-long battle the Legion beat off the attack with such effect that when the Army resumed its march at the end of July the war chief of the Indians was at first disposed to accept Wayne's offer of peace. Reinforced by some 1,400 mounted Militia, which brought his force up to about 3,000 men, Wayne advanced to within a few miles of Fort Miami, a post recently established by the British on the site of what is now Toledo, Ohio. There, on 20 August 1794, almost within sight of the British guns, the Indians again attacked. Wayne's men held their ground; then, with a furious bayonet charge they drove the enemy out of the cover of fallen trees that gave the Battle of Fallen Timbers its name. In the open prairie the Indians were at the mercy of Wayne's mounted volunteers, and in less than an hour the rout was complete. Wayne's operations constitute an historical example illustrating the successful application of the principles of objective, security, mass, and maneuver.

Ignoring the protests of the British commander at Fort Miami, Wayne stayed where he was for several days burning the Indian villages and destroying crops. Then, having accomplished his mission, he led the Legion back to Cincinnati. The western tribes, their resistance broken, finally agreed to make peace and cede their lands in Ohio to the United States by the Treaty of Greenville, 3 August 1795. Their submission had been hastened by news that England was about to evacuate the frontier posts and British troops soon withdrew from United States territory.

The Militia. During these formative years, the prevailing view was that the brunt of an invasion would be met by, and the general security of the country could be safely entrusted to, the Militia, provided the Militia was well organized and well trained. Time and again Washington pointed out that the only alternative to a large standing army was an effective militia, but the efforts of President Washington, Knox, and Hamilton to make the Militia more effective by bringing it more under the control of the Federal Government failed. The problem was the amount of discipline and training required by the extremely complicated tactics of that day. Without such training no troops could be expected to employ the formal linear tactics successfully. When permitted to fight in less standardized fashion—either from behind fortifications or as irregulars—Militiamen gave a good account of themselves. Stronger ties of loyalties to the states than to the Federal Government resulted in a strict interpretation of the constitutional provision that specifically reserved to the states the "Authority of training the Militia according to the discipline prescribed by Congress." Congress in the Act of May 8, 1792 went no further than prescribing General von Steuben's system of discipline and field exercises as the rules to be followed by the Militia; the extent and thoroughness of the training was left completely to the states. The result was that, in the vital matter of training, the Militia was neither uniform nor well regulated.

The authority to employ Militia for suppressing insurrection and executing the laws of Congress, which the new Constitution gave to the Federal Government, was first exercised in 1794, when President Washington sent a force of Militia into western Pennsylvania, under Maj. Gen. Henry Lee, to enforce the laws. No resistance was encountered. As a show of force, the demonstration was impressive: as an indication of the military value of the Militia in an emergency, it was inconclusive.

Military Realities, 1783–1797. The policies and Military Establishment of the new nation developed realistically, guided by certain factors often overlooked by present day critics. First, there was little actual military threat to the United States from a foreign nation. Britain had no desire or design to reconquer its lost colonies, although Britain, as well as Spain, sought to curb the United States from expanding beyond the borders established by the Treaty of 1783. The military alliance that bound the United States to England's archrival, France, was a potential source of danger, but England and France were at peace until 1793. Second, the jealousy of the individual states toward one another and toward the Federal Government made it difficult to establish a Federal army and defeated efforts to institute Federal regulation of the Militia beyond the minimum permitted by the Constitution. Third, the Federal Government, plagued by financial problems, was faced with the necessity of paring expenditures to the bone. Fourth and finally, there was extreme reluctance on the part of Americans to serve in the Army, either as Regular soldiers or as volunteers, for more than a very brief period. At no time was it possible to recruit enough men to bring the Regular Army up to authorized strength. In view of these factors, a larger military establishment was not feasible, even though the well-trained Militia, which was to take the place of a large standing army, was lacking.

While the United States was launching a new government, France had undergone a revolution, as a result of which Europe became embroiled in war. When Great Britain in 1793 joined the coalition against France, the strategic position of the United States was made precarious. At first France hoped the United States would be a friendly neutral, if not an ally, and would permit French privateers to fit out and recruit crews in American ports. Britain clamped down a blockade and in the first year of the war seized at least 300 American merchant vessels. Jay's Treaty eased the mounting crisis in Anglo-American relations. By acquiescing in the British doctrine of contraband, the United States obtained a settlement of some of the long-standing problems, including the evacuation of the frontier posts, but only at the expense of domestic unity and peaceful relations with the French. Regarding Jay's Treaty as evidence of a pro-British policy on the part of the United States, France retaliated by seizing American vessels that were trading with the British, by sending secret agents to stir up the Creek Indians along the southern frontier, and by meddling in American politics in an attempt to bring about the defeat of the "pro-British" administration. If the European war had made possible the settlement of old differences with England and Spain, at the same time it created new and serious problems of its own. As soon as Europe went to war, both France and England adopted a course of action that threatened the peace of America. This was the legacy that President Washington handed over to his successor, John Adams, in 1797.

In 1797 the Army had an authorized strength of about 3,300 officers and men but an actual strength of about 3,000. The Legion type of organization and the troops that had been added for the temporary emergency in 1792 had been dropped by an act of 30 May 1796, and the Army had returned to a regimental type of organization with four regiments of infantry of eight companies each, a corps of artillerists and engineers consisting of four battalions, and two companies of light dragoons. It corresponded very closely to the force that Hamilton's committee had recommended to Congress in 1783. Each company was smaller in size than that of the Legion had been, and the four battalions of riflemen authorized for the Legion were discontinued.

During 1796 and early 1797 there was something of a redeployment into the Southwest, so that in the latter year nine companies of infantry, about two companies of artillery, and the entire force of dragoons were stationed along the southwestern frontier. Up in the old Northwest there were five infantry companies at Detroit and smaller detachments at a dozen scattered forts elsewhere in the territory. Fort Washington, at Cincinnati, was the major installation and had perhaps a full regiment as a garrison. A program of harbor defense construction at the important seaports had been started in 1794 under the supervision of French technicians who had fled their country after the overthrow of the monarchy. By 1797 there were small harbor defense garrisons at New York, Philadelphia, Baltimore, Norfolk, Wilmington, N. C., and Charleston. The rest of the Army was stationed along the Canadian border from the lakes eastward and at the older posts like West Point, Carlisle, and Fort Pitt.

There was no navy. Congress in 1794 had approved the building of six powerful frigates but had hesitated to provide funds. By 1797 work on three of the ships had been pushed slowly along. The Treasury Department had 10 small revenue cutters, built in 1791, but they were by this time considered too small and inadequate for the protection of the revenue, let alone to defend the coasts or protect American shipping.

President Adams and the "Undeclared War" With France. When the French continued to attack American vessels and refused to receive the newly appointed American Minister to Paris, President Adams called Congress into special session to consider national defense. Recognizing the nature of the threat, Adams particularly urged that immediate steps be taken to provide a navy. He also recommended that Congress provide for improved harbor defenses and additional cavalry, that the Militia law of 1792 be revised to provide for a better organization and training, and that the President be authorized to call out an emergency force, although he saw no immediate need for it. The naval recommendations were passed, but, except for a modest appropriation for harbor defenses and an act authorizing the President to call out 80,000 Militia for a maximum term of three months, Congress voted down the military recommendations.

By the spring of 1798 the country had become thoroughly aroused, and when President Adams recommended an expanded defense program Congress did somewhat better by it. Again the naval increases recommended by the President and the Secretary of War were speedily passed, and a separate Navy Department was created. Of the three regiments—one of infantry, one of artillery, and one of cavalry—which the administration recommended adding to the Regular Army, Congress authorized the additional artillery but failed to approve the cavalry. With respect to the infantry regiment, the Secretary of War proposed to Congress that the regiment act in the double capacity of marines and infantrymen. But instead of creating a regiment that would be a Jack-of-all-trades, Congress voted the U. S. Marine Corps into existence, making it part of the Army or the Navy according to whether the marines served on land or on shipboard. The number of companies in each of the four regular infantry regiments was increased from 8 to 10; a sizable sum for harbor defenses and ordnance was voted; and a "Provisional Army"—the emergency force that Adams had suggested the year before—was authorized.

The defects of short-term enlistments were avoided by setting the duration of the "existing differences between the United States and the French Republic" as the term of enlistment for the Provisional Army. However, when the President again asked for an increase in the Regular Army, Congress instead gave him authority to accept privately armed and equipped volunteer units for short-term service. Adams never made use of this authority, but went ahead with the plans to raise the 12 infantry regiments and 1 cavalry regiment that made up the Provisional Army. Washington was persuaded to come out of retirement to accept command as lieutenant general. Alexander Hamilton was appointed senior major general. By the beginning of 1799 the officers had been appointed and in May 1799 recruiting began. By the time the Provisional Army was disbanded in June 1800, about 4,100 men had been mobilized, assembled in camps, and given from 6 to 12 months' training. Preparation of new drill regulations, to replace Von Steuben's, was begun under Hamilton's direction, but before the task was finished the French crisis had ended and the Provisional Army was discharged.

By the beginning of 1799 the infant Navy had grown to a respectable size. Three of the new frigates and about 30 other ships were in service under orders to take any French armed vessels they encountered. In the space of two years, 111 French privateers were captured and 4 sunk; and more than 70 American merchantmen that had been taken by the French were recovered.

The growing naval might of the United States and the possibility that the United States might join Britain in a full-scale war helped to persuade the French Government to agree to negotiations. Furthermore, the French had been pressing Spain to give Louisiana back to France as a step towards restoring the French colonial empire in America, and for this venture peace with the United States was necessary. On 30 September 1800 a treaty was signed in which France agreed to recognize American neutrality and to refrain from seizing American vessels that were not carrying contraband. On the very next day, 1 October 1800, France and Spain signed a secret treaty turning Louisiana over to France, and a few months later England and her allies made peace with France.

The Navy Under Jefferson. President Jefferson took office in 1801 committed to a policy of peace and economy. With Europe at peace and our own relations with France and England better than they had been for 10 years past, Jefferson proceeded to economize. The hatchet fell on the Navy first. On the last day of the Adams administration Congress had authorized the sale of all but 13 of the Navy's vessels, and of these only 6 had to be kept in commission. Jefferson lost no time in carrying out the wishes of Congress. The Navy that had acquitted itself so well in the quasi-war with France was immediately sold, except for the frigates and a few of the other larger ships. The smaller vessels that Jefferson disposed of were exactly what the Navy needed when war with the Barbary pirates broke out a few months later.

The Jeffersonian Army. The Army did not feel the effect of the economy drive until March 1802, when Jefferson had been in office for a year. Until then the Military Establishment was much as Adams had left it after the Provisional Army troops had been discharged, with an authorized strength of 5,438 officers and men. Its actual strength was about 4,000 officers and men. In the reduction of March 1802 the total strength of the Army was cut back to 3,220 officers and men, approximately what it had been in 1797 when Adams took office; but it was now more than 50 percent stronger in artillery. The cavalry arm was eliminated. This remained the regular peacetime establishment until the war with England in 1812. Additional forces were authorized in 1808 and 1812, but they were special, emergency forces not being considered a part of the Regular peacetime establishment.

Ever since the Revolution, the Army had faced a lack of trained technicians, particularly in engineering science, and had depended largely upon foreign experts. To remedy this unsatisfactory situation, Washington, Knox, Hamilton, and others had recommended the establishment of a military school. During Washington's administration, the rank of cadet was created in the Corps of Artillerists and Engineers. Two cadets were assigned to each company for instruction. Formal establishment of the Military Academy came in 1802. In the reorganization of the Army under Jefferson in March 1802 the engineers were separated from the artillery and the Corps of Engineers consisting of 10 cadets and 7 officers was created, which was to be stationed at West Point and to constitute the Military Academy. Within a few years the Academy became a center of study for the military sciences in general and a source of trained engineer officers. By 1812 the Academy could list 89 graduates. Sixty-five of them were still in the Army and had an important part in building fortifications during the war.

The Army and Westward Expansion. Not long after Jefferson became President, rumors—confirmed in 1802 by the French Government—reached America that France had acquired Louisiana from Spain. The news was upsetting. In the first place, many Americans, including Jefferson, had believed that when Spain lost its weak hold on the colonies the United States would automatically fall heir to them. But with a strong power like France in possession, it was useless to wait for the colonies to fall into the lap of the United States. In the second place, a new problem of security was raised. Up to this time the Mississippi Valley had not been particularly regarded as an invasion route. The problem of frontier defense had been chiefly one of pacifying the Indians, keeping the western territories from breaking away, and preventing American settlers from molesting the Spanish. Now, with France, a strong, aggressive nation, as backdoor neighbor, the frontier problem became tied up with the question of security against possible foreign threats. In the third place, the transfer of Louisiana to France was accompanied by restraints on American trade down the Mississippi. American settlers had been permitted by Spain to send their goods down the river and to store them at New Orleans. At the urging of France, Spain, just before transferring the colony, revoked the privilege of storing goods at New Orleans, an action which made it almost impossible for Americans to send goods out by this route. These considerations persuaded Jefferson to inquire about the possibility of purchasing New Orleans from France, and when Napoleon, anticipating the renewal of the war in Europe, offered to sell the whole of Louisiana, Jefferson quickly accepted. Thus in 1803 the size of the United States was suddenly doubled. The Army was called upon to provide small garrisons for New Orleans and the other former Spanish posts on the lower Mississippi, and preparations for exploring the newly acquired territory were hastened. Brig. Gen. James Wilkinson, who had survived his own rascalities and the various reorganizations of the Army to become the senior officer, was appointed Governor of the Louisiana Territory (map 14).

A year before the purchase of Louisiana, Jefferson, with the reluctant consent of the Spanish Government, had decided to send an exploring party into the unknown territory west of the Mississippi. The acquisition of this territory now made such an exploration even more desirable. To lead the expedition, Jefferson chose Capt. Meriwether Lewis and Lt. William Clark, both of whom had served under General Wayne in the Northwest. Leaving St. Louis in the spring of 1804, the party, including 27 enlisted men, traveled up the Missouri River, crossed the Rocky Mountains, and followed the Columbia River down to the Pacific, which was reached after much hardship in November 1805. On the return journey the party explored the region of central Montana and returned to St. Louis in September 1806.

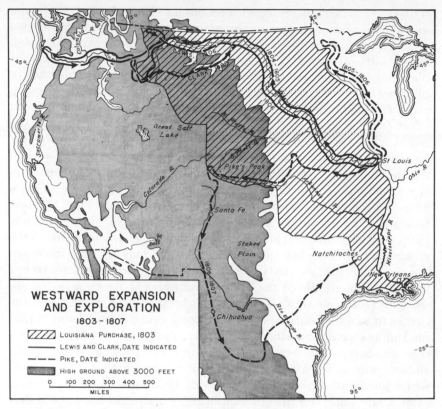

WESTWARD EXPANSION
AND EXPLORATION
1803 - 1807

///// LOUISIANA PURCHASE, 1803
——— LEWIS AND CLARK, DATE INDICATED
- - - PIKE, DATE INDICATED
▓▓▓ HIGH GROUND ABOVE 3000 FEET

0 100 200 300 400 500
MILES

Map 14. Westward expansion and exploration, 1803–1807

While Lewis and Clark were exploring beyond the Missouri, General Wilkinson sent out Capt. Zebulon M. Pike on a similar expedition to the headwaters of the Mississippi. In 1807 Wilkinson organized another expedition. This time he sent Captain Pike, accompanied by the general's son, Lt. James B. Wilkinson, and 19 soldiers, westward into what is now Colorado. After exploring the region around the peak that now bears his name, Pike encountered some Spaniards and his party was taken to Santa Fe. From there they were escorted down into Mexico, then back across Texas to Natchitoches, where, once more in American territory, they were released. The Lewis and Clark expedition and those of Captain Pike remain as great epics of the West, and at the time they contributed much to the geographic and scientific knowledge of the country.

The Battle of Tippecanoe. After the Battle of Fallen Timbers, settlers had pushed rapidly into Ohio and beyond into lands still claimed by the Indians. In an effort to resist the encroachments, a tribal confederacy was organized by Tecumseh, chief of the Shawnees, and his brother, the Prophet. The Governor of the Indiana Territory,

William H. Harrison, rejected Tecumseh's demands that the white settlers keep out. Urged on by the settlers, Governor Harrison decided in the summer of 1811 to strike at the Indians before they could descend on the settlements. His scheme was approved by the Secretary of War and 300 Regular infantry were placed under his command, in addition to about 650 Militia, including mounted riflemen. Moving north from Vincennes at the end of September 1811, Harrison built a fort on the edge of the Indian country and then continued on to the neighborhood of Tecumseh's principal village (map 13). Halting his force about a mile west of the village, Harrison on 6 November invited the Indians to a conference. The troops were encamped in the form of a trapezoid around their wagons and baggage on a piece of high wooded ground that rose above the marshy prairies. On the side facing the Indian village were a battalion of the Regulars and three companies of Militia. Along the opposite side, facing away from the village, were another battalion of Regulars and four Militia companies. The mounted riflemen were posted on the flanks, except for three troops located in the middle of the camp. Acting as spokesman in the absence of Tecumseh, who was in the South attempting to persuade the Creeks to join the confederacy, the Prophet apparently promised that the Indians would not attack while Harrison's proposal for a conference was being considered; but that night the Prophet whipped the Indians into a frenzy and incited them into action. The Indians struck just before dawn. Harrison's situation was very similar to that of St. Clair, and for a time there was grave danger of his force suffering the same fate. Furious hand-to-hand combat followed the Indians' wild charge, which at first had threatened to overrun the camp. Although taken by surprise, the soldiers rallied and then counterattacked. The end came when the cavalry charged in on the Indians and drove them from the field. The troops pushed forward to the Indian village and, finding it deserted, burned it. The entire force then started back to Vincennes, where it was disbanded. Harrison had lost 39 men killed and missing and had 151 wounded, of whom 29 died.

The engagement by no means solved the frontier problem in the northwest. The outbreak of war with England eight months later overshadowed any permanent effects of the battle, but in after years a tradition grew up which helped to elevate Harrison to the presidency in 1841.

The American Reaction to the Napoleonic Wars. The brief period of peace in Europe ended and the second round of the great conflict between England and France began in 1803, shortly after the purchase of Louisiana. It was a much more serious affair than the earlier war, which had almost drawn the United States into the line-up against France. Both Britain and France adopted policies under which American merchant shipping, whether carrying contraband or not, was subject to search and seizure. In an attempt to insulate America from the war in Europe President Jefferson and his successor, James Madison, tried to keep American merchant vessels at home. Jefferson's Embargo Act, which came into effect on 22 December 1807, prohibited trade with all foreign countries. It was replaced by the Non-Intercourse Act of 1809, which prohibited trade only with England and France. The Non-Intercourse Act was, in turn, replaced by an act in May 1810, known as Macon's Bill No. 2, which reopened trade with England and France but provided that, if either of those coun tries repealed its restrictive measures and the other failed to follow suit, the Non-Intercourse Act would be put into effect against the nation that continued its restrictions.

The legislation failed to keep the United States from becoming embroiled in the war and was unsuccessful in forcing England and France to respect neutral trade. Neither the Jefferson administration nor that of Madison recognized that, under the new scheme of economic warfare being waged by both England and France, the American measures were in effect provocative acts, bound to bring the United States into the war on one side or the other.

Jefferson's Embargo Act and, to a lesser extent, the Non-Intercourse Act of 1809 did succeed in crippling American trade, something that neither Britain nor France had succeeded in doing. As a result, the American people, who were already divided by sectional jealousies and by the French crisis during Adams' administration, were so thoroughly disunited that the Government could not count on the loyalty and support of a sizable part of the population.

In February 1808, two months after the embargo went into effect, President Jefferson submitted to Congress a proposal for augmenting the Army. He made two requests: (1) a volunteer force of 24,000 men who would be required to serve 12 months out of any 24 in a 5-year period and to take 2 or 3 months' training every year during the period; (2) an addition to the Regular Army consisting of five infantry regiments, one rifle regiment, one light artillery regiment, and one regiment of light dragoons, which would add 6,000 men to the forces. Congress on 12 April 1808 authorized the eight additional regiments but rejected the volunteer force. Two years later, in January 1810, the actual strength of the Army totaled 6,954 officers and men, of whom 2,765 belonged to the three regiments of the Regular peacetime establishment and 4,189 to the eight new regiments. Probably as an economy measure, the light dragoons of the additional force were equipped as light infantry and were not mounted until the outbreak of the War of 1812. Relations with Britain were rapidly deteriorating by January 1810, and President Madison recommended that a volunteer force of 20,000 men be raised. Congress, apparently satisfied with the existing Militia system, again refused to vote a volunteer force. No further additions to the Army were authorized until January 1812, when Congress voted 13 additional regiments totaling about 25,700 officers and men and authorized the President to call 50,000 Militiamen into service.

Six months later, on 18 June 1812, Congress declared war against England. A Senate proposal to declare war also against France failed to pass by only two votes.

Summary. The years from 1783 to 1812 were a formative period in which the new nation faced the tasks of disbanding its wartime Army, of organizing a new government and a permanent peacetime military establishment, and of making an adequate response to the emergency situations that arose. Sectional jealousy, partisan politics, fiscal difficulties, and widespread distrust of a large standing army complicated the efforts of the Government to solve its military problems. The first serious external threat to the security of the United States arose when France and England went to war. It developed as a result of the vulnerability of American commerce, a situation for which Jefferson had no remedy except to withdraw American shipping from the seas. Madison's response was an even more dangerous policy of economic coercion. Neither policy was adequate preparation for the war into which the United States was drifting.

QUESTIONS

1. What two important effects resulted from Shays' Rebellion?
2. What are the military powers of Congress under the Constitution? of the President?
3. Why did Wayne succeeed against the Indians, whereas St. Clair and Harmar failed?
4. In what task was the Army chiefly occupied from 1803 to 1808?
5. How did the measures taken by President Adams to meet an external threat differ from those adopted by President Madison?

Reading List

Jacobs, J. R. *The Beginnings of the U. S. Army.* Princeton, 1947.
Agar, Herbert. *The Formative Years.* Boston, 1947. 2 vols.
Wildes, Harry E. *Anthony Wayne.* New York, 1941.
Brooks, Noah. *Henry Knox.* New York, 1900.

CHAPTER 7

WAR OF 1812

The Origins. The immediate origins of the War of 1812 can be found in the seizure of American ships, the insults and injuries to American seamen by the British Navy, and problems of the American frontier. The British outrages at sea took two distinct forms. One was the seizure and forced sale of merchant ships and their cargoes for allegedly violating the British blockade of Europe. Although France had declared a counterblockade of the British Isles and had seized American ships, England was the chief offender because its Navy had greater command of the seas. The second, more insulting, type of outrage was the seizure of men from American vessels for forced service in the Royal Navy. The pretext for impressment was the search for deserters, who, it was claimed, had taken employment on American vessels.

To the country at large the seizure of American seamen was a much more serious matter than the loss of cargoes. Finally, when a British naval vessel in June 1807 attacked and disabled the USS *Chesapeake* and impressed several members of the crew, a general wave of indignation rose in which even the maritime interests joined. This was an insult to the flag, and had Jefferson chosen that moment to go to war with England he would have had a united country behind him. As it was, he decided to clamp down an embargo on American trade. In New England, scores of prosperous shipowners were ruined, and a number of thriving little seaports were thrown into an economic depression from which few of them recovered. While the rest of the country remembered the *Chesapeake* affair and stored up resentment against Britain, maritime New England transferred its anger to Jefferson and his party.

The seat of anti-British fever was in the Northwest and the lower Ohio valley, where the frontiersmen had no doubt that their troubles with the Indians were the result of British intrigue. Stories of British Army muskets and equipment being found on the field were circulated after every Indian raid. By 1812 the westerners were convinced that their problems could best be solved by throwing the British out of Canada. By this time, also, the balance of political power was shifting westward; ambitious party leaders had no choice but to align themselves with the "War Hawks," and 1812 was a presidential election year.

President Madison's attempt to use economic pressure to force England to repeal its obnoxious blockade almost succeeded. The revival of the Non-Intercourse Act against Britain, prohibiting all trade with England and its colonies, coincided with a failure of the grain harvest in England and with a growing need of American provisions to supply the British troops fighting in Spain. As a result, on 16 June 1812 the British Foreign Minister announced that the blockade would be relaxed as far as American shipping was concerned. Had there been an Atlantic cable, war might have been averted. President Madison had sent a message to Congress on 1 June listing all the complaints against England and asking for a declaration of war. Dividing along sectional lines, the House had voted for war on 4 June, but the Senate did not approve until 18 June and then by only six votes.

The Opposing Forces. *American strength.* At the outbreak of the war the United States had a total population of about 7,700,000 people. A series of border forts garrisoned by very small detachments of the Regular Army stretched along the Canadian boundary. The most important of these were Fort Michilimackinac, on the straits between Lake Michigan and Lake Huron, Fort Dearborn, near the present Chicago, Fort Detroit, and forts along the Niagara River and Lake Ontario, at Buffalo, Fort Niagara, Oswego, and Sacketts Harbor (map 15). The actual strength of the Army in June 1812 totaled approximately 11,744 officers and men, which included an estimated 5,000 recruits enlisted for the additional force authorized the preceding January. The Navy consisted of 20 vessels: the 3 large 44-gun frigates, 3 smaller frigates of the *Constellation* class rated at 38 guns, and 14 others. They mounted an aggregate of slightly more than 500 guns. In addition, there were 62 small gunboats in commission, but they proved to be of little value. The Army's supply of muskets and ordnance was adequate. In the six months before declaring war, Congress had readily authorized preparations for it, while at the same time refusing to appropriate funds for carrying out the preparations adequately. In the spring of 1812 two of the separate service departments necessary for a greatly enlarged military establishment had been provided. In March a civilian Commissary-General of Purchases and a Quartermaster Department had been created and given the function of procuring and purchasing all military stores and articles of supply, camp equipage, and transport. In May Congress had made provision for an Ordnance Department, responsible for the inspection and testing of all ordnance, cannon balls, shells, and shot, the construction of gun carriages and ammunition wagons, and the preparation and inspection of the "public powder." The Corps of Engineers was enlarged by the addition of a company of bombardiers, sappers, and miners, and the Military Academy at West Point was expanded and reorganized. In addition to increasing the Regular

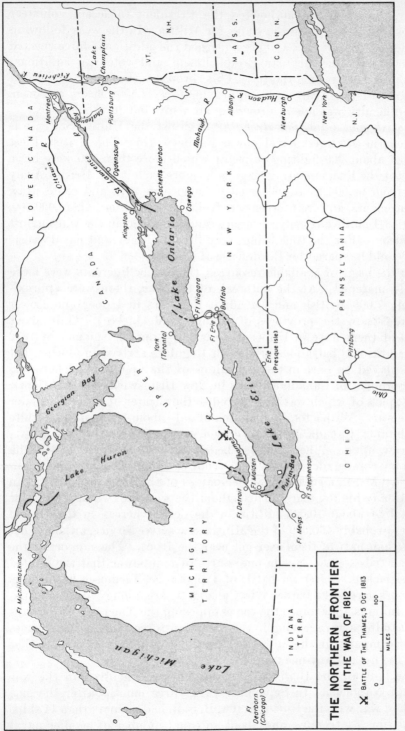

The map legend reads:

**THE NORTHERN FRONTIER
IN THE WAR OF 1812**

X   BATTLE OF THE THAMES, 5 OCT 1813

0   100

MILES

Map 15.   The Northern Frontier in the War of 1812.

Army, Congress had authorized the President to accept volunteer forces and to call upon the states for Militia. In the week following the declaration of war, Congress merged the additional force enacted in 1808 with the Regular Establishment and voted an additional eight regiments of infantry. This brought the total *authorized* strength of the Army up to approximately 44,500 officers and men. The difficulty was not in providing an army, but in raising one.

British and Canadian strength. Against the United States was ranged the strongest naval power in the world. The British Fleet totaled about 600 fighting ships, of which more than 100 were large ships of the line, mounting 60 guns or more each. The British Army had from 90,000 to 100,000 men in service in 1812 and could draw replacements and reinforcement from a population of 18,000,000. Most of Britain's resources were tied up, however, in the war against Napoleon. For the time being, very little military and naval assistance could be spared for the defense of Canada.

On the basis of available resources, the two belligerents were more evenly matched. At the outbreak of the war, there were approximately 7,000 British and Canadian Regulars in Upper and Lower Canada (now the provinces of Ontario and Quebec). Only about 1,600 of them were in Upper Canada. During the summer of 1812 two additional battalions of British Regulars arrived in Quebec, but they played no part in the campaigns of the first year. There was one regiment of Canadian troops in New Brunswick, on the Atlantic coast, part of which was transferred to the theater of operations later in the war. With a total population of only about half a million white inhabitants, Canada itself had only a very small reservoir of Militia to draw upon. When the war began, Maj. Gen. Isaac Brock, the military commander and civil governor of Upper Canada, had available 800 Militiamen, the flank companies of the organized Militia, in addition to his Regulars. Throughout the war, the two provinces put a total of about 10,000 Militia in the field, whereas in the United States probably 450,000 of the Militia saw active service, although not more than half of them ever got near the front. The support of the Indian tribes gave Canada one source of manpower that the United States lacked. After the battle of Tippecanoe, Tecumseh had led his warriors across the border into Canada, where, along with the Canadian Indians, they joined the forces opposing the Americans. Perhaps 3,500 Indians were serving in the Canadian forces during the Thames River campaign in the fall of 1813, probably the largest number that took the field at any one time.

The bulk of the British Navy was likewise involved in the war against Napoleon. In September 1812, three months after the outbreak of war with the United States, Britain had no more than 11 ships of the line, 34 frigates, and about an equal number of smaller naval vessels in the western Atlantic. These were all that could be spared for operations in American waters, which involved the tremendous task of escorting British merchant shipping, protecting the St. Lawrence River, blockading American ports, and at the same time hunting down the American frigates.

American and British weaknesses. An important element of weakness in the American position was the disunity of the country. In the New England States public opinion ranged from mere apathy to actively expressed opposition to the war. A good many Massachusetts and Connecticut shipowners fitted out privateers—privately owned and armed vessels that were commissioned to take enemy ships—but New England contributed little else to the prosecution of the war, while continuing to sell grain and provisions to the British.

Canada was not faced with the same problem. Nevertheless, many inhabitants of Upper Canada were recent immigrants from the United States who had no great desire to take up arms against their former homeland, and there were other Canadians who thought that the superiority of the United States in numbers and materiel strength made any defense hopeless. That General Brock, the British commander, was able to overcome this spirit of defeatism is a tribute to his leadership.

The Strategic Pattern. The fundamental strategy was simple enough. Americans could scarcely wait for a declaration of war before undertaking the conquest of Canada. Likewise, on the naval side, American strategy was to take the offensive immediately: to set loose on the high seas a swarm of privateers and the small Navy for the purpose of destroying British commerce. The old invasion route to Canada by way of Lake Champlain and the Richelieu River led directly to the most populous and most important part of the enemy's territory. The capture of Montreal would have cut the line of communication upon which the British defense of Upper Canada depended, and the fall of that province would have been inevitable. But this invasion route was near the center of disaffection in the United States, and little local support in the shape of men and supplies could be expected. The West, where enthusiasm for the war ran high and where the Canadian forces were weak, offered a safer, if less strategically sound, theater of operations. The initial assaults were therefore delivered across the Detroit River and across the Niagara River between Lake Erie and Lake Ontario. To attack in this theater was a striking violation of the principles of objective and economy of force.

The war progressed through three distinct stages. The first, lasting until the spring of 1813, saw England so hard pressed in Europe that neither men nor ships in any great number could be spared for the conflict in North America. The United States was free to take the initiative, to invade Canada, and to send out cruisers and privateers against enemy shipping. The second stage, lasting from early 1813 to the beginning of 1814, was one in which England was able to establish a tight blockade but still could not materially reinforce the troops in Canada. In this stage the American Army, gaining experience, won its first successes. The third stage, in 1814, was marked by the constant arrival in North America of British Regulars and naval reinforcements which enabled the enemy to raid the American coast, almost at will, and to take the offensive in several quarters. At the same time, in this final stage of the war, American forces fought their best fights and won their most brilliant victories.

The First Campaigns. *Fall of Forts Michilimackinac, Detroit, and Dearborn.* The first blows of the war were struck in the Detroit area and at Fort Michilimackinac. Brig. Gen. William Hull, Governor of Michigan Territory, was given command of operations in that area. He arrived at Fort Detroit on 5 July 1812 with a force of about 1,500 Ohio Militiamen and 300 Regulars, which he led across the river into Canada a week later (map 15). At that time the whole enemy force on the Detroit frontier amounted to about 150 British Regulars, 300 Canadian Militiamen, and some 250 Indians led by Tecumseh. Most of the enemy were at Fort Malden, about 20 miles south of Detroit, on the Canadian side of the river. General Hull had been a dashing young officer in the Revolution, but age and its infirmities had by this time made him cautious and timid. Instead of moving directly against Fort Malden, Hull issued a bombastic proclamation to the people of Canada and stayed at the river landing almost opposite Detroit. He sent out several small raiding detachments along the Thames and Detroit Rivers, one of which returned after skirmishing with the British outposts near Fort Malden. In the meantime, General Brock, who was both energetic and able, had sent a small party of British Regulars, Canadians, and Indians across the river from Malden to cut General Hull's communications with Ohio. By this time Hull, discouraged by the loss of Fort Michilimackinac and of the news that the enemy in Fort Malden had received reinforcements (which he overestimated tenfold) and fearing that Detroit would be completely cut off from its base of supplies, on 7 August began to withdraw his force back across the river into Fort Detroit. The last American had scarcely returned before the first men of Brock's force appeared and began setting up artillery opposite Detroit. By 15 August five guns were in position and opened fire on the fort with considerable effect. The next morning Brock led his troops—about 700 British and Canadians and some 600 Indians—across the river, but, before he could launch an assault, Hull surrendered. Militiamen were released under parole; Hull and the Regulars were sent as prisoners to Montreal. Later paroled, General Hull returned to face a court-martial for his conduct of the campaign, was sentenced to be shot, and was immediately pardoned. Brock's campaign against Hull amply demonstrates the principles of offensive and objective.

On 15 August, the day before the surrender of Detroit, Fort Dearborn had also been lost. On that day, acting on orders from General Hull, the small garrison at Dearborn had evacuated the post and started out across the Michigan peninsula to Detroit, but it was almost immediately attacked and wiped out by a band of Indians, who then destroyed the fort.

With the fall of Forts Michilimackinac, Detroit, and Dearborn, the entire territory north and west of Ohio fell into enemy control. The settlements in Indiana lay open to attack. The neighboring tribes of Indians hastened to join the winning side, while the Canadians in the upper province quickly lost the spirit of defeatism with which they had reacted to the outbreak of the war.

The Niagara Campaign—defeat at Queenston. Immediately after taking Detroit, Brock transferred most of his forces to the Niagara frontier where, at Lewiston, a force of New York Militiamen was assembled under the command of Maj. Gen. Stephen van Rensselaer (map 16). General van Rensselaer owed his appointment not to any military experience, of which he had none, but to his family position. Untrained and inept as he was in military art, Van Rensselaer at least fought the enemy—more than could be said of the Regular Army commander in that theater, Brig. Gen. Alexander Smyth. By the beginning of October, Van Rensselaer had about 2,300 Militiamen at Lewiston. General Smyth had 1,650 Regulars and nearly 400 Militiamen at Buffalo, but he refused to cooperate with a Militia general. Another force of Regulars, about 1,300 strong, was at Fort Niagara. Opposite Van Rensselaer's camp lay the Canadian town of Queenston, protected by a fortified battery on the steep heights between the town and the Niagara River and defended by about 300 men, mostly British Regulars. After one attempt had been called off, Van Rensselaer began crossing the river during the early morning hours of 13 October 1812. The first echelon of about 300 men, mostly Regulars, were pinned down for a time on the river bank below the heights, but, finding a path that had been left unguarded, the troops clambered to the summit, surprised the enemy, and drove them down into Queenston. A counterattack by the British, in which General Brock was killed, was repulsed. During the morning 600 or more reinforcements were ferried across the river, but less than half of them joined the troops holding the heights. Most of Van Rensselaer's Militiamen flatly refused to cross, and General Smyth ignored his request for aid. Meanwhile, British and Canadian reinforcements had arrived in Queenston. Van Rensselaer's men, tired and outnum-

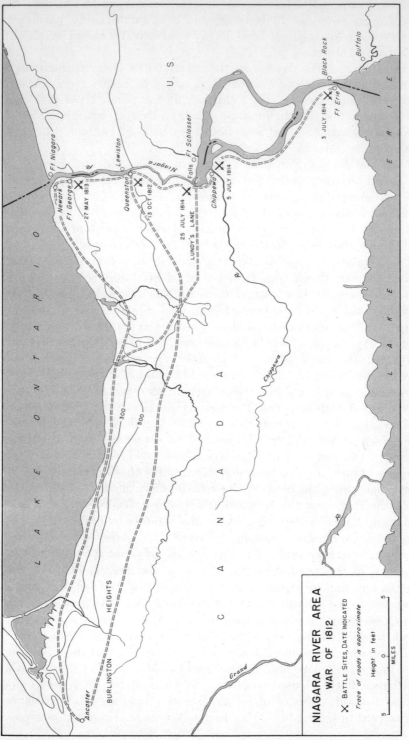

Map 16. Niagara river area, War of 1812.

bered, put up a stiff resistance on the heights, but in the end were overwhelmed—90 Americans were killed and nearly 1,000 captured.

Winter Stalemate. After the defeat at Queenston, Van Rensselaer resigned and was succeeded by the unreliable General Smyth who spent his time composing windy proclamations. Disgusted at being marched down to the river on several occasions only to be marched back to camp again, the new army, which had assembled after the battle of Queenston, gradually melted away. The men who remained lost all sense of discipline, and finally at the end of November the Volunteers were ordered home and the Regulars went into winter quarters. General Smyth's request for leave was hastily granted and three months later his name was quietly dropped from the Army rolls.

Except for minor raids across the frozen St. Lawrence, there was no further fighting along the New York frontier until the following spring. During the Niagara campaign the largest force then under arms, commanded by Maj. Gen. Henry Dearborn, had been held in the neighborhood of Albany, more than 250 miles from the scene of operations. Dearborn had had a good record in the Revolutionary War and had served as Secretary of War during the Jefferson administration. Persuaded to accept the command of the northern theater, except for Hull's forces, he was, nevertheless, in doubt as to the extent of his authority. But when it was clarified he was reluctant to exercise it. Proposing to move his army, which included seven regiments of Regulars with artillery and dragoons, against Montreal in conjunction with a simultaneous operation across the Niagara River, Dearborn was content to wait for his subordinates to make the first move. When Van Rensselaer made his attempt against Queenston, Dearborn, who was still in the vicinity of Albany, showed no sign of marching towards Canada. At the beginning of November he sent a large force north to Plattsburg and announced that he would personally lead the army into Montreal, but he got no farther than the boundary. At that point he turned around and marched his troops back to Plattsburg, where they went into winter quarters.

The War at Sea. If the land campaigns of 1812 reflected little credit on the Army, the war at sea brought lasting glory to the infant Navy. Capt. Isaac Hull became the first hero of the war, when as commander of the *Constitution* he outfought and sank the British frigate *Guerriere*. Captain Hull's victory was the first of a series of single-ship actions in which the big 44-gun frigates *Constitution* and *United States* humbled the pride of the Royal Navy. At the same time, American privateers were picking off English merchant vessels by the hundreds. Altogether nearly 1,000 British vessels were captured by American privateers during the war. Having need of American foodstuffs, Britain was at first willing to take advantage of

New England's opposition to the war by not extending the blockade to the New England coast; but by the beginning of 1814, the whole American coast was effectively blockaded. Of the 22 American warships that had managed to get to sea, only the *Constitution* and 4 smaller vessels were still operating when the war ended. Likewise, except for a flurry of activity in European waters during the summer and fall of 1814, most of the American privateers had been bottled up in port or driven off the seas. The Navy had, however, boosted American morale in the early dark days of the war, and the few privateers that managed to slip past the blockade had good hunting to the end.

1813—The Second Year. On land, the objects of the American plan of campaign for 1813 were the recapture of Detroit and an attack on Canada across Lake Ontario (map 15). For the Detroit campaign, the American troops were placed under the command of Brig. Gen. William H. Harrison, Governor of the Indiana Territory and the hero of Tippecanoe. The difficulties of a winter campaign were tremendous, but the country demanded action. Harrison therefore started north towards Lake Erie at the end of October 1812 with some 6,500 men. A sizable detachment, amounting to about 1,000 men, pushed on to a point nearly opposite Fort Malden, where they were defeated and brutally massacred by a slightly larger force of Canadians and Indians. Harrison then decided to suspend operations for the winter. Building two forts—Meigs and Stephenson— he posted his army near the Michigan border at the western end of Lake Erie.

Capture of York. The Ontario campaign was entrusted to General Dearborn, who was ordered to move his army from Plattsburg to Sackett's Harbor, where Commodore Isaac Chauncey had been assembling a fleet. Dearborn was to move across the lake to Kingston, capture it and destroy the British flotilla there, then proceed to York (now Toronto), the capital of Upper Canada, to capture the stores at that place, and finally he was to cooperate with a force from Buffalo in seizing the forts on the Canadian side of the Niagara River. When the time came to move, Dearborn and Chauncey, hearing a rumor that the British forces in Kingston had been reinforced, decided to bypass that objective and attack York directly. About 1,700 men were embarked and sailed up Lake Ontario without incident, arriving off York before daybreak on 27 April. Dearborn, who was in poor health, turned over the command of the assault to Brig. Gen. Zebulon Pike, the explorer of the Southwest. The landing, about four miles west of the town, was unopposed. The British garrison of about 600 men, which occupied a fortification about halfway between the town and the landing, was overwhelmed after sharp resistance; but just as the Americans were pushing through the fort towards the town, a powder magazine or mine exploded, killing or disabling many Americans and a number of British soldiers. Among those killed was General Pike. Remnants of the garrison fled towards Kingston, 150 miles to the east. The losses were heavy on both sides—almost 20 percent of Dearborn's forces had been killed or wounded. With General Dearborn incapacitated and General Pike dead, the troops apparently got out of hand. Public buildings in York were looted or burned and the provincial records destroyed. After holding the town for about a week, Dearborn's force recrossed the lake to Niagara to join an attack against the forts on the Canadian side of the Niagara River.

Sackett's Harbor defended. Meanwhile, Sackett's Harbor had been almost stripped of troops for the raid on York and for reinforcing the army at Fort Niagara. At Kingston, across the lake, Sir George Prevost, the Governor General of Canada, had assembled a force of 800 British Regulars in addition to Militia. Taking advantage of the absence of Chauncey's fleet, which was at the other end of the lake, Prevost on the night of 26–27 May launched an attack on Sackett's Harbor with his entire force of Regulars. The town was defended by about 400 men from several outfits of the Regular Army and approximately 750 Militiamen, under the command of Brig. Gen. Jacob Brown of the New York Militia. Brown posted his men in two lines in front of a fortified battery to cover a possible landing. The British landed under heavy fire, pressed rapidly forward, routed the first line, and pushed the second back into the prepared defenses. There the Americans held. The British then tried two frontal assaults but were repulsed with heavy losses. While they were re-forming for a third attack, General Brown, displaying courage, initiative, and determination, rallied the Militia and sent them towards the rear of the enemy's right flank. This was the turning point. In danger of being cut off, the British hurriedly withdrew to their ships and sailed back to Kingston, having suffered serious losses.

Fort George taken. On the same day that Prevost sailed against Sackett's Harbor, General Dearborn at the western end of Lake Ontario was invading Canada with an army of 4,000 men. The operation began with a well-executed and stubbornly resisted amphibious assault led by Col. Winfield Scott and Comdr. Oliver Hazard Perry, USN, with Chauncey's fleet providing fire support. Outnumbered more than two to one, the British retreated, abandoning Fort George and Queenston to the Americans (map 16). An immediate pursuit might have sealed the victory, but Dearborn, lacking energy and drive, waited several days and then sent a part of his command, some 2,000 men, after the enemy. The detachment advanced to within 10 miles of the British and camped for the night with slight regard for security. During the night a force of about 700 British attacked the camp and thoroughly routed the Americans. Some two weeks later, on 24 June, a smaller detachment, which had ventured 15 miles outside the fort, surrendered to a force of British and Indians that was half as large. After these reverses there was no further action of consequence on the Niagara front until the end of the year. Dearborn, again incapacitated by illness, resigned his commission in early July. Both armies were hard hit by disease and the American forces were further reduced by the renewal of the war in the west and by an attempt against Montreal.

The Battle of Lake Erie. Hull's disaster at Detroit in 1812 and Harrison's unsuccessful winter campaign had clearly shown that any offensive action in that quarter depended upon first gaining control of Lake Erie. To build a fleet and seize control of the lake was the task that had been assigned to Commander Perry. Throughout the spring and summer of 1813, except for the time he had joined Dearborn's force, Perry had been busy at Presque Isle assembling his fleet, guns, and crews. By the beginning of August his force was superior to that of the British in every respect except long-range armament. Sailing up the lake, he anchored in Put-in-Bay, near the line still held by General Harrison in the vicinity of Forts Meigs and Stephenson, and there on 10 September Perry met the British fleet, defeated it, and gained control of Lake Erie.

The Battle of the Thames. As soon as the damage to Perry's ships and the captured British vessels had been repaired, Harrison embarked his army and sailed against Fort Malden. A regiment of Kentucky mounted riflemen, commanded by Col. R. M. Johnson, moved along the shore of the lake toward Detroit. Outnumbered on land and open to attack from the water, the British abandoned both Forts Malden and Detroit and retreated eastward. After leaving a detachment to garrison the forts, Harrison set out after the enemy with Colonel Johnson's cavalry regiment, five brigades of Kentucky volunteers, and a part of the 27th Infantry, a force of about 3,500 men. On 5 October he made contact with the British on the banks of the Thames River about 85 miles from Malden (map 15). The enemy numbered about 2,900, of whom about 900 were British Regulars, and the remainder Indians under Tecumseh. Instead of attacking with infantry in the traditional line-against-line fashion, Harrison ordered Colonel Johnson to make a mounted attack. The maneuver succeeded completely. Unable to withstand the hard-riding Kentuckians, the British surrendered in droves. The Indians were routed and Tecumseh, who had brought so much trouble to the western frontier, was killed. Among those who distinguished themselves on this day was Commander Perry, who had ridden in the front rank of Johnson's charge.

As a result of the victory, Lake Erie became an American lake. The Indian confederacy was shattered. The American position on the Detroit frontier was reestablished, a large portion of Canadian territory was brought under American control, and all threat to that position was eliminated.   There was no further fighting in this quarter for the rest of the war.   The success of Harrison's operations illustrates the principles of cooperation, the offensive, and mass.

The small remnant of the British force that had escaped capture at the Thames—no more than 250 men and a few Indians—made its way overland to the head of Lake Ontario.   Harrison, after discharging his Kentucky Volunteers and arranging for the defenses of the Michigan Territory, sailed after them with the remainder of his army.   He arrived at the Niagara frontier at an opportune time, since the American forces in that theater were being called upon for men to support a two-pronged drive against Montreal.

Another attack on Montreal.   The expedition against Montreal in the fall of 1813 was one of the biggest fiascoes of the war.   It involved a simultaneous drive by two forces: one, an army of about 4,000 men assembled at Plattsburg on Lake Champlain under the command of Brig. Gen. Wade Hampton; and another, of about 6,000 men, which was to attack down the St. Lawrence River from Sackett's Harbor under the command of Maj. Gen. James Wilkinson.   Relations between Hampton and Wilkinson were strained, with the two generals scarcely on speaking terms and no one on the spot to command the two of them.   Neither had sufficient strength to capture Montreal without the other's aid; each lacked confidence in the other; and both suspected that they were being left in the lurch by the War Department.   At first contact with the British, about halfway down the Chateaugay River, Hampton retreated and, after falling back all the way to Plattsburg, resigned from the Army.   Wilkinson, after having a detachment of about 2,000 men severely mauled in an engagement just north of Ogdensburg, also abandoned his part of the operation and followed Hampton into Plattsburg.

Reverses at Niagara.   In the meantime, during December 1813, the British took advantage of the weakened state of American forces on the Niagara frontier to recapture Fort George and to cross the river and take Fort Niagara, which remained in British hands until the end of the war.   Before evacuating Fort George the Americans had burned the town of Newark and part of Queenston.   In retaliation the British, after assaulting Fort Niagara with unusual ferocity, loosed their Indian allies on the surrounding countryside and burned the town of Buffalo and the nearby village of Black Rock.

Operation in the South.   During 1813 a new theater of war had opened in the South.   While the "War Hawks" of the Ohio Valley had urged war in the hope of conquering Canada, the people of Georgia, Tennessee, and the Mississippi Territory had been entertaining similar designs against Florida, a Spanish possession (map 17).   The fact that in Europe, Spain and England were fighting against a common enemy, Napoleon, presented the southern "War Hawks" with an excuse for invading Florida.   One of the most ardent expansionists in the south was

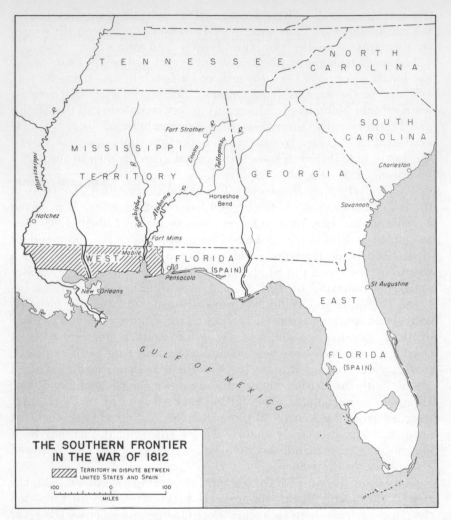

Map 17. *The southern frontier in the War of 1812.*

Andrew Jackson, commander of the state Militia of Tennessee, who wrote the Secretary of War that he would "rejoice at the opportunity of placing the American eagle on the ramparts of Mobile, Pensacola, and Fort St. Augustine," and for this purpose Tennessee had raised a force of 2,000 men under Jackson's command. Congress, after much debate, approved only an expedition into that portion of the Gulf Coast which was in dispute between the United States and Spain, into West Florida as it was called, and refused to entrust the venture to the Tennesseans. Just before he went north to take part in the Montreal expedition, General Wilkinson led his Regulars into the disputed part of West Florida and without meeting any resistance occupied Mobile, while the Tennessee army was left cooling its heels in Natchez.

Inspired by Tecumseh's early successes, the Creek Indians took to the war path in the summer of 1813 with a series of outrages that culminated in the massacre of more than 500 men, women, and children at Fort Mims. Jackson, with characteristic energy, reassembled his army, which had been dismissed after Congress rejected its services for an attack on Florida, and moved into the Mississippi Territory. His own energy added to his problems, for he completely outran his primitive supply system and dangerously extended his line of communication. The hardships of the campaign and one near defeat at the hands of the Indians destroyed any enthusiasm the Militia might have had for continuing in service. Jackson was compelled to entrench at Fort Strother, on the Coosa River, and remain there for several months until the arrival of a regiment of the Regular Army gave him the means to deal with the situation. At the end of March 1814 he decided that he had sufficient strength for a decisive blow against the Indians, who had gathered a force of about 900 warriors and many women and children in a fortified camp at the Horseshoe Bend of the Tallapoosa River. Jackson had about 2,000 Militiamen and Volunteers, nearly 600 Regulars, a few pieces of artillery, and several hundred friendly Indians. The attack was completely successful. A bayonet charge led by the Regulars routed the Indians, who were ruthlessly hunted down and all but a hundred or so of the warriors killed. "I lament that two or three women and children were killed by accident," Jackson later reported. The remaining hostile tribes fled into Spanish territory. The most important result of the campaign was the appointment of Jackson to major general in the Regular Army. The war against the Creeks had no direct bearing on the outcome of the war with Britain, but for that matter neither had any of the campaigns in the North so far.

1814—The Last Year of the War. *Organizational changes.* In March 1813 Congress had authorized an expansion of the Army staff. An adjutant general's department, an inspector general's department, a surgeon general, and an apothecary general were re-created and eight topographical engineers were assigned to the staff. In early 1814, Congress increased the Army to 45 infantry regiments, 4 regiments of riflemen, 3 of artillery, 2 of light dragoons, and 1 of light artillery. The number of general officers was fixed at 8 major generals and 16 brigadier generals in addition to the generals created by brevet.

After the setbacks at the end of 1813, a lull had descended on the northern frontier. In March 1814 Wilkinson made a foray from Plattsburg with about 4,000 men and managed to penetrate about eight miles into Canada before being stopped by some 200 British and Canadian troops supported by gunboats on the Richelieu River (map 15). It was an even more miserable failure than his attempt of the preceding fall. As a result of these and earlier setbacks, most of the senior generals were replaced by younger, more active officers—a

Maj. Gen. Andrew Jackson.

change that came too late to affect the outcome of the war. Jacob
Brown, who had been commissioned a brigadier general in the Regular Army after his heroic defense of Sackett's Harbor, was promoted
to major general and placed in command of the Niagara-Lake Ontario
theater. Command of the Lake Champlain frontier and promotion to
major general was given to 38-year-old George Izard, who had been
educated for a military career but later failed to fulfill expectations.
Six new brigadier generals were appointed from the ablest, but not
necessarily most senior, colonels in the Regular Army, among them
Winfield Scott, who had distinguished himself at the battle of Queenston Heights and who was now placed in command at Buffalo. During
the spring of 1814 Scott threw himself energetically into the task of
drilling and training his new recruits.

    The Battle of Chippewa. British control of Lake Ontario, which
had been achieved by feverish construction activity during the pre-

Scott's Brigade at Chippewa, 5 July 1814.

vious winter, obliged the Secretary of War to recommend operations
from Buffalo. Disagreement within the President's cabinet delayed
adoption of a plan until June. By this time Commodore Chauncey's
naval force at Sackett's Harbor was expected to be strong enough to
challenge the British fleet and a coordinated attack on the Niagara peninsula was decided upon (map 16). General Brown was instructed
to cross the Niagara River in the vicinity of Fort Erie and, after assaulting the fort, to move against Fort George and Newark or to seize
and hold a bridge over the Chippewa River as he saw fit.

Brown accordingly crossed the Niagara River on 3 July with his
whole force, about 3,500 men, took Fort Erie and then advanced
toward the Chippewa River, 16 miles away. There a smaller British
force, including 1,500 Regulars, had gathered to oppose the American
Army. General Brown posted his army in a strong position behind a
broad ditch or creek with his right flank resting on the Niagara River
and his left protected by a swamp. In front of the American position
was an open plain, beyond which flowed the Chippewa River, and
on the other side of the river were the British.

In celebration of Independence Day, General Scott had promised
his brigade a grand parade on the plain. The next day, 5 July, he
formed his brigade, numbering about 1,300 men, but on moving
forward he discovered that they would have a battle instead of a
parade, for the British Regulars had crossed the river without being
discovered and were lined up on the opposite edge of the plain. Scott
ordered his men to charge and the British advanced to meet it. Alter-
nately stopping to fire and then moving forward, closing the gaps
torn by the volleys and artillery fire, the two lines approached each
other. They came together first at the flanks, while about 60 or 80
yards apart at the center, and at this point the British line crumbled
and broke. By the time a second brigade sent forward by General
Brown reached the battlefield, the British had withdrawn across

141

the Chippewa River and were retreating towards Ancaster, on Lake Ontario. Scott's casualties amounted to 48 killed and 227 wounded; British losses were 137 killed and 304 wounded.

Battle of Lundy's Lane. Brown followed the retreating British as far as Queenston, where he halted to await the arrival of Commodore Chauncey's fleet. After waiting two weeks for Chauncey, who failed to cooperate in the campaign, Brown withdrew to Chippewa, proposing to strike out across country to Ancaster by way of a crossroad known as Lundy's Lane from which he could reach the Burlington Heights at the head of Lake Ontario and the rear of the British.

Meanwhile the British had drawn reinforcements from York and Kingston and more troops were on the way from Lower Canada. Sixteen thousand British veterans, fresh from Wellington's victories against the French in Europe, had just arrived in Canada, too late to participate in the Niagara campaign but in good time to permit the redeployment of the troops that had been defending the upper St. Lawrence. By the time General Brown decided to pull back from Queenston, the British force at Ancaster amounted to about 2,200 men under General Riall; another 1,500 British troops were gathered at Fort George and Fort Niagara at the mouth of the Niagara River.

As soon as Brown began his withdrawal, Riall sent forward about 1,000 men along Lundy's Lane, the very route by which General Brown intended to advance against Burlington Heights; another force of more than 600 British moved out from Fort George and followed Brown along the Queenston road; while a third enemy force of about 400 men moved along the American side of the Niagara River from Fort Niagara. Riall's advance force reached the junction of Lundy's Lane and the Queenston road on the night of 24–25 July, the same night that Brown reached Chippewa, about three miles distant. Very much concerned that the British force on the opposite side of the Niagara would cut off his line of communication and entirely unaware of Riall's force at Lundy's Lane, General Brown on 25 July ordered Scott to take his brigade back along the road towards Queenston in the hope of drawing back the British force on the other side of the Niagara; but that force in the meantime had crossed the river and joined Riall's men at Lundy's Lane. Scott had not gone far when much to his surprise he discovered himself face to face with the enemy.

The ensuing battle, most of which took place after nightfall, was the hardest fought, most stubbornly contested engagement of the war. For two hours Scott attacked and threw back the counter-attacks of a numerically superior force of British, who, moreover, had the advantage in position. Then both sides were reinforced. With Brown's whole force engaged, the Americans now had about 2,900 men on the field against approximately the same number of British. At this point the British were forced back from their position and their artillery was captured.   The battle then continued without material advantage to either side until just before midnight, when General Brown ordered the exhausted Americans to fall back to the camp across the Chippewa River.   The enemy, equally if not more exhausted, remained where they were, unable to follow.   Casualties on both sides had been heavy and about equal.   The loss among officers was especially heavy.   On the American side, both General Brown and General Scott were severely wounded, Scott so badly that he saw no further service during the war.   On the British side, General Riall and his superior, General Drummond, who had arrived with the reinforcements, were wounded and Riall was taken prisoner.

Both sides claimed Lundy's Lane as a victory, as well they might, but the fact is that Brown's invasion of Canada was halted.   Commodore Chauncey, who failed to prevent the British from making use of Lake Ontario for supply and reinforcements, contributed to the unfavorable outcome.   In contrast to the splendid cooperation between Harrison and Perry on Lake Erie, relations between Brown and Chauncey were far from satisfactory.   A few days after the Battle of Lundy's Lane the American army withdrew to Fort Erie and held this outpost on Canadian soil until early in November.

Siege of Fort Erie.   Reinforced after Lundy's Lane, the British laid siege to Fort Erie at the beginning of August but abandoned the effort on 21 September after suffering extremely heavy casualties.   Shortly afterwards General Izard arrived with reinforcements from Plattsburg and advanced as far as Chippewa, where the British were strongly entrenched.   After a few minor skirmishes, he decided to cease operations for the winter.   The works at Fort Erie were destroyed and the Army withdrew to American soil on 5 November.

Campaigns on the Chesapeake.   During the summer of 1814 the British had been able not only to reinforce Canada but also to stage several raids on the American coast.   Eastport, Maine, on Passamaquoddy Bay, and Castine, at the mouth of the Penobscot River, were occupied without resistance.   This operation was something more than a raid since Eastport lay in disputed territory and it was no secret that Britain wanted a rectification of the boundary.   No such political object was attached to the British forays in the region of Chesapeake Bay.

In the spring of 1813 Hampton, Va., at the mouth of the bay and Havre-de-Grace, Md., at its head, had been pillaged and burned by the British.   Now, in the summer of 1814, a force of some 4,000 British troops under Maj. Gen. Robert Ross landed on the right bank of the Patuxent River and marched on Washington.   At the Battle of Bladensburg, Ross easily dispersed a mixed force of about 5,000 that had been hastily gathered together to defend the Capital.   The British then entered Washington, burned the Capitol, the White House, and other public buildings, and returned to their ships.   Baltimore was next on the schedule, but that city had been given time to prepare its defenses. The approach to Baltimore by land was covered by a rather formidable line of redoubts; the harbor was guarded by Fort McHenry and blocked by a line of sunken gunboats. The Maryland Militia delayed the invaders and caused them considerable loss, including General Ross, who was killed. When the fleet failed to reduce Fort McHenry, the assault on the city was called off. Inspired by the sight of the American flag still flying over the fort after the bombardment, a young Washington attorney, Francis Scott Key, who was being detained on one of the British vessels, was moved to write a poem "The Star-Spangled Banner." It was soon set to a popular tune of the day and became the American national anthem.

| *Macdonough's Victory on Lake Champlain.* Two days before the attack on Baltimore, the British had suffered a much more serious repulse on Lake Champlain. After the departure of General Izard for the Niagara front, there had remained at Plattsburg a force of about 3,300 men under the command of Brig. Gen. Alexander Macomb. Supporting them was a small fleet under Commodore Thomas Macdonough. Across the border in Canada was an army of British veterans of the Napoleonic wars, more than 16,000 strong. At the beginning of September 1814, Sir George Prevost, the Governor General of Canada, was ready to invade the United States. Moving slowly up the Richelieu River toward Lake Champlain, he crossed the border and on 6 September arrived before Plattsburg with about 11,000 men. There he waited for almost a week until his naval support was ready to join the attack. With Militia reinforcements, Macomb now had about 4,500 men manning a strong line of redoubts and blockhouses that faced a small river. Macdonough had anchored his vessels in Plattsburg Bay, out of gunshot from the British, but in a position to resist an assault on the American line. On 11 September the British flotilla appeared and Prevost ordered a joint attack. There was no numerical disparity between the naval forces, but an important one in the quality of the seamen. Macdonough's ships were manned by well-trained seamen and gunners, the British ships by hastily recruited French-Canadian Militia and soldiers, with only a sprinkling of regular seamen. As the enemy vessels came into the bay the wind died and the British were exposed to a heavy raking fire from Macdonough's long guns. The British worked their way in, came to anchor, and the two anchored fleets began slugging at each other, broadside by broadside. At the end the British commander was dead and his ships battered into submission. Prevost immediately called off the land attack and withdrew to Canada the next day.

Macdonough's victory ended the gravest threat that had arisen so far. More important was the impetus given to peace negotiations then under way. News of the two setbacks—Baltimore and Plattsburg—reached England simultaneously, aggravating the war weari-

Battle of New Orleans, 8 January 1815.

ness of the British and bolstering the efforts of the American peace commissioner to obtain satisfactory terms.

Battle of New Orleans. The progress of the peace negotiations influenced the British to continue an operation that General Ross, before his repulse and death at Baltimore, had been instructed to carry out: namely, a descent upon the Gulf Coast, the object of which was the capture of New Orleans and a possible severing of Louisiana from the United States (map 17). Maj. Gen. Sir Edward Pakenham was sent to America to take command of the expedition. On Christmas Day, 1814, Pakenham arrived at the mouth of the Mississippi to find his troops disposed on a narrow isthmus below New Orleans between the Mississippi River and a cypress swamp. They had landed two weeks earlier at a shallow lagoon some ten miles east of New Orleans and had already fought one engagement. In this encounter, on 23 December, General Jackson, who had taken command of the defenses on 1 December, almost succeeded in cutting off an advance detachment of 2,000 British, but, after a three-hour fight in which casualties on both sides were heavy, he was compelled to retire behind fortifications covering New Orleans.

The main American position was on the east bank of the Mississippi extending along a ditch stretching from the river to a swamp. Behind the ditch Jackson had raised earthworks and strengthened them with bales of cotton. The defenses were manned by about 3,500 men with another 1,000 in reserve. More than 20 pieces of artillery, including a battery of 9 heavy guns on the opposite bank of the Mississippi and the guns of a schooner, were prepared to support the American defenses.

After trying an artillery duel on 1 January, which the American gunners won, Pakenham decided on a frontal assault in combination with an attack against the American troops on the west bank. The main assault was to be delivered by about 5,300 men, while about 600 men under Lt. Col. William Thornton were to cross the river and clear the west bank. For the main attack, Jackson was ready.

As the British columns appeared out of the early morning mist on 8 January, they were met with murderous fire, first from the artillery, then from the muskets and rifles of Jackson's infantry. The British were mowed down by the hundreds. Pakenham and one other general were killed and a third general badly wounded. More than 2,000 of the British were casualties; the American losses were trifling. It was an excellent illustration of the principle of mass achieved by fire power. As the main attack ended, Thornton's force on the west bank began its advance on the American position. Jackson had made inadequate preparations to meet a move in this quarter until the British began their movement, and by then it was too late. The heavy guns of a battery posted on the west bank were not placed to command an attack along that side of the river and only about 800 Militia, divided in two groups a mile apart, were in position to oppose Thornton. The Americans resisted stubbornly, inflicting greater losses than they suffered, but the British pressed on, routed them, and overran the battery. Had the British continued their advance Jackson's position would have been indeed critical, but Pakenham's successor in command, appalled by the defeat of the main assault, ordered Thornton to withdraw from the west bank and rejoin the main force. Jackson failed to take the offensive. For 10 days the shattered remnant of Pakenham's army remained in camp unmolested by the Americans, and then reembarked and sailed away.

Jackson's fears that the attack would be renewed in some other quarter were realized when the British appeared off Mobile on 8 February. After the small fort that guarded the entrance to the harbor had capitulated, the way into the city lay open; but on 14 February news arrived that a peace treaty had been signed on 14 December 1814, three weeks before the battle of New Orleans was fought.

Summary. The artillery contributed conspicuously to American successes in the War of 1812 at Chippewa, at Sackett's Harbor, at the siege of Fort Erie, and at New Orleans. American superiority in gunnery was even more marked in the naval war, in Perry's victory on Lake Erie and Macdonough's victory at Plattsburg, and in the cruiser battles on the high seas. If sufficient numbers of infantry had been as well trained as the artillery the course of the war might have been entirely different. As it was, training and experience demonstrated their value in the conduct of the troops during the Niagara campaigns of 1814.

The small Corps of Engineers, a branch which owed its efficiency partly to the services of foreign experts but chiefly to the United States Military Academy, also made important contributions. Graduates of the Academy completed the fortifications at Fort Erie, built Fort Meigs, planned the harbor defenses of Norfolk and New York, and directed the fortifications at Plattsburg.

Gunnery and engineering skill would have been of no avail without competent and experienced leaders. They were not available at the beginning, but by 1814 such leaders had been found. Officers like Winfield Scott, Jacob Brown, and Andrew Jackson proved worthy successors to the heroes of the Revolution.

QUESTIONS

1. What preparations were made by Congress for waging war with England in the matter of military organization? in the matter of providing adequate armed forces?

2. What strategic error was represented in the American plan for invading Canada at the outset of the war?

3. Why was General Brown's invasion of Canada in the summer of 1814 unsuccessful?

4. What was the significance of Macdonough's victory at Plattsburg?

Reading List

Adams, Henry. *The War of 1812*. Edited by H. A. DeWeerd. Washington, 1944.

Beirne, Francis F. *The War of 1812*. New York, 1949.

James, Marquis. *Andrew Jackson: The Border Captain*. Indianapolis, 1933.

Mahan, Alfred T. *Sea Power in its Relation to the War of 1812*. Baltimore, 1915.

Pratt, Julius W. *Expansionists of 1812*. New York, 1925.

From the British point of view, the 1812–1815 conflict in America had been an annoying diversion, merely a sideshow to the tremendous Napoleonic conflict in Europe. Military developments in America as well as in Europe must be judged in the light of the entire experience.

Innovations of the Napoleonic Period. The American War of 1812 had been waged along traditional 18th century lines to a much greater extent than the war in Europe. In America only a small part of the total population was directly involved in the military effort. Armies were small and the fighting took place only on the perimeter of the country. With a few minor exceptions, the campaigns were either retaliatory raids or actions designed to establish a better bargaining position for the peace negotiations. There was little attempt on either side to destroy the other's capacity for continuing the war, and tactics and weapons were much the same as they had been for many years past.

On the other hand, the Napoleonic wars in Europe represented a departure from traditional concepts in several important particulars. France, very early in the wars, found it necessary to resort to conscription, and for the first time in modern history an entire nation was mobilized. Not only was the whole populace made subject to call for military service, but all the resources of the country were made subject to the demands of war. This had the effect of greatly expanding the scope of war, of reviving the old tactical issue of "masses" versus "lines" and of stimulating the search for more destructive weapons. Linear tactics, an advance by thin lines, had been well adapted to the highly trained professional armies of the 18th century which won their battles by maneuver rather than by destroying their opponents. The huge conscript armies of Napoleon lacked the training and experience necessary for the successful employment of linear tactics. Napoleon's armies therefore adopted the massed column as their formation for attack. Although Napoleon thus gained the advantage of sheer weight of numbers, he sacrificed the flexibility and mobility which the linear formation permitted. To offset the difficulty of adjusting his massed columns to the various battle situations that might develop, Napoleon made far greater use of skirmishers than had been customary in the past. The very size of the armies affected tactics by placing a premium on the means of killing rather than merely capturing the enemy or forcing him to retire. Napoleon, in addition to exploiting the terrific impact of his massed infantry columns, attempted to blast the opposing force with concentrated artillery fire. In massing his guns he applied a technique of siege operations to field warfare, and by giving his artillery an unprecedented degree of mobility he was able to move his concentrations of cannon to that part of the battlefield on which the most critical action was taking place. Thus Napoleon applied the principle of mass in terms of firepower while utilizing the shock effect of his infantry columns.

As a result of the demands for increased firepower and the natural desires of professional men to improve their craft, there were several important technical developments during the Napoleonic period. Shrapnel, which combined the principles of canister and explosive shells and which had been invented during the 1790's, came into use in this period. Although more accurate and of longer range than grapeshot, shrapnel was, like the early shells, unpredictable, subject to the dangerous habit of bursting in the muzzle. Grape, canister, and solid shot continued to be the mainstay of the artillery. Experiments conducted in 1804 by the British Army resulted in the development of a rocket, which aroused immediate interest, far out of proportion to its destructiveness. The principal value of the rockets, particularly against untrained troops, was in their demoralizing effect. After 1815 the British lost their monopoly in rockets. In the United States an improved version was developed and employed during the Mexican War. The most important technical development of the Napoleonic period was the invention of the percussion cap in 1807, which when used in place of the flintlock to detonate the powder charge of muskets was found to reduce misfires and increase the range of the piece. The percussion cap also facilitated the development of breechloaders and repeating guns. After 1820 the American Army gradually converted its muskets from flintlock to percussion cap. The Colt revolver, using a percussion cap, was perfected in 1835. A few of them were used two years later in the Second Seminole War, but the first real test of Colt's "six-shooter" came in the Mexican War.

The Post-1815 Reaction in Europe. After 1815 the western world settled down to enjoy the longest period of peace it had seen in at least 200 years. In Europe the rise of liberalism and the rapid progress of the industrial revolution brought with them an aversion to war, while the appalling loss of life and the destruction caused by the Napoleonic wars produced a reaction not only against war in general but against the new type of war in particular. On the professional level the new tactics found many opponents. To some students of military art, Napoleon's tactics were but crude hammer blows compared to the neat rapier thrusts of 18th century armies. Furthermore, the issue of line versus massed column had not really been settled, for Napoleon had after all lost the war and the British ascribed their victories to their "thin red lines."

Those who sought to return to the "good old days," while at the same time retaining the best features of Napoleonic warfare, found support in the writings of one of the two eminent military thinkers of the time, Maj. Gen. Antoine H. Jomini. In his first work, published in 1804, Jomini formulated certain fundamental principles of military operations based in the main on his analysis of the Seven Years' War. His greatest work, published in 1838, reaffirmed his belief that the practice of war could be reduced to a set of general principles which could be applied to all situations. In his insistence that the rules of logic rather than the laws of probability guided war and in his emphasis on the strategic importance of gaining and controlling territory, Jomini was a man of the 18th century and stood on different ground from that of his great contemporary, Maj. Gen. Karl von Clausewitz. It was the latter's misfortune that during this period the climate of opinion in Europe was more receptive to the views of Jomini. Jomini's analysis of the Napoleonic wars in terms of basic principles and of classic, traditional warfare greatly influenced military thought.

Postwar Reduction and Reorganization. In February 1815, at the end of the War of 1812, the Regular Army totaled about 33,000 men. A reduction of 20,000 was recommended by President Madison as soon as hostilities ended. In April 1815 the Acting Secretary of War, Alexander J. Dallas, convened a board of general officers to consider the postwar military establishment. Congress finally fixed the ceiling strength at 10,000 men in addition to the Corps of Engineers, which was not changed. Eight regiments of infantry, 1 light artillery regiment, and 8 battalions of artillery were authorized; among the units that were abolished was the regiment of light dragoons. At this same time provision was made for a "general staff," which should not be confused with the current concept of a general staff. The 1815 general staff, which was under the direction of the Secretary of War, was comprised of 2 major generals, each with 2 aides; 4 brigadier generals, each with 1 aide; an adjutant and inspector general, 2 adjutant generals, and 4 brigade inspectors; a quartermaster general, 2 deputy quartermaster generals, and 4 brigade quartermasters; a judge advocate; chaplains; and the superintendent and staff of the Military Academy. Also provided were the following departments: Ordance, Medical, Pay, and Purchasing. A territorial organization of the United States was prescribed with two divisions: the division of the north, under Maj. Gen. Jacob Brown, included four military territorial departments; the division of the south, under Maj. Gen. Andrew Jackson, comprised five military territorial departments.

John C. Calhoun and the War Department. Two major problems faced Secretary of War Calhoun when he took office in the fall of 1817: first, the problem of reorganizing the peacetime establishment, and second, that of meeting an outbreak of border warfare in the South. Neither problem was new, but Calhoun brought more energy and ability to bear on them than any Secretary had displayed since the days of Secretary of War Knox. In repetition of the experience of the Washington and Adams administrations, the Army after 1815 could not be maintained at full strength; Congress, as it had in the past, showed a disposition to cut the authorized strength back to the actual strength. At the end of 1817 the actual strength had fallen to about 8,200 men. A year later, in November 1818, it amounted to 7,676 officers and men.

Almost from the very moment he took office, Calhoun was faced with Congressional proposals to cut the strength of the Army, abolish the general staff, and discontinue the Military Academy at West Point. The old maxim that a large standing army was dangerous to the liberty of a country was responsible for much distrust of the staff. The Military Academy was in the throes of disorder over the dismissal of its superintendent. Above all, there was the normal desire to economize after the tremendous expense of war. Nevertheless, Calhoun was able to stave off Congressional action until 1821. He pointed out that, in proportion to the wealth and population of the country and to the number of military posts that required garrisons, the Military Establishment in 1815 was relatively smaller than that of 1802. A reduction in the staff, Calhoun argued, would have serious consequences. "It is in every service," he stated, "invariably the last in attaining perfection; and if neglected in peace, when there is leisure, it will be impossible in the midst of the hurry and bustle of war to bring it to perfection." By the fall of 1820 Calhoun's political opponents were able to muster enough support in Congress to pass an act reducing the Army to 6,000 men. Secretary Calhoun suggested that the reduction, if it had to come, could be effected by reducing the enlisted personnel of each company to half strength. In time of war this army could be quickly expanded to a force of approximately 19,000 officers and men. Congress rejected Calhoun's plan, however, and reduced not only the company strength but also the number of regiments. The Act of March 2, 1821, which provided for the reduction, fixed the size of the Army at four artillery regiments and seven infantry regiments. Each company of infantry was to consist of 42 privates, a drop of 26 from the previous figure. The Ordnance Department, by the same act, was merged with the artillery, and only one major general was provided for. The latter provision meant the retirement of General Jackson, who preferred appointment as Governor of Florida to demotion. The northern and southern territorial divisions were abolished and replaced by an Eastern and a Western Department, under the respective commands of General Scott and Brig. Gen. Edmund P. Gaines. One of the serious deficiencies in the War Department during the War of 1812 had been the lack of a senior line officer in the chain of command or as adviser to the Secretary of War and the President. Calhoun rectified this mistake by bringing Maj. Gen. Jacob Brown to Washington in a position which later became known as Commanding General of the Army.

Among Calhoun's accomplishments during his tenure as Secretary of War were the following: the line of military posts and trading houses was extended into the Indian territories west of the Mississippi (map 18), the supply and purchasing services of the Army were overhauled, and an improved diet was provided for the soldiers; under Calhoun's direction, General Scott prepared a new manual of infantry tactics, which Congress eventually adopted as the standard manual for both Regular Army and Militia. Calhoun also proposed a "school of practice" for men in service, out of which in 1824 grew the Artillery School at Fort Monroe. Unlike modern service schools, which instruct individuals, the Artillery School began by instructing an entire unit at a time, the unit being assigned to the station for a year's tour of duty. From a long-range point of view, one of Calhoun's most important measures was an order requiring Army surgeons to keep detailed day-to-day weather records at all posts. When these records were compiled 20 years later, they constituted the basic data for the first scientific study of weather in the United States and the most complete data of the sort in the world.

The First Seminole War. Before Calhoun had been at the head of the War Department a full week he found it necessary to order the Army into action on the southern frontier. The Seminole Indians in lower Georgia had for some time been engaging in sporadic raids and murders, retreating after each foray into Florida where they came under the protection of the Spanish flag. The climax was reached when 50 Americans were murdered near an Army post in Georgia. Orders were sent to General Gaines permitting him to cross into Florida after the Indians but not to attack them if they took shelter at a Spanish post. In the following month, December 1817, General Jackson himself took command of the operations, and, interpreting the War Department's instructions as permission to launch a full-scale invasion, Jackson proceeded to recruit a force of about 1,500 volunteers from Kentucky, Tennessee, and Georgia and an additional 1,500 friendly Creek Indians. For three months Jackson swept across northern Florida, burning Indian villages, cleaning up the nests of marauders, and at the same time sweeping the Spaniards out of Spanish Florida. The news put Washington in a furor. Not only had Jackson, in violation of the Constitution, raised a military force and

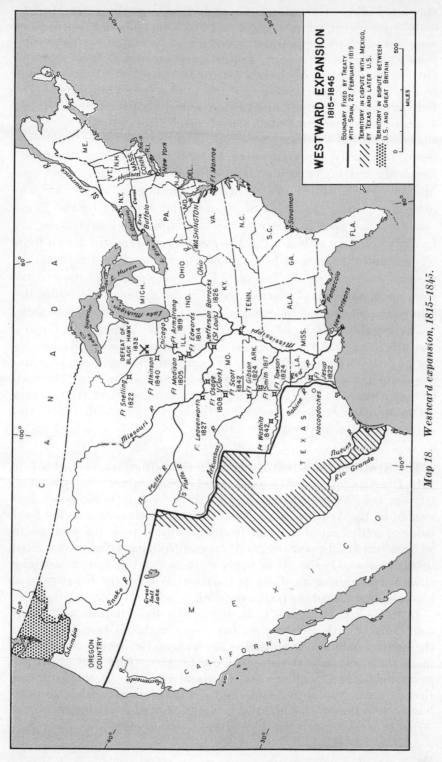

Map 18. *Westward expansion, 1815–1845.*

appointed officers (including a Creek Indian brigadier general) without Congressional authorization, but his operations had jeopardized some ticklish diplomatic negotiations with Spain and American relations with England. Among the prisoners taken by Jackson were two British subjects, one of them a former lieutenant of Marines, whom he executed for inciting the Seminoles and selling them arms. The British Minister to the United States entered a prompt protest, but after investigation the British Government disavowed the actions of the two men and let the matter drop. The Spanish Government protested vigorously, especially over Jackson's high-handed capture of Pensacola and his expulsion of the Spanish authorities. President Monroe was placed in a difficult situation, for negotiations with Spain toward acquiring the whole of Florida and agreeing on the Texas boundary had been in progress for some time. A compromise was finally worked out by which the American forces were withdrawn from Florida and the captured forts restored to Spain without repudiating General Jackson. On 22 February 1819, two weeks after the evacuation, Spain ceded all of Florida to the United States and in return the United States accepted the Sabine River as its southwestern boundary.

The Spanish Treaty of 1819, known as the Adams-Onis Treaty, was a landmark in the expansion of the United States. Except for the lingering dispute with Great Britain over the northeastern boundary, which was settled in 1842, the United States now had title to all territory east of the Mississippi River. West of that river, Spain was eliminated as a contender for the northwest Pacific coast and Americans claims to it were strengthened.

The Army on the Great Plains. In the pattern established before 1812, the Army pushed westward ahead of the settlers, surveying, fortifying, and building roads. The stockades and forts built and garrisoned by the Army in Iowa, Nebraska, and Kansas became the footholds of settlement in the wild frontier. Just outside the walls could be found gristmills, sawmills, and blacksmith shops, all of them erected by the troops. On the site of many of these frontier forts flourishing cities were to grow up, their foundations laid by the brave men in blue who first blazed the trail westward.

In 1832 Capt. Benjamin L. E. Bonneville and a detachment of 110 men from the 7th Infantry set out to study the western Indians in their native habitat. Disguised as fur traders, Bonneville and his men made their way into the heart of the Rockies where they spent five years among the Nez Perce and Flathead Indians. It was a venture that required courage and hard work. The information they accumulated about Indian customs and behavior was of great benefit to the Army in its dealings with the Indians in after years.

In 1842 2d Lt. John C. Fremont of the Topographical Engineers was sent out in command of another expedition. His mission was to explore and map the Platte River country for the benefit of emigrants moving over the Oregon Trail. Results were so valuable that the next year Fremont was again sent out, this time to try to find an easier route to the west coast. After exploring the region of the Great Salt Lake and descending the Snake and Columbia Rivers, he reached Sacramento. Returning, he crossed the Rockies at Denver and arrived back at his starting point in Kansas City, Mo., in August 1844.

A battalion of mounted rangers had been organized in 1832, which was expanded the following year into a regiment of dragoons—the first cavalry to appear in the Regular Army since 1815. Their purpose was to protect the overland routes pushing into California and Oregon. One detachment of five companies under Col. Stephen W. Kearny left Fort Leavenworth, Kans., on 18 May 1845 and returned 99 days later, having covered 2,200 miles.

Territorial expansion inevitably brought conflicts with the Indians. The Sac and Fox Indians, who had been pushed out of their tribal lands in western Illinois into the prairies west of the Mississippi River, began to show signs of restlessness in 1831 and started to move back to their old home. Their chief, Black Hawk, following the example of Tecumseh, tried to organize a confederacy of the various tribes and sought an alliance with the British in Canada; but the British were no longer interested in stirring up the Indians. Although blocked in his diplomacy, Black Hawk led his people, including about 500 warriors, across the Mississippi into Illinois. Brig. Gen. Henry Atkinson in command at Fort Leavenworth was ordered to take the field with Regulars of the 6th Infantry; the Governor of Illinois called out a large force of Militia, most of them mounted; and General Scott was rushed from the east coast with about 1,000 infantry and artillery. After an inconclusive brush between a detachment of the Militia and Black Hawk's warriors, most of the Illinois volunteers returned home, leaving General Atkinson and his Regulars to deal with the Indians. On 2 August 1832, Atkinson, with about 500 Regulars and as many volunteers as he had been able to collect, caught up with the Indians at the confluence of the Bad Axe River and the Mississippi. In a three-hour battle, in which more than 150 of the Indians were killed and wounded, Atkinson dispersed the foe. Black Hawk himself was taken prisoner. Five days after the battle General Scott arrived on the scene, having covered the 1,800 miles from Fort Monroe in the unbelievably short space of 18 days. Only a small remnant of his force arrived with him. He had moved by water to New York, then up the Hudson and through the Erie Canal to Buffalo. At Buffalo the force embarked on four steamers for Chicago, but Asiatic cholera broke out and by the time Chicago was reached, one third of the force had died or was incapacitated by the disease. Many others deserted in panic and helped to spread the epidemic.

The Second Seminole War—1836–1842. The First Seminole War had been different from other Indian wars in that it was an episode of the disintegration of the Spanish Empire and part of the unfinished business of the War of 1812. The Second Seminole War, like the other Indian wars, began when the Seminoles, after giving up their lands by treaty, refused to move out. Only a few troops were stationed in Florida. They were badly reduced in December 1835 when a detachment of 110 Regulars was ambushed and slain, and a second detachment of Florida volunteers and a few Regulars was severely mauled. Although the part of Florida where hostilities were taking place was in the Western Department, commanded by General Gaines, the War Department immediately sent General Scott to direct the operations against the Seminoles, principally because Gaines was expected to have his hands full with troubles that were brewing along the Texas frontier. While Scott was at Savannah assembling an army and planning an impressive three-pronged offensive, Gaines had raised a force of about 1,000 men, mostly Louisiana volunteers, and embarked for Florida without waiting for instructions from the War Department. When he did receive word of Scott's appointment, Gaines ignored it, commandeered supplies that had been reserved for Scott, continued his advance, was attacked, and was saved only by the timely arrival of one of Scott's subordinates with reinforcements and more supplies. Gaines then returned to New Orleans, reporting that he had brought peace to Florida. Gaines was wrong. General Scott took to the field several months later with a smaller force than he had originally planned, but he was unable to come to grips with any sizable force of Indians, and was transferred when the public became aroused over a slur he had cast on the fighting qualities of volunteers. Over the next six years, three other commanders—Maj. Gen. Thomas S. Jesup, Brig. Gen. Zachary Taylor, and Brig. Gen. Walker A. Armistead—tried and failed to drive the Seminoles out of their dismal bogs and palmetto swamps. Finally, a campaign of extermination, like those waged by the early colonists, succeeded in routing the Indians out of the swamps and permitted the war to be officially ended. A total of something less than 5,000 Regulars and perhaps 20,000 short-term volunteers had been engaged in the effort against approximately 1,000 Seminole warriors. Nearly 1,500 men had lost their lives in battle or from disease in order that 3,200 half-starved Indians might be shipped west.

The Removal of the Cherokees. Midway in the Seminole War trouble developed with the Creek Indians of southern Georgia and the Cherokees farther north. After a brief, bloodless campaign the

Creeks were forced to surrender and move west of the Mississippi; the Cherokees presented a more formidable problem. More numerous than the Creeks, civilized, led by educated chiefs, the Cherokees had adopted the white man's customs and had many friends in Washington. But gold had been discovered on the Cherokee lands and the whites were determined to turn the Indians out. In the summer of 1838 General Scott was instructed to remove the 15,000 Cherokees to lands in the present State of Oklahoma. With two regiments of Regulars and a force of Georgia volunteers, Scott moved into the Cherokee country. Although the situation was tense, he succeeded, through tact and careful attention to the Indians' comfort, in persuading most of them to emigrate peacefully. It was another chore of the sort to which the Army was becoming accustomed.

A Professionally Competent Army. To meet the needs of the Seminole War, Congress in 1838 had authorized an increase in the strength of the Army. The first substantial increase since the War of 1812, it brought the authorized strength up to nearly 13,000 by expanding the existing regiments and adding a new regiment of infantry. As it stood then the Army consisted of eight regiments of infantry, four of artillery, two of dragoons (the second of which had been authorized in 1836), and the Corps of Engineers. Immediately after the Seminole War officially ended the authorized strength was cut back to about 8,600 men by reducing the rank and file strength of the regiments. One of the regiments of dragoons was dismounted and converted into a rifle regiment, only to be remounted two years later, in April 1844. Actual strength continued to be about 50 to 60 percent of the authorized strength. In 1845, on the eve of the Mexican War, the Army numbered only 5,300 men. Nevertheless, the principle of an expansible army appears to have become firmly established in place of the elimination of units and the creation of new ones.

To provide men and replacements, a badly needed reform of the recruiting system had been made in 1822. Until then, all recruiting had been done by the individual regiments, with widely unequal and not generally successful results. In an effort to bring the Army up to strength, General Brown in July 1822 instructed General Scott, commander of the Eastern Department, to open recruiting depots at New York, Philadelphia, and Baltimore for the purpose of enlisting men for the Army at large, not for specific units. The men accepted at these depots were given some training and then assigned to regiments on orders from the War Department. The General Recruiting Service, as it was known, immediately proved more successful than regimental recruiting. In the two years following its establishment, six additional depots were opened, three of them in the Western Department. During its first three years of operation, the recruiting service enlisted about 68 percent more men than the regiments recruited. Regimental recruiting continued along with the new system and in times of emergency the General Recruiting Service also faced competition from newly raised volunteer units, but the system had been established on a solid footing and proved its worth when the Mexican War made rapid expansion of the Army necessary.

Progress was also made in maintaining a corps of professionally trained officers. The Military Academy at West Point survived the disorganization and neglect brought by the War of 1812 and the removal of the wartime superintendent, Capt. Alden Partridge. The difficulties incident to the superintendent's removal seem to have stemmed primarily from his interference with the faculty. Although popular with the cadets, he was a poor administrator. Under his successor, Capt. Sylvanus Thayer, the Academy flourished. His great achievement was in organizing the academic course, a program of progressive instruction in French, mathematics, chemistry, and the other physical sciences, and engineering, which presented these subjects as professional tools as well as for their cultural value. Among the early textbooks were Jomini's *Treatise on Grand Tactics* and other classics of the military art. Thayer brought order to the disorder into which the Academy had fallen, allayed much of the opposition to the Academy within the Army, and established its traditions. Partridge, after his dismissal, resigned from the Army and returned to his native Vermont, where he organized the first private military academy in the country. In 1824 Norwich University, which Partridge's academy later became, had 162 cadets in residence as compared to about 260 at West Point. Whereas West Point aimed at producing professional soldiers, Norwich was the school of the citizen-soldier. To this extent, the ideas of Captain Partridge departed from the military trend of his day and were instead more nearly akin to the American Militia tradition and to the warfare of the Napoleonic period. The pattern of education that Partridge first established at Norwich soon spread, and it is the heritage in which the 2,000,000 college men who have served in ROTC units have shared. West Point was nevertheless the major source for a permanent peacetime officer corps. By 1845 approximately five hundred graduates of the West Point institution were in active service. Another five hundred had resigned to enter civilian life, where they helped in building the first railroads and telegraph systems, laid out the new towns on the frontier, and constructed highways, canals, and bridges, but, like the Norwich graduates, they were available when their country called.

Coast and Harbor Defense. Although Indian affairs and a developing crisis along the Texas border occupied the immediate attention of the Army during most of the 30 years after 1815, the major problem of national defense involved the possibility of war with either England or France. The execution of a systematic and extensive program of harbor fortifications and the manning of the completed forts was the Army's responsibility. It was a weighty responsibility, since the coastline was long and the harbors and seaports were many. The fact that local workmen found employment on the construction projects generally meant that it was not difficult to obtain funds from Congress. Annual appropriations for the purpose varied from $400,000 to $600,000. In 1826, 18 harbors and ports from the Penobscot River in Maine to the mouth of the Mississippi had been fortified with a total of 31 works of varying size. Although some were fairly elaborate, the fortifications consisted in general of sloping earthworks covered with grass and backed by stone or brick walls. By 1843 the harbor defense program had been extended to 35 or 40 coastal areas at which places 69 fortifications either existed or were under construction. Naval armaments had made strides during this period and the harbor defense program attempted to keep pace, but the more revolutionary changes were to come later, after 1850. The two noticeable changes in the 1830's and 1840's were the greater emphasis on heavy guns (24- and 32-pounders and 8-inch heavy howitzers) and the declining importance attached to protecting the landward approaches to the forts.

The Texas Issue. The military problems of the United States were complicated by the crumbling of the Spanish empire in America. Where this process created a vacuum, as in Florida and Louisiana, the United States had moved in. Elsewhere the process was hastened by the outbreak of revolution in the Spanish colonies, and in 1822, after the ratification of the Adams-Onis Treaty, the United States became the first nation of the world to recognize the independence of Spain's former colonies, including Mexico. Claiming as its northern boundary the line fixed by the Adams-Onis Treaty, Mexico adopted an immigration policy designed to attract American settlers to the uninhabited plains of Texas. Between the years 1825 and 1830, approximately 15,000 immigrants with several thousand Negro slaves poured into northern Mexico from the United States. In the end the policy was unsuccessful in cementing Texas to Mexico. The refusal of the United States to confirm the Adams-Onis boundary with Mexico, the persistent efforts of the United States to purchase part of Texas, the inability of American immigrants to cut their old ties completely, and the instability of Mexican politics resulted in 1830 in a reversal of Mexican policy, expressed in severe restrictions on immigration and land ownership. The resulting discontent among the Texans flared into open revolt in 1835, and in the following year Texas proclaimed its independence. The Mexicans, under Gen. Antonio Lopez de Santa

Ana, moved against the rebels and destroyed the garrison in the Alamo after a heroic siege that lasted 13 days. American volunteers rushed across the Sabine River to help the Texans, and for about five months during the summer and fall of 1836 a regiment of the Regular Army occupied the town of Nacogdoches, some 50 miles south of the boundary. On 21 April 1836 the Texan general Sam Houston, with 743 raw troops, decisively defeated a force of about 1,600 veteran Mexicans under Santa Ana, who was captured the next day. The United States, in March 1837, recognized Texas as an independent republic and exchanged diplomatic representatives. France recognized the independence of Texas in 1839, and Great Britain extended recognition in 1840.

In declaring their independence, most Texans meant only independence from Mexican rule. They hoped and expected that they would speedily be annexed to the United States, but the annexation question immediately became tied up with the slavery controversy in the United States. Northerners saw it as an attempt of the South to extend slavery. Texas became an issue of sectional and partisan politics. For nearly 10 years, therefore, Texas existed as an independent nation. Refusing to recognize Texan independence, Mexico made sporadic attempts to recover its lost province. Border raids marked by extreme ruthlessness and ferocity by both Texans and Mexicans kept the country in constant turmoil, particularly along the Rio Grande River.

Summary. The 30 years following the end of the War of 1812 were marked by a growing trend toward a professional army, capable of being expanded in time of war. This trend was based in part on the lessons of the Napoleonic Wars and the reaction to those wars, and in part on necessity. The Army, kept fairly small by Congressional limitations and by the difficulty of obtaining recruits, had to be made into a professionally competent force, one that made up in quality what it lacked in quantity. The influence of the United States Military Academy made itself increasingly felt in the growth of a professional officer corps. Advances in naval armament during this period made corresponding improvements in the coast and harbor defenses necessary, which in turn required the services of increasing numbers of trained engineers and artillerymen.

At the same time the Army was faced with tasks to which the energies of a much larger force could have been profitably devoted. The two Seminole Wars, the Black Hawk War, the removal of Indians, and the exploration of the West kept a large part of the Army almost constantly occupied in these years. During the final decade of the period war with Mexico over the Texas question became more and more threatening. By 1845 the bulk of the Regular Army was along the Sabine River keeping watch over the troubled situation.

QUESTIONS

1. What effect did Napoleon's application of the principle of mass have upon military thought after 1815?

2. What in the way of a compromise did the Act of March 2, 1821, represent?

3. What important developments in military education took place between 1815 and 1845?

4. What were the principal defense problems between 1815 and 1845, and how were they met?

Reading List

Beers, Henry P. *The Western Military Frontier, 1815–1846.* Philadelphia, 1935.

Forman, Sidney. *West Point.* New York, 1950.

James, Marquis. *The Raven: A Biography of Sam Houston.* Indianapolis, 1929.

Pelzer, Louis. *Marches of the Dragoons in the Mississippi Valley.* Iowa City, 1917.

Prucha, F. P. *Broadax and Bayonet.* Madison, Wis., 1953.

CHAPTER 9

THE MEXICAN WAR

Causes and Considerations. War with Mexico was the result of the annexation of Texas to the United States on 1 March 1845, at which time the United States inherited the Texans' conflict with Mexico. President Tyler had revived the annexation issue in the spring of 1844 as a political buildup for the presidential election of that year. He sent an annexation treaty to Congress, but it was held up in the Senate until after the nominating conventions and then defeated because it had become identified with the proslavery interests of the South. The victory of the Democratic Party candidate, James K. Polk, although he won by only a slender margin, was interpreted as a mandate from the people for the annexation of Texas, since Polk and his party had come out strongly in favor of annexation and expansion. Three days before Polk was inaugurated Congress jointly resolved to admit Texas into the Union. The Mexican Government, which had served notice on the United States that the annexation of Texas would be considered an act of war, immediately broke off diplomatic relations. Polk then dispatched troops into Texas and deployed the Navy along the Mexican coast. By midsummer of 1845, nearly 4,000 troops of the Regular Army plus a few mounted volunteers had been assembled between the Sabine and Nueces Rivers, under the command of Brig. Gen. Zachary Taylor, with advance headquarters at Corpus Christi.

Meanwhile, Polk was attempting to restore diplomatic dealings with Mexico. When Texas was part of Mexico, the southern boundary of the province had been the Neuces River, but on declaring independence the Texans had claimed the Rio Grande as their boundary. Now Polk sent a representative to Mexico with an offer to release Mexico from the payment of old claims in return for recognition of the Rio Grande as the southern boundary of the United States. Mexico refused to receive the American representative, and as soon as the news reached Washington President Polk ordered General Taylor to move into the disputed territory and establish himself on the Rio Grande.

"The Army of Observation." Taylor led his command south to Point Isabel, while a fleet of supply vessels followed along the coast. Establishing his main base at Point Isabel, Taylor went on to the Rio Grande with almost his entire force and proceeded to build a fort

162

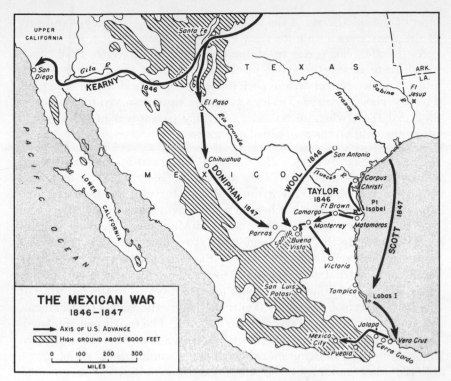

Map 19. The Mexican War, 1846–1847.

opposite the Mexican town of Matamoros. He rejected the Mexican commander's demand that the Americans retire forthwith to Corpus Christi, and for almost two months the two forces watched each other across the river while both continued their preparations for whatever might happen. Taylor's troops were Regulars: the 3d, 5th, 6th, 7th, and 8th Infantry Regiments, Maj. Samuel Ringgold's "Flying Artillery" and parts of two other artillery regiments, and a regiment of dragoons. All were understrength. Many of the enlisted men were of foreign birth—English, Irish, Germans, and Poles. An indeterminate number of them were unable to resist the temptation of exchanging their army pay of seven dollars a month for the free land and immunity that Mexico offered to American deserters, a problem against which General Scott also had to contend later in the war. Except for a few companies armed with the new percussion cap musket, Taylor's men carried flintlocks that were little different from those used in the Revolution and the War of 1812. The troops were well officered, although few had ever commanded as large a body of men as they had under them on the Rio Grande. The elite of the army, at least it considered itself such, was the light, mobile horse artillery, trained in rapid battlefield maneuver. Commanded by Major Ringgold, the horse artillery was led by young officers, graduates of West Point, as indeed

163

most of the subalterns of the Regular Army were. The eyes and ears of the army were a volunteer force of Texas Rangers.

As the Mexican forces in Matamoros grew in strength, they began to infiltrate across the river, north and south of the American fort, and one or two patrol actions took place between Mexicans and Texans. The first clash in which Taylor's Regulars were involved took place on 25 April 1846, when an American cavalry patrol was attacked north of the fort and all the men killed or captured.

The Opening Battles. *Palo Alto.* Concerned by the threat to his lightly held base and line of communication, General Taylor on 1 May withdrew the bulk of the army to Point Isabel. To hold the fort opposite Matamoros he left behind a small detachment of artillery and the 7th Infantry, under the command of Maj. Jacob Brown, with instructions to fire the heavy siege guns at regular intervals if the fort were attacked and in need of help. Early in the morning of 3 May the Mexican artillery opened on the fort with heavy cannon and mortar fire. The bombardment continued for two days. On the morning of 5 May the garrison found itself surrounded by thousands of Mexicans, apparently moving into position for assault. The continued bombardment was causing damage and there had been a few casualties. Brown decided, on the following morning, to begin sounding his signal guns. All that day and night the small garrison waited in uncertainty, momentarily expecting to be attacked and wondering whether General Taylor had heard the signal guns. Major Brown fell, mortally wounded, and ammunition began to run low. During the night of 7 May there was much activity in the Mexican camp; bugles sounded, but there was no assault. The next morning large numbers of the enemy were seen moving off in the direction of Point Isabel. It could mean only one thing to the weary Americans.

General Taylor had heard the guns and on the afternoon of 7 May had started back with about 2,300 men to relieve the fort. The next morning, when a little more than halfway to the fort, his army came face to face with the enemy. The Mexicans, outnumbering Taylor by at least two to one and perhaps numbering as many as 6,000 men, were forming a line of battle to bar the road, their right flank on an elevation known as the Palo Alto and their left ending in a marshy area closely covered with scrub growth. Moving unhesitatingly to join battle, Taylor ordered his artillery to open fire to cover the deployment of his infantry into battle. The gun drill of the artillery was smooth and rapid and the fire was deadly. A Mexican column that was still moving into position was cut to pieces. The Mexican artillery in the center replied and for over an hour the battle raged as a cannon duel. Then the Mexicans tried two wide flank attacks. First Lt. Randolph Ridgely's artillery raced around the line to meet and throw back one of the attacks. On the other flank, the 5th and 3d

Infantry Regiments, forming in squares, scattered the Mexican cavalry. The dry grass had been set on fire by the gunfire and a cloud of black smoke obscured the battlefield. Under the cover of this smoke screen, the American artillery moved into a new position and opened a destructive fire on the right flank of the Mexican line, throwing it into confusion. Now, in the growing dusk, the Mexicans tried one last attack, their infantry advancing in line with flags flying and the band playing but the American artillery tore the line to pieces and the battle ended as it had begun, with an artillery duel. As the guns ceased to fire in the darkness, the Mexicans fell back beyond the Palo Alto. The American action at Palo Alto illustrates the successful use of fire power as a substitute for manpower in the application of the principle of mass.

General Taylor had lost only 9 men killed, 1 of whom was Major Ringgold, the artillery commander, for whom Fort Ringgold was later named, and 47 wounded. The Mexicans had over 700 casualties, of whom about 320 were killed, but replacements and reinforcements kept coming in from Matamoros.

Reseca de la Palma. The next morning Taylor resumed his march after sending out a strong advance party to locate the enemy. Word came back that the Mexicans were in a defensive position a few miles down the road, in a dry river bed (the Reseca de la Palma) that lay athwart the road along which Taylor was moving. It was a strong position. The Reseca provided natural breastworks for the Mexican infantry, whose flanks were protected by lagoons of standing water and thickets of cactus. The enemy artillery was in a position from which it could rake the main approach along the road.

Taylor ordered the "flying artillery" to advance and engage the Mexican batteries and sent two infantry regiments forward on each side of the road in support of the artillery. In spite of heavy enemy fire the infantry formed in line and worked its way painfully through the brush. Losing sight of each other, the various units moved independently but their adherence to standard procedure gave the over-all effect of close coordination. Lieutenant Ridgely, who had taken over Ringgold's command, was having difficulty with one Mexican battery placed squarely on the road, and Taylor sent in his dragoons. Charging down the road, the cavalry drove the Mexicans from their guns, crossed the Reseca, turned, and discovered that the enemy artillerymen were back at their posts. But before the cavalry could charge the battery from the rear, Taylor's infantry had taken it. The road was open. In the meantime the American infantry had turned the enemy's left flank and the whole Mexican line broke and fled. The rout became a race to the Rio Grande, which the Mexicans won.

In the second day's battle, Taylor's losses amounted to 33 men killed and 89 wounded. The enemy had suffered severely—well over a thou-

Battle of Resaca de la Palma, 9 May 1846.

sand men were killed and wounded and many more were drowned attempting to cross the Rio Grande. Second Lt. Ulysses S. Grant, who had been given temporary command of an infantry company on the second day, noted that the Mexican soldier was brave and would put up a good fight if well led. But they had not been well led and their marksmanship had been poor because of excessive powder charges in their musket cartridges. On the American side, the leadership was of such high calibre as to demonstrate the value of West Point and the necessity of discipline. Palo Alto had been primarily an artillery battle, but at Resaca de la Palma the infantry bore the brunt of the fighting. Taylor, whose leadership in battle had already earned him two brevet promotions, was advanced to major general, and many of his subordinates were also promoted.

For want of boats to cross the Rio Grande, Taylor was compelled to stay until 18 May at the fort, which was later named Fort Brown in honor of its gallant commander. A year before,he had requested the War Department to provide him with a ponton train for river crossings, but he had never received the equipment. It took him 10 days to collect a few boats and find a ferry and on 18 May he began to move into Matamoros. The Mexican Army had disappeared into the interior. A mounted detachment penetrated 60 miles to the south and returned with information that a move in force would be impossible because of the lack of water and forage in that direction.

166

Congress Declares War. On 9 May, the day of the battle of Reseca de la Palma, President Polk called a cabinet meeting to discuss the Mexican situation. No news had come from Texas for some weeks. For all that Polk and the cabinet knew the Mexicans were going to permit General Taylor to remain on the banks of the Rio Grande unmolested. Polk suggested that he might draw up a war message for Congress on the basis of Mexico's refusal to pay the old American claims, and only Secretary of Navy George Bancroft insisted on waiting until the Mexicans committed an act of hostility against Taylor's forces. That evening a message came from the War Department telling of the skirmish of 25 April, in which the American cavalry patrol had been wiped out. Polk immediately drafted a message declaring that a state of war existed. Congress passed the declaration, and President Polk signed it on 13 May. Congress then appropriated $10,000,000, doubled the strength of the Regular Army by setting the enlisted strength of a company at 100 men, authorized the President to call for Volunteer units to a maximum of 50,000 men for a term of one year or the duration of the war, added a regiment of mounted riflemen to the Regular Army, and authorized the President to charter or purchase such vessels as might be suitable for the public service.

The United States went into the war without the pronounced sectional division that had existed during the War of 1812. There was some opposition to the Mexican War and a noticeable falling off of ardor the farther one went from the Rio Grande, but the opposition was primarily on partisan grounds. The President established a quota of volunteers for each state, and the news of Taylor's victories helped to counteract the lack of enthusiasm. Nevertheless, some indication of popular attitude can be had from the fact that in the course of the War Texas and the Mississippi Valley furnished 49,000 volunteers, and the Thirteen Original States sent only 13,000. This was but natural for the states of the Southwest were nearer the scene of action.

Grand Strategy. The President had gone into the war with at least one object clearly in view—to seize all of Mexico north of the Rio Grande and the Gila River and westward to the Pacific. After he discussed with General Scott, Commanding General of the Army, how this was to be done, the outlines of a huge three-pronged thrust emerged (map 19). Taylor, it was decided, should advance against Monterrey while another force advanced from San Antonio against Chihuahua. A third movement was to start from Fort Leavenworth, where a force mostly of Militia and Volunteers was being concentrated under the command of Col. Stephen W. Kearny, and was to be aimed at Sante Fe. Its ultimate objective was California. The Navy was to blockade the east coast of Mexico from Tampico to Yucatán and capture the California coast in conjunction with Kearny. The campaign that eventually ended the war—the landing at Vera Cruz and the move on Mexico City—was a later addition to the plan.

General Scott, an experienced campaigner, realized the magnitude of the task. Mexico had a population of approximately 7,000,000 inhabitants. Its Regular Army, which included 15 infantry regiments and 4 artillery brigades, had about 30,000 names on the muster rolls, and the Central Government had more or less control over a large territorial Militia. Particularly impressive to foreign observers was the Mexican light cavalry, armed with lance, carbine, and sword, of which there were 15 regiments. Twenty years of intermittent revolution and civil turmoil had given the Mexican soldiers plenty of experience in the field. Climate, geography, and disease were all on the side of the Mexicans. While President Polk had talked about a "quick war," Scott plunged into the intricate and stupendous problems of supply, transportation, communications, and mobilization, which had to be solved before operations on a grand scale could be conducted with any chance of success.

The Monterey Campaign. All through June and July volunteers and supplies poured into Matamoros. The new troops, units such as the Mississippi Rifles, commanded by Taylor's son-in-law, Col. Jefferson Davis, made up in exuberance and spirit what they lacked in training and experience, but fortunately discipline was likewise not one of the enemy's strong points. Some training, although not enough to satisfy all the Regular officers, was given the new arrivals while Taylor waited for boats to take the army up river and for the summer rains to stop.

Instead of striking across the barren country directly for Monterey, Taylor had decided to move by boat and wagon train up the Rio Grande to the town of Camargo, 130 miles above Matamoros. From Camargo, a road led 150 miles southwest to Monterey and the other key cities of northern Mexico. By the end of July Quartermaster General Thomas S. Jesup had been able to send Taylor enough shallow draft river steamboats to begin the move, and by mid-August 20 steamers were in operation between Matamoros and Camargo. But the ravages of disease, the necessity of keeping holding forces at critical points along the river, and a shortage of wagons limited the size of the force that started for Monterey at the end of August to a little more than 6,000 men, of whom about two-thirds were Regulars.

On 17 September 1846 Taylor arrived before Monterey. A force of from 7,300 to 9,000 Mexicans defended the city, against which Taylor promptly moved to attack. He had organized his command into three divisions: one of Volunteers, and the other two of Regulars. Sending one of his divisions of Regulars around to the west side of the city to cut off the road to Saltillo and then to attack from that side, Taylor moved in on the eastern outskirts with the remainder of his force. After two days of hard fighting both attacks succeeded in driving into the city proper. Then followed two more days of fighting such as Americans had never before experienced, except for the few Continentals that had pushed into Quebec with Montgomery and Arnold back in 1775. As in most Mexican cities, the houses of Monterey were strongly built of stone and adobe, forming solid walls along narrow streets that led to a central plaza. Each street was easily converted into a fortress. Painfully but relentlessly Taylor's men blasted down walls, chased the enemy troops from house to house and off the flat rooftops, and finally pushed them into the plaza. On 24 September the Mexican commander offered to surrender the city on condition that his troops be allowed to withdraw unimpeded and that an eight-week armistice go into effect. General Taylor agreed, and Monterey was in his hands.

President Polk and the administration received the news of the surrender terms with chagrin and disappointment, and promptly repudiated the armistice. In justice to Taylor it should be noted that it had been a tremendous feat to win the stronghold on any terms, that he had had a long line of communications to secure, and that, as far as he knew, his mission was not to win the war but merely to hold northern Mexico. By the time Taylor learned that he was expected to defeat the enemy in the field, not win cities, the armistice had almost expired.

While Taylor waited in Monterey, the other prongs of the grand operation had been put in motion. Kearny had taken Santa Fe and with a small force was on his way across the deserts and rugged mountains to California. Brig. Gen. John E. Wool with about 2,000 men was on the march from San Antonio, but instead of Chihuahua his objective now was the town of Parras, situated in a fertile region from which supplies for Taylor's army could be drawn. With General Wool approaching Parras, Taylor in mid-November sent one of his divisions forward from Monterey to occupy the city of Saltillo, a provincial capital and important road junction on the routes to Parras and México City. Another detachment occupied the city of Victoria, capital of the province of Tamaulipas and about halfway between Monterey and the port of Tampico, which had been taken and occupied by an American naval force. Thus at the beginning of December a large part of northern Mexico had come under American control. Kearny and his dragoons had reached San Diego after one of the most extraordinary marches in American history, to find that a naval squadron had already seized the California ports with the questionable help of a force of California volunteers.

Maj. Gen. Zachary Taylor.

Maj. Gen. Winfield Scott.

A New Strategic Objective—Mexico City. A strike at the heart of Mexico and the capture of its capital, Mexico City, and the defeat of the Mexican Army had been under discussion ever since Taylor's victories along the Rio Grande. The points at issue were who should command the expedition and what route should be taken. In June, while Taylor had been preparing to move against Monterrey, Scott had expected to take personal command of the army of the Rio Grande and he had written to Taylor to press on into the heart of the enemy's country and take "the High Road to the capital of Mexico." The Secretary of War hastened to reassure Taylor that if such an invasion appeared to be too difficult the War Department would consider making the attempt by way of Tampico or Vera Cruz, or some other place along the coast. General Scott, after deciding not to leave Washington for the time being and on further study of the logistical and communications problems, began to urge approval of the Vera Cruz project. Taylor, too, after taking Monterrey, recommended an assault by way of Vera Cruz. Political decisions had delayed the appointment of the commander, and by this time Taylor was even less acceptable than Scott to the administration. Finally, in mid-November, it was reluctantly decided to give General Scott command of the Vera Cruz expedition.

Scott in methodical fashion had proceeded to draw up the requirements for the campaign. There would be needed 15,000 to 25,000 men, most of them Regulars. During the next two months the able and hardworking Quartermaster General labored mightily to assemble supplies, munitions, and transports, while Scott proceeded to Camargo to see what troops he could detach from Taylor's Army. With the center of action shifting, there seemed to be no necessity for a large force in northern Mexico. Scott therefore detached practically all of Taylor's Regulars—about 4,000 men—and an equal number of Volunteers, who were ordered to rendezvous at Tampico and at the mouth of the Brazos River in Texas. Taylor was left with less than 5,000 men, all of them Volunteers except two squadrons of dragoons and a small force of artillery.

Buena Vista. The President of Mexico, General Santa Ana, had taken the field in person and had assembled in the neighborhood of San Luis Potosi an army of approximately 20,000 men. Word of Scott's expedition had leaked out to the newspapers and was known in Mexico City almost as soon as the preparations got under way. A captured dispatch revealed to Santa Ana the plans for depleting Taylor's army. The opportunity thus presented could not be ignored, and Santa Ana decided to strike northward against Taylor's weakened forces. Taylor was understandably concerned with his situation but ignorant of Santa Ana's intention. He assumed, as did General Scott and the War Department, that the Mexicans would make their main effort at Vera Cruz. Early in February 1847 Taylor moved all his troops except a small garrison out of Saltillo into a camp 18 miles south of the city. General Wool, who had been brought from Parras when Taylor's force was reduced and who had been occupying a position at Buena Vista, about three miles nearer Saltillo, was moved forward to the new camp a few days later. No tactical significance was attached to the shift. Taylor merely thought it would improve the morale of his troops to move them a few miles in the direction of the enemy and he also hoped that it would persuade the inhabitants of Saltillo, who had been driven away by frequent alarms, to return to the city. As late as 14 February Taylor considered a Mexican advance on his position improbable.

A week later, on 21 February, an American scouting party came into camp with news that a force of several thousand Mexicans was approaching. It turned out to be the leading elements of Santa Ana's army. Taylor immediately drew back to Buena Vista, where the terrain offered better possibilities for defense, and prepared to engage the Mexicans.

At Buena Vista the high valley along which Santa Ana was approaching narrowed to a defile flanked by the shoulders of a rugged mountain ridge. The road from the south followed a stream up the valley and through the defile, and then continued over the ridge in the direction of Saltillo. As Santa Ana came up the valley he saw the bulk of the American forces posted on the ridges to the right of the road. At the head of the defile Taylor had placed a battery of artillery and a regiment of Indiana Volunteers. To the left of the defile, the right flank of the Americans was held by a Kentucky regiment. About 4,800 men were in position. Taylor had gone on to Saltillo with the Mississippi Rifle Regiment and a squadron of dragoons, leaving General Wool in command at Buena Vista. Santa Ana had perhaps 15,000 men on the scene.

The Mexican general decided to make his main effort against the American left flank. The first day, 22 February 1847, was largely devoted to an attempt on the part of the Mexicans to outflank the American position. A brigade of Mexican light infantry moved toward a ridge the Americans had not occupied on the extreme left, seized it, and pushed back a force of dismounted American cavalry and riflemen who tried to counter the move, while a force of about 1,500 Mexican cavalry made a wide sweep along mountain roads toward Saltillo and the American rear. The next day, at dawn, the battle opened in earnest with an attempt by the Americans to restore the left, which the Mexicans repulsed and countered by sending a division up the road against the American position at the head of the defile. Santa Ana's tactics were French, an advance by column. Maj. Braxton Bragg's artillerymen and the Indiana infantry could ask for no better target and quickly broke up the attack. There was no further action in this sector of the field. Now Santa Ana launched his grand assault on the American left, an attack by a column of two divisions. For half an hour the Americans—360 men of the 2d Indiana Regiment and a battery of 3 cannons—withstood the assault, pouring a heavy fire into the massed columns. The commander then ordered a withdrawal. The men turned, then broke and ran. Two adjoining regiments of mounted Volunteers joined the flight and ran almost all the way back to Saltillo. A third regiment retired in good order to another position along the ridge. At this critical point the artillery came at a gallop from the right flank and went into action on the exposed left, and almost simultaneously General Taylor arrived on the scene from Saltillo with Jefferson Davis' Mississippi Rifles and about half the men of the Indiana regiment whom he had rallied on the way. At the same time the Kentucky regiment came over from the right flank and joined the fight. The combined grape, canister, and musket fire of the Americans was more than the dense Mexican columns could stand, and they began to fall back. There was a lull in the battle. The Americans now took the initiative against what they believed to be a thoroughly shaken foe, only to be met by an entire, fresh division of Mexicans, Santa Ana's last reserves. Bragg's artillery was again hastily thrown into the breach. The first volley of canister stopped the enemy only a few yards from the muzzles of the guns. The next volley threw the Mexicans back in disorder, and the arrival of troops from the Mississippi and Indiana regiments at this point ended the battle. Santa Ana ordered a withdrawal to Taylor's old camp a few miles to the south. Apprehensive of what the next day would bring, the weary Americans rested that night on the battlefield with their arms beside them. But Santa Ana had had enough.

He had lost 1,500 to 2,000 men killed and wounded. The cavalry column that he had sent against Saltillo had been defeated and thrown back. His army was completely demoralized. There was nothing to do but retreat to San Luis Potosi. Taylor's losses had been 264 men killed, 450 wounded, and 26 missing. His men had won the hardest battle that was to be fought in the entire war; their leaders had exhibited courage, initiative, and resourcefulness and many of them were rewarded with brevet promotion.

Buena Vista ended any further Mexican threat against the Rio Grande and secured the American hold on Mexico's northern provinces. There was only one other action in that theater during the rest of the war, a fight that took place in Chihuahua less than a week after Taylor's victory at Buena Vista. A force of 900 Missouri volunteers under Col. Alexander W. Doniphan, detached from Kearny's command, had set out from Santa Fe early in February to pacify the region of the upper Rio Grande. Crossing the river at El Paso, Doniphan soon encountered a well-entrenched force of approximately 3,000 Mexicans, mostly local Militia, and defeated them with great slaughter, killing 300 and wounding 500 while losing only 2 men killed and 7 wounded. Doniphan's force then continued to Parras and Saltillo and back to the United States by way of Camargo, an epic march of about 1,000 miles.

The March on Mexico City. General Scott's army for the invasion of central Mexico had been assembling at the mouth of the Brazos River and at Tampico. Including the detachments drawn from General Taylor, most of which were at Tampico, Scott had 13,660 men, of whom 5,741 were Regulars. On 15 February 1847 advance elements left the Brazos for the rendezvous on Lobos Island, about 50 miles south of Tampico, from which the entire force sailed for Vera Cruz on 2 March. A beach two miles south of the city was chosen for the landing after a reconnaissance by Scott and his staff in which the small vessel carrying the party narrowly escaped being struck by shells from the citadel. Had it been sunk the stream of American military history might have taken an entirely different course, for in addition to the commanding general the party on board included a number of young officers—Joseph E. Johnston, Pierre G. T. Beauregard, George G. Meade, and Robert E. Lee. At 1800 on the evening of 9 March the landing commenced, and in the space of four hours more than 10,000 men went ashore in the heavy surf boats that had been brought along for the purpose. Not a shot was fired. The Mexican commander, having only about 4,300 men with which to defend the place, had decided to keep his entire force behind the city's walls.

Landing at Vera Cruz. This was the first major amphibious landing of the U. S. Army.

To avoid casualties, Scott chose to take the city by siege and bombardment rather than by assault, but the seven mortars with which he was provided proved ineffective against the heavy stone walls and bastions of the citadel. The commander of the American naval forces, Commodore Matthew C. Perry, cooperated with the Army in the same exemplary manner his brother, Oliver Hazard Perry, had with General Harrison on Lake Erie. He loaned Scott six heavy naval guns and crews. With these weapons the walls were easily breached and the defenders were soon demoralized. On 27 March 1847 Vera Cruz capitulated.

Because the yellow fever season was approaching, Scott was anxious to move forward into the interior uplands where the climate was more healthful, but he was not able to collect enough pack mules and transport for an advance until 8 April.

The first resistance was encountered at Cerro Gordo, about 30 miles from Vera Cruz, where Santa Ana with a newly raised army of approximately 12,000 men was occupying a strongly entrenched position in the mountain passes through which ran the road to Jalapa and Mexico City. A reconnaissance led by Captain Lee disclosed that the Mexican left flank was vulnerable. Scott decided to split his force and send two of his three divisions around Santa Ana's left to cut the only road by which the Mexicans could withdraw, while the third division, a Volunteer outfit, made a frontal assault. The flanking movement won the day. Finding themselves surrounded, the Mexicans surrendered in droves, although they had beaten off the frontal attack. It was a smashing victory for Scott, demonstrating the principles of the offensive, security, and maneuver. At a cost of only 431 men killed and wounded Scott had taken 3,000 prisoners, 4,000 muskets, and 43 cannon and had inflicted casualties of 1,000 to 1,200 on the Mexicans. Santa Ana and the remnants of his army fled into the mountains. Scott moved on to Jalapa without delay.

The Americans were now about 60 miles from Vera Cruz. The capital of Mexico was 170 miles farther on, but the road lay open. Nevertheless, an immediate advance faced a number of difficulties. Scott had expected to replenish his provisions and forage at Jalapa, but in this he was disappointed. The army's supply of ready cash was running low. Most of the cavalry had to be detailed to escort wagon trains to and from Vera Cruz. Scott had heard nothing from General Taylor, only rumors that Taylor's army was at San Luis Potosi preparing to advance on the capital, and his own planning was thus made more difficult. The extremes of climate and unbalanced rations had sent large numbers of troops to the hospital. At the end of May, Scott reported, more than 3,200 sick and wounded soldiers were in hospital. Most important of all factors, the term of enlistment of seven of Scott's Volunteer regiments was about to expire. Wounds, sickness, and the departure of the Volunteers reduced the army to 5,820 effective noncommissioned officers and privates.

During the month after the battle at Cerro Gordo, Scott pushed cautiously forward to Puebla, where he stayed until the beginning of August awaiting reinforcements and the outcome of an attempt to negotiate a peace. Influenced no doubt by Taylor's armistice after Monterrey, perhaps by a desire to salvage some of the glory for the Democratic administration, and by the conviction that the military arm of the Government was not the proper instrument for negotiating with the Mexican Government, the President had dispatched a State Department official, Nicholas P. Trist, with instructions to accompany Scott and to handle all peace negotiations. Scott had protested vigorously at the appointment and, for a time, refused to have anything to do with Trist, but during the stay at Puebla the two men patched up their differences and decided that Santa Ana might be more quickly persuaded to acknowledge defeat if something material were offered as an inducement. The Mexican President agreed that for $10,000 down and $1,000,000 to be paid when a treaty was ratified he would discuss peace terms. However, after the down payment was safely in hand, Santa Ana discovered that he could not prevail upon the Mexican Congress to repeal a law it had passed making it high treason for any official to treat with the Americans. It was clear that Scott would have to move closer to the capital of Mexico before Santa Ana would seriously consider terms of a peace.

By the beginning of August, Scott, after leaving a small garrison in Puebla, had nearly 10,000 men available for the advance on Mexico City. His force was not sufficiently large to provide at the same time protection for the road to Vera Cruz, so Scott decided upon a step of great daring, nothing less than to strike out from his base and abandon his line of communications with the coast. On 7 August the leading division moved out of Puebla towards Mexico City. Within a week the army had climbed up to the high and broad plateau on which the city lay and had come in sight of the outer defenses.

In front of Mexico City, in the direction from which Scott was approaching, lay three large lakes surrounded by low marshes. The roads leading to the city gates passed through these marshes over raised causeways guarded at their intersections by strongly fortified positions. Out of the marshy lowland rose an occasional steep hill which the Mexicans had likewise fortified. The most formidable of them was the citadel of Chapultepec, a massive stone fortress on top of a 200-foot hill situated about a mile from the city proper. In these positions in and around the city Santa Ana had disposed his army.

Two brisk and bloody actions were fought on 19–20 August, as a result of which the Mexicans were pushed back to the defenses just outside the city walls. An apparent disposition on the part of the Mexican Government to consider peace terms encouraged Scott to propose an armistice. Santa Ana quickly agreed. For two weeks Trist and representatives of the Mexican Government discussed terms until it became clear that the Mexicans would not accept what Trist was prepared to offer and were merely making use of the armistice as a breathing spell. On 6 September Scott called a halt to the discussions and prepared to assault the city. Two days later the most important outwork of Chapultepec was taken and the citadel itself fell on 13 September. This was the end. Scott's troops pushed on from Chapultepec and on the same night a small vanguard entered the gates of the city. At dawn on 14 September the Mexican authorities sent out a white flag. The garrison, led by Santa Ana, had slipped away during the night, but it had ceased to be an effective fighting force. Santa Ana promptly abdicated the Presidency and shortly afterwards the last remnant of his army, about 1,500 volunteers, was completely defeated while attempting to capture an American supply train on the road from Vera Cruz.

The End of the War. For two months the only responsible government in Mexico was the American military government under Scott. The collection of the revenues, the suppression of disorder, the administration of justice, all the details of governing the country were in the hands of the Army. When the Mexicans finally organized a government with which Commissioner Trist could negotiate a peace treaty, dispatches arrived from Washington instructing Trist to return to the United States and ordering Scott to resume the war. Knowing that now the Mexicans were sincerely desirous of ending the war and realizing that the Government in Washington was unaware of the true situation, both Trist and Scott decided to continue the negotiations.

On 2 February 1848 the Treaty of Guadelupe Hidalgo was signed. Mexico recognized the Rio Grande as the boundary of Texas and ceded New Mexico (including the present states of Arizona, New Mexico, Utah, and Nevada, a small corner of present day Wyoming, and the western and southern portions of Colorado), and Upper California (the present state of California) to the United States. The United States on its part agreed to pay Mexico $15,000,000 and to assume the unpaid claims against Mexico. Resisting public demands that the whole of Mexico be annexed and refusing to repudiate Trist and the treaty, President Polk promptly sent the treaty to the Senate, which ratified it after bitter debate. On 1 August 1848 the last American soldiers stepped aboard their transports at Vera Cruz and quitted Mexican soil.

Summary. In the conduct of military operations the United States had come a long way since the War of 1812, although the nature of the opposition doubtless accounted for some of the apparent improvement. The American Army was better trained and disciplined in 1846 and 1847 than it had been in a comparable stage of the earlier wars. There was less reliance on short-term Militia calls and more reliance on Volunteers. The Volunteers that were raised were for the most part given some intensive training before being sent into battle, but their 12-month term of enlistment still proved to be too short to permit the planning of campaigns without considering this factor as an important limitation. The generalship of Scott and Taylor was of higher calibre than that displayed in the War of 1812, in its first stages at least. Nevertheless, both Scott and Taylor were severely critized by some of their contemporaries, and each has had his partisans among later writers.

The supporting arms and services were generally of high quality. The artillery, consisting almost entirely of Regulars, turned the tide at critical points in several battles. The success of the horse artillery demonstrated the value of mobility and justified the training that had been given the artillery in this respect in the years before the war. The engineers had little opportunity to display their technical knowledge in the building of defensive works except at Fort Brown, for the Americans were taking the offensive in every engagement except Buena Vista. The engineers made their principal contribution as the eyes of Scott's army. A careful reconnaissance of the enemy position, conducted by the engineers, was generally insisted on by Scott before engaging in battle. The Quartermaster Department was faced with a tremendous task. The theater of operations was greater and the lines of communications more extended than in either of the earlier major wars. Considering the unprecedented demands, the logistical arrangements worked out with a minimum of confusion.

The Mexican War was unique in a number of ways. For the first time an American army engaged in house-to-house fighting in city streets. For the first time American forces were transported overseas to fight in a climate and over terrain entirely different from that to which they were accustomed. Although operations on the Great Lakes during the War of 1812 had involved amphibious landings and the use of water routes for transport and supply, the landing at Vera Cruz and the use of transport vessels by both Taylor and Scott in the Mexican War far surpassed those earlier operations. The use of steam-propelled vessels had facilitated troop movements during the Black Hawk and Seminole Indian Wars; they were for the first time extensively used by an American army in the Mexican War. Finally, in the Mexican War an American army for the first time was required to establish and administer a system of military government over a defeated people.

QUESTIONS

1. What advantages over the Mexicans did General Taylor have at the Battles of Palo Alto and Resaca de la Palma? What disadvantages did he have?

2. What was the general object of American strategy at the outbreak of the war? How was it to be achieved?

3. How was the news of Taylor's victory at Monterrey received by the administration in Washington? Why?

4. What was the importance of the Battle of Buena Vista?

5. What factors influenced General Scott's plan of campaign immediately after the battle of Cerro Gordo?

6. What arrangement was made to insure the cooperation of General Scott in establishing a peace satisfactory to the administration? How well did the arrangement work?

Reading List

Bill, Alfred H. *Rehearsal for Conflict.* New York, 1947.

Elliott, Charles W. *Winfield Scott: The Soldier and the Man.* New York, 1937.

Hamilton, Holman. *Zachary Taylor.* Indianapolis, 1941.

Henry, Robert S. *The Story of the Mexican War.* Indianapolis, 1950.

Smith, Justin H. *The War With Mexico.* New York, 1919. 2 vols.

CHAPTER 10

1848–1860

The Peacetime Army: Organization and Operations. The brief interval of peace between the end of the Mexican War and the beginning of the Civil War in 1861 saw the Army reduced at a time when it was assuming vastly greater responsibilities. The settlement of the Oregon boundary question and the victory over Mexico added to the United States a wide stretch of territory—much of it wild, rough, and inhospitable. Further, the rich lands on the Pacific coast enhanced by the discovery of gold in California in 1849 lured an increasing number of emigrants to essay the long hard trip across the plains, which were populated by such hardy, warlike Indian tribes as the Cheyennes, Blackfeet, Sioux, Pawnees, Utes, Comanches, and Apaches. These tribes, whose braves totaled an estimated 40,000, loved fighting and plunder, and their males were trained to be fighters from infancy. The Army protected the emigrants and settlers by guarding the several transcontinental wagon routes and by keeping the tribes in check throughout the vast spaces between the Mexican and Canadian borders. At the same time the Army was responsible for coastal fortifications and for exploring and surveying the new regions. In addition, the years 1848–1860 saw a resolute and intelligent effort to acquire for the Army newer, more efficient weapons that developing 19th century technology made possible and to revise tactical doctrine to fit the new weapons.

Return to Peacetime establishment. With the signing of the peace treaty with Mexico and the return of the soldiers to American soil, reduction of the Army began. The Volunteers were discharged and returned to their homes. The Regiment of Mounted Rifles was retained as part of the Regular Establishment, but all the other new regiments were mustered out. The Mounted Rifles regiment was at once ordered overland to Oregon, but many of its members took advantage of a wartime law which permitted Regulars to receive discharges at the conclusion of hostilities. As a result, the depleted regiment had to wait for recruits at Fort Leavenworth, Kans., until 10 May 1849, when it started its 2,000-mile trek. By the end of 1848 the Army had reverted to peacetime strength and status. But as the Indian frontier was a scene of constant unrest and active campaigns, the word "peace" was for the Army a somewhat erroneous term. Authorized strength totaled 9,878 officers and enlisted men. Because of the time and distance involved in sending recruits from the East to the frontier posts to replace casualties and discharged men, actual strength always lagged behind authorized strength, so that staff and line of the Army usually totaled several hundred less than authorized. Altogether 446 officers and enlisted men were authorized for the general staff, the Corps of Engineers and Topographical Engineers, and the various administrative services. In the tactical organizations, the two dragoon regiments together were allowed a total of 72 officers and 1.230 enlisted men; the Mounted Rifles, 36 officers and 765 enlisted men; the four artillery regiments, 216 officers and 2,600 enlisted men; and the eight infantry regiments, 288 officers and 4,192 enlisted men. There were 50 privates per company in the dragoons, 64 in the Mounted Rifles, and 42 in the artillery and infantry. Administratively, the Army was divided into three divisions. The Eastern Division, under General Scott, who as senior officer was also General in Chief with headquarters in New York City, embraced four departments, mainly consisting of forts and posts on the eastern seaboard and in the Great Lakes region. The Western Division, under Maj. Gen. Zachary Taylor, consisted of nine departments and included Florida, Alabama, Iowa, Wisconsin, Missouri, Texas, New Mexico, Arkansas, the Indian Country, and the Oregon Trail. Col. and Brevet Brig. Gen. Persifor F. Smith commanded the Pacific Division, which embraced California and Oregon.

A Small Increase. The manifold responsibilities involved in keeping the Indians in check and protecting the emigrants naturally stretched the small army very thin. Thirty-two new posts were established in the new territories, chiefly along the Oregon and Santa Fe Trails, before the end of 1849, and four-fifths of the Army found employment on the frontier. Further, the enlisted strength of 9,439 authorized in 1849 was smaller than the 1815 peacetime establishment by 2,499 men. It was weakened by the lag between discharges and enlistments and by the fact that, after gold was discovered in California, many soldiers stationed there deserted to look for the precious metal. Of 1,200 soldiers in 1849, 500 risked imprisonment to desert and hunt for riches, and commanders eventually sought to reduce desertion by granting short furloughs to soldiers desiring to become temporary prospectors. In a further effort to solve the problem, Congress authorized extra pay for officers and enlisted men stationed on the west coast; and in 1852 this provision was extended to those serving in the Territory of New Mexico. In 1854, when enlisted pay was increased and longevity pay was authorized, Congress continued the system of extra pay for service beyond the Rocky Mountains.

In 1849 General Scott, seriously concerned over the Army's relative weakness, recommended that the number of enlisted men be doubled either by creating new units or by augmenting existing ones, and he presented to the Secretary of War a scheme by which the Army could be expanded to 18,007 men.   George W. Crawford, Secretary of War under President Zachary Taylor, accepted Scott's recommendations in part and urged them on Taylor, who concurred.   As a result, Congress on 17 June 1850 approved enlarging the companies serving on the frontier to 74 privates and also accepted Crawford's recommendation that some of the infantry units serving on the Texas plains be mounted to enable them to cope with the well-mounted, hard-riding Indians. Thereafter, 90 of the 158 companies were enlarged, so that at the end of 1850 the Army was authorized 12,927 officers and enlisted men.

New regiments.   Neither the enlargement of the company nor the mounting of the infantry proved completely satisfactory.   General Scott disapproved the latter, pointing out that it was hard on the horses and spoiled the men as infantry without making them into good cavalrymen.   He and the various Secretaries of War did not always agree on the precise methods by which enlargement should be attained, but they all agreed that the Army was too small to carry out its missions.   When Jefferson Davis, a West Point graduate, Volunteer regimental commander in the Mexican War, successful Mississippi planter, and former Senator, became Secretary of War under President Franklin Pierce in 1853, he strongly urged a larger Army, one that could be expanded to 27,818 men in time of war by enlarging the company to 128 men.   Davis desired new mounted regiments for frontier service, pointing out, like his predecessors, that only highly mobile units could hope to handle the Indians.   Congress acted, and on 3 March 1855 four new regiments were authorized.   Thus were organized the 1st and 2d Cavalry Regiments and the 9th and 10th Infantry Regiments. The mounted arm thus consisted of dragoons, mounted rifles, and cavalry until the Civil War, when the older names were discarded. All mounted regiments were then called cavalry, and numbers were changed in accordance with regimental seniority.   At Davis' insistence the new infantry units were armed with percussion cap, muzzle-loading rifles instead of smooth bore muskets.   At the close of 1855 the Army numbered 15,752, with an authorized total of 17,867 men, which was slightly under its approximate strength at the outbreak of the Civil War.

Decline of the Militia.   The militia system based on compulsory service of all able-bodied men had continued to deteriorate.   Public indifference and apathy on the part of state authorities blocked any effort of the Federal Government to strengthen and improve it.   Many states either failed to organize the militia or neglected to report its strength to the War Department.   Some, notably New York, Massachusetts, Virginia, and Louisiana, managed to maintain creditable organizations, but in general only by absorbing the Volunteer units.

The Indian Wars.   The years 1848–1860 saw a constant succession of marches, expeditions, and campaigns against the Indians.   During the decade of the fifties there were no less than 22 distinct "wars," ranging from Florida to Arizona, and from the Missouri River to Oregon. In the year 1857 alone the Army sent out 37 separate expeditions that involved actual combat, plus many others that accomplished their missions without shedding blood. The extent of the campaigns can be seen from the fact that in 1858 each regiment of the Army marched an average distance of 1,234 miles, and every expedition carried with it all its requirements from horseshoe nails to artillery.

All this was done in rough terrain in a part of the country where local procurement was nonexistent. Supplying the various frontier posts entailed great effort. In former years these posts had been located on or near navigable rivers, but now the frontier posts were as far as 1,000 miles from inland waterways. All goods had to be hauled in wagons or carried by pack train.

Merely getting troops to the frontier posts was a major effort. To reach the west coast from the Mississippi River region required three months of arduous overland travel; every day's march required a tactical formation; every night's bivouac required all-round security. There were two alternate methods of reaching the West from the Atlantic coast: the long, rough sea voyage around Cape Horn, or by ship to Panama, overland across the jungled isthmus, thence by ship to the west coast. These alternatives were also hazardous and unpleasant. In 1853 the chartered steamer *San Francisco*, loaded with 3d Field Artillery soldiers, their wives, and children, sank at the outset of a voyage from New York City around Cape Horn. It carried about 200 people to their deaths. The journey over the disease-ridden isthmus was also bad. One regiment lost 107 men to cholera and various fevers acquired in Panama.

Despite all these difficulties, however, the scattered garrisons and units of the Army substantially carried out their missions. Although the frontier would not and could not be completely pacified until the area was more densely settled, the emigrant wagon trains were, in the main, well protected. Indian forays against isolated settlements could not be stopped completely, but they were kept down in part by the Indian's knowledge that a foray was always followed by retaliatory action. Further, the constant warfare and alerts kept the individual units of the Army in a high state of tactical efficiency, although the necessity for garrisoning many dispersed posts (in 1857 there were 68 large, permanent forts, and 70 temporary forts) made brigade and division maneuvers impossible, and there were no brigade headquarters in the Army until the Civil War.

The Utah Expedition. Indians were not the only source of trouble. To the Utah Territory had immigrated the main body of The Church of Jesus Christ of Latter Day Saints, more popularly called the Mormons. Almost immediately after his inauguration as President in March 1857, President Buchanan received reports that the Mormons were defying Federal authority. Although this was not strictly true Buchanan believed it and acted accordingly. When he sent civil officials to the territory, he decided to send with them a strong body of troops. About 2,500 men—eight companies of the 2d Dragoons, the 5th and 10th Infantry Regiments, and two artillery batteries—went out under command of Col. Albert Sidney Johnston. But before the column could enter the Great Salt Lake Valley, the alarmed Mormons skillfully separated the wagon train from the troops, burned the wagons, and captured many horses. Johnston's isolated force was compelled to spend the winter in the Rockies on short rations. In the spring of 1858 more troops started out from Fort Leavenworth—the 1st Cavalry, the remaining companies of the 2d Dragoons, two companies of light artillery, the 6th and 7th Infantry Regiments, detachments from the Mounted Rifles and the 3d Infantry, and a battalion of volunteers—to bring Johnston's strength to 5,500. But agreement with the Mormons was reached, and most of the troops were sent elsewhere before reaching Utah. But as late as 1860 the Army still had 828 men in the Department of Utah.

Construction and exploration. Fighting, though of primary importance, did not absorb all the Army's energies. During this period the Engineers were busy with the seacoast fortifications and improving rivers and harbors. The method of building forts during this period underwent some changes. The sloping, grass-covered glacis was abandoned in favor of vertical granite walls with the expectation that the guns of the fort would prevent assault from landing and that long-range cannonading would decide the action. In 1853 responsibility for building the north and south wings of the Capitol Building in Washington, D. C., was transferred from the Interior Department to the Army Engineers. Capt. Montgomery C. Meigs, who became Army Quartermaster General during the Civil War, directed the work and made extensive studies in acoustics, heating, and ventilation in the course of building the Senate and House Chambers. At the same time he supervised initial construction of the Washington Aqueduct designed to carry water from the Great Falls of the Potomac to the District of Columbia. The Topographical Engineers were constantly busy with surveys and exploration, generally in hostile Indian country, where every exploring party was a military expedition. The most significant and far-reaching explorations began in 1853, when Congress authorized comprehensive explorations to discover the best railway routes from the Mississippi River to the Far West. Several parties went out, one of which was wiped out by Indians in Utah in October. The reports of the expeditions resulted in recommendation of four routes which were substantially those eventually followed by the Northern Pacific, the Union Pacific, the

Topographical Engineer Surveying Expedition—exploring the Colorado River region in the vicinity of Chimney Peak.

Kansas Pacific, and the Southern Pacific when those railroads were built after the Civil War. Largely as a result of Jefferson Davis' recommendation, the United States bought from Mexico a tract of land south of the Gila River in New Mexico (the Gadsden Purchase) to provide a route that skirted the Rocky Mountains.

Use of camels. The difficulties of supplying the isolated frontier posts in the arid regions of the Southwest brought forth an interesting experiment in the use of camels. Davis conceived the idea that the camel, which for centuries had been used as a pack and riding animal in the deserts of Asia and Africa, might help solve the problem. Obtaining a small appropriation from Congress, he had about 30 camels purchased and shipped to Texas in 1856. Experience showed that a camel could carry twice what a horse could pull in a wagon and could walk surefootedly over ground no wagon could traverse. John B. Floyd, Secretary of War from 1857 to 1860 under Buchanan, was so enthusiastic that he asked Congress for money to buy 1,000 of the beasts, but Congress refused to appropriate the funds. Nevertheless, the original camels and their descendants carried supplies in the Southwest until the Civil War, and some are reported to have carried the Confederate mails in Texas. The Civil War interrupted the U. S. Army's experiment, and the construction of the transcontinental railways afterward rendered the camel unnecessary. Some were turned loose to roam the wilderness, and others were sold to circuses.

Weapons and Tactics. *The rifle and rifle ammunition.* Rifles, with their superior range and accuracy, had been used for military purposes in America during the 18th century, but their slow rate of fire compared with that of the musket had made it inadvisable to issue them to infantry of the line. But because of improvements the rifle had been gradually replacing the smooth bore musket for some time, as the existence of the Mounted Rifles, Davis' Mississippi Rifles in the Mexican War, and the addition of two rifle regiments to the Army in 1855 bear witness. Nineteenth century technological developments had made possible an accurate, dependable muzzle-loading rifle with at least as fast a rate of fire as the smooth bore musket. The earlier introduction of the percussion cap had made the musket much more reliable. The application of this principle, together with the Minié ball, made the rifle, or rifled musket, a good military weapon. The Minié ball, perfected by a French officer, was adopted by the U. S. Army in 1855. This ball was cylindro-conoidal in shape and consisted of a lead shell tapering forward from its hollow base. To load and fire, the soldier bit open the paper cartridge, poured the powder down the barrel, rammed in the paper to seat the charge, and then rammed the bullet home. He then put the cap in place, full-cocked the piece, aimed, and fired. Sparks from the cap fired the powder. The force of the explosion expanded the hollow base of the bullet to fit the rifling, and the bullet left the barrel with considerably accuracy. Its maximum range was about 1,000–1,200 yards, and its effective range was about 400–600 yards as compared with 100–200 yards for smooth bore muskets. Rate of fire was a theoretical three rounds a minute, but it was seldom attained in practice. In 1855 manufacture of smooth bore muskets in national armories was stopped. The armories then began making only rifles and, in addition, started converting smooth bores into rifles with the intention of arming the Regular Army and the Militia with them. The work took time. By the end of 1858 the Springfield and Harper's Ferry Armories had manufactured but 4,000 of the new type of rifle, the Springfield .58. When the Civil War began most state troops still had smooth bores, and both Federal and Confederate governments scoured the European markets for suitable weapons.

Breechloaders. Like rifling, the principle of breech-loading to permit much more rapid rates of fire was an old one, but it could not be put into practice until metallurgy and methods of accurate measurement had developed to a state which made possible a tight-fitting, but easymoving, bolt that would withstand the force of a propellant charge and at the same time operate a firing pin. Many breechloaders were on the market in the 1850's and the Army began testing all available models, although it had not completed its tests before 1861. In 1860 Secretary Floyd prophesied that the breechloader would replace the muzzle-loader just as surely as the percussion cap supplanted flint and steel. Effective breech-loading rifles required metallic rather than paper cartridges to prevent the escape of gases at the breech. Metallic cartridges were invented in 1856 but were not produced in large numbers until after 1861.

Artillery developments. Field artillery ammunition did not change substantially after the Mexican War. Grape and canister, shell (high explosive and shrapnel), and solid shot were still standard. The outstanding new development came in the introduction of rifling into both field and coast artillery—during the fifties wrought-iron carriages were being substituted for wooden ones in the Coast Artillery. As in the case of small arms, rifling greatly increased the accuracy and more than doubled the effective range of weapons, but rifled guns did not immediately supplant the smooth bores. During this period there was introduced a new artillery piece for the light batteries—the 12-pound bronze cannon called the "Napoleon" after Napoleon III. A smooth bore, it was a substantial improvement over older models. Capt. Robert P. Parrott's rifled cannon was developed in 1851 but did not come into use on an appreciable scale until the Civil War. Another muzzle-loader, the Parrott rifle was made of cast iron with its breech reinforced by an iron band. Its projectiles employed both percussion and time fuzes. Development of an elongated, expanding projectile—which resulted from the application of the Minié principle to artillery—did much to further the use of rifled artillery, and led to a great improvement in accuracy and effectiveness.

Tactical principles. In retrospect, it is clear that tactical doctrine did not entirely keep pace with the development of weapons, although some efforts were made in that direction. As Secretary of War, Davis prescribed light infantry tactics for all infantry units in an attempt to put the lessons of the Mexican War into practice and to fit tactical doctrine to the new weapons. In general, this meant reducing the line of the infantry from three to two ranks and placing increased emphasis on skirmishers, but tactics remained basically those of the 18th century. Formations were rigid; men stood shoulder to shoulder (it was very difficult to load a muzzle-loader lying down) in ranks, and intervals between units were small. These relatively dense formations would, in the early days of the Civil War, offer inviting targets to the field artillery and to riflemen. But some changes in tactics had been made, and the shock of battle in the Civil War would effect more.

Books and schooling. The great amount of operational activity and the development of new weapons were accompanied by an increased intellectual activity. Constant efforts were made to keep improving the curriculum, standards of instructions, and physical plant at the U. S. Military Academy, where such great names as Robert E. Lee and Dennis Mahan, author of many works on engineering and fortification, appeared on the roster of staff and faculty. To the great satisfaction of professional artillerymen, the Artillery School of Practice was reopened at Fort Monroe. Jefferson Davis sent Majs. R. Delafield and A. Mordecai and Capt. George B. McClellan to Europe to study all aspects of the Crimean War in particular and of European military institutions and developments in general. Such volumes as Scott's *Instructions for Field Artillery* (1845), the *General Regulations for the Army of the United States* (1847), *Hardee's Tactics*, and the new volume on infantry tactics sponsored by Davis were made available to Army officers and a few others, but not enough were obtained to furnish copies to the Militia. A number of military schools had been founded throughout the country, with the South having a slight edge, an advantage that was to provide trained officers to the Confederate Army when the Civil War broke out.

Drift Toward War. During the decade of the fifties the slavery problem increased in intensity, and, in the absence of reasonably acceptable solutions, the Nation ran its apparently inexorable course toward civil war. Tensions mounted alarmingly in the 1850's. The Compromise of 1850 failed to achieve sectional harmony; the return of fugitive slaves to their owners resulted in riots and violence. Open warfare broke out in the Kansas Territory between antislavery and proslavery factions, and in 1856 four companies were sent from Fort Leavenworth to Lawrence, Lecompton, and Topeka to stop the fighting. Secretary Davis approved further action, and Brevet Maj. Gen. Persifor F. Smith used nearly all the 1st Cavalry and the 2d Dragoons and part of the 6th Infantry to keep the peace. He succeeded in stopping the fighting without bloodshed. John Brown, who had won notoriety in "bleeding" Kansas, seized Harper's Ferry in a mad attempt to foment a slave uprising. He was subdued by a detachment of marines from Washington and the local Militia, all under command of Col. Robert E. Lee. Alarmed Southerners believed, inaccurately, that Brown typified Northern opinion.

By the end of the decade people spoke everywhere of the possibility of civil war, although it seems probable that the majority of Americans wanted to avoid it. The Army, drawing its officers from all sections of the country, became affected by the Secessionist and pro-Unionist fervors. There was actually no way to prepare military plans to meet the crisis. Civil wars are almost impossible to plan for. Further, the Army's general staff—the War Department bureaus— was an administrative body. No one person, office, or committee was charged directly with the primary responsibility for strategic planning, and not until the Civil War was more than half over would the Federal Union devise effective machinery for strategic planning and efficient, centralized command. Further, it is unlikely that the Army could have prepared plans to coerce dissident states even if machinery had existed. When the Southern states began seceding, President Buchanan showed that he had no policy by doing nothing. Moreover, the men who served as Secretaries of War from 1853 until the end of 1860 not only opposed the Federal Government's right to coerce a state but joined the Confederacy themselves. Davis became president. Floyd, resigning with his accounts in a mess, became a brigadier general in the Confederate Army. He was replaced as Secretary by the pro-Union Joseph Holt, but it was too late to accomplish anything.

On the other hand, the charges that Davis and Floyd purposely hamstrung the Army and posted an undue number of men in the South are false. In fact, Davis was in a great measure responsible for strengthening the Army by adding four regiments to its roster and by adopting the rifle and Minié ball. The charges against Floyd derived from some of his foolish and untruthful boasts after he joined the Confederate Army. As the table below shows, the changes in troop assignments to the various departments, which replaced the divisions, did not change, proportionately, very much between 1853 and the end of 1860. The most significant changes resulted from the larger numbers sent to the west coast, which was not slave territory.

Comparative Distribution of Troops: 1853 and 1860

Department	1853	1860
Total	9, 099	14, 072
Department of the East	1, 087	929
Department of the West	1, 507	2, 808
Department of Texas	3, 294	2, 949
Department of New Mexico	1, 611	3, 104
Department of the Pacific	1, 600	(*)
Department of Utah	(*)	828
Department of Oregon	(*)	2, 236
Department of California	(*)	1, 218

* Not in existence.

QUESTIONS

1. Compare Jefferson Davis' plans for expanding the Army with those of John C. Calhoun.

2. Explain why the Army had difficulty in keeping its actual strength up to authorized strength.

3. Aside from fighting Indians, what other contributions did the Army make?

4. In what ways was the rifle superior to the smooth bore?

Reading List

Strode, Hudson. *Jefferson Davis, American Patriot: 1808–1861.* New York, 1955. Pp. 245–296.

CHAPTER 11

THE CIVIL WAR—1861

Introduction. *Military significance of the Civil War.* In the Western World the American Civil War was, after the Napoleonic struggles, the largest and longest major conflict in the 19th century. Fierce and bloody, it has proved of interest to diverse groups of Americans and foreigners alike. Intensely dramatic, it was the last American war wherein infantry attacked in the open in dense formations. Conversely, it was extremely modern, for the recent improvements in technology and manufacturing, plus new inventions, put new types of materiel at the disposal of commanders, increased the range and accuracy of older weapons, and made possible the sustained mobilization and deployment of mass armies. Thus the Civil War saw the employment of railroads, balloons, telegraphs, steamships, armorplate, revolving turrets, rifled artillery, long-range rifles, and even breechloaders. Not all these were new but most were used on an unprecedented scale. The war was a gory struggle between economies that would be won by the side which could most resolutely and skillfully bring to bear superior economic resources and manpower. Finally, since this massive war was fought within the boundaries of the United States, and on different occasions under the eyes of the rival commanders in chief, it proved an exacting test of the American political system and of all the components of the United States armed forces, together with their existing command and staff organizations. Introducing new dimensions and problems into warfare, it strongly affected military policy and thought in the United States and abroad.

Secession. The election of Abraham Lincoln to the Presidency in 1860 triggered the states of the deep South into enacting ordinances of secession and taking possession of Federal property, including forts, arsenals, and navy yards, within their borders. By February 1861 seven states—South Carolina, Georgia, Alabama, Florida, Mississippi, Louisiana, and Texas—had declared themselves out of the Union (map 20). A provisional government calling itself the Confederate States of America was established at Montgomery, Ala. The President, Jefferson Davis, was a U. S. Military Academy graduate. Like Mr. Lincoln, he had seen service in the Black Hawk War. Subsequently Davis had resigned from the Army to become a planter, distinguished himself as a regimental commander in the Mexican War, and had served as United States Senator and Secretary of War. In February he called for the services of 100,000 volunteers to serve for 12 months. By the time Mr. Lincoln took the Presidential oath on 4 March 1861, the

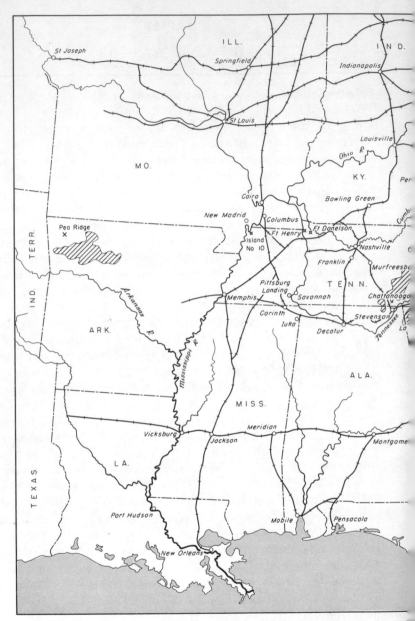

Map 20.—Area of operati

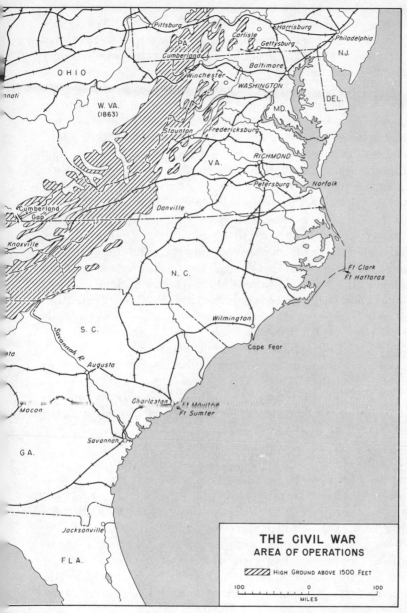

THE CIVIL WAR
AREA OF OPERATIONS

▨ HIGH GROUND ABOVE 1500 FEET

100   0   100
MILES

Civil War.

only places within the Confederacy that were effectively controlled by the U. S. Government were Fort Pickens at Pensacola and Fort Sumter in Charleston harbor. Eight slave states—Delaware, Maryland, Virginia, North Carolina, Kentucky, Tennessee, Missouri, and Arkansas—remained within the Union but strongly secessionist opinion prevailed in several of them. The actions of the dissident states were strongly affecting the Regular Army, which on 1 January 1861 consisted of 1,098 officers and 15,304 enlisted men mostly stationed in the West to ensure peace on the Indian frontier. Most, but not all, of the Southern-born officers resigned their commissions and offered their services to the Confederate government. Some Northern-born officers joined the Confederates, but most stayed in the U. S. Army. The enlisted men could not resign. Almost to a man, they stuck steadfast to their oaths. About one-third of the officers resigned to "go South."

Fort Sumter. President Lincoln was determined to maintain the Union and to hold Fort Sumter and Fort Pickens. But he had to move cautiously. He was anxious to avert civil war, eager to avoid any act that would drive the eight remaining slave-holding states out of the Union, and well aware that he was not backed by a unanimous public opinion in the North. Major Robert Anderson, Sumter's commander, had earlier withdrawn his tiny garrison from the indefensible Fort Moultrie in Charleston Harbor. Since then he had been virtually besieged by a growing Confederate force. In January 1861 an unarmed supply vessel attempted to bring in reinforcements and supplies for Anderson's men, but was fired on by Confederate batteries and withdrew. President Lincoln, after receiving conflicting counsel from his civilian and military advisers, decided to succor the fort and dispatched a seaborne expedition. He so notified the governor of South Carolina. But the Confederates lost patience. On 12 April 1861, after Anderson had rejected a demand for his surrender, Confederate cannon which ringed the harbor's shore began a 34-hour bombardment. Fort Sumter returned fire in earnest, but the result was inevitable. Anderson surrendered with the honors of war. (Fort Pickens was successfully reinforced.) On Sunday, 14 April, his 90-man garrison saluted the United States flag and marched aboard ship for New York. This incident was minute in itself, but the rashness of the Confederates in committing an overt act of war removed many difficulties from Lincoln's path. It crystallized a large body of Northern opinion in favor of preservation of the Union, and gave the President the resolution to act swiftly and decisively.

Call for Militia. Acting under authority vested in him by the Militia Act of 1795, Lincoln immediately called upon the governors of the loyal states to furnish 75,000 Militiamen to suppress the rebellion. These men were to serve for three months, the maximum time possible under the law. The response from most of the states was so enthusiastic that nearly 100,000 men were offered. On the other hand, the President's decision to use force led Virginia, North Carolina, Tennessee, and Arkansas to join the Confederacy. (Virginia's western counties refused to secede, however, and remained in the Union.) Virginia's secession lost to the United States the services of Col. Robert E. Lee, a distinguished officer whom Brevet Lt. Gen. Winfield Scott, General in Chief of the Army, had decided should have the field command of the forces in the event of war. Colonel Lee, though personally opposed to slavery and to secession, felt that he could not honorably fight against Virginia, his native state. He resigned from the U. S. Army, joined the forces of Virginia, and shortly thereafter rose to the rank of general in the Confederate army.

Call for Volunteers. Now that war seemed inevitable, and with four more states in the Confederacy, Lincoln declared a blockade of the entire Confederate coast line and called a special session of Congress to begin on 4 July 1861. Correctly anticipating that Congress would approve his actions, he acted on his own authority and established 40 regiments of U. S. Volunteers (42,034 men) to serve for three years or for the duration of the war, and called for men to serve in the regiments. He also increased the Regular Army by 1 field artillery regiment, 1 cavalry regiment, and 8 infantry regiments (actually 9 were added), or 22,714 men, and the Navy by 18,000 men. The discrepancy in numbers is explained by the fact that the previously existing Regular infantry regiments, like those of the Militia and the new U. S. Volunteers, were 1-battalion regiments, while the new Regular infantry regiments were to have 3 battalions of about 800 men each. As it turned out, however, the 3-battalion regiments were never recruited up to strength. Until the end of the war, despite increased inducements to join the Regulars, men preferred the larger bonuses, laxer discipline, and more neighborly atmosphere of the Volunteers. The response to the various Presidential calls was so enthusiastic that men poured into the state and Federal camps faster than they could be housed, equipped, and trained. Mr. Lincoln was forced to ask the governors to slow down the induction of recruits. The task of raising and organizing the troops was initially handled by the Treasury, while the War Department provided arms and supplies. The War Department did not control the raising of the armies until 1862. Actually, the mobilization of forces in 1861, although accompanied by confusion that resulted from the inexperience of the War and Treasury Departments, Army, states, and recruits, was accomplished at a scale and speed which compare favorably with those of the First and Second World Wars. It is obvious that President Lincoln did not, despite the warnings of General Scott, anticipate the length or scale of the war which faced him. But his foresight was remarkable; he was calling into being far larger forces than the United States had ever before possessed.

Appointment of officers. In raising these forces he used methods that were time-honored in the United States, but which hind-sight shows were not necessarily the most efficient. As a result the combat efficiency and state of training of the new units varied from good to very poor. Some of the state Militia regiments were well trained and equipped; others were regiments in name only. The soldiers of the green Volunteer regiments often elected their own company officers; these in turn were supposed to select all the field-grade officers except the regimental commanders, who were appointed by the state governors. In other instances the governors commissioned all officers. Similar practices had always been followed among United States volunteer forces. These practices were based in part on the belief that soldiering, whether on the level of the squad or the regiment, was something that a man of good sense and good will could easily master. The results were the same as in earlier wars, but intensified, for warfare had grown more complex, and the duties of an officer or noncommissioned officer could not be learned in a day. Although many of the newly made officers proved enthusiastic, devoted to duty, quick, and eager to learn, many incompetents were also commissioned. Before the end of 1861, however, officers were being required to prove their qualifications before examining boards, a practice which Congress soon made mandatory. Those found unfit were allowed to resign. The President, frequently acting upon the advice of governors and members of Congress, commissioned all U. S. Volunteer officers above the rank of colonel. Some commissions went to leading politicians in order to provide a broader base of support from the various Northern political factions. Some of these, such as John A. Logan and Francis P. Blair, Jr., proved quite competent and were to distinguish themselves later, while others were only hindrances. The majority of the first generals' commissions in the Volunteers went to Regulars on active duty, to former Regulars like George B. McClellan who had resigned from the Army to pursue civilian careers, and to those who had held Volunteer commissions in the Mexican War. The Confederacy never gave higher than a brigade command to a volunteer officer until he had proved himself in battle.

The Regular Army. The Regular Army, in 1861 and for the duration of the war, was kept intact. This policy has often been criticized on the ground that the Regular units should have been broken into cadres and used to train the Volunteers (which after First Bull Run poured in by the hundreds of thousands), but such a course was impractical in 1861 because the President did not foresee a long war and because the Regular units were needed on the frontier until trained men could replace them. Further, the effect on morale that might have resulted from breaking up units that possessed all the *esprit de corps* that accompanies a long and distinguished regimental history does not seem to have occurred to the critics. It is true that until

Volunteer commissions were opened to all Regulars in 1862, some were promoted very slowly in comparison with inexperienced Volunteers who began their military careers as full colonels. But the slow promotion probably worked to the Regular's advantage, for he thus obtained tactical experience in command of small units before being catapulted into command of large ones. Ulysses S. Grant and William T. Sherman, for example, both Military Academy graduates who had resigned from the peacetime army, had specifically asked for regimental commands, for which they felt qualified, rather than the higher rank that might easily have been theirs.

Replacements. The Confederate Army, though often hamstrung by States' rights views that insisted that Virginians be commanded only by Virginians, Georgians by Georgians, etc., and by the Southern governors' demands for troops as home guards, devised a replacement system that stood it in good stead until the closing days of the war. On the other hand, except for the Wisconsin Volunteers and the Regulars, the U. S. forces never devised an efficient, automatic replacement system. As battle losses mounted and the ranks of the veteran regiments thinned, they were forced to send men back to their home states on recruiting duty. The state governors preferred to create new regiments, while old battle-tested regiments declined to company strength.

The Contending Forces. *Economic strength and manpower.* The two sides, the United States of America and the Confederate States of America, readied themselves for battle in the spring of 1861. The preponderance of productive capacity, manpower, and agricultural potential lay on the side of the North. The South was primarily agricultural, but the North's crops were worth more annually in dollars than the South's. Further, the South's agriculture was concentrated on cotton and, to a lesser extent, tobacco. In seapower, in railroads, in highways, in material wealth, and in factories devoted to the production of iron and munitions the North was vastly superior to the South. This disparity became all the more important as the ever-tightening Federal blockade gradually cut the Confederacy off from foreign imports. The number of horses and mules in the North outnumbered those of the South, a factor of considerable importance in a war wherein most supplies were carried by wagon from the railhead to the troops, and wherein the mounted arm was so important, and wherein all field artillery was horsedrawn. The free Northern States had a white population of 18,936,579; Southern whites numbered 5,449,647, but as the 3,521,111 slaves contributed materially to the Southern economy, their numbers must also be taken into account. The four border slave states of Delaware, Maryland, Kentucky, and Missouri had a white population of 2,589,533, with 429,401 slaves. These states furnished men to both sides in about equal numbers. The disparities in populations are reflected by the size of the armies that were raised. The United States put into the field some 1,556,000 men (there were about 2,900,000 total enlistments, with reenlistments accounting for the discrepancy). Figures for the Confederate armies are not so exact, but it seems probable that between 800,000 and 900,-000 men wore the gray uniform. The Mississippi River, navigable from St. Louis to New Orleans, made the South vulnerable to invasion. Not all advantages lay with the North. Inland the South possessed interior lines. She had a long coast line which would make difficult an effective blockade. And she possessed, besides a military tradition, a proportionately larger number of men who were familiar with firearms and horses than the North. The view often implied, on the other hand, that the Northern Armies consisted of city-bred millhands and clerks is false. Three-fourths of the Northern population was rural, and the average Union soldier was farm-bred. As the war went on, the armies on both sides demonstrated a high degree of military skill and bravery. Man for man, they became almost evenly matched, and their battles were among the bloodiest in modern history.

Leadership. In leadership the South possessed initial advantages. Many of the most competent and experienced officers were Southerners. The senior officers who stayed in the U. S. Army were almost uniformly too old for field command, so that commands of large units were often abruptly given to men who had never before led more than a company, and many of them naturally fumbled their jobs. The great Union generals of 1864–1865 started the war in relatively low ranks. In Jefferson Davis the Confederacy had as President one of the most brilliant and experienced men in public life. But the advantages that accrued from his military training and experience were largely illusory. For most of the war he commanded all the Confederate forces in person in addition to all his other Presidential duties. But he had never experienced the problems inherent in waging war on a large scale. His specific military knowledge made him prone to try to do too much himself and to look after details that his subordinates should have handled. On the other hand Mr. Lincoln, whose only military experience came as a company commander in the Black Hawk War, knew that he lacked military knowledge, and made every effort to acquire it. With his keen knowledge of men and his ability to learn and to grow he developed into an outstanding war leader. One of his major problems as President was his search for one man who could and would serve as field commander of the armies, and in a sense the story of the Civil War from the Northern side can be told in terms of Lincoln's search.

Hope of foreign aid. Mr. Davis and his advisers also thought that the sympathy, or even intervention, of foreign nations would more than compensate for the Confederacy's lack of material resources.

This hope, largely illusory from the start, became less and less likely with the emancipation of the slaves, with every Northern victory on land, and with the increasing effectiveness of the Union Navy's blockade.

Strategy and geography. But the South possessed one tremendous military advantage *vis à vis* the North. It could win by doing nothing, if the North did not attack. To win its war the North had to take the offensive and subdue a valorous people zealously fighting for what it considered to be its liberty, its honor, its very existence. Militarily, then, unless the South chose to conquer the North, or the North to abandon the South, the theater of war lay below the Mason-Dixon Line. Geography, in the form of the Appalachian Mountains and the Mississippi River, divided the South into three theaters of operation: the Eastern, between the mountains and the Atlantic; the Western, between the mountains and the Mississippi; and the Trans-Mississippi (map 20). The last saw constant and bitter fighting for the four years of war, but the fighting had little or no effect on the final outcome. The Western and Eastern Theaters were decisive. In the West, control of the Cumberland, Tennessee, and Mississippi Rivers, of the railroads, and of the Gulf ports, coupled with destruction of the Confederate armies, were the main Union strategic objectives. In the East, the main objectives were similar: seizure of the major ports, control of the waterways and railways, and destruction of the armies. In an era of poor land communications, control of navigable waterways was of tremendous significance. The importance of waterways to the North can easily be seen from the fact that all the major Union armies were named for rivers. In the Eastern Theater the purely military problem was complicated by the fact that the rival capital cities faced each other across a 100-mile stretch of rolling country that rivers and streams formed into cross compartments. (After Virginia seceded the Confederates moved their capital to Richmond.) Richmond, a railroad center and the site of the only iron works in the South at the outbreak of war (the guns and armor for the *Merrimac* were made here) had some purely military value, as did Washington, which possessed the largest naval gun factory on the continent. But the psychological importance of Washington to Northern prestige and morale was too great to allow the Confederates to capture it, even if it had no purely military value. The Confederates felt similarly about Richmond. Thus a lunge in the direction of one capital was sure to bring out a contending army. These generalizations about geography and strategic objectives anticipate a great deal, for they were not entirely clear to either side in that hectic spring of 1861. Most Southerners, underestimating the North's devotion to the cause of Union and its military capacity, thought in terms of no war, or a short easy one, or of foreign intervention. Many in the North also thought in terms of a short war that would end with the capture of Richmond.

General Scott's plan. This view was in sharp contrast to that held by General Scott, who as General in Chief was the ranking officer of the U. S. Army. He commanded all the military departments and field armies, and was the chief military adviser to the Secretary of War and the President. The old veteran, who moved his headquarters to Washington to be in close touch with the President, recommended that time be taken to train an army of 85,000 men, and that a stringent naval blockade of the entire coast line be enforced to strangle the South economically. Then the Army should advance down the Mississippi to divide and conquer the Confederacy. This was the concept which the press ridiculed as the "Anaconda Plan." It was the general plan by which the North won the war, although its manpower estimates were too modest.

Campaign of Bull Run (Manassas). *The situation.* With the partly trained Militia, the almost untrained Volunteers, and one new battalion of Regulars defending Washington in July 1861, the total Federal forces at hand numbered about 50,000 men. They were commanded by Brig. Gen. Irwin A. McDowell, recently promoted from the rank of major. Almost three months had elapsed since the President had called out the Militiamen, whose terms of service were now about to expire. Similarly, General Beauregard had, to defend Richmond, posted about 20,000 Confederates at Manassas, a road and rail junction some 30 miles southwest of the Federal capital (map 21). (Until the U. S. Navy could be expanded, a seaborne advance against Richmond was out of the question.) In the Shenandoah Valley Brig. Gen. Joseph E. Johnston commanded some 11,000 Confederate soldiers. At Martinsburg, 18,000 Union troops under Brig. Gen. Robert E. Patterson were charged with responsibility for keeping Johnston in place. Other Federal and Confederate forces, including a Federal unit under Maj. Gen. Benjamin F. Butler at Fort Monroe, were holding various ports, junctions, and mountain passes.

Training and organization. Neither side was yet well trained. The Confederates had started earlier and probably had a slight edge over the Federals. McDowell had less than three months to train his soldiers, but might have accomplished more with a better staff and higher degree of organization. He tried to do too much himself; he had no chief of staff and not enough staff officers to help him. Further, the highest headquarters under him was that of the regiment until just before he marched out to fight, when he organized his regiments into five infantry divisions of two to four brigades each, save the 4th Division which had nine regiments but no brigade headquarters.

Federal preparation. Northern public opinion, as demonstrated by newspaper editorials and speeches in Congress, demanded immediate action in the form of an advance against Richmond. General Scott had warned against starting a campaign before the troops were fully trained. But President Lincoln, either bowing to popular pressure or pretending to, and certainly anxious to use the three months' Militiamen before their terms expired, aware that the Confederates were far from seasoned, and cherishing the belief that one defeat would make the South quit, wanted action. Scott, whose opinion was perhaps influenced by erroneous intelligence reports that indicated Washington was in danger of attack, acceded. McDowell was therefore directed to prepare a plan of operations. In brief, his plan as accepted in late June called for Butler and Patterson to prevent the Confederate forces facing them from reinforcing Beauregard while McDowell, with about 30,000 troops committed to the assault and 10,000 in reserve, advanced against Manassas to outflank Beauregard's position. The plan was a good one but it was badly executed.

The advance. It was 16 July before McDowell had enough men and moved out, trailed by Congressmen, newspapermen, and hucksters, along the Warrenton Turnpike (now U. S. Route 29) (Map 22). Everything depended on a rapid march, if the Union troops were to hit Beauregard before anyone could reinforce him. But the 35,000 troops—the largest army assembled on the North American continent up to then—marched slowly, and frequently straggled; McDowell did not force the troops to speed up. It was 18 July before the Army had covered the 20 miles to Centreville, about 4 miles east of the Stone Bridge over Bull Run. From there McDowell's advance guard pushed the Confederate outposts back. The Warrenton Pike crossed Bull Run over the Stone Bridge, and numerous dirt roads led to the fords. The country was fairly rough, cut by streams, and thickly wooded, so that it provided good defensive positions. While McDowell's main body waited at Centreville for the Army wagon trains, his leading division advanced against the fords, found them stoutly defended, and retired. Sure that his green troops could not force their way over Bull Run under fire, McDowell tarried for two more days, 19 and 20 July. He concentrated his troops while engineers reconnoitered for an undefended ford. When they found one that seemed undefended at Sudley Springs, northwest of the Stone Bridge, McDowell decided to envelop the Confederate left flank on 21 July and destroy the Manassas Gap Railway to keep Johnston from reinforcing Beauregard from the Valley. This was a good idea, but the Confederates had moved too fast.

Confederate dispositions. On 17 July spies in Washington told Beauregard of McDowell's move. He at once telegraphed the information to Richmond. Davis, also using the telegraph, ordered up reinforcements from Richmond and Acquia Creek, and directed Johnston to proceed to Manassas from the Valley at once. By adroit maneuvering, and by employing a cavalry screen led by a promising young colonel named J. E. B. Stuart, Johnston slipped away from Patterson, and shipped 9,000 effectives by rail to Manassas by 20 July, the day

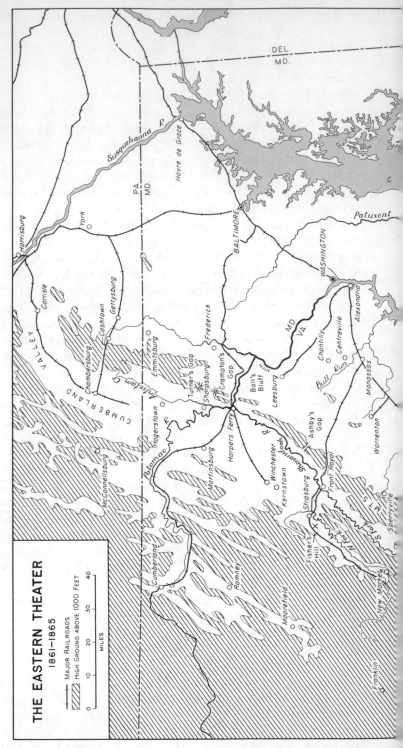

THE EASTERN THEATER
1861–1865

‡ MAJOR RAILROADS
▨ HIGH GROUND ABOVE 1000 FEET

0 10 20 30 40
MILES

Map 21. T

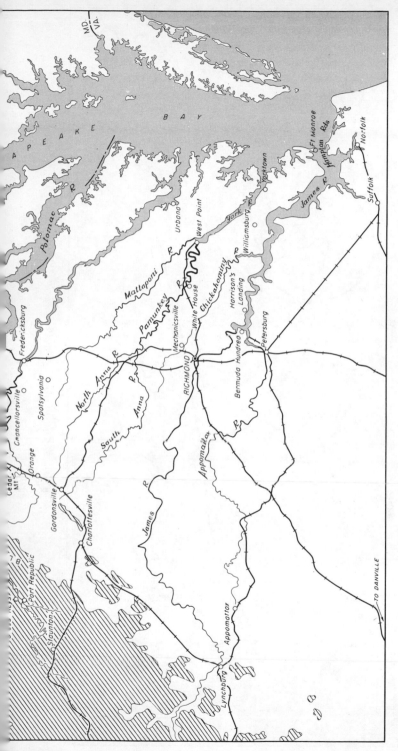

...ern theater.

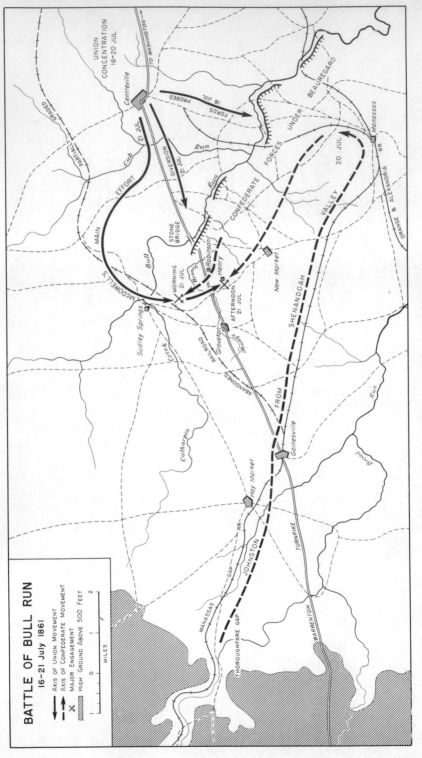

Map 22. Battle of Bull Run, 16–21 July 1861.

BATTLE OF BULL RUN

16–21 July 1861

Axis of Union Movement

Axis of Confederate Movement

X   Major Engagement

High Ground Above 500 Feet

MILES

0   1   2

before McDowell attacked. The combination of such new tools as the telegraph and the railroad coupled with such classic techniques as skillful maneuvers and a cavalry screen gave the Confederates mobility, surprise, and mass at the critical points. Beauregard had already deployed six and one-half brigades to defend the fords, and the timely reinforcements gave him four more. Johnston ranked him, but as Beauregard had already prepared a battle plan Johnston let him control the battle.

McDowell's tactical plan. Holding one division plus one brigade and artillery at Centreville in reserve, McDowell planned a diversionary attack by one division in the vicinity of the Stone Bridge. The main effort was to be executed by two divisions, under McDowell's direct command, which were to advance in column to the right, cross the Run at Sudley Springs, and envelop the enemy flank and rear. Once the main body had forced the Confederates away from the Stone Bridge, the diversionary division would cross and join the attack.

The battle. McDowell's leading division, the one scheduled to make the diversionary attack, moved out slowly along the Warrenton Pike on the morning of 21 July. It delayed the movement of the two enveloping divisions. The diversionary attack against the Stone Bridge was feebly executed. The Confederates were not deceived. McDowell's enveloping column reached Sudley Springs at 0900, rather than 0700 as originally scheduled, and drove southeast. Beauregard, warned by courier and by a wig-wag flag signaler, made ready. At first the Federal attack went well, and forced the Confederates across the Pike to the vicinity of the Henry and Robinson houses. Here on a flat-crested ridge they rallied on the brigade led by Brig. Gen. Thomas J. Jackson, who on this day won the nickname "Stonewall." The troops fought bitterly for about two hours, as McDowell collected 10,000 men to attack 7,000 Confederates. But Beauregard was able to counterattack with fresh troops, some of whom wore blue uniforms and were thought to be comrades by the Federals until too late. This was enough. The Federal units lost cohesion; individually and in groups soldiers left the field. Panic broke out among some who fled and did not stop until they had reached Washington. This gave rise to the notion that virtually the entire Army was routed. In reality several of the Volunteer and Militia regiments marched away in an orderly manner. The withdrawal was steadily covered by the battalion of Regulars, whose conduct seems all the more exemplary in light of the fact that it had not much more training or experience, though it doubtless had sterner discipline, than the Volunteers. As in so many Civil War battles there was no pursuit, except for some harassing by cavalry and artillery. Stonewall Jackson, who was slightly wounded in the battle, vowed he could take Washington with 5,000 fresh men. This is doubtful, because the Confederates were almost as disorganized as the Federals, and there were no logistic preparations for an advance. Further, the 5,000 men would somehow have had to deal with the Regular battalion, the Volunteers and Militia who had not panicked, and McDowell's reserve division which had not been engaged.

Summary. Bull Run was not an important action in itself, but it highlights many of the problems and deficiencies that were typical of the first years of war. A clash between large, ill-trained bodies of recruits, it was disorderly and confused. Plans called for envelopments, but most attacks were frontal. The principle of security was frequently disregarded; reconnaissance was poorly carried out. Neither commander was able to employ his whole force effectively. Of McDowell's 35,000, only 18,500 crossed Bull Run, to suffer about 2,900 casualties, including missing. Beauregard, with about 32,000 men, got only 18,000 into action and lost about 2,000. Instead of placing himself in the army's rear where he could exercise effective control, McDowell led the enveloping column and acted more like a subordinate than an army commander as he valorously led individual regiments into the attack. Even Sherman could not put his brigade in action as a unit, but committed his regiments piecemeal. Similarly, Beauregard rode up and down the front, encouraging individual units and men. Some of his orders were vague and confusing, and others were never delivered. The confusion that arose from the welter of uniforms led to the adoption of gray for all Confederate troops, and blue for the Federals. Further, the Confederate flag, the "Stars and Bars," had looked dangerously like the Stars and Stripes when no wind was blowing. The Confederate Armies thereupon adopted the famous battle flag with the Cross of St. Andrew. Aside from all the deficiencies noted and from the case of the Federal Militia unit, which marched to the rear to the sound of gunfire on 21 July when its term of service expired, Bull Run was particularly notable for the employment of the telegraph and the railroad for military purposes.

Increased Mobilization. *Military legislation.* The campaign of First Bull Run had consequences that were felt far beyond the Henry House area, for now the Northern leaders began to grasp the nature and scope of the struggle, and more than redoubled their efforts. Conversely, the deceptively easy victory convinced some Southerners that little more would be required. President Lincoln and Congress set to with a will to raise and train the vast armies that would be required. On 22 July the President signed a bill which authorized enlistment of 500,000 volunteers to be raised by the machinery of the several states to serve for three-year terms, except that at the end of six months the soldier had the option of discharge or continuing his enlistment. This law also rigidly fixed the ratio of field artillery and cavalry to infantry, and authorized brigades of four or more regiments, with three or more brigades per division. No corps were established, and initially only 24 general officers were provided for. (Both these deficiencies were later rectified.) Three days later the law was amended to provide for the enlistment of 500,000 volunteers for the duration of the war. The response was enthusiastic. With recruits pouring in, it was obvious that the Army's prewar staff and administrative machinery was too small for its tasks. In August Congress therefore provided for an Assistant Secretary of War and a chief of Ordnance, and authorized additional inspectors general, surgeons and assistant surgeons, adjutants general, commissaries, engineers, topographical engineers, quartermasters, and ordnance officers, as well as the employment of medical cadets and female nurses, and called for the appointment of one Christian chaplain for each regiment. Jewish chaplains were provided for in 1862.

Command. McDowell had done his best but President Lincoln decided the task of commanding the forces around Washington—shortly thereafter designated the Army of the Potomac—was beyond him. On Scott's advice Maj. Gen. George B. McClellan, who had just won acclaim by a series of small but heartening victories in West Virginia, was appointed to command the Army of the Potomac. Before the year was out Scott took advantage of a new law and retired from active service. Lincoln named McClellan as General in Chief at once. Acting on McClellan's assurances that he could handle two jobs, he retained him in command of the Army of the Potomac. McClellan, wearing two hats in different echelons, was thus subordinate to himself. To anticipate slightly, President Lincoln took a long step toward successful prosecution of the war in January 1862 when he dismissed his first Secretary of War, the lax, inefficient Simon Cameron. To the Secretaryship he named Edwin McM. Stanton, who was nationally known as a trial lawyer. Self-confident, arrogant, irascible, abrupt to the point of rudeness, and contemptuous of professional military men, Stanton was also fiercely energetic, incorruptible, and efficient. Respecting few men and fearing none, he did his best to stamp out favoritism, and tried to make sure that war contracts were honestly negotiated and faithfully filled. Under his administration the poor arms, faulty ammunition, and shoddy clothing and equipment of Cameron's day largely disappeared; Stanton insisted that the U. S. Army receive the best available, and no campaign by any Union army ever failed for want of supplies. Few of his contemporaries liked him, but almost all respected him.

Organization. By the end of 1861 the Volunteers had been organized into 560 regiments of infantry, 82 of cavalry, and 15 of field artillery. Actual strength of the Regular Army totaled 19,871 men. Following established usage and the statutory requirements, McClellan organized the Army of the Potomac into 10,000-man divisions, each consisting of 3 infantry brigades, 1 cavalry regiment, and four 6-gun field artillery batteries. Other armies followed suit. The assignment of a cavalry regiment to each division was never fully carried out, for cavalrymen were used for a multiplicity of duties—as pickets, wagon train escorts, and messengers. This practice contrasted with that of the Army of Northern Virginia, as Johnston's command came to be called after Bull Run, wherein cavalry was treated as a separate arm and grouped, first as a division and finally as a corps. It was 1863 before the cavalry of the Army of the Potomac was finally concentrated. Artillery was being standardized, the favorite field pieces being the 3-inch Parrott rifle and the 12-pound bronze smoothbore "Napoleon." McClellan planned, once corps were activated, to withdraw one-half the guns from each division as corps artillery, and to maintain a strong force of artillery directly under army command. By spring of 1862, at Lincoln's insistence, the Army of the Potomac was organized into four corps. The haste and shortages of 1861 had caused the infantry to be armed with a variety of foreign and American arms, including obsolete smoothbore muskets, but the caliber .58, single-shot, muzzle-loading, percussion-cap, Springfield rifle was the standard weapon and was being issued as fast as it became available.

Staff organization. Staff organization followed the conventional pattern of the day. The Civil War general staff, both in the War Department and in the field armies, consisted of what today would largely be called administrative and technical services. In the War Department, the staff consisted mainly of the heads of bureaus: The Adjutant General, The Inspector General, The Quartermaster General, The Surgeon General, The Judge Advocate, the Chief of Ordnance, The Commissary General, The Paymaster General, the Chief of Engineers, the Chief of Topographical Engineers, and the Chief Signal Officer. War Department organization expanded a great deal but changed little in form during the war. In addition to the Assistant Secretary of War authorized by Congress in 1861, two more were appointed by Presidential authority the next year. The Judge Advocate's Office became a bureau in 1862, and the head became The Judge Advocate General. The Signal Corps received bureau status in 1863, the same year that the Corps of Topographical Engineers was merged with the Corps of Engineers, and the Provost Marshal General's Department was created to administer the draft (enrollment) act. In the Army of the Potomac, as in other Union armies, full colonels and general officers filled the jobs of chief of staff, adjutant-general, quartermaster, commissary, chief engineer, chief of artillery, and director of railway transportation. Union staff organization was generally superior to that of the Confederate armies, whose staffs too often functioned only as messengers and clerks.

Ball's Bluff and the Joint Congressional Committee on the Conduct of the War. Except for the capture of Forts Hatteras and and Clark, N. C., and of Port Royal, S. C., and the drawn battle at

Wilson's Creek, Mo., in August, there were no significant ground actions in the Eastern or Western Theaters during the latter half of 1861. A badly executed reconnaissance at Ball's Bluff on the Potomac by a Union detachment on 21 October, however, had results that were far-reaching. A Volunteer officer and former Senator, Col. Edward D. Baker, was killed, and a congressional committee decided to investigate. Out of this investigation came the Joint Congressional Committee on the Conduct of the War, which by searching out graft and inefficiency was to do valuable work but was to vex the President and most of the generals until hostilities ended. Composed of extreme antislavery men without military knowledge or experience, it probed the battles, tried to force all its views regarding statecraft and military strategy on the President, and put forward its own candidates for high command. It judged commanders' qualifications, not by their military abilities, but by their views on slavery and abolition. Suspicious of proslavery men and men of moderate views, it considered that the only generals fit for office were those who had been abolitionists before 1861. Curiously, had a Confederate congressional committee set up such prewar standards, Robert E. Lee would necessarily have been judged unfit for command.

Summary. As 1861 drew to a close, both sides were earnestly preparing for a hard war. Field operations so far had not been significant, but the Federals and Confederates were raising and training armies on a scale without precedent in America.

QUESTIONS

1. Analyze critically the Union's methods of raising and training troops in 1861. What were the major faults? Were there any advantages?

2. How were volunteer officers commissioned? Comment critically.

3. Compare and contrast the war potentials of the contending sides.

4. Describe briefly the main geographic features of the theaters of operations, and show their influence upon strategy.

5. Describe General McDowell's plan for the advance to Manassas. Why did the plan fail to achieve victory?

6. Comment critically on the military deficiencies—both Union and Confederate—demonstrated by Bull Run.

7. Describe the organization of the Army of the Potomac.

Reading List

See reading list at end of chapter 14.

CHAPTER 12

THE CIVIL WAR—1862

Orders From the President. The winter of 1861–1862 wore on. McClellan, a perfectionist, was prone to exaggerate his difficulties and the enemy's strength, and to minimize the enemy's problems. He drilled and trained his army, while the western forces under his general command seemed to be accomplishing little. The President again grew impatient for offensive action. In an effort to push matters he took over command himself and issued his General War Order No. 1 on 27 January 1862. This order, besides superfluously telling the armies to obey existing orders, directed that a general movement of the U. S. land and sea forces against the Confederacy be launched on 22 February 1862. Lincoln's issuance of orders for offensives several weeks in advance, without considering what the weather and the roads might be like, has been scoffed at frequently. But the modern student, who takes in his stride the massive advance planning that characterized World Wars I and II, will not think that a directive calling for future operations is unusual, although issuance of tactical orders is not normally a function exercised by the President. If the President had had a modern staff officer to advise him, he probably would have ordered the General in Chief to advance "at a time and a date to be announced later," and specified that "D-day for planning purposes will be 22 February 1862." He apparently only issued the order to get McClellan to agree to move. But even before he issued his order, important movements in the Western Theater had begun.

Western Operations. *Federal forces.* Union forces beyond the Appalachians were organized into two separate commands in early 1862. One was under Brig. Gen. Don Carlos Buell with headquarters at Louisville, Ky. The second was commanded by Maj. Gen. Henry W. Halleck, whose headquarters was at St. Louis, Mo.

Confederate dispositions. Facing Buell and Halleck were 43,000 scattered and ill-equipped Confederate troops under Gen. Albert Sidney Johnston. Charged with the mission of keeping the Federals out of Kentucky, and holding Tennessee and the Mississippi River, they occupied a long line of forts and camps extending from Cumberland Gap in western Virginia through Bowling Green, Ky., to New Madrid and Island No. 10 on the Mississippi. With most of the roads in the region virtually impassable in winter, rivers and railroads provided Johnston with a line of communications. To protect a lateral railroad where it crossed the rivers in Tennessee, the Confederates had built Fort Henry on the Tennessee River and Fort Donelson on the Cumberland River (map 20).

Fort Henry. Halleck and Buell were supposed to be cooperating with one another, but so far had not done so effectively. Without any assurances from Buell, Halleck, in early February of 1862, decided to effect a strategic penetration of the center of Johnston's line. He sent 17,000 men under Brig. Gen. Ulysses S. Grant, supported and transported by armored gunboats and river craft under Flag Officer Andrew H. Foote, up the Tennessee River to seize Fort Henry. Grant landed near the fort and moved overland. On his approach the Confederate commander sent most of his men to Fort Donelson. On 6 February, after the gunboats had shelled Fort Henry, he surrendered before Grant's troops arrived.

Fort Donelson. General Grant was no rhetorician. Sparing with words, he never bombarded his troops with Napoleonic manifestos like McClellan. But his actions combined Field Marshal Haig's "sincere desire to engage the enemy" with Lord Nelson's "Lose not an hour." He therefore turned against Fort Donelson at once. The river craft carried some of the troops down the Tennessee to its confluence with the Cumberland, thence up the latter to Fort Donelson. The rest of the troops moved through the sleet, snow, and mud of the Tennessee winter across the 10-mile neck of land separating the forts. Reinforced up to a strength of about 25,000, Grant's army invested Fort Donelson on the evening of 12 February. Johnston, sure that the fall of Donelson would jeopardize his entrenched camp at Bowling Green, hurried 12,000 reinforcements to Fort Donelson, and retired toward Nashville with 14,000 men. Even without reinforcements, Fort Donelson was a strong position. Standing 100 feet above the river, it embraced an area of about 100 acres; the river and two creeks formed a moat that completely surrounded it. Grant and Foote first attempted to reduce it by the gunboat bombardment that had succeeded so well at Fort Henry, but the gunboats were handled roughly and suffered such severe damage that they withdrew. Grant then prepared for a long siege, as he did not think his troops well enough trained to assault successfully. But the Confederates essayed a sortie which failed. Grant thereupon attacked successfully, then sent his famous unconditional surrender message to his old friend, Brig. Gen. Simon B. Buckner. Some Confederate troops escaped, including Brig. Gen. John B. Floyd, the fort's nominal commander and a former Secretary of War, but 11,500 men surrendered on 16 February. Meanwhile Buell had advanced on learning of Fort Henry's surrender. He reached Bowling Green the day Fort Donelson fell. Grant's bold advance, coupled with Buell's move, cracked the Confederate Cumberland Gap-Bowling Green-Mississippi River line and forced the Confederates out of Kentucky and much of Tennessee. Johnston withdrew to Corinth, Miss., averaging 14 miles a day on the march.

Shiloh—preliminary movements. As theater commander Halleck naturally received much credit for these victories. President Lincoln decided to unify command of all the western armies, and on 11 March Halleck was given the command. That general, with the nickname "Old Brains," was well known as a master of the theory and literature of war. Lincoln's decision gave him command of more than 100,000 men, organized into four armies—Brig. Gen. Samuel Curtis' Army of the Southwest in Missouri and Arkansas, Grant's Army of the Tennessee, Buell's Army of the Ohio, and Maj. Gen. John Pope's Army of the Mississippi. While Pope, in cooperation with Foote's naval forces, attacked New Madrid and Island No. 10, Halleck decided to concentrate Grant's and Buell's armies and move against Johnston's Army of the Mississippi in Corinth. He ordered Buell to Savannah on the Tennessee and dispatched Grant's troops up the Tennessee to Pittsburg Landing, about nine miles from Savannah. Johnston, meanwhile, had received some reinforcements, though not all he needed. High water and Curtis' Army, which defeated Confederate forces at Pea Ridge, Ark., delayed the movement of some troops from Arkansas. Well aware of the Federals' movements, Johnston decided to attack Grant at Pittsburg Landing, where Shiloh Church was located, before Buell could join him (map 23). His army, 40,000 strong, marched out of Corinth on the afternoon of 3 April. Two dirt roads led through thick forests to Shiloh, 22 miles away, but heavy rains turned them into bogs. It was late afternoon of 5 April before the Confederates reached a point about two miles from Grant's front. Johnston postponed his attack until the morning of 6 April, and the delay proved fatal to his hopes. Grant's forces were encamped, in accordance with the principles of the day, in line of battle. Two divisions in front held a 2-mile sector, with two more in supporting positions behind, and one in reserve. A sixth, on the point of joining the main body, was about six miles away. The position was not a good one. The army was pocketed, with the river at its back and a creek on each flank. As the army was on an offensive mission, it had not entrenched. Grant has often been criticized for this omission, but entrenchment was not common at that stage of the war. Aside from the entrenchment question, the fact that the principle of security was disregarded is inescapable. There were no cavalry outposts in front, and very little patrolling had been carried out. The Federals were completely unaware that a Confederate army of 40,000 men was spending the night of 5–6 April just two miles away. Further, Grant seems to have naively accepted some rumors, perpetrated by Johnston, about the deteriorating morale of his troops. The Forts Henry and Donel-

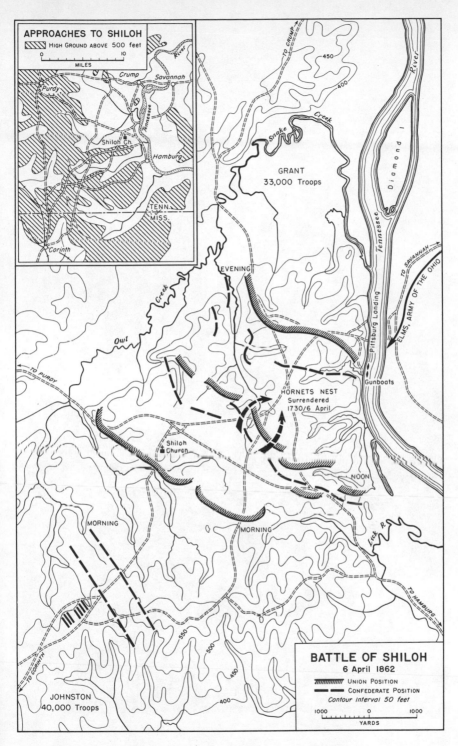

APPROACHES TO SHILOH

▨ HIGH GROUND ABOVE 500 feet

0 _____ 10
MILES

Crump

Savannah

River

Purdy

Tennessee

Shiloh Ch.

Hamburg

TENN.

MISS.

Corinth

GRANT
33,000 Troops

Snake Creek

Diamond I

Tennessee River

450

400

EVENING

TO CRUMP

Owl Creek

TO PURDY

Pittsburg Landing

TO SAVANNAH

ELMS, ARMY OF THE OHIO

Gunboats

HORNETS NEST
Surrendered
1730/6 April

Shiloh
Church

NOON

MORNING

MORNING

Lick R.

TO HAMBURG

550

500

450

400

TO CORINTH

JOHNSTON
40,000 Troops

BATTLE OF SHILOH
6 April 1862

▨▨▨ UNION POSITION
━ ━ ━ CONFEDERATE POSITION
Contour Interval 50 feet

1000   0   1000
YARDS

Map 23.   Battle of Shiloh, 6 April 1862.

211

Lt. Gen. Ulysses S. Grant in 1864.

son victories apparently engendered an overconfident feeling in the army, which like Johnston's was only partly trained.

Shiloh—the battle. Johnston's men burst out of the woods early on 6 April, so early that men turned out into their company streets from their tents to fight. Some fled to the safety of the river, but most of the regiments fought stubbornly and yielded ground slowly. By afternoon the Confederates had attained successes all along the line. But the attackers became badly disorganized. Johnston's formation for the attack had been awkward. He had formed his three corps into one column with each corps deployed with divisions in line, so that each corps stretched across the whole battlefront, one behind the other. Such a formation could not be effectively controlled by either army or corps commanders. Johnston himself was mortally wounded in leading a local assault. General Beauregard, Johnston's successor, suspended the attack for the day and attempted to straighten out and reorganize his command. As the day ended Grant's sixth division and advance elements of Buell's army reached Shiloh. Next morning Grant counterattacked, regained the lost ground, and the Confederates withdrew to Corinth. There was no pursuit. Shiloh was the bloodiest battle fought in North America up to that time. Of 63,000 Federals, 13,000 were casualties. The Confederates lost 11,000. Fortunate indeed for the Federals had been Lincoln's decision to unify the command in Halleck, for this act had guaranteed Buell's presence and prevented Johnston from defeating the Union armies in detail. Grant came in for much denunciation for being surprised, but President Lincoln loyally sustained him. "I can't spare this man; he fights."

Island No. 10 and New Orleans. Halleck was a master of military maxims, but in sending Pope against Island No. 10 and New Madrid he ignored the wisdom of going after one objective at a time: that is to say, he did not apply the principles of objective, mass, and economy of force. Had all Halleck's forces been present, he might have destroyed Beauregard. As it was, Pope and Foote took Island No. 10 and New Madrid on 7 April, whereupon Halleck's great force ponderously advanced against Corinth. Remembering Shiloh, Halleck entrenched every night, and it was 30 May before he reached his objective. As might be expected, Beauregard had already left. Meanwhile Capt. David G. Farragut, with 8 steam sloops and 15 wooden gunboats, had sailed up the Mississippi from the Gulf of Mexico. He cracked a boom across the river and ran a gantlet of fire from armored rams, fire rafts, river boats and two forts, to land General Butler's soldiers in New Orleans.

Strategic results. Except for the battle of Perryville, Ky., in October, and the bloody action at Murfreesboro (Stone's River) on the last day of the year, wherein the Confederates partly undid the earlier

Union victories, little was accomplished by either side in the West for the rest of the year. Not all Union objectives had been secured, but the results were impressive. Missouri, Kentucky, and western Tennessee were in Union hands, and the Federals controlled most of the Mississippi River. The only points on the river that the Confederates still held were in the vicinity of Vicksburg and Port Hudson. These gave them communications with Louisiana, Arkansas, and Texas.

Eastern Theater. *Objectives—command.* Meanwhile the Eastern Theater had seen a long series of complex, closely interrelated operations. As the year 1862 began, the plans prepared by the Washington authorities and the Army of the Potomac were aimed at capture of Richmond rather than destruction of the army commanded by Joseph E. Johnston, now a full general. Precise methods of reaching Richmond differed. President Lincoln favored an overland advance which would always keep an army between the Confederates and Washington. McClellan agreed at first, then changed his views in favor of a waterborne move by the Army of the Potomac to Urbana on the Rappahannock, whence he could drive to Richmond before Johnston could move from the region of Manassas to intercept him (map 21). The Washington fortifications, McClellan reasoned, would be adequate to protect the Capital with the field army away. Johnston, however, rendered this plan obsolete; he withdrew from Manassas to Fredericksburg, halfway between Washington and Richmond, and thereby placed his army astride McClellan's prospective route of advance. To give his army some field experience, McClellan in early March moved it to the deserted Confederate camps around Manassas, thence back to Alexandria, Va. While he was in the field with his troops, President Lincoln relieved him as General in Chief, doubtless on the ground that he could not directly command one army in the field and at the same time supervise operations of all the armies of the United States. Lincoln did not appoint a successor. For a time he and Stanton took over personal direction of the ground forces, and in this capacity they received advice from a newly constituted Army board consisting of the elderly Maj. Gen. Ethan A. Hitchcock and the chiefs of the War Department bureaus.

Plans. When events overtook the Urbana scheme, McClellan began advocating a seaborne move to Fort Monroe, Va., at the tip of the peninsula formed by the York and the James Rivers, to be followed by an overland advance up the peninsula. If the troops moved fast, he maintained, they could cover the 70 miles to Richmond before Johnston could concentrate his forces to stop them. Had Richmond been a true strategic objective, this plan had much to recommend it. It made use of Fort Monroe; it took advantage of Federal control of the seas. (On 9 March the *Monitor* successfully neutralized the *Merrimac*, which withdrew to Norfolk.) Naval vessels in the York River could support McClellan as he advanced from Monroe to White House on the Pamunkey River. There were fewer rivers to cross than by the overland route. But the terrain of the peninsula was tangled and swampy. Where McClellan expected to find good roads, there were only dirt tracks. Mr. Lincoln never liked this plan, but gave McClellan his approval subject to the proviso that McClellan leave behind the number of men that his corps commanders considered adequate to insure the safety of Washington and hold Manassas. McClellan gave the President his assurances, but failed to take the President into his confidence by pointing out that he considered the Federal troops in the Shenandoah Valley to be covering Washington. In listing the forces he had left behind, he also counted some men twice and included several units in Pennsylvania that were not under his command, a piece of carelessness that was to cost him dearly.

Preliminary movements. Embarkation for the Peninsular Campaign began at Alexandria on 17 March 1862, and by 4 April advance elements of the Army of the Potomac had moved out of Fort Monroe against Yorktown. The day before, however, the commander of the Washington defenses reported that he had insufficient force to protect the city. In addition, Stonewall Jackson had become active in the Shenandoah Valley. Lincoln thereupon told Stanton to detain one of the two corps which were awaiting embarkation at Alexandria. Stanton held General McDowell's, which numbered 30,000 men. (McClellan later received two divisions from this corps: the first in April, the second in June.)

Jackson's Valley Campaign. *The battles.* Recognizing McClellan's threat to Richmond, the Confederate garrison at Yorktown made ready to delay McClellan while Johnston hurried his army to the peninsula. In Richmond, meanwhile, Confederate authorities had determined on a spectacularly bold diversion. Robert E. Lee, who had received rapid promotions and was now a full general, had assumed office as military adviser to Jefferson Davis on 13 March, and subsequent events bore the imprint of his daring hand. He was not in active command, however, but rather was charged with the conduct of operations of the Confederate armies under Davis' direction. With a small force Stonewall Jackson attacked Federal troops at Kernstown on 23 March and suffered defeat. But it was a strategic victory, for by calling attention to Jackson's threat to Harper's Ferry and perhaps to Washington, it diverted forces from McClellan. The equivalent of three Federal divisions was sent to the valley at once to destroy Jackson. Davis and Lee, noting the reaction in Washington, sent Jackson reinforcements in April. Lincoln and Stanton, using the telegraph and what military knowledge they had, devised plans to bottle him up and destroy him. But Federal forces in the valley were not under a locally unified command; they moved too slowly; one force did not obey orders strictly; and the orders from Washington tended to be too detailed and did not always take time and distance, or logistics, into account. And in Stonewall Jackson the Union troops were contending against one of the most outstanding field commanders America has ever produced. By mobility and maneuver induced by rapid marches, and by surprise, deception, and hard fighting, Jackson neutralized and defeated in detail Federal forces with a total strength three times larger than his own. In a classic campaign, he made two and a half round trips up and down the Shenandoah Valley, and from 23 March to 9 June 1862 fought six battles: Kernstown, McDowell, Front Royal, Winchester, Cross Keys, and Port Republic. All but Kernstown were victories.

Diversion of McDowell. Jackson also prevented another strong Federal force from joining McClellan. When Johnston left Fredericksburg for the peninsula, Lincoln and Stanton appointed McDowell as commander of the new Department of the Rappahannock and sent him southward from Washington by land. On 14 May, when McDowell with 40,000 men had reached Fredericksburg, McClellan asked that these men proceed by water to join him on the peninsula. Lincoln acceded on 17 May, but directed McDowell to march the 65 miles by land so as not to uncover Washington. His instructions to McDowell were complicated, and, rather than assigning him to McClellan's command, they directed him to cooperate with McClellan. But on Sunday, 25 May, as the movement was about to begin, Lincoln decided to use part of McDowell's force in the effort to destroy Jackson. He sent 20,000 men to the valley, where they stayed, accomplishing little, until the end of June, and by then the Peninsular Campaign had ended in failure.

The Peninsular Campaign. *From Fort Monroe to Fair Oaks.* When McClellan personally reached the peninsula in early April, he decided not to wait for his whole army but to begin the advance at once in order to gain time and ground before Johnston could concentrate. Using civilian detectives as intelligence agents, he consistently overestimated Confederate strength, and thought himself outnumbered. He wanted 155,000 men for the operation. His exact strength during the campaign is subject to dispute, but Union forces committed appear to total that number, though not that many were ever present at one time. Further, McClellan was overgenerous in granting furloughs, so that large numbers of men assigned to units of the Army of the Potomac were actually visiting their homes during the fighting. The Confederate Maj. Gen. John B. Magruder, a student of drama and master of deception, was holding Yorktown with some 10 to 15 thousand men. By clever ruses and deceptive maneuvers he so dazzled McClellan that the latter, instead of brushing Magruder aside, spent a month in a siege. As a result, Johnston was able to move his army, which now was equal to two-thirds of McClellan's, to

Gen. Robert E. Lee.

Yorktown before McClellan attacked. McClellan emplaced heavy guns and constructed complicated siegeworks, and planned to assault on 5 May. But Johnston, who wanted to fight the decisive action closer to Richmond, decamped on 3 May and withdrew slowly up the peninsula. His cavalry, under Brig. Gen. J. E. B. Stuart, covered the rear. Led by Federal cavalry, the Army of the Potomac set out in pursuit. At Williamsburg, on 5 May, McClellan's advance elements made contact with the Confederate rear guard under Maj. Gen. James Longstreet, who successfully delayed the Federals while Johnston pulled his wagon trains back to safety and continued his withdrawal. McClellan pursued in leisurely fashion. By 16 May, two days after requesting McDowell's force, he established his headquarters and main base at White House on the Pamunkey River. By 25 May two corps of the Army of the Potomac had turned southwest toward Richmond and crossed the Chickahominy River. The remaining three corps were on the north side of the river with the expectation of making contact with McDowell. Men of the two corps south of the river could see the spires of Richmond, but Johnston's army was in front of them (map 24).

Battle of Fair Oaks (Seven Pines). The Chickahominy, which divided the Army of the Potomac, was usually a sluggish, shallow stream, but drenching rains on 30 May made it unfordable. McClellan had provided bridges, but the rains washed out most of them and weakened the others, and the two parts of the army were effectively separated. Johnston decided to grasp this chance to defeat the Federals in detail. He struck on 31 May near Fair Oaks. His plans called for his whole force to concentrate against the isolated corps south of the Chickahominy, but his staff and subordinate commanders were not up to the task of executing them. Assaulting columns became confused, and attacks were delivered piecemeal. The Federals, after some initial reverses, held their ground and bloodily repulsed the Confederates.

General Lee's plan. When Johnston suffered a severe wound at Fair Oaks, President Davis replaced him with General Lee. While McClellan waited for the weather to clear and prepared to cover his advance against Richmond with his superior artillery, Lee pulled back closer to Richmond and started fortifications. Lee did not mean to defend Richmond passively; fortifications would enable him to protect Richmond with a relatively small force while he used the main body of his army offensively in an attempt to cut off and destroy the Army of the Potomac. He ordered Jackson out of the Shenandoah Valley toward Richmond with all possible speed. Jackson eluded his pursuers and traveled by rail, wagon, and on foot in such secrecy that the Federals did not know where he was until his troops were about to deliver their first attack.

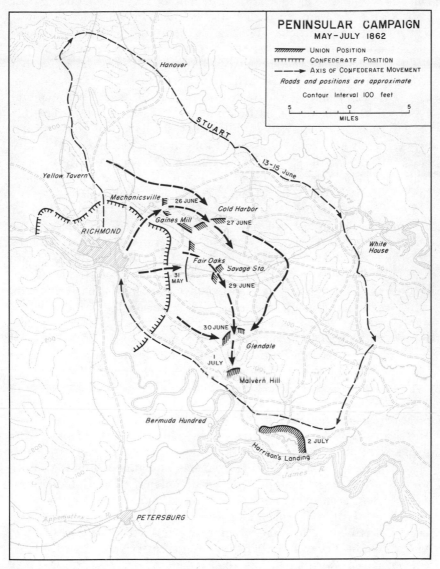

Map 24. Peninsular campaign, May–July 1862.

The Seven Days' Battles—first phase. Lee struck before McClellan resumed his advance. At Mechanicsville, on 26 June, he attempted to roll up McClellan's right flank north of the Chickahominy and cut the line of communications between it and the base at White House. One division was to assault frontally, another from the flank, against Brig. Gen. Fitz-John Porter's V Corps. Again the conception was better than the execution. Timing and coordination were off; Jackson, of all people, was slow; the V Corps defended stoutly during the day. McClellan thereupon withdrew the V Corps southeast to a stronger position at Gaines' Mill (1st Cold Harbor). Porter's men dug field entrenchments and made ready. Lee massed 57,000 men and assaulted 34,000 Federals on 27 June. The fighting was severe, for on both sides the troops were equally well trained and valorous. Numbers told, however, and the Federal line broke. Darkness fell before Lee could exploit the opportunity, and Porter's corps took advantage of the night to cross to the south bank of the Chickahominy where the main body of the Army of the Potomac was encamped.

The Seven Days' Battles—the change of base. With his line of communications to White House thus cut, and with the James River now open to the U. S. Navy (the Confederates had blown up the *Merrimac* on 11 May), McClellan decided to abandon White House and shift his base to Harrison's Landing on the south side of the peninsula. This move, which involved 90,000 men, the artillery train, 3,100 wagons, and 2,500 head of cattle, began on the night of 27–28 June, and was accomplished by using two roads. Lee, having lost contact with McClellan, pushed forward, but was held off by Federal rear guards at Savage Station on 29 June and at Fraser's Farm or Glendale on the last day of the month.

The Seven Days' Battles—final phase. By the first day of July McClellan had concentrated the Army of the Potomac in a strong position on a commanding plateau at Malvern Hill, northwest of Harrison's Landing. There was a good field of fire to the front. The flanks were protected by streams. Massed artillery, ready to sweep all approaches, lay in supporting positions, and gunboats on the James were ready to fire in support of the left flank. The Confederates' assembly area, somewhat more than three to four hundred yards north of Malvern Hill, was broken and wooded, traversed by a swamp, and barely passable. When, on the morning of 1 July, Lee's attempt to knock out the Federal artillery by counterbattery fire failed, he decided that Malvern Hill was too strong to attack. But at 1500, when a shifting of Federal troops deceived him into thinking that they were withdrawing, he changed his mind and attacked. Again staff work and control were poor. The assaults, which were all frontal, were delivered piecemeal by only part of the army, and the Union artillery halted them and shattered the attacking units. This failure to carry out the principle of concentration cost heavily. Lee lost 5,000 casualties in this, the last action of the Peninsular Campaign. Next day, 2 July, the Army of the Potomac fell back to Harrison's Landing and dug in. After reconnoitering McClellan's position on 3 July, Lee ordered his exhausted men back to the Richmond lines for rest and reorganization.

Summary. Casualties on both sides in the Peninsular Campaign—during which Brig. Gen. Daniel C. Butterfield devised the bugle call "Taps"—were heavy. The Federals lost some 15,849 men killed, wounded, and missing. The Confederates, who had done most of the attacking, lost 20,614 men out of a total of 95,481 men engaged. The improvement in the training and discipline of the two armies since the disorganized fight at Bull Run was notable. Also significant was the fact that the higher commands had not yet thoroughly mastered their jobs. Except for McClellan's defensive action at Malvern Hill, which was largely conducted by his corps commanders, neither side had been able to bring an entire army into coordinated action.

Campaign of Manassas.* *New commanders and revised strategy.* Now President Lincoln abandoned the idea of exercising command over the Union armies in person, and decided to delegate it again to a military professional. On 11 July 1862 he selected as new General in Chief Henry W. Halleck who had won acclaim from the victories in the West. (He did not at once appoint a successor in the West, which was to suffer from divided command for a time.) It was Lincoln's intention that Halleck exercise field command himself, and direct the various Federal armies in close concert to take advantage of the North's superior strength. If all Federal armies coordinated their efforts, Lincoln reasoned, they could strike where the Confederacy was weak or force it to strengthen one army at the expense of another, and eventually wear the Confederacy down, destroy the various armies, and win the war. Lincoln was destined to be disappointed by Halleck, who seldom attempted to exercise field command or assume responsibility for strategic direction of the armies. He acted more as military adviser to the President than as a commander, but in this advisory capacity he performed a valuable function by serving as a channel of communication between the President and the field commanders. He translated the President's ideas into terms the generals could comprehend, and expressed the soldiers' views in language that the President understood.

Shortly before Lincoln appointed Halleck, he had also decided to consolidate the various Union forces in the Shenandoah Valley and other parts of western Virginia—some 45,000 men—as the Army of Virginia. To command this force he appointed the victor of Island No. 10, General Pope. On 26 June Lincoln, acting on the ad-

---

*The Confederates called this Second Manassas. It is also commonly called Second Bull Run.

vice of Pope or perhaps Scott, directed Pope to threaten the Confederate forces in the Shenandoah Valley and divert pressure from McClellan on the peninsula. But when Jackson left the valley, Pope's mission was altered. He was told to help relieve McClellan by marching southwestward up the valley, then turning east against Richmond. Thus, when Halleck took over as General in Chief, Pope's scattered army was in western Virginia. The Army of the Potomac, close to 100,000 strong, was at Harrison's Landing. Between them lay Richmond and Lee's Army of Northern Virginia. President Lincoln had never heartily favored the peninsular concept, and by then seemed to have lost confidence in McClellan's resolution in spite of the latter's desire to stay on the peninsula and take another crack at Richmond. Despite the fact that the two Union armies vastly outnumbered Lee, the President and Halleck were concerned by the dispersion of forces, and on 3 August Halleck ordered McClellan to withdraw by water from the peninsula to Aquia Creek on the Potomac and to effect a speedy junction at Fredericksburg with Pope. Embarkation began on 14 August. Pope, meanwhile, acting on orders from Washington which aimed at concentrating the two Union armies between Washington and Richmond, began posting the Army of Virginia in the region of Sperryville and Warrenton, with the exception of one division which was defending the depot at Falmouth across the Rappahannock from Fredericksburg (map 21).

Preliminary movements. Lee, dauntless and resolute, well knew that his Army of Northern Virginia was in a dangerous position between Pope and McClellan, and in an equally dangerous position if McClellan and Pope united. Pope's presence in western Virginia had already forced him to divert a strong force eventually totaling 24,000 men under Stonewall Jackson. Jackson's column left Richmond on 13 July, marched northwest, and reached Gordonsville on 19 July with the intention of blocking Pope. Jackson then decided to strike the advance elements of Pope's Army of Virginia before Pope could bring up the rest. He encountered part of the II Corps under Maj. Gen. Nathaniel P. Banks at Cedar Mountain on 9 August. Banks attacked and drove Jackson back; but Jackson received reinforcements, and Banks had no reserve. Stonewall drove Banks from the field, but did not pursue because he discovered that the rest of Pope's army was close at hand. He and Pope then waited in position until 15 August. Lee, knowing that McClellan was leaving Harrison's Landing, had meanwhile marched out of Richmond with the rest of the Army of Northern Virginia, and arrived at Gordonsville on 15 August. He now had about 55,000 men to Pope's 45,000, and resolved to outflank and cut off Pope before the whole of McClellan's vast army could be brought to bear.

Pope's Railway Line before the battle of Manassas.

The captured orders. Pope was thus dangerously exposed, for the Federal authorities seem to have expected Lee to stay near Richmond. But in a stroke of luck induced by boldness Union cavalrymen nearly captured Stuart, who was now a major general. He escaped, but they did capture his adjutant with copies of Lee's orders which were promptly forwarded to Pope. Seeing his danger, Pope withdrew the Army of Virginia to the north bank of the Rappahannock astride the Orange and Alexandria Railroad. Several days of feints and maneuvers followed as Lee probed for openings across the fords of the Rappahannock. Then Stuart's troopers overran Pope's headquarters in a dashing raid. They seized documents which showed that two corps of the Army of the Potomac (V Corps, under Porter, and III Corps under Maj. Gen. Stuart P. Heintzelman) were marching west from Aquia and would join Pope within two days, as would a reserve division from the III Corps (McDowell) of the Army of Virginia. These forces totaled 20,000, and the rest of the Army of the Potomac, Lee learned, was at Aquia Creek and Alexandria within five days march. To add to Lee's problems, heavy rains caused the Rappahannock to rise so high in the vicinity of the railroad that it could not be forded. Lee acted quickly and boldly to escape the threatening disaster. To divert Pope, he sent Jackson on 25 August off on a wide turning movement through Thoroughfare Gap in the Bull Run Mountains around the right (north) flank of the Army of Virginia, and next day followed the same route with the divisions commanded by Maj. Gen. James Longstreet.

The battle—28-29 August 1862. Pope took note of Jackson's move, but first assumed that it was pointed toward the Shenandoah Valley. Then Jackson, covering nearly 60 miles in two days, came in behind Pope at Manassas on 26 August, destroyed supplies there, and moved westward. Pope marched and countermarched his forces for two days trying to find the elusive Jackson. Stonewall turned on 28 August and attacked Pope at Groveton, then made ready for defense. Next day, Pope, whose dispositions failed to take Lee's other force into account, walked into Lee's trap, which was designed to lure him into battle before the corps from the Army of the Potomac could arrive in strength. Pope attacked Jackson, whose divisions held a strong position behind the embankment of the abandoned railroad, but again the attack consisted of a series of piecemeal frontal assaults, which were all repulsed with heavy casualties (map 22). By then Porter's corps had reached the field, and was disposed on Pope's left (south) astride the Gainesville-Manassas Road. Pope ordered Porter to roll up Jackson's right (south) flank, but this proved an impossibility as Longstreet's column had burst through Thoroughfare Gap and deployed on Jackson's right in such position that Porter would have had to advance directly across Longstreet's front to reach Jackson. (Pope's Chief of Staff later preferred charges of willful disobedience against Porter, who was court-martialed and dismissed from the service, but restored to rank during Grant's Presidency.)

The battle—30 August 1862. Next day, 30 August, passed uneventfully until about noon when Pope attacked north of the Warrenton Pike. Massed Confederate artillery broke the first assault, but the Federals pushed on valiantly until Lee sent some of Longstreet's troops to bolster Jackson, who drove back the attackers. Longstreet then pushed east toward Bald Hill, southwest of the Henry House, which commanded the entire battlefield including the Warrenton Pike. When Pope sent men to hold this vital eminence, Jackson pushed back the weakened force on his front. Pope, who had fought hard but with less skill than his opponents, admitted defeat and led his army back to Washington, fighting an enveloping Confederate force at Chantilly on the way. The troops reached the capital defenses about 3 September. Lee, by great daring and rapid movement coupled with the fact that the Confederate forces were unified under his command, had successfully defeated one formidable Union army in the presence of another even larger one. Halleck, as General in Chief, had not taken the field to coordinate Pope and McClellan, although he did take a more active role in the conduct of field operations during Second Bull Run than he ever did again.

Changes in command. On 1 September, as the Army of Virginia was withdrawing to Washington, Halleck, acting on Lincoln's instructions, gave McClellan command of all forces in the area of the capital, including the Army of the Potomac and Pope's army. The President, desiring to use McClellan's admitted talents in training and reorganizing the battered Eastern armies, had become convinced that the bitter personal feelings that existed between McClellan and Pope would make it impossible for them to serve effectively in the same theater. He had known both Pope and his father before the war, but he gave the general short shrift. On 5 September, Halleck by the President's order dissolved the Army of Virginia and assigned its component units to the Army of the Potomac. He sent Pope to a command in Minnesota. The Union authorities expected that McClellan would be able to devote several months to training and reorganization, but Lee disappointed these hopes.

Campaign of Antietam (Sharpsburg). *Confederate plans.* Up to now, the Confederates in the East had been following defensive strategy, though tactically they frequently assumed the offensive. But now Davis and Lee, for a complicated set of political and military reasons, determined to take the offensive and invade the North. On the political side, they thought a successful invasion would strengthen the numerous advocates of peace as well as the downright disloyal "Copperheads" in the North. Miscalculating public opinion in Maryland, they expected that an invasion might bring about secession of that state. Further, they imagined that successful invasion might evoke recognition, or even forcible intervention to break the naval blockade, by Great Britain and France. This last hope was only a hope. Emperor Napoleon III was primarily interested in advancing his Mexican schemes; he considered both recognition and intervention, but would not move without British support. Britain, which followed the policy of recognizing *de facto* governments, would undoubtedly have eventually recognized the Confederacy had it won the war. But the British Government never seriously considered premature recognition, never considered intervention at all, and throughout the war declared itself neutral and respected the Union blockade. On the military side, invasion gave Lee a chance to defeat or destroy the Army of the Potomac and uncover such cities as Washington, Baltimore, and Philadelphia, and to cut Federal communications with the states to the west.

Approach marches. The Army of Northern Virginia, which was organized into two infantry commands (Longstreet's, consisting of five divisions, and Jackson's of four divisions) plus Stuart's three brigades of cavalry, and the reserve artillery, now numbered about 55,000 effectives. Lee did not stop for rest after Manassas but moved out of Chantilly, northward across the Potomac near Leesburg, on 4 September and on to Frederick, Md. There he rested for two days (map 21). The Union garrison at Harper's Ferry, however, threatened his line of supply and retreat. Lee sent Jackson's column back across the Potomac against the garrison and some of Longstreet's men posted themselves on the heights on the north side of the Potomac overlooking Harper's Ferry. The remainder of Lee's army crossed South Mountain (the local name for the Blue Ridge Mountains) by way of Turner's and Crampton's Gaps and headed for Hagerstown, about 25 miles northwest of Frederick, with Stuart's cavalry screening the right flank. In the meantime McClellan's cavalry had reported Lee's general location. McClellan marched the Army of the Potomac—90,000 men organized into six corps—northwest from Washington to Frederick, which was reached on 12 September.

The captured orders. Then came a stroke of luck for McClellan. Lee, in assigning missions to his command, had detached Maj. Gen. D. H. Hill's division from Jackson and attached it to Longstreet, and had sent copies of his orders, which prescribed routes, objectives, and times of arrival, to Jackson, Longstreet, and Hill. But, in the abscence of the modern "distribution list" which shows exactly how many copies of a document are prepared and to whom they go, Jackson was not sure that Hill had received the order. He therefore made an additional copy of Lee's order and sent it to Hill. One of Hill's orders, wrapped around some cigars, was somehow left behind in an abandoned camp to be picked up on 13 September by Union soldiers and rushed to McClellan. This gave McClellan an unmatched opportunity to defeat Lee's scattered forces in detail if he pushed fast through the gaps. But he did not start the troops moving until next morning, and did not urge them on. Lee, informed of the lost order, sent all available forces to hold the gaps, so that it was nightfall on the 14th before McClellan got through to the west side of South Mountain.

The battle. Lee then retreated to Sharpsburg on Antietam Creek. He reached there on 15 September and decided to fight. The decision was bold to the point of recklessness, for Lee was pinned in between Antietam Creek and the Potomac River with no room for maneuver. And he was greatly outnumbered. Jackson had taken Harper's Ferry the same day and was marching hard to join him, but his leading elements would not arrive until 16 September. Fortunately for Lee, McClellan delayed his attack until 17 September, when he launched an uncoordinated series of assaults which drove back the Confederates in places and came within an inch of breaking their line. But McClellan, having committed five corps to the attack, would not commit his reserve—the V Corps, under Porter. Jackson's last division arrived in time to head off the final assault, and at the day's end Lee still held most of his ground. As in nearly all Civil War battles, casualties were heavy. Of 70,000 Federal troops engaged, 13,000 were killed, wounded, or missing. The 40,000 Confederates lost 8,000. McClellan did not resume the attack the next day, and Lee withdrew unmolested to Virginia. McClellan went leisurely southward.

The Emancipation Proclamation. Tactically, Antietam was about a draw, but the fact that Lee was forced to call off the invasion made it a strategic victory and gave President Lincoln an opportunity to strike at the Confederacy, psychologically and economically, by issuing the Emancipation Proclamation on 22 September. Mr. Lincoln, though opposed to slavery and its extension to the western territories, was not an abolitionist. He had stated publicly and privately that the war was being fought over union or secession, with the slavery question only incidental. But in anticipation of the total war and of the psychological warfare techniques of the 20th century, he had for some time desired to free the slaves of the Confederate states in order to weaken their economies and to appeal to antislavery opinion in Europe. He had been waiting for the opportune moment that a Union victory would give him, and decided that Antietam was suitable. On 22 September 1862, he acted on his authority as Commander in Chief and issued the Proclamation which stated that all slaves in states or districts in rebellion against the United States on 1 January 1863 would be thenceforward and forever free. As is known, the Proclamation set no slaves free on the day it took effect. Negroes in the four slave states in the Union were not touched, nor were the slaves in those Confederate areas that had been subjugated by Union bayonets. And it had no immediate effect behind the Confederate lines, except to cause a good deal of excitement. (In the closing days of the war, Mr. Davis was vainly to offer emancipation of the slaves in return for foreign recognition.) But thereafter, as Union armies penetrated the South, the newly freed people deserted the farms and plantations and flocked to the colors. Many of them worked as laborers, but by the war's end 100,000 Negroes were regularly enrolled as U. S. Volunteers.

The Fredericksburg Campaign. *McClellan's relief.* In early November the Army of Northern Virginia was divided between Culpeper, south of the Bull Run Mountains and east of the Blue Ridge, and Winchester in the valley. McClellan was at Warrenton making ready to attack Lee. But his military career was about to end. His slowness, his failure to accomplish more at Antietam, and perhaps his rather arrogant habit of offering gratuitous political advice to his superiors, coupled with the intense anti-McClellan views of the Joint Congressional Committee on the Conduct of the War, convinced Lincoln that he could retain him no longer. Therefore he relieved him as commander of the Army of the Potomac on 7 November. Maj. Gen. Ambrose E. Burnside, who had won some distinction in operations that gained control of ports on the North Carolina coast and who had led a corps at Antietam, was named in his place. Burnside accepted the post with reluctance.

Burnside's plan of campaign. Abandoning McClellan's plan to strike at Culpeper, Burnside evolved a plan to demonstrate with part of his army while the main body advanced rapidly to Falmouth on the north bank of the Rappahannock, crossed the river on ponton bridges, seized Fredericksburg, and moved along the railroad toward Richmond. If successful, this move would interpose the 120,000–man Army of the Potomac between Lee and his principal base. To achieve greater ease of tactical control, Burnside created three headquarters higher than corps—the Right, Center, and Left Grand Divisions under Maj. Gens. Edwin V. Sumner, Joseph Hooker and William B. Franklin, respectively—with two corps plus cavalry assigned to each grand division. In reserve was the XI Corps, but it took no part in the action. Success of Burnside's plan depended on speed; he had to get across the river and take the high ground behind (southwest of) Fredericksburg before Lee could get there (map 25).

Preliminary movements. Things went well at first. The Right Grand Division reached Falmouth on 17 November, ahead of Lee, and was followed shortly by most of the rest of the army with one important exception—the ponton trains. These were at Harper's Ferry, and for a set of complicated and largely inexplicable reasons did not reach Falmouth until 25 November. The Rappahannock could have been forded, but Burnside feared that rain or snow might flood the river and cut off the troops on the far bank. Meanwhile Lee, who had organized the Army of Northern Virginia into two corps under lieutenant generals, plus cavalry and reserve artillery, had detected Burnside's movement and deduced his intentions. He rushed the I Corps under Longstreet from Culpeper to the high ground behind Fredericksburg. Jackson followed from Winchester, and by the time Burnside was ready there were 78,500 Confederate soldiers waiting to receive the attack. At this point Burnside might well have changed his plan, since it was based on the assumption that there would be little or no opposition to his river crossing and seizure of the high ground. Malvern Hill had shown the folly of frontal assaults against such positions as the Confederates had prepared but still Burnside decided to carry on.

Tactical plans. Briefly, Burnside initially directed the Right Grand Division to cross on three ponton bridges at Fredericksburg and attack Marye's Heights, a steep eminence about one mile from the river, while the entire Left went over farther downstream and pushed against the Confederate positions on a long, low-wooded ridge southeast of the Heights. But on the morning of 13 December he altered this plan, and decided to send only a part of the Left Grand Division against the low ridge, held by Jackson's corps. Part of the Center Grand Division was to support the crossing; the rest was in army reserve. Brig. Gen. Henry J. Hunt, Burnside's artillery chief, posted 147 guns on the heights on the Union side of the river to cover the crossing and support

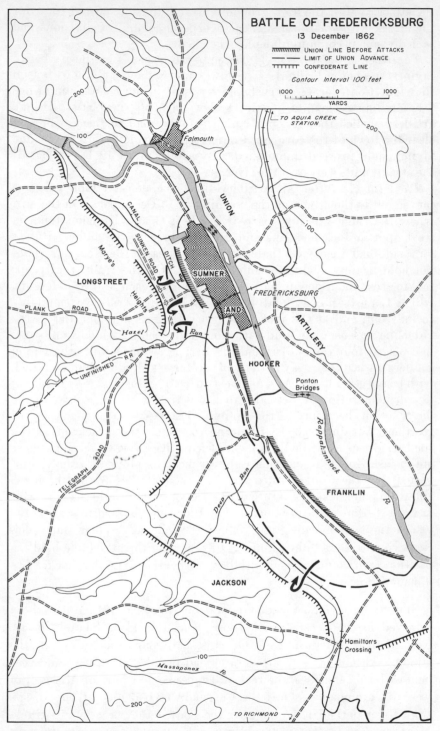

Map. 25. Battle of Fredericksburg, 13 December 1862.

the attack against the high ground. Grand divisions would form for the attack with corps abreast, each corps in column of divisions and each division in columns of deployed brigades.

The river crossing. On 11 December Burnside's engineers began laying the ponton bridges. There was no trouble on the left, but on the right Confederate sharpshooters posted in houses and buildings (the civilian occupants had left) shot them off the boats. Hunt's artillery shelled the city, but Union infantry had to ferry over and clear the town of the covering Confederate brigade before the bridge laying could proceed unmolested. By afternoon of 12 December all the assault units were over the river.

The attack. After an artillery duel, the dense Union columns moved out to the attack on the morning of 13 December. On the left, where the ridge was low, part of the Left Grand Division found a weak spot in Jackson's line and drove in to seize the ridge. But as Burnside had weakened that part of the assault the Federals could not hold against Jackson's counterattack. On the right, the troops had to cross about one mile of open ground to reach Marye's Heights, which Longstreet was holding. In addition, a drainage canal lay to its front, and at the foot of Marye's Heights and parallel to the ridgeline was a sunken road with stone walls behind which Longstreet had posted four ranks of riflemen. In a series of assaults the Union soldiers pushed their way to the foot of Marye's Heights, but all failed, with heavy casualties. As a demonstration of valor it was exemplary; as a demonstration of tactical skill it was tragic. In the course of the day's action the Army of the Potomac lost 12,600 men, the Army of Northern Virginia, 5,300. Planning to resume the attack on 14 December, Burnside pulled his men back to the river. Jackson, whose enthusiasm for war sometimes approached the point of frenzy, suggested that the Confederates strip off their clothes for better identification and strike the Army of the Potomac in a night attack. But Lee knew from a captured order that Burnside planned to resume the attack the next morning and vetoed the scheme. When Burnside's corps commanders talked him out of renewing the attack, he held his position for two days, then withdrew across the Rappahannock. Lee did not follow.

Summary. And so ended operations in 1862. Much had been achieved in the West: Forts Henry and Donelson, Island No. 10, New Madrid, Corinth, New Orleans. Missouri was safely in the Union. Although the Confederates had invaded Kentucky and still held eastern Tennessee, the rest of Tennessee and part of Mississippi were in Union hands. Only the Vicksburg forts denied all the Mississippi River to the Union and gave the Confederacy access to its trans-Mississippi states (map 26). In the Eastern Theater no strategic

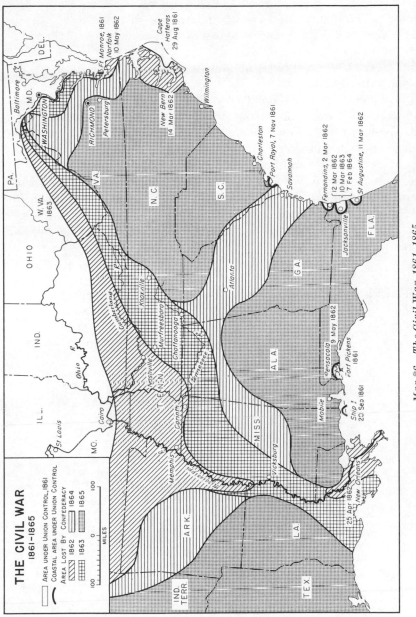

Map 26. *The Civil War, 1861–1865.*

231

decision had been reached, although 10 large-scale battles had been fought.

QUESTIONS

1. Explain the strategic results of the captures of Forts Henry and Donelson, and of the other western operations in 1862.

2. Comment critically on the battle of Shiloh in terms of the principles of war.

3. Discuss the advantages of McClellan's peninsular plan. Were there any disadvantages?

4. Comment critically on the Peninsular and Shenandoah Valley Campaigns (March–June 1862) in terms of the principles of war.

5. Explain briefly how Lee, in the Manassas Campaign, was able to defeat the Union forces.

6. Why did Davis and Lee decide to invade Maryland? What were the results of the invasion and subsequent withdrawal? Why, with all his advantages, did McClellan fail to achieve more than he did in the Antietam Campaign?

7. Analyze the factors which led to the Union repulse at Fredericksburg.

Reading List

See reading list at end of chapter 14.

CHAPTER 13

THE CIVIL WAR—1863

Conscription. Civil War battles were bloody and costly, but even so the death rates from disease in both armies were higher than those from battle casualties. Thus the year 1863 had found the ranks of both armies seriously depleted. In 1862 the Confederate Congress passed a draft or conscription law. Mr. Lincoln asked for 300,000 more volunteers on 2 July 1862. This time only 85,000 men responded immediately. Therefore, on 3 March 1863 Congress passed the Enrollment Act, the first national draft law in United States history. This law made able-bodied males between 20 and 45 years of age liable for national military service. The Enrollment Act was not popular, as the New York riots demonstrated after Gettysburg. Both the Confederate and the U. S. laws were undemocratic in that they did not apply equally to all individuals. They provided for exemptions that made it possible for many to escape military service entirely. Comparatively few men were drafted into the Federal service, but by stimulating volunteering the Enrollment Act had its desired effect.

The Medal of Honor. The year 1863 saw the awarding of the highest United States decoration, the Medal of Honor. The Congress authorized it on 12 July 1862, and the first medals were given by Secretary Stanton in 1863 to Pvt. Jacob Parrott and five other soldiers. They had demonstrated extraordinary valor in a daring raid behind the Confederate lines near Chattanooga. Since 1863 the award of this medal has remained the highest honor the United States can bestow upon any individual in the Army.

Welfare. Throughout the western world the 19th century, with its many humanitarian movements, saw a general improvement in the lot of the individual soldier, and the U. S. soldier was no exception. The more severe forms of corporal punishment were abolished in the Army in 1861. Although Civil War medical science was primitive in comparison with that of the mid-20th century, an effort was made to extend medical services in the Army beyond the mere treatment of battle wounds. As an auxiliary to the regular medical service, the volunteer U. S. Sanitary Commission fitted out hospital ships and hospital units, provided male and, for the first time in the U. S. Army, female nurses, and furnished clothing and fancier foods than the regular rations. Similarly, the U. S. Christian Commission augmented the efforts of the regimental chaplains and even provided, besides song books and Bibles, some coffee bars and reading rooms.

Tactics. By 1863 the war had entered what Sherman called its professional phase. The troops were well trained and had had ample experience in combat. The high commanders had pretty well mastered their jobs, and were deploying their forces fairly skillfully in accordance with the day's tactical principles. Further, by now the increased range and accuracy of weapons, together with the nature of the terrain, had induced some alteration in tactics, alterations which were embodied in a revised infantry manual published in 1863.

Infantry. The infantry usually marched in column but attacked and defended in a line of two ranks. The brigade was the basic maneuvering unit, and it formed for the attack with regiments in a two-rank line. The division usually attacked in column of brigades, the second 150 to 300 yards behind the first, the third a similar distance behind the second. Terrain and skirmishers protected the flanks if no units were posted on either side. As the war wore on the number of skirmishers in front, who were used to drive in the enemy outposts and cover the approach of the brigades in formation, was increased so much that the skirmishers were almost a complete line in themselves. As most men were using single-shot muzzle-loaders, they still had to stand shoulder to shoulder in order to load conveniently and to get enough firepower. But intervals between units were increased. Attacks started in close order, but troops often scattered for cover and concealment when they came under fire, and thereafter advanced by short rushes supported by fire from neighboring units. The generals attempted to combine frontal assaults with envelopments and flanking movements, but the difficulty of timing and coordinating the movements of such large bodies of men in broken terrain made intricate maneuvers very difficult. Most assaults, therefore, were delivered frontally with fixed bayonets, and throughout the war most of them failed. The reasons for these failures lie in the longer range and greater effectiveness of Civil War rifles and field artillery and in the enthusiasm and skill with which the soldiers entrenched and used such features as ditches, trees, logs, and stone walls.

Field artillery. The infantry's main support was provided by field artillery. Rifled guns of relatively long range were available, but the standard pieces were the 6-pound and 12-pound smoothbore, muzzle-loading, bronze "Napoleons" with ranges varying from 320 to 1,660 yards. The troops preferred the older to the rifled guns for several reasons. Rifled cannon were harder to clean; their projectiles were not as effective; their greater range could not always be effectively used because development of a good indirect fire control system would have to await the invention of the field telephone and the radio—the telegraph was generally used strategically, not tactically;

and finally, the rifled guns had flat trajectories, while the higher trajectories of the smoothbores enabled gunners to put fire on reverse slopes. Smoothbore projectiles were the same as those used in the Mexican War: solid shot, shell, canister, and shrapnel.

Cavalry. Cavalrymen, armed with saber, pistol, and breech-loading carbine, were dragoons that rode to the scene of battle but usually fought on foot. The broken and heavily wooded terrain of most battles were poor country for mounted action, and there were only a few fights between mounted men with drawn sabers. And the range and accuracy of the Springfield .58 rifle made it next to impossible for mounted men to attack infantry in position. With their superior speed and mobility, cavalrymen were particularly useful for screening, reconnaissance, and in advance guard actions in which they seized and held important hills, river lines, and road junctions pending the arrival of infantry. In these engagements they dismounted and fought with their breech-loading carbines, which had a faster rate of fire but shorter range than the infantry rifle. These generalizations regarding tactics find ample illustration in the great battles of 1863.

The Vicksburg Campaign. *Command and strategy.* When Halleck went east in 1862 to become General in Chief, Maj. Gen. Ulysses S. Grant was left as commander of the District of West Tennessee with about 42,000 men. To recapitulate slightly, in 1862 the Army's victories in the West had gained control of most of the important points on the banks of the Mississippi. At the same time Flag Officer Andrew H. Foote, pushing down the river, and Capt. David G. Farragut, steaming up from New Orleans, had cleared most of the stream. Only the posts in the Vicksburg and Port Hudson areas prevented the Union from controlling the entire length of the Mississippi and splitting the Confederacy in two (map 20). Farragut tried to seize Vicksburg in May and again in June 1862, but the Confederates easily repulsed him. In the autumn of 1862 Grant decided to capture it, but President Lincoln and Secretary Stanton devised a scheme which even now their most fervent admirers do not try to defend. The President, of course, had always seen the importance of controlling the Mississippi, and, after the battles of Iuka and Corinth in the latter part of 1862, he and Stanton prepared plans to advance simultaneously northward from New Orleans and southward from Tennessee. But they wrote vague orders without consulting General in Chief Halleck. They planned to give command of the northbound expedition to General Banks, who had replaced Butler as commander of the Department of the Gulf. Command of the southbound expedition was to go to Maj. Gen. John A. McClernand, a relatively untried Volunteer officer who won an unenviable reputation as an intriguer. Further, McClernand was to operate within Grant's department but independently of him. When Halleck found out about the Lincoln-Stanton plan, he persuaded the President to put Grant in command of the southbound expedition and to make McClernand one of his subordinates.

The first attempt. Grant first tried a combined land and water expedition in December 1862–January 1863. He sent Sherman out, but the Confederates raided and cut the 200-mile-long line of communications. For this reason, and perhaps to keep close rein on McClernand who ranked Sherman, Grant then determined on a river expedition which he would lead in person. He resolved to use his entire force, three corps totaling 45,000 men. McClernand led XIII Corps; Maj. Gen. William T. Sherman, XV Corps; Maj. Gen. James B. McPherson, XVII Corps. During the ensuing campaign Grant received two more corps as reinforcements, and his total strength reached 75,000.

Terrain and enemy strength. Vicksburg was almost a perfect location for defense (map 27). At that point on the river, bluffs rose as high as 250 feet above the water and extended for about 100 miles from north to south. North of Vicksburg lay the Yazoo River and its delta, a gloomy stretch of watery, swampy bottom land extending 175 miles from north to south, 60 miles from east to west. The ground immediately south of Vicksburg was almost as swampy and impassable. The Confederates had fortified the bluffs from Haynes' Bluff on the Yazoo, some 10 miles above Vicksburg, to Grand Gulf at the mouth of the Big Black River about 40 miles below. Vicksburg could not be assaulted from the river, and sailing past it was extremely risky. The river formed a great U here, and Vicksburg's guns threatened any craft that tried to slip by. For the Union troops to attack successfully, they would have to get to the high, dry ground east of town. This would put them right in Confederate territory between two enemy forces. Lt. Gen. John C. Pemberton commanded some 30,000 men in Vicksburg, while the Confederate supreme commander in the area, General Johnston (now recovered from his wound) concentrated forces at Jackson, Miss., 40 miles east of Vicksburg.

Canal digging. During late winter and early spring, with the rains falling, the streams high, and the swamps at their wettest and muddiest, overland movement was impossible. Grant set his army, now again designated the Army of the Tennessee, to work digging canals. All canals had as their objects the clearing of an approach by which troops could sail to a point near the high ground east of the river without being fired on by Vicksburg's guns, and all were failures. That Grant kept on trying in the face of such discouragements is a tribute to his dogged persistence, and that Lincoln supported him is a tribute to his wisdom and resolution.

The new plan. In March, working in close cooperation with the local naval commander, Flag Officer David D. Porter, Grant evolved

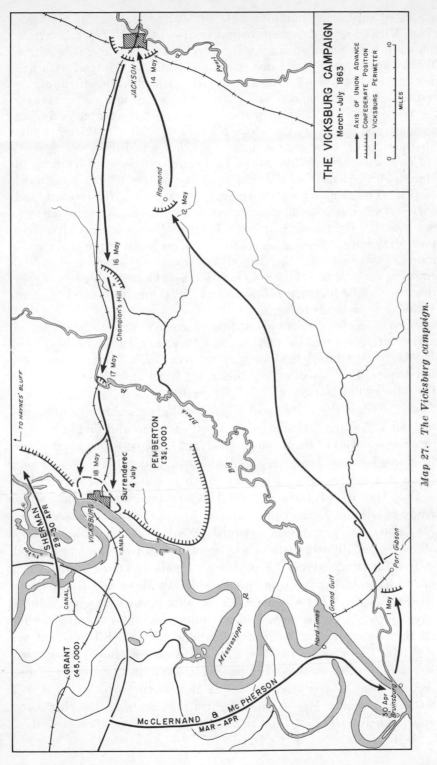

Map 27. *The Vicksburg campaign.*

a plan of surpassing boldness. He decided to use part of his force above Vicksburg to demonstrate and to divert the Confederates while the main body marched southward overland on the west side of the Mississippi, crossed to the east bank, and struck out inland with five days' rations to live off a hostile country without a line of supply or retreat. Porter's gunboats and other craft, which up to now were on the river north of Vicksburg, were to slip past the batteries during darkness and then ferry the troops over from the west to the east bank. Sherman thought the campaign too risky, but was proven wrong.

The move south. While Sherman demonstrated near Vicksburg in March, McClernand's and McPherson's corps started their southward march. The rains let up in April, the waters slightly receded, and overland movement became somewhat easier. Even so, the march took one month. On the night of 16–17 April, Porter led his river fleet past Vicksburg, whose guns started a heavy bombardment once the move was discovered. Luckily, all but one transport made it safely. Starting on 30 April, Porter's craft ferried the troops eastward over the river at Bruinsburg below Grand Gulf, and the march against Vicksburg was ready to begin.

The approach. Grant's army, less Sherman's corps which followed a week later, captured Port Gibson on 1 May, then waited for Sherman. Pemberton tried to defend too wide an area; he had not concentrated but dispersed his forces at Vicksburg, the Big Black River, and along the railroad line to Jackson, Miss., where Johnston was gathering more troops. Grant therefore decided he must defeat Johnston before attacking Vicksburg. He moved out northeastward and fought his way into Raymond on 12 May, a move which put him in position to interpose his force between Johnston and Pemberton and cut the Confederate line of communications. Next day Sherman and McPherson marched against the city of Jackson, with McClernand following in reserve, ready to hold off Pemberton. The leading corps took Jackson on 14 May, and drove its garrison eastward. While Sherman occupied Jackson to fend off Johnston, the other two corps faced about westward and started for Pemberton and Vicksburg. Pemberton tried to hold them off, and fought hard at Champion's Hill (16 May) and Black River Bridge (17 May) but was defeated and shut up in Vicksburg. In 18 days, Grant's army had marched 200 miles and won 4 victories, living off the country except for 5 days' rations all the while. Grant assaulted Vicksburg on 18 May, and again on 22 May. When both attacks failed, he established a base on the Yazoo 12 miles away and began a siege. After the attack of 22 May, during which he sent in a misleading report, McClernand slighted the efforts of the other corps and publicly criticized the army commander. Grant replaced him with Maj. Gen. Edward O. C. Ord.

Assault on Vicksburg by 1st Battalion, 13th Infantry on 18 May 1863.

The surrender. The rest was now a matter of time, as Sherman readily kept Johnston away and the Federals advanced their approaches toward the Confederate works. Food was short and the troops and civilians inside Vicksburg were soon reduced to eating mules and other less conventional fare. Shells pounded the city. The front lines were close, and the Federals threw hand grenades into the Confederate works. The Confederates had no grenades, but occasionally managed to fling back Federal grenades before they exploded. By 1 July the Union troops had completed their approaches and were ready for another assault. But Vicksburg was starving and Pemberton asked for terms. Grant offered to parole all prisoners, and Vicksburg surrendered on Independence Day. Since Grant was out of telegraphic contact with Washington, the news reached the President via naval channels on 7 July, the day before General Banks' 15,000-man army, having advanced up from New Orleans, captured Port Hudson, La. The whole river was now repossessed by the Union, the Confederacy sliced in two.

The Eastern Theater, January–May 1863. *Hooker replaces Burnside.* Accomplishments in the Western Theater during the first seven months of 1863 were magnificently impressive. Those in the east during the same period were dramatic but indecisive. After the battle of Fredericksburg, Burnside's Army of the Potomac went into winter quarters on the north bank of the Rappahannock, while the main body of Lee's Army of Northern Virginia held Fredericksburg and guarded the railway line to Richmond. Lee dispatched Longstreet on a supply collecting expedition to southeastern Vir-

239

ginia. During January Burnside's subordinates, who almost to a man disapproved of their commanding general, intrigued against him in an unsoldierly way and went out of channels to present their grievances to Congress and the President. When Burnside heard of this, he went to Mr. Lincoln and asked that he be relieved of command, or that virtually all his subordinate general officers be removed. The President accepted the first alternative, and on 25 January 1863 replaced Burnside with Maj. Gen. Joseph Hooker. The new commander had won a good reputation as an intrepid and competent division and corps commander. He was highly favored by the Committee on the Conduct of the War, but Lincoln made the appointment without asking for outside advice. In appointing Hooker the President wrote him his famous frank, fatherly letter in which he warned Hooker against rashness and overambition, reproached him for intriguing against Burnside, and concluded by asking for victories. Under Hooker's able administration, discipline and training improved. Morale, which had fallen after Fredericksburg, rose as Hooker regularized the furlough system and saw to it that rations of good quality, supplied by the War Department, were delivered to his front-line troops. Abolishing Burnside's grand divisions, Hooker returned to the orthodox corps, of which he had seven of about 15,000 men each. He also took a long step toward improving his army by reorganizing the cavalry, which up to now had been assigned a multiplicity of diverse duties and was split up into small attachments. Hooker regarded cavalry as a combat arm of full stature, and he concentrated his cavalry units in a corps of three divisions under Brig. Gen. George Stoneman.

Chancellorsville—opening phase. With Lee holding Fredericksburg, Hooker, whose strength totaled about 134,000 men, planned a double envelopment which would place strong Union forces on each of Lee's flanks (map 28). He ordered three of his infantry corps to move secretly up the Rappahannock and ford the stream, while two more corps, having conspicuously remained opposite Fredericksburg, crossed below the town. Two more corps were in reserve. The cavalry corps, less one division which was to screen the move, was to raid Lee's rear to divert him. Hooker's plan was good, but he executed it poorly. The three corps secretly moved up the river on 27 April and two days later crossed the Rappahannock and advanced to the principal road junction of Chancellorsville. They were now in the Virginia Wilderness, a low, flat area of scrub timber and narrow dirt roads in which movement and visibility were extremely limited. That same day, 29 April, two corps under Maj. Gen. John Sedgwick crossed the Rappahannock below Fredericksburg. The two remaining corps then moved up to join Hooker at Chancellorsville. So far everything had gone according to plan,

Winter Quarters, Army of the Potomac.

save that Stoneman's raid failed to divert Lee. One of Stuart's brigades kept Stoneman under surveillance while the main body of the cavalry stayed with Lee and provided him with much more information about Hooker than Hooker ever obtained about Lee. But Hooker now had strong forces on each of Lee's flanks, and his western force of three corps turned east against Lee. He had won the first round. General Lee, with 60,000 men, had been preparing plans to invade the North once again, but Hooker's action forestalled them. By morning of 30 April Lee was aware of what was up and knew that he was threatened by double envelopment. A less bold and resolute man would have retreated southward at once, and with such ample justification that only the captious would have found fault. But Lee, here as at Manassas, used the offensive, maneuver, and surprise to compensate for his inferior numbers. Instead of retreating, he left a part of his army to hold Marye's Heights at Fredericksburg and started for Chancellorsville with the main body.

Chancellorsville—Hooker's position. When Lee began to move, Hooker changed his plan and decided to assume the defensive. He established a line in the forest, felled trees for an abatis, and constructed earth-and-log breastworks. The line faced generally south. The left (east) flank was refused toward the Rappahannock but the right (west) flank was weak, unsupported, and did not rest on any strong natural feature.

Chancellorsville—Lee's plan. Lee brought his main body up and on 1 May made contact with Hooker's strong left. That day Stuart's cavalry discovered the location of Hooker's vulnerable right flank and late that afternoon brought the news, together with information about

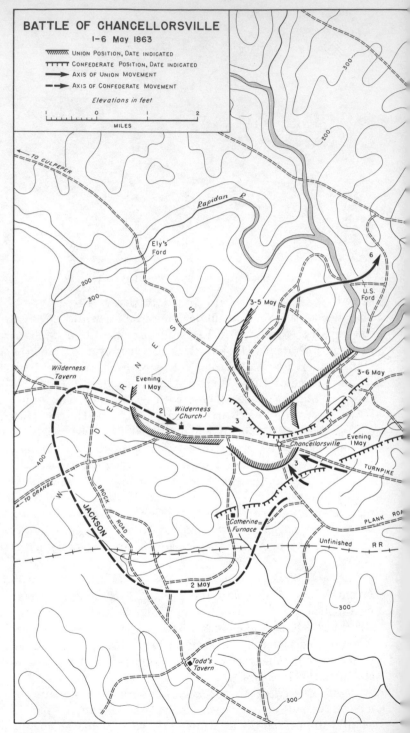

Map 28. Bat

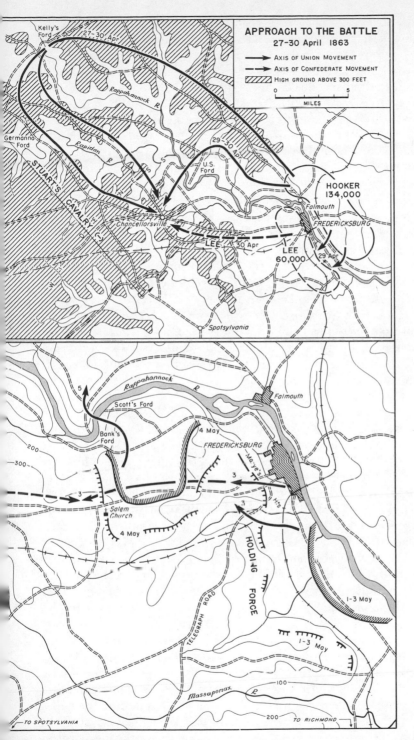

APPROACH TO THE BATTLE
27-30 April 1863

→ AXIS OF UNION MOVEMENT
--→ AXIS OF CONFEDERATE MOVEMENT
//// HIGH GROUND ABOVE 300 FEET

0   5
MILES

Kelly's Ford
27-30 Apr.

Rappahannock R.

Germanna Ford
Rapidan R.

STUART'S CAVALRY

29-30 Apr.
U.S. Ford

Chancellorsville

LEE   30 Apr

HOOKER
134,000

Falmouth
FREDERICKSBURG

LEE
60,000

29 Apr

Spotsylvania

Rappahannock R.

Scott's Ford

Falmouth

Bank's Ford

4 May

FREDERICKSBURG

200

300

Marye's Hts.

3

Salem Church

3

4 May

3

HOLDING FORCE

1-3 May

TELEGRAPH ROAD

1-3 May

100

Massaponax R.

TO SPOTSYLVANIA

200   TO RICHMOND

ellorsville, 1 May 1863

243

the roads, to Lee. Conferring that night with Stonewall Jackson, Lee made another bold decision. Facing an army much greater than his own, an army that was threatening to envelop and destroy him, he decided to divide his army and envelop the envelopers. Accordingly, Lee committed about 20,000 men against Hooker's left to hold it in place while Jackson with 25,000 men made a wide 15-mile swing to get beyond the right flank. At first glance Lee's decision looks like a violation of the principles of mass and concentration, but reflection shows that it was not. Lee's two forces were initially separated, but their common objective was the Army of the Potomac, and their ultimate routes converged on a common center.

Chancellorsville—the Battle: 2 May 1863. Jackson's force, in a 10-mile-long column, moved out at daybreak of 2 May, marching southwest first, then swinging northwest to get in position. The Federals noted the beginning of his march and realized something was afoot but were unable to intercept Jackson or determine his intentions. In late afternoon Jackson, marching on the Brock Road, reached the Orange Turnpike near Wilderness Tavern. He was now west of Hooker's right flank. Here the woods thinned out a little, and it was possible to form a line. Time was running short, so Jackson hastily deployed his force in column of divisions, with each division deployed in line with brigades abreast, the same kind of formation Johnston had used at Shiloh. Shortly after 1700 Stonewall's leading division, shrieking the wild Rebel Yell, struck and drove Maj. Gen. Oliver O. Howard's XI Corps out of position. Jackson pressed forward but was halted by a combination of darkness, fresh Union troops, and the disorganization of his own. As Jackson and his staff returned to the Confederate lines in darkness after a reconnaissance, soldiers of a North Carolina regiment failed to recognize the party and fired on it. Jackson was severely wounded and died eight days later. At the time Jackson was wounded, command of the Confederate II Corps passed to Maj. Gen. Ambrose P. Hill, but he was quickly wounded and replaced by Stuart. During the night of 2–3 May Stuart reformed his lines. Hooker launched local counterattacks against Stuart's right, which at first attained some success, but on the morning of 3 May withdrew his whole line, although his position had been advantageous, for he had had a strong force between Lee's two divided and weaker forces.

Chancellorsville—3 May 1863. Stuart renewed the attack during the morning as Hooker pulled his line back. The two wings of Lee's army made contact and pressed forward. During the morning a Confederate shell struck a pillar of the Chancellor house, Hooker's headquarters, while the general was on the porch. A piece of the pillar hit him on the head, knocked him down, and from then on until the end of the battle he was dazed and incapable of exercising effective command. But he did not relinquish it, and neither the next senior

Maj. Gen. J. E. B. Stuart.   Lt. Gen. Thomas J. Jackson.

general nor the surgeon dared declare him unfit. Meanwhile Sedgwick, who shortly after Jackson's attack had received orders to proceed through Fredericksburg to Chancellorsville, had assaulted
Marye's Heights. He carried them about noon of 3 May after a
morning-long fight. Lee then detached troops against Sedgwick,
pressed him on his front and rear, and forced him off the road and
northward over the river. Lee now made ready for a full-scale assault
against the Army of the Potomac on 6 May, but on Hooker's orders
the army withdrew to the north bank of the Rappahannock before the
attack. Total Union casualties numbered about 17,000; the Confederates lost 13,000. The two armies returned to positions on the opposite
sides of the Rappahannock.

Chancellorsville—Summary. Chancellorsville was doubtless Robert E. Lee's most brilliant battle. Starting from an initial disadvantage, he had outwitted, outmaneuvered, outflanked, and outfought
a force more than twice as large as his own. Yet in essence it was
Hooker he had beaten, not the Army of the Potomac, for the majority
of the men had not been committed at all. It was the general who
failed, not his subordinates. Some time before the battle, Mr. Lincoln
had told Hooker in his next fight to "put in all your men." In his
homely way the President was advising Hooker to apply the principles of mass and concentration in order to win decisively. Hooker
was a talented tactical commander with a good reputation. His major
fault as an army commander—one he shared with several other Union
and Confederate generals—was that while he could effectively lead
a body of troops under his own eyes, he could not use maps and reports to evaluate and control situations that were beyond his range
of vision.

The Gettysburg Campaign: June–July 1863. *Strategy.* With
the great victory at Chancellorsville, the Confederate cause in the
Eastern Theater looked exceptionally bright. If 60,000 men could

beat 134,000, then the Confederacy's inferiority in manpower was surely offset by superior generalship and skill at arms. Vicksburg was not yet under siege, although Grant had ferried his army over to the east bank of the Mississippi. If Davis and Lee were over-optimistic, they can hardly be blamed. Prior to Chancellorsville Davis, Lee, Longstreet and others had been considering strategy for the year. Davis and Lee favored another invasion of the North for the same political and military reasons that led to the invasion in 1862. Longstreet, on the other hand, was concerned over the Federal threats in the West. He proposed going on the defensive in Virginia and advised taking advantage of the Confederacy's railroads and interior lines to send part of the Army of Northern Virginia to Tennessee to clear out the Union armies there and relieve the pressure on Vicks-burg. But he was overruled, and Lee made ready to move into Penn-sylvania. By now Union strategy in the East was clearly defined: to continue operations against Conferedate seaports—an attempt to seize Fort Sumter on 7 April had failed—and to destroy Lee's army. The President's orders made clear that the destruction of the Army of Northern Virginia was the major objective of the Army of the Potomac. Richmond was only incidental. The Confederate deci-sion to invade brought about the battle of Gettysburg. This fight was one of the most dramatic and most typical of the 2,000-odd land engagements of the Civil War.

Strength and organization. On 30 June 1863 the Army of the Potomac numbered 115,256 officers and enlisted men, with 362 guns. It consisted of 51 infantry brigades organized into 19 divisions, which in turn were organized into 7 infantry corps. The cavalry corps had 3 divisions. Field artillery, 67 batteries, was assigned by brigades to the corps, except for army reserve artillery. The Army of North-ern Virginia, numbering 76,224 men and 272 guns in late May, now consisted of 3 infantry corps, each led by a lieutenant general, and Stuart's cavalry division. (The Confederacy was much more gen-erous with rank than was the U. S. Army.) In each corps were 3 divisions, and most divisions had 4 brigades. Of the 15 field artillery battalions of 4 batteries each, 5 battalions were attached to each corps under command of the corp's artillery chiefs.

Preliminary movements: Meade replaces Hooker. In early June General Lee began moving his units away from Fredericksburg. In his advance he used the Shenandoah and Cumberland Valleys, for by holding the east-west mountain passes he could readily cover his ap-proach route and line of communications (map 21). Hooker got wind of the move; he noted the weakening of the Fredericksburg defenses, and on 9 June his cavalry, now commanded by Maj. Gen. Alfred Pleasonton, surprised Stuart at Brandy Station, Va. Here on an open plain was fought one of the few mounted, saber-swinging, cut-

and-thrust cavalry combats of the Civil War. Up to now the Confederate cavalry had been superior, but Union cavalry was improving and Stuart was lucky to hold his position. The Federals learned that Confederate infantrymen were west of the Blue Ridge heading north, and Hooker started to move to protect Washington and Baltimore and to attempt to destroy Lee. Earlier Hooker had actually proposed seizing Richmond while Lee went north; Lincoln, however, telling him his true objective was Lee's army, had vetoed the scheme. As the Army of Northern Virginia moved through the valleys and deployed into Pennsylvania, the Army of the Potomac moved north on a broad front to the east. It crossed the Potomac near Leesburg on 25 and 26 June. By now Lee, forced to disperse by the exigencies of scanty supplies, had extended his infantry corps from McConnelsburg and Chambersburg on the west to Carlisle in the north, York on the east.

After Brandy Station, and some sharp clashes in the mountain passes, Stuart moved through Ashby's Gap in the Blue Ridge and set forth on another dramatic ride around the Union Army. With only vague instructions and acting largely on his own initiative, he proved of little use to Lee. It was only on the afternoon of 2 July, with his troopers so weary they were almost falling from their saddles, that Stuart rejoined Lee in the vicinity of Gettysburg, too late to have an important influence on the battle. His absence had deprived Lee of prompt, accurate information about the Army of the Potomac. When on 28 June Lee did learn from Longstreet that the Army of the Potomac was north of the river, he ordered his Army to concentrate at once between Gettysburg and Cashtown.

After Chancellorsville Lincoln, though advised to drop Hooker, had kept him in command of the Army of the Potomac on the ground that he would not throw away a gun because it had missed fire once. But now Hooker, while advancing northward, became embroiled in an argument with General in Chief Halleck; Hooker wanted to abandon Harper's Ferry and attach its garrison to his command, but Halleck insisted, and for good tactical and logistical reasons, that Harper's Ferry be held. Hooker requested relief and was quickly removed. Appointed in his place was a corps commander, Maj. Gen. George G. Meade, who at 0300, 28 June, received word of his promotion, which would entail all the vast problems inherent in assuming command of a great army while it was moving toward the enemy. Meade, who was to command the Army of the Potomac for the rest of the war, started north on a broad front at once, but within the next two days decided to fight a defensive action in Maryland and issued orders to that effect. However, not all his commanders received the order, and events overruled him.

The first encounter: 30 June 1863. During the afternoon of 30 June the advance guard of the Union 1st Cavalry Division, covering the left of Meade's army, encountered Confederates from Lee's III Corps (Lt. Gen. A. P. Hill) in Gettysburg. In the vicinity of the village were strong tactical positions, and Gettysburg was the junction of 12 roads which led to Harrisburg, Philadelphia, Baltimore, Washington, and to the mountain passes to the west, which were controlled by Lee. The rest was inevitable; the local commanders sent reports and recommendations to their superiors, who forwarded them upward, so that both armies, still widely dispersed, started moving toward Gettysburg.

Terrain. About ½ mile west of Gettysburg, and extending southwestward for about 4 miles, lay Seminary Hill and Seminary Ridge (map 29). About ½ mile south of town, and 80 feet above it, was Cemetery Hill, connected by an east-west saddle to Culp's Hill, a 100-foot high knoll ½ mile to the east. Stretching south from Cemetery Hill, and about 1 mile east of Seminary Hill, was Cemetery Ridge. It ran south for 1¾ miles but sloped down to level ground north of Little Round Top and east of the later famous peach orchard and wheat field near the Emmitsburg Road. The western slope of Cemetery Ridge was open. On the south were three steep, rocky, wooded knolls—Little Round Top, Round Top, and the Devil's Den. (The last name has been applied both to a hill and to a ravine.) Round Top was highest but of less tactical significance than the others because it lay beyond effective rifle range of Little Round Top and was too steep for field artillery. Little Round Top lay 500 yards north of Round Top. There were numerous rail fences and stone walls. The Culp's Hill-Cemetery Hill-Cemetery Ridge-Little Round Top position had great defensive strength; each part supported the others.

Action of 1 July. The Union cavalrymen, dismounted, fought a delaying action against advance troops of Hill's III Corps northwest of Gettysburg until Meade's I Corps arrived. Elements of the XI Corps soon followed, but by now the Confederate II Corps (Lt. Gen. Richard S. Ewell) came down from the north and drove the Federals back through Gettysburg. The Federals held firm on Cemetery and Culp's Hills. Lee, who reached the field about 1400, decided to wait for Longstreet's I Corps, which was still several miles west of Gettysburg, before renewing the attack. He hoped to assault early on 2 July before the rest of Meade's army could concentrate. The Confederate positions extended in a great curve from northeast of Culp's Hill westward through Gettysburg, thence south on Seminary Ridge. The Federals, with interior lines, held the key points of Culp's Hill, Cemetery Hill, Cemetery Ridge, and Little Round Top. Elements of Meade's III and XII corps had begun reaching the field in the afternoon.

Action of 2 July. More and more Union troops marched in. Four whole corps and ⅔ of two more were present by 0900, 2 July; 6 corps were on hand by noon, as well as the reserve artillery, and the VI Corps, having made a 34-mile forced march, began arriving at 1400.

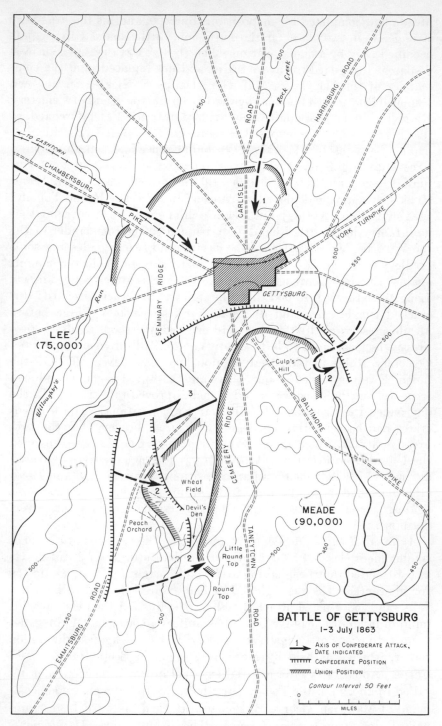

TO CASHTOWN

CHAMBERSBURG

PIKE

CARLISLE ROAD

Rock Creek

HARRISBURG ROAD

YORK TURNPIKE

500

550

Run

SEMINARY RIDGE

GETTYSBURG

Culp's Hill

500

550

LEE
(75,000)

Willoughby's

3

2

Wheat
Field

Devil's
Den

Peach
Orchard

CEMETERY RIDGE

BALTIMORE

TANEYTOWN ROAD

PIKE

MEADE
(90,000)

2

Little
Round
Top

Round
Top

EMMITSBURG ROAD

500

550

450

450

500

500

BATTLE OF GETTYSBURG
1–3 July 1863

1 ──▶ Axis of Confederate Attack,
Date indicated

┬┬┬┬┬ Confederate Position

||||||| Union Position

Contour Interval 50 Feet

0   1

MILES

Map 29.   Battle of Gettysburg.

Meade had completed his dispositions by 0900, and his line was very strong save in two places: in the confusion, Little Round Top was left occupied only by a signal station when the 1st Cavalry Division was dispatched to guard the army trains and not replaced; and the commander of the III Corps, Maj. Gen. Daniel E. Sickles, on his own responsibility moved his line forward from the south end of Cemetery Ridge to higher, more defensible ground near the Peach Orchard, so that his corps lay in an exposed salient. On the Confederate side, Lee had not been able to attack early; reconnaissance took time, and Longstreet's leading division, which was to make the attack, did not arrive until afternoon. Not until 1500 did the attack start, when Longstreet's men, having deployed, advanced toward Little Round Top and the Devil's Den. At this point Meade's chief engineer, discovering that no infantry held Little Round Top, persuaded the commander of the the V Corps, Maj. Gen. George Sykes, to send two brigades and some artillery to the knoll. They arrived just in time to hold the summit against a furious Confederate attack. When this attack bogged down, Longstreet threw a second division against the Peach Orchard; this cracked Sickles' line and drove as far as Cemetery Ridge before Meade's reserves halted it. Lee had ordered his troops to attack progressively from right to left, so now one of Hill's divisions assaulted Cemetery Ridge in piecemeal fashion, but was driven off. On the north Ewell attacked about 1800 and captured some abandoned trenches, but the stone walls and trenches proved too strong. As the day ended the Federals held all their main positions. The Confederates had been fighting hard and with great bravery, but the progressive attack, which ignored the principle of mass, never engaged the Union front decisively at any point. The assaults were delivered against stoutly defended, prepared positions; Malvern Hill and Fredericksburg had shown this to be folly, although perhaps Lee's successes against prepared positions at Chancellorsville led him into over-optimism.

Action of 3 July. Meade, after requesting the opinions of his corps commanders, decided to defend, rather than attack, on 3 July. He also estimated that Lee, having attacked his right and left, would try for his center. He was right. Lee had at first planned to launch a full-scale, coordinated attack all along the line but then changed his mind in favor of a massive frontal assault by 15,000 men—10 brigades from 4 divisions of Longstreet's and Hill's corps—against the Union center, which was held by Maj. Gen. Winfield Scott Hancock's II Corps. About 1400, after an artillery duel in which the Confederates failed to knock out the Federal artillery, the 15,000 men, under command of Maj. Gen. George E. Pickett, attacked eastward from Seminary Ridge along a mile of front. The assault force—47 regiments altogether—moved at a walk until it reached the Cemetery Ridge, then broke into a run. Union artillery, especially 40 Napoleons on the south end of Cemetery Ridge and some rifled guns on Little Round Top, opened fire, enfiladed the gray ranks, and forced Pickett's right over to the north. Despite heavy casualties the Confederates kept their formation until they came within rifle and canister range of the II Corps, and by then the lines and units were intermingled. Union riflemen, shooting from behind stone walls, opened up on the formation. The four brigades composing the left of Pickett's first line were heavily hit but actually reached and crossed the stone wall defended by Brig. Gen. John Gibbon's 2d Division of II Corps, only to be quickly cut down or captured. Pickett's survivors withdrew to Seminary Ridge, and the fighting was over except for a suicidal mounted charge by Union Cavalry which Longstreet's right flank units easily halted.

Casualties. Of 90,000 effective Union troops and 75,000 Confederates, there were more more than 51,000 casualties. The Army of the Potomac lost 3,155 killed, 14,529 wounded, and 5,365 prisoners and missing. Of the Army of Northern Virginia, 3,903 were killed, 18,735 wounded, and 5,425 missing and prisoners.

The aftermath. Both sides had fought hard and with great valor. Meade, new to army command, had conducted an able, resolute defense but by going almost completely without sleep during the whole campaign had exhausted himself and doubtless reduced his capacity for effective command in the days that followed. If Chancellorsville was Lee's best battle, Gettysburg was clearly his worst; but the reverse did not unnerve him or reduce his effectiveness as a commander. The invasion had patently failed, and he retired at once toward the Potomac. As that river was flooded, it was several days before he was able to cross. Mr. Lincoln, naturally pleased over Meade's defensive victory and elated over Grant's capture of Vicksburg, thought the war would end in 1863 if Meade launched a resolute pursuit and destroyed the Army of Northern Virginia on the north bank of the Potomac. But Meade, who might have been suffering from what today would be called combat fatigue, did not move at once, and Lee safely returned to Virginia on 13 July. Gettysburg was the last important action in the Eastern Theater during 1863. A Federal attempt to take Charleston failed in September; Lee and Meade maneuvered against each other in Virginia, but there was no more fighting. After Gettysburg and Vicksburg the center of strategic gravity shifted to Tennessee.

Chickamauga Campaign. *Union strategy.* With the fall of Vicksburg Grant suggested to Washington that he move against the port of Mobile, Ala. The idea had merit, but larger considerations had to prevail. With the Mississippi under Federal control and the naval blockade tightening, Mr. Lincoln wished to tidy up peripheral matters before sending any armies into the interior of the Confederacy. Specifically, he desired to send an expedition to Texas in order to insure it against possible French aggression, for troops of Napoleon III were then conquering Mexico in the name of Prince Maximilian of Austria. Some of Grant's troops were needed for the Texas expedition, which was led by the Gulf Department commander, General Banks. Meanwhile, in Tennessee, Maj. Gen. William S. Rosecrans had replaced Buell at the head of the Army of the Cumberland. (No one had yet replaced Halleck as supreme commander in the West.) Lincoln and Halleck had urged Rosecrans to undertake some form of activity to support Grant's Vicksburg campaign, but Rosecrans did not start moving until June, when Vicksburg lay under siege. Lincoln had long wished to push an army into the strongly Unionist east part of Tennessee and now prodded Rosecrans, who began an advance from Murfreesboro to Chattanooga during July 1863.

Importance of Chattanooga. Chattanooga's location made it one of the most important cities in the South (map 20). It was a main junction on the Richmond, Knoxville, and Memphis Railroad. Further, here the Tennessee River cuts through the parallel ridges of the Appalachian Mountains and forms a natural gateway to either north or south. By holding Chattanooga the Confederates could threaten the Ohio River and could prevent a Union penetration of the southeastern part of the Confederacy. If the Union armies pushed through Chattanooga, they would be in position to attack Savannah, Ga., or even Richmond from the rear.

Confederate strategy: Longstreet's move. After Gettysburg Longstreet had his way, for Davis approved his proposal to ship troops by rail from Virginia to Tennessee to strengthen the Army of Tennessee under Gen. Braxton Bragg. Longstreet's move, involving 10,000 men and 6 field artillery batteries, began on 9 September. But a force under Burnside, now commanding the Department of the Ohio, which was not part of Rosecrans' command, had penetrated the Cumberland Gap and driven the Confederates from Knoxville; Longstreet had to go around by way of Augusta and Atlanta, Ga., and did not reach Bragg before Rosecrans had crossed the Tennessee and started southward.

Preliminary movements. Rosecrans, with his army, had reached the north bank of the Tennessee River near Stevenson, Ala., on 20 August. By 4 September he was over and on his way toward Chattanooga. He planned to get in behind Bragg from the southwest and bottle him up in Chattanooga, but Bragg saw through the scheme and slipped away southward. Rosecrans then resolved to pursue, a decision that would have been wise if Bragg had been retreating in disorder. There were few passes through the mountains and no good lateral roads. Rosecrans' army, which consisted of XX Corps under

Maj. Gen. Alexander McD. Cook, XIV under Maj. Gen. George H. Thomas, XXI under Maj. Gen. Thomas L. Crittenden, and the Reserve under Maj. Gen. Gordon Granger, was dispersed in three columns over a 40-mile front in order to make use of the various passes. Bragg concentrated his army about 10 September at Lafayette, Ga., some 22 miles south of Chattanooga. As his force was three times as large as any one of the Union columns, Bragg hopefully anticipated that he could defeat Rosecrans in detail. But his intelligence service failed him; he thought there were two, rather than three Union columns, and prepared plans accordingly. He first planned to strike what he thought was Rosecrans' right—actually the center—then the left, but his subordinates did not support him loyally and the attack was not made.

Rosecrans concentrates: Bragg delays. By 12 September Rosecrans was aware that Bragg was not retreating in disorder but was getting ready to fight. He ordered an immediate concentration, but this would take several days. In the meantime, his corps were vulnerable. Bragg was usually speedy in executing attacks but this time he delayed. Planning to push Rosecrans southward from Chattanooga, he decided to wait for Longstreet in order to concentrate his whole force to hit what he thought were two Federal corps. By 17 September he was occupying a position east of, and parallel to, Chickamauga Creek (map 30).

Attack of 18 September 1863. When Longstreet's three leading brigades arrived on 18 September, Bragg decided to cross the creek and attack. But the Federals, with two corps now almost concentrated, defended the fords so stoutly that only a few units got over that day. During the night of 18–19 September more slipped across, and by morning of the 19th about three-fourths of Bragg's men were over.

Action of 19 September 1863. Thomas' corps, in the center, had joined its flanks to the corps on the left, and the third Union corps arrived on the 19th. Bragg thus encountered a much stronger force than he had anticipated. The battlefield was heavily wooded, with few landmarks, and units had some difficulty maintaining direction. Fighting went on throughout the day; all units were engaged but in piecemeal fashion. The Federal lines were broken several times, but counterattacks restored all positions. By nightfall the Federals still controlled the roads to Chattanooga. That night Lee's "War-horse," Longstreet, arrived in person with two more brigades. As he went looking for Bragg to report to him, he got lost in the woods. Encountering some soldiers, he asked them what unit they belonged to. When they replied with numbers—Confederate divisions were named for their commanders—he realized he was in the presence of Union

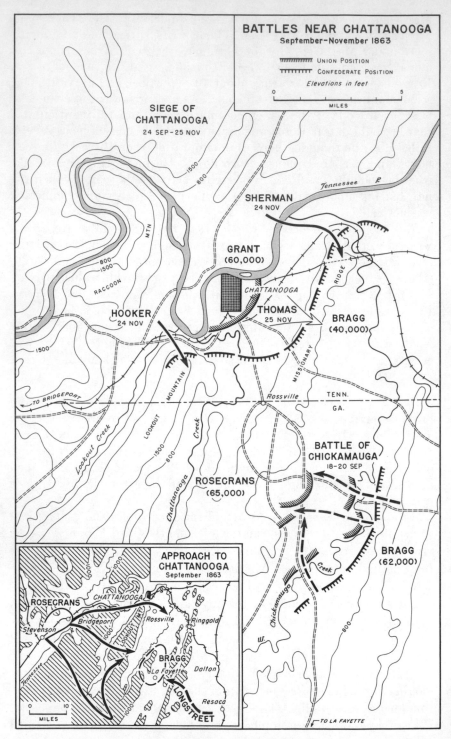

Map 30. Battles Near Chattanooga.

troops, hastily rode off in the darkness, and eventually found Bragg. During the night Rosecrans withdrew slightly and dug in.

Action of 20 September 1863. Bragg decided to renew the attack the next day and to attack progressively from right to left. The right wing—three corps under Maj. Gen. the Rt. Rev. Leonidas Polk, who had been Protestant Episcopal Bishop of Louisiana—was to attack first, followed by the left, which consisted of three corps under Longstreet. The attack began about 0900 and hit Thomas' corps first. When Rosecrans received an erroneous report that one of his units was not supported, he ordered another unit to move in and help. But he had become confused, and designated a unit which was already in line of battle. When this force obediently abandoned its position, Longstreet, just beginning his attack, saw the hole and drove into it at once. Thomas' right was bent back, and troops beyond the gap were driven over Missionary Ridge. Some units retreated in disorder all the way to Chattanooga and swept Rosecrans along with them for about half the distance. Rosecrans, considering he had been defeated, went on to Chattanooga to organize it for defense. Thomas, with about two-thirds of the disorganized army, stood fast and checked Longstreet with a counterattack delivered on foot by a brigade of mounted infantry armed with repeating rifles. The attacks continued all day. Thomas refused both flanks, so that his line was U-shaped. His resolute stand and the valorous performance of the 19th Infantry won for him and the unit the title "Rock of Chickamauga."

The withdrawal. Bragg concluded that no decisive results could be attained that day. Thomas withdrew unmolested from the field that night to a blocking position extending from Missionary Ridge west to Lookout Mountain. Next day he retired into Chattanooga.

Further Battles Around Chattanooga. *The siege.* Rosecrans' army, having started out offensively, was now shut up in Chattanooga, as Bragg took up positions on Lookout Mountain and Missionary Ridge. Burnside, in eastern Tennessee, was too far away to render immediate aid. There were no strong Confederate units north of Chattanooga, but Rosecrans' line of communications was cut anyway. The Nashville and Chattanooga Railroad did not run directly into the city but reached the river at Stevenson, crossed at Bridgeport southwest of Chattanooga, and ran through Confederate territory into town. River steamers could get only to within eight miles of Chattanooga; beyond the Tennessee River was too swift and narrow. Supplies therefore came over the mountains in wagons, but starting 30 September Confederate cavalry under Maj. Gen. Joseph W. Wheeler, one of Bragg's cavalry corps commanders, raided as far north as Murfreesboro. He was heavily attacked by Union cavalry and failed in his effort to tear up the railroad, but he managed to destroy many precious wagons. With the mountain roads breaking down under the heavy traffic in wet weather, rations ran short. Men went hungry and horses and mules began to die of starvation. Rosecrans started preparations to reopen his line of communications by means of an overland route. But this was dominated by Confederate troops on Raccoon and Lookout Mountains. Additional troops to clear these positions were required if the Army of the Cumberland was to eat regularly.

Dispatch of Hooker. Rosecrans' problems had been receiving earnest consideration in Washington. On 23 September the President met with Secretary Stanton, General Halleck, and others to determine what could be done. As General Meade in the east was not then active, they decided to detach two corps, or 20,000 men, from the Army of the Potomac and send them by rail to Tennessee under command of General Hooker, who had been without active command since his relief. The forces selected were XI and XII Corps and 10 artillery batteries. The 1,200-mile journey involved four changes of trains, owing to differing gauges and lack of track connections. Meade received orders to start the movement on 24 September, the same day Bragg's army established itself in front of Chattanooga. The first railway train left Washington on the Baltimore and Ohio the next afternoon; the last departed on 29 September.

Grant to command in the West. Chickamauga had caused Stanton and his associates to lose confidence in Rosecrans. For some time Lincoln had been dubious about Rosecrans, who, he said, acted "like a duck hit on the head" after Chickamauga, but he did not immediately choose a successor. Finally, about mid-October, he decided to unify command of all the western armies, and to vest it in General Grant, who still commanded the Army of the Tennessee. On 17 or 18 October Stanton met Grant in Louisville and gave him two sets of orders which allowed him some discretion in selecting subordinates. Grant was appointed commander of the Military Division of the Mississippi, which embraced the Departments and Armies of the Ohio, Cumberland, and Tennessee, and included the vast area from the Alleghenies to the Mississippi River north of Banks' Gulf Department. Thomas replaced Rosecrans, and Sherman was appointed to command Grant's old army.

Opening the "cracker line." Now that Hooker had arrived, the line of communications, or the "cracker line" to the troops, could be reopened. On 26 October Hooker crossed the Tennessee at Bridgeport and attacked eastward. Within two days he had taken the spurs of the mountains, and the supply line was open once more.

Grant resumes the offensive. In early November Bragg weakened his besieging army by sending Longstreet's force after Burnside in eastern Tennessee. This reduced his strength to about 40,000, and at about the same time Sherman arrived with Grant's old Army of the Tennessee. The troops immediately at hand under Grant—

Lookout Mountain, scene of the battle above the clouds, 24 November 1863.

Thomas' Army of Cumberland, Sherman's Army of the Tennessee, and Hooker's two corps from the Army of the Potomac—now numbered about 60,000. Grant characteristically decided to resume the offensive with his entire force.

Lookout Mountain and Missionary Ridge. Hooker took Lookout Mountain on 24 November. On the same day Sherman crossed the Tennessee at the mouth of Chickamauga Creek and gained positions on the north end of Missionary Ridge. He attacked southward along the Ridge on 25 November but failed to gain. Grant's plan had initially provided for Thomas to attack the western face of Missionary Ridge only after Hooker had pushed southeastward from Lookout Mountain and enveloped Bragg's left. But Grant's mind was flexible, and when Sherman's attack stalled he switched plans. To help Sherman, he directed Thomas to take the rifle pits at the foot of the west slope of Missionary Ridge. These rifle pits were the first of three lines of Confederate trenches. Thomas' troops drove forward and seized the pits, and then themselves took control of this phase of the battle. Coming under fire from the pits upward

257

and in front of them, they kept going. When Grant observed this movement he was at first concerned but, when he saw it succeeding, he gave it additional support. Thomas' troops drove up all the way to the top, and in the afternoon Hooker swept the southern end of Missionary Ridge; the Union troops then had the unusual experience of seeing a Confederate army in precipitate retreat. Grant pursued Bragg the next day, but one Confederate division skillfully halted the pursuit while Bragg retreated and concentrated his Army.

Results. This victory cleared practically all of Tennessee for the Union, as Longstreet shortly returned to Virginia. Further, it opened the way for invasion of the lower south and in Chattanooga provided a base for the invasion. So ended operations in 1863, a year notable for the great victories at Vicksburg and Gettysburg, as well as at Chattanooga. Victory for the Union was not yet assured, but it was in sight, although it could only be won by arduous and skillful fighting. In retrospect, it is clear that the Confederacy had lost the war, but the Confederates were not disposed to admit that fact.

QUESTIONS

1. Explain how the muzzle-loading rifle affected infantry tactics.
2. Explain the role of cavalry in the Civil War. Why was it virtually impossible for cavalry to attack infantry in prepared positions?
3. Analyze Grant's strategic and tactical problems in the Vicksburg Campaign. What principles of war are illustrated by these operations?
4. Explain Hooker's plan for Chancellorsville, and Lee's plan for countering it. Why, in your opinion, was Hooker defeated?
5. List and explain the principles of war illustrated by the battle of Gettysburg. Use both positive and negative examples.
6. Explain the strategic significance of Chattanooga. What was accomplished by Grant's victories in November 1863?

Reading List

See reading list at end of chapter 14.

CHAPTER 14

THE CIVIL WAR—1864–1865

High Command and Strategy. *Appointment of Grant.* In February 1864 Congress revived the rank of lieutenant general, which until then had been held by only two U. S. Army officers: George Washington and Winfield Scott. President Lincoln promoted Grant to lieutenant general on 9 March, relieved Halleck as General in Chief, and put Grant in his place. Sherman succeeded to Grant's western command of three armies. As indicated previously, Lincoln for years had been seeking a man who would accept responsibility and effectively control all the Union armies, operating them in concert with one another to bring the superior resources of the Union to bear against the South, win decisive victories, and end the war. McClellan and Halleck had disappointed him, but in Grant he found the man he wanted—a man who possessed the requisite military knowledge, intelligence, strategic vision, leadership, resolution, and strength of will and character for such high responsibility.

Lincoln and Grant. Strategy for winning the war was developed by Lincoln and Grant in personal conference during the spring of 1864. Grant decided to establish his headquarters in the Eastern Theater, but elected to accompany Meade's Army of the Potomac in its southward advance rather than occupy a Washington office. But he was never very far from the capital, and the President visited him frequently. And the telegraph kept him in constant touch with Lincoln. The President gave Grant much wider latitude in exercising strategic control over the armies than he had given to McClellan and Halleck, doubtless because Grant was willing to accept responsibility and because Lincoln had confidence in Grant's ability and resolution.

The system of command. The organizational machinery which Lincoln and Grant devised to control the armies was remarkable for its smooth efficiency, and it was perhaps the best system, in its day, in both Europe or America. Briefly, Grant, as General in Chief, reported to Stanton and to the President, keeping them informed on the broad aspects of his strategic plans and informing them in advance of the armies' requirements in men and munitions. For the conduct of operations he maintained a small staff at his headquarters in the field. Grant's job, administratively, was very large, for under him were 17 different field commands that embraced more than half a million men.   Grant dealt directly with Meade; he used Halleck, who now loyally stepped down and assumed a new post as Army Chief of Staff in Washington, as a channel of communication with the other army commanders.   Halleck eased the heavy burden of studying the army commanders' reports and plans for Grant by preparing brief digests, so that Grant's time was not taken up by too many routine details.   As during the whole course of the war, men and munitions were sent forward to the armies by the General Staff (the Bureaus) in Washington, which under Stanton's keen and exacting supervision functioned efficiently.

Grant's generalship.   As a military commander, Grant was married to the principle of the offensive.   He was not a profound student of the literature of war, but his operations were models of the application of the principles of war.   He was a keen judge of military men and made the utmost use of their abilities.   He learned from experience in his rise from regimental to supreme command, and if he sometimes made mistakes he rarely repeated them.   He was calm in crisis and in victory; reversals and disappointments did not unbalance his cool judgment.   Although a rigorous trainer and strict disciplinarian, he was not a perfectionist like McClellan.   He always did his effective best to carry out orders with available forces without fretting superiors by complaints, excuses, or impossible demands.   On the technical side, if he was not a great or original tactician, he was capable of mastering every situation he encountered during the war. He knew how to deploy and maneuver massive forces on the map as well as under his own eye, and he mastered logistics.   He also saw that in modern war destruction of the enemy's economic resources is as necessary as destruction of his armies, and he applied the principle. Although never popular with his troops in McClellan's showy way, he won their respect, for he exemplified the old principle that the best way for a commander to get along with his troops is to show them that he knows more than they do.

Strategic plans.   Grant's plans called for the Union armies to move toward a common center in a vast, concentrated effort that for size and distance was hitherto unsurpassed in modern war.   As Grant saw it, in the absence of effective, centralized control before 1864, the Union armies had not pulled together but had acted like a balky team.   The Confederates had been able to use their interior lines and railroads to shift troops from one theater to another, but Grant intended to stop that.   He planned to hold Lee with the Army of the Potomac, attempting to defeat the Army of Northern Virginia in a decisive engagement, while the western armies executed a wide, swinging movement through the South which would, in effect, envelop the whole country east of the Mississippi.   Grant ordered the Army of the Potomac to drive southward against Lee, giving him no respite whatever but rather seeking a decisive battle to destroy him and always fighting so as to win by attrition if other means failed. At the same time he directed Butler, who now commanded the Army of the James at Fort Monroe, to advance up the peninsula. Butler was to menace Richmond, capture it if possible, and destroy the railroads south of the city in order to cut Lee's main supply route. If Butler captured Richmond, then Lee could not retire into the city's entrenchments. Maj. Gen. Franz Sigel, commanding a small force in the Shenandoah Valley, was to lead a raid up the valley, possibly divert the Confederates away from Richmond, and perhaps get at Lee from the rear. In the West the three armies under Sherman were to advance southward from Chattanooga to break up and destroy the Army of Tennessee, which was now commanded by Johnston, then push into the Confederacy's interior and damage its war-making resources. After Chattanooga Grant had still wanted to attack Mobile, Ala., but Lincoln had overruled him because he did not wish to risk exposing east Tennessee to invasion. Grant then desired Banks, the Gulf commander, to proceed from New Orleans to Mobile in concert with Sherman's operations so as to seize the line Chattanooga-Mobile, but this never came off. Banks, acting on vague orders from Halleck, had started up the Red River in March 1864 toward Shreveport and was defeated by Lt. Gen. Richard Taylor. Farragut's fleet was to capture Mobile Bay in August 1864. In the spring of 1864, then, Grant mapped his strategy to stop minor, uncoordinated movements and to use the vast might of the Union in one integrated effort. As Lincoln described the scheme, "Those not skinning can hold a leg." This general plan governed operations until the end of the war. During this period it is the strategic moves of the armies, rather than tactical details, which are most instructive. Aside from a much larger emphasis on entrenchments and some increased use of breech-loading rifles (the Gatling machine gun was also employed experimentally), there were no tactical innovations after 1863.

The Army of the Potomac—May–June 1864. *Strength and organization.*

In May 1864 the Army of the Potomac consisted of three infantry and one cavalry corps, and was thus more easily controlled than when it had had six or seven corps. Hancock led the II Corps; Maj. Gen. Gouverneur K. Warren the V Corps, and Sedgwick, the VI Corps. There were about 25,000 in each infantry corps. In addition, Burnside's IX Corps, of 20,000 men, had been brought east. Burnside operated directly under Grant for a time, then was assigned to Meade's army. Butler's Army of the James numbered 25,000. Commanding the 12,000-man cavalry corps was Maj. Gen. Philip H. Sheridan, an energetic young man and a rising star in the west whom Grant brought east on Halleck's recommendation. Meade had again dispersed the cavalry and used the troopers as messengers, pickets, and train guards, but Sheridan, after a good deal of argument, eventually succeeded in concentrating it as a combat arm. Lee's Army of Northern Virginia,

Maj. Gen. William T. Sherman.   Maj. Gen. Philip H. Sheridan.

about 70,000 strong, was also organized into three infantry and one cavalry corps under the same commanders that had fought at Gettysbur. Longstreet led the I Corps; Ewell, the II Corps; and Hill, the III Corps. Stuart commanded the cavalry.

The Wilderness. Meade's and Sherman's widely separated armies moved out to the attack on the morning of 4 May 1864. The Army of the Potomac crossed the Rapidan River and attempted to slip around Lee's right (east) flank to envelop him and defeat him decisively while Butler cut his line of communications (map 31). Grant had decided to go by Lee's right, rather than his left, so as to use the Potomac River to ease the supply problem. Even so, the army trains numbered 4,000 wagons. Grant had to accept the disadvantages inherent in such a move. There was less room for maneuver, and he was forced to advance through the wilderness where Hooker had come to grief the year before. As the army halted near Chancellorsville to allow the wagon trains to get through on 5 May, Lee struck at Meade's right (west) flank. Grant and Meade swung the troops into line and fought back hard. The fighting, consisting of assault, defense, and counterattack, was close and desperate in the thickets. Artillery could not be brought to bear effectively since there were few open spaces and observation was limited. The dry woods caught fire, and some of the wounded died miserably in the flames. Lee attacked again on 6 May and drove the Federals back. Longstreet suffered such a severe wound in the neck that day, inflicted in error by his own men, that he was out of action until October. In the course of the battle Lee, his fighting blood aroused to white heat, attempted to lead an assault in person, but the Texas brigade in question insisted that he go to the rear. Neither side renewed the fight on 7 May.

Push to Spotsylvania—Yellow Tavern. Now was time of crisis in Grant's execution of strategy. He had been worsted, though not really beaten, by Lee, a much more formidable antagonist than Bragg or

262

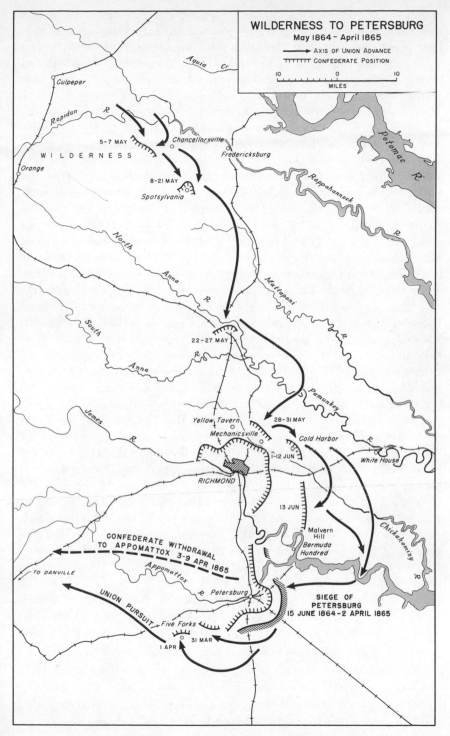

Map 31. Wilderness to Petersburg.

Pemberton. After an encounter with Lee, other Union commanders had usually retired and tried to postpone any further clashes with that great general. But Grant showed his courage, resolution, and solid grasp of the value of the offensive by remaining unruffled and renewing his attempt to push south to get around Lee's flank and interpose the Army of the Potomac between Lee and Richmond. On 7 May he drove south toward Spotsylvania, a key road junction. Lee detected the move and, using roads generally parallel to Grant's, also raced toward Spotsylvania. Some of his cavalry units harassed and slowed Grant, so that Lee got there first and quickly built strong earth-and-log trenches on commanding ground which covered the roads leading to Richmond. Sheridan's cavalry would have been useful to Grant in this race, but Meade had dissipated the cavalry corps' strength by using two divisions to guard his already well-protected trains. This provoked a showdown argument between Meade and Sheridan which the General in Chief resolved in favor of Sheridan. Grant agreed to concentrate the cavalry and give Sheridan a free hand when the latter promised to stop raids by Stuart's cavalry. Sheridan thereupon led his corps southward in a long raid toward Richmond which had as its objective a decisive action with Stuart. Sheridan succeeded. He fought a running series of engagements that culminated in the victory at Yellow Tavern, in which the gallant Stuart was mortally wounded. The South was already short of horses and mules, and Sheridan's 16-day raid ended forever the offensive power of the cavalry of the Army of Northern Virginia.

Action at Spotsylvania. From 9 to 20 May the Army of the Potomac and the IX Corps struck at Lee's fortifications but were bloodily beaten back. On two separate occasions the Federals actually broke through the trenches and split Lee's army in two, but in each case the attackers became disorganized, supporting elements did not or could not come to their aid, and Confederate counterattacks were delivered with such ferocity that the gains could neither be exploited nor held. Sedgwick was killed by a rifle bullet early in the action; Maj. Gen. Horatio G. Wright took his place. On 20 May Grant decided the line was too strong to attack and sideslipped south again, still trying to envelop Lee's right flank.

North Anna—Cold Harbor. With inferior forces, Lee skillfully avoided Grant's trap and refused to come out from behind entrenchments to get beaten in decisive open battle. He retired to the North Anna River and built positions that Grant decided were too strong to attack. Grant then moved left (south) again. Butler, meanwhile, had advanced up the peninsula toward Richmond but did not capture it and did not cut Lee's railroads, for Beauregard outmaneuvered him in May and bottled him up at Bermuda Hundred between the James and the Appomattox Rivers. Lee therefore easily made his way into the Richmond defenses with his right flank on the Chickahominy and his center at Cold Harbor, the site of the Gaines' Mill action in 1862. With the armies facing each other along six to eight miles of front on 3 June, Grant ordered an assault against Lee's center at Cold Harbor. The attack was badly planned, though bravely executed. The Confederates repulsed it with gory efficiency, and Grant later regretted that he had ever made the attempt.

Crossing the James. Thus far Grant, though fighting constantly, had scarcely achieved a single major objective in the east. He had inflicted some 25,000 to 30,000 casualties on Lee. But Federal casualties in that bloody summer numbered 55,000 to 60,000, and the newspapers were calling Grant a butcher. Lincoln, in July, had to call for another half million volunteers; deficiencies were to be made up by the draft. But Grant had achieved more than met a superficial glance. His heavy casualties could be made good, whereas the Confederates could not afford theirs. Southern manpower was running short. And Grant had kept Lee on the defensive and had prevented him from sending any troops to help Johnston in his fight against Sherman. Since Butler had utterly failed to accomplish his missions—he was later relieved, as was Banks—and since Lee was strongly entrenched in Richmond, Grant now altered his plan. He decided to cross the James River east of Richmond to drive against Petersburg, through which ran all the railways and main roads connecting Richmond with the south. If he could take Petersburg, he could either starve Lee into surrender or force him out of his trenches to fight. All the corps were assembled on the north bank of the deep, wide James by 14 June and crossed over a 2,100-foot pontoon bridge, the longest up to that time in modern history. Lee, expecting Grant to attack between the Chickahominy and James Rivers, did not interfere with the move.

Petersburg. Grant's leading elements, having crossed the river and deployed, came up in front of Petersburg on 15 June. Inasmuch as Lee had been deceived about Grant's intentions, the city was held by but a handful of Confederate soldiers under Beauregard and could have been taken handily on 15 June. But the commanders on the spot had not understood Grant's intentions either. They dawdled, so that Lee found out what was up and quickly moved into Petersburg. A heavy assault on 18 June failed, and on the last day of July a great mine tunneled under the Confederate works was exploded. It blew a large breach in the Confederate line, but the succeeding infantry assault was poorly managed. It failed, with over 4,000 casualties. Grant thereupon undertook siege operations, an effort which continued on into the next year. It was position warfare, a war of trenches and sieges, conducted ironically enough by two masters of mobile warfare. Mortars were used extensively, and heavy siege guns were mounted on railway cars and brought up. Grant extended his lines to the left, in

Guns and Fortifications at Petersburg, 1864.

a westerly direction, as he still sought to get around Lee's right, and operated against Lee's left to prevent him from shortening his line and achieving a higher degree of concentration. Lee moved his lines to counter Grant, so that the two commanders were, in effect, manuevering their fortifications.

Early's Raid. While Grant and Lee were hammering each other in the vicinity of Richmond, Federal troops had been moving up the Shenandoah Valley to threaten Lee from the rear. Now that he was firmly in place at Petersburg and could spare some troops, Lee decided to ease the pressure by sending Maj. Gen. Jubal A. Early with one corps to raid northward through the Shenandoah Valley. Entering the valley from the south in early July, Early advanced. Maj. Gen. David Hunter, who had replaced Sigel and received confusing orders from Washington, retired up the valley, but when he reached the Potomac he turned west into the safety of the mountains and uncovered Washington. Early saw his chance and drove through Maryland toward the capital. Delayed by a Union force on 9 July, he reached the northern outskirts of the city on 11 July and skirmished briskly in the vicinity of Fort Stevens. He did not know that an interested spectator in a black frock coat and tall silk hat stood behind the fort's parapet—the Commander in Chief of all the armed forces of the United States, Abraham Lincoln. That same day elements of Wright's VI Corps, hastily dispatched by Grant, reached Washington. Early, who was only raiding, realized he was engaging troops of the Army of the Potomac and made off the next day. Although he was outnumbered by Union forces in the vicinity, he escaped safely.

Sheridan's Valley Campaign. *Unity of command.* Up to then Grant had not been paying close attention to the forces in the Shenandoah Valley, but on President Lincoln's instructions he exerted his authority. He decided that Early had eluded the superior forces because they had not been under a single commander. He therefore abolished the four separate departments in the vicinity of Washington and formed them into one command embracing Washington, western Maryland, and the Shenandoah Valley. After discussing the problem with Lincoln and General Hunter, with their concurrence he put Sheridan in command in August with orders to follow Early to the death.

Operations. Sheridan spent the rest of the year in the valley. Employing and coordinating his infantry, cavalry, and artillery in a manner that has won the admiration of military students ever since, he met and defeated Early at Winchester and Fisher's Hill in September, and shattered him at Cedar Creek in October (map 21). To stop further raids and prevent the crops of that fertile valley from being used to feed Lee's army, Sheridan devastated it.

Sherman's Advance to Atlanta. *Strength and organization.* While Grant and Meade were fighting Lee and Sheridan was pursuing Early and burning the Shenandoah Valley, Sherman with his great force of three armies had been advancing from Chattanooga to Atlanta (map 32). In May 1864 Sherman's command included the Army of the Tennessee, now under Maj. Gen. James B. McPherson, consisting of three corps; General Thomas' Army of the Cumberland of three corps; Maj. Gen. John M. Schofield's Army of the Ohio of one corps; and Maj. Gen. George Stoneman's cavalry command of four cavalry divisions—a total force of about 105,000 men. Facing him were two corps of the Army of Tennessee under Johnston. This force was shortly joined by Polk's Army of Mississippi to bring Johnston's whole force, including Wheeler's cavalry, to about 65,000 men. Sherman's mission was the destruction of Johnston's armies and the capture of Atlanta, Ga., which, after Richmond, was the most important industrial center in the South.

Johnston's delaying tactics. Sherman moved out on 4 May 1864, the same day the Army of the Potomac crossed the Rapidan. Johnston, realizing how seriously he was outnumbered, decided to go on the defensive, preserve his forces intact, hold Atlanta, and delay Sherman as long as possible. There was always the hope that the North would grow weary of the costly struggle and that some advocate of peaceful settlement might defeat Abraham Lincoln in the election of 1864. From 4 May through mid-July, the two forces maneuvered against each other. There were daily fights but few large-scale actions. As Sherman pushed south, Johnston would take up a strong position and force Sherman to halt, deploy, and reconnoiter. Sherman would then outflank Johnston, who in turn would retire to a new line and start the process all over again. On 27 June Sherman, unable to maneuver because the roads were muddy and seriously concerned by the unrest in his armies brought about by constant and

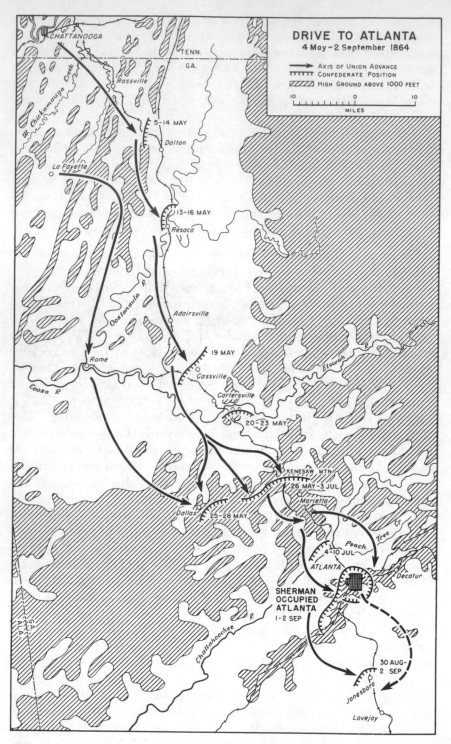

Map 32. Drive to Atlanta.

apparently fruitless marching, decided to assault Johnston at Kenesaw Mountain. This attack against prepared positions, which followed the costly failure at Cold Harbor, was beaten back. Sherman returned to maneuver and forced Johnston back to positions in front of Atlanta.

Hood replaces Johnston. Johnston had done his part well. He had accomplished his missions and had so slowed Sherman that he had covered only 100 miles in 74 days. Johnston, his forces intact, was holding strong positions in front of Atlanta, his main base. But by now Jefferson Davis had grown impatient with Johnston and his tactics of cautious delay. In July he replaced him with Maj. Gen. John B. Hood, a much more impetuous commander.

Capture of Atlanta. On 20 July, while Sherman was executing a wide turning movement around the northeast side of Atlanta, Hood left his fortifications and attacked at Peach Tree Creek. When Sherman beat him off, Hood pulled back into the city. While Sherman made ready to invest, Hood attacked again and failed again. During this action McPherson, for whom Fort McPherson, Ga., was later named, was killed; he was replaced by Maj. Gen. Oliver O. Howard. Sherman now tried cavalry raids to cut the railroads, just as Johnston had during the advance from Chattanooga, but Sherman's raids had as little success as Johnston's. Stoneman was captured during one of them. Sherman then began extending fortifications on 31 August. Hood, who had dissipated his striking power in his assaults, gave up and retired to northwest Alabama, and Sherman marched into Atlanta on 1 and 2 September.

The March to the Sea. *Strategy.* The fall of Atlanta and Hood's withdrawal raised the question of Sherman's next mission, and he proved himself an able strategist as well as a consummately bold and aggressive commander by his new proposals. Abandoning the idea of catching up with Hood, he suggested that he send two corps of about 30,000 men back to Thomas at Nashville, where Thomas would raise and train more men and be in position to hold Tennessee and deal with Hood if he came north. It was the final part of Sherman's plan that demonstrated his boldness and originality, for he proposed to employ mobility and aggressiveness to carry the offensive against the economy of the Confederacy. He recommended that he take four corps of about 62,000 men, cut his communications, live off the country, and march to the seacoast through the very heart of the Confederacy, meanwhile devastating and laying waste all farms, railways, and storehouses in his path. When he reached the coast, he reasoned, he could get to a port and make contact with U. S. naval forces. Neither Grant nor Lincoln was hidebound in thought, but their reaction to the plan was less than enthusiastic. That they accepted it at all was proof of their confidence in Sherman.

Sherman's Men Destroying Railroads, Atlanta 1864.   To destroy the rails soldiers heated them over burning ties, then twisted them with crowbars.

The march.   After destroying Atlanta's military installations—much of the city itself was burned either by accident or design—the troops set forth on 12 November and headed for Savannah, Ga. They planned to live off the country but carried a 20-day emergency supply of rations in the wagon train.   Operating on a 60-mile-wide front, they systematically burned and destroyed crops, cotton gins, cattle, railways, and storehouses as they marched along.   There was no fighting, and the march became something of a rowdy excursion.   As might be expected from troops engaged in a mission of destruction with their spirits not tempered by the presence of a Confederate army, discipline, which was never overly strong in Civil War armies, seems to have broken down.   As a consequence, in addition to the destruction carried out officially by Sherman's orders, there was a good deal of looting.   Sherman's campaign anticipated the economic warfare and strategic bombardments of the 20th century, but the victims of his ideas can hardly be blamed if they regarded Sherman's strategy as an excuse for simple thievery.

Capture of Savannah.   Sherman's army, having disappeared from Grant's view, turned up in front of Savannah on 10 December. Confederate forces evacuated the city on 21 December, and Sherman offered it as a Christmas present to the Nation.

The Nashville Campaign.   *Hood's approach.*   The two corps Sherman sent to Thomas, IV and XXII Corps, were under Schofield's command.   While they were on their way, the aggressive Hood pushed north again and with 30,000 men attacked Schofield at Frank-

270

lin, Tenn. (map 20). The battle, which opened after 1600 on 30 November and ended at dusk, was short, sharp, and furious. Schofield beat Hood off, inflicting 6,000 casualties and losing 2,300. Next day Schofield brought his men into Nashville.

Battle of Nashville. General Thomas, the Rock of Chickamauga, belonged to the last bootlace school of soldiering. In comparison with Grant and Sherman, he was slow. But he was also sure. He had collected and trained troops and horses and had made ready to attack Hood on 10 December, but a snow and sleet storm on 9 December made any movement impossible. Grant meanwhile became so impatient that he did not accept Thomas' assurances that he would strike, and soon, and decided to relieve him of command. He actually started for Nashville in person. But before he arrived the weather improved; Thomas hit Hood on 15 December and drove him back in an attack that military students have regarded as virtually faultless. He then renewed the fight and drove Hood from the field in almost complete disorder, and his cavalry carried out one of the most effective pursuits of the whole war. A scattering of Hood's men got back across the Tennessee, but his army was never again an offensive threat.

The Final Campaigns. *Strategy.* From then on the strategic problem simply resolved itself into a continuance of the operations of 1864. Grant and Meade hung on to Lee. The General in Chief and Sherman decided that the latter could accomplish more by marching overland from Savannah toward the Army of the Potomac, tearing up communications as he went, than by taking ships to Virginia. Sherman started north in January 1865. Schofield's force, unemployed after Nashville, came east by rail, took ship, and landed on Cape Fear, N. C., in March. The Confederacy was clearly about to fall.

The last battles—Five Forks. Sherman moved through Wilmington, N. C., the Confederacy's last port, in February 1865, then pushed on. Johnston, newly reappointed to a command, had the mission of stopping him, but could not. During these closing days of the war the Confederate Congress conferred supreme command of all the Confederate armies on Lee, but it was an empty honor. He could not control events. At Petersburg, toward the end of March, Grant renewed his efforts to get at Lee's right (west) flank. By now Sheridan's cavalry and the VI Corps had returned from the Shenandoah Valley, and the total force immediately under Grant numbered 101,000 infantry, 14,700 cavalry, and 9,000 artillery. Lee had 46,000 infantry, 6,000 cavalry, and 5,000 artillery. On 29 March Grant began his move to the left. Sheridan and the cavalry pushed out ahead by way of Dinwiddie Court House in order to strike at Burke's Station where the Southside and Danville Railroads intersect, while Grant's main body moved to envelop Lee's right. But Lee caught on and moved west. General Hill, who never stood on the defense if there was a chance to attack, took his corps out of its trenches and assaulted the Union left in the swampy forests around White Oak Road. He pushed General Warren's V Corps back at first, but Warren counterattacked and by 31 March had driven Hill back to his trenches. Next day Sheridan advanced to Five Forks, a road junction southwest of Petersburg, and there encountered a strong Confederate force under General Pickett—cavalry plus two infantry divisions—which Lee had dispatched to forestall Sheridan. Pickett attacked and drove Sheridan back to Dinwiddie Court House, but there Sheridan dug in and halted him. Pickett then entrenched at Five Forks instead of pulling back to make contact with Hill, whose failure to destroy Warren had left a gap between him and Pickett, with Warren's corps in between. Sheridan, still formally the commander of the Army of the Shenandoah, had authority from Grant to take control over any nearby infantry corps of the Army of the Potomac. He desired Warren to fall upon Pickett's exposed rear and destroy him. But Warren moved too slowly and Pickett consolidated his position. Next day Sheridan attacked again but failed to destroy Pickett because Warren moved his corps too slowly and put most of it in the wrong place. Sheridan, another devotee of the offensive principle who would not tolerate failure to engage the enemy, summarily relieved him of command.

Retreat and pursuit. Grant renewed his attack against Lee's right on 2 April. The assault broke the Confederate line and forced it back northward. The Federals took the line of the Southside Railroad, and the Confederates withdrew toward Petersburg. Lee then pulled Longstreet's corps away from Richmond to hold the line, and in this day's action Hill was killed. With his line stretched very thin, Lee was forced to abandon Richmond and the Petersburg fortifications. Lee struck out and raced west toward the Danville Railroad, hoping to get to Lynchburg or Danville, break loose, and eventually join forces with Johnston. But Grant had him in the open at last. He pursued relentlessly and speedily, with troops behind (east of) Lee and south of him on his left flank. And Sheridan dashed ahead with the cavalry to cut Lee off. A running fight ensued from 2 through 6 April. Ewell's corps was cut off and captured at Sailor's Creek. Lee's rations ran out; his men began deserting and straggling by the thousands. Finally, Sheridan pushed his men to Appomattox Court House, squarely athwart Lee's line of retreat. This decided the issue.

The Surrender. Lee resolved that he could accomplish nothing by more fighting. Sadly, he went to Grant. The two great leaders met at the McLean house in Appomattox on 9 April 1865. The handsome, well-tailored Lee, the very epitome of Southern chivalry, asked

Grant for terms. Reserving all political questions for his own decision, Lincoln had authorized Grant to treat only purely military matters. Grant, though physically less impressive than Lee, was equally chivalrous. He accepted Lee's surrender, allowed the Confederates to keep their horses and mules, furnished rations to the Army of Northern Virginia, and forbade the soldiers of the Army of the Potomac to cheer or fire salutes in celebration of victory over their old antagonists. Johnston surrendered to Sherman in April, after the assassination of the President. Other Confederate forces gave up the struggle, and the grim fighting was over.

Casualties. In this costly war, the Union side lost 138,154 men killed incident to battle. This figure seems huge, but is scarcely half the 221,374 who died of other causes, bringing the total Union dead to 359,528. Wounded in action were 280,040 men. Figures for the Confederacy are less exact, but at least 74,524 were killed incident to battle, 59,297 died of disease, and from 25,976 to 30,716 died in Northern prisons.

Conclusion. Although in many respects, infantry tactics for example, the Civil War was similar to those of the 18th century, it was remarkably modern in other ways: railways, telegraph, steamships, armor, rifled artillery and small arms, trenches, economic warfare—all these have a contemporary ring. And the war was vast. The armies were larger, the degree of industrial mobilization higher, the battlefields more spacious than the modern world had yet seen. For these reasons, and because its battles so well illustrate the principles of war and furnish so many excellent examples of both good and bad leadership, the Civil War furnishes a fertile field of study and reflection to the military student.

QUESTIONS

1. Explain the system of command developed by the Union in 1864-1865, and analyze the broad strategy employed by the Union.

2. Compare and contrast Grant's generalship with that of McClellan, or of Hooker.

3. Explain the reasons for Grant's decision to cross the James River and go for Petersburg in June 1864.

4. Discuss the reasons for Johnston's tactics against Sherman, May-July 1864.

5. Explain Sherman's reasons for the march from Atlanta to the seacoast.

6. Explain why the Civil War is usually regarded as the first great modern war.

Ballard, Colin R. *The Military Genius of Abraham Lincoln.* Cleveland and New York, 1952.

Blackford, William W. *War Years with Jeb Stuart.* New York, 1945.

Cleaves, Freeman. *The Rock of Chickamauga: The Life of General George H. Thomas.* Norman, Okla., 1948.

Freeman, Douglas S. *R. E. Lee: A Biography.* New York 1934–1935. 4 vols.

———————————. *Lee's Lieutenants: A Study in Command.* New York, 1942–1944. 3 vols.

Fuller, J. F. C. *The Generalship of Ulysses S. Grant.* New York, 1929.

———————————. *Grant and Lee: A Study in Personality and Generalship.* New York, 1933.

Hassler, Warren W., Jr. *General George B. McClellan: Shield of the Union.* Baton Rouge, 1957.

Harrington, Fred Harvey. *Fighting Politician: Major General N. P. Banks.* Philadelphia, 1948.

Henderson, G. F. R. *Stonewall Jackson and the American Civil War.* London and New York, 1949.

Henry, Robert Selph. *"First With the Most" Forrest.* Indianapolis, 1944.

Lewis, Lloyd. *Sherman: Fighting Prophet.* New York, 1932.

Maurice, Sir Frederick. *Statesmen and Soldiers of the Civil War: A Study of the Conduct of War.* Boston, 1926.

Mitchell, Joseph B. *Decisive Battles of the Civil War.* New York, 1955.

O'Connor, Richard. *Sheridan: The Inevitable.* Indianapolis, 1953.

Rhodes, James Ford. *History of the Civil War. 1861–1865.* New York, 1935.

Sanger, Donald Bridgman, and Thomas Robson Hay. *James Longstreet.* Baton Rouge, 1952.

Thomas, Benjamin P. *Abraham Lincoln.* New York, 1952.

Thomason, John W. *Jeb Stuart.* New York, 1930.

U. S. Army. *The Medal of Honor of the United States Army.* Washington, 1948.

Williams, Kenneth P. *Lincoln Finds a General: A Military Study of the Civil War.* New York, 1949–1952. 3 vols.

Williams, T. Harry. *Beauregard: Napoleon in Gray.* Baton Rouge, 1954.

———————————. *Lincoln and His Generals.* New York, 1952.

Wiley, Bell I. *The Life of Billy Yank: The Common Soldier of the Union.* Indianapolis, 1952.

———————————. *The Life of Johnny Reb: The Common Soldier of the Confederacy.* Indianapolis, 1943.

CHAPTER 15
1865–1898

Demobilization. The ink on the surrender document at Appomattox was scarcely dry before the people were demanding the immediate demobilization of the Union Army. Out of the 1,034,064 volunteers that remained to be mustered out on 1 May 1865, more than 800,000 had been demobilized by November. Taking into consideration the vastly increased responsibilities of the Army, General Grant proposed that a standing army of 80,000 men be maintained. The Secretary of War whittled the estimate down to a force of 50,000 which without the addition of new units could be expanded to 82,600. By September 1866 the strength of the Regular Army had dwindled to 38,545, but in the following year it climbed to 53,962, a postwar peak from which it thereafter steadily declined. In 1874 Congress set the maximum strength of the Army at 25,000, a figure which was to be maintained until the emergency brought about by the war with Spain.

Reorganization. *The War Department.* Ever since 1821, when the first Commanding General of the Army had been appointed, an anomalous situation had existed in the War Department. The Commanding General of the Army, who could not be removed before retirement except by court-martial, was responsible for the efficiency, discipline, and conduct of the troops. The Secretary of War was responsible for the administrative and technical services—he controlled the purse, and the bureau chiefs reported directly to him. Generally a civilian, with little experience in military matters and with limited tenure, the Secretary was dependent for guidance upon the bureau chiefs, especially The Adjutant General, who became very powerful inasmuch as he issued the orders. As a consequence, there was no clearly defined line of command in the War Department. The extent of the ability of the Commanding General to command the Army and perform his duties was completely dependent upon the support that he received from the President and the Secretary of War.

In order to rectify this all but impossible situation, General Grant in January 1866 proposed to Secretary of War Stanton that the Office of The Adjutant General be placed under the control of the Commanding General. Under this arrangement, the Commanding General would be responsible to the President through the Secretary of War on all Army matters. No action was taken at that time, but

275

when Grant became President in March 1869 he issued an order putting his plan into operation. However, because the order conflicted with the statutes that created the individual bureaus and aroused much opposition, it was revoked within less than a month. Throughout the rest of the period Congress constantly investigated and probed the organization of the War Department, but nothing was ever done on the various proposals to reorganize it and no further progress was made toward the creation of a true General Staff. As a result, there was no machinery that would permit the systematic preparation of war plans.

The Army. In July 1866 the peacetime strength of the Army was set at 5 regiments of artillery, 10 of cavalry, and 45 of infantry. Each artillery and cavalry regiment was composed of 12 companies, and each infantry of 10. Also, provision was made for 1,000 Indian scouts. The Army was organized into 19 territorial departments and 5 geographical divisions, but this number was to fluctuate considerably in the ensuing decades. In 1869 the number of regiments was reduced to 25. On 30 June 1878 the Regular Army consisted of 2,153 officers and 23,254 enlisted men organized into 5 regiments of artillery, 10 of cavalry, and 25 of infantry. This organization was to exist until 1898.

After the reconstruction period, most of the American Army was widely dispersed in small units along the frontier. A garrison usually consisted of one company of infantry and one of cavalry, but frequently a single company was the only protection for many miles of territory. Under such conditions there could be little uniformity within regiments. For example, in 1882 the troops of the entire 10 cavalry regiments of the Army were distributed among 55 posts in the Indian country. Maj. Gen. John M. Schofield described the military establishment thus scattered over such a vast area as a "police force and not an army". Despite its smallness and disperson, the post-Civil War Army had to perform three important missions—(1) elimination of the threat posed by the government of Emperor Maximilian in Mexico; (2) occupation of the southern states; and (3) suppression of dissident Indians and restoration of order on the Western frontier.

Maximilian and Mexico. *Background.* Through the enunciation of the Monroe Doctrine in 1823, the United States had warned the nations of Europe that it would consider an attempt to secure any part of the American continents as an unfriendly act. Napoleon III of France saw in the American Civil War an opportunity for profitable fishing in forbidden waters. In 1861, with the United States locked in strife, he seized the occasion to secure Mexico. His troops, and those of Great Britain, marched into the country with the ostensible purpose of restoring order and collecting debts owed their nationals.

The British, recognizing the imperialist design of Napoleon for what it was, withdrew. The United States protested the French action but was powerless to take a hand. Then the surrender at Appomattox completely changed the picture.

American action. As early as the middle of May 1865, General Sheridan with an army of about 50,000 men was ordered to Texas. Although he took no aggressive action, Sheridan's force posed a threat that was not lost on the Maximilian government or upon its sponsor. Finally, in 1866 the United States flatly demanded that Napoleon III recall his soldiers. In spite of the fact that the French Emperor was beset with other problems, the military power of the United States had an important bearing upon his decision to comply with this demand by withdrawing French troops in January 1867. The remaining forces of Maximilian were later defeated by the Mexicans; his government was overthrown; and he was executed. The Mexican republic under Benito Juarez was restored.

Occupation of the South. *Military government.* While Sheridan's forces were deployed along the Mexican border, other Army units were engaged in occupation duties in the South. It was not Lincoln's intention to impose a harsh and lengthy military occupation on the South, and if he had lived it is likely that reconstruction would have followed a different course. Before the termination of hostilities, the President had laid out a moderate program. After Lincoln's death, President Andrew Johnson endeavored to follow his policies. He appointed civil governors over the states that had lately been in rebellion. When Congress assembled in December 1865, most of these states had accepted Johnson's program, had completed their civil government, and were in readiness for readmission to the Union. But Congress was not pleased. The members felt that the Chief Executive had usurped powers that rightly belonged to Congress. In various pieces of legislation they undid all that had been done and placed the South under military control.

The period of reconstruction in the South can be broken into two distinct phases. During the first, which lasted until 1870, the South was under military government. Ten of the former Confederate states were divided into five military districts, each commanded by a major-general. During the second phase, in which civil control was restored, the Army was used to maintain law and order and to uphold the civil authority. In 1877 occupation responsibilities were terminated, and Army troops remaining in the South performed the usual garrison duties.

The Freedmen's Bureau. One of the least-wanted tasks given the Army was the administration of the Freedmen's Bureau created by Congress on 3 March 1865. Later granted very wide powers, the Bureau was originally designed to help former slaves adjust to a life of freedom. It furnished food and clothing to needy Negroes and helped them find employment. It secured homesteads for the Negroes on public lands, protected their rights on labor contracts, established schools and hospitals for them, and protected their civil rights in unfriendly Southern communities. The commissioner of the Freedmen's Bureau was Maj. Gen. Oliver O. Howard, who divided the South into 10 districts, each with an assistant commissioner in charge. A considerable number of Army officers were employed by the Bureau to carry out its assigned task.

The Indian Wars. The third important mission confronting the Army in the decades after the Civil War was the protection of the white settlers that were thronging to the trans-Mississippi West as the railroad steadily pushed its way through the hostile Indian country (map 33). From 1865 to 1891 there were 13 different campaigns and at least 1,067 separate engagements with the Indians. The principal tribes involved were the Comanches, Modocs, Apaches, Northern Cheyenne, Sioux, Nez Perce, Bannocks, Piutes, and Utes.

In 1849 the administration of Indian affairs had been taken away from the War Department and entrusted to the Department of the

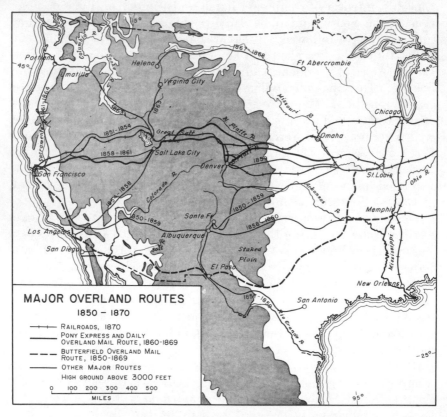

Map 33. Major overland routes, 1850–1870.

Interior, whose agents either were inexperienced in the administration of Indian affairs or deliberately cheated their charges. Even under conditions of hostility, these agents furnished Indians with the latest models of repeating rifles and plenty of ammunition, either because it was financially profitable to do so or because they naively believed that the Indians wanted the weapons only to kill buffalo.

Only after the work of the Indian agent had failed and the Indians were on the warpath was the Army called in. A campaign against the Indians was an unpleasant assignment: the press was apt to be deeply critical of the Army whether it won or not; the requisite campaigning resulted in a very high percentage of deaths and permanent maiming not only as a direct result of the fighting but also from many nonbattle causes such as freezing and sunstroke; and a campaign meant long absences from the small pleasures of post life and from families who had to remain behind in the dangerously undermanned forts.

The Army wanted authority over the Indian agencies because it believed it could remove abuses and establish controls that would keep the Indians confined to their reservations and thus eliminate the necessity for costly and arduous campaigns. There were many honest and able administrators in the Army. For example, Maj. Gen. George Crook during a few years of Army administration gave the Southwest peace from Apache depredations. Crook was impartial, resourceful, and courageous; he possessed initiative and looked out for the welfare of his men and animals. His word, once given, could be depended upon. The Indians recognized Army officers as stern but eminently just men, unlike many United States citizens who did not hesitate to break treaties that guaranteed the Indians certain lands.

The major difficulty with the Indians resulted from the fact that they belonged to tribes with quasi-sovereign rights and could not be dealt with as individuals. All too often when some members of a tribe went on the warpath or committed acts which the white men considered crimes, the practice was to call on the Army. This, in turn resulted in a campaign against an entire tribe, guilty and innocent alike. There was no legal armed force except the Army to oppose hostile Indian bands, and the Army had no power to act except in compliance with orders from higher authorities. It was not until the passage of the Dawes Act in 1887 that a firm Indian policy was established. Under the provisions of this act, the tribes were dissolved as legal entities and the tribal lands distributed among the constituent members. This act resolved one of the great causes of Indian unrest.

The Indians. There were about 250,000 Indians in the Rocky Mountain regions and the Great Plains directly in the path of the white westward expansion. About 175,000 of them were organized in 99 tribes between the Rockies and the Mississippi River. Each of the plains area tribes was loosely organized into 4 to 12 warrior societies of varying rank, strength, and prominence.

The tribes set great store by bravery and warlike attributes. From earliest youth, the male Indian was trained to be a warrior; he was taught to endure hardship and pain unflinchingly and how to use his weapons—rifle, bow and arrow, knife, and tomahawk. In addition, his horsemanship was magnificent. The Army officers against whom the Indian fought were generous in their praise of his fine soldiership and tactics.

Army tactics. The Army employed various tactics during the Indian Wars to achieve victory. One tactic frequently employed was that of converging columns. General Crook, however, found that converging columns never seemed able to entrap the extremely fast and elusive Apache bands. He therefore organized small, fast-moving columns of selected soldiers under orders never to give up the trail. His successor, Brig. Gen. Nelson A. Miles, had better success with converging columns.

Another tactic employed was that of intersecting the trail, or the supposed trail, of the hostile tribesmen. During the Nez Perces Campaign Generals Howard and Miles, Col. John Gibbon, Col. Samuel D. Sturgis, and others all tried unsuccessfully to intersect the 1,600-mile trail of Chief Joseph and cut him off.

During this period the tactics of both mounted and dismounted troops were changed. In dismounted tactics the number of ranks in fighting formations was reduced to two, and in mounted tactics to one. Movements, especially those of the cavalry, were thus greatly simplified, since formations could quickly be changed by wheeling by twos or fours. With the companies of the period greatly under-strength, this change was especially applicable to Indian fighting.

Frequently the troops would close in on an unsuspecting village during the night and then attack at dawn, preferably from several directions in order to cut off all the escape routes of the Indians. Although this method of attack was generally successful, there was danger that a large enemy force could defeat one Army force after another, especially when the several elements could not communicate with each other or were beyond supporting distance.

The Indian campaigns—1862. After a Sioux uprising in Minnesota in 1862 had been suppressed, most of the Sioux nation moved westward into the Dakotas. Col. Andrew Carrington, 18th Infantry, in 1866 built and garrisoned posts on the Bozeman trail, which led through the Sioux country toward the gold mines of Montana in the vicinity of Virginia City (map 34). The Indians vigorously protested the encroachments and harassed the new garrisons. On 21 December

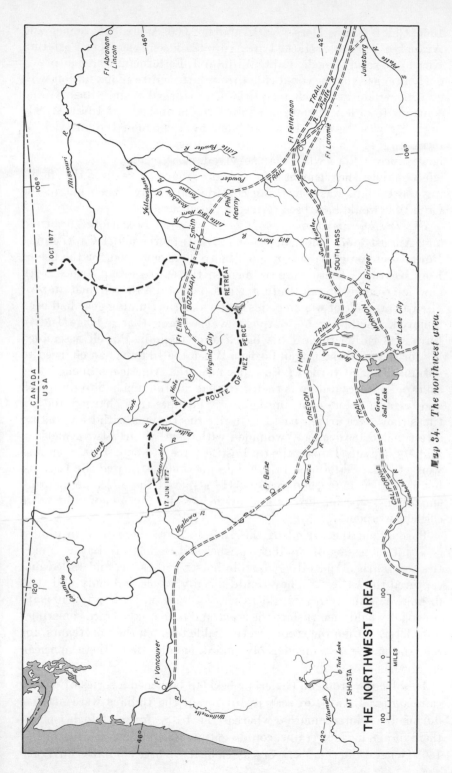

Map 34. The northwest area.

THE NORTHWEST AREA

MILES
100   0   100

1866 Chief Crazy Horse, with about 2,000 Sioux, Cheyenne, and Arapahoe warriors, attacked an Army train sent out from Fort Phil Kearny to secure wood. Capt. William J. Fetterman, who had previously bragged that he could ride through the entire Sioux nation with 80 men, was ordered out to relieve the besieged train. Rashly, and contrary to orders, he moved against the main body of Indians. He probably was drawn into an ambush by a common Indian trick of retreating with a small body into a killing ground surrounded by a larger force. Not a white man survived. The incident had a sobering effect on the rasher elements of the Army; they now realized that fighting the Indians was something considerably more than what in the Civil War would have been termed a patrol action.

The Indian campaigns—1867. The "Wagon Box Fight" occurred on 2 August 1867. Elements of the 27th Infantry under Capt. James Powell were on guard as some of the soldiers cut wood for the use of Fort Kearny. There were 32 men in the entire group armed with new long-range breech-loading rifles. Captain Powell had improvised a barricade of wagon beds from which the running gear had been removed. Suddenly his outposts warned him that a large Indian force was riding toward his barricade. Captain Powell assembled his force behind the wagon boxes. When the Indians had charged to within about 50 yards of Powell's men, the Americans opened fire. So rapid and accurate was their fire that the Indians had to pull back and re-form before charging again. Six times they charged and six times they were driven back. Finally the Indians withdrew, taking an estimated 180 dead and wounded with them. Thirty-two American soldiers had stood up against a hostile force of about 1,500 men and won. Unlike Fetterman, Powell had not underestimated the Indians, but was dismounted and ready. He achieved the effect of mass by employing superior fire power made possible by a new and more efficient weapon.

Throughout the period of the Indian Wars there was an almost constant succession of small skirmishes and raids by Indian war parties that burned and pillaged, stole horses and cattle, and killed and captured the settlers. They would usually attack suddenly and then disappear. The Army would learn of a raid only after it had happened; it would then rush to the scene and take up the trail, sometimes days later. Often the troops were unable to catch the miscreants, for the Indians were considerably more mobile than the American cavalrymen.

To solve the problem, General Sheridan launched a series of winter campaigns. Because of scarcity of forage the Indians were inactive during the winter months, whereas the U. S. forces, which carried their forage in their trains, could continue operations. In the fall of 1868 General Sheridan's troops assembled. Three columns converged

"Wagon Box Fight," near Fort Phil Kearny, Wyo., 2 August 1867.

on the Cheyennes, Arapahoes, and Kiowas in the upper Arkansas region with the purpose of driving them back to their reservations. This was accomplished partly by successful operations and partly by a threat to kill two Kiowa chiefs who had been held as hostages.

The Indian campaigns 1872–1873. The Indian raids continued for several years more. In 1872 a campaign was launched against the Modocs on the Pacific coast. The Modocs had been removed from their lands and placed on the same reservation as the Klamaths, their enemies. Being stronger, the Klamaths bullied the Modocs and in general made life intolerable for them. As a consequence, the Modocs quit the reservation and went back to their tribal lands, only to be expelled by the white settlers. The Modocs refused to obey the order of the Indian agent to return to the Klamath reservation.

The commanding officer of the Department of the Columbia, Brig. Gen. Edward R. S. Canby, was a friend of the Indians; he wished to settle the matter by placing the Modocs on a separate reservation. However, the Commissioner of Indian Affairs insisted that the Army disarm the Modocs and return them to their old reservation. Capt. James Jackson with Company B, 1st Cavalry, received the assignment. At dawn on 29 November 1872 his troops surrounded the Indian band under its chief, Captain Jack. The Modocs surrendered a few old muzzle-loaders, but, when an attempt was made to arrest the leaders, pistol-firing broke out. Each side suffered a few casualties. The Indians withdrew into the easily defensible lava beds east of Mount Shasta, where they were reinforced to a strength of about 120 men. Well-armed and provisioned from caches they had stored there the entrenched Modocs successfully resisted an attack by a hastily organized force of about 400 men—half Regulars and half civilians.

Contrary to the recommendation of General Canby, the Indian

Bureau appointed a peace commission with Canby as its head. Because of mutual distrust and suspicion, the commission did not meet with Captain Jack and his party until April 1873. The Indians came armed; General Canby and another commissioner were killed.

Brig. Gen. Jefferson C. Davis, who succeeded General Canby as departmental commander, renewed the campaign. Mortar fire delivered by crews from the 4th Artillery drove the Indians away from their water supply, Tule Lake. The Indians were defeated, and on the first day of June 1873 the last of the Modocs surrendered. This time the earlier recommendations of General Canby were followed, and the Modocs were given a new reservation.

The Indian campaigns—Battle of Little Big Horn. The next important campaign was against the Sioux and Cheyenne. In November 1875 the Indian Inspector reported to the Commissioner of Indian Affairs that these Indians were getting out of hand and recommended that they be sent back to their reservations. When they refused to return, it became necessary for the Army to take action. In February 1876 General Sheridan planned an attack employing three converging columns—south, west, and east under General Crook and Colonels Gibbon and Custer respectively. Gibbon and Custer were under the command of Brig. Gen. Alfred H. Terry, the commander of the Department of the Dakotas. General Crook was in command of the Department of the Platte.

In late February 1876 General Crook concentrated 10 troops from the 2d and 3d Cavalry and 2 companies of the 4th Infantry at Fort Fetterman, and on 1 March moved out toward the Powder River. During the night the cavalry, under Col. Joseph J. Reynolds, preceding Crook's column, located a Cheyenne village near the mouth of the Little Powder River. At dawn Reynold's force attacked from three directions, driving the Indians out, destroying over 100 lodges with ammunition stores, and capturing a large band of ponies, before the Cheyennes recovered from their initial surprise and fought back. By then the troopers were suffering greatly in the extreme cold, having removed their heavier clothing. Colonel Reynolds suddenly ordered a withdrawal leaving behind his dead and, it is alleged, one wounded. The Indians pursued, harassing the troops, and during the night recaptured their ponies. General Crook arrived shortly after, but because of the inclement weather, the defeat of Reynolds, and the encumbrance of 6 wounded and 66 frost-bitten men, he was forced to return to his fort.

In the meantime General Terry had not moved out, having been held back by the severity of the weather and the necessity of assembling the 7th Cavalry. Not until the latter part of May did General Crook again move out from Fort Fetterman, this time with 15 companies of cavalry and 5 companies of infantry. He reached the Tongue River, where he left his trains, and then moved to and across the

Rosebud. On 17 June he encountered a Sioux–Cheyenne force of about 1,500 under Chief Crazy Horse. The fight was indecisive; 11 dead Indians were found on the field, and Crook lost 9 killed and 21 wounded. General Crook then returned to his trains and awaited supplies and reinforcement. Meanwhile, the two columns under General Terry had finally started. Colonel Gibbon with 450 men—6 companies of infantry and 4 companies of cavalry—marched east from Fort Ellis in Montana along the north bank of the Yellowstone River to the mouth of the Big Horn where General Terry ordered him to halt.

A larger force of about 12 companies of cavalry and 6 companies of infantry moved out of Fort Abraham Lincoln and on 7 June established a supply camp at the confluence of the Powder and Yellowstone Rivers. A six-company reconnaissance party under Maj. Marcus A. Reno found a heavily traveled Indian trail that led south along the Rosebud and then west across the mountains apparently toward the Little Big Horn River.

With this information General Terry outlined a plan in a meeting at the mouth of the Rosebud. Colonel Custer was to take all of the 7th Cavalry and follow the trail found by the reconnaissance party. If he found that the trail led to the Little Big Horn, Custer was not to follow it but was to sidestep south in order to prevent the Indians from escaping around his left and give the slower-moving infantry under Colonel Gibbon more time to move up. General Terry was to join Colonel Gibbon's force and move south along the Big Horn to a junction with Custer at some point on the Little Big Horn

Custer followed the Indian trail up the Rosebud for about 20 miles and found that it did lead to the Little Big Horn River. For some unknown reason he did not then sidestep south according to plan. Instead, he continued toward the Little Big Horn, where he found a large Indian encampment with an estimated strength of 2,500 warriors. Disregarding the principles of mass, maneuver, and security, he attacked alone over unfamiliar terrain, not knowing the strength of the Indian party or General Crook's action on the Rosebud eight days earlier. In addition, Custer separated his attacking force into three battalions, each beyond supporting distance of the other. Major Reno with three companies was sent into the valley at the point where the trail met the river. Custer was to attempt to enter the valley about three miles lower down. Capt. Frederick W. Benteen was to scout the country to the left.

Reno's three companies forded the river, dismounted, and fought on foot. Overwhelmed by numbers, they were forced to withdraw back over the river and take a position on the high bluffs overlooking it. Here Reno was joined by Captain Benteen, who with three companies had been about two miles to the left of Reno when the fight started and had been ordered by Custer to return. When he came to the river,

Benteen, seeing it would be impossible to force a crossing because of the large number of Indians blocking the way, joined Reno's hard-pressed force on the bluffs. They were soon surrounded by an over-whelming Indian force that took up a commanding position overlook-ing the troops. A bitter fight ensued in which the cavalry suffered severe casualties. Upon the approach of General Terry and Colonel Gibbon, the Indians withdrew.

The movements of Custer and his five companies of cavalry are shrouded in mystery. All that is definitely known is that the entire command moved into an ambush, dismounted, and was destroyed by the Indians. A single horse, Comanche, survived and, for the rest of his days, appeared saddled but riderless at all 7th Cavalry parades.

The Indians had secured a resounding victory over the U. S. Army almost without parallel in Army history. Custer's violation of the principles of maneuver and security had cost dearly.

It was imperative that the U. S. Army immediately take steps to rectify the situation. All posts in the military division of the Missouri were stripped for reinforcements, 24 companies of artillery were re-equipped as infantry, Generals Terry and Crook were reinforced, and the Indians on the Sioux reservations were disarmed and dismounted. General Sheridan then launched a series of expeditions that lasted through that winter and the next. Most of the Sioux were driven back into their reservations, but a small group under Chief Sitting Bull fled to Canada. At this time Congress authorized an increase of cavalry but at the expense of the other arms—2,500 cavalrymen could be added but the total strength of the Army was not to exceed the authorized strength of 25,000.

The Indian campaigns—1877. In the summer of 1877 a campaign was launched against the Nez Perce Indians, a hitherto peaceful tribe. Angered by being forced out of the Wallowa Valley and by the murder of their chief's brother, a group of the Nez Perces raided a white set-tlement and killed 20 settlers. Although Chief Joseph had counseled peace with the white men, he saw that war was inevitable and joined his tribesmen. The Nez Perces were well trained and disciplined, and Chief Joseph was an excellent tactician. An Army force of over 90 men, sent out to bring the recalcitrant tribesmen back to the reserva-tion, ran into a well-planned ambush in White Bird Canyon to the east of the Wallowa Valley and was routed.

General Howard, the commander of the Department of the Colum-bia, then took the field with a force of about 400 men from the infantry, cavalry, and artillery. He caught up with the Indians at the Clear-water River on 11 July 1877. In the engagement that ensued Chief Joseph and his men, though they fought well, were forced back over the river. Moving east over the Lolo Trail, they encountered a trail-block of about 140 soldiers and civilians. Chief Joseph, using trails unknown to the whites, managed to evade the block and proceeded south along the Bitter Root River, leaving Howard's force far behind. At the Big Hole Basin, Chief Joseph rested his tribe, thinking he had outdistanced the Army. Colonel Gibbon, however, alerted by telegraph, moved in with six infantry companies and some volunteers—a total force of about 200 men. At dawn Gibbon attacked the unguarded camp from three directions and took it within 20 minutes. Chief Joseph, displaying remarkable energy and ability, rallied his warriors for a counterattack and soon had his adversaries on the defensive. For three days the Indians besieged Gibbon and his men, who were saved by the arrival of General Howard. Chief Joseph and his band escaped.

Though other engagements were fought as General Howard continued his pursuit, the end was in sight. At dawn on 30 September 1877 Col. Nelson A. Miles with 6 companies of infantry, 5 cavalry companies, and 2 field guns attacked Chief Joseph's camp in the Bear Paw Mountains. Though surprised, the Indians soon recovered and dug in. On 4 October, after a four-day battle, Chief Joseph and the remnants of his band surrendered. In 11 weeks, he had moved his tribe 1,600 miles, engaged 10 separate U. S. commands in 13 battles and skirmishes, and in nearly every instance had either defeated them or fought them to a standstill. General Sherman rightly termed the struggle "one of the most extraordinary Indian Wars of which there is any record".

The Indian campaigns in the Southwest. Other equally arduous campaigns were in the meantime being undertaken against the Apache Indians in the Southwest. This tribe was notorious for extreme cruelty as well as for cunning and endurance. Bitter warfare had long existed between the Apaches and the white settlers, neither of whom gave or asked for quarter.

In 1871 Colonel Crook assumed command of the Department of Arizona. His policies for dealing with Indians on the warpath and for administering the Indian reservations were very successful. He used Apache Indians as scouts, issued strict instructions that a column in pursuit must never give up an Indian trail, and strongly emphasized the use, care, and training of mule pack transport. The troops were trained by long conditioning marches and longer reconnaissances.

In 1874, when Crook was ordered north, Arizona was at peace. The Indian Bureau took over the reservations and started to concentrate the Indians, a process that stirred them up and caused trouble. The Apache chiefs, Victorio, Geronimo, and others, started to shuttle back and forth across the international boundary between the United States and Mexico and committed many depredations. The Army sent out numerous punitive expeditions, but nothing decisive was achieved as long as the American troops had to stay on their side of the border. In 1880 Victorio was captured and killed by the Mexicans on their side of the border. Two years later a treaty was signed by the American

Three American Cavalrymen in their last stand against the Indians.

and Mexican Governments permitting troops of either country to cross over the boundary in unpopulated regions when in hot pursuit.

General Crook, in the Southwest again after his Sioux campaigns, decided to take advantage of the treaty to punish the Apache Chato, who had been actively raiding up and down the border. In May 1882 a cavalry troop started out in pursuit and located Chato's camp 200 miles south of the border. Although the troop was unable to capture the camp, the Apaches decided that they had had enough. Geronimo, Chato, and the other chiefs surrendered and returned to their reservation in southeastern Arizona. The administrators of this reservation were Army officers, who kept the Indians quiet for two years.

In May 1885, when the reservation was again under control of the Indian Bureau, Geronimo and his tribesmen slipped off the reservation. Twenty troops of cavalry moved toward the border in a fruitless effort to intercept the Apaches. The pursuit continued into Mexico, and in January 1886 Capt. Emmet Crawford with 80 Apache scouts located and attacked the principal hostile camp about 200 miles south of the border. He forced the Indians to agree to parley, but an unexpected attack by Mexican irregulars killed Crawford and the negotiations were delayed. Later, at a conference near the border with General Crook, Geronimo agreed to surrender if certain conditions were granted. Crook acquiesced. Shortly thereafter Geronimo broke his pledge and disappeared with some of his band into the Sierra Madres.

General Sheridan, who did not like the terms to which General Crook had agreed, held that the flight of Geronimo negated the agreement with those Apaches who remained. Crook, who felt that he had given his word, asked to be relieved and was succeeded by General Miles.

Maj. Gen. Nelson A. Miles.　　　　　*Maj. Gen. George Crook.*

Miles set up a system of observation posts located on high peaks, connected by heliograph, and covering the critical area. He then sent small, mobile columns into Mexico. One of these, under Capt. Henry W. Lawton, pursued Geronimo more than 2,000 miles and deep into Mexico. In two skirmishes Lawton captured much of Geronimo's ammunition and supplies, and many of his horses, though the Indians themselves escaped. Finally Lt. Charles B. Gatewood, who was highly respected by the Apaches, secured the surrender of Geronimo by going almost alone to the chief's camp and persuading the Indians to come in and hold a surrender conference with General Miles.

In the winter of 1889–90 the preachings of an Indian mystic in Nevada threatened to start a general Indian war. The Sioux were particularly influenced, for they had long been dissatisfied. They streamed off their reservation into the Bad Lands by the hundreds. About half of the U. S. Army went after them. The large number of troops employed left the Indians little alternative but to return to their reservations, and in January 1891 the danger subsided. This was the last of the Indian Wars.

The Indian Wars gave the Army a rich tradition and a heritage that was to contribute much to its *esprit de corps*. They left the Army lean and hard and provided excellent training for the junior officers who were to lead it in the coming years.

Measures for Improving the Army. *The manuals.* In 1867 the War Department adopted Lt. Col. Emory Upton's manual, *Infantry Tactics*, as a basis for training the infantry. The new system prescribed a much simpler and more efficient type of drill, which a recruit could learn in a much shorter period of time than it took him to master the one previously in use. The cavalry later adopted this manual for the training of its troopers.

Schools. During this period great advances were made in the professional education of the officers and men in the art and science of warfare. In the middle of July 1866 Congress, recognizing the Military Academy's broadening military responsibilities outside the field of engineering, specified that the superintendent of the Military Academy, who had previously been an engineer, could come from any branch of the service. West Point thereafter changed from a strictly scientific school to one of general education and training for all branches of the Army.

In the latter part of 1867 General Grant reestablished the Artillery School at Fort Monroe. Two years later a Light Battery School was opened at Fort Riley, Kans., but it was discontinued in 1871 because of the Indian Wars. It reopened in 1892 as the School for Cavalry and Light Artillery. In 1868 an officer from each of the territorial departments was sent to Washington to secure signal instruction from the Chief Signal Officer; the curriculum was later broadened to include courses in meteorology. An event of far-reaching importance was the establishment of the School of Application for Infantry and Cavalry at Fort Leavenworth, Kans., in 1881. This school was the precursor of the Command and General Staff College. Students at that school pursued a two-year course of instruction. When the scope of instruction at the Military Academy was enlarged, a new school was established in 1885 for the education of the engineers. This school at Willets Point, N. Y., was officially designated the Engineer School of Application.

Congress in 1866 passed an act that required all permanent camps or garrisons to maintain schools for enlisted men. In 1894 an important step forward was made when it was required that henceforward all recruits would have to be able to read and write.

Military instruction in the colleges. The outbreak of the Civil War brought to a head the idea of introducing military instruction into certain tax-supported colleges. The Morrill Act, approved on 2 July 1862, granted public lands for the establishment of colleges and provided that military tactics should be a part of the curriculum of these colleges. In October 1865, the War Department first authorized an Army officer to accept a professorship of Military Science and Tactics. In the years that followed the number of officers so detailed steadily increased, until in 1893 there were 79 colleges and universities giving military instruction. In that year, a recommendation of the Secretary of War that military instruction be extended to the high schools of the large cities was adopted.

Commissioned personnel. Following the Civil War many officers, who had received brevet promotions considerably higher than they held in the Regular Army, reverted to their peacetime ranks. Although these officers retained their brevet commissions it was without additional compensation. Promotion was very slow and the Army stagnated. Certain Army officers themselves were the first to realize the need for improvement. Among the measures they sponsored was the establishment of the service journals beginning in 1878. Since then the journals have had an important professional impact upon the military profession.

Taking cognizance of the situation, the War Department issued orders establishing a Bureau of Information in the Adjutant General's office, which became the predecessor of the Military Intelligence Division of the General Staff, ordered the establishment of post schools or lyceums throughout the Army, and instituted an annual efficiency report for all officers to facilitate the elimination of the inefficient and to facilitate the selection of qualified officers for preferred assignments.

Still later Congress took a hand in the matter by requiring examinations for promotion, by making retirement mandatory for all officers at the age of 64, and by authorizing a liberal allowance for shipment of professional books.

All of these innovations had a salutary effect upon the officer corps and represent the beginning of many changes that were to take place in later periods for the improvement of the Army.

The National Guard. At the close of the Civil War, the militia of the states had sunk to a very low point and it was difficult to obtain recruits. By 1868, however, many of the officers who had served with distinction in the war again interested themselves in the militia of the several states. The militia soon showed a marked improvement in discipline and training, and inefficient organizations were disbanded. Public interest began to revive as the states recognized their responsibility for the proper arming and equipping of their militia.

As a consequence of property losses sustained by Pennsylvania in riots in Pittsburgh, that state completely reorganized its National Guard and modeled it after the Regular Army. Many of the other states followed suit. In this period, Connecticut was the first state to organize camps of instruction. By the 1880's practically all of the states had established camps of instruction for their National Guardsmen.

Technological developments. The Civil War was the last war in which the muzzle-loading rifle was used to any great extent. As early as January 1866, a board of officers recommended that breechloaders be adopted. By the end of 1867, 50,000 Civil War rifles had been converted to breechloaders. There were other changes which culminated in the adoption of the famous breechloader—the Springfield, Model 1873. The new rifle—55 inches long, 4 inches shorter than its predecessor—had a greater muzzle velocity and range. Its greatest deficiency was that it was a single shot. Although the troops on the plains complained that their Indian adversaries had repeaters, the Army was slow in making any change. It was not until 1892 that it adopted a repeating rifle, the Danish Krag-Jorgensen, which held five cartridges. The Krag cartridge was the first adopted by the Army that used smokeless powder. During this period the modern machine gun, which later was to revolutionize warfare, was invented by Hiram Maxim. The United States Army experimented with this weapon as early as 1888.

As a result of the Franco-Prussian War, the nations of the world, including the United States, adopted a breech-loading cannon. The effect was to accelerate the rate of fire which could be attained by the artillery. Although the United States adopted breechloaders in 1881, muzzle-loaders were still issued as late as the turn of the century. The normal artillery gunnery practice in this period was direct fire—that is, fire at a target visible to the gun crew. Indirect fire did not become the normal practice until the early years of the 20th century.

Civil Functions of the Army. The Army in the years between the Civil and Spanish-American Wars was a major factor in the building up of the Nation. Its civil duties were not only numerous and varied but also generally unheralded and unsung.

The Army in Alaska. The United States purchased Alaska from Russia by the Treaty of 30 March 1867, and the Army was sent there to establish a military occupation, or to act as a temporary caretaker, until Congress provided some form of civil government. As events turned out, the Army remained in charge of the territory for 10 years. During this period the Army explored the country, set up several posts, maintained law and order, and regulated the affairs of the native population. In June 1877 the last of the troops were withdrawn, and military control over the territory ceased. For the next 20 years there were no troops in Alaska except for exploring parties.

Civil functions. It is impossible to enumerate the many and varied peacetime assignments of the Army in this period. In the year 1872 alone, the Army Engineers were engaged in coastal fortifications; river and harbor improvements and the surveys for them; the protection of the navigable waters of the United States; the geodetic and hydrographic survey of the Great Lakes; surveys for the defense of the coasts; military surveys into the interior; geographical and geological explorations; construction of public buildings and grounds in the District of Columbia (in this period the Army completed many public buildings including the Capitol, the Washington Monument, and the State, War and Navy Building); the construction of lighthouses; and the demarcation of the boundary between the United States and Canada. The Army maintained a vast network of meteorological stations scattered throughout the country for the securing and distribution of the latest information on the weather. In the tremendous expansion of the railroads after the Civil War, the Army played an important role. Many of the engineers who superintended the construction of the trans-Mississippi railroads were former Army officers.

Summary. At the end of the Civil War, the United States had one of the largest and most efficient armies in the world. Even though the volunteers were soon discharged and the Regular Army was sharply reduced, the potential power of the United States was sufficient to compel the French Emperor to abandon his support of the Maximilian government in Mexico. During most of this period, the Regular Army numbered around 25,000 men. Although small numerically, it was always in excellent condition because of the training and experience gained in the Indian Wars.

This period witnessed a great renaissance in the training of both officers and men. The Military Academy continued to be the fundamental school for officers of all of the services, and additional schools were established for the advanced training of officers in their fields of specialization. At the same time, the education of the enlisted men was not neglected. Progress was made in providing the troops with modern weapons but much remained to be done.

The Army made many substantial contributions to the civil aspects of the American economy. The explorations, surveys, and works on the rivers and harbors and the railroads were of first importance, the beneficial effects of which are still being felt.

There was, however, a dark side of the picture. Because of the smallness of the Army and its wide dispersal, most of the officers had had no training in the handling of units even as large as a regiment. There were a few veterans of the Civil War in the Army but these were advanced in years. Moreover, the power and insularity of the bureau chiefs stifled all initiative. Under such a system, no effective plans could be made for war and mobilization. The archaic organization of the War Department was to demonstrate its complete inefficiency in the war that was soon to follow.

QUESTIONS

1. Discuss the significance of American military power with respect to the dispute with France over Maximilian's Mexican Empire.

2. Trace the development of the ROTC from the passage of the Morrill Act of 1862.

3. Show how the violation of the principles of war resulted in the disaster at Little Big Horn.

4. Compare the tactics of the Indians with those of the U. S. Army.

5. Discuss the effects of the growth of bureaucracy on the development of the U. S. Army.

6. What military advances, technical and professional, were made between 1865–98?

Reading List

Downey, Fairfax. *Indian-Fighting Army.* New York, 1944.

Fee, Chester Anders. *Chief Joseph: The Biography of a Great Indian.* New York, 1936.

Howard, O. O. *My Life and Experiences Among Our Hostile Indians.* Hartford, 1917.

Randall, James A. *Civil War and Reconstruction.* New York, 1937.

Rister, Carl Coke. *Border Command, General Phil Sheridan in the West.* Norman, 1944.

Schmidt, M. F. and D. Brown. *Fighting Indians of the West.* New York, 1948.

Sheridan, Philip H. *Personal Memoirs.* New York, 1888. 2 vols.

Stewart, Edgar I. *Custer's Luck.* Norman, 1955.

Wellman, Paul I. *Indian Wars of the West.* New York, 1953.

CHAPTER 16

THE WAR WITH SPAIN—THE PHILIPPINE INSURRECTION—THE CHINA RELIEF EXPEDITION

Introduction. Few periods in American history have witnessed a greater and more significant change of direction in national policy than the one around the turn of the century. The United States entered it still provincial in thought and policies and emerged a world power. With the disappearance of the frontier (officially in the 1890 census) the energy that had gone into westward expansion sought new outlets. Most of it went into industrial and internal development, but enough was left over for ventures beyond the sea.

The Pacific. In 1884 the United States acquired a coaling and naval maintenance station at Pearl Harbor in Hawaii. Later when the Hawaiian queen, Liliuokalani, sought to reorganize her government and end the concession, local Americans with the support of a naval force set up a provisional government and negotiated a treaty of annexation with the United States. But for the objections of President Grover Cleveland, who opposed the use of high-handed methods in international affairs, Hawaii would have been annexed in 1893 instead of 1898 during the Spanish-American War. The year 1889 saw the assertion of American interest in the Samoan Islands after a local uprising involving a pro-German faction. The firm stand taken by the United States in the dispute prevented the immediate partition of the islands and led to a tripartite agreement between England, Germany, and the United States which recognized the independence of the islands but placed the real authority in the hands of officials chosen by the three powers. Ten years later the United States joined Germany in partitioning the islands, the American share being the island of Tutuila.

The Caribbean. Of more immediate concern to most Americans was the area in and around the Caribbean. No other region, with the possible exception of Canada, was as vital to the future of the United States. It was awareness of this fact that led Richard Olney, Secretary of State under Cleveland, to reassert the Monroe Doctrine in a dispute between England and Venezuela over the boundary of British Guiana in 1895. His position—and particularly the strong language in which it was stated—shocked the British and other Europeans as well, but it received almost unanimous support from the American people. Their reaction indicated that they sensed the strategic importance of the Caribbean area and were ready to make its problems their own.

Insurrection in Cuba. This feeling was demonstrated to an even greater degree when an insurrection broke out in the island of Cuba in 1895, incited and kept alive in part by a Cuban Junta operating in the United States. The American people, normally sympathetic to the aspirations of colonials for independence, favored the insurgent cause, but the administration at first maintained strict neutrality. Sympathy for the Cubans mounted when Spain adopted stern measures to deal with the revolt. In January 1896, the Spanish Government sent Gen. Valeriano Weyler to the island as successor to the conciliatory governor and commander in chief, Gen. Martinez Campos. The new Governor was a man of entirely different stamp. He met the depredations and terroristic methods of the insurgents by introducing his harsh reconcentration system. Under it, noncombatants (men, women, and children) were herded into concentration camps and garrisoned towns and prohibited from leaving them under pain of death and forfeiture of property. Without sufficient supplies to keep them alive, they perished miserably by the thousands. The policy of meeting terrorism with ruthlessness further alienated American public opinion. Unscrupulous newspapers in the United States seized upon the sad conditions in Cuba to inflame public opinion and increase their circulations. The Spanish commander was universally called "Butcher" Weyler, while the Cuban insurgents were portrayed as high-minded patriots struggling for freedom from the Spanish yoke. Politicians, anxious to ride the wave of popular emotion, joined the parade, vying with each other in denouncing Spanish decadence and brutality, and demanding intervention. A few saw in the crisis an opportunity for the United States, not only to acquire outposts and naval bases in the Caribbean, but also to play a bigger role in world politics. While Cleveland was President the demands for intervention and war with Spain made little headway. His successor, William McKinley, also opposed war, but his ambiguous policy and lack of firmness enabled the advocates of war to determine the course of events.

The De Lome letter. Their success was made easier by two events that took place early in 1898. The first was the publication of a private letter written by Dupuy de Lome, the Spanish Minister to the United States. This letter, purloined from the Post Office in Havana, characterized President McKinley as "a weakling . . . a bidder for the admiration of the crowd" and "a would-be politician who tries to leave a door open behind him while keeping on good terms with the jingoes of his own party." Public indigation in the United States ran high over the affront to the President, which the speedy resignation of De Lome did little to calm. It was viewed as a national insult.

The sinking of the Maine. The other incident was the sinking of the *Maine* in Havana harbor after an explosion which ripped the vessel apart and killed 260 members of the crew. Although the cause of the disaster was never definitely established, there was little doubt in the minds of most Americans that Spanish treachery was responsible. Newspapers the country over demanded war and the country rang with the cry, "Remember the Maine", and the tune, "There'll Be a Hot Time in the Old Town Tonight".

The Spanish-American War. *The outbreak of war.* Caught in a storm of public emotion which it had done little to combat, the administration made weak, last minute efforts to avert conflict. But a peaceful solution was no longer possible. An ultimatum sent to Spain on 27 March demanded the end of the reconcentration policy, an amnesty, and the right of the United States to act as arbitrator between the Spanish Government and the insurgents. Spain seemed ready to agree to such terms, provided a way could be found to do so without bringing about the overthrow of the Spanish monarchy. This required time and patience on the part of the American public and their representatives in Congress, but both had run out.

On 19 April Congress passed a joint resolution proclaiming Cuba free and independent and authorizing the President to use land and naval forces to expel Spain from the island. Attached to the resolution was the "Teller Amendment", which altruistically disclaimed "any disposition or intention to exercise sovereignty, jurisdiction or control" over Cuba following the elimination of Spanish authority.

The joint resolution, when signed by McKinley the next day, amounted to a declaration of war. It was followed immediately by a Presidential order to blockade Cuba, and by 22 April an American squadron was off Havana. On the same day Congress voted to double the size of the Regular Army and empowered the President to issue a call for 125,000 Volunteers from the several states.

Unpreparedness. When war broke out the Regular Army numbered slightly over 28,000, scattered around the country among many different posts. Individually the troops were well trained, but the Army as a whole was unprepared for war in practically every other respect. It lacked a mobilization plan, a well-organized high command, and experience and doctrine in combined operations. Units larger than a regiment were nonexistent, and those of regimental size were rarely assembled in one place. Only a few older officers had ever seen a unit as large as a brigade and still fewer had any experience in commanding one. As for the National Guard, it numbered around 100,000 men, composed mostly of infantry units, whose training, discipline, and equipment were, with rare exceptions, lamentable. Few had any acquaintance with military matters beyond close order drill and company administration. Equipment of all sorts was either scarce or obsolete. None had yet fired smokeless powder ammunition and few were to do so at any time during the war. To make matters worse, the organization of the National Guard varied from state to state, and so, to all intents and purposes, there were as many different armies as there were states. All were exceedingly jealous of their peculiar prerogatives and suspicious of any move that might be interpreted as bringing them under Regular Army control. There was also a question about the legality of sending the National Guard abroad to serve. Before it could be done, existing law would have to be changed and the process might take considerable time. In the light of these conditions and the unfortunate experience with National Guard units in the Civil War, their absorption into the Army as units was considered unwise. The Volunteer bill passed on 22 April, therefore, was so framed that National Guard units could serve as state Volunteer units with the sanction of the respective governors.

Confusion in mobilization. Early in April, as war was approaching, Maj. Gen. Nelson Miles, Commanding General of the Army, urged the concentration of the entire Regular Army at Chickamauga Park, Ga., where it could be "equipped, drilled, disciplined and instructed in brigades and divisions and prepared for war service." But Russell A. Alger, the Secretary of War, who was hardly on speaking terms with Miles, had different ideas. Alger had been a general officer in the Civil War and considered himself fully competent to run the Army. Disregarding the advice of the Commanding General, he ordered the cavalry and artillery to Chickamauga and the infantry to New Orleans, Tampa, and Mobile. What his orders meant in negating training in combined arms did not seem to bother him at first, his main purpose apparently being the concentration of the infantry at points where they could make a quick descent upon Cuba (map 35). Like many others, Alger believed that Spain would withdraw from the island at the show of force and that the war would end in a few weeks without any fighting. Most military experts were less optimistic and pointed out that the Spanish Army was in a position to make a stand and that months, rather than weeks, would be required to drive it from Cuba.

General Miles also preferred a small force of about 80,000 men to a large one predominantly composed of volunteers. Such an army, he believed, would be more effective because it could be more quickly trained and equipped. As events proved, he was right, but the administration, Congress, and the people thought otherwise. In response to public demand, the number of volunteers that could be called was soon raised from 125,000 to 267,000. The fact that about a mil-

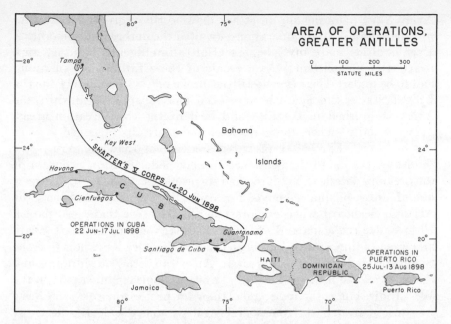

Map 35. Area of operations, Greater Antilles.

lion men offered their services indicated that the war was looked upon as a glorious national picnic that nearly everyone wanted to attend. Not until the volunteers were exposed to the hardships of camp life in the South did enthusiasm decline. There instead of picnic conditions they found utter confusion. Volunteer officers were untrained, equipment and supplies short, sanitary conditions disgraceful, food tainted, medical service woefully inadequate, and weapons and ammunition obsolete. Thousands lacked such essentials as underwear, socks, and shoes, and those who were clothed in uniforms wore woolens designed for use on the western plains, not for wear in southern camps during the summer or campaigns in the tropics. The Regular Army fared better than the volunteers, but most of it also failed to receive proper clothing before the fighting was over.

Lack of operational plans. Logically, the long period of strained relations with Spain should have produced some plan for military operations in Cuba, which everyone could see would become the scene of operations in case of hostilities. Actually, there was no plan. The preparation of war plans is the duty of a general staff, not of officers burdened with routine administrative duties, and there was no true general staff. Consequently the Nation went to war without any coordinated plan and quite ignorant of such basic matters as the strength, disposition, and capabilities of the Spanish on the island or of the Cuban insurgents, whose ally the United States automatically would become the moment war broke out. Nor was much thought given before the war to organizing for amphibious warfare. Joint

Army-Navy planning for an attack on a hostile shore, the most complicated of all military operations, awaited the outbreak of hostilities. Even accurate maps of Cuba, essential to intelligent planning, were practically nonexistent. As a result of these failures all planning had to be undertaken after hostilities broke out. Fortunately for the United States, the Spanish were even more inept. Meanwhile the Army languished in the filth and heat of the concentration areas, growing daily sicker, more restless, and more disillusioned.

The Navy. Far better prepared for combat than the Army was the Navy, thanks to the construction and modernization program of the previous decade. Yet it too had its problems. The main one grew out of unreasonable demands for protection from cities along the Atlantic Seaboard when rumors reached America that the Spanish Fleet under the command of Adm. Pascual Cervera had left Spain and was heading for the American coast. Navy leaders knew that the Spanish squadron was no threat to American cities or shipping and that it would be lucky to reach the safety of some Spanish port in the West Indies but as the fears and clamor for protection grew, the Navy was forced to depart from sound strategy and divide the fleet. A "Flying Squadron" under the command of Commodore Winfield S. Schley was detached from the main fleet and directed to watch for the enemy and prevent an attack on the eastern coast. To create a feeling of security, obsolete Civil War vessels that were utterly useless for defense were anchored in ports. Meanwhile the main fleet, operating from Key West as a base, blockaded northern Cuba and prepared to engage the Spanish Fleet should it show up in Caribbean waters.

Manila Bay. While attention was focused on Cuba and the whereabouts of Admiral Cervera's fleet, events of tremendous importance were shaping up in the Far East. The eve of war found an American squadron of six vessels under Commodore George Dewey in Hong Kong taking on coal and other supplies in preparation for a quick descent on the Philippine Islands where a Spanish Fleet was known to be. Obliged to leave the neutral port when word of war was received, Dewey steamed for the Philippines in accord with the principle that war made every Spanish possession a legitimate objective. On the night of 30 April after a previous reconnaissance of Subic Bay to ascertain if the Spanish Fleet was there, he boldly entered Manila Bay (See map 43). The next morning he located the Spanish vessels at Cavite and immediately gave battle. The action that followed lasted all morning, and when it was over the entire Spanish Fleet was either sunk or reduced to burning wreckage without the loss of a single American ship or life. Within a few days, the land batteries controlling Manila harbor also fell to Dewey, but the city itself held out. To take it a land force would be necessary and Dewey at once requested it. Meanwhile, he blockaded the port and encouraged Emilio Aguinaldo, whom he had brought in from exile in China, and his Filipino insurgents to hem in the Spanish on land, pending the arrival of American troops. Despite his naval victory and Filipino support, Dewey's position was not a happy one. He was a month's sailing time from the nearest home port with only 1,700 men of his own, scarcely enough to man his vessels.

Difficulties in Manila Bay. Dewey's problems were not made any easier by the arrival of English, French, and German warships, ostensibly to protect their nationals from the insurgents, but also to be on hand to pick up loose territory in case the United States should decide against taking over control of the islands after the collapse of Spanish power. The Germans in particular were suspected of having such ambitions, a suspicion that was increased by the actions of the German commander, Rear Adm. Otto von Dietrichs, who persistently violated Dewey's blockade rules. For a while it appeared that a serious incident involving the German and American Fleets was in the making, but Dewey's patience and firmness prevented it from arising. The situation improved when the policy of the United States not to abandon the islands became clear and the German Fleet departed Philippine waters, under orders from Berlin.

Santiago becomes the objective. Meanwhile Cervera's fleet, which had caused so much excitement along the Atlantic seaboard, slipped into Santiago Bay. Composed of four armored cruisers and two destroyers, and commanded by a man who saw only ruin ahead, it had sailed across the Atlantic directly into the center of operations, skillfully eluding a superior hostile fleet. As a naval achievement, the voyage was an unqualified success. But this success was the Spanish Fleet's first and last. In entering Santiago Bay, Cervera had virtually sealed the fate of his fleet. His move brought the American Fleet together and gave the armed forces a definite objective.

Naval blockade. The Navy at once blockaded the port and dispatched a force of marines to establish a naval base on Guantanamo Bay. After a minor action, the first on Cuban soil involving Americans, the site was taken. At the same time the forts and batteries commanding the entrance to Santiago Bay were subjected to naval bombardment, but without success. Fearful of Spanish coast defenses and mines, Rear Adm. William T. Sampson hesitated to risk his ships in running the channel. Instead, he sought to prevent the escape of Cervera's fleet by ordering the collier *Merrimac* sunk across the channel. The attempt failed, despite the heroic conduct of Lt. (jg.) Richmond P. Hobson, who was in charge of the project. Sampson now was confronted with the problem of forcing an entrance into the bay or calling for land forces to take the batteries that his ships could not silence. He decided to call for assistance.

The Army moves to Cuba. Eager to get the Army into action, the War Department at once directed Maj. Gen. William R. Shafter to embark from Tampa for Cuba. His orders gave him the choice of moving directly on the forts dominating the entrance to Santiago Bay or driving into the interior to take Santiago from the rear. To issue orders to move an Army to Cuba was one thing : to get it there was quite another. For weeks harassed and bewildered officers and War Department officials struggled with the problem of getting the expedition under way. Meanwhile the Army lingered impatiently in Tampa. A worse place could hardly have been chosen, for the port had but one pier and was served only by a single track railroad.

On 11 June, the embarkation of some 17,000 men finally got started. It lasted four days, an operation which if properly organized could have been done easily in eight hours. But the embarkation was anything but organized. No detailed and coordinated plan existed and no staff was on hand to direct the movement. Little attention was given to proper loading for a combat mission. Men, supplies, and equipment were loaded into ships helter-skelter without regard to the order in which they might have to be discharged in case resistance was encountered during the landing. So confused did the embarkation become that some regiments actually took matters into their own hands, commandeering railroad cars and equipment meant for other units and even fighting on the pier in an effort to board transports. Yet somehow, someway, men and supplies were loaded and the expedition finally got under way.

By 20 June, it reached a point off Santiago. Shafter immediately conferred with Sampson, who urged him to land his troops near the fort on the east side of the entrance to the bay, storm it, and then drive the Spanish from the battery positions on the opposite side. The Navy could then sweep the mines from the channel and enter Santiago Bay to engage the Spanish fleet. Shafter, after looking at the fort perched on a hill rising sharply from the sea to a height of 230 feet, concluded that it was too difficult a position to take without heavy artillery. He decided, instead, to follow the advice of Gen. Calixto Garcia, commander of the Cuban insurgents in the area, and land his army at Daiquiri, 18 miles east of Santiago Bay (map 36). After making a feint west of the bay to throw the Spanish off guard, the force began to move ashore, following a heavy naval shelling of the landscape aimed at driving out any Spaniards who might be in the neighborhood. Fortunately the area was undefended. By failing to oppose the landing, the Spanish lost a splendid opportunity for the debarkation was if anything more disorganized and confused than the embarkation at Tampa.

The landing. That a landing could have been effected in the face of determined resistance is extremely doubtful. No plans had been made for an amphibious assault and units got ashore as best they could, with or without equipment. Many captains of chartered merchant ships refused to take their vessels inshore, and some, in fright, actually fled the scene and had to be rounded up by the Navy. Horses were gotten ashore by the simple expedient of dropping them overboard and letting them swim. Unfortunately some swam out to sea and were lost before someone hit upon the scheme of stringing them together and leading them ashore with boats. The expedition that should have been landed in hours actually took days, but thanks to Spanish military inefficiency catastrophe was avoided.

Shafter moves on Santiago. After the landing of some 6,000 troops on the first day, the march on the city of Santiago began despite the criticism of the Navy, which still hoped the force would move against the positions guarding the entrance to the bay. Shafter's plan was simple enough : a quick drive toward Santiago by the most direct route, which meant by the one road leading to the city through Siboney, a village on the coast. About 12,000 Spanish troops were thought to be in entrenched lines around Santiago, but their exact location was not known. On 23 June, Brig. Gen. Henry W. Lawton, commanding the vanguard, reached Siboney and captured it without difficulty. His orders directed him to establish a perimeter defense behind the beach so that further debarkation operations could be moved to that area. This was done, and Siboney from that time on became the base for the operation. While Lawton was reorganizing to continue the advance as directed, Brig. Gen. Joseph W. Wheeler, a veteran of the Confederate Army, stole a march on him and pushed on toward Santiago with his dismounted cavalry division. At Las Guasimas, he ran into the rear guard of a retiring Spanish force, which inflicted some casualties. No serious delay was suffered, however, since the Spanish had no intention of making a stand beyond Santiago's outer defenses.

Shafter's plan. The most important of these defenses were along a series of ridges, known collectively as San Juan, and in the village of El Caney to the north. To prevent the city from being reinforced and to cut its water supply, Shafter decided to attack El Caney first and then follow with a frontal assault on the San Juan positions. Only 2 hours were allowed for the capture of El Caney, an estimate that proved much too little. General Lawton, who was to take the fortified village, moved out on time, but because of poor roads and difficult terrain conditions he was unable to begin the assault on schedule.

San Juan. The force assigned to take the San Juan heights, commanded by Maj. Gen. Jacob F. Kent, waited more than two hours for the El Caney attack to get under way before beginning its attack. It was a poorly coordinated effort, and within a short time units of the attacking force became badly disorganized. Part of the confusion resulted from the heavy artillery fire that a Signal Corps captive balloon brought upon the troops as it was being towed along in the ad-

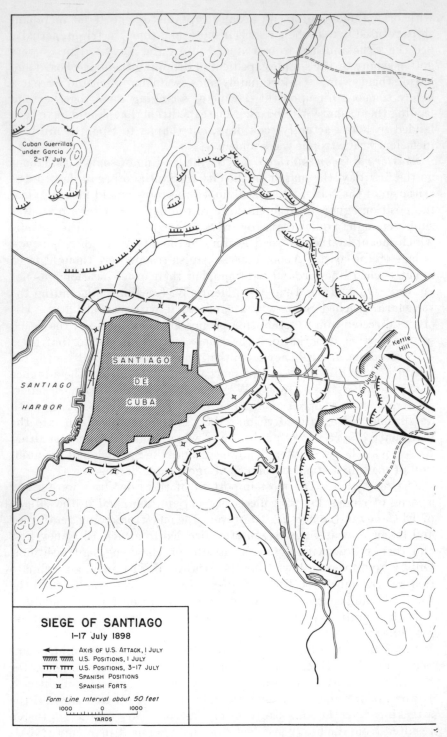

Cuban Guerrillas
under Garcia
2-17 July

SANTIAGO
HARBOR

SANTIAGO
DE
CUBA

Kettle
Hill

San Juan Hill

SIEGE OF SANTIAGO
1-17 July 1898

⟵ AXIS OF U.S. ATTACK, 1 JULY
🏳🏳🏳 U.S. POSITIONS, 1 JULY
🏳🏳🏳 U.S. POSITIONS, 3-17 JULY
🏳🏳🏳 SPANISH POSITIONS
⌗ SPANISH FORTS

Form Line Interval about 50 feet

1000   0   1000
YARDS

Map 36. Siege of Santiago,

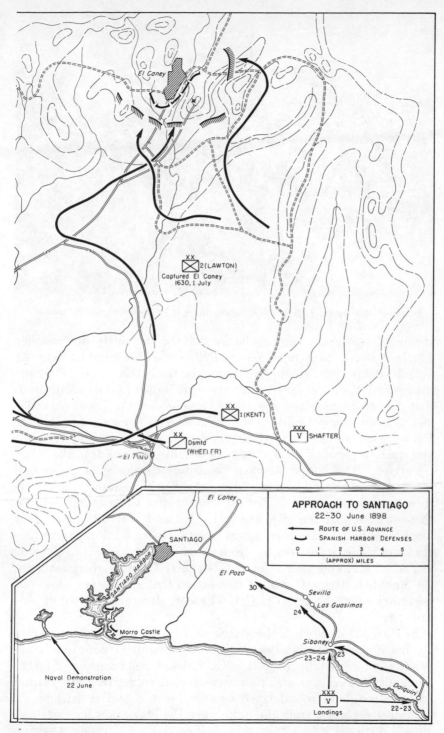

El Caney

XX
2 (LAWTON)
Captured El Caney
1630, 1 July

XX
1 (KENT)

XXX
V SHAFTER

XX
Dsmtd
(WHEELER)

El Pozo

APPROACH TO SANTIAGO
22–30 June 1898

→ ROUTE OF U.S. ADVANCE
⌣ SPANISH HARBOR DEFENSES

0 1 2 3 4 5
(APPROX) MILES

El Caney

SANTIAGO

SANTIAGO HARBOR

El Pozo

30

Sevilla

24

Las Guasimas

Morro Castle

Siboney

23-24

23

Naval Demonstration
22 June

XXX
V
Landings

Daiquiri

22-23

1–17 July 1898

Battle of San Juan, 1 July 1898. Note the use of Gatlings in the assault.

vancing front line. Another factor was the extremely hot weather. The heat nearly prostrated General Shafter, who weighed over 300 pounds, and prevented him from directing the battle. Poor communications and inadequate staff work also contributed to the lack of direction. Subordinate officers rose to the occasion, however, restored order, and stormed enemy positions with a medley of troops. Lt. John H. Parker, commander of a Gatling gun detachment, for example, sought and received permission to move his guns into line and join the infantry attack. This use of weapons heretofore considered suitable only in the defense proved highly successful. The close support given the infantry helped establish fire superiority and contributed much to the restoration of the offensive spirit, without which the San Juan heights could not have been taken. Kettle Hill, a knob separate from the main ridge, was taken by dismounted cavalry units including the 1st, 3d, 6, 9th, and 10th (Colored) Regular Cavalry Regiments and the Rough Riders. It was in this action that the former Assistant Secretary of the Navy, Lt. Col. Theodore Roosevelt, distinguished himself.

El Caney. Meanwhile the attack on El Caney finally got started. At first it made little headway. Some 500 Spanish troops in a strong position protected by barbed wire, resisted stubbornly until their ammunition gave out and they were forced to retire. The capture of the stronghold was delayed because Lawton had to withdraw a volunteer regiment from the fight when the black powder cartridges it used betrayed its position, bringing heavy enemy fire on American lines, and because he deployed his artillery initially in such a manner that it could not properly support the advance. Late in the battle the artillery was moved forward to positions from which it could effectively shell enemy defenses. The attack then proceeded at a more rapid pace. With the fall of the village all the outer defenses of Santiago were in American hands. Shafter now faced the problem of what to do next.

Siege of Santiago. Before him lay the enemy's well-organized second line of defense, and behind that, the more formidable inner defenses, strongly protected by barbed wire. Despite his victory, Shafter's position was not an enviable one. The troops were exposed to enemy fire which they could not return effectively, and malaria, yellow fever, and the approaching hurricane season threatened their health and safety. To attempt to storm the city without sufficient artillery to blast a way through the barbed wire and batter entrenched positions would be suicidal. Shafter's first inclination was to withdraw to higher ground about 4 miles from the city, but this move was vetoed by the War Department.

Army-Navy differences. Shafter next tried to persuade the Navy to run the channel and attack the city from the bay, but neither Sampson nor his superiors in the Navy Department in Washington would risk the fleet in running batteries that they had called upon the Army to take. No one person below the President himself had command authority over both Army and Navy forces in the area, and since McKinley was not inclined to exercise it the Army-Navy differences threatened to develop into a public debate between spokesmen of the two services. In fact, the debate had already begun when Spanish action brought it to an abrupt halt.

Destruction of the Spanish Fleet. While Shafter and Sampson were worrying about their problems, the Spaniards faced far more serious ones. In Santiago ammunition and food were low and there was little hope of getting more of either. Near-famine conditions prevailed, seriously affecting the health and morale of both troops and inhabitants. Despite the strength of their defensive position, it seemed to the Spanish leaders after San Juan and El Caney that the fall of the city was inevitable. But there was one hope. Since Santiago had become a military objective only because Cervera's fleet had found refuge in its harbor, the departure of the fleet for some other Cuban port probably would induce the U. S. Navy to follow and possibly the Army also. At all events there was nothing to be gained by leaving the fleet in the port and letting it fall into the hands of the enemy without a fight. Admiral Cervera's superiors in Madrid therefore ordered him to attempt to escape with his fleet as soon as the fall of the city seemed imminent. Cervera objected, considering escape hopeless, but finally obeyed orders. Suddenly on the morning of 3 July, while Sampson and Shafter were in conference ashore discussing their differences, the Spanish Fleet emerged from the narrows of the bay and made for the open sea hoping to reach the port of Cienfuegos. A dramatic running battle ensued which ended in the complete destruction of the entire enemy fleet. The victory was decisive and ended whatever hopes the Spanish still had of holding out successfully in Santiago.

Surrender of Santiago. A few days later General Shafter and Gen. Jose Toral, the defender of Santiago, met between the lines to discuss the fate of the city. Shafter convinced Toral that honorable surrender was his only course. The U. S. general personally would have permitted the Spanish garrison to withdraw from the city without arms, but Washington insisted on unconditional surrender. Toral at first refused to capitulate on that basis but finally agreed, after a long-range naval bombardment of Santiago which caused more fright than damage. On 16 July terms were signed. They provided for the surrender of 11,500 troops in the city and some 12,000 others situated at Guantanamo, San Luis, and other places, 25 to 60 miles away. The next day a formal surrender ceremony was held which ended in a round of handshaking between the erstwhile enemies.

Campaign in Puerto Rico. After the fall of Santiago, General Miles who had arrived in Cuba to take personal command of the Army, moved into Puerto Rico with 3,000 men. His original plan was to land at Cape Fajardo on the northeastern corner of the island, establish a base there to which reinforcements could be sent, and then move on San Juan, the capital on the north coast. While at sea, he decided to land at Guanica on the southeastern coast instead. Why he changed plans is not clear, but there is good reason to believe he was motivated as much by a desire to dispense with the services of the Navy in an operation against San Juan as to deceive the enemy. At all events, no harm was done for the landing met no opposition. The city of Ponce, just east of Guanica, was taken next without trouble and immediately turned into an Army Base. Meanwhile additional troops under Maj. Gen. John R. Brooke were landed at Guayama, also on the south coast. Within a short time the island was overrun by four columns. There was some light resistance, but the population as a whole received American troops with enthusiasm. One problem arose—to get enough American flags with which to bedeck government buildings and properly celebrate the expected annexation to the United States. Campaigning in Puerto Rico was indeed a picnic. There was little bloodshed, no serious hardship, and plenty of fun. No wonder units still in the United States clamored for a chance to get into action before the peace treaty put an end to the adventure.

The plight of the Army in Cuba. After the surrender of Santiago the Army met its worst problems in Cuba. These were caused not by

Spanish troops but by more deadly enemies—malaria, typhoid, and yellow fever. So serious did the danger become that a group of senior officers drew up a joint letter addressed to General Shafter in which they called for the immediate evacuation of the Army from Cuba. While this "round robin" letter was being dispatched to General Shafter it was also leaked to the press, with the result that officials in Washington read the letter in the newspapers before they were acquainted with its contents through the commanding general in Cuba. Its publication caused a sensation, coming as it did, just when peace negotiations were beginning. The whole business was very unmilitary, very indiscreet, and very embarrassing to General Shafter, but it did bring action. American troops were immediately brought back and placed in an isolated camp on Montauk Point at the tip of Long Island. Some 20,000 of the 35,000 who passed through the camp were ill, but most of them eventually regained their health. It was at Montauk Point that the troops finally were able to shed their woolen clothing and don cotton uniforms.

Battle of Manila. The last military action of the war was the battle for Manila. In response to Dewey's request for 5,000 men, the War Department started at once to organize a force with Maj. Gen. Wesley Merritt in command. On 1 July, the first contingent of 2,500 arrived in Manila. This was gradually built up until it reached 11,000 shortly after Merritt arrived on 25 July. As American strength increased, dependence on Filipino insurgents decreased. Their leader, Aguinaldo, who had hoped for recognition of his Philippine Republic, was far from pleased with the American build-up. Relations grew strained as it became clear that the American leaders were determined to take Manila with a minimum of Filipino aid. A partial reason for this determination was that the Spanish early in the siege indicated a willingness to surrender the city, provided it was not exposed to undisciplined insurgents afterward. But the main reason was that the administration was trying to make up its mind about the future of the islands and did not want to be handicapped by obligations or commitments to a native government. Both Dewey and Merritt therefore had to adjust their actions to a policy in the making. This was not an easy thing to do. It meant resistance to insurgent aspirations and demands without bringing matters to a breaking point. To make matters more difficult, the insurgents held a line around Manila between the U. S. lines and the city walls. Before an advance on the city could be arranged without the insurgents, their positions would have to be occupied by American troops. With skill and tact, this feat was accomplished by the end of July, the Filipinos leaving reluctantly but peacefully. Plans for the final assault thereafter moved rapidly, if a negotiated operation can be called an assault. At all events, the arrangement for a bloodless action was completed and everything seemed to be in perfect order when the attack began. But something happened: just what no one knows. In general the advance became confused in the rice paddies before the city. Insurgent bands moving on the flanks became intermingled with American troops, and as they approached the Spanish forward positions firing broke out. The American firing stopped when the Spanish failed to reply, but the insurgent fire continued. It seemed for a time that the token assault would become a serious affair, but after some difficulty the firing was reduced sufficiently to permit the Spanish to capitulate. The fact that the war had ended two days before was not known in Manila, for the cable that Dewey had cut when he steamed for Manila was not yet back in operation. The Filipino units that had entered the city were induced to leave, and on 14 August formal surrender terms were signed.

The Philippine Insurrection. The collapse of Spanish power and the approaching cession of the islands to the United States brought a rapid deterioration of Filipino-American relations. Aguinaldo and his followers were as determined as ever to be free, and on 4 February, as the Treaty of Paris was about to be ratified by the Senate, hostilities broke out around Manila. The Army, having eliminated the Spanish, was now faced with the far more serious task of suppressing a native revolt. For this Maj. Gen. Elwell S. Otis, who succeeded General Merritt, had some 21,000 men on hand. Since many of these were volunteers about to be returned to the United States, he could count on only 12,000 effectives. His control in the islands at the time scarcely extended beyond Manila, the insurgents holding a semicircular line of blockhouses around the city with a force estimated by some to be as high as 40,000. Just what sparked the hostilities of 4 February is not known. Whatever the cause, the reaction of the Army was immediate and determined. In a battle which lasted two days the insurgents lost about 3,000 men and the Army of Occupation 250.

The outbreak convinced the United States that a larger force was needed to meet the challenge to its control. Ten volunteer regiments were raised, and within seven months nearly 35,000 reinforcements were on their way to the islands. The fighting that followed was fashioned by terrain, climate, and differences in weapons. Because of shortages in firearms the Filipinos resorted to guerilla warfare rather than open battle. In jungle country devoid of roads, movement was difficult and surprise and ambush easy. The natives fought with bolos as often as with rifles, and their attacks were met with small arms fire and bayonet charge. Gatling guns, used effectively against the Spanish, were too unwieldy for jungle warfare. For the same reason, little artillery was used.

Until reinforcements arrived General Otis could not undertake an all-out offensive, but he did not remain idle. A few points were seized in February and March 1898, including Malolos, the insurgent capital, and the islands of Panay, Cebu, and Negros. By April, Otis was ready to undertake a general offensive in Luzon, the center of insurgent resistance. It began with a two-pronged advance—one under General Lawton on Santa Cruz; the other under Maj. Gen. Arthur MacArthur up the central plain from Malolos toward San Fernando. Both drives were successful, and by mid-May organized resistance in Central Luzon was seriously weakened. A shortage in manpower and the approaching rainy season then temporarily halted the offensive. In October it was resumed. To cut off Aguinaldo's retreat to the mountain fastnesses of Northern Luzon, Otis planned to continue the advance up the central plain with his main force and send two smaller forces around each flank, the one on the right by way of the Lingayen Gulf. The operation failed to trap the insurgent leader, but it dispersed much of his band. Aguinaldo himself was not taken until March 1901. In Southern Luzon progress was equally successful, and by March 1900 it and the neighboring Visayas were both brought under control. Mindanao and the Sulu Archipelago, inhabited by the warlike Moros, were occupied next, and organized resistance ended, but not the fighting. In some respects the 13 months between May 1900 and June 1901 were the most difficult of the insurrection. Fighting was bitter and brutal with little quarter given or asked. Over 1,000 separate engagements were fought, and the casualties surpassed those of the earlier period. When these months of fighting ended, except for spasmodic outbreaks which lasted for years, the insurrection was over. The experience of the Army in the Indian Wars where scouting, speed, surprise, self-reliance, and individual initiative were essential to success proved invaluable in suppressing the insurrection. In fact the Philippine campaign was an extension of that experience. It proved so excellent a training school that man for man the men and officers who went through it became the equal of the best soldiers in the world.

The China Relief Expedition. *The Boxer Uprising.* Over a period of decades China had gradually grown weak and inept in both domestic and foreign affairs. Since weakness invites exploitation imperialistic powers helped themselves to Chinese territory from time to time and extorted favorable economic and commercial concessions. Realizing that the continuing raids on Chinese sovereignty would eventually jeopardize its growing trade in the Far East, the United States formally proposed an "Open Door" policy in September 1899 aimed at equalizing commercial opportunity and preserving the integrity of China as a nation. Most of the powers accepted the proposal, Great Britain and Germany almost at once. But the new policy came too late to halt the growth of violent antiforeign sentiment in China.

Rise of antiforeign feeling. Aroused by the ruthless exploitation of their country, many Chinese readily accepted the preachings of the "Boxers," fanatical members of a secret society dedicated to the extermination of "foreign devils" and the eradication of their influence. Under the leadership of Prince Tuan and encouraged by the reactionary Dowager Empress, the Boxers and their supporters proceeded to carry out their program. Hundreds of hated foreigners and Chinese Christians were slain. A climax was reached on 20 June 1900 when the German Minister was murdered in cold blood while on his way to protest against the indignities of the Boxers. Convinced by the incident that they were no longer safe in Peking, many foreigners and Chinese converts took refuge in the legation compound, where they were immediately besieged by thousands of Chinese including some troops from the Chinese Army.

Relief expedition formed. The powers reacted at once by organizing a relief expedition. Because the United States was involved in military operations in the nearby Philippines, it was in a position to make a substantial contribution to the international force. Manila became a main base and, by agreement with Japan, Nagasaki was used as a secondary base. The latter proved very valuable as a distribution point for men and supplies from the states. In less than three weeks after receiving their orders, the 9th Infantry and a battalion of marines were landed at Taku, the Chinese port closest to Peking. Maj. Gen. Adna R. Chaffee, commander of the United States force, and others soon joined them, bringing the American contingent up to 2,500 men, surpassed in strength only by the Russians and Japanese. On 13 July the expedition, composed of American, British, French, Japanese, and Russian troops, attacked and took the walled city of Tientsin after a 15-hour battle during which the city was badly damaged. Its fall opened the way to Peking 75 miles away.

The march on Peking. Early in August the allied force, now numbering about 18,000 men, began its advance on the capital through a region infested with Boxers and their sympathizers. Several sharp skirmishes were fought. Losses were serious, but by 12 August the Allies were at the gates of Peking. There seems to have been no one in supreme command at the time, for decisions were made by Council. As might have been expected, the national components of the force tended to act independently. The chief offenders were the Russians and Japanese. The former, although slow during the march, jumped the gun in the assault on Peking, attacking the Tong-Pien-Men Gate on the east side of the Outer City a day before scheduled. After forcing an entrance, the Russians were thrown into confusion and had to be rescued by their allies.

Scaling the Tartar Wall, Peking, 14 August 1899.

The fall of Peking. On 14 August the expedition succeeded in taking the Outer City, thereby insuring the relief of the beleaguered legations. In this action two companies of the 14th Infantry scaled the Tartar wall and covered the British as they entered the city in force. A final assault on the Inner or "Forbidden City" was made the next day after an American artillery unit known as "Reilley's Battery" blasted the gates that blocked the entrance. With the fall of the "Forbidden City" the important military operations came to an end. Order was restored in Peking, but not without unnecessary violence and much looting by some of the European contingents, which did not add to the reputation of foreigners in China. Mopping-up operations also were undertaken in the provinces, particularly Chih-li where Boxer influence was still strong. Meanwhile reinforcements, including a large contingent from Germany, continued to arrive. An international army of occupation, commanded by Field Marshal Count Alfred von Waldersee, was set up which in a few months succeeded in wiping out the last traces of resistance in the provinces.

The settlement. Thoroughly beaten but still a power in China, the Dowager Empress proposed peace through her emissaries. She offered to indemnify and reaffirm the old commercial concessions in return for a cessation of hostilities and the withdrawal of foreign troops. After months of negotiations terms were signed. Among other things, China agreed to punish those implicated in the uprising, set up an exclusive reservation for foreign legations in Peking, permit the military occupation of the Tientsin-Peking railway line by an international force, and pay an indemnity of $333,000,000. All the powers except the United States united in exacting outrageous reparations, hoping thereby to keep China in economic bondage. The U. S. Government was content with approximately $25,000,000 to cover the damages suffered by Americans during the uprising. Only half of this amount was ever claimed and the rest was remitted in 1908 with the understanding that the Chinese Government would use it to establish a fund for the education of Chinese students in the United States and for educational and scientific work in China.

In return for the concessions made by the Chinese Government, the powers agreed to evacuate all troops but legation guards by the fall of 1901. All of them did so except Russia, which continued to maintain a strong force in southern Manchuria and the province of Chih-li. In so doing it ignored the principles of the "Open Door" and incurred the suspicions of the other powers, particularly Japan and England. It was alarm over Russia's undisguised imperialist intentions in China that brought about the Anglo-Japanese alliance in 1902 and eventually the Russo-Japanese war in 1904.

Summary. The United States entered the war with Spain with great confidence but little preparation. The cause was lofty and enthusiasm unparalleled. Few Americans at the outset had any notion that the limited campaign envisioned in Cuba and Caribbean waters would almost immediately be expanded by an aggressive Navy to include operations on the other side of the world. None, not even the wisest and best informed, foresaw that a war undertaken to liberate the "heroic Cubans" from the yoke of a decadent colonial power would end with the United States itself engaged in suppressing a colonial insurrection.

The military operations against Spain, despite lack of planning, poor coordination between the services, and general confusion, adhered to the principles of the offensive. They were carried through to a successful conclusion by an army composed of regulars and volunteers, without a single defeat. Apart from luck and the inefficiency and weakness of the enemy on land and sea, this success must be attributed to the initiative, courage, and endurance of the American soldier and his immediate superiors. They took the bungling in high places in stride and demonstrated an aptitude for improvisation equal to the highest traditions of the Army. But for the high quality of the men the war might well have dragged out for many weary months instead of ending in a little over three.

Although the campaigns to establish United States authority in the Philippines required considerable effort and time, the ultimate outcome was never in doubt. The confined area of operations, lack of roads, jungle conditions, rugged terrain, and guerilla tactics of the insurgents made maneuvering with large balanced forces impossible. War was waged in the pattern of the Indian wars of the past except that the infantryman rather than the cavalryman was cast in the leading role. As a school for developing soldiers and leaders, the Philippine battles were unsurpassed.

Because the Army was involved in the Philippines, it was possible for the United States to assume its responsibility as a world power quickly when trouble broke out in China in early 1900. The American contribution was out of proportion to the number of troops sent, adding respect and force to the voice of the United States in all diplomatic discussions thereafter aimed at settling Far Eastern problems.

QUESTIONS

1. Discuss the underlying and immediate causes of the War with Spain.

2. What was the military objective of the United States when the War with Spain broke out? What happened that led it to be expanded?

3. Describe the expansion of the Army after the outbreak of hostilities against Spain and the problems that it created.

4. Discuss operations in Cuba from the time of the original landings until the capitulation of the Spanish forces at Santiago.

5. In what way did military operations against the insurgents in the Philippines differ from those against the Spanish in Cuba?

6. Discuss the role of the United States Army in the China Relief Expedition.

Reading List

Chadwick, French E.   *The Relations Between the United States and Spain*.   New York, 1909–1911.   3 vols.

Davis, Richard H.   *The Cuban and Puerto Rican Campaigns*.   New York, 1898.

Dennett, Tyler.   *Americans in Eastern Asia*.   New York, 1922.

Latane, J. H.   *America as a World Power*.   New York and London, 1907.

Mahan, Alfred T.   *Lessons of the War with Spain*.   Boston, 1899.

Millis, Walter.   *The Martial Spirit*.   Cambridge, 1931.

Sexton, William T.   *Soldier in the Sun*.   Harrisburg, 1939.

CHAPTER 17

1898–1917

Introduction. *Changing times.* The end of the 19th and the beginning of the 20th century witnessed not only the rise of the United States to world power but also the intensification of international rivalry throughout the world. Most of the great powers sought to strengthen their alliances and alignments and improve their diplomatic positions. These developments reflected, among other things, startling technological and industrial progress, particularly the rise of mass production with its ever increasing pressure for new markets and sources of raw materials. Indicative of the changing emphasis in international affairs and the conduct of diplomacy were new terms such as "The Open Door", "The White Man's Burden", *"Drang nach Osten"*, "Dollar Diplomacy", and "Power Politics".

By 1907 the rivalry among the European powers crystallized to the point where two groups, the Triple Alliance, composed of Germany, Austria-Hungary, and Italy, and the so-called Triple Entente, France, England, and Russia, faced each other in uncertain peace. Smaller countries tended to gravitate toward one camp or the other, the direction they moved determined in large part by fear, economic pressure, national ambitions, ancient animosities, and racial, linguistic, and historical ties. To support national policies, armies and navies were reorganized and expanded, new weapons introduced, tactics altered, and training intensified. The unprecedented arms race that resulted matched the struggle for commercial dominance and continually threatened to upset the delicate balance of power in international affairs. Quite unaware of the signs of approaching catastrophe, the peoples of the Western World moved rapidly down the road to war despite the efforts of some of their leaders to relieve tensions through international conferences and diplomatic negotiations.

Although not directly aligned with either of the two great European groups, the United States nevertheless was caught in the continuous struggle for power and began to give increased attention to the development of its military establishment. As a nation with newly acquired overseas possessions, it emphasized the strengthening of the Navy as its first line of defense but did not entirely neglect the Army.

The new Navy. Even before the war against Spain, the necessity for a stronger navy to defend the extensive seacoast of the United

States and its overseas trade found sufficient support among the American people and their representatives in Congress to create a respectable naval force. Along with its small but modern fleet, the Navy also had, thanks to the historical studies and teachings of the brilliant Capt. Alfred Mahan, a body of sound strategic doctrine and tactical principles governing the use of sea power. What the Navy could do was dramatically demonstrated at Manila Bay and off Santiago, and from that time on a "Big Navy" policy, championed in the political field by such men as Theodore Roosevelt and Henry Cabot Lodge, rarely lacked popular support. The goal of the advocates of a "Big Navy" was a navy second only to that of Great Britain, which meant one stronger than that of Germany. While the United States Navy never quite attained the position of second rank before World War I, it became powerful enough to dominate home and adjacent waters.

Naval lessons learned. During the War with Spain the country learned much about the conduct of sea warfare. For one thing it discovered that steam-propelled vessels were seriously limited by their capacity to refuel. This limitation emphasized the need of coaling stations and naval bases under the American flag in areas of likely operations where warships could be refueled and repaired without running afoul of the time limitations imposed in such matters by international law. Naval experience also exposed the folly of dividing the fleet as was done when the "Flying Squadron" was split from the main flotilla in response to unreasonable demands for protection from cities along the Atlantic seaboard. The failure of the fleet to reduce the Spanish coast defenses in Cuba and Puerto Rico proved that no navy, operating alone far distant from home bases, could successfully attack the United States if it was protected by coast defense guns of caliber equal to those of a hostile fleet. These lessons and many more were later confirmed by the results of the Russo-Japanese war, the only other war in the period between the close of the Spanish-American War and World War I in which sea power played a decisive part.

The strategic significance of the Philippines. The decision of the American people to reject anti-imperialism in the election of 1900 indicated a willingness to hold on to the Philippines. But what the retention of the islands implied strategically was doubtless lost on most of the public. The acquisition of an outpost in the western Pacific plunged the Nation into Far Eastern affairs and committed it to the defense of territory thousands of miles away. To hold so remote a region successfully required not only a substantial army and a large navy but also a secure line of communications. The opportunity to establish the latter presented itself at the close of the war when Spain, heavily in debt, decided to liquidate her remaining Pacific possessions, but the United States did not act. Uninterested in the islands between Hawaii and the Philippines, except Guam, the United States raised no objections to Germany's purchase of them in 1899. This might not have been serious had not Germany in 1918 lost them to Japan, whose strategic position in the western Pacific made it far more dangerous to U. S. interests in that area than any Atlantic power. Few suspected the strategic implications of the fateful decision to retain the Philippines, followed by the failure to establish an adequate line of communications to the islands and later to prevent vital sections of the natural line from falling into the hands of a potentially dangerous foe.

Technological Developments. *General.* In response to the technical and industrial progress and the rising international tensions, implements of war underwent rapid change around the turn of the century, forcing reforms in military organization, administration, and tactics. The new era found governments more willing than before to spend a larger portion of their national income on armaments and to give increasing attention to new ideas and weapons. In the navies of the world, ships became heavier and faster and the guns they mounted more powerful. Following the lead of Great Britain other nations made the "Dreadnought" class of battleship the backbone of their fleets, supported by fast cruisers and destroyers and a new instrument of destruction—the submarine, armed with the deadly torpedo. The advances on sea were paralleled by those on land. Armies began to pay serious attention to developments in small arms, particularly the machine gun; they improved their artillery and ammunition; and they harnessed such new equipment as the motor vehicle, telephone, wireless telegraph, and airplane to their use.

Small arms. The Krag-Jorgensen rifle, with which a part of the United States Infantry was armed in the Spanish-American War and the Philippine Insurrection, gave way in 1903 to the improved bolt-action magazine-type Springfield rifle. In it the Army now had a rifle which was probably the best in the world. About the same time, the .45-caliber automatic pistol was developed for close fighting. Its adoption was based on experience in the Philippines which pointed to the need of a side arm capable of stopping an attacking bolo-throwing fanatic in his tracks. More significant was the further development of the rapid-firing machine gun. The first to find wide acceptance, it will be recalled, was the Gatling gun. In the 1880's a true automatic weapon using the recoil from a fired cartridge to bring the next into firing position was invented by Hiram Maxim. About the same time John M. Browning invented a machine gun that utilized escaping gas from a fired shot to actuate a mechanism that brought another shell into place. Some automatic weapons were employed in the Spanish-American War, the Boer War, the Russo-Japanese War, and the Balkan Wars, but it was not until World War I that their deadly effectiveness was fully demonstrated. In the hands of well-trained crews, the machine gun and its smaller counterpart, the automatic rifle, tended to strengthen the defense rather than the offense, until countered by the widespread use of armor.

Artillery. No munitions underwent greater changes in the late 19th and early 20th centuries than artillery and artillery ammunition. Muzzle-loading cannon typical of most Civil War artillery gradually gave way to breechloaders. Smokeless powder was introduced, permitting a more rapid rate of fire since it eliminated the need of awaiting the clearing of smoke clouds from muzzle blasts after each round. When the hydropneumatic recoil system was adopted for artillery, still greater speed and accuracy were attained. This mechanism overcame the backward roll that displaced the artillery piece from its position, thereby permitting it to be fired immediately following a quick check for proper orientation on the target.

Improvement in explosives and the machining of guns and shells made not only for greater accuracy but longer range as well. This in turn permitted indirect fire by a variety of guns. Artillery was divided in general into three classes: mortars, howitzers, and guns. Each class varied according to the trajectory of the projectile it fired. For example, a mortar lobbed shells at short range in a high curve usually over high obstructions; a gun discharged projectiles in a flat curve; while the howitzer delivered its shells in a curve between the two. These differences in artillery were of little significance in the days when ranges were short, but as new and more powerful explosives made longer ranges and greater penetrating power possible, mortars temporarily fell into disuse, to be revived later in World War I as an infantry weapon for close fighting in trench warfare. Howitzers and guns on the other hand were standardized, the former for fire against enemy positions in defiladed areas, the latter with their longer range and high penetrating power for use against more distant targets. Neither required a cannoneer to see his target.

Internal combustion engines. Probably no product of the new industrial age influenced military thought and activity more profoundly than did the internal combustion engine. The impact of this great invention was felt all along the line—in strategy, in tactics, in organization, and in supply. It revolutionized transportation and made possible the airplane and the armored vehicle. More than any other single invention, it is responsible for the mechanized armies of today.

Tactical Developments. *The twilight of horse cavalry.* The startling rise in the effectiveness of infantry and artillery weapons tended to restrict the role of cavalry and decrease its importance in certain areas. Against an enemy armed with machine guns and rapid firing artillery, the heavy cavalry charge, which occasionally in the past had proved decisive in battle, could no longer prevail. Although still effective for reconnaissance, for combat in open country against a poorly equipped foe, and for dismounted action, cavalry was gradually relegated to a secondary role in Europe. But it still played an important part in secondary theaters where American troops were engaged. Until the development of armor, in western Europe at least, infantry and artillery dominated the battlefield.

The balance swings to the defense. Throughout history the balance between the power of the offense and defense has fluctuated as a result of some weapon or group of weapons which tend to favor one or the other. This advantage exists until countered by some other development, either technical or tactical. Often the shift in balance is not recognized until proved in combat. Such was the case on the eve of World War I. The newly developed automatic weapons and rapid firing artillery with their intense fire power had already tilted the scales in favor of the defense, but the shift did not become known until it was demonstrated on the Western Front in World War I. Except in the first months of the war, neither side was able, as will be seen, to win much ground against the other until the spring of 1918 when the Germans effectively countered the defensive weapons with new offensive tactics. That the Germans did finally collapse was mainly due to the effects of the blockade, attrition, and the overwhelming superiority of the Allies in arms, ammunition, and manpower. The British and French also developed a counterweapon in the tank, but it was not mechanically efficient or produced in sufficient numbers during World War I to become decisive.

The United States Army After the Spanish-American War. *Size.* In the demobilization that followed the War with Spain the Army suffered less loss of strength than in previous postwar periods, partly because the United States still had military commitments, particularly in the Philippines. There was also a growing realization on the part of the American people that the Nation, as a world power, could not longer afford to allow its defenses to wither away completely. To be sure, victory was won, but over a decadent enemy that had not seriously tested the ability of the United States to fight a major war. After the first flush of triumph had passed this fact gradually impressed itself on a sobered public mind and the U. S. Government began to focus its attention on the weaknesses displayed during the war and on the responsibilities that accompanied the Nation's new position in world affairs.

Changes in organization. No one appreciated what these responsibilities meant in terms of national defense more than Elihu Root, who as Secretary of War immediately on taking office set himself the task of preparing the Army for its new role. After studying its experiences in the recent war, he became convinced that most of the mistakes made could be traced directly to faulty military organization. The division of authority, in existence since the early 19th century, under which the Commanding General of the Army exercised discipline and control over the troops in the field while the Secretary of War, working through his bureau chiefs, handled administration and fiscal matters, struck him as the underlying cause of the friction and confusion that marked the conduct of the war. This conviction led him to propose the first of his great reforms: the elimination of dual control over the Army and the restoration of command in strictly military matters to the Army. He would create a Chief of Staff who would take the place of the Commanding General of the Army and be the responsible advisor and executive agent of the President through his Secretary of War. The formulation of Army policy, however, would remain under civil authority. Despite the opposition of diehards, Congress accepted Root's proposal in February 1903. But to pass a law was one thing; to change a system, hallowed by tradition, was another. It required time for reeducation. The subordination of the bureau chiefs, in particular, proved to be a difficult task and was not quickly accomplished.

The General Staff. The second reform recommended by Root was the creation of a General Staff Corps, a group of selected officers free to devote full time to matters of policy and the preparation of military plans. In all previous national emergencies, Root pointed out, plans were drawn up hastily by officers staggering under the load of other duties, with the result that they were woefully inadequate to meet crises when they arose. Again Congress listened and adopted Root's recommendation. The Army now, for the first time in its history, was in a position to develop a group of officers capable of scientific planning for war in time of peace. One of the early products of the new General Staff was the first Field Service Regulations published in 1905. Pioneer work on these regulations and the principles of war had been going on at the Leavenworth schools for quite a few years before that time.

As might have been expected, there were at first misconceptions about the duties of General Staff officers which led some of them to interfere in the affairs of others. Gradually, however, the true functions of the General Staff came to be understood, thanks in part to the educational program that Root sponsored. On setting up a unified command in a theater of operations where both Army and Navy might be involved, Root made no recommendations. It remained, as in the past, a matter which depended on the judgment of the Chief Executive.

Branch and Special Staff reforms. To stay abreast of new ideas and requirements, several reforms affecting the noncombat services and the Special Staff also were introduced. The Medical Department was reorganized gradually to include a Medical Corps, a Hospital Corps, an Army Nurse Corps, a Dental Corps, and a Medical Reserve Corps, the last designed to attract civilian physicians to serve during national emergencies. In 1912 the Subsistence and Pay Department was combined with the Quartermaster to create the Quartermaster Corps. An attempt was also made in that year to establish an Enlisted Reserve Corps, but without success, largely because the framers of the legislation did not provide for the payment, promotion, or training of the Reservists. How complete the failure was is indicated by the fact that only 16 enlisted men were enrolled in the Enlisted Reserve Corps by 1914.

Army schools. To raise the professional qualifications of the Army, annual maneuvers for units of regimental and occasionally larger size were prescribed. The Army schools which had been in existence before the Spanish-American War were reorganized and a number of new schools were established for advanced and specialized study. In 1901 the Leavenworth school was reorganized as the General Service and Staff College to train officers in the use of combined arms and to prepare them for staff and command positions in large units. In November 1903, the Army War College opened its doors, providing a much-needed institution for the education of experienced officers in the problems of the War Department and of high command in the field. The influence of these schools was constructive and far reaching. An Army signal school was established in 1905, indicating the growing military importance of rapid signal communications. Other branch schools followed: the Field Artillery School in 1911 and the School of Musketry in 1913.

Employment of the Regular Army. Because of the disturbance in the Philippines and the need of troops to protect and garrison Alaska, Hawaii, and other overseas areas, a large part of the Regular Army served abroad after 1898. Even after the Philippine Insurrection was officially declared suppressed in mid-1902, American troops could not be withdrawn, for much remained to be done in stamping out scattered resistance and organizing and directing a native force known as the Philippine Scouts. While the size of the Regular Army in peacetime was increased officially to 100,000 officers and men organized into 30 infantry and 15 cavalry regiments supported by a corps of artillery, it did not reach that number and continued to be too small to meet alone the requirements of both home defense and commitments abroad. Congress therefore decided to fill the deficiency in defense needs by strengthening the National Guard.

Changes in the National Guard. The Militia Act of 1903 provided the National Guard with Federal funds, prescribed drill at least twice a month, supplemented the drill periods with short annual training periods, and patterned the Guard's organization and equipment after the Regular Army's. Still, no National Guard unit could be called into Federal service without the consent of the Governor of the state, and then not for more than nine months; no Guardsman could be ordered to such service unless he volunteered; and no Guard officer could be removed by any agency of the Federal government. These restrictions left the National Guard relatively free from Federal control. Between 1908 and 1914 additional changes were introduced. The main ones were the right of the President to prescribe the length of Federal service and, with the advice and consent of the Senate, to appoint all officers of the Guard while in Federal service.

To improve training and to break down the barriers that had plagued relations between the Regular Army and the militia since the birth of the Nation, joint maneuvers were held from time to time after 1902. While these maneuvers failed to produce all the results sought, they encouraged coordination between the two components and helped to create a better integrated, more harmonious defense force, capable of immediate participation in a major conflict.

In response to changing functions, the artillery in 1907 was divided into the Coast Artillery Corps and the Field Artillery. The purpose of the former was to plot and prepare underwater mine fields and to man the heavy guns in the new harbor defenses that had been constructed to protect American ports against hostile fleets. Its mission was not unlike that of the Navy. The Field Artillery on the other hand remained in the field army with its main mission, the support of the infantry in battle, unchanged. In the light of the differences that had developed in mission, equipment, and operations the change was a logical and necessary one at the time.

Plans for larger tactical units. Experience in the Spanish-American War, observations of developments abroad, and annual maneuvers all pointed to the need of permanent, self-sufficient units, composed of the combined arms. Regiments, the largest peacetime units then in existence, afforded no training in the command of large units or in meeting the special problems of supply and administration created by brigades and divisions. In 1910 the General Staff drew up a plan for three permanent infantry divisions composed of designated Regular Army and National Guard regiments. Because of the difficulties that arose shortly thereafter along the Mexican border, the plan could not be put into operation. Instead, a provisional "maneuver division" was hastily organized, and its component units were ordered to the border in the hope that an immediate show of force would discourage further disturbances.

What actually happened was disappointing. No division could be quickly assembled. Regular Army troops had to be collected from widely scattered points in the continental United States, and every post, depot, and arsenal had to be denuded to scrape up the necessary equipment. Even so, when the "maneuver division" was finally brought together it was far from fully operational since none of its regiments were up to strength or adequately armed. Field artillery ammunition supply, for example, was so low that there was scarcely enough in the entire country to meet the needs of a single day of normal combat even in accordance with a ratio of field artillery to infantry which, under existing organizational concepts, was considered much too low. Fortunately, the efficiency of the "maneuver division" was not put to any battle test, and within a short time it was possible to break it up and return component units to their home stations. It would have been far wiser to relocate these units in a few places, as many responsible military leaders at the time advocated, but political considerations prevailed and they were again distributed among some 50 posts around the country. Since the average strength of the garrison at these posts was only 700 men, continued practice in the use of combined arms and the handling of large units was impossible. An effort was made to organize the scattered posts so that their garrisons could join one of three paper divisions, but this was hardly more than a short step in the direction of the mobile, well-trained and well-equipped force required.

Conservative estimates by the General Staff at the time placed the defense need at over 500,000 men, with provisions for the immediate mobilization of an additional 300,000 in case of a national emergency. Reasonable as these estimates may seem today, they were far too high to receive approval at the time. It was to take the outbreak of war in Europe to persuade Congress that additional increases in the strength of the Army were actually necessary. Yet the early border experiences and the staff studies on organization made during the period were not without value. When in 1913 trouble with Mexico, arising out of chronic revolutionary conditions in that country, again led to a military concentration along the border, the lessons learned in the earlier mobilization were so well applied that in less than a week a division was assembled ready for movement to any danger spot.

The beginning of the Air Service. Interest in aeronautics in the Army goes back to the captive balloons used during the Civil War. Interest in heavier than air flying equipment, powered by the internal combustion engine also began early, in fact long before a successful flight was made. In 1898 the War Department subsidized Dr. Samuel P. Langley's experiments, only to discontinue them in 1903 when his ill-fated plane crashed into the Potomac River. Attempts on the part of Wilbur and Orville Wright to prove that their machine could pass army tests successfully were at first rebuffed, and it was not until late in 1908 that their creation was given a trial. The results of the test indicated that the Army had a promising new weapon within its grasp. But when Congress was asked for funds to further its development, the request was denied.

Meanwhile other nations were paying considerably more attention to the weapon that was to influence warfare so profoundly. By 1913,

France, Russia, Germany, and England were spending millions annually on aviation. Even Mexico was spending $400,000 yearly at a time when the United States was devoting only $125,000 to aviation. The result of such niggardly appropriations was that on the eve of one of the greatest wars in history the United States Army had but 6 planes and 16 trained pilots. A hope that this lack of parity with other nations might be overcome rapidly arose in July 1914 when Congress authorized the creation of an Aviation Section in the Signal Corps composed of 60 officers and 260 enlisted men. But this group accomplished little, partly because the young air enthusiasts in it received only grudging and tardy support from their superiors. Consequently, only a few planes were available on the Mexican border in 1916, most of which broke down. When the United States entered World War I as a belligerent, the Army discovered that it had been left far behind in aviation by startling developments abroad, not only in equipment but in organization and doctrine as well. American pilots were required to learn as they fought in foreign aircraft, for not a single American fighter plane reached the Western Front before the armistice, despite the millions of dollars poured into the effort to catch up with the other powers.

Cuban Occupation. The close of the war with Spain did not settle the Cuban problem which had caused it. As a result of years of misrule and fighting, conditions in the island were in a deplorable state when the fighting ended. Under the provisions of the Teller Amendment, it will be recalled, the United States was committed to turning Cuba over to its people. But to have withdrawn from the island before economic and political stability was established would have been both folly and evasion of responsibility. A provisional government supported by an army of occupation therefore was set up immediately headed first by Maj. Gen. John R. Brooke and later by Maj. Gen. Leonard Wood. It began at once the many tasks involved in the tremendous job of rehabilitation and reform: feeding and clothing the starving; caring for the sick; cleaning up the accumulated filth of centuries in the cities; restoring agricultural and commercial activity; disbanding the Cuban Army and paying its veterans; organizing municipal governments, local guards, and courts; building roads and other public works; establishing schools; and, in general, preparing the people for self-government. One of the greatest achievements of the Provisional Government was the elimination of yellow fever by the Army Medical Department. This was made possible by the discovery that the dread disease was carried by mosquitoes.

When stability was finally restored, a constitutent assembly was convened which, under the chairmanship of General Wood, drew up an organic law for the island patterned after the Constitution of the United States. Into it, several clauses known as the Platt Amendment were incorporated, limiting the amount of debt Cuba could contract, granting the United States naval bases at Guantanamo and Bahia Honda, and giving the United States the right to intervene to preserve "Cuban independence" and maintain a government "adequate to the protection of life, property and individual liberty". In 1902, after a general election and the inauguration of the Republic's first President, the occupation came to an end. These provisions were later incorporated into a Treaty of Relations between the United States and the Republic of Cuba. Events soon proved that the period of tutelage in self-government had been too short. Thrice thereafter—in 1906, in 1912, and again in 1917 during World War I—the United States had to intervene to reestablish law and order. Each time the occupying force was withdrawn as soon as order was restored. In 1934 a new Treaty of Relations abrogating the restrictions on Cuba's sovereignty imposed by the earlier treaty, was concluded. Under it the United States retained the right to maintain its naval base at Guantanamo. Despite past interventions and the limitations placed on the island's sovereignty by the Platt Amendment (relinquished in 1934), Cubans today generally agree that the attitude of the United States toward their land has been one of unselfish helpfulness.

The Panama Canal. A logical result of the emergence of the United States as a world power with a primary interest in the Caribbean was the construction of an interocean canal. The strategic need of such a waterway was deeply impressed upon the American people during the Spanish-American War by the long voyage of the battleship *Oregon* from Puget Sound on the west coast around South America to Cuban waters where it arrived just in time to participate in the destruction of Cervera's fleet off Santiago. President Roosevelt therefore was widely supported when he rather arbitrarily set diplomatic and political machinery in motion to acquire the sole right to complete a canal in Panama, begun earlier by a defunct French company headed by Ferdinand de Lesseps, builder of the Suez Canal. Toward the end of 1903, all political obstacles had been overcome sufficiently to permit work on the project to begin as soon as Congress appropriated funds and a final decision was made as to who should do the work.

After considerable deliberation and negotiations with a civilian engineering firm the conclusion was reached that building a canal was a job for the Army rather than private enterprise. A commission of Army officers under Col. George W. Goethals, who served as Chairman and Chief Engineer and a little later as Civil Governor of the Canal Zone as well, was set up to supervise the task of construction. An able soldier and expert administrator, Goethals pushed construction to completion in eight years. In this task he was ably supported by the Medical Department in the Canal Zone headed by

Col. William C. Gorgas. By rigidly applying the principles of field sanitation and the knowledge acquired in the Cuban Occupation, malaria was quickly brought under control, yellow fever, the curse of the Tropics, was wiped out, and the Canal Zone was transformed from a pest hole to a healthy and attractive place for human habitation. Without the splendid work of the Medical Department, it is doubtful that Goethals would have had the success he did. Today, the canal stands as a lasting monument to the technical ability, discipline, and efficiency of the Army working at its best in the fulfillment of a peacetime mission. Its completion partially freed the Nation of the heavy cost of maintaining an enormous fleet in both the Atlantic and Pacific since it permitted vessels to move quickly to any point of need in either ocean. On the other hand, it created a strategic point in the continental defense system which required for protection the strongest and most up-to-date facilities manned by permanent highly trained garrisons.

Mexico in Turmoil. *The United States becomes involved.* As has already been noted, internal trouble in Mexico led to serious border disturbances which threatened to upset the peace between that country and the United States. In 1913 Gen. Victoriano Huerta, who had become President of Mexico after the assassination of President Francisco Madera, found himself faced with an uprising led by former supporters of Madera. To add to Huerta's difficulties, President Woodrow Wilson upon assumption of office adopted a policy of "watchful waiting"; withheld recognition of Huerta because of the manner in which he had come to power, thereby altering a long-standing recognition policy; and permitted the sale of arms to Huerta's chief opponents, Gen. Venustiano Carranza and Francisco Villa. Resentful of this treatment, some of Huerta's followers arrested U. S. sailors while in the port of Tampico. They were soon released with an expression of regret from the dictator, but Rear Adm. Henry T. Mayo, commanding the U. S. Fleet, was not satisfied and demanded an additional apology in the form of a salute to the American flag. This Huerta refused to do unless the Mexican flag was saluted in return. The demand having been made by Admiral Mayo, President Wilson supported it. The policy of "watchful waiting" was temporarily abandoned, and the port of Vera Cruz was occupied after a bombardment that cost many lives. War with Mexico seemed inevitable but was avoided when Huerta resigned and Carranza, whom Wilson favored, became President. Carranza had hardly assumed office when his erstwhile ally, "Pancho" Villa, started another revolution, during which he managed to win control of most of northern Mexico.

The Punitive Expedition. Despite Carranza's precarious hold on Mexico, President Wilson decided to recognize his government. It

Punitive Expedition in Mexico. Brig. Gen. John J. Pershing, right foreground.

was now the turn of Villa to show resentment, which he did by creating border incidents. The chief one was a surprise attack by some 1,500 men against Columbus, N. M., on 9 March 1916. A number of American troops and civilians were killed in the raid, and considerable property was destroyed before units of the 13th Cavalry drove off the band. The following day, President Wilson ordered Brig. Gen. John J. Pershing into Mexico to assist the Mexican Government in taking Villa.

On 15 March the punitive expedition entered Mexico in "hot pursuit". It chased Villa through unfriendly territory for hundreds of miles, never quite catching up with him but managing to disperse most of his followers. Although Carranza could not suppress Villa, he soon showed that he had no desire to have the United States do the job for him. He protested the continued presence of American troops in Mexico and insisted on their withdrawal. This attitude, plus the orders from the War Department forbidding attacks on Mexicans that were not followers of Villa, made it extremely difficult for Pershing to deal effectively with other hostile Mexicans who blocked his path without running the danger of precipitating war. Some clashes with government troops actually took place. The most important one was the fight at Carrizal in which scores were killed or wounded. The action once again created a critical situation and led President Wilson to call 75,000 National Guardsmen into Federal service to help police the border. War probably would have broken out then and there but for the bitter struggle raging in Europe. Anxious not to become involved in Mexico at a time when relations with Germany were deteriorating, Wilson agreed to submit the disputes arising out of the punitive expedition to a joint commission for settlement. Some time later the commission ruled, among other things, that the American unit commander involved in the Carrizal affair was at fault. In January 1917, as the relations between the United States and Germany approached the critical stage, the expedition was withdrawn.

Military benefits from border experience. Although Pershing failed to capture Villa, the activities of the American troops in Mexico and along the border were not wasted effort. The dispersal of Villa's band put an end to serious border incidents. More important from a military point of view was the intensive training in the field received by both the Regular Army and the National Guard on the border and in Mexico. Many defects in the Military Establishment, especially in the National Guard, were uncovered in time to correct them before the Army was thrown into the cauldron of war in Europe. One other result that can be attributed to the experiences of the Army on the border, in part at least, was the passage of much-needed new legislation affecting national defense.

National Defense Act of 1916. In June 1916 Congress passed a National Defense Act which made possible the retention of the National Guard on the border as long as necessary by empowering the President, when authorized by Congress, to call it into Federal service for the duration of a national emergency, not merely for the nine months permitted under the act of 1903. Congress also reasserted the principle embodied in law since 1792 that all able-bodied men between the ages of 18 and 45 were subject to military service. In reaffirming this principle, Congress made possible the translation of an indefinite military obligation, about which most Americans were uninformed, into compulsory service in time of war, thereby paving the way for the passage of the Selective Service Act of May 1917. The National Defense Act also provided for an Officers' Reserve Corps and an Enlisted Reserve Corps, the latter to be formed from men who wished to enroll after completing active duty. Maximum Regular Army strength was increased to about 288,000 men, organized into 65 infantry, 25 cavalry, and 21 artillery regiments, 91 coast artillery companies, and the necessary service units to support them. To fill the recognized need for large-sized tactical organizations in being rather than on paper, these units were assigned to brigades and divisions. In the same act, National Guard strength up to 425,000 men was authorized. It also provided for fuller support of military training in colleges and summer camps, an important and necessary step to meet the need for officers in an expanding army. The flaw in the bill was the provision which required increases to be spread over a period of five years. Failure to provide for immediate enlargement left the Army with only some 5,000 officers and 123,000 men in the Regular Army and 8,500 officers and 123,000 men in the National Guard on the eve of America's entry into World War I.

The Preparedness Campaign.   Conscious of the dangers in continued military weakness, many Americans began to urge immediate steps to prepare the Nation for any eventuality as soon as war broke out in Europe in 1914.   Summer camps fostered by General Wood were established as early as 1913.   Young men could attend these camps without compensation in order to prepare themselves for future leadership in the Army.   The first of the summer camps was at Plattsburg Barracks, N. Y., and so the movement came to be called the "Plattsburg Idea".   It proved to be one of the most significant military developments of the time.   Those who attended the camps not only learned something about military drill and discipline but became ardent supporters of preparedness, preaching the gospel of universal military training and service whenever the opportunity arose.   The movement won wide support and doubtless played an important part in lining up public opinion behind the National Defense Act of 1916 and in preparing the American people for the acceptance of wartime universal military service.   Its success might have been even greater had it not been pictured by antiwar groups as too closely associated with those who were working to put the United States into the European conflict on the side of the Allies.   In fact, the whole preparedness movement suffered because many of its leading advocates were also ardently in favor of intervention at a time when a large part of the American public still preferred to remain neutral.

Summary.   The period between 1900 and the outbreak of World War I was one of great industrial and commercial growth and increased competition for world markets.   To further national interests, diplomatic activity was intensified and armies and navies were expanded to unprecedented peacetime size.   The result was an armament race and a heightening of tension between the powers.   Increased technical knowledge and mass production methods combined to produce new, more abundant, and more deadly weapons, raising manyfold man's capacity both to destroy his enemy and to defend himself.

The United States, in accord with the times, sought to advance its interests by both diplomatic effort and military strength.   Because the Navy was the first line of defense and was essential to protect the newly acquired possessions in the Caribbean, the Pacific, and the Far East, it received more attention than the Army.   By 1914 it was the third largest in the world, only slightly behind Germany.   But the Army was not allowed to wither away, mainly because of overseas commitments.   Organizationally, it underwent considerable change, partly in adjustment to new weapons but more in the interest of greater efficiency.   The confusion and many defects that came to light during the Spanish-American War proved the need for reform. Under the leadership of Elihu Root dual control over the Army was eliminated; a General Staff Corps was created; and new schools were established for the instruction of officers and men.   National Guard training was improved and its organization and equipment were brought into line with that of the Regular Army, a development that helped to create a more harmonious and effective Army. Other organizational changes were made from time to time, some of them basic, but little was done except on paper to organize units larger than a regiment. The result was continued inadequate field training in the use of combined arms and the handling of brigades and divisions. But for the mobilization and shakedown on the Mexican border, the Army would have entered World War I with no more experience in such matters than in previous wars.

Among the achievements during the period between the War with Spain and World War I, in which the Army can take just pride, the reconstruction work in Cuba, the building of the Panama Canal, and the maintenance of order on the Mexican border deserve mention. The first two showed the Army engaged in a peaceful constructive activity, wiping out disease and establishing order. On the Mexican border, the Army put an end to incidents without involving the Nation in war. The experience gained proved invaluable. Without it the Army in World War I would have been far less successful than it was.

QUESTIONS

1. What new weapons came into more general use in armies and navies after 1900? What forces in the world were responsible for their adoption?

2. Explain Root's Army reform program.

3. Describe the nonmilitary activities of the Army in Cuba and Panama.

4. What effect did the acquisition of the Philippines have on (1) American foreign policy, (2) strategy?

5. Explain the impact of the Mexican border experiences on Army organization and training.

6. What were the major provisions of the National Defense Act of 1916?

7. Discuss the preparedness campaign.

Reading List

Bishop, J. B. *Panama Gateway*. New York, 1915.

Chapman, Charles E. *A History of the Cuban Republic*. New York, 1927.

Dennett, Tyler. *The Americans in Eastern Asia*. New York, 1922.

Hackett, C. W. *The Mexican Revolution and the United States, 1910–1926*. New York, 1926.

Jones, Chester Lloyd. *The United States and the Caribbean*. New York, 1929.

Rippey, J. F. *The United States and Mexico*. New York, 1931.

CHAPTER 18

WORLD WAR I

Outbreak of War. Shortly after the beginning of trouble with Mexico, the long period of peace between the armed camps in Europe suddenly ended and the Continent burst into flame. The spark that set it off was the assassination of the heir to the Austro-Hungarian throne by a fanatical Serbian nationalist in Sarajevo on 28 June 1914. Supported by the German Government, which believed a localized settlement possible, the Austro-Hungarian Government sent an ultimatum to Serbia, making demands that were rejected; whereupon Austria-Hungary declared war. Events moved swiftly and by 4 August, Germany, France, Russia, England, and Belgium were drawn into the struggle, while Italy, a lukewarm member of the Triple Alliance, declared itself neutral. Before the conflict ended, many other nations were drawn into it. Turkey and Bulgaria joined Austria-Hungary and Germany, while Japan, Italy, China, the United States, and others joined the Allies. Europe was the center of military activity, but campaigns were also fought in Asia and Africa, and almost every ocean witnessed some naval activity. All told, about 65,000,000 men were mobilized, of whom 10,000,000 were killed. In lives lost and wealth expended no previous war in history approached it in magnitude.

German Miscalculations. German strategy in case of war on two fronts called for the quick destruction of the French armies in the west before Russia could mobilize, then a rapid shifting of forces to the east and the defeat of the Russian armies at will. During the first few weeks of World War I it appeared that the German plan might succeed. But the Germans made two serious mistakes. The first was the modification of the "Schlieffen Plan," prepared years before the war by Germany's famous Chief of Staff, Count Alfred von Schlieffen. That war plan had aimed at encircling the French armies by a wide sweep through the Low Countries and northern France and then crushing them against fixed German fortifications in Lorraine. But the Germans, by withdrawing units from the right flank to bolster the Eastern Front and shifting troops to the center, found themselves in the summer and fall of 1914 incapable of enveloping the French. The weakening of the right flank has since been cited as a classic example of the violation of the principle that mass should be concentrated in the force that is to deliver the main blow.

The second major German error was the underestimation of the time it would take the Russian Army to mobilize and launch an attack on Germany. The Russians began to move much sooner than the Germans expected. To meet the danger, the Germans withdrew two corps from the west and sent them to the Eastern Front. Before they arrived the Germans had already destroyed the Russian armies in the battles of Tannenberg and Masurian Lakes in August and September 1915. Had the two corps been retained in the west where they were badly needed, it might not have been necessary for the Germans to withdraw to positions behind the Aisne River after losing the critical Battle of the Marne in September.

Stabilized Warfare Begins. After the Battle of the Marne the Allies vigorously attacked the Germans on the Aisne but failed to dent their skillfully chosen and well-organized positions, evidence that the technical developments of the prewar period tended to favor the defense rather than the offense at least under conditions where narrow fronts with protected flanks made wide envelopments impossible. More and more, leaders on both sides awakened to the fact that a transition from open to stabilized warfare was at hand in western Europe and that the expected short war was destined to become a prolonged one (map 37).

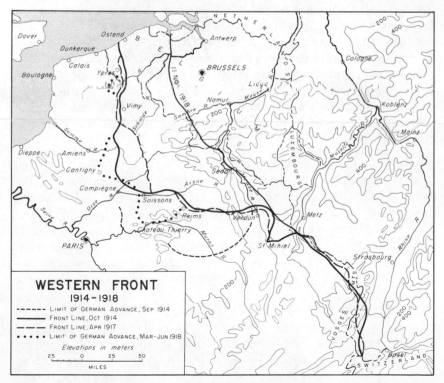

Map 37.   Western Front, 1914–1918.

The Race to the Sea. The stalemate along the Aisne was followed by a "race to the sea," in which each side sought to envelop the northern flank of the other in successive battles. By October the race was over, neither side having won. Fortunately for the Allies they retained all the channel ports west of Ostend. Loss of these ports would have seriously handicapped England in supplying her forces on the Continent and would have given the Germans valuable bases for future naval operations.

Stalemate on the Western Front. With the flanks of both opposing armies securely protected by the sea on the north and by neutral Switzerland on the south, the only hope of victory for either side lay in a successful penetration of the line of the other. The story of the war on the Western Front from that time until the end of hostilities deals largely with the efforts of first one belligerent and then the other to break through its opponent's defense system. Against a well-dug-in defender, skillfully coordinating terrain with firepower, no attacker, however high his offensive spirit, could hope to prevail without first attaining overwhelming superiority in men and weapons. Such principles of war as maneuver, economy of force, and surprise could be applied only in a limited manner; that of mass became dominant. Because of superior long-range artillery and greater skill in the use of field fortifications, barbed-wire, machine-guns, mortars, and grenades, the Germans initially enjoyed an advantage in the new type of warfare. To overcome it, the Allies had to raise and train vast armies and produce munitions and supplies on an unprecedented scale. In industrial potential, economic strength, and manpower the advantage was distinctly with the Allies. The unanswered question was: could it be transferred to the battlefield in time to prevent the Germans from breaking the deadlock and winning a decision?

Effect on Tactics and Weapons. New tactics, too, were required to break the stalemate. In attacking across the "no-man's land" between the hostile lines in the face of artillery, mortar, and machine-gun fire, troops on both sides learned to advance in waves, first moving out in platoon and section columns and then deploying in assault lines characterized by wide intervals between men as they encountered defensive small arms fire. As the war progressed new weapons also came into use. Chief among the offensive weapons developed were gas and tanks.

The Germans first used gas on the Eastern Front at Bolinov in early 1915 but without great success for cold weather spoiled its effectiveness. They first used it on the Western Front in April 1915 against the British at Ypres. Here chlorine gas, disseminated from cannisters and carried by a favorable breeze, caused great confusion among the exposed troops on a five-mile front. But the Germans were totally unprepared to exploit the surprise created by the green vapor. This was a strategic blunder, for complete surprise was wasted merely to attain a local victory. Both sides thereafter rapidly developed a variety of gases of toxic and lacrymatory nature which they delivered mostly in shells fired by artillery and also defensive measures against them.

The tank was first developed by the British and French as a weapon to penetrate barbed-wire entaglements and overwhelm enemy machine gun nests. The British tank was a ponderous vehicle invented by General Swinton of the Royal Engineers who had obtained some of his ideas from American farm tractors. It weighed 27 tons and had a cruising range of 25 miles in battle. Its weakness, aside from its limited range, was that it was unwieldy and subject to frequent mechanical failures. The 7-ton Renault tank, developed by the French, was lighter but faster. Both depended on close coordination with advancing infantry for success. The British first used tanks in the Somme area in September 1916 in an effort to break the deadlock on the Western Front. In a surprise attack the tanks had spectacular success initially but failed to penetrate the German lines. By using tanks prematurely the British lost the full effect of the surprise. Over a year elapsed before the tank was properly employed, by which time the enemy had developed a defense against it. In another surprise attack near Cambrai 476 tanks, followed closely by infantry and covered by a smoke screen, smashed through the German forward positions. But a breakdown in Allied tank-infantry teamwork, coupled with new German defense tactics and the obstacle of the St. Quentin Canal, enabled the Germans to break up the attack.

The Impact of the War on the United States. It was natural for the American people, drawn as they were from many nations and chiefly from those at war, to display an intense interest in the struggle in Europe. Ignoring the admonition of President Wilson to remain "impartial in thought as well as in action", most Americans soon took sides. The side they chose was determined as much by emotion, engendered by blood, racial, cultural, and economic ties, and political affinity and propaganda as by knowledge of the underlying causes of the conflict. Yet despite the strong passions exhibited, there was at first little desire to become involved. The tradition of non-involvement in European affairs was still too firmly fixed in the American mind, but, as time went on and the conflict grew more violent and bitter, the spirit of neutrality gradually weakened.

From the start both sides interfered with the trade of nonbelligerents. The British Navy dominated the seas and blockaded not only Germany but neutral European nations as well. The British arbitrarily added to the list of prohibited items many commodities not normally considered contraband of war under international law, blacklisted firms suspected of trading directly or indirectly with the Central Powers, and ordered neutral shipping into British ports for search. Germany, unable to use its surface fleet, resorted to submarines to stop the flow of supplies to the Allies, thereby inaugurating a new type of blockade, the legality of which was at once questioned. To meet this threat, Great Britain armed merchant vessels and directed them to fire at submarines on sight. Contending that the protection of international law did not extend to armed merchantmen, Germany retaliated by ordering enemy cargo ships sunk without warning. As was to be expected, the Germans could not avoid errors of identification, one of which resulted in an attack on the American ship *Gulflight*. A climax was reached in 1915 when the British liner *Lusitania* was sunk off the coast of Ireland with the loss of 1,195 lives, including 124 Americans.

The United States protested the violation of neutral rights by both belligerents but in stronger terms to Germany since its actions involved the destruction of life. In April 1916, after President Wilson threatened to break off diplomatic relations unless it discontinued unrestricted submarine warfare, Germany agreed not to sink passenger ships and to warn all other vessels before attacking them, provided they offered no resistance. For a while the promise was kept and tension eased. But early in 1917, following Allied rejection of a peace offer, Germany announced a return to unrestricted submarine warfare in a zone covering the approaches to Great Britain and France; whereupon the United States at once severed diplomatic relations.

The succession of events now hastened the United States along the road to war. Early in March American opinion was shocked by the publication of an intercepted German message to the Mexican Government, the Zimmerman note, which proposed an alliance between Germany and Mexico if the United States entered the war. Shortly afterwards, President Wilson announced that American merchant ships would be armed, and on the same day an American ship was sunk under circumstances which for the first time permitted no excuse whatever on grounds of error. In the next few days four more American ships fell victim to German U-boats. Six Americans lost their lives. With public opinion thoroughly aroused, Congress on 6 April 1917 declared war on Germany.

German Hope for Ultimate Victory. In returning to unrestricted submarine warfare, the German Government was fully aware that it risked war with the United States. It had taken the risk largely because German naval leaders were confident that unrestricted submarine warfare would bring the Allies to their knees before American arms could become a decisive factor. The decline in Allied morale also gave Germany hope of ultimate victory. France, Italy, and Russia were all showing signs of war weariness, and the Germans had every reason to believe that Russia at least might soon be eliminated from the war, permitting them to concentrate most of their military strength in the west.

The German leaders miscalculated, however, in believing that America's entry into the war would bring no significant increase in material aid to the Allies, that no army could be raised in time to render a substantial contribution on the battlefield, and that no solution to the menace of the submarine could be found. Events proved their reasoning wrong on all points. The United States, stimulated by actual war, raised a formidable military force, increased the output of its factories and farms tremendously, and built ships faster than German U-boats could destroy them. The United States Navy joined the Allied war effort on the seas, making possible an effective convoy system that in time nullified the German submarine campaign. Because of these developments, Germany's one remaining hope of victory lay in the early elimination of Russia from the war and the defeat of the French and British before American troops could turn the tide of battle.

The Collapse of Russia. The German Army, therefore, went on the defensive in the west during 1917, shortened its lines to save manpower, and concentrated its strength in the east where a revolutionary Russian government headed by Alexander Kerensky had launched a last offensive. When it failed, the Germans counterattacked. The Russian armies disintegrated rapidly; the Kerensky government was itself overthrown; and by November the Bolsheviks under Lenin and Trotsky, who had come to power with the connivance of Germany, agreed to talk peace. After several months of haggling over terms, during which the Germans advanced to the outskirts of St. Petersburg, the Bolsheviks on 3 March 1918 signed a treaty at Brest Litovsk taking their country out of the war. Russia's collapse brought some economic relief to the Germans, who were suffering from the strangling effect of the Allied blockade, and released enough men and guns to enable them to gain a temporary numerical superiority on the Western Front for the first time since the early days of the war.

American Military Activity Begins. Shortly after entering the war the United States dispatched advance elements of an expeditionary force under Maj. Gen. John J. Pershing to France, where they arrived in June 1917. The choice of Pershing proved to be an excellent one; he was professionally competent, a natural leader, a thorough organizer, and a strict disciplinarian. During his career in the Army he had carried out every mission given him with imagination and vigor.

After studying Allied needs in men and arms, Pershing advised the War Department to prepare to send 1,000,000 trained men to Europe within a year and to lay plans for raising a total force of 3,000,000—a figure that was later increased to 4,000,000 by the War

337

Maj. Gen. John J. Pershing landing in France.

Department. The strength of the Army at the time was about 200,000 men, 65,000 of whom were National Guardsmen in Federal service. To increase the Army twentyfold and train it was a tremendous task, one that would require considerable time even under the most favorable conditions.

Hope and Disillusionment. Many uninformed people had visions of hundreds of thousands of "Yankees" pouring into France within a short time to give the Allies the overwhelming numerical superiority needed to drive the invader across the Rhine and bring the war to a close. As the months passed with the arrival of nothing more than a token force, Allied morale, already shaken by bad news from Russia and Italy and the disaster suffered by the French in the Second Battle of the Aisne, declined rapidly. The high hopes of the spring and summer of 1917 gave way to disillusionment, often in circles where only shortly before confidence had been strongest. What many failed to appreciate was that raising a military force of several million men involved more than merely calling men to the colors. For such a task existing facilities, equipment, and instructors were completely inadequate.

Mobilization. *The Selective Service Act.* It was clear from the start that the time-honored volunteer system could not provide all the men needed by the Army. A form of conscription was required. But conscription was not popular, many Americans believing that compulsory service was unbefitting a free people, particularly if administered by military authority. Newton D. Baker, the Secretary of War, hoped to overcome this opposition by placing the draft machinery in the hands of civilian boards. Based on Baker's proposal, Congress passed the Selective Service Act on 19 May 1917. The act established the National Army and required all males between the ages of 21 and 30 to register for service. Later, the age was raised to 45. The law also permitted volunteering for the Regular Army, National Guard, Marine Corps, and Navy. It specifically prohibited the twin evils of the Civil War period, the hiring of substitutes and the payment of bounties to induce enlistments.

Conscription. On 5 June 1917 the first million men registered for service, and from this initial reservoir of manpower conscripts were chosen by lot. Within three months, the first draftees, numbering 180,000, were selected, screened, and sent to training camps. Other contingents followed periodically thereafter until the end of the war, when conscription was suspended. About 67 percent of the men serving in the Army during World War I were brought in under the Selective Service Act. Under the system, 2,810,296 men were selected and delivered to the armed forces in less than 18 months.

Officering the National Army. The selection and training of officers for the National Army was a far more difficult task than providing men for the ranks. When war broke out there were less than 9,000 officers in Federal service. About 200,000 were needed. In previous wars appointments directly from civilian life had largely met officer requirements, often to the detriment of the men in the ranks. In World War I the Army attempted to select prospective officers on the basis of proved leadership and capacity to command. Only specialists, such as doctors and individuals qualified for duty in supply and technical services, received direct commissions. Officers for other assignments were obtained from qualified enlisted men of the Regular Army, from the Reserve Officers' Training Corps and Student Army Training Corps in colleges and universities, and from officer training camps and schools in division cantonments. The last two produced most of the officers commissioned during the war. Candidates for commissions were carefully selected for the camps and then subjected to intensive training for a period of about three months. Those who made the grade, about 60 percent of the number originally enrolled, were commissioned in the new National Army. Their capacity for leadership far exceeded that of the average officer of the Army in any previous war. It was largely these new officers who led the troops that broke the "Hindenburg Line" in 1918, winning by their deeds the respect of friend and foe alike.

Organization. Reports from observers in Europe early in the war convinced the War Department that the existing organization of the Army, particularly the infantry division, was not suited to the type of war that was being fought on the Western Front. A division capable of greater and longer-sustained driving power was needed. On the recommendation of General Pershing the strength of the infantry division was therefore increased to 27,000 men—later 28,000—and the division was reorganized into two infantry brigades of two regiments each, a field artillery brigade, a regiment of combat engineers, three machine gun battalions, and supporting service troops. These changes made the American infantry division roughly twice the size of the British, French, and German infantry divisions of the time. The enlarged division, though unwieldy and difficult to control, had tremendous striking and staying power, the characteristics that experience proved were most needed to crash through enemy defenses on the Western Front.

The War Department organized 62 divisions during World War I. At the close of the war 43 of these had been sent to France and 19 others were in various stages of organization and training. At first the National Guard and National Army divisions comprised men from particular areas, but, as fillers and replacements from all parts of the land were assigned to these divisions, they became almost as thoroughly mixed as the Regular Army divisions.

Other organizational changes came about as the result of the introduction of new weapons. The War Department assigned the antiaircraft mission, which derived from the use of the airplane in war, to the coast artillery rather than the field artillery largely because the coast artillery had training in firing on moving objects and because the field artillery was expected to need all its resources in fulfilling its traditional mission. The War Department also created special units either to handle or to defend against gas, flame throwers, tanks, and other new weapons.

Logistical Problems. Probably the most difficult organizational problem that the Army had to deal with in World War I was the establishment of a smooth-functioning logistical system for both the Zone of Interior and the theater of operations. World War I turned out to be a vast undertaking in which the resources of the Nation were mobilized as never before. Because of great natural wealth, experience in mass production, and the aptitude of the people for getting things done, the United States had a greater capacity for producing munitions of war than any other nation. But it was one thing to produce goods for peacetime use, quite another for war purposes. The war created new requirements and demanded a speeding up of procurement, production, and distribution. To estimate the military requirements and to accelerate the machinery of production and distribution placed a premium on planning and organization. It meant not only the mobilization of the financial and industrial power of the United States but also its coordination with that of the Allies. This was a herculean task that taxed the ability and strength of America and the patience of the Allies to the utmost.

Production of arms. In the United States most of 1917 was devoted to the retooling and expansion of industrial plants, to the construction of barracks and facilities to house troops, and to estimating requirements and letting contracts. New weapons were slow in rolling from factories, and many of the first men drafted were trained with dummy or obsolete weapons. To speed up the arming of troops, the War Department adopted the British Lee-Enfield rifle modified to take U. S. ammunition. Manufacture of the Springfield .03 rifle was curtailed, and the 600,000 available were issued to Regular Army units only. The British and French supplied machine guns and automatic rifles for most of the Army. But those troops reaching France after 1 July 1918 were armed with Browning machine guns and automatic rifles. These proved to be far more reliable and effective than those bought from the Allies. The artillery used by the Army was acquired in large part from the French. Planes and tanks were furnished by both France and Great Britain. The United States did produce an excellent 12-cylinder Liberty airplane engine, which was put into the British De Havilland 4, an observation and daytime bombing plane. The United States succeeded in manufacturing some aircraft for war purposes, but, on the whole, its plane production program was unsuccessful, particularly in the categories of fighters and bombers. For those, the United States remained dependent on the Allies throughout the war despite untold millions spent on development. This failure in plane output was largely attributable to the fact that the government did not maintain its lead in aviation and to constant changes in design after production had begun.

Transportation. Transportation is one of the most critical elements in any logistics system. The shipment of some 2,000,000 men across 3,000 miles of ocean was the major movement problem confronting the United States in World War I. The problem was the more difficult because there was no previous experience to guide those dealing with a task of such magnitude. Success demanded an unprecedented number of ships of all kinds, the organization of ports, the construction of piers, warehouses, roads, railroads, and planning and coordination all along the line of communications from the source of production to the point of delivery in the theater of operations. Under the circumstances it would have been a miracle had everything proceeded smoothly.

When the United States entered World War I, the shipping situation was critical owing to losses inflicted by enemy submarines. Following the introduction of the convoy system, losses were cut sharply. To further reduce the strain on Allied shipping, the United States curtailed imports drastically, reduced the turnaround time of vessels by one-half, and initiated a mass construction program of standardized cargo ships. It also used British vessels, interned German liners, and some ships seized from the Dutch.

The movement of troops overseas was accomplished with less difficulty and confusion than the shipment of cargo. Poor planning, lack of vision, and inadequate control over rail shipments resulted in the glutting of the ports on both sides of the Atlantic as the load increased. The situation became so bad in the United States that the Government finally had to take over and operate the railroads. In France the confusion, though partly the result of unclarified command and the low morale among service troops, was mainly attributable to the lack of an expansible organization for handling the tremendous increase in the volume of supplies. Realizing the importance of the problem, General Pershing reorganized the Services of Supply and assigned Maj. Gen. James G. Harbord, one of his ablest officers, to this command. By firm action and intelligent planning, Harbord succeeded in clarifying command responsibility, restoring morale, and clearing the ports, thereby saving the American Expeditionary Forces from the complete supply breakdown that threatened.

Utilization of American Troops. Shortly after the first contingent of American troops arrived in France, the Allies began to exert pressure to have them fed into their armies ostensibly for training purposes. Actually they sought replacements to bolster the sagging strength of their battalions. General Pershing, with the full support of the War Department, opposed the demands on the grounds that integration would destroy confidence and national pride, two main characteristics in a successful fighting force, and prevent the training of his higher officers in command and staff responsibilities. The commander of the AEF was not so obstinate in his view, however, that he clung to it at the cost of Allied defeat, for he offered the unrestricted use of his troops in the crisis created by the German breakthrough in March 1918. Instead of allowing his troops to be parceled out, Pershing sought and obtained an area near Lorraine where his forces could concentrate, train, and eventually fight. The buildup was slow at first, but it speeded up rapidly during the spring and summer of 1918.

Staff Training in the AEF. The size and complexity of the AEF convinced General Pershing that success in battle would be impossible without efficient staff work. This required a large number of trained officers using a common system under uniform methods. After studying British and French staffs, Pershing adopted an organization largely patterned after that of the French. The staff had three main divisions, a general staff, a technical staff, and an administrative staff. The general staff was divided into sections which varied in number depending upon the size of the command. For Pershing's headquarters (GHQ) and army headquarters there were five sections: G–1, Administration; G–2, Intelligence; G–3, Operations; G–4, Coordination (supply replacements); and G–5, Training. In corps and division headquarters the number of general staff sections was limited to three. A chief of staff was responsible for the coordination of the general staff and the technical and administrative staffs at all headquarters down to and including the division.

To train staff officers Pershing set up a staff college near Chaumont and directed that only graduates of the school would be assigned to vacancies in staff positions. The result was that uniformity soon supplanted variety in staff organization and operations. It made possible the skillful management of the largest force of U. S. troops ever assembled in the field up to that time.

Germans Renew the Offensive. *Plans.* By the end of 1917 German hopes of winning the war through unrestricted submarine warfare were fading. But there still was time for the Germans to strike a decisive blow in the west before the full strength of American arms could be brought to bear. Many troops were available as a result of the collapse of Russia, and Germany decided to resume the offensive. Field Marshal Erich von Ludendorff, now virtually in command of the German Army, selected the Somme area for the attack, hoping that a breakthrough there would drive a wedge between the French and the British and that a British defeat would cause the French to lose heart and agree to peace.

German tactics. In addition to surprise, the Germans banked heavily on the effectiveness of the new tactics they had developed to penetrate strongly entrenched positions. The Hutier tactics, named after the German general who developed and first applied them in the siege of Riga, had proved highly successful at Caporetto in Italy and against the British at Cambrai in 1917. The German tactics called for a short, intensive artillery shelling of previously spotted positions to neutralize them without destroying surprise. This artillery preparation was followed by an immediate infantry assault in which battle groups, armed mostly with machine guns and automatic rifles, advanced closely behind a rolling barrage that moved forward at a predetermined rate varying according to the terrain. In the first phase of the attack, assault troops infiltrated and isolated known centers of resistance within range of their artillery. The attack then entered a second phase marked by a rapid advance without regard to flank security. Enemy positions that had not been wiped out were bypassed and left for succeeding units to mop up. To enable the infantry to cope with local resistance that small arms fire could not overcome, light artillery was attached to assault battalions. Accompanying guns fired pointblank at definite targets such as machine gun nests, tanks, and pillboxes—a tactical use of horse-drawn artillery heretofore considered suicidal in trench warfare. To avoid loss of momentum, assault divisions were pushed to the limit before being relieved.

The new tactics put a premium on courage, physical stamina, initiative, and coordination. Only troops intensively trained as battle groups could carry them out successfully. Fortunately for the Allies, the Germans were too short of time and reserves and too limited in equipment to indoctrinate all their divisions in the new methods. This forced Ludendorff to select only the best divisions, to withdraw them from the line, and to put them through an intensive course of instruction. Live ammunition was used in training to accustom the troops to follow closely behind a rolling barrage. As a result of thorough preparation, confidence and morale rose rapidly throughout the German·Army. But more was needed. Ludendorff, recognizing that no offensive could hope to succeed on the Western Front without surprise, ordered elaborate security measures and even chose his army commanders from among those who had previously won laurels in surprise attacks. Among them was Lt. Gen. Oskar von Hutier.

The Somme offensive. On 21 March the first blow fell with shattering force on the British. Their lines were pierced, and for a time it looked as though the German advance might develop into a pursuit. By 26 March Amiens, a strategically located rail center, was in serious danger (map 37). If it fell, continued cooperation between the French and British armies would be difficult if not impossible. In the crisis Ludendorff hurled 20 fresh divisions into the battle, but they were repulsed mainly because they were untrained in the Hutier tactics. On 27 March a gap was created between the French and British armies, but German troops, now exhausted and out of supplies, were unable to exploit the situation. Allied reserves moved rapidly into the threatened area by rail and succeeded in plugging the gap. By the end of the month the German drive had lost its momentum, bogged down in mud and debris. By 5 April the offensive was definitely over. Tactically the Germans had won a brilliant victory. Leading units had succeeded in breaking through the Allied positions and had advanced 40 miles in 8 days, taking 70,000 prisoners and 1,100 guns and inflicting about 200,000 casualties. But strategically the offensive was not successful. The British Army, although seriously battered, was not destroyed; Amiens was not captured; and lateral communications between the Allies were not disrupted. For their gains the Germans had paid a high price in human life, particularly in the shock divisions whose trained men could least be spared. Equally harmful to German chances of ultimate victory was the unity of Allied command achieved as a result of the crisis on the Somme.

Unity of command. General Pershing and others had long advocated acceptance of the basic military principle of unity of command. Past experience in coalition warfare had indicated that the reconciliation of national interests, traditions, and methods was most difficult to achieve. World War I proved to be no exception. A first step towards unity of command had been taken after the collapse of the Italian armies at Caporetto when a Supreme War Council, composed of the prime ministers of Great Britain, France, and Italy and a representative of the United States, was organized to give over-all direction to the Allied military effort. But command authority vested in a committee of political leaders proved to be no answer to the problem. This had been demonstrated when the council failed in its attempt to create a general reserve of 30 divisions because Field Marshal Sir Douglas Haig, the British commander in chief, refused to contribute his quota of 6 divisions. Expressing himself as able to "deal with a man but not a committee", Haig instead made an agreement with Gen. Henri P. J. B. Petain which committed each to go to the assistance of the other in case of need. The arrangement had hardly been made when the Germans struck on the Somme. Facing defeat, Haig called on Petain for support. The French commander, fearing the next blow would fall on his own army, responded with only a few units. Angry and aroused by what he considered inadequate support under the agreement, Haig immediately called for the appointment of a "determined general who would fight" as supreme commander. An inter-Allied conference, hurriedly convened at Doullens on 26 March 1918, gave Marshal Ferdinand Foch command over the British and French armies operating in the vicinity of Amiens. At a later conference Foch's authority was made permanent and extended to include all the Allied forces. For the first time in the war, the Allies had unity of command, qualified though it was by the proviso that each national commander could appeal a decision of the Supreme Commander to his home government in case he believed the vital interests of his country at stake.

The Lys offensive. Despite the indecisive battle on the Somme, Gen. Erich Ludendorff clung to his basic plan to destroy the British Army before dealing with the French and the Americans. This time he chose to strike in the Lys area in Flanders, north of the previous point of attack. On 9 April the Germans again applied their new tactics. As before, they succeeded initially in overrunning British positions and inflicting heavy damage. So desperate was the situation that Haig issued a "backs to the wall" order, urging his troops to fight to the end. He also appealed to Foch for help, thus putting the principle of unity of command to its first great test. The Supreme Commander, convinced that the British could hold and determined to regain the initiative, refused to commit his reserves to battle. His decision proved to be sound. The British held, and, as on the Somme, the Germans failed to win a decision. Again their tactical performance was excellent, though not equal to that in the previous offensive. The battle also betrayed a weakness in the German Army not heretofore discernible. For the first time, discipline collapsed to a serious degree as the troops overran British food dumps and took precious time out during a critical phase of the battle to loot. The long blockade was beginning to affect even the iron-disciplined Germany Army. By 29 April, having committed 46 divisions to action, General Ludendorff called off the offensive. For a few weeks quiet reigned on the Western Front punctuated only by local attacks, air battles, and a long-range artillery bombardment of Paris.

The Aisne offensive. Still hoping to defeat the British and roll them back to the channel ports, Ludendorff planned to renew the battle in Flanders as soon as he had regrouped his forces. To attain surprise, he decided on a diversionary attack on the Chemin des Dames, a dominant ridge east of the Aisne River. The position had become a quiet sector to which battle-weary Allied divisions were sent to recuperate. So confident was the local commander in the natural strength of his area that he failed to organize a defense in depth, which Petain had urged upon him and which experience had shown was the best way to counteract the Hutier tactics. Even so, an attack on such a strong position as the Chemin des Dames was exceedingly dangerous. Its success demanded complete surprise. The Germans therefore prepared their attack with even greater secrecy than before. On 27 May the assault began following a short but intensive shelling of Allied lines. The bombardment was the more effective because much of the defending force had been deployed well forward by the local commander. By the end of the first day the Germans had reached all their objectives, advancing 13 miles and taking most of the bridges across the Aisne before the French could destroy them. This unexpected success led Ludendorff to change his plans. What he had conceived as a diversionary attack to prevent the French from supporting the British, he now decided to turn into a major offensive. He rushed reserves forward and ordered the advance to continue in the hope that the momentum of the attack would enable the Germans to establish bridgeheads across the Marne for future use should he decide on a drive toward Paris.

Chateau Thierry. By 29 May the Germans reached Chateau Thierry, less than 40 miles from Paris, and the situation looked very dark indeed for the Allies. In the crisis the French commander appealed to Pershing for help. He responded with two divisions. The 3d Division was rushed to the scene by rail and motor, arriving just as the Germans prepared to cross the Marne. In a three-day battle beginning 1 June every German effort to establish a bridgehead was repulsed. West of Chateau Thierry, the 2d Division, including a brigade of marines, was committed to action along the Chateau Thierry-Paris road. There, too, the Germans were checked in a series of bitterly fought local actions which culminated in an

American attack that recaptured Belleau Wood and the villages of Bouresches and Vaux. The price paid at Belleau Wood was high, but the action changed German opinion on the combat effectiveness of American troops from one of open skepticism to respect.

Though checked, the offensive on the Aisne was a tactical success for the Germans. But it left them in a dangerous salient, its western side supplied mainly by an exposed railroad that ran close to the Allied lines and through the town of Soissons. Ludendorff held on to this weak position because of the adverse effect a withdrawal would have on German morale. The decision to stay led later to a counter-offensive in which American forces played a leading role.

Cantigny—The First American Offensive. Meanwhile, in another sector, American troops undertook their first offensive. Following the German attack on the Somme the 1st Division was assigned an active sector west of the farthest point of German advance. This was considered the hottest spot in the line. On high ground to the front lay the village of Cantigny, which afforded the Germans good observation of Allied lines and concealed their own activities. Its capture would reverse the situation and give a much-needed boost to Allied morale. On 28 May, as the Germans broke through on the Aisne, the 1st Division, supported by American and French artillery and French tanks and flame throwers, launched its attack. Success was immediate and complete. Cantigny was not only taken but held against strong German counterattacks. This engagement, though only a local affair, proved the ability of the American soldier to fight offensively and bolstered sagging Allied morale.

Moyen-Montdidier. *The last German offensive.* As a result of their first three offensives of 1918, the Germans had driven three salients into the Allied defenses. Although the supply line of each salient was vulnerable, Ludendorff still retained the initiative and held to his basic plan—the defeat of the British in Flanders. He decided to begin with a diversionary attack, this time in the Moyen-Montdidier area. By attacking there, he hoped to widen the base of the Marne salient and to tie down Allied reserves by threatening Paris. On 9 June he struck with two armies. Gains were slight and costs heavy, because this time the element of surprise was absent and French defenses were organized in depth.

German morale declines. With the failure to achieve a decisive victory in the offensives launched with such high expectations, German morale suffered a sharp decline. The blockade was choking the economic life out of Germany, a country never self-sufficient in raw materials and other essentials. While victory was in sight, the German people suffered privations without much complaint, but, as the casualty lists grew longer and news from the front offered little hope, discontent arose. Taking advantage of the opportunity to further undermine German morale the Allies redoubled their propaganda activity by showering the German front lines and cities with leaflets from the air. But Ludendorff continued to reject all demands for peace negotiations in the hope that one more offensive would bring victory.

To retain the initiative he had to act soon, for the balance in manpower was shifting rapidly to the Allies as American troops arrived by the hundreds of thousands monthly permitting Foch to create the strategic reserve needed to assume the offensive. The Germans planned two attacks. The first was to pinch off Rheims which, if successful, would protect the supply of the Marne salient and draw in Allied reserves. The second, to take place 10 days later and much larger in concept, was a renewed attack on the British Army in Flanders. As events turned out the second was never undertaken. The attack on Rheims failed to achieve surprise. General preparations, usually well-kept secrets in the past, leaked out of Berlin or were spotted from the air, while detailed plans were learned from captured prisoners. This information enabled Foch to rearrange his reserves and take other defensive measures before the Germans struck.

In anticipation of an attack the Allies were deployed in depth with a main line of resistance about 2,500 yards behind an outpost line. Between the two lines fortified positions had been established to break up the attack. Artillery was also deployed in depth so that it could support both the outpost and the main line, while reserves were held in readiness to counterattack in case of a breakthrough. As a result of these defensive preparations, the enemy was himself surprised when he launched his offensive on 15 July and was stopped far short of his objective. Two American divisions, the 3d and the 42d, participated in the battle winning high praise for their conduct. The failure of this offensive, which, although planned only as a diversion, German troops had come to regard as "a Peace Offensive", had a demoralizing effect on them. It convinced Foch that the time for a counterstroke had come at last.

The Aisne-Marne Offensive. The area chosen for the Allied offensive was the Marne salient. Assault units were to attack along its entire front with the main blow directed at the northwest base of the salient near Soissons. Spearheading the attack was the French XX Corps composed of the U. S. 1st and 2d Divisions and the French 1st Moroccan Division. Since U. S. divisions were numerically stronger, the force actually was four-fifths American. Troop concentrations were carried out with the utmost secrecy some distance behind the lines. Only at the last moment were assault units rushed forward, one United States division moving at night over muddy roads and then into jump-off position at double time.

The attack was launched early in the morning of 18 July behind a heavy barrage. Surprise was complete, and the initial assault was so powerful that it quickly overran the German front lines and forward artillery positions. By 0800 Allied troops had advanced three miles and captured the high ground south of Soissons, thus assuring the fall of that stronghold and the ultimate success of the battle. Elsewhere along the front Allied forces, heavily reinforced with American divisions, made uniform progress. Realizing his position had become untenable, Crown Prince Wilhelm, who commanded the German armies in the area, ordered a gradual withdrawal from the salient. In order to save supplies and equipment, the Germans prepared successive defensive positions and stubbornly and skillfully defended them. By 3 August, with the salient evacuated, the Germans were in strong positions behind the Aisne and Vesle Rivers. Attempts on the part of the U. S. 4th and 32d Divisions to drive them from these positions failed and the offensive was over.

The battle had numerous and far-reaching results. It eliminated the German threat to Paris, upset Ludendorff's cherished plan to attack the British again in Flanders, gave the Allies important rail communications, demonstrated beyond further doubt the effectiveness of American troops on the offensive, firmly established Allied unity of command, and so dimmed German aspirations for victory that even Ludendorff thereafter no longer hoped for more than a stalemate. Most important of all, the initiative passed to the Allies.

A Separate American Army. The conduct of American troops in the Aisne-Marne offensive strengthened Pershing's case for an independent American army and a separate sector on the Western Front. This had been the original plan, but it had lapsed in the crisis produced by the German offensives. As the danger passed, Pershing pressed the issue again. Foch was sympathetic and, after a series of conferences, agreed to the organization of the U. S. First Army and assigned it a sector in the St. Mihiel area. Within a short time most of the American divisions then in France were assembled there. Three remained under French command along the Vesle, where they were badly needed.

Allied Plans. While the battle to flatten the German salient on the Marne was at its height, Foch called a conference of his commanders to plan future Allied operations. He proposed first to reduce the three main German salients in order to improve lateral communications between Allied sectors, shorten the line, and set the stage for a general offensive. He assigned the reduction of the St. Mihiel salient to Pershing, who had requested it. Since joint effort was gradually reducing the Marne salient at the time, the only question remaining was who would deal with the Amiens salient. The final decision called for a joint British-French operation under Haig's direction.

The Amiens Offensive. Marshal Haig decided on a simple converging attack directed at the center of the salient with the British Fourth Army attacking from the northwest while the French First Army hit from the southwest. Haig had nearly 600 tanks and chose to make full use of them. In order to avoid betraying the time of the attack, he planned no artillery preparation and deliberately delayed the attack of the French Army, which was equipped with only a few tanks, until the British advance was well under way. On 8 August the British struck with 10 divisions in the line; 45 minutes later, on schedule, the French moved in with 8 divisions. The mass of British infantry, advancing with the tanks behind a rolling barrage, shattered the German lines capturing 1,600 prisoners and 200 guns in the first two hours. An hour later advance elements, including cavalry, had penetrated German defenses to the extent of nine miles, forcing a general withdrawal to lines held by the Germans in 1915. The French advance, while not as spectacular, nevertheless contributed to the success of the engagement. As Ludendorff said, it was a "Black Day" for the German Army, although it finally succeded in holding. Eager to exploit the advantage gained, Foch urged Haig to continue the attack, but the British commander, realizing that he was up against a well-integrated defense system which could be broken only after long and heavy artillery preparation, recommended an attack farther north between Amiens and Miraumont. To this Foch reluctantly agreed. The new drive opened on 21 August but encountered a stubborn defense in depth and counterattacks which soon brought it to a halt. But since Haig had committed only part of his force, he was still able to apply pressure elsewhere along his line. By the end of August he had forced the Germans back to the original positions from which they had started their offensive. The Amiens salient had disappeared.

St. Mihiel. The elimination of the Amiens salient left only one major salient still in the hands of the enemy. Its reduction had been assigned to the American army. Pershing lost no time in preparing for the attack. He faced numerous problems, including shortages in artillery, aircraft, and tanks. Borrowing needed units and equipment from the French, he made up some deficiencies. The offensive was about to be launched when Foch, anxious to take advantage of the successes around Amiens before the Germans recovered, proposed to reduce the size of the St. Mihiel operation Pershing had planned and to disperse excess American units among the French and British armies. To exploit the recent successes was, of course, sound, and Pershing fully appreciated that, but he now obstinately refused to permit his army to fight except as an independent force. Two days later he agreed to a new plan that left his force intact but limited the objective of the St. Mihiel operation so that the American army could

Renault Tanks followed by Infantry breaking through barbed wire entanglements.

undertake a major offensive between the Meuse River and the Argonne Forest about 10 days later.

The plan committed Pershing and his staff to the task of preparing and launching two offensives within 23 days in areas 40 miles apart, a tough assignment never before attempted on the Western Front by a single army. However, it was a mission which, if successful, would establish the reputation of the American army. The original plan for the St. Mihiel offensive was quickly modified. It now called for a simultaneous attack on the two sides of the triangular-shaped salient. One American corps was to attack the western face, delivering its main blow fairly close to the base of the triangle, while two corps attacked the southern face, with their main blow falling half way between the base and apex. (See inset, map 38.) Both forces were to meet approximately in the center of the salient pinching off all enemy forces caught in its nose. A French corps was to make a secondary attack against the nose and exploit whatever success the two main attacks achieved.

Supported by 3,000 guns, largely French, 1,500 planes, mostly British and French, and 267 French light tanks, the American attack opened. Everywhere the Germans, who had been preparing to evacuate the salient, gave way, and by the end of the first day the Americans had reached all their objectives. The advance might have gone farther, but Pershing called a halt because of the coming Meuse-Argonne offensive. It was the first major World War I victory won by the American Army under its own command. This operation eliminated the danger to the rear of the Allied strongholds of Nancy and Verdun, improved Allied lateral communications, and deprived the Germans of excellent defensive positions covering the approaches to the fortress of Metz and the coal mines of Briey.

Plans for a General Offensive. Even before the reduction of the St. Mihiel salient, Foch had come to believe that a general offensive aimed at driving the enemy across the borders was possible before winter slowed down operations. The Allies now had unquestioned superiority in men and equipment, and their morale was high as the result of the victories in the Aisne-Marne and Amiens areas, while that of the Germans was showing increasing signs of decline. Only a rapid and orderly evacuation, combined with systematic destruction of roads, railroads, and bridges, could prevent German defeat. But retreat would mean the abandonment of vast stores of supplies and equipment accumulated since 1914. To prevent an orderly German withdrawal, Foch planned an offensive that would yield two key railroad junctions that tied in enemy lateral rail communications with those from Germany. Two powerful converging attacks were to be made, one by the British, the other by the American army with Aulnoye and Mezieres as their respective objectives. To mount their operations, the British, weakened in reserves by the earlier German offensive, had to scrape the bottom of their manpower barrel and draw on units being prepared for an all-out effort in 1919. Leaders in the British Government grumbled but finally agreed. To further the success of the two main blows, the French armies were to exert pressure all along their line and protect the flanks of both British and American armies while a newly created Belgian-French-British army group in the north, commanded by King Albert of Belgium, drove toward Ghent. The date set for the commencement of the offensive was the last week in September. This barely allowed time for preparations, particularly for the Americans who still had the reductions of the St. Mihiel salient to accomplish.

The Meuse-Argonne Offensive. *Preparations.* For the next few weeks the U. S. First Army was busy planning operations and switching troops in and out of the concentration area between Verdun and the Argonne Forest (map 38). The task was complicated by the fact that many U. S. divisions were engaged in the St. Mihiel battle at the time and because all movements had to be made at night in order to avoid observation by the enemy. All told about 820,000 troops with their equipment were involved, 220,000 French moving out of the area as 400,000 Americans moved in. As a logistical operation it was a brilliant success for which a young staff officer, Col. George C. Marshall, won well-deserved acclaim. Since the Germans had no exposed flanks, Pershing had to plan a frontal attack powerful enough to effect a breakthrough. Terrain features and objectives led him to

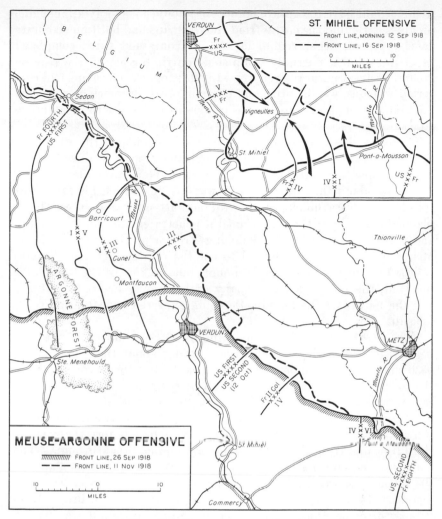

Map 38. Meuse-Argonne offensive.

decide to make his main attack between the Meuse River and the western edge of the Argonne Forest, a zone roughly 20 miles in width. He massed three corps in the area disposed in line. Each corps was to attack with two divisions in the assault and one in reserve. Three other divisions were held as an army reserve available for use where needed as the battle developed.

The country through which the attack was to be made favored the defense. On the east were the heights of the Meuse, which afforded the enemy excellent observation; on the west was the Argonne Forest, high, rugged, and heavily wooded. In the center a ridge running north and south dominated the valley of the Meuse to the east and the valley of the Aire to the west. On the ridge were the heavily fortified positions of Montfaucon, Cunel, and Barricourt, which American troops would have to capture before they could make any appreciable progress. Behind the entire front the Germans had built an elaborate defense system organized in depth. It contained three completed main lines and a partially completed fourth farther to the rear on ground of great natural strength. In addition, the Germans had converted villages, woods, hills, and other natural obstacles between the lines into strong points to serve as centers of resistance to break up an attack.

Strong as this defense system was, Pershing hoped the weight of the attack would carry his army through the first three lines without loss of momentum and enable him to open up German flanks to attack and bring about that state of open warfare for which his army was trained. In case quick success did not attend his first effort, he planned to continue the attack until it penetrated the enemy defenses and then to join with the advancing French at Granpre, cross the Meuse, and advance northward to cut the strategic Sedan-Mezieres railroad. The plan was simple enough, but, because of the large force involved, the inexperience of many of his newly arrived divisions, and the nature of the terrain, Pershing expected coordination to be difficult.

First phase. Early in the morning of 26 September the offensive began with an artillery preparation lasting about three hours. At 0530 the infantry jumped off. The assault divisions promptly took the forward positions and by the end of the first day had made excellent progress everywhere except in two places, Montfaucon and the Argonne Forest. In the next few days the first two defense lines were captured, but the advance ground to a halt before the enemy's third line, upsetting Perishing's hope for a quick breakthrough. The battle now entered its second phase. The reasons for the collapse of the initial assault, other than stubborn enemy resistance, were numerous. Tank support proved ineffective, and supply broke down because of congestion and poor roads. More important was the inexperience of the divisions that were receiving their first taste of battle. Three had to be replaced by veteran outfits as soon as a lull in the battle permitted, not an easy task considering the condition of the roads serving the front lines. Nevertheless, it was accomplished by 1 October, and the stage was set for a renewal of the attack.

Second phase. Between 4 October and the end of the month the U. S. First Army slowly drove its way through the third German line. Casualties mounted as the enemy threw in reserves and stubbornly contested every defensible position. Gains were limited but significant because the gruelling struggle forced the enemy to draw units from other parts of the front and commit them to battle. In the air the enemy introduced the "battle squadron" to strafe front-line troops, and Col. William Mitchell made the first large-scale bombing raid upsetting enemy preparations for a counterattack. During this

Infantry in Action, Meuse-Argonne Offensive.

period the Argonne Forest was cleared and the attack was extended
east of the Meuse River. By mid-October enough divisions were in
action to necessitate the organization of the U. S. Second Army under
the command of Maj. Gen. Robert L. Bullard; Maj. Gen. Hunter
Liggett was appointed to command the First Army and General Pershing then assumed command of the army group.

Third phase. Having finally penetrated the third main enemy line,
the Americans were in a position to reap the harvest of success. Fresh
outfits replaced exhausted divisions; most of the Allied units serving
with the AEF were released and withdrawn; roads were built and re
paired; and the supply system was improved. The Germans in the
meantime had so strengthened their fourth line that it, too, had to be
penetrated before open warfare was possible. On 1 November the attack reopened with the usual artillery preparation. The infantry
assault that followed was highly successful; V Corps in the center advanced six miles in the first day, forcing the Germans to withdraw in a
hurry to save their units west of the Meuse. Three days later units of
III Corps crossed the river and headed toward Montmedy. By 7 November the heights before Sedan were seized, denying the Germans
the use of the Sedan-Mezieres railroad. Sedan could probably have
been taken by the First Army shortly thereafter had not Foch altered
its left boundary to permit the French to capture the city which had
witnessed the capitulation of the French Army to the Prussians in
1870. Even so, certain American units attempting to enter Sedan
first, displayed a bad example of initiative and confused the situation
by moving across the line of advance of other friendly units. Pershing
next planned a coordinated attack in the direction of Montmedy.

Troops were moving into position for this attack when the armistice put an end to further hostilities.

The Meuse-Argonne offensive was one of the greatest and most decisive battles ever fought by the U. S. Army. The prize was the vital Sedan-Mezieres area with its strategic lines of communications, the loss of which would mean the collapse of the entire German front. Almost a million and a quarter American troops were engaged in the offensive before it ended. The price paid was heavy, some 120,000 casualties, but the military results were decisive. In a desperate effort to hold, Ludendorff was forced to pour his rapidly diminishing reserves into the battle thereby making it possible for Allied arms to register spectacular gains elsewhere on the Western Front. In the end he failed. The dogged persistence of the American platoons, companies, and battalions led by young commanders who not many months before had been college students or young business and professional men met and defeated the best enemy troops and broke the so-called "Hindenburg Line". When it collapsed, the prospect of complete defeat forced the German military leaders to advise an immediate armistice.

Other Allied Offensives. The successes gained by the AEF in the Meuse-Argonne offensive were matched by the Allies on other sectors of the front. By 5 October the British had penetrated the true "Hindenburg Line", and a month later took Aulnoye, the other strategic rail junction upon which German supply depended. In their offensive they had the use of two American divisions, the 27th and the 30th, which participated in some of the bloodiest fighting of the war. In Flanders King Albert's Belgian-British-French army pushed ahead until it slid to a temporary halt in Belgian mud. As soon as ground conditions improved, King Albert's army renewed the attack regaining the entire coast of Belgium before the armistice. During the last 10 days of this operation two American divisions, the 37th and 91st, saw action. The French, whose mission was to apply pressure in the center between the American and British zones, did this so well that their armies made rapid progress as the German lines fell back. In this offensive two American divisions, the 2d and 36th, participated. All along the Western Front success was so gratifying that a major operation against Metz seemed possible before the end of the year. Plans for the attack to begin on 15 November were well under way when the armistice came.

Germany Surrenders. Disheartened by the inability of his armies to hold the Allied attacks, Ludendorff on 2 October informed his government that Germany could not win and advised it to seek peace. The Imperial Government reacted immediately by notifying President Wilson of its willingness to accept terms based on his earlier announced "Fourteen Points". Wilson could not respond at once,

356

for he was not sure that all the Allies were willing to negotiate with the Imperial Government. Meanwhile, the fighting continued with disastrous results for the Germans. An offensive in Italy in late October forced the Germans to reinforce that tottering front. At the same time the Allies continued to advance all along the Western Front. A last desperate plan of the German Navy to break out and challenge the British Grand Fleet failed because the German sailors mutinied and seized the port of Kiel. Within a few days several other cities in northern Germany fell to the mutineers, who set up soldiers and sailors committees reminiscent of the events in Russia 18 months before.

Early in the crisis Ludendorff was relieved. A German republic was proclaimed and the Kaiser fled to Holland. German emissaries crossed the lines to discuss terms with Allied representatives in a railroad car near Compiegne. After several days of negotiation, agreement was reached on an armistice which took effect at 1100 on 11 November. It provided for: (1) the withdrawal of the German armies from occupied territory within two weeks; (2) the surrender of most of Germany's artillery, machine guns, planes, rolling stock, and trucks; (3) the immediate return of Allied prisoners of war; (4) the evacuation of the west bank of the Rhine; (5) the demilitarization of a six-mile strip on the east bank; (6) the relinquishment to the Allies of Mainz, Coblenz, and Cologne as bridgeheads; (7) the surrender of all submarines; and (8) the internment of the German fleet in neutral or Allied ports. These military and naval terms were supplemented by equally severe economic and political provisions.

Allied forces moved in to occupy the west bank of the Rhine and the three designated bridgeheads. President Wilson at first was reluctant to occupy any territory, but under urging he agreed to permit the American army to take over the area around Coblenz.

Replacements. The victories in the gruelling battles in which American troops participated during the summer and fall of 1918 were costly. Casualties ran high, many divisions losing over 5,000 men. To keep them at fighting strength required a continuous flow of replacements from the rear based on anticipated losses. Originally the War Department had planned to receive and train recruits in depot brigades established in the 16 cantonments that had been built in the United States for National Army divisions. This system broke down within a short time because the depot brigades had to devote almost all their time to receiving draftees. This led the War Department to direct the breaking up of some existing units to meet shortages in others. That practice seriously lowered the morale of the units raided and disrupted the training of all concerned. In France the results were particularly harmful. Unable to rely on an adequate flow of replacements, Pershing was forced to break up whole divisions and to skeletonize many units engaged in essential services in rear areas to make up his battle losses. The effect on morale and efficiency was serious. Men were fed into front-line units, often without adequate training for combat. Whatever spirit and pride they may have had in their former outfits was destroyed when they were assigned to other units to serve under different officers and in positions for which they were not trained. As a result, efficiency declined and losses in battle increased needlessly. Complaints from the field finally forced the War Department to face the realities of the replacement problem. In April 1918 replacement training centers opened in the United States for the sole purpose of training men as replacements to make up estimated losses and to fill vacancies in the services. Had the system been introduced sooner it might have worked, but, as General Pershing said, "the change came too late to be of material benefit". Fortunately for the combat divisions, the war ended before shortages in replacements created a disastrous crisis.

Summary. The shots fired by a Serbian fanatic in a little Bosnian town precipitated a great war which ended with Allied victory but with all western Europe greatly weakened. The system of alliances in which the powers had become enmeshed proved unequal to the task of maintaining peace, and what began as a local war between an empire and a troublesome Balkan neighbor developed almost overnight into a conflict that engulfed most of the Continent. Before it ended few nations in the world were spared the horrors of war and none escaped its effect. In the end three great empires collapsed and several new states were born. New and powerful social, economic, and political forces arose out of the wreckage and confusion to confound the period that followed. The Central Powers, although confronted with a war on two fronts, won many initial successes mainly because they were better organized, trained, equipped and led, and because they had the advantage of interior lines. They managed to overrun the Balkans, retain the Dardanelles, eliminate Russia, and occupy much of France and Belgium in the west and part of Italy in the south. The entrance of the United States into the war as an active belligerent did not restore the balance immediately, but as time went on the power of American arms began to tell.

For the first time since the establishment of the Nation the United States departed from its traditional policy of noninvolvement in European affairs. Resources, industry, accumulated wealth, and manpower were harnessed in a war effort as never before in history. The U. S. Navy joined with the British Navy in cutting losses, eliminating the menace of unrestricted submarine warfare, imposing a stranglehold on the economic life of the Central Powers, and in transporting the U. S. Army to Europe. The U. S. Army, raised largely by conscription, was slow getting into action but, once there, it gave an impressive account of itself. For the first time since the Civil War vast numbers of men were mobilized, put into uniform, equipped, trained, and committed to battle. Unprepared though the Army was when the war broke out, it grew and learned rapidly. By the summer of 1918 enough men and supplies had arrived at the Western Front to turn the tide of battle in favor of the Allies. In the Meuse-Argonne offensive American troops fought the greatest battle in which the Army had been engaged up to that time. They met and beat the best troops in Europe in a dogged, gruelling battle which convinced the enemy that further resistance was useless. Many costly mistakes were made, particularly in the field of logistics, airplane production, and replacements, but many things were done well. Conscription was introduced and handled inexpensively and justly; officers were selected on the basis of merit and qualifications; the complexities of trench warfare were mastered without sacrifice of fundamental operational concepts; morale was kept at a high level both in the Army and on the home front; and finally, mobilization was handled with speed and without serious impairment of the Army's efficiency or disruption of the Nation's economic life.

QUESTIONS

1. Discuss two strategic blunders the Germans made which cost them a possible victory.

2. What reasoning led the Germans to reintroduce unrestricted submarine warfare?

3. Explain Army logistical problems in the United States and in France. What steps were taken to solve them?

4. What were Pershing's views on: (1) the use of American troops, (2) unity of command, (3) open warfare, (4) Army organization, (5) replacements?

5. Explain the German offensives of 1918 and the role of United States forces in Foch's counteroffensive.

Reading List

Edmonds, James E. *A Short History of World War I.* London, 1951.

Fay, Sidney. *The Origins of the World War.* New York, 1930. 2 vols.

Harbord, James G. *The American Army in France.* Boston, 1936.

Infantry School. *Infantry in Battle.* Washington, 1934.

March, Peyton C. *The Nation at War.* Garden City, 1932.

Millis, Walter, *The Road to War.* Boston, 1935.

Pershing, John J. *My experiences in the World War.* 2 vols. New York, 1931.

United States Military Academy. *A Short Military History of World War I.* West Point, 1950.

CHAPTER 19

1919–1941

Military Policy. The Army of the United States, which totaled 3,710,563 on 11 November 1918, was reduced to about 19,500 officers and 245,000 enlisted men by the beginning of 1920. During that interval the War Department had urged the establishment of a permanent Regular force of about 600,000 and of a three-month universal military training system that would permit a rapid expansion of this force to meet the requirements of a new major war. The Congress and American public opinion rejected this proposal. It was hard to believe that the defeat of Germany and the exhaustion of the other European powers did not guarantee that there would be no major war on land for years to come. The possibility of war with Japan was recognized, but American leaders assumed that such a war, if it came, would be primarily naval in character. Indeed, the fundamental factor in the military policy of the United States during the next two decades was reliance on the United States Navy as the first line of national defense. Another basic factor that determined the character of the peacetime Army was the decision of the United States not to join the League of Nations and therefore to reject participation in an active and cooperative world security system to maintain peace. The American people soon showed themselves unwilling to support an army in being any larger than that required to defend the continental United States and its overseas territories and possessions, to keep alive a knowledge of the military arts, and to train inexpensive and voluntary civilian components. Since the Army had huge stocks of munitions left over from its belated production for World War I, the principal concern of the War Department until the 1930's was manpower to fulfill these peacetime missions.

Demobilization. Demobilization planning began less than a month before the armistice. When the fighting ended, almost all of the officers and men in the Army became eligible for discharge. The War Department had to decide how to muster out these men as quickly and equitably as possible without unduly disrupting the national economy and at the same time to maintain an effective force for occupation and other postwar duties. It decided in favor of the traditional method of demobilization by units as the one best calculated to achieve these ends. Units in the United States were moved to 30 demobilization centers located throughout the country, so that men after processing could be discharged near their homes. Units overseas were brought back just as rapidly as shipping space could be found for them, processed through debarkation centers operated by the Transportation Service, and then sent to the demobilization centers for discharge. In practice, the unit system was supplemented by a great many individual discharges and by the release of certain occupational groups, notably railroad workers and anthracite coal miners. In the first full month of demobilization the Army released about 650,000 officers and men, and within nine months nearly 3,250,000 were demobilized without seriously disturbing the American economy. A demobilization of war industry and disposal of surplus materiel paralleled the release of personnel, but the War Department kept a large reserve of weapons for peacetime or new emergency use. Despite the lack of much advance planning, demobilization was accomplished reasonably well. The Army was concerned at the outset because it had no authority to enlist men to replace those discharged. A law of 28 February 1919 permitted enlistments in the Regular Army for either one or three years, and by the end of 1919 the active Army was almost entirely a Regular volunteer force.

Immediate Duties. The military duties of the Army abroad and at home did not cease with the armistice. The United States had agreed to join Great Britain and France in a military occupation of western Germany, and for political rather than military reasons it had also joined in sending expeditionary forces into Russia. At home during 1919 and 1920 Army forces continued the guard on the border of Mexico required by revolutionary disturbances in that country, and, because of the lack of National Guard forces (not yet reorganized), the active Army had to supply troops on numerous occasions to help suppress domestic disorders arising chiefly out of labor disputes and race conflicts in a restless postwar America.

German occupation. The newly activated U. S. Third Army, under Maj. Gen. Joseph T. Dickman, crossed into Germany on 1 December 1918 to occupy a small segment of territory along the Rhine River centering on Coblenz. As many as nine divisions participated in the occupation during the spring of 1919. American troops had no unusual difficulties with the German populace, and soon after the peace conference ended in May 1919 the occupation forces were rapidly reduced. They numbered about 15,000 at the beginning of 1920. After rejecting the Treaty of Versailles, the United States remained technically at war with Germany until the summer of 1921, when a separate peace was signed. Thereafter, the occupying force was gradually withdrawn, and the last thousand troops left for home on 24 January 1923.

Russian expeditions. The revolutionary turmoil in Russia in 1918 induced President Wilson in August to direct Army participation in expeditions of United States and Allied forces that penetrated the Murmansk-Archangel region of European Russia and into Siberia via Vladivostock. The north Russian force, containing about 5,000 American troops under British command, suffered heavy casualties while guarding war supplies and communication lines south of the Arctic ports mentioned, before being withdrawn in June 1919. The Siberian force of about 10,000 under Maj. Gen. William S. Graves had many trying experiences in attempting to rescue Czech troops and curb Japanese expansionist tendencies between August 1918 and April 1920. Together these two forces suffered about as many combat casualties as the Army expeditionary force of similar size had sustained in Cuba in 1898. After the withdrawals from Germany and Russia, the only Army forces stationed on foreign soil until 1941 were the garrison of about 1,000 maintained at Tientsin, China, from 1912 until 1938, and a force of similar strength dispatched from the Philippines to Shanghai for four months' duty in 1932. The Marine Corps, rather than the Army, provided the other small foreign garrisons and expeditionary forces required after World War I, particularly in the Caribbean area.

National Defense Act of 1920. After many months of careful consideration, unfortunately not backed by any widespread popular interest, Congress passed a sweeping amendment of the National Defense Act of 1916. The new National Defense Act of 4 June 1920, which governed the organization and regulation of the Army until 1950, has been widely acknowledged to be the most constructive piece of military legislation ever adopted in the United States. It rejected the theory of an expansible Regular Army urged since the days of John C. Calhoun. Instead, it established the Army of the United States as an organization of three components, the professional Regular Army, the civilian National Guard, and the civilian Organized Reserves (Officers' and Enlisted Reserve Corps). Each component was to be so regulated in peacetime that it could contribute its appropriate share of troops in a war emergency. The act was in effect an acknowledgment that throughout its history the United States had been unable to maintain a standing peacetime force capable of sufficient expansion to meet the demands of a great war, and that in practice it had therefore been necessary to raise new armies of civilian-soldiers to achieve a large scale mobilization. In contrast to earlier practice, the training of civilian components now became a major peacetime task of the Regular Army, and principally for this reason the Army was authorized an officer strength of 17,717—more than three times the actual officer strength of the Regular Army before World War I. At least half of the new officers were to be non-Regulars who had served during the war. The act also provided that officer promotions, except for doctors and chaplains, were henceforth to be made from a list, a step that equalized opportunity for advancement throughout most of the Army. The Regular Army was authorized a maximum enlisted strength of 280,000, but the actual strength would depend on the amount of money voted in annual appropriations. The act authorized the Army to continue all of its arm and service branches established before 1917 and to add three new branches, the Air Service, the Chemical Warfare Service, and a Finance Department, the first two reflecting new combat techniques demonstrated in World War I. The Tank Corps of World War I, representing a new arm, was absorbed by the Infantry. The act specifically charged the War Department with mobilization planning and preparations for the event of war. It assigned the military aspects of this responsibility to the Chief of Staff and the General Staff and the planning and supervision of industrial procurement to the Assistant Secretary of War.

Organization. World War I experience both in Washington and in France had greatly strengthened the position and authority of the General Staff. In 1921 General Pershing became Chief of Staff, and under his direction the War Department General Staff was reorganized to include five divisions: G–1, dealing with personnel; G–2, with intelligence; G–3, with training and operations; G–4, with supply; and a new War Plans Division that dealt with strategic planning and related preparations for the event of war. These divisions assisted the Chief of Staff in his supervision of the military branches of the War Department and of the field forces. The field forces in the continental United States were put under the command and administration of nine corps areas approximately equal in population, and those overseas in Panama, Hawaii, and the Philippines under departments with similar authority. The division rather than the regiment became the basic Army unit, especially in mobilization planning, and each corps area was allocated six infantry divisions—one Regular Army, two National Guard, and three Reserve. The defense act had contemplated a higher organization of divisions into corps and armies, but no such tactical organizations existed in fact for many years. The principal organizational change in the 1920's came in 1926 with the establishment of the Air Corps as an equal combat arm and with provision for its enlargement and modernization.

Army school system. Between 1920 and 1941 education for and within the Army received far greater attention than ever before. This reflected the emphasis in the National Defense Act on preparedness in peacetime as well as the increasing complexity of modern war. The United States Military Academy and the Reserve Officers' Training Corps program furnished most of the basic schooling for new officers. Thirty-one special service schools provided branch training. The largest of these was the Infantry School, located at Fort Benning, Ga., at the close of World War I. These branch schools trained officers and enlisted men of the civilian components as well as those of the Regular Army and, in addition, furnished training through extension courses. Three general service schools provided the capstone of the Army educational system. The oldest of them, located at Fort Leavenworth, Kans., and known after 1928 as the Command and General Staff School, provided officers with the requisite training for divisional command and General staff positions. In Washington the Army War College and, after 1924, the Army Industrial College trained senior officers of demonstrated ability for the most responsible command and staff positions. In establishing the Industrial College the Army recognized the high importance of logistical training for the conduct of modern warfare.

Civilian Components. One of the major purposes of the National Defense Act was to promote the integration of the Regular Army and the civilian components by establishing uniformity in training and professional standards. In practice this purpose fell considerably short of full realization; nevertheless, the new military system saw an unprecedented amount of military training of civilians in peacetime. It brought the Regular out of his traditional isolation from the civilian community, and it acquainted large numbers of civilians with the problems and views of the professional soldier. All together, the civilian components and the groups in training that contributed to their ranks had an average strength of about 400,000 between the wars. The end result of the civilian training program was an orderly and effective mobilization of National Guard and Reserve elements into the active Army in 1940 and 1941.

National Guard. The absorption of the National Guard into the Army during World War I left the states without any Guard units after the armistice. The act of 1920 contemplated a National Guard of 436,000, but its actual peacetime strength was stabilized at about 180,000. This force relieved the Regular Army of any duty in curbing domestic disturbances within the states from 1921 until 1941, and stood ready for immediate induction into the active Army whenever necessary. The War Department, in addition to supplying Regular officers for instruction and large quantities of surplus World War I materiel for equipment, applied about one-tenth of its military budget to the support of the Guard in the years between wars. Guardsmen engaged in 48 armory drills and 15 days of field training each year. Though not comparable to active Army units in readiness for war, the Guard was much better prepared by 1939 than it had been when mobilized for Mexican border duty in 1916. Numerically, the National Guard was the largest component of the Army of the United States between 1922 and 1939.

Organized Reserves. The civilian community had, of course, a very large number of trained officers and enlisted men after World

War I, and this assured the Nation a natural reservoir of manpower for the Army for a decade or more after the war. Only a very few of these men joined the Enlisted Reserve Corps, but large numbers of officers maintained their commissions in the Officers' Reserve Corps through five-year periods, during which they received further training through school and extension courses and in brief tours of active duty. The composition of the Officers' Reserve Corps, which numbered about 100,000 between the wars, gradually changed as its ranks were refilled by men newly commissioned after training in Reserve Officers' Training Corps or in the Citizens' Military Training Camp program.

Reserve Officers' Training Corps. The National Defense Act of 1920 gave impetus to a greatly enlarged and better-regulated ROTC program. By 1928 there were ROTC units in 325 schools, about 225 of them being senior units enrolling 85,000 students in colleges and universities. Regular Army officers detailed as professors of military science and tactics instructed these units, and about 6,000 men graduating from them were commissioned each year in the Officers' Reserve Corps. The ROTC also contributed large numbers of officers and enlisted men to National Guard units. This inexpensive program paid rich dividends when the Nation again mobilized to meet the threat of war in 1940 and 1941.

Citizens' Military Training Camps. The Army's CMTC program, a very modest alternative to the universal military training system proposed in 1919, provided about 30,000 young volunteers with four weeks of military training in summer camps each year. Those who completed four years of CMTC training became eligible for Reserve commissions, the CMTC thus providing another, though much smaller, source for the rolls of the Officers' Reserve Corps and the National Guard.

National Policy. For 15 years, from 1921 to 1936, the American people, their representatives in Congress, and their Presidents thought that the United States could and should avoid future wars with other major powers. They believed this could be done by maintaining a minimum of defensive military strength, avoiding entangling commitments with Old World nations, and yet using American good offices to promote international peace and the limitation of armaments. The United States took the initiative in 1921 in calling a conference in Washington to consider the limitation of armaments. The naval treaty of 1922 produced by the conference temporarily checked a race for naval supremacy. It froze capital ship strengths of the United States, Great Britain, and Japan in a 5–5–3 ratio for a number of years. This ratio and restrictions on new naval base construction assured that neither the United States nor Japan could operate offensively in the Pacific as long as the treaty provisions were respected.

But if Japan should violate the treaty and attack the Philippine Islands, the practical effect would be that the United States could not defend them. On the other hand, a general agreement among the western nations and Japan to maintain the *status quo* in the Pacific and in China offered fair assurance against a Japanese war of aggression, but only as long as the Western Powers did not themselves become embroiled in the European-Atlantic area. In 1928 the United States and France joined in drafting the Pact of Paris, which renounced war as an instrument of national policy. Thereafter, the United States announced to the world that, if other powers did likewise, it would limit its armed forces to those necessary to maintain internal order and defend national territory against aggression and invasion. About this same time the chief of the Army's War Plans Division advised the Chief of Staff that the defense of frontiers was precisely the cardinal task for which the Army had been organized, equipped, and trained. There was no real conflict between national policy and the Army's conception of its mission during the 1920's and early 1930's. But in the Army's opinion the Government and the American public, in their antipathy to war, failed to support even minimum needs for national defense.

Regular Army. When the National Defense Act was adopted in June 1920, the Regular Army numbered about 200,000—about two-thirds the maximum strength authorized in the act. In January 1921 Congress directed a reduction in enlisted strength to 175,000 and in June 1921 to 150,000. A year later Congress limited the active Army to 12,000 commissioned officers and 125,000 enlisted men, not including the 7,000 or so in the Philippine Scouts. Regular Army strength was stabilized at about this level until 1936. Appropriations for the military expenses of the War Department also became stabilized during this same period, amounting to about $300,000,000 a year. This was about half of what a full implementation of the National Defense Act had been estimated to cost. The United States spent rather less on its Army than on its Navy during these years, in line with the national policy of depending on the Navy as the first line of defense. War Department officials, especially in the early 1920's, repeatedly expressed alarm over the failure of Congress to appropriate enough money to carry out the terms of the National Defense Act. They believed that it was essential for minimum defense needs to have a Regular Army with an enlisted strength of 150,000 or, after the Air Corps Act of 1926, of 165,000. As the Chief of Staff pointed out in 1933, the United States ranked 17th among the nations in active Army strength, although foreign observers rated its newly equipped Army Air Corps 2d or 3d in actual power.

Equipment. In equipment the Air Corps offered a marked contrast to the rest of the Army. For almost two decades ground units had to get along as best they could with weapons left over from World War I. The Army was well aware that these old weapons were becoming increasingly obsolete and that new ones were needed. For example, the Chief of Staff in 1933 described the Army's tanks—except for a dozen experimental models—as completely useless for employment against any modern unit on the battlefield. Although handicapped by very small appropriations for research and development, Army arsenals and laboratories worked continuously during the 1920's and 1930's to devise new items of equipment and to improve old ones. Service boards, links between branch schools and headquarters, tested pilot models and determined the doctrine for their employment so that it could be incorporated into training manuals. But not much new equipment was forthcoming for ground units in the field until after Army appropriations began to rise in 1936.

Tactical units. For a number of years only about one-fourth of the officers and one-half of the enlisted men of the Regular Army were available for assignment to tactical units in the continental United States. Many units existed only on paper; almost all had only skeletonized strength. Instead of nine infantry divisions, there were actually three. In May 1927 one of the infantry divisions, a cavalry brigade, and 200 planes participated in a combined arms maneuver in Texas, but for the most part Regular units had to train as battalions or companies. The continued dispersion of skeletonized divisions, brigades, and regiments among a large number of posts, many of them relics of the Indian wars, was a serious hindrance to the training of Regulars, although helpful in training the civilian components. Efforts to abandon small posts continued to meet with stubborn opposition from local interests and their elected representatives in Congress. In the infantry, for example, the 24 regiments available in the United States for field service in 1932 were spread among 45 posts, with a battalion or less at 34. Most of the organic transportation of these units was of World War I vintage, and the Army did not have the money to concentrate units for training by other means. Nor were there large posts in which they could be housed. The best training of larger units occurred overseas in the fairly sizable garrisons maintained by the Army in Hawaii, the Philippines, and Panama. In the early 1930's the great depression had the immediate effect of cuts in appropriations and pay, which further reduced the readiness of Army units for military service.

Nonmilitary Tasks. The most conspicuous employment of the Army within the United States during these years of peace was a variety of nonmilitary tasks that only the Army had the resources and the organization to tackle quickly. In floods and blizzards and hurricanes it was the Army that was first on the spot with cots and blankets and food. In another direction, Army Engineers expanded their work on rivers and harbors for the improvement of navigation and flood control. For four months in 1934 the Air Corps, on orders from the President, took over the carrying of the air mail for the Post Office Department. The most important and immediately disruptive of these nonmilitary duties began in the spring of 1933, after Congress passed an act that put large numbers of jobless young men into reforestation and other reclamation work. President Roosevelt directed the Army to mobilize these men and thereafter to run their camps without in any way making the Civilian Conservation Corps (CCC) program a military project in disguise. Within seven weeks the Army mobilized 310,000 men in 1,315 camps. For more than a year the War Department had to keep about 3,000 Regular officers and many noncommissioned officers assigned to this task, and in order to do this the Army had to strip tactical units of their leadership. Unit training was brought to a standstill, and the readiness of units for immediate military employment was almost destroyed. In the second half of 1934 the War Department called a large number of Reserve officers to active duty to replace the Regulars, and by August 1935, 9,300 Reserve officers (not counted in active Army strength) were serving with the CCC. A good many of them continued to serve with the CCC until 1941, but the Army never wanted to introduce military training into the program because the CCC camps were small and isolated. Despite its initial and serious interference with normal Army operations, the CCC program had a longer-range beneficial effect on military preparedness. It furnished many thousands of Reserve officers with valuable training, and it gave nonmilitary but disciplined training to many hundreds of thousands of young men who were to become soldiers and sailors in World War II.

New Threats Abroad. The clouds of war began to form again in 1931 when the Japanese seized Manchuria and then defied the efforts of the League of Nations and the United States to pry them loose. In 1933 Japan quit the League and a year later announced that it would no longer be bound by the naval limitation treaties after they expired in 1936. In Europe, Hitler came to power in 1933, and by 1936 Germany had denounced the Treaty of Versailles, embarked on rearmament, and occupied the demilitarized Rhineland. Hitler's partner in dictatorship, Italy's Mussolini, began his career of aggression by attacking Ethiopia in 1934. In the face of these developments the United States made significant adjustments in its foreign policy; it recognized Soviet Russia in 1933; voted eventual independence for the Philippines in 1934, liquidated its protectorates in the Caribbean area, and in Latin America actively pursued the Good Neighbor policy. No radical change in American military policy followed. But beginning in 1935 the armed forces received substantially larger appropriations that permitted them to improve their readiness for action. Army improvements during the next three years reflected not only the increasingly critical international situation but also the careful planning of the War Department during General Douglas MacArthur's tour as Chief of Staff from 1930 to 1935. His recommendations led to a reorganization of the combat forces and a modest increase in their size, and were accompanied by more realistic planning for using the manpower and industrial might of the United States for war if that should become necessary.

The Army Strengthened. The central objective of the Chief of Staff's recommendations had been to establish a small, hard-hitting force ready for emergency use. In line with this objective the Army wanted to mechanize and motorize its Regular combat units as soon as it could and to fill their ranks so that they could be trained effectively. The Army also needed a new organization, to control the training of larger units and teams of combined arms in peacetime, and to command them if war came. For these purposes the War Department between 1932 and 1935 created four army headquarters and a General Headquarters Air Force organization in the continental United States under command of the Chief of Staff. Under the supervision of these headquarters, beginning in the summer of 1935, Regular and National Guard divisions and other units trained together each year in summer maneuvers and other exercises. Significant joint Army-Navy exercises had been held even earlier in the spring of 1932. In 1935 Congress authorized the Regular Army to increase its enlisted strength to the long-sought goal of 165,000. This increase was accompanied during the following years by substantially greater expenditures for equipment and housing, so that by 1938 the Regular Army was considerably stronger and more nearly ready for action than it had been in the early 1930's. But in the meantime the strength and power of foreign armies had been increasing even more rapidly.

Emphasis on the offensive. In the slow rebuilding of the 1930's the Army concentrated on equipping and training its combat units for mobile warfare rather than for the static warfare that had characterized operations on the Western Front in World War I. Even so, its concept of mobility at that time later proved to be too limited. Through research the Army managed to acquire some new weapons that promised increased fire power and mobility as soon as equipment could be produced in quantity. In 1936 the Army adopted the Garand semiautomatic rifle to replace the 1903 Springfield, and during the 1930's it perfected the mobile 105-mm howitzer that became the principal divisional artillery piece of World War II. It also developed light and medium tanks that were much faster than the lumbering models of World War I. In units, horses gave way to motors as rapidly as new vehicles could be acquired, but here, too, there were inadequate plans for new mechanized units. To increase the maneuverability of its principal ground unit, the division, the Army decided after field tests to triangularize the infantry division by reducing the number of its infantry regiments from four to three, and to make it more mobile by using motor transportation only.

Mobilization Planning. Modern war is so complex and modern armies are so demanding in equipment that industrial mobilization for war must precede the large-scale employment of manpower by at least two years if a war is to be fought effectively. The Army's Industrial Mobilization Plan of 1930 established the basic principles for harnessing the Nation's economic strength to war needs, and revisions of this plan to 1939 improved the pattern. Manpower planning culminated in the Protective Mobilization Plan of 1937, prepared under the direction of Gen. Malin Craig, then Chief of Staff. Under this plan the first step was to be the induction of the National Guard to provide, with the Regular Army, an Initial Protective Force of about 400,000. The Navy plus this defensive force would then protect the Nation while the Army engaged in an orderly expansion to planned strengths of one, two, and four million, as necessary. With the development of mobilization planning there evolved for the first time before actual hostilities a definite training plan, which included the location, size, and scheduling of replacement training centers, unit training centers, and schools, detailed unit and individual training programs, and the production of a variety of training manuals. While these plans were useful in guiding the mobilization that began in the summer of 1940, it turned out that the planners had set their sights too low. They assumed a maximum mobilization of World War I dimensions, whereas World War II was to call forth more than twice as many men for the Army and proportionately an even greater industrial effort. The plans also assumed, until 1939, that mobilization for war would come more or less suddenly instead of relatively slowly during many months of nominal peace.

The Beginnings of World War II. *Background.* The German annexation of Austria in March 1938 followed by the Munich crisis in September of the same year awakened the United States and the other democratic nations to the imminence of another great world conflict. The new conflict had already begun in the Far East, where Japan had invaded China in 1937. After Germany seized Czechoslovakia in March 1939, war in Europe became inevitable because Great Britain and France decided that they must fight rather than yield anything more to Hitler. At the last moment Germany made a deal with the Soviet Union that provided for a partition of Poland and a Soviet free hand in the Baltic states and Finland. Then Germany invaded Poland on 1 September 1939. When France and Great Britain responded by declaring war on Germany, they embarked on a war they could not hope to win without aid from the United States.

The American response. An overwhelming majority of the American people wanted to stay out of war if they could. This sentiment necessarily governed the actions of the United States Government and the prewar preparations of the armed forces between 1938 and 1941. President Franklin D. Roosevelt and his advisers, fully aware of the dangers of the situation, launched the Nation on a limited preparedness program at the beginning of 1939. By then the technological improvement of the airplane had introduced a new factor into the military calculations of the United States. The moment was approaching when it would be feasible for a hostile Old World power to establish air bases in the Western Hemisphere, from which the Panama Canal—the key to American naval defense—or the continental United States itself might be attacked. Such a development would destroy the oceanic security that the American nation had long enjoyed. The primary emphasis in 1939 was therefore on increasing the striking power of the Army Air Corps. At the same time Army and Navy officers collaborated in drafting the RAINBOW plans that were to guide the preparations of the American armed forces. The focus of these plans in 1939 and 1940 was on hemisphere defense. After the European war started, the President proclaimed a limited emergency and authorized increases in Regular Army and National Guard enlisted strengths to 227,000 and 235,000, respectively. At his urging, Congress gave limited support to the western democracies by ending the prohibition on munitions sales to nations at war embodied in the Neutrality Act of 1937. British and French orders for munitions, in turn, helped to prepare American industry for the large-scale war production that was to come. When the quick destruction of Poland was followed by a lull in the war, the tempo of America's own defense preparations slackened. The Army concentrated on making its Regular force ready for emergency action by providing it with full and modern equipment as quickly as possible, and by engaging 70,000 troops in the first genuine corps and army maneuvers in American military history. How adequate the Army was would be determined by whether France and Great Britain survived. The successful German seizure of Denmark and Norway in April 1940, followed by the quick defeat of the Low Countries and France and the grave threat to Great Britain, forced the United States in June to adopt a new and greatly enlarged program for defense, for it then looked as if the Nation might eventually have to face the aggressors of the Old World almost alone.

Mobilization for Defense. *Hemisphere defense.* Under the leadership of Chief of Staff General George C. Marshall and, after July, of Secretary of War Henry L. Stimson, the Army embarked in the summer of 1940 on a large expansion program designed to protect the United States and the rest of the Western Hemisphere against the forces of aggression that had been unleashed in the Old World. Army expansion was matched by a naval program designed to give the United States a "two-ocean" Navy strong enough to deal simultaneously with the Japanese Fleet in the Pacific and the naval strength that Germany and its new war partner Italy might acquire in the Atlantic if they defeated Great Britain. Both expansion programs had the overwhelming support of the American people, who though still strongly opposed to entering the war were now convinced that the danger to the United States was very real. Congressional appropriations between May and September 1940 reflected this conviction. The Army received six billion dollars for its needs during the succeeding year—a sum about equal to what had been granted for the support of its military activities during the preceding 16 years. The munitions program approved for the Army on 30 June 1940 called for procurement by October 1941 of all items needed to equip and maintain a 1,200,000-man force, including a greatly enlarged and modernized Army Air Corps.

Manpower. To fill the ranks of this new Army, Congress on 27 August approved induction of the National Guard into Federal service and the calling up of the Organized Reserves. Then it authorized the first peacetime draft of untrained civilian manpower in the Nation's history in passing the Selective Service and Training Act of 16 September 1940. Selectees, Reserve officers to train them, and units of the National Guard, were brought into service as rapidly as the Army could construct camps to house them. During the last six months of 1940 the active Army more than doubled in strength, and by mid-1941 it numbered nearly one and a half million officers and men.

Organization. A new organization, General Headquarters, took charge of training the Army in July 1940. In the same month the Army established a separate Armored Force and subsequently Antiaircraft and Tank Destroyer Commands, which, with the Infantry, Field Artillery, Coast Artillery, and Cavalry, increased the number of ground combat arms to seven. The existing branch schools and a new Armored Force School concentrated during 1940 and 1941 on improving the fitness of National Guard and Reserve officers for active duty, and in early 1941 the War Department established officer candidate schools to train men selected from the ranks for junior leadership positions. In October 1940 the four field armies assumed command of ground units in the continental United States and thereafter trained them under the supervision of General Headquarters. The corps area commands became administrative and service organizations. Major overseas garrisons were strengthened, and the Army established new commands to supervise the garrisoning of Puerto Rico and Alaska, where there had been almost no Army troops for many years. In June

Gen. George C. Marshall.

1941 the War Department established the Army Air Forces to train and administer air units in the United States. In July it began the transformation of General Headquarters into an operational post for General Marshall as Commanding General of the Field Forces. By the autumn of 1941 the Army had 27 infantry, 5 armored, and 2 cavalry divisions, 35 air groups, and a host of supporting units in training in the continental United States. Many of these units were still unready for action, in part because the United States had shared much of its old and new military equipment with the nations that were actively fighting the Axis triumvirate of Germany, Italy, and Japan.

Foreign Aid. President Roosevelt had directed the transfer of large stocks of Army World War I weapons to Great Britain in June

1940, and in September the United States and Britain had agreed to an exchange of destroyers for offshore Atlantic bases. Open collaboration with Canada from August 1940 onward led eventually to strong U. S. support of the Canadian war effort, Canada having followed Great Britain into war in September 1939. The foreign aid program culminated in the Lend-Lease Act of March 1941, which openly avowed the intention of the United States to become an "arsenal of democracy" against aggression. The fundamental purpose of foreign aid was to help contain the military might of the Axis powers until the United States could complete its own protective mobilization.

Toward War. By early 1941 it appeared to Army and Navy leaders and to President Roosevelt that the United States might soon be drawn into full participation in the conflict. Assuming the probability of simultaneous operations in the Pacific and in the Atlantic, they agreed that Germany was the greater menace and that if the United States did enter the war it ought to concentrate on the defeat of Germany first. This principle was accepted in staff conversations between American and British military representatives in February and March 1941. During the spring of 1941 the United States decided to accept responsibility for the development and operation of military air routes across the North Atlantic via Greenland and across the South Atlantic via Brazil. The actual projection of American military power across the Atlantic began with the initial movement of American forces to Iceland in July 1941, followed two months later by a sizable Army expeditionary force. In August the President and Prime Minister Churchill met in Newfoundland and drafted the Atlantic Charter, which defined the general terms of a just peace for the world. By October the United States Navy, with some assistance from Army aircraft, had joined with British and Canadian forces in warring against the depredations of German submarines in the North Atlantic. In the meantime, American policy toward Japan had stiffened, and in July 1941 the Army decided to reinforce the Philippines against the threat of Japanese attack. For their part, the Japanese, while negotiating with the United States, decided in September to embark on a war of conquest in Asia and the East Indies as soon as possible and to try to immobilize American naval opposition by an opening air strike against the great American naval base of Pearl Harbor in Hawaii.

Summary. After World War I the United States had returned to its traditional custom of maintaining a small standing Army in time of peace. In marked contrast with earlier peacetime periods, the Army after 1920 concentrated on training the civilian components that were to provide the immediate reinforcement and the trained leadership for a large expansion if war threatened. The ROTC program became the keystone of this system, since it contributed so much of the junior leadership on which an efficient expansion of the Army depended. In further contrast with traditional practice the War Department had also engaged in continuous planning for war, however remote its prospect. When the world situation darkened in the 1930's, the Army began a slow build-up of strength that changed into partial mobilization when the outlook suddenly worsened in the summer of 1940. Regulars, National Guardsmen, Reserves, selectees, and volunteers were fused during 1941 into a new Army, as large in numbers as the combined forces of North and South in the Civil War. Although raised for defense, this Army was trained and its equipment designed for offensive operations, providing a sure base for wartime expansion and ultimate victory in World War II.

QUESTIONS

1. Why did the United States reject a system of universal military training after World War I?

2. What duties did the Army have to perform overseas after World War I?

3. Discuss the organization of the Army of the United States as prescribed by the National Defense Act of 1920.

4. Describe the nature and purposes of the Army educational sys-system.

5. What important nonmilitary tasks were performed by the Army during this period?

6. How effective were the mobilization plans drafted by the Army during the 1930's?

7. Discuss foreign aid as a factor in American preparations for defense, 1939–1941.

8. Compare the Army of December 1941 with the Army of April 1917.

Reading List

ARMY AIR FORCES IN WORLD WAR II:
 Craven, Wesley F. and James L. Cate. *Plans and Early Operations.* Chicago, 1948.
 Langer, William L., and S. Everett Gleason. *The Challenge to Isolation.* New York, 1952.
 ------------. *The Undeclared War.* New York, 1953.
UNITED STATES ARMY IN WORLD WAR II:
 Greenfield, Kent R., Robert R. Palmer and Bell I. Wiley. *The Organization of Ground Combat Troops.* Washington, 1947.
 Watson, Mark S. *Chief of Staff: Prewar Plans and Preparations.* Washington, 1950.

CHAPTER 20

WORLD WAR II—THE DEFENSE PHASE

The Outbreak of War. Unknown to American political or military leaders, strong Japanese forces had concentrated in November 1941 for attacks on the two main centers of American power in the Pacific, Hawaii and the Philippines. Without warning, in the early morning of 7 December, powerful carrier-borne air forces smashed the Pacific Fleet at anchor in Pearl Harbor, Hawaii. The same day (8 December in this longitude), about noon, Formosa-based bombers caught the bulk of the U. S. Far East Air Force lined up on Clark and Iba Fields, not far from Manila in central Luzon, and virtually destroyed it.

Burning Ships at Pearl Harbor, 7 December 1941.

The attack on Pearl Harbor was one of the most brilliant tactical feats of the war. From six carriers which had advanced undetected to a position 200 miles north of Oahu, some 350 aircraft came in through the morning mist, achieving complete tactical surprise. They bombed and strafed the neatly aligned planes on Hickam and Wheeler Fields, and carefully singled out major units of the Navy's Battle Force at anchor in the harbor. Fortunately, the Fleet's three carriers were away at the time, and the attackers failed to hit the oil tanks and naval repair shops on shore. But the blow was devastating enough. Almost 200 aircraft were destroyed, all eight battleships were sunk or badly damaged, besides numerous other vessels, and total casualties came to about 3,400, mostly killed. Japanese losses were only 29 aircraft and 5 midget submarines. The operation admirably combined the principles of surprise, objective, mass, and, in preparations and approach to the target, security and maneuver. In its larger strategic context, it also exemplified the principles of the offensive and economy of force. The Joint Committee investigating the attack called it the "greatest military and naval disaster in our Nation's history."

These two attacks—on Pearl Harbor and the Philippines—effectively wiped out American striking power in the Pacific. The Philippines and other American possessions in the western Pacific were isolated, their loss a foregone conclusion. The Hawaiian Islands and Alaska lay open to invasion; the Panama Canal and the cities, factories, and shipyards of the West Coast were vulnerable to raids from the sea and air. Months would pass before the United States could regain the capacity for the most limited kind of offensive action against its oriental enemy. As Japanese forces moved swiftly southward against the Philippines, Malaya, and the Netherlands Indies, Japan's Axis partners, Germany and Italy, promptly declared war on the United States, thus ending the uncertainty whether this country would become a full-fledged belligerent in the European War. For the first time in its history, the United States was embarked upon an all-out two-front war.

Meanwhile Britain was battling to maintain its hold on the eastern Mediterranean region, which lay athwart the historic lifeline to possessions and Commonwealth associates in the Far East. Late in 1940 small British forces based in Egypt gained important successes against Italian armies in Libya, and the Greeks in the winter of 1940-41 resoundingly defeated an invading Italian army and chased it back into Albania. But German armies quickly came to the aid of their Italian ally. In April 1941 the famous panzer divisions, supported by overwhelming air power, swept through the Balkans, crushing the Yugoslav and Greek armies and a British expeditionary force hastily dispatched to aid the latter. The following month German airborne forces descended on the island of Crete and swamped its British and Greek defenders in a spectacular, though costly, blitz. In Libya, meanwhile, a powerful German-Italian army under Field Marshal Erwin Rommel drove the British back across the Egyptian border, isolating a large garrison in Tobruk and threatening the Nile Delta. Against these disasters Britain could count only the final expulsion of the Italians from the Red Sea area and of the Vichy French from Syria, the suppression of pro-German uprisings in Iraq, and the achievement of a precarious naval ascendancy in the eastern and western portions of the Mediterranean. During the remainder of 1941 the British gradually built up strength in eastern Libya and late in the year they succeeded in relieving Tobruk and pushing Rommel back to his original starting point at El Agheila.

The war in Europe. Since mid-1940 the military fortunes of the anti-Axis powers had declined as the European war expanded. Germany had crushed all her Continental European opponents in the west, and then attempted late in 1940 to destroy Britain's air forces as a prelude to an invasion across the English Channel. In the air battles over Britain in September 1940 the Royal Air Force won a brilliant victory. But during the following winter and spring the waning threat of invasion had been replaced by the equally deadly and more persistent menace of economic strangulation. German aircraft pulverized Britain's ports and inland cities, while U-boats, surface raiders, and mines decimated shipping. By 1941 the imports on which the United Kingdom depended for existence had dwindled to less than two-thirds of their pre-war volume, and the British people faced the prospect of ultimate starvation.

In June 1941, however, the storm center of the war had moved elsewhere. Only slightly delayed by the conquest of the Balkans, Hitler on 22 June 1941 hurled German might against the Soviet Union, the only remaining power on the European continent capable of challenging his ascendancy. By early December, when the onset of winter and stiffening Soviet resistance finally brought the advance to a halt, the German armies had driven to the suburbs of Moscow, inflicted huge losses on the Red Army, and occupied a vast expanse of European Russia embracing its most densely populated and industrialized regions. This, as it turned out, was the high tide of German success in World War II; Hitler, like Napoleon, was to meet disaster on the wind-swept plains of Russia. But in December 1941 few were willing to predict so much. British and United States leaders assembling in Washington at the end of that month to concert plans for dealing with the crisis had to reckon with the probability that in the year to come, unless the Western Allies could somehow force Germany to divert substantial forces from the eastern front, the German steamroller would complete the destruction of the Soviet armies. Hitler would then be able, with the resources and enslaved peoples of all Europe at his feet, to throw his full power against the West.

The Victory Program. American military leaders had already given thought to this grim prospect, and to the implications it held for America's role in the war. In the "Victory Program," drawn up by the Army and Navy at the President's behest during the summer of 1941, the leaders of the two services had set forth in some detail the strategy and the means they considered necessary to win ultimate victory if, as they expected, Soviet Russia succumbed to the Axis onslaught. The strategy was the one laid down in the RAINBOW 5 War Plan—wear Germany down by bombing, blockade, subversion, and limited offensives, while mobilizing the strength needed to invade the European continent and to defeat Germany on her own ground. Japan meanwhile would be contained by air and sea power, local defense forces, China's inexhaustible manpower, and Russia's Siberian divisions. With Germany out of the running, Japan's defeat or collapse would soon follow. As for the means, America would have to provide them in large part, for the British were already weary and their resources were limited. The United States would serve not merely, to use the President's catchy phrase, as the "arsenal of democracy," supplying weapons to arm its allies, but also as the main source of the armies without which wars, above all this war, could not be won. Army leaders envisaged the eventual mobilization of 215 grand divisions, 61 of them armored, and 239 combat air groups, making a grand total, with supporting forces, of 8.8 million men. Five million of these would be hurled against the European Axis. It was emphasized that victory over the Axis powers would require a maximum military effort and full mobilization of America's immense industrial resources.

Yet the Victory Program was merely an expression of professional military views, not a statement of national military policy. That policy, on the eve of Pearl Harbor, was still ostensibly hemisphere defense. The pace of rearmament and mobilization, in the summer and fall of 1941, was actually slowing down. The Army expected to reach the end of its planned expansion (to 1.8 million men) by the following March. Thereafter, even though the troops would still be far short of their minimum training allowances of equipment, the plan was to divert the bulk of the new weapons coming off production lines to British, Soviet, and other anti-Axis forces. No more than 16 divisions were to be readied for overseas service. Plans were afoot to demobilize the National Guard and abandon conscription. All this pointed to a policy of making the American contribution to the defeat of the Axis, as Walter Lippmann put it, one "basically of Navy, Air, and manufacturing," something a great deal less than the all-out effort envisaged in the Victory Program. Public and Congressional sentiment, moreover, still clung to the hope that the country would not have to intervene in the war at all, as evidenced by the near defeat of the bill to extend Selective Service, the continuation of the prohibition against sending selectees outside the Western Hemisphere, and the apathetic public response to submarine attacks on American destroyers in September and October.

Reaction to war. The Japanese attack on Pearl Harbor and the Philippines changed the entire picture. A wave of patriotic indignation over Japanese duplicity and brutality swept the country. Isolationism, suddenly unpopular, virtually evaporated as a public issue, and all parties closed ranks in support of the war effort. The President, early in January, dramatized the magnitude of the effort now demanded by proclaiming a new set of production goals—60,000 airplanes in 1942 and 125,000 in 1943; 45,000 tanks in 1942 and 75,000 in 1943; 20,000 antiaircraft guns in 1942 and 35,000 in 1943; half a million machine guns in 1942 and as many more in 1943; and 8 million deadweight tons of merchant shipping in 1942 and 10 million in 1943. Vanished were the twin illusions that America could serve only as an arsenal of democracy, contributing weapons without the men to wield them, or, conversely, that the nation could rely solely on its own fighting forces, leaving other anti-Axis nations to shift for themselves. "We must not only provide munitions for our own fighting forces," Roosevelt advised Secretary of War Stimson, "but vast quantities to be used against the enemy in every appropriate theater of war." A new Victory Program boosted the Army's ultimate mobilization goal to ten million men, and the War Department planned to have 71 divisions and 115 combat air groups organized by the end of 1942, with a total of 3.6 million men under arms. As an Army planner had predicted back in the spring of 1941, the United States now seemed destined to become "the final reserve of the democracies both in manpower and munitions."

"Germany first." Late in December President Roosevelt and Prime Minister Churchill met with their advisers in Washington (the ARCADIA Conference) to establish the bases of coalition strategy and concert immediate measures to meet the military crisis. They faced an agonizing dilemma. Prompt steps had to be taken to stem the spreading tide of Japanese conquest. On the other hand, it seemed likely that the coming year might see the collapse of Soviet resistance and of the British position in the Middle East. In this difficult situation the Allied leaders made a far-reaching decision, which decisively shaped the whole course of the war. Reaffirming the principle laid down in the ABC Conversations ten months earlier, they agreed that the first and main effort must go into defeating Germany, the more formidable enemy. Japan's turn would come later. Defeating Germany, it was recognized, would involve a prolonged process of "closing and tightening the ring" about Fortress Europe. Operations in 1942 would have to be defensive and preparatory, though limited offensives might be undertaken if the opportunity offered. Not until 1943 at the earliest could the Allies contemplate a return to the European Continent, "across the Mediterranean, from Turkey into the Balkans, or by landings in Western Europe."

The high command. Another important action taken at the ARCADIA Conference was the establishment of the Combined Chiefs of Staff (CCS). This was a committee consisting of the professional military chiefs of both countries, responsible to the President and Prime Minister for planning and directing the grand strategy of the coalition. Its American members were the Army Chief of Staff, General Marshall; the Chief of Naval Operations, Admiral Stark (replaced early in 1942 by Admiral Ernest J. King); and the Chief (later Commanding General) of the Army Air Forces, General Henry H. Arnold. In July 1942 a fourth member was added, the President's personal chief of staff, Admiral William D. Leahy. Since the CCS normally sat in Washington, the British Chiefs of Staff, making up its British component, attended in person only at important conferences with the heads of state. In the intervals they were represented in Washington by the four senior members of the permanent British Joint Staff Mission, headed until late in 1944 by Field Marshal Sir John Dill, the former Chief of the British Imperial General Staff. Under the CCS a system of primarily military subordinate committees grew up, assisting the CCS in such fields as strategic and logistical planning, transportation, and communications.

For control of American forces, Army planners suggested soon after Pearl Harbor the creation of a supreme U. S. military commander, who would be responsible to the President and be assisted by a joint Army-Navy general staff. This scheme was rejected owing to the Navy's objections. Instead, by February 1942 the Joint Chiefs of Staff (JCS), consisting of the U. S. members of the CCS, had emerged as the highest authority in the U. S. military hierarchy (though never formally chartered as such), and responsible directly to the President. The old Joint Board remained nominally in existence. Like the CCS, the JCS in time developed a machinery of planning and working committees, the most important of which were the Joint Staff Planners (JPS), the Joint Strategic Survey Committee (JSSC), and the Joint Logistics Committee (JLC). No executive machinery was created at either the CCS or JCS level. The CCS ordinarily named either the British Chiefs or the U. S. Joint Chiefs to act as its executive agent, and these in turn employed the established machinery of the service departments.

Command and administration overseas. In the spring of 1942 Britain and the United States agreed on a world-wide division of strategic responsibility. The U. S. Joint Chiefs of Staff were to be primarily responsible for the war in the Pacific, and the British Chiefs for the Middle East-Indian Ocean region, while the European-Mediterranean-Atlantic area would be a combined responsibility of both powers. China was designated a separate theater commanded by its chief of state, Chiang Kai-shek, though within the United States sphere of responsibility. In the Pacific, the JCS established two main theaters, the Southwest Pacific Area (SWPA) and the Pacific Ocean Area (POA), the former under General Mac-Arthur, the latter under Admiral Chester W. Nimitz. POA was further subdivided into North, Central, and South Pacific areas, the first two directly controlled by Nimitz, the third by his deputy, Admiral William F. Halsey, Jr. (map 41). Later in 1942, the United States air and service troops operating in China, India, and northern Burma were organized as U. S. Army Forces, China-Burma-India, under Lt. Gen. Joseph W. Stilwell. On various other far-flung lines of communications U. S. Army forces, mostly air and service troops during 1942, were organized under similar theater commands. In June Lt. Gen. Dwight D. Eisenhower arrived in England to take command of the newly established European Theater of Operations, and after the landings in North Africa late in the year a new United States theater was organized in that region.

It had been decided at the ARCADIA Conference that Allied forces in each overseas theater would operate, as far as possible, under a single commander, and this principle was subsequently applied in most theaters. Within theaters, subordinate unified commands were created, in some cases, for Allied ground, naval, or air forces, and most frequently, for task forces formed to carry out a specific operation or campaign. The authority of Allied theater commanders over national forces was always restricted with respect to areas and missions, and, as a last resort, senior national commanders in each theater could appeal to their own governments against specific orders or policies of the theater commander. In practice, this right of appeal was rarely invoked.

In essence, unified command at the Allied level gave the commander control of certain specific forces for operational purposes, rather than jurisdiction over a given geographical area. Administration of national forces and the allocation of resources were usually handled through separate national channels. In certain cases, inter-Allied boards or committees, responsible to the Allied theater commander, controlled the common use of critical resources (such as petroleum products) or facilities (such as railways and shipping) within a theater. Administration of U. S. forces overseas also generally followed separate Army and Navy channels, except in the Pacific where, from 1943 on, supply, transportation, and certain other services were jointly administered to a limited degree.

Reorganization of the War Department. Even before Pearl Harbor it had become evident that the peacetime organization of the War Department General Staff, dating back to 1921, was an inadequate instrument for directing a major war effort. Originally a small coordinating and planning body, the General Staff, and especially its

War Plans and Supply Divisions, rapidly expanded during the emergency period into a large operating organization, increasingly immersed in the details of supervision to the detriment of its planning and policy-making functions. The Chief of Staff, to whom some 61 officers and agencies had direct access, carried an especially heavy burden.

Three additional features of the organization demanded remedy. One was the continued subordination of the Army Air Forces to General Staff supervision, which conflicted with its drive for autonomy. Another was the anomalous position of General Headquarters (GHQ), whose role as command post for the field forces and responsibilities in the fields of training and logistics clashed with the authority of the General Staff at numerous points. Finally, the division of supply responsibilities between the Supply Division (G4) and the Office of the Undersecretary of War—with requirements and distribution assigned to the former and procurement to the latter— was breaking down under the pressures of mobilization.

Spurred by the Pearl Harbor disaster, which seemed to accentuate the need for better staff coordination in Washington, General Marshall on 9 March put into effect a sweeping reorganization of the War Department. Under the new plan, which underwent little change during the war years, the General Staff, except for the War Plans and Intelligence Divisions, was drastically whittled down and limited in function to broad planning and policy guidance. An expanded War Plans Division, soon renamed Operations Division (OPD), became General Marshall's command post and, in effect, a superior general staff for the direction of overseas operations. The Army Air Force gained almost complete autonomy, administering its own personnel and training, and those aspects of supply that were peculiar to air operations. Its planning staff also became mainly responsible for direction of air operations overseas.

Two new Zone of Interior commands were created, the Army Ground Forces (AGF) and the Services of Supply, later renamed the Army Service Forces (ASF). The former, headed by Lt. Gen. Lesley J. McNair, took over the training mission of GHQ, now abolished, and absorbed the ground combat arms. To the ASF, commanded by Lt. Gen. Brehon B. Somervell, were subordinated the supply (renamed technical) and administrative services, the nine corps areas, and most of the Army posts and installations throughout the United States, including the ports of embarkation through which troops and supplies flowed to the forces overseas. In supply matters, Somervell now reported to two masters, the Chief of Staff for requirements and distribution, and the Undersecretary of War, Mr. Robert P. Patterson, for procurement. His subordination to the latter was, in reality, only nominal since most of Patterson's organization was transferred bodily to Somervell's headquarters. Except for materiel peculiar to the Army Air Forces, the ASF thus became the Army's central agency for supply in the United States. It drew up the Army's "shopping list" of requirements, the Army Supply Program; through the seven technical services (Quartermaster, Ordnance, Signal, Chemical, Engineer, Medical, and Transportation) it procured most of the Army's supplies and equipment; it distributed this materiel to the Army at home and abroad, as well as to foreign allies under lend-lease; it operated the Army's fleet of transports; it trained specialists and service units to perform various specialized jobs. General Somervell himself became General Marshall's principal logistical adviser.

Immediate measures. All this looked to the future. In the first few weeks after Pearl Harbor, while the Navy was salvaging what it could from the wreckage at Pearl Harbor and striving to combat German submarines in the western Atlantic, the War Department made desperate efforts to bolster the defenses of Hawaii, the Philippines, the Panama Canal, Alaska, and the U. S. West Coast. It also initiated some of the movements to North Atlantic bases, including Iceland, scheduled under RAINBOW 5. By the end of December, the immediate danger of an attack on the Hawaii-Alaska-Panama triangle seemed to have waned, and the emphasis shifted to measures to stave off further disasters in the Far East. It was decided at ARCADIA that the Allies would attempt to hold the Japanese north and east of the line of the Malay Peninsula and the Netherlands Indies and to reestablish communications with the Philippines to the north. To coordinate operations in this vast theater the Allied leaders created the ABDA (American-British-Dutch-Australian) Command, including the Netherlands Indies, Malaya, Burma, and the Philippines. British Lt. Gen. Sir Archibald P. Wavell was placed in overall command. Through India from the west and Australia from the east, the Allies hoped in a short time to build up a shield of air power stout enough to blunt the Japanese thrust.

Japaneses conquests. For a time it seemed as though nothing could stop the Japanese juggernaut. In less than three weeks after Pearl Harbor, the isolated American outposts of Wake and Guam fell to the invaders, the British garrison of Hong Kong was overwhelmed, and powerful land, sea, and air forces were converging on Malaya and the Netherlands Indies. Picked jungle-trained troops drove down the Malay Peninsula toward the great fortress of Singapore, infiltrating and outflanking successive British positions. Two of the most formidable warships in the British Navy, the battleship *Prince of Wales* and the battle cruiser *Repulse*, were sunk by Japanese torpedo planes off the east coast of Malaya, a loss that destroyed the Allies' last hope of effectively opposing Japan's naval power in the

Far East. Attacked from the land side, Singapore and its 70,000 troops surrendered on 15 February 1942. Meanwhile the Japanese had invaded the Netherlands Indies from the north, west, and east. In a series of actions during January and February, the weak Dutch and Australian naval forces, joined by the U. S. Asiatic Fleet withdrawing from the Philippines, were destroyed piecemeal, only four American destroyers escaping south to Australia. On 9 March the last Allied ground and air forces in the Netherlands Indies, almost 100,000 men (mostly Indonesian troops) surrendered to the invaders. In Burma, the day before, the British had been forced under heavy bombing to evacuate Rangoon and retreat northward. Before the end of April the Japanese had completed the occupation of Burma, driving the British westward into India and Chinese forces under U. S. Lt. Gen. Joseph W. Stilwell back into China. In the process they had won possession of a huge section of the Burma Road, the only land connection between China and India. Henceforth, and until late in the war, communication between between China and its allies was to be limited to the air ferry from India over the "hump" of the Himalayan Mountains. During the late spring strong Japanese naval forces reached the coastal cities of India and even attacked Britain's naval base on Ceylon.

By May 1942 the Japanese had thus gained control of all southeastern Asia—Burma, Malaya, Thailand, and French Indo-China—and the Malay Archipelago, while farther to the east they had won strong lodgments on the islands of New Guinea and New Britain and in the Solomons, flanking the approaches to Australia and New Zealand from the United States. This immense empire had been won at remarkably little cost, through an effective combination of superior air and sea power and only a handful of well-trained ground divisions. The Japanese had seized and held the initiative while keeping their opponents off balance. They had concentrated their strength for the capture of key objectives such as airfields and road junctions and for the destruction of major enemy forces, while diverting only minimum forces on secondary missions, thus giving an impression of overwhelming numerical strength. They had frequently gained the advantage of surprise, and had baffled their enemies by their speed and skill in maneuver. The whole whirlwind campaign, in short, had provided Japan's enemies with a capsule course of instruction in the principles of war.

Fall of the Philippines. Only in the Philippines, almost on Japan's southern doorstep, was the timetable of conquest delayed. When the Japanese struck, the defending forces in the islands numbered more than 130,000, including the Philippine Army which, though mobilized to a strength of ten divisions, was ill-trained and ill-equipped. Of the U. S. Army contingent of 31,000, more than a third consisted of the Philippine Scouts, most of whom were part of the Regular Army Philippine Division, the core of the mobile defense forces. The Far East Air Force, before the Japanese attack, had a total of 277 aircraft of all types, mostly obsolescent but including 35 new heavy bombers. Admiral Thomas C. Hart's Asiatic Fleet, based on the Philippines, consisted of 3 cruisers, 13 old destroyers, 6 gunboats, 6 motor torpedo boats, 32 patrol bombers, and 29 submarines; a regiment of Marines, withdrawn from Shanghai, also joined the defending forces late in November 1941. Before the end of December, however, American air and naval power in the Philippines had virtually ceased to exist. The handful of bombers surviving the early attacks had been evacuated to Australia, and the bulk of the Asiatic Fleet, its base facilities in ruins, had withdrawn southward to help in the defense of the Netherlands Indies.

The main Japanese invasion of the Philippines, following preliminary landings, began on 22 December 1941. While numerically inferior to the defenders, the invading force of two divisions with supporting units was well trained and equipped and enjoyed complete mastery in the air and on the sea. The attack centered on Luzon, the northernmost and largest island of the archipelago, where all but a small fraction of the defending forces were concentrated. The main landings were made on the beaches of Lingayen Gulf, in the northwest, and Lamon Bay in the southeast. General MacArthur's plan was to meet and destroy the invaders on the beaches, but his troops were unable to prevent the enemy from gaining secure lodgments. On 23 December MacArthur ordered a general withdrawal into the mountainous Bataan Peninsula, across Manila Bay from the capital city. Manila itself was occupied by the Japanese without resistance. The retreat into Bataan was a complex operation, involving converging movements over difficult terrain, into a cramped assembly area from which only two roads led into the peninsula itself. Under constant enemy attack, the maneuver was executed with consummate skill, and at considerable cost to the attackers. Yet American and Filipino losses were heavy, and the unavoidable abandonment of large stocks of supplies foredoomed the defenders of Bataan to ultimate defeat in the siege that followed. An ominous portent was the cutting of food rations by half on the last day of the retreat.

By 7 January 1942 General MacArthur's forces held well-prepared positions across the upper part of the Bataan Peninsula. Their presence there, and on Corregidor and its satellite island fortresses guarding the entrance to Manila Bay, denied the enemy the use of the Bay throughout the siege. In the first major enemy offensive, launched early in January, the "battling bastards of Bataan" at first gave ground, but thereafter handled the Japanese so roughly that attacks ceased altogether from mid-February until April, while the enemy reorganized and heavily reinforced. The defenders were, however, too weak to seize the initiative themselves.

General MacArthur, meanwhile, was ordered by the President to leave his post and go to Australia in order to take command of Allied operations against the Japanese in the southwest Pacific. In mid-March he and a small party made their way through the Japanese lines by motor torpedo boat to Mindanao, and from there were flown to Australia. Command of the forces in the Philippines devolved upon Lt. Gen. Jonathan M. Wainwright.

By April the troops on Bataan were subsisting on about 15 ounces of food daily, less than a quarter of the peacetime ration. Their diet, consisting mostly of rice supplemented by carabao, mule, monkey, or lizard meat, was gravely deficient in vitamins and provided less than 1,000 calories a day, barely enough to sustain life. Weakened by hunger and poor diet, thousands succumbed to malaria, dengue, scurvy, beriberi, and amoebic dysentery, which the shortage of medical supplies, especially quinine, made it impossible to control. Desperate efforts were made to send food, medicine, ammunition, and other supplies through the Japanese blockade to the beleaguered forces. But during the early weeks, before the enemy cordon had tightened, it proved impossible, despite promises of lavish pay and bonuses, to muster the necessary ships and crews. Even so, sizable stocks were accumulated in the southern islands, but only about 1,000 tons of rations ever reached Manila Bay. Shipments in converted destroyers from the United States were too late and too few, and only insignificant quantities could be brought in by submarine and aircraft.

At the beginning of April the Japanese, behind a pulverizing artillery barrage, attacked again. The American lines crumpled, and in a few days the defending forces virtually disintegrated. On 9 April Maj. Gen. Edward P. King, Jr., commanding the forces on Bataan, surrendered. For almost another month the garrison on Corregidor and the other islands, swelled by refugees from Bataan, held out under air bombardment and almost continuous plunging fire from heavy artillery massed on adjacent shores and heights—one of the most intense artillery bombardments, for so small a target, of the entire war. On the night of 5 May, after a final terrific five-day barrage, Japanese assault troops won a foothold on Corregidor, and the following night, when it had become apparent that further resistance was useless, General Wainwright surrendered unconditionally. Under his orders, which the Japanese forced him to broadcast, other American commanders in the Philippines capitulated one by one. By early June, except for scattered guerilla detachments in the hills, all organized resistance in the islands had ceased.

The Means at Hand. After more than a year and a half of rearming, the United States in December 1941 was still in no position to carry the war to its enemies, and was ill-prepared even to defend itself at home. On 7 December the Army numbered some 1,644,000 men (including about 120,000 officers), organized into 4 armies, 37 divisions (30 infantry, 5 armored, 2 cavalry), and over 40 combat air groups. Three of the divisions were overseas (2 in Hawaii, one in the Philippines), with other garrison forces totaling a little less than 200,000—only about half their authorized war strength. By spreading equipment and ammunition thin, a substantial force might have been put into the field, to repel an attack on the Continental United States; 17 of the divisions at home were rated as technically ready for combat. But these divisions lacked the supporting units and the training necessary to weld them into corps and armies. More serious still, they were inadequately equipped with many weapons that recent operations in Europe had shown to be indispensable—for example, tank and antitank guns, antiaircraft artillery, radios and radar— and some of these shortages were aggravated by shortages of auxiliary equipment like fire-control mechanisms.

Above all, ammunition of all kinds was so scarce that the War Department was unwilling to commit more than one division and a single antiaircraft regiment for service in any theater where combat operations seemed imminent. Only one division-size task force, in fact, was sent to the far Pacific before April 1942. Against air attacks, too, the country's defenses were meager. Along the Pacific coast the Army had only 45 modern fighter planes ready to fly, and only 12 three-inch antiaircraft guns to defend the whole Los Angeles area. On the east coast there were only 54 Army fighter planes ready for action. The total number of modern fighter aircraft available was less than 1,000. Fortunately, there was no real threat of an invasion in force, and the rapidly expanding output of munitions from American factories promised to remedy most of these weaknesses within a few months. Furthermore, temporary diversions of lend-lease equipment, especially aircraft, helped to bolster the overall defense posture within the first few weeks after Pearl Harbor. The Army hoped by April to have as many as 13 divisions equipped and supplied with ammunition for combat.

Shipping and the war at sea. To deploy these forces overseas was another matter. Although the U. S. Merchant Marine ranked second only to Great Britain's and the country possessed an immense shipbuilding capacity, the process of chartering, assembling, and preparing shipping for the movement of troops and military cargo took time. Time was also needed to schedule and organize convoys, and, owing to the desperate shortage of escort vessels, troop movements had to be widely spaced. Convoying and evasive routing, in themselves, greatly reduced the effective capacity of shipping. Moreover, vast distances separated United States ports from the areas threatened

Convoy en route to North Africa.

by Japan, and to these areas went the bulk of the forces deployed overseas during the months immediately following Pearl Harbor. Through March 1942, as a result, the outflow of troops to overseas bases averaged only about 50,000 per month, as compared with upwards of 250,000 during 1944, when shipping was fully mobilized and plentiful and the sea lanes were secure.

There seemed a real danger early in 1942, however, that German U-boats might succeed in reducing transatlantic deployment to a trickle—not so much by attacking troop transports, most of which could outrun their attackers, as by sinking the slow cargo ships on which the forces overseas depended for support. Hard on the heels of Germany's declaration of war, the U-boats struck at the virtually unprotected shipping lanes in the western Atlantic, and subsequently extended their attacks to the Gulf and Caribbean areas and the mouth of the St. Lawrence. During the spring of 1942 tankers and freighters were torpedoed in plain view of vacationers on east-coast beaches, and coastal cities dimmed or extinguished their lights in order that ships might not provide silhouetted targets for the U-boats. The Navy lacked the means to cope with the peril. In late December 1941 it had only 20 assorted surface vessels and about a hundred aircraft to protect the whole North Atlantic coastal frontier. During the winter and spring these were supplemented by another hundred Army planes of longer range, several armed British trawlers, and as many improvised craft as could be pressed into service. But the toll of ship sinkings increased. In March 788,000 deadweight tons of Allied and neutral dry cargo shipping were lost, in June 936,000 tons. Tanker losses reached an all-time peak of 375,000 tons in March, leading to complete suspension of coastal tanker movements and gasoline rationing in the seaboard states. During the first six months of 1942 losses of Allied shipping were almost as heavy as during the whole of 1941 and exceeded new construction by almost 2.8 million deadweight tons. Although the United States was able by May to balance its own current losses by building new ships, Britain and other allied countries continued until the following August to lose more than they could build, and another year passed before new construction offset cumulative losses.

Slowly and with many setbacks a system of countermeasures was developed. Convoying of coastal shipping, with ships sailing only by day, began in the spring of 1942. North-south traffic between United States and Caribbean and South American ports was also convoyed, on schedules interlocked with those of the transatlantic convoys. The latter, during 1942, were protected in the western half of the Atlantic by the United States and Canadian navies, in the eastern half by the British. Troops were transported across the Atlantic either without escort in large, speedy liners like the *Queen Elizabeth* and *Queen Mary*—which between them carried almost a quarter of all U. S. troops sent to Europe—or in heavily escorted convoys. Throughout the war, not a single loaded troop transport was sunk on the United Kingdom run. The slow merchant ships were convoyed in large groups according to speed.

But with responsibility for United States anti-submarine operations divided between the Navy and Army Air Forces, effective cooperation was hampered by sharp disagreement over organization and methods, and available resources throughout 1942 were inadequate. The U-boats, meanwhile, were operating with deadly effect and in growing numbers. Late in the year they began to hunt in packs, resupplied at sea by large cargo submarines ("milch cows"). The Allied convoys to Murmansk and other northern Soviet ports suffered especially heavy losses on their long passage around the top of the Scandinavian Peninsula. One of these convoys, in June 1942, lost 22 out of its 33 freighters. In November shipping losses from all causes soared above 1.1 million deadweight tons—the peak, as it turned out, for the entire war, but few at the time dared so to predict.

Early deployment—the Pacific. In the Pacific, fortunately, the principal barriers to deployment of U. S. forces were distance and lack of prepared bases, not enemy submarines. Japan's small fleet of undersea craft made little effort to prey on the Allied sea lanes and probably, over the vast reaches of the Pacific, could not have inflicted serious damage in any case. The principal goal of American deployment to the Pacific during most of 1942, following the initial reinforcement of Hawaii and the Panama Canal, was to build up a base in Australia and secure the chain of islands leading to it.

Australia was a vast, thinly populated, and, except in its southeastern portion, largely undeveloped island continent, 7,000 miles and almost a month's sail from the U. S. west coast. It had provided a haven for some 4,000 American troops who on 7 December had been at sea bound for the Philippines, and in January a task force of division size (POPPY Force) was hastily assembled and dispatched to New Caledonia to guard its eastern approaches. During the first few weeks the main effort of the small American forces went into sending relief supplies to the Philippines and aircraft and troops to Java to stem the Japanese invasion. Beginning in March, as the futility of these efforts became evident, and coincident with the arrival of General MacArthur to assume command of all Allied forces in the Southwest Pacific, the construction of base facilities and the buildup of balanced air and ground forces got under way in earnest.

This buildup had as its first object the defense of Australia itself, for at the end of January the Japanese had occupied Rabaul on New Britain Island, thus posing an immediate threat to Port Moresby, the weakly held Australian base in southeastern New Guinea. In February President Roosevelt pledged American help in countering this threat, and in March and April two Infantry Divisions (the 41st and 32d) left the United States for the Southwest Pacific. At the same time, construction of air and refueling bases was being rushed to completion in the South Pacific islands that formed stepping stones along the ocean routes to Australia and New Zealand. The western anchor of this chain, New Caledonia, was secured in February with the arrival of the powerful POPPY Force. In subsequent weeks Army and Marine Garrisons and reinforcements were sent to various other islands along the line, culminating with the arrival of the 37th Division in the Fiji Islands in June.

These moves came none too soon, for during the spring the Japanese, following their occupation of Rabaul, pushed into the southern Solomons, within easy striking distance of the American bases on Espiritu Santo and New Caledonia. They also occupied the northeastern coast of New Guinea, just across the narrow Papuan Peninsula from Port Moresby, which the Americans and Australians were developing into a major advanced base in preparation for an eventual offensive northward. Thus, the stage was set for a major test of strength in the Pacific—American forces spread thinly along an immense arc from Hawaii to Australia, with outposts far to the north in Alaska; the Japanese securely in possession of the vast areas north and west of the arc and prepared, with the advantage of interior lines, to strike in force at any point. The first test came in May, when the Japanese made a major bid for naval supremacy in the South Pacific. This was successfully countered in the great carrier battle of the Coral Sea. Thereupon the Japanese struck eastward, hoping to destroy the U. S. Pacific Fleet and to seize Midway. A diversionary attack on Dutch Harbor, the main U. S. base in Alaska, caused considerable damage, and the Japanese were able to occupy the islands of Kiska and Attu in the foggy Aleutian chain. But the main Japanese forces, far to the south, were crushingly defeated, with especially heavy losses in carriers and aircraft. The Battle of Midway in June 1942 was one of the truly decisive engagements of the war. By seriously weakening Japan's mobile striking forces, Midway left the Japanese virtually helpless to prevent the consolidation of American positions and the eventual development of overwhelming military supremacy throughout the Pacific. Only two months later, in fact, American forces took the first step on the long "road back" by landing on Guadalcanal in the southern Solomons.

The Atlantic. Although the RAINBOW 5 plan was put into effect immediately after Pearl Harbor, the desperate situation in the Pacific and Far East and the shortage of shipping and escorts ruled out most of the scheduled Atlantic, Caribbean, and South American deployments. In January reinforcements were sent to Iceland and a token force to Northern Ireland, and by June two full divisions (the 34th Infantry and the 1st Armored) had reached the latter destination, while the remainder of the 5th Infantry had arrived in Iceland, completing the relief of the U. S. Marine brigade and most of the British garrison. No more divisions sailed eastward until August. Meanwhile, garrisons in the Atlantic and Caribbean were being built up to war strength. But plans to occupy the Azores, Canaries, and Cape Verdes, and to capture Dakar on the west African coast, went by the board, primarily for lack of shipping. Also abandoned after lengthy discussion was a project (GYMNAST), proposed by Prime Minister Churchill at the ARCADIA Conference, for an Anglo-American occupation of French North Africa.

Thus, despite the reaffirmation of the "Germany-first" strategy at ARCADIA, the great bulk of American forces sent overseas during the first half of 1942 went to the theaters of the war against Japan. Of the eight Army divisions that left the country before August, five went to the Pacific. Including two more already in Hawaii, and a Marine division at sea bound for New Zealand (eventually for the landings on Guadalcanal in August), eight divisions were deployed against Japan in July 1942. Sixty percent of the approximately 520,000 Army troops in overseas bases were in the Pacific (including Alaska) and the newly established China-Burma-India theater; the remainder were almost all in Caribbean and western Atlantic garrisons. Of 2,200 Army aircraft overseas, about 1,300 were in the Pacific (including Alaska) and Far East, 900 in the western Atlantic and Latin America. Not until August did the U. S. Air Forces in the British Isles attain sufficient strength to fly a single independent bombing mission over northern France.

Planning for a Cross-Channel Invasion. The Army's leaders and planners, schooled in a tradition that emphasized the principles of mass and the offensive, had been fretting over this trend since early in the year. Late in January Brig. Gen. Dwight D. Eisenhower, whom General Marshall had assigned to handle the crisis in the Pacific, noted worriedly, "We've got to go to Europe and fight—and we've got to quit wasting resources all over the world." In the joint committees Army planners urged that as soon as the situation could be stabilized in the Southwest Pacific, U. S. forces should begin to concentrate in the British Isles for an offensive against Germany. Secretary Stimson and others were pressing the same views on the President. In the middle of March the JCS approved this course of action, and in April, at the President's order, General Marshall and Harry Hopkins went to London to seek British approval.

Logistical considerations heavily favored both the general strategy of concentration against Germany and the specific plan of invading northwestern Europe from a base in the British Isles. Because the target area was close to the main sources of British and American power, two to three times as many forces could be hurled against northwestern Europe, with a given amount of shipping, as could be supported in operations against Japan. Britain itself was a highly industrialized country, fully mobilized after two and a half years of war, and well shielded by air and naval power—a ready-made base for a land invasion and for air attacks on Germany's vitals. While invading forces were assembling, moreover, they would serve to garrison the British Isles. Finally, an invasion across the English Channel would involve the only short water crossing to the Continent from a base already available and would thrust directly at the heart of Fortress Europe via the main historic invasion routes.

Even so, the plan was a desperate gamble. If northwestern Europe offered the Allies a position of strength, the Germans, too, would be strong there, close to their own heartland, served by the superb rail and road net of Western and Central Europe, shielded by submarines based along the entire length of Europe's Atlantic front. The limited range of fighter aircraft based in southern England narrowly restricted the choice of landing areas. Much hinged on Russia, where for the present the bulk of Germany's land forces were pinned down. If Russia collapsed, an invasion from the West would be a suicidal venture. The invasion must therefore be launched before the Soviet armies were crushed and, moreover, in sufficient strength to draw substantial German forces away from the eastern front in order to avert that very catastrophe. On the face of it, these two requirements seemed to cancel each other. For Allied planners had little hope that the Russians could stand up under another summer's onslaught, and it was obvious, in view of the scarcity of shipping, that any attack the

Western Allies could mount by the coming summer or early fall would be hardly more than a pin prick. The best solution General Marshall's planners could offer to this dilemma was to set the invasion for the spring of 1943 (ROUNDUP), in the hope that until then, through air bombardment of Germany and a continued flow of war material to the Soviet armies, they could help the latter stave off defeat. If these measures should fail, and Soviet resistance seemed about to collapse, then, with whatever forces were on hand, the Allies would have to invade the Continent in 1942 (SLEDGEHAMMER)—and no later than September, before bad weather closed down over the Channel. The same course would be followed in the unlikely event that Germany itself showed signs of serious weakness in 1942.

In London, Hopkins and General Marshall found the British delighted that the United States was ready to commit itself to a major offensive against Germany in 1943. The British readily agreed that preparations should begin immediately for an invasion the following spring, and undertook to provide more than half the shipping needed to move about a million American troops and immense quantities of war material to the United Kingdom. They warned, however, that their first concern at present was to maintain their position in the Middle East, where, late in January, Rommel's revitalized Afrika Korps had inflicted a serious reverse on the Eighth Army. Both sides were now feverishly building up for a new offensive. The British also expressed deep misgivings over the proposed emergency cross-Channel operation in the fall.

On the American side, too, there were strong reservations. Admiral King did not contest in principle the "Germany-first" strategy. But he was determined not to allow preparations for the cross-Channel invasion to jeopardize "vital needs" in the Pacific, by which, as he candidly stated early in May, he meant the ability of U. S. forces "to hold what we have against any attack that the Japanese are capable of launching." Only the President's peremptory order on 6 May that the invasion buildup in Britain must not be slowed down (it had, indeed, scarcely begun) prevented a large-scale diversion of forces and shipping to the Pacific to counter the Japanese offensive that culminated in the great naval battles of the Coral Sea and Midway. The President himself made it clear, on the other hand, that aid to the Soviet Union must continue on a mounting scale, whatever the cost to BOLERO in material and shipping. And even Army leaders were unwilling to assign shipping for the movement until the scheduled buildup of garrisons in the Western Hemisphere and various other overseas stations had been completed, which, it was estimated, would not be until August at the earliest. Until then British shipping would have to carry the main burden.

The invasion buildup starts—and stops. Not until June, therefore, did the first shipload of American troops under the new plan set sail for England in the great British luxury liner, *Queen Eliza-beth*. Almost simultaneously a new crisis erupted in the Middle East. At the end of May, after a four-month lull, Rommel seized the initiative and swept around the southern flank of the British Eighth Army holding strong positions in eastern Libya from Gazala on the coast south to Bir Hacheim. After two weeks of hard fighting, in which the British seemed to be holding their own, Rommel succeeded in taking Bir Hacheim, the southern anchor of the British line. During the next few days British armor, committed piecemeal in an effort to cover a withdrawal to the northeast, was virtually wiped out by skillfully concealed German 88-mm antitank guns. The Eighth Army once again retreated across the Egyptian frontier, and on 21 June Tobruk, which the British had expected, as in 1941, to hold out behind Axis lines, was captured with its garrison and large stores of trucks, gasoline, and other supplies.

News of this disaster reached Prime Minister Churchill in Washington, where he had gone early in the month to tell the President that the British were unwilling to go through with an emergency cross-Channel landing late in 1942. General Marshall immediately offered to send an armored division to help the hard-pressed British in Egypt, but it was decided, for the present, to limit American aid to emergency shipments of tanks, artillery, and the ground components of three combat air groups. This required the diversion of a substantial amount of U. K. shipping from the North Atlantic for many weeks on the long voyage around the Cape of Good Hope. But the heaviest impact on the invasion buildup in the United Kingdom resulted from the diversion of British shipping to the Middle East, and the retention there of shipping the British had earmarked for the buildup. For the time being, British participation in the BOLERO program virtually ceased.

By the end of August, with only seven months to go before the invasion was to be launched, only about 170,000 American troops were in or on their way to the British Isles, and the shipment of equipment and supplies, particularly for the development of cantonments, air fields, and base facilities, was hopelessly behind schedule. There seemed little likelihood that enough shipping would be available to complete the movement across the Atlantic of a million troops, with the 10 to 15 million tons of cargo that must accompany them, by April 1943 as scheduled. And even if the shipping could have been found, Britain's ports and inland transportation system would have been swamped long before the influx reached its peak. Thus, by the late summer of 1942, a spring 1943 ROUNDUP appeared to be a logistical impossibility.

Torch Replaces Sledgehammer-Roundup. By this time, in fact, American military leaders had already given up hope for a cross-

Channel invasion in spring of 1943, though not primarily because of the lag in the buildup program. In June the British had decided that SLEDGEHAMMER, for which they had never had any enthusiasm, could not be undertaken except in a situation which offered good prospects of success—i.e. if the Germans should seem about to collapse. At the moment, with the German summer offensive just starting to roll toward the Caucasus and lower Don, such a situation did not appear to be an imminent possibility. The British decision was influenced in part by the alarming lag in deliveries of American landing craft, of which less than two-thirds of the promised quota for the operation was expected to materialize. The British also argued that the confusion and losses attendant upon executing SLEDGEHAMMER, and the cost of supporting the beachhead once established, were likely to disrupt preparations for the main invasion the following spring. Since SLEDGEHAMMER, if carried out, would have to be, in the main, a British undertaking, their veto was decisive. SLEDGEHAMMER was cancelled.

As a substitute, the British proposed a less risky venture—landings in French North Africa—which they were confident could be accomplished in stride, without harm to ROUNDUP. To Stimson, Marshall, King, and Arnold this proposal was anathema. Failure would be a costly, perhaps fatal rebuff to Allied prestige. Success might be even more dangerous, the Americans feared, for it might lead the Allies step by step into a protracted series of operations around the southern periphery of Europe, which could not be decisive and would only postpone the final test of strength with Germany. At the very least, an invasion of North Africa would, the Americans were convinced, rule out a spring 1943 ROUNDUP. The Army planners preferred the safer alternative of simply reinforcing the British in Egypt.

The British proposal was, nevertheless, a shrewd one, for it was no secret that President Roosevelt had long ago set his heart on this very undertaking. He was determined, besides, that American ground forces must go into action somewhere in the European area before the end of 1942. Already half persuaded, he hardly needed Churchill's enthusiastic rhetoric to win him over to the new project. When General Marshall suggested, as an alternative, that the United States should immediately go on the defensive in Europe and turn all-out against Japan, Roosevelt brusquely rejected the idea.

In mid-July, Hopkins, Marshall, and King went to London under orders from the President to reach agreement with the British on some operation in 1942. After a vain effort to persuade the British to reconsider SLEDGEHAMMER, the Americans reluctantly agreed on 24 July to the North Africa operation, now christened TORCH, to be launched before the end of October. The President, overruling

Marshall's suggestion that final decision be postponed until mid-September in order to permit a re-appraisal of the Russian situation, cabled Hopkins that he was "delighted" and that the orders were now "full speed ahead." Into the final agreement, however, Marshall and King wrote their own conviction that the decision on TORCH "in all probability" ruled out ROUNDUP for 1943 and meant further that the Allies had accepted "a defensive, encircling line of action" in the European-Mediterranean war.

QUESTIONS

1. Describe the state of American military preparations on the eve of Pearl Harbor. Toward what kind and degree of participation in the war were these preparations aimed? What were the views of Army leaders on American participation in the war?

2. Discuss Japanese operations in 1942 in terms of the principles of war.

3. How and with what limitations was "unity of command" reflected in (a) the Anglo-American coalition, (b) the wartime organization of the American High Command, (c) the wartime organization of the War Department, and (d) the wartime organization of U. S. forces overseas?

4. How did the American and British approaches to strategy differ, and why? In what respects did American and British strategists agree, and in what respects did they differ, in 1942, on the conduct of the war in Europe?

5. What were the arguments for and against the invasion of northwest Africa late in 1942?

6. Do you believe that a cross-Channel invasion of Europe would have been feasible in spring of 1943? Explain.

Reading List

See reading list at end of Chapter 21.

CHAPTER 21

GRAND STRATEGY AND THE HOME FRONT

Coordinating Machinery. By mid-summer of 1942 the United States, having blunted the immediate Japanese threat, was ready to launch limited attacks in the Pacific and, with Great Britain, in North Africa in order to gain positions for the offensives that were to follow. At home the machinery of mobilization, training, and production, was now running in high gear, transforming the raw ingredients of manpower and materials into trained soldiers, ships, weapons, equipment, and supplies. These were the tools with which the strategists had to work, and the quantities that could be produced and delivered to the fighting fronts set limits within which strategy had to operate.

During 1942 a vast new apparatus for control of the nation's economic mobilization came into being. Its keystone was the War Production Board (WPB), established in January 1942 to coordinate industrial mobilization through controls over the allocation and use of raw materials, machine tools, and facilities—powers similar to those of the War Industries Board in World War I. The authority of the WPB did not extend, however, to the actual procurement— that is, purchasing and production—of munitions and other war materials. This was carried out directly by the Army's technical services (including the Air Materiel Command), the Navy's bureaus, and other procuring agencies. Mobilization of the nation's shipyards for mass production of merchant shipping became the wartime task of the Maritime Commission, established in the mid-1930's to modernize the American merchant marine. In February 1942 the President created the War Shipping Administration (WSA), headed by the Maritime Commission's chairman, Admiral Emory S. Land, to operate, maintain, and allocate United States merchant shipping. Close cooperation between WSA and the British Ministry of War Transport resulted in efficient pooling of the two merchant fleets, comprising the bulk of the world's mercantile tonnage.

Manpower for the armed services was provided through the Selective Service System, while the War Manpower Commission, the U. S. Employment Service, and various regional agencies attempted to coordinate the distribution and use of total manpower resources. This coordination was never as efficient or thoroughgoing as that of the nation's material resources, and in the latter war years manpower shortages became the most serious single limitation on the war effort.

The Office of Price Administration combated inflation through price fixing and other controls, and other agencies dealt with such critical commodities as food, petroleum products, and rubber. In the spring of 1943 most of the mobilization agencies were subordinated to a new coordinating unit, the Office of War Mobilization (later renamed Office of War Mobilization and Reconversion) headed by former Justice James F. Byrnes. Through these and many other agencies the Federal government sought to provide guidance or controls for virtually every segment of the wartime economy.

Lend Lease. Under the Lend-Lease Act of March 1941 the War Department turned over to Allied countries approximately $25 billion worth of war materials. About 58 percent went to Britain, 23 percent to Russia, 8 percent to France, 7 percent to China, and the remainder to other countries. Included in these supplies were some 37,000 light and medium tanks, nearly 800,000 trucks, and 3,400 locomotives. The Army Service Forces was the Army's operating agency for administering this program, and from 1942 on military lend-lease requirements were included with U. S. Army requirements in the Army Supply Program.

Theoretically U. S. munitions production along with that of the British Empire was placed in a "common pool" and distributed according to strategic need. Allocations were made by two Munitions Assignments Boards, each representing both countries and responsible to the CCS. One board, sitting in Washington, allocated U. S. production, while the London board allocated British production. These two boards made allocations to other Allied countries as well as to the United States and Britain. Supplies for the Soviet Union, however, were governed by a separate diplomatic protocol, and the boards seldom attempted to alter their provisions in making assignments.

As far as munitions were concerned, the "common pool" consisted largely of American-produced material, since Britain had little to distribute. In a broader frame of reference, however, British contributions of shipping to U. S. military services and the manifold reciprocal aid ("reverse" lend-lease) services and supplies provided for American forces in the United Kingdom, Australia, and New Zealand went far to even the balance. The British early sought to establish the principle that American munitions should be allocated to them in one block for all British "protege" countries—e. g. other members of the Empire (except Canada) and the small Middle East countries. Eventually the Americans rejected this method. In practice, too, assignments of munitions came to be made on the "residual" principle, according to which each partner had first call on its own output.

French rearmament became a major program from 1943 on, under agreements reached at the Casablanca Conference in January between President Roosevelt and General Giraud, the leader of French forces

Medium tanks on assembly line in a war production plant, 1942.

cooperating with the Allies in North Africa. Shipments under this program were made to the North African theater along with cargo for U. S. forces, and were distributed by the theater commander who was empowered, in emergencies, to allot material to his forces as he saw fit. Eleven French divisions were to have been equipped under the original program; these were later reduced to eight, but additional forces were equipped in metropolitan France following the Allied invasion. In Australia General MacArthur, who enjoyed to an exceptional degree the confidence of the Australian Government, exercised discretionary powers over the distribution of both military and civilian lend-lease material. Similar powers, somewhat more ambiguously defined, were exercised by General Stilwell over Chinese defense supplies.

War Production in 1942. During 1942 American factories and shipyards poured out a veritable torrent of munitions. The aggregate value of all munitions, construction, and other war material produced in this year was $58.7 billion, more than three and a half times that of the previous year's production, and it engrossed about 31 percent of the total national output, as against only 9 percent in 1941. While the President's production goals, proclaimed in January, were met only in a few instances, the performance came far closer to realizing them than most people had thought possible. In merchant shipping the goal of 8 million deadweight tons was actually reached and passed. The most spectacular performance was the launching of almost 600 new Liberty ships, work horses of the sea lanes. Sixty thousand military aircraft were delivered, more than doubling the 1941 output, and trebling it in airframe weight, since the trend was toward heavier planes. Also included in the munitions output for

1942 were more than 1.5 million rifles and carbines, 677,000 machine-guns, 25,000 light and medium tanks, 91,000 artillery pieces (excluding mortars), over 600,000 trucks, 275,000 radios, and about 9.5 billion rounds of small arms ammunition. For the resurgent Navy, American shipyards launched 4 new battleships, 1 aircraft carrier, 8 cruisers, 81 destroyers, 34 submarines, 295 subchasers, 231 minecraft, and almost 7,000 amphibious landing vessels of various sizes ranging from the big ocean-going tank landing ships down to the smallest beaching craft.

The Feasibility Dispute. Impressive though this achievement was, it fell short of what the military authorities believed could have been accomplished. Between them and the civilian experts of the War Production Board a sharp conflict arose over the framing of the great war supply programs. The WPB experts were alarmed at the tendency of the military services to place demands on industry far in excess of the country's estimated productive capacity as limited by available raw materials, facilities, and labor. They suspected further that stated military requirements were heavily inflated estimates, not based on concrete strategic plans. Under WPB pressure the supply programs for 1942 were successively scaled down, but their goals late in the year still stood substantially higher than the levels actually attained.

The conflict came to a head over the supply programs for 1943. As formulated in late summer of 1942, these programs set objectives for munitions and war construction totaling almost $93 billion, which, with the addition of expected outlays for military pay, food, and other items, would have raised monthly expenditures for all war purposes, by the end of 1943, to about 75 percent of the total national production of goods and services. No war economy, the WPB economists declared, could support such a load, and they insisted that the 1943 supply programs would have to be drastically cut back. They urged further that a supreme war production council be created, consisting of representatives responsible for "military strategy, production strategy, and social and political strategy," with authority to overrule even the JCS on questions of war production.

The Cutback in Military Supply. This last proposal General Somervell wrathfully called "an inchoate mass of words." He disputed the accuracy of the WPB estimate of national productive capacity, and contended that a reduction of the 1943 goals would cause relaxation of efforts throughout the war economy. Undersecretary of War Patterson, however, supported the WPB argument that over-ambitious production goals would throw schedules out of line and cause maldistribution of materials, thus actually reducing output. Somervell accordingly compromised. At his suggestion, WPB Chairman Donald Nelson told the JCS that the 1943 program would have to be scaled down to the neighborhood of $75 billion, leaving to them the determination of which parts of the program should be eliminated or postponed. Nothing more was said about a supreme war production council. Late in November the JCS submitted to Nelson a reduced supply program totaling about $80 billion, which the WPB accepted as probably feasible.

The dispute settled once and for all the authority of the WPB to determine the overall feasibility of the military supply programs, from the point of view of their impact on the whole economy and, more specifically, on the civilian economy. The determination of military requirements, on the other hand, and their adjustment to limitations of materials, facilities, and labor remained functions of the military services and the JCS.

Strategy, Supply, and Mobilization. The apportionment of the cuts in the 1943 supply programs reflected more fundamental decisions on the role the United States was to play in the war. It was evident that, while this country would remain the major "arsenal of democracy," it could no longer be regarded as a limitless source of munitions. At the same time the limits of American manpower were also becoming visible. The pool of unemployed that had cushioned the shock of mobilization for three years was now almost exhausted. Industrial expansion was slowing down, labor was becoming tight in many areas, and in November the President placed a ceiling of 8.2 million officers and men upon the Army's expansion during 1943, intimating at the same time that this limit would probably hold for the duration of the war. General Marshall and his colleagues on the JCS were still determined that America must make a major contribution in fighting forces and leadership to the defeat of the Axis. But the postponement of the invasion of northwestern Europe, together with the indicated limitations on American resources and manpower, made it necessary to reconsider the nature of that contribution.

The reduced supply programs underlined the character of the change. The cuts fell most heavily on the ground munitions program, which was reduced by more than one-fifth, and on lend-lease to nations other than Russia. Some reductions were also made in naval ship construction, but recently instituted programs for building escort vessels and small aircraft carriers ("baby flattops") to combat enemy submarines were left intact. The merchant shipbuilding program was actually enlarged to make full use of the immense shipyard capacity developed during 1942. The aircraft program was reduced only 10 percent. It had been decided, in short, to produce first of all the tools needed to defeat the U-boats and secure the sea lanes for the deployment of American forces overseas, and at the same time to insure that ample shipping would be available for this purpose. Soviet armies must be assured a continuous flow of munitions to enable them to stave off the Germans for another year or more. Meanwhile, air power must be built up and brought to bear as rapidly as possible, while the slower mobilization and deployment of ground forces was under way—heavy bombers to batter the German homeland, carrier-borne aircraft to restore mobility and striking power to the forces in the Pacific. The ground army, finally, must be shaped to operate, for at least the coming year and a half, in relatively small packages at the end of long lines of communications, in jungles and deserts, on tropical islets, in arctic regions, and in devastated or underdeveloped areas. Its units must be compact, versatile, and easily transportable, but also mobile and able to hit hard. Every ton of shipping, as General McNair declared, must deliver the maximum of fighting power.

The Wartime Army. By the end of 1942 the U. S. Army had grown to a strength of 5.4 million men. Although this was still well under the ceiling of 8.2 million set by the President in November, the mobilization of ground combat elements was already nearing completion. Seventy-three divisions were now in being, and no more than 100 were expected to be activated. In June 1943 this goal was again reduced to 90 divisions, with an overall strength ceiling of 7.7 million—a far cry from the heavily mechanized force of 215 divisions which the framers of the Victory Program in 1941 had considered none too large to take on the German Army. In the event, the U. S. Army in 1945 reached a peak strength of 8.3 million men and 89 divisions. The last division was activated in August 1943.

Actually the strength of ground combat units in the Army increased hardly at all after 1942, even though 16 divisions and some 350 separate artillery and engineer battalions were added after that date. These additional units had to be formed by means of redistribution and economies within existing personnel allotments in the same categories. Since the Army as a whole increased by almost 3 million men after 1942, its ground combat elements (even including replacements) declined from over half of the Army's total strength at the beginning of 1942 to about a third in the spring of 1945. Actually it was no mean achievement merely to maintain the Army's combat units at full strength during the heavy fighting of 1944 and 1945. Neither the Germans nor the Japanese were able to do as much.

Training. Mindful of the untrained divisions sent overseas in World War I, General Marshall from the first set as his goal thorough and realistic training of large units in the United States, culminating in large-scale maneuvers by corps and armies like those staged in the fall of 1941. Since all divisions had been activated by August 1943 and the mass deployment of the army overseas did not begin until late in that year, most divisions were thoroughly trained. The major threat to an orderly training program came in 1944 when many trained divisions had to be skeletonized (and later brought up to strength with raw recruits) in order to meet the demand for trained replacements. Equipment shortages were a serious obstacle to effective training in 1942 and early 1943, as was also the shortage of trained commissioned and noncommissioned officers to provide cadres.

Ground force reorganization. In 1942 and 1943 the Army's ground forces underwent drastic reorganization and streamlining. Troop basis cuts reduced the planned number of armored divisions from 20 to 16, eliminated all motorized divisions, and cut back tank destroyer and antiaircraft units. The armored corps disappeared. Armored and infantry divisions were reduced in personnel and equipment. Tanks taken from armored divisions were organized into separate tank battalions, to be attached to divisions as needed, and motor transport was pooled under corps or army headquarters, for greater flexibility.

The division remained the basic fighting team of arms and services combined in proportions designed for continuous offensive action under normal battle conditions. Its triangular organization was retained. The infantry division contained three regiments, and included, besides four artillery battalions (three armed with 105-mm howitzers, one with 155-mm howitzers), a reconnaissance troop (scout cars and light tanks) and antitank, engineer, ordnance, signal, quartermaster, and medical units. Each regiment could readily be teamed with an artillery battalion. Reinforced with other elements of the division, or with elements assigned by corps or army headquarters, they formed the regimental combat team. To it, in turn, could be attached other elements as needed to perform a particular task. The total strength of the infantry division was reduced from its prewar 15,503 to 14,037.

The armored division, as organized in 1942, was based on two tank regiments and one armored infantry regiment, plus three battalions of armored artillery and an armored reconnaissance battalion. This arrangement was calculated to produce two combat commands, with varying proportions of tanks and infantry in division reserve. The armored division also included supporting elements corresponding to those in the infantry division but motorized to increase mobility. In the armored division as reorganized in 1943, battalions replaced regiments. The new model contained three medium tank battalions, three armored infantry battalions, and three armored artillery battalions. These, with supporting elements, could be combined readily into three combat commands ("A," "B," and "Reserve"). The total strength of the armored division was reduced from 14,419 to 10,670. Two armored divisions remained "heavy" divisions, with the old organization, until the end of the war.

The only other special type of division retained in 1943 was the airborne division. Based on one parachute regiment and two glider-borne regiments, it was designed as a miniature infantry division, with lighter, more easily transportable artillery and the minimum of vehicles and service elements needed to keep it fighting after an airdrop until it could be reinforced. Its strength was only 8,500 until early 1945 when it was raised to 12,979.

Underlying all this were the basic aims of making ground forces mobile, flexible, and easily transportable, by increasing the proportion of standardized and interchangeable units in less rigid tactical combinations. Nor did this involve any sacrifice of effective power. Army leaders were convinced, and experience on the whole proved, that these units could not only move faster and farther, but could also strike even harder than the units they replaced.

The manpower squeeze of 1944. In 1944 the manpower shortage became nation-wide. The Army, under the double pressure of accelerated deployment schedules and heavy demands for replacements for battle casualties, was driven to heroic measures. The Army Specialized Training Program, which had absorbed 150,000 soldiers in college study, was dissolved, and the aviation cadet training program was drastically curtailed. As the Army moved overseas, many posts were consolidated or closed, releasing large numbers of overhead personnel. Margins of over-strength and basic privates in tactical units were eliminated or reduced. Coast artillery units were converted to heavy artillery, hundreds of antiaircraft units were dissolved, and nondivisional infantry regiments became a source of infantry replacements. To meet the threat of the German counteroffensive in the Ardennes in December 1944, the handful of divisions remaining in this country, most of them earmarked for the Pacific, were rushed to Europe, leaving the United States without a strategic reserve.

At the end of the war in Europe the ground army comprised 68 infantry, 16 armored, and 5 airborne divisions.

The air arm. The extent to which the Army depended on its air arm to confer striking power and mobility is suggested by the enormous growth of the Army Air Forces—from about 400,000 men at the beginning of 1942 to a peak of over 2.4 million early in 1944. At the end of the war in Europe it had 243 organized groups in being, and a numerical strength of 2.3 million men. More than 1.5 million of the world-wide AAF strength in March 1945 consisted of service troops, troops in training, and overhead.

Service troops and overhead. After 1942 the growth of the ground army also was very largely in services and administrative elements. By March 1945 these comprised 2.1 million (not counting hospital patients and casuals en route), of the ground army's 5.9 million personnel. This growth reflected both the global character of the war, with its long lines of communications, and the immense numbers of noncombatant specialists needed to operate and service the equipment of a modern mechanized army. They were a manifestation, too, of the American people's insistence on providing the American citizen soldier with something like his accustomed standard of living. Less tangible and more difficult to control was the demand for large administrative and coordinating staffs, a demand that was self-generating since administrators themselves had to be administered and coordinators coordinated. One of the most conspicuous phenomena of global war was the big headquarters. In the European Theater in 1944 "overhead" personnel, largely in higher headquarters, numbered some 114,000 men. On the eve of V–E Day, with overseas deployment for the two-front war complete, almost 1.3 million men remained in the United States in War Department, AGF, ASF, and AAF overhead agencies to operate the Zone of Interior establishment.

The demand for noncombatant personnel was swelled by the assignment to the Army of certain administrative tasks. One was the administration of military lend-lease. Another was the development of the atomic bomb, the super-secret, two-billion-dollar "Manhattan Project" assigned to the Corps of Engineers. Two of the Army's overseas commands—the China-Burma-India Theater and the Persian Gulf Command—had missions that were largely logistical in character. From the first the Pacific theaters generated the heaviest demands for service troops, to build, operate, and service the manifold facilities needed by a modern army in regions where these were virtually nonexistent. To a lesser degree these needs were also present in the Mediterranean, and operations against the Germans everywhere involved the task of repairing the ruin wrought by an enemy who made a science of destruction. Big construction projects like the Alcan Highway (from western Canada to Alaska) and the Ledo Road in Burma added to the burden. To carry out the Army's vast procurement program—to compute requirements, negotiate contracts, and expedite production—called for a horde of highly trained administrators, mostly civilian businessmen whom the Army put into uniform.

Thus, for every three fighting men in the ground army, there were two technicians and administrators somewhere behind, engaged in functions other than that of killing the enemy. Behind the fighting front, too, stretched the "pipeline," filled with what General McNair once called "the invisible horde of people going here and there but seemingly never arriving." In March 1945 casuals en route or in process of assignment numbered 300,000. Far more numerous were the replacements, who at this time totaled 800,000 in the ground army; AAF replacements numbered 300,000. Almost no provision had been made for replacements in the early troop basis. The necessity of providing spaces for them in the Army's total allotment of manpower went far to account for the difference between the 215 divisions in the original Victory Program and the 89 actually organized.

Casualties. Replacements did not add to the effective strength of the Army, but only kept it from declining. The number of soldiers in hospitals in World War II seldom fell below 200,000, and at the beginning of 1945 it reached a peak of almost half a million. Some 280,000 of these were overseas, representing over 5 percent of the Army's forces overseas. Roughly a third of the overseas hospital population at this time were battle casualties. Throughout the war, the Army suffered a total of 936,000 battle casualties, including 235,000 dead; to the latter must be added 83,400 nonbattle deaths. The Army's dead represented about 3 percent of the 10,420,000 men who served in its ranks during World War II.

The Casablanca Conference. By the beginning of 1943 the U. S. Army, supported by large reserves and a mobilized economy at home, and with a million troops overseas, was ready to embark on major operations on both fronts. In mid-January Roosevelt, Churchill, and the Combined Chiefs of Staff met at Casablanca in Morocco, where U. S. forces had landed more than two months earlier, to map plans for an offensive strategy in the coming year. Already the Allies had made important gains. All German forces in North Africa were now hemmed into Tunisia, and in the Pacific the Americans had won a foothold in the southern Solomon Islands and were on the offensive in New Guinea. In Russia, too, the German drive had been halted, and in the ruins of Stalingrad on the Volga a whole army had been isolated and now faced annihilation. Reflecting the prevailing optimism, and in order to reassure the Russians that no "deal" would be made with the Axis powers, President Roosevelt announced that the Allies were determined to exact "unconditional surrender" from their enemies.

Agreeing that a cross-Channel invasion probably could not be launched in 1943, the Allied leaders decided to follow up the expected early conclusion of the Tunisian campaign with landings on Sicily in June or July. Conquest of this island would not only remove the last major barrier to passage of shipping through the Mediterranean, but would also provide a springboard for invading Italy—though the Americans, fearing further postponement of the cross-Channel invasion, refused to commit themselves definitely to that undertaking. It was generally hoped, in fact, that Italy would collapse without being invaded. The Allies also decided to begin immediately an intensive strategic bombing offensive against Germany from bases in Britain, and to accelerate the lagging buildup of American air power and invasion forces in the British Isles.

While thus planning to step up the tempo of the war in Europe, the Americans also served notice on the British that they intended to allot more resources to the war against Japan in order to prevent the Japanese from consolidating their new empire while the Western

Ships under construction, Los Angeles Port of Embarkation.

Allies were tied down in Europe. The JCS had, in fact, already diverted to the Pacific considerable numbers of aircraft, landing craft, and ships originally earmarked for Europe. Admiral King at this time unveiled a scheme for a drive across the central Pacific toward Japan, to complement the advance of MacArthur's and Halsey's forces in the south and southwest.

The Shipping Crisis of Spring 1943. Developments in the weeks following rapidly dissipated the optimism that had prevailed at Casablanca. A German counteroffensive sent American forces in Tunisia reeling back, and the planned capture of the Japanese fortress of Rabaul on New Britain had to be postponed to 1944 for lack of shipping, aircraft, and troops. Even more serious was the sudden intensification of the U-boat offensive in the Atlantic, which in March took a toll of more than a million deadweight tons of shipping. The British, whose shipping throughout 1942 had suffered proportionately heavier losses than the American, now faced a crisis at home as a result of a cumulative lag in essential imports of food and raw materials. In November 1942 the President had promised Churchill that the expanding output of U. S. shipyards would be shared with Britain as needed to support its war effort, but military demands had caused a temporary reduction in this instance. In March 1943 British officials informed Washington that many more ships would be needed during the coming spring and summer to bolster their faltering war economy and to enable them to participate fully in forthcoming campaigns in the Mediterranean and Burma.

The President's decision. In planning their deployments for 1943 the American staffs had seriously underestimated the amount of U. S. shipping that would have to be contributed to British services.

409

The JCS warned the President that the new British demand, if granted, might cripple the whole offensive strategy of the Western Allies during 1943, and suggested that the British could easily tighten their belts a little more without undue harm to their economy. But the President was advised by Lewis Douglas, Deputy War Shipping Administrator, that American military requirements for shipping were habitually overestimated and that the British economy was truly in serious straits. Accordingly he overruled the JCS—one of the few such instances during the war—and promised the British the shipping requested.

Aftermath of the crisis. Subsequent developments largely vindicated the President's judgment. Without the large infusion of American shipping into British services that began in late spring of 1943, Britain could not have made the major contribution it did make to the defeat of the European Axis. Nor did this drain upon U. S. merchant shipping cause any appreciable diminution in Allied efforts elsewhere, except in southeastern Asia, where it was partly responsible for the failure to carry out the planned invasion of Burma late in 1943. On all other fronts, in 1943, the Allies forged ahead. In this year also the Anglo-American strategic bombing offensive became a mighty scourge of Germany's war industry, while hundreds of ships shuttled across the North Atlantic carrying American troops and material to Britain.

Victory over the U-Boats. That the Western Allies, despite the planners' gloomy predictions in March 1943, were able to sustain the offensive on all major fronts during this year, was in some measure an achievement of American shipyards. The output of merchant shipping in 1943 was prodigious—over 1,200 Libertys and half as many merchant ships of other types, and in all, more than 18.5 million deadweight tons. This was the peak performance of the war, but only because the JCS, when asked to endorse an even larger building program for 1944, decided that more shipyard capacity than heretofore could safely be devoted to faster and more specialized vessels which took longer to build. In mid-1943 merchant shipping ceased to be a bottleneck.

This flood of new shipping swamped the German U-boat offensive even as Allied counterattacks by sea and air, in the spring of 1943, were defeating it in a military sense. After November 1942 the U-boats were never again able to sink ships as rapidly as they were being built, and in April 1943 the tide of battle began to turn. At the President's peremptory order, responsibility for all United States antisubmarine operations was centered in the Navy and coordinated from Washington. The British and Canadian navies assumed responsibility for protecting the convoys on the main North Atlantic routes between Britain and North America, while the U. S. Navy convoyed shipping between the United States and North African ports. By late spring new escort vessels and small aircraft carriers were appearing in considerable numbers, and long-range Liberator bombers provided air cover over the middle stretch of the North Atlantic routes. Aircraft were armed with rockets and improved radar detection devices. Fifty-five U-boats were destroyed in April and May, as against only 85 during the entire preceding year. During the same months the curve of Allied shipping losses plummeted downward, and in June the beaten remnants of the enemy withdrew from the North Atlantic altogether. That summer Allied aircraft played havoc with them on the approaches to their bases in the Bay of Biscay. In the last three months of 1943 the Germans scored only 47 ship sinkings, while losing 53 U-boats.

The sea battles of spring 1943 were not only decisive, but, as it turned out, marked the last gasp of the German undersea offensive. In the following year the Germans put into action a number of submarines equipped with breather tubes ("Schnorkel"), which enabled them to remain submerged for long periods, and early in 1945 they brought out an improved craft of great speed and range. But these developments came too late to influence the outcome.

The Trident Conference (May 1943). While the battle was still raging in the Atlantic sea lanes, but with victory clearly in sight, Allied leaders met at Washington in May 1943 for the third of the great wartime conferences. The recent crushing defeat of the Axis in Tunisia seemed an omen of successes to come. The U. S. Chiefs of Staff brought to the conference a grand design for accelerating the war against Japan in 1943 and 1944. United States forces in the Pacific would converge on the Philippines from two directions, along the route of the Solomons, Bismarck Archipelago, and New Guinea coast, and through the central Pacific via the Marshalls, Carolines, and Marianas. To all this the British agreed with little debate, but they objected to the proposal of a large-scale land invasion of Burma (ANAKIM), primarily by their own forces, during the coming winter. The British favored, instead, expansion of the air lift over the "Hump" in support of General Chennault's air forces in China, and only limited ground and amphibious operations in Burma during 1944. On these points, in general, the British had their way, although Stilwell's engineers pushed doggedly ahead with the building of the Ledo Road. Despite subsequent modifications in the plan, operations in Southeast Asia were to remain a subsidiary phase of the war against Japan.

Plans for a cross-Channel invasion. The U. S. Chiefs of Staff were also determined to push preparations for a cross-Channel invasion in the spring of 1944, and were more than ever unwilling to become involved in further major undertakings in the Mediterranean. They insisted, therefore, that no additional resources must be committed to the Mediterranean, though they agreed in principle to limited operations following the conquest of Sicily, aimed at eliminating Italy from the war and pinning down German forces.   For their part, the British raised no objection to going ahead with cross-Channel invasion preparations, and readily agreed to a target date of 1 May 1944.   They also pledged themselves to provide almost half the shipping needed. While it was evident that neither the available shipping nor reception facilities in England would permit the assembling of invasion forces on the scale envisaged in the old ROUNDUP plan, the Allied leaders hoped that with overwhelming air superiority an operation on a smaller scale would be feasible.   Staff calculations indicated that by May 1944 about 29 United States, British, and Canadian divisions would be ready in England to cross the Channel, including 7 battle-tested divisions (4 U.S. and 3 British) which were to be transferred from the Mediterranean.   After these forces had carved out a lodgment, additional divisions from the United States would flood in behind them.

Landing Craft and Amphibious Strategy.   It was also evident at the TRIDENT Conference that with the landing ships and craft likely to be available the following spring, only a small assault force could be landed on the Normandy coast to spearhead the cross-Channel invasion.   Through 1943 and the greater part of 1944, in fact, Allied strategy, which depended so heavily on amphibious assaults against ememy-held coasts, was to be shaped in large measure by the availability of the specialized ships and craft needed to land troops and equipment on a defended beach.   Both Britain and the United States produced the smaller types of craft, as well as the assault transports that carried them and the attacking forces to launching positions off a hostile shore.   But, by mutual agreement, all but a handful of the ocean-going landing ships—especially the LST's (landing ships, tank) and LCI(L)'s (landing craft, Infantry, large)—which could cross long stretches of water and beach themselves, were built in the United States.   Here also were constructed amphibious wheeled and tracked vehicles, like the 2½-ton Dukw and the "amtrack" (LVT), which, like amphibians, could navigate both on water and on land.

The first landing craft program.   Production of all these vessels in the United States had been slow in getting under way in 1942. With the cancellation or postponement of the planned cross-Channel attacks, the program had lost much of its urgency, and late in the year, over British protests, some portions of it were cancelled.   In spring of 1943 production of all types was cut sharply back.   Yet, for all its faltering beginnings and early termination, the results of this first wave of production were impressive.   In the year ending

LST discharging cargo over a ponton causeway, Gela, Sicily.

in April 1943, 8,719 vessels of all types were turned out, including 214 of the indispensable LST's, and totaling 512,333 light displacement tons. Together with the smaller but substantial output of British yards and factories, the program, down to the middle of 1943, proved generally adequate. Even in 1942, before production had hit its stride, no serious shortages of craft hampered the relatively small-scale landings at Dieppe, on Guadalcanal, or in North Africa, and in July 1943 it was even possible, without drawing on vessels assigned to the Pacific, to land eight Allied divisions simultaneously on Sicily—in some respects the most massive amphibious undertaking of the entire war.

But the great armada assembled for the invasion of Sicily was a wasting asset. Losses in this and subsequent operations, together with ordinary wear and tear, were expected to cut it down to half or less by the following spring. American production, currently at a low ebb, was almost all alloted to the Pacific. U. S. Navy officials, moreover, resolutely opposed any major increases in production of landing ships and craft, which competed for the steel, engines, and facilities needed to build escorts and other combatant vessels. The TRIDENT planners could, therefore, reckon on only about enough assault lift in the cross-Channel attack to land three divisions at once, with perhaps two more afloat in reserve.

The Quebec (QUADRANT) Conference (August 1943). Three months after TRIDENT the Allied leaders met again, this time at Quebec. Much had happened in the interim. In July Soviet armies had successfully contained a German offensive against Kursk on the southern front, and almost simultaneously launched one of their own farther north. By the end of August they had pushed the Germans back some 200 miles to the line of the Dnieper and were forging ahead along the entire front. In the Mediterranean, Mussolini's regime had fallen, and the Italian Government had opened secret negotiations for an armistice, though the Germans were moving swiftly to take over control of the peninsula from the demoralized Italian forces. On 16 August, the day before the Allies completed the conquest of Sicily, General Eisenhower with CCS approval ordered the execution of plans to invade the mainland with multiple landings around the southern end of the peninsula.

At the Quebec meetings, in mid-August, the Allied leaders considered an outline plan for the cross-Channel operation (now named OVERLORD), submitted by an Anglo-American planning staff in London headed by Lt. Gen. Sir Frederick Morgan. As ordered at TRIDENT, Morgan had provided for an initial assault by only about three divisions (with a two-division followup) based on the expected availability of landing craft. He emphasized that with so small a force success could be hoped for only if German forces in the area did not exceed a specified strength. Prime Minister Churchill bluntly called for an immediate increase in American landing craft production to overcome the deficiency, pledging at the same time a maximum output in his own country. The British also proposed to transfer to OVERLORD more of their own landing craft from the Mediterranean, as a result of unexpectedly light losses in Sicily, and they increased their contribution of troop shipping for the build-up of American invasion forces in England.

Conceding that the OVERLORD assault, as planned, was dangerously weak, the JCS still would make no commitment at this time to increase production of landing craft, and they refused to go along with the British in transferring additional craft to OVERLORD for the Mediterranean. Any "surplus" in the latter area they proposed to use to mount either a diversionary threat or an actual invasion of southern France at about the same time as OVERLORD, even though only about a one-division lift seemed likely to be available. It was expected that this operation, if attempted, would be carried out by American-equipped French troops. As for Italy, it was agreed that General Eisenhower's forces should advance to Rome and as far beyond as feasible until the Germans dug in for a determined stand. OVERLORD's role as the primary effort against the European Axis in 1944, with a target date of 1 May, was reaffirmed. Plans were also approved for an earlier move across the Channel (RANKIN) in the event of a German collapse; a Soviet collapse, by this time, was considered altogether unlikely.

The Pacific War and the new landing craft program. During the summer months of 1943 American and Australian forces in the Pacific made rapid advances. It had been decided that Rabaul would be bypassed, not captured, and that the central Pacific offensive would be opened in November with an attack on the Gilbert Islands. All this meant a marked acceleration of earlier timetables, and foreshadowed a heavy demand for amphibious shipping of all kinds, especially in 1944 before shipping could be redeployed from Europe after the Normandy landings. By September 1943, too, with victory over the U-boats assured, the Navy was cutting back its escort and antisubmarine vessel programs, thus releasing yards for construction of landing ships, and the outlook for steel was brighter. In September and October, accordingly, the Navy ordered large increases in production of landing ships and craft, including two types especially designed for Pacific operations—the landing ship, medium (LSM) and the armored landing vehicle, tracked or "amtrack." Complementing this program, the Navy in November launched another large program of assault transports, also peculiarly adapted to amphibious operations in the Pacific. All this new construction, starting almost from scratch late in 1943, was not expected to reach heavy volume output until mid-1944 (assault transports even later), too late to benefit OVERLORD or planned Mediterranean operations. Production of the most critical types, LST's and LCI(L)'s, did not, in fact, rise substantially until March and April 1944. The real impact of the new programs was to be felt in the big amphibious operations of late 1944 and 1945 in the far Pacific.

Setbacks in the Mediterranean. After the landings in southern Italy early in September 1943, Allied forces pushed rapidly up the peninsula, quickly capturing Naples and the airfields at Foggia. Sardinia and Corsica yielded almost without a struggle. At the beginning of October, however, the German High Command decided to stand fast south of Rome instead of retreating to northern Italy. Fresh divisions were rushed southward and by early November the Allied advance had bogged down in the mountains southeast of Rome. In the race to build up strength the Allies, despite air and naval superiority, were at a disadvantage, since rail and road communications in southern Italy were primitive and good ports were few; Naples wrecked by demolitions, could not handle heavy traffic until November. In this period, too, seven British and U. S. divisions were being withdrawn for OVERLORD. Impending withdrawals of landing craft for the same operation would further reduce the rate of buildup and also eliminate the possibility of outflanking the enemy by amphibious landings in his rear. During October, too, the Germans launched a violent counterattack against British forces which a short time earlier had gained lodgments in the Dodecanese Islands off the southwestern coast of Turkey. Since General Eisenhower could not at this critical juncture risk a large-scale diversion of air forces from Italy, the

British were unable to regain the initiative and were driven out of the Dodecanese with heavy losses—their most severe defeat since the fall of Tobruk in June 1942.

The Cairo-Tehran (Sextant-Eureka) Conferences (November-December 1943). These setbacks in the Mediterranean brought to a head the long-smoldering differences between the Americans and British over European strategy. At the first Cairo Conference (28 November–December 1943) the British bluntly charged that American insistence upon the "sanctity of OVERLORD"—i. e., rigid adherence to the scheduled target date of 1 May 1944—might indefinitely prolong the present stalemate in the Mediterranean and thereby imperil OVERLORD's own chances of success. They wanted (a) to hold in the Mediterranean the large contingent of LST's earmarked for OVERLORD long enough to permit a major amphibious "end run" around the German right flank south of Rome and thus break the deadlock on that front; (b) to push beyond Rome as far as the Pisa-Rimini line; (c) to extend more aid to the Balkan guerilla forces in the form of weapons, technical assistance, supplies, and commando raids; (d) to try to bring Turkey into the war before the end of the year; and (e), with Turkish consent, to open the Dardanelles and Bosphorus to Allied shipping. The opening move, provided Turkey's support were assured, would be an attack about February 1944 on the largest of the Dodecanese Islands, Rhodes, commanding the approaches to the Aegean and the Straits. To accomplish this would mean postponing OVERLORD, probably to about 1 July 1944. In addition, the British proposed a unified command, under a British officer, for the whole Mediterranean region.

The latter demand the Americans were already prepared to concede, in return for the appointment of a U. S. commander for OVERLORD. Before the end of the year, in fact, President Roosevelt announced the appointment of General Eisenhower as Supreme Commander for OVERLORD, and about the same time General Sir Henry Maitland Wilson became the Supreme Allied commander in the Mediterranean. The JCS also found little to quarrel with in the British proposals regarding the campaign in Italy and aid to the Balkan guerillas. Eisenhower's request for retention of 68 OVERLORD LST's until mid-January was readily granted, and he was authorized to proceed with plans for amphibious landings south of Rome.

But the Americans were wary of further British ventures in the Aegean, in view of recent defeats there, and feared that even if Turkey could be persuaded to enter the war, the Turks might require more aid than the Allies were prepared to give. Above all, they dreaded any involvement in the eastern Mediterranean that might lead to military operations in the Balkans, a land of inhospitable terrain, primitive communications, and turbulent peoples. The proposal to

416

postpone OVERLORD strengthened American suspicions that the British had no intention of going through with the cross-Channel invasion, but planned to subordinate it indefinitely to peripheral and indecisive campaigns in the Mediterranean that would serve their own long-range political ends. The JCS also resisted an alternative British proposal that the assault shipping needed for the Rhodes operation be taken from Southeast Asia, since this would necessitate postponing or canceling planned amphibious landings on the Burma coast in connection with the land campaign in the spring. The presence at the Cairo Conference of the Chinese Nationalist leader, Chiang Kai-shek, who had the ear of President Roosevelt, made acceptance of this scheme doubly difficult. Since the British would not abandon their Aegean plans, a deadlock resulted.

At Tehran, where Roosevelt, Churchill, and the CCS had their first war-time meeting (28 November–1 December 1943) with Marshal Stalin, the deadlock was broken. The Soviet leader's emphatic insistence that OVERLORD be made the "basic" operation in 1944 induced Churchill to agree, as a compromise, to a target date of late May or early June for OVERLORD. Roosevelt and Churchill also promised Stalin that they would launch a complementary invasion of southern France at about the same time as OVERLORD, but declined to abandon other planned operations in the Mediterranean, which Stalin had bluntly characterized as diversionary. Stalin, for his part, agreed to support Turkey if it intervened. Back at Cairo, following the Tehran Conference, Churchill was able to persuade Roosevelt to give up his insistence on a major amphibious operation in Burma, even at the cost of postponing the reconquest of Burma. The assault shipping earmarked for the operation was immediately ordered back to European waters, and the British proceeded with preparations for the attack on Rhodes. It was further decided that the southern France operation (ANVIL) would be spearheaded by at least a two-division assault, for which Admiral King promised to provide an additional complement of landing ships and craft.

Thus, at the end of the Cairo-Tehran Conferences, the stage seemed set for the final converging onslaughts on Fortress Europe. Allied military fortunes stood high. The Soviet winter offensive had driven the Germans back along the whole central and southern front, isolating the Crimea, recovering most of the northern Ukraine, and dangerously pinching the great Dnieper salient in the south. Depleted German armies everywhere were being swamped by the immense weight of Soviet manpower, backed by a fully mobilized industry and the swelling flow of war materials from the West. German weakness in Russia owed much, moreover, to the increasing pressure of British, American, and partisan forces in the West. About 70 German divisions were pinned down in the Mediterranean and northwest-

Wartime conference at Tehran.

ern Europe, and the Allied strategic bombing offensive had forced Hitler to concentrate the bulk of his dwindling air forces and tens of thousands of antiaircraft guns for the defense of the homeland. At the same time United States offensives in the Pacific were gaining momentum. On all fronts except Italy and Burma the Allies were advancing. Germany's defeat was now predicted for October 1944, and the JCS were working on plans to defeat Japan within the year following.

Deployment and Production. During 1943 U. S. forces overseas had been built up to a total of 3.7 million men—Army, Navy, and Marines—of whom slightly more than half were arrayed against Japan. The Army's overseas deployment, however—2.3 million, including 30 divisions and 134 combat air groups—had gone predominantly into the European and Mediterranean Theaters. The buildup of American invasion forces in England, spurting forward during the closing months of 1943, had passed the halfway mark toward its D-day goal of 1.4 million men. With 11 U. S. divisions and 52 combat air groups now in the British Isles, as against only 6 divisions and 41 groups in the Mediterranean, the strategic concept of concentration in northwestern Europe had at long last become a reality.

By this time, the mobilized strength of the United States clearly overshadowed that of its chief partner. Britain still had more divisions overseas and in contact with the enemy than the United States (and would have until March 1944), but its manpower and industry were fully mobilized, and it faced the inevitable prospect of declining industrial output and dwindling armed forces. American armed forces, though approaching the limits of planned expansion, were mostly uncommitted, awaiting deployment overseas, and American war industry had by now achieved a productivity that, for most types of munitions, actually surpassed all foreseeable needs. A survey of prospective resources at the end of the Cairo-Tehran Conferences revealed that, except for landing ships, no material shortages serious enough to hamper military operations seemèd likely to develop.

In the main, these expectations were borne out. "Supply," indeed, often failed to meet "demand" during 1944 and 1945, in the sense that the enemy theoretically might have been defeated sooner had more tanks, guns, ships, and planes been available, along with trained soldiers to use them. But in practice, operations were planned and objectives defined with an eye to the means prospectively available, so that real demand exceeded supply only when means were seriously overestimated or needs underestimated. Such miscalculations sometimes occurred. During the winter of 1944-45, for example, an acute shortage of ammunition developed in northwestern Europe and Italy as a result of unexpectedly heavy fighting, distribution failures, and premature cutbacks in production; fortunately, it was of short duration. Merchant shipping, too, became tight late in 1944 owing to the immobilization of hundreds of ships awaiting discharge in forward areas where port facilities were inadequate, and the retention of many more for local use, particularly in the Pacific, in interisland or operational services. Ultimately the log-jam was broken by a Presidential order prohibiting the use of ocean-going vessels for storage purposes and by strict curbs on overseas retentions. In the summer of 1945, again, the combined demands of civil relief in Europe and of redeployment and buildup for the final offensives against Japan threatened a major world-wide shipping shortage, which, owing to the abrupt termination of hostilities in August, never materialized.

In general, however, the Western Allies during 1944 and 1945 had more of most types of munitions than they could use or distribute effectively. Distribution and use, in turn, were limited less often by the physical means of movement or by local "bottleneck" shortages of certain types of equipment, than by such factors as manpower shortages, difficult terrain, or the sheer inertia of administration. As a result, the path of Allied victory was littered by huge stocks of war material left to rust and rot in rear areas and along lines of communications.

The Ordeal of Anvil. The Cairo-Tehran decisions on Mediterranean strategy were soon overtaken by events. Before the end of December 1943 British plans for an attack on Rhodes had to be abandoned owing to a sudden demand by the Turks for more military aid, in return for intervention, than the British were willing to provide. The landings south of Rome were finally carried out late in

January 1944, but the landing forces were immediately hemmed in by the Germans. Not until late in the spring was the beleaguered beachhead finally linked up with the U. S. Fifth Army advancing from the south, and Rome fell to the Allies only on 4 June, two days before the Normandy invasion.

ANVIL, the planned invasion of southern France, also came under fire early in 1944. Soon after his appointment as OVERLORD commander, General Eisenhower, who had already advocated a three-division assault for ANVIL, concluded that the OVERLORD assault as planned was also too weak and should be increased to five divisions. His deputy, Field Marshal Montgomery, and the British Chiefs of Staff, held that this could only be done at the expense of ANVIL, which would have to be canceled or reduced to a one-division threat. The United States Chiefs believed, on the contrary, that a five-division assault could be mounted with the lift already assigned to OVERLORD. While this question was being debated, the tieup of assault shipping supplying the Anzio beachhead was complicating its redeployment for both ANVIL and OVERLORD, and the drive on Rome was making little headway. British commanders in the theater feared that the withdrawal of troops for ANVIL, which must begin in April, would cripple the offensive in Italy. In any case, they argued, ANVIL's purposes would be better served by a vigorous drive up the Italian peninsula, using a small assault lift for flanking operations. The British Chiefs and eventually Eisenhower himself supported this view. Though the JCS disagreed, they consented late in March 1944 to postpone ANVIL to July. Most of its assault shipping was transferred to England.

On 6 June 1944 Allied troops landed in Normandy and the great invasion began. ANVIL had been eliminated as a complement to OVERLORD, but the debate over the operation's merits went on. While it was under way, the JCS in April ordered a new contingent of landing ships and craft to the Mediterranean, thus insuring that a substantial amphibious operation could be mounted there sometime during the summer. By the latter part of June the Normandy invasion seemed to have bogged down, while in Italy the Germans were in pellmell retreat north of Rome. British and United States views hardened into clearcut disagreement. The JCS, and now Eisenhower, too, insisted that it was imperative to seize Marseilles and drive up the Rhone Valley, threatening the Germans from the rear and opening an avenue for bringing the still uncommitted mass of the American Army into battle. Churchill and the British Chiefs were equally convinced that more damage could be inflicted on Germany by the destruction of her armies north of Rome and the additional forces that would be sent to defend the Po Valley. They proposed to make complementary landings on the Istrian Peninsula, and General

Alexander, the British commander in Italy, even hoped to cross the Julian Alps into the Hungarian plain and join hands with the advancing Russians. If the ANVIL divisions were now withdrawn from Italy, the British warned, the Germans might be able to hold fast along the northern Apennines. But this time the Americans held firm and on 2 July orders went to the Mediterranean to execute ANVIL on 15 August.

The last gasp in the debate over ANVIL came early in August. Allied forces had broken out of the Normandy beachhead and armored columns were already racing into Brittany. At this juncture Churchill made an eleventh-hour attempt to have the forces assigned to ANVIL (now renamed DRAGOON) diverted to the Breton ports, where they might hope to land unopposed and join the main front sooner. But the Americans again presented a solid front and on 15 August a combined United States and French army invaded southern France.

In the event, both sides were proved to have been at least partly right. DRAGOON was a resounding success. The landings were virtually unopposed and the Allies swept rapidly up the Rhone Valley to a junction with Eisenhower's forces on 11 September. Subsequently a substantial number of divisions from the United States were routed through Marseilles to the main front. On the other hand, DRAGOON had no effect in drawing German forces away from the Normandy front, which had already begun to disintegrate. The German divisions in southern France had to withdraw, in fact, in order to avoid being trapped by Allied armies advancing from the west. In northern Italy, by contrast, the withdrawal of divisions for DRAGOON seriously weakened the Allies at the very moment the Germans were being heavily reinforced, and contributed significantly to the Allies' failure to break through to the Po Valley before winter weather halted active operations.

The Second Quebec Conference (Octagon) (12–16 September 1944). In mid-September, however, Germany's defeat seemed imminent. In the east the Soviet steamroller was grinding inexorably through the Baltic States, Poland, and Romania. Finland was out of the war, Bulgaria had switched sides, and the Germans were trying to extricate themselves from the Balkans. American, British, and French armies in the west had driven the Germans in disorder across France and had come up against the Siegfried Line and the German frontier. In Italy the Allies were assaulting the last barriers to the Po Valley.

When the Western leaders assembled at Quebec in the middle of the month, therefore, the great issues of European strategy seemed to have been settled. The JCS now concurred in the British design, bitterly opposed a few weeks earlier, of a thrust into northeastern

Italy aiming ultimately at Vienna, and were willing to turn over some of the DRAGOON assault shipping for landings in Istria. Agreement was reached on assignment of occupation zones to U. S. and British forces in Germany, and on resumption of CCS control of the Allied strategic air forces in Europe, hitherto under Eisenhower's command. But the main interest had shifted to the war against Japan. Large forces, British and United States, were scheduled to be transferred soon from Europe to the Pacific and Burma fronts. Plans were approved for a spring offensive in Burma, including a British amphibious attack on Rangoon using assault shipping to be transferred from the Mediterranean. Churchill's offer of the British Fleet to take part in the main operations against Japan in the Pacific was accepted by the President without qualification, and it was agreed more generally that Royal Air Force heavy bombers would be used. But the JCS, worried over the problem of bases, refused to commit themselves definitely to large-scale British naval participation in Pacific operations.

Conclusion. As it happened, the optimism voiced at Quebec proved premature. The war in Europe was to drag on for another seven months, correspondingly delaying the redeployment of forces to the Pacific and Far East. But the grand design of the war in Europe had been fixed, and a brief debate at the Malta Conference (30 January–2 February 1945) over strategy and command arrangements for the final drive into Germany had little effect on the theater commander's plans and none on the final outcome. This was the last top-level airing of British-United States differences over European strategy. In the war against Japan, now reaching its climax, Britain had only a minor role. After the late summer of 1944 grand strategy yielded to operational strategy, and the important decisions were made by commanders in the theaters. At this point, therefore, it is appropriate to turn from the realm of high commands and war councils and, in the next two chapters, to trace the actual course of operations in the war in North Africa and Europe and the war against Japan.

QUESTIONS

1. Analyze the United States-British debate over strategy in Europe with reference to—(a) the division of resources between the war in Europe and the war against Japan; (b) the timing of the cross-Channel invasion; (c) the relation of operations in the Mediterranean to preparations for the cross-Channel invasion; (d) operations in the Mediterranean following the Normandy landings; (e) political and postwar objectives; and (f) the principles of war.

2. How and to what extent was Allied grand strategy in World War II shaped by the availability of merchant shipping? of landing craft?

3. What were the military factors influencing the relations between the Soviet Union and the Western Allies in World War II?

4. How did the reduction of military supply programs late in 1942 affect United States strategy and the American contribution to the Allied war effort?

5. What were the chief issues discussed at the Cairo-Tehran Conferences of November–December 1943? What decisions were reached? In the light of later developments, how would you assess the influence of the Cairo-Tehran Conferences on the conduct of the war?

Reading List for Chapters 20 and 21

Ballantine, Duncan S., *Naval Logistics in the Second World War.* Princeton, 1947.

Bureau of the Budget, *The United States at War.* Washington, 1946.

Churchill, Winston S., *The Second World War.* 6 vols., Boston, 1948–1952.

Connery, Robert H., *The Navy and the Industrial Mobilization.* Princeton, 1951.

Ehrman, John, *Grand Strategy.* Vols. V and VI in *History of the Second World War, United Kingdom Military Series,* ed. by J. R. M. Butler. London, 1956.

Feis, Herbert, *Churchill, Roosevelt, Stalin: The War They Waged and the Peace They Sought.* Princeton, 1957.

Fuller, John F. C., *The Second World War.* New York, 1949.

Guderian, Heinz, *Panzer Leader.* New York, 1957.

Lord, Walter H., *Day of Infamy.* New York, 1957.

Millis, Walter, with Harvey C. Mansfield and Harold Stein, *Arms and the State.* New York, 1958.

Morison, Samuel E., *The Battle of the Atlantic; The Rising Sun in the Pacific; Coral Sea, Midway, and Submarine Actions; The Atlantic Battle Won.* All in *History of U. S. Naval Operations in World War II.* 12 volumes, Boston, 1947–1958.

Morison, Samuel E., *Strategy and Compromise.* New York, 1958.

Sherwood, Robert, *Roosevelt and Hopkins, An Intimate History.* New York, 1950.

Shugg, Roger W., and Harvey A. De Weerd, *World War II, A Concise History.* Washington, 1946.

Somers, Herman M., *Presidential Agency.* Cambridge, 1950.

U. S. Military Academy, *A Military History of World War II.* 2 vols., West Point, 1953.

THE U. S. ARMY IN WORLD WAR II:
  Cline, Ray S., *Washington Command Post: The Operations Division.* Washington, 1951.

Green, Constance M., Harry C. Thomson, and Peter C. Roots, *The Ordnance Department: Planning Munitions for War*. Washington, 1955.

Greenfield, Kent R., Robert P. Palmer, and Bell I. Wiley, *The Organization of Ground Combat Troops*. Washington, 1947.

Leighton, Richard M. and Robert W. Coakley, *Global Logistics and Strategy, 1940–1943*. Washington, 1955.

Matloff, Maurice and Edwin M. Snell, *Strategic Planning for Coalition Warfare, 1941–1942*. Washington, 1953.

Millett, John D., *The Organization and Role of the Army Service Forces*. Washington, 1954.

Morton, Louis, *The Fall of the Philippines*. Washington, 1953.

Romanus, Charles F. and Riley Sunderland, *Stilwell's Command Problems*. Washington, 1956.

Romanus, Charles F. and Riley Sunderland, *Stilwell's Mission to China*. Washington, 1953.

Watson, Mark S., *Chief of Staff: Prewar Plans and Preparations*. Washington, 1950.

CHAPTER 22

WORLD WAR II—THE WAR AGAINST GERMANY AND ITALY

American Role in Allied Strategy. With the invasion of North Africa (Operation TORCH), the U. S. Army in late 1942 entered upon active offensive operations that were to be sustained at a strategic level in the Mediterranean and in Europe until the final defeat of Germany. More than a million Americans were to participate in the Mediterranean war and more than four million were engaged on the European Continent, exclusive of Italy. Alongside them were to march British, French, Canadian, and other Allied troops in the greatest demonstration of coalition warfare the world has ever known, while on another front the Russians were to contribute enormously to eventual Allied victory.

The North African Campaign (8 November 1942–10 May 1943). Given the assignment to invade North Africa only at the end of July 1942, the U. S. Army was ready to carry it out by November of the same year. In light of the limited resources available in the first year of war, the time for preparation was painfully brief.

The enemy position. In North Africa the Germans and their Italian allies controlled a narrow but strategic strip along the Mediterranean coast between Tunisia and Egypt (map 39). Impassible desert bounded the strip on the south. Numbering some 100,000 men in November, the German-Italian army in the Libyan Desert was commanded by a battle-tested German leader, Field Marshal Erwin Rommel. In conjunction with Axis possession of the northern shores of the Mediterranean, Rommel's hold on North Africa denied much of the Mediterranean to Allied shipping and posed constant threats to Egypt, the Near East, and French-dominated Tunisia, Algeria, and Morocco in northwest Africa. The position of the French, who stood between the Allied invasion force and the real enemy, was enigmatic. After the armistice which followed French defeat by the Germans in 1940, the loyalties of the French forces had become split among factions. How each or all of these factions would react to the Allied landings in North Africa could not be predicted.

Objectives. TORCH was primarily designed to utilize ready Allied strength in an operation to relieve pressure against the Russians. But it had several other objectives—(1) to gain French Morocco, Algeria, and Tunisia as a base for enlisting the French Empire in the war, (2) to assist the British in the Libyan Desert in destroying the Axis forces in North Africa, and (3) to open the Mediterranean to

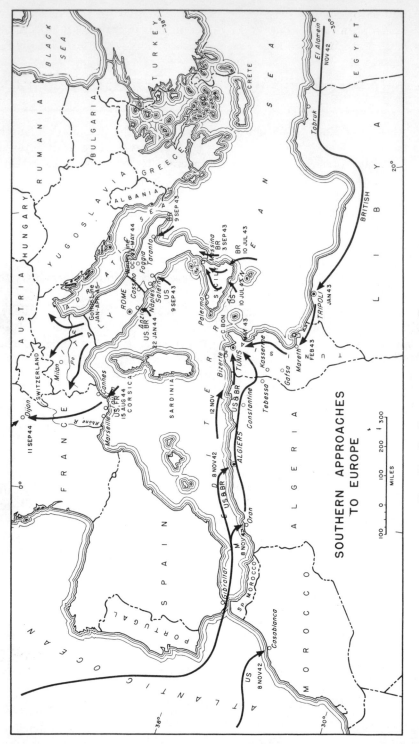

Map 39. Southern approaches to Europe.

Allied shipping and prepare the way for further operations against the European Axis. The method by which these objectives were to be accomplished involved concentric attacks. While Gen. Sir Harold R. L. Alexander, British Commander in Chief in the Middle East, struck from Egypt with the veteran British Eighth Army under Lt. Gen. Bernard L. Montgomery, a combined British-U. S. force was to invade French North Africa and hit the enemy's rear. Since the Americans would furnish most of the forces in the invasion of northwest Africa, overall command went to an American, General Eisenhower, who already was in England supervising the assembly of United States forces for the projected cross-Channel invasion.

Strategic surprise. It was especially important to achieve strategic as well as tactical surprise in the North African invasion, for the Allies were well aware that if the Germans learned of the plan in advance it would be possible for them to occupy and defend Tunisia, Algeria, and Morocco and thereby seal the Mediterranean at the Strait of Gibraltar. It was also important to gain French approval of the invasion, not only to avoid the casualties likely in a fight with the French but also to permit a swift occupation of all the French-dominated provinces before the Germans could move in from the east. Yet to apprise the French of the plan in the hope of gaining assistance—or at least neutrality—was to risk the possibility of one or more of the dissident French factions revealing the plan to the Germans. This peculiar situation hampered tactical planning and preparations up to the very moment of the assault.

Choice of landing sites. In selecting beaches for the invasion, U. S. planners insisted upon landing on the Atlantic coast of Morocco lest the Germans seal the Strait of Gibraltar and cut off support to forces put ashore on the Mediterranean coast. Because both troops and shipping were limited, this insistence restricted the number and the size of landings possible inside the Mediterranean. Though both British and Americans wanted to land as close as possible to Tunisia, they had to consider that Axis aircraft might intervene decisively, if landings were made within fighter range of Sicily and Sardinia. Making their decision on the side of security, the Allies planned simultaneous landings at three points—in Morocco, near the Atlantic port of Casablanca, and in Algeria, near the ports of Oran and Algiers. When the success of these landings was assured, a fast convoy was to land additional troops closer to the eastern border of Algeria, and a ground column was to move eastward into Tunisia in hope of getting there before the Germans could move in more than a token force. Some idea of the immensity of the distances involved is evident in the fact that from Casablanca to Tunis is more than a thousand miles.

The landings. On 23 October, at the eastern end of the Mediterranean, Montgomery's Eighth Army auspiciously opened an offensive at El Alamein after soundly defeating a prior Axis offensive led by

Rommel. A little over two weeks later, before daylight on 8 November, the U. S. Navy put U. S. Army forces ashore near Casablanca, while the British Navy put other United States troops and contingents of British troops ashore near Oran and Algiers. The entire invasion force consisted of over 400 warships, 1,000 planes, and some 107,000 men, including a battalion of paratroopers making the first United States combat jump of the war. The troops at Oran and Algiers had sailed from the British Isles. Those at Casablanca had come directly from the United States, the only instance in World War II in which a force of more than division size was combat loaded in U. S. ports for landing directly on a hostile invasion beach.

French resistance. Though the Allies achieved strategic surprise, the French in every case but one fought back at the invasion beaches. The dissidence among the French factions limited the effectiveness of the opposition in some instances, but the fact of any resistance endangered the entire operation because of the delay it imposed on the move by land into Tunisia. Indeed, the French possessed sufficient strength—more than 100,000 men plus considerable naval forces—even to defeat the invasion. Three days passed before an agreement could be reached with the French and resistance brought to an end. The incongruity of Frenchmen fighting against Americans and British can be explained in part by attempts of some of the French to live up to the 1940 armistice in hope of forestalling German occupation of southern France, which was still nominally under French control, and in part by the need for secrecy that had prevented the Allies from enlisting the support of all French factions before the landings.

The drive into Tunisia. On 11 November, after French support on the Allied side was assured, an Allied column headed for Tunisia. The Germans, in the meantime, had begun to move into Tunisia in force across the narrow body of water between Sicily and Tunisia, and successfully defeated the Allied drive on Tunis. The Axis eventually brought in more than 150,000 troops. The major ports of Bizerte and Tunis were for the moment out of Allied reach. The German situation was further improved when Rommel's troops from the east, falling back before Montgomery's Eighth Army, eventually established themselves behind the Mareth Line in southeastern Tunisia in contact with the German reinforcements, now brought to Army strength.

Counteroffensive. Rommel's forces now held a giant beachhead in Tunisia and were prepared for offensive action. On 14 February 1943 strong German armored units sallied forth from passes in central Tunisia on the front of the U. S. II Corps, commanded by Maj. Gen. Lloyd R. Fredendall, in an attempt to turn the south flank of the British First Army (Lt. Gen. Kenneth A. N. Anderson) and capture the base of operations that the Allies had built up around Tebessa. In a series of sharp armored actions the Germans defeated the Allies

A U. S. TANK DESTROYER MOVES UP to the front in Maknassy, Tunisia Sector.

and forced a withdrawal by American troops back through Kasserine Pass and the valley beyond. By 21 February they had achieved a spectacular advance of almost a hundred miles before determined countermeasures by American and Anglo-American forces brought them to a halt on 22 February, still short of their objectives. The counteroffensive having failed, the Germans withdrew to their original positions. By the middle of March two lesser enemy offensives—one farther north against the British First Army, the other from the Mareth Line against the British Eighth Army—also had failed.

Allied offensives. Having defeated all Axis measures, the Allies resumed the offensive. In southern Tunisia the U. S. II Corps, commanded now by Lt. Gen. George S. Patton, Jr., attacked toward the flank and rear of the Mareth Line, while to the south General Montgomery sent elements of the British Eighth Army through the desert to outflank the Axis position and then to break through into the eastern coastal region of central Tunisia. Close liaison between the two Allied forces was then established. Within a month the Allies had compressed all Axis troops into a small bridgehead covering the Cape Bon Peninsula at the northeastern tip of Tunisia. For the final attack in these operations, the U. S. II Corps passed to the command of Maj. Gen. Omar N. Bradley, so that General Patton could prepare for the Sicilian campaign. In massive attack the Allies pushed through to the ports of Bizerte and Tunis. The last of some 275,000 Germans and Italians surrendered on the Cape Bon Peninsula on 10 May.

Analysis. Though obviously slowed by the initial resistance of the French, victory in North Africa had been achieved in less than seven months. It meant much in terms of the outcome of the war and, indeed, may be considered the turning point in the war in Europe. The victory opened the Mediterranean to Allied shipping. In eliminating the German North African armies, it provided the Allies with positions from which to attack the "underbelly" of Europe. Also, a French Army had been reborn. Perhaps equally important, American troops and commanders had gained experience in both combat and logistical operations, and the stage was set for the campaigns that were to follow.

The Sicilian Campaign (10 July–17 August 1943). Allied leaders having decided in January 1943 at the Casablanca Conference to invade Sicily, military commanders had begun to plan the campaign and assemble their forces even before the Tunisian campaign was over. The decision to invade Sicily (Operation HUSKY) had been taken in large measure because of the realization that a cross-Channel attack could not be launched in 1943. On the other hand, the immense resources already accumulated in the Mediterranean might well be used against the enemy in Sicily and perhaps in Italy. These operations, it was hoped, would divert German strength from the Russian front, knock Italy, the junior Axis partner, out of the war, and assure control of the Mediterranean.

The forces and the target date. Allied ground forces were assembled for Operation HUSKY under the 15th Army Group, commanded by General Alexander. General Alexander's command included Montgomery's British Eighth Army and a newly created U. S. Seventh Army under General Patton. The total invasion force numbered some 160,000 men. D-day was set for 10 July, a date that allowed time to solve the mammoth training and logistical problems involved in mounting the operation and took advantage of the favorable phase of the moon. The question of moonlight figured prominently in the planning because an entire U. S. airborne division was to be dropped behind the invasion beaches in hope of forestalling enemy reaction to the landings.

Tactical surprise. Because Sicily was an obvious objective after North Africa, complete strategic surprise was impossible. Yet a noteworthy feature of the operation was the achievement of tactical surprise. For weeks before D-day, Allied planes bombarded the western part of Sicily in hope of concealing the Allied intention to land on the southern and eastern coasts. As events developed, this program failed to draw sizable enemy strength to the west, but it did prompt considerable dispersion of German armor, thereby delaying quick, concentrated counterattacks. The event that contributed most to surprise was the result of chance. As the huge armada of invasion craft steamed toward Sicily, winds of near gale proportions arose in the Mediterranean. This made the landings exceedingly difficult because of heavy surf, but it put the beach defenders off their guard.

Tactical objectives. The major objective in Sicily was Messina, the gateway to the narrow body of water between Sicily and Italy, the enemy's escape route to the Italian mainland. Yet chances of a successful seaborne assault directly against the objective were slim because of the narrowness of the Strait of Messina and the distance from Allied airfields. The Allies instead put their faith in the principles of security and maneuver. Landing on the southern and eastern coasts, they intended to strike first for dominating ground in the east-central part of the island. Having secured a firm base, complete with a number of airfields, they would then launch the final attack on Messina.

Drive to Palermo. After recovering from initial surprise, the Germans concentrated in the east opposite the British, thereby closing the most direct route to Messina. With the British Eighth Army held up by the German concentration in the Catania area, the U. S. Seventh Army moved rapidly toward Palermo. Looking upon the British line as a kind of large-scale holding attack, Patton sent a mobile provisional corps, under Maj. Gen. Geoffrey Keyes, to the northwest to cut Sicily in two. The Provisional Corps captured the port of Palermo only 12 days after the first landings. This broke the morale of a large (170,000) Italian garrison on the island and placed U. S. forces in position to attack from the west to break the deadlock opposite the British.

Victory in Sicily. In August, when a final assault against the German line was being readied, the Germans began to withdraw across the Strait of Messina. Although the Allies commanded the sea and the air, the Germans nevertheless managed to evacuate much of their strength; some 40,000 German troops escaped to the Italian mainland. When on 17 August, 30 days after the Sicilian campaign began, U. S. patrols pushed into Messina, the Germans had incurred some 10,000 casualties of all types. Italian losses can only be estimated, but, including captured, may have been close to 100,000. Allied casualties were 31,158.

The Italian Campaign (3 September 1943–2 May 1945). Loss of Sicily and the proximity of Allied forces to the Italian mainland contributed to the overthrow of the Mussolini government. The capitulation of Italy became a matter of negotiation and time. Though Sardinia and Corsica had been regarded as potential Allied objectives after Sicily, it became apparent that an invasion of Italy would be more advantageous. It would facilitate Italian surrender and at the same time tie down maximum German forces and prevent their deployment either to the Russian front or to the defenses of western France, the latter scheduled to be hit by the cross-Channel attack in the spring of 1944. Invasion of Italy would also provide airfields from which the Allies might bomb Germany and the Balkans.

A triple assault. On 3 September a British force crossed the Strait of Messina and landed on the toe of the Italian boot as a prelude to a long overland movement toward the eventual objective of airfields around Foggia. On 8 September, the surrender of Italy was announced and the Allies came into possession of the Italian fleet. On the following day, while a British fleet steamed into the harbor of Taranto and put a division ashore in the arch of the Italian boot, the U. S. Fifth Army under Lt. Gen. Mark W. Clark made the main effort of the Allied invasion by landing on beaches along the Gulf of Salerno.

Crisis at Salerno. Reacting in strength against the Salerno invasion, the Germans two days after the landing began a vigorous counterattack which threatened to push the Allies into the sea. For four days, the issue was in doubt. Reinforcement of the ground troops, hard fighting, liberal use of air support, and unstinting use of naval gunfire at last repulsed the German attack. On 15 September the crisis was surmounted as the Germans began to withdraw. The next day patrols of the U. S. Fifth and British Eighth Armies met southeast of Salerno and united the British and American fronts. Two weeks later the Allies took Naples, thereby gaining an excellent harbor, and Foggia and its airfields. Establishing a line of communications based on ports along the Adriatic coast, the British deployed their forces in the eastern part of Italy. The Fifth Army, based on Naples, deployed in the western part.

A shift in emphasis. Up to the fall of 1943 the war in the Mediterranean had made heavy demands upon the buildup in England for a cross-Channel invasion in 1944. Now the situation was reversed; troops and resources were withdrawn or withheld from the Mediterranean for use in the invasion of the Continent. Though hard fighting was not to end in Italy for a long time, and the Italian Campaign was to continue to tie down some 20-odd German divisions, the Mediterranean war in many aspects began to look like a poor relation of the projected cross-Channel attack. When the U. S. Fifth and British Eighth Armies renewed their push northward from Naples and Foggia in October 1943, they had between them only 11 divisions. It required hard and skillful fighting for the Allies to continue the northward advance. A particular problem arose from the mountainous nature of the Italian terrain and the narrowness of the peninsula, both of which severely restricted maneuver and favored the defense.

The Winter Line and Anzio. The renewed offensive in October 1943 broke a strong German delaying position at the Volturno River, about 20 miles north of Naples, and carried the Allies as far as the so-called Winter Line anchored on Cassino, which the Germans had been hurriedly preparing about 75 miles south of Rome. The Allied army group commander, Field Marshal Sir Harold Alexander, then planned an operation by which he hoped to overcome the restrictions on maneuver imposed by the terrain and the skillful German defense. His plan was to envelop the German line with a flanking movement by sea. Since an obvious objective of the Italian campaign was Rome—an objective of more political importance than military— Alexander proposed that Clark's Fifth U. S. Army make an amphibious landing on the beaches near Anzio, some thirty miles south of Rome. By threatening or cutting the German lines of communication behind the Winter Line, the Anzio force was to facilitate a Fifth Army advance up the Liri valley, the most obvious military route to Rome.

Strengthening the line with a French corps equipped with American arms, General Clark pulled out the U. S. VI Corps to make the envelopment. While the VI Corps sailed toward Anzio, the Fifth Army launched a massive attack against the Winter Line, hoping thereby not only to divert the Germans from Anzio but also to gain access to the Liri valley. Only the first object was attained. The VI Corps landed at Anzio unopposed, but the Fifth Army was denied entrance into the Liri. From positions anchored on the town of Cassino and the heights around the abbey of Monte Cassino, the Germans prevented American troops from crossing the Rapido River and breaking the Winter Line.

At Cassino, subsequent attacks by the Allies in February and March failed to force a penetration. Meanwhile, the Anzio force, isolated in its beachhead some 60 miles from the main front, fought to retain its hold on the Italian coast. A German counterattack, designed to annihilate the Anzio force, reached a peak of intensity on 17 February. Only a magnificent defense by U. S. infantrymen, supported by artillery, tanks, planes, and naval gunfire, at last brought the counterattack to a halt.

The fall of Rome. Through the rest of the winter and early spring, the U. S. Fifth and British Eighth Armies regrouped and reorganized in preparation for another assault against the Winter Line. On 11 May, both armies synchronized their efforts and drove toward Rome. When they reached supporting distance of Anzio, the VI Corps also began to attack. The Italian capital fell on 4 June, two days before the Allies crossed the Channel to invade France.

Tank-Infantry Team entering Rome, 4 June 1944. Burning vehicle is a German Tiger tank.

Final operations in Italy. Allied forces in Italy, although reduced in strength after relinquishing a number of divisions scheduled for use in France, nevertheless stuck assiduously to the principle of the offensive.   Pursuing the enemy to the Gothic Line in the rugged North Apennine Mountains, they initiated in September a three-month campaign that broke the new position after some of the toughest fighting of the war.   In the spring of 1945 they pushed across the Po Valley, and in the latter days of the war, made spectacular advances ending in the surrender of the German forces in Italy on 2 May 1945.

Results of the campaign. Less loudly sung than other campaigns of World War II, the Italian Campaign nevertheless played a vital role in determining the outcome of the war.   It was begun at a time when the Russians still needed help and when Allied ability to exert direct military pressure was limited.   By persisting in Italy, the Allies with a minimum of strength tied down a German force that might have upset the balance in France.   U. S. casualties in Italy totaled approxi mately 114,000.   Nowhere in World War II was the principle of the offensive pursued with more doggedness in the face of excruciating problems of terrain, weather, and limited manpower.

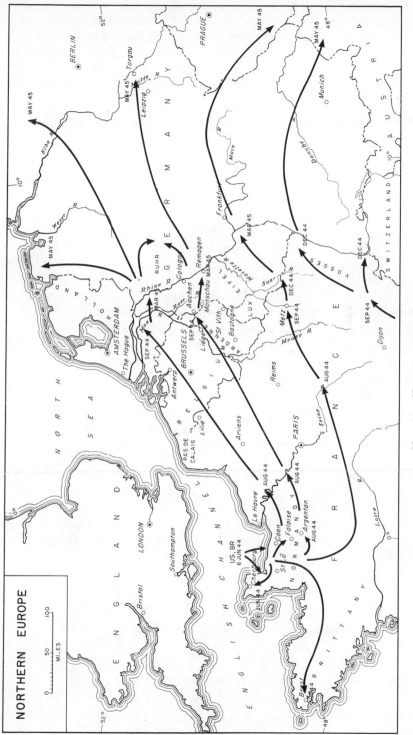

Map 40. Northern Europe.

European Theater of Operations. *Cross-Channel attack.* **That** major campaigns could be fought in the Mediterranean area and in the Pacific at the same time that preparations for the biggest amphibious operation in history were proceeding in the United Kingdom testified to the massive resources the Allied nations now were accumulating for winning the war. The build-up was easily the most tremendous single logistical undertaking of all time. Even before D-day the program required transporting some 1,200,000 men across the submarine-infested Atlantic to the United Kingdom and providing for their shelter, hospitalization, supply, training, and general welfare. It required 20,000,000 square feet of covering, storage, and shop space, and 44,000,000 square feet of open storage. Parks were planned for 50,000 military vehicles. More than 20,000 railroad cars and 1,000 locomotives were shipped to the United Kingdom. The air forces required tremendous facilities, including 163 airfields. All the while these preparations were under way, the great strategic air bombardment of Germany was proceeding and the German Air Force was being knocked from the skies.

Command. General Eisenhower was named Supreme Commander of the Allied armies for the invasion of the Continent. To coordinate forces during the landing and until Eisenhower should assume direct command on the Continent, British General Montgomery was designated as ground commander. The armies involved were the British Second Army under Lt. Gen. Sir Miles C. Dempsey and the U. S. First Army under Lt. Gen. Omar N. Bradley.

Preliminary air program. While the strategic air campaign against Germany continued unabated, the Allied air forces began a new air offensive three months before D-day to pave the way for the invasion. The purpose was to restrict the enemy's ability to shift reserves, that is, to isolate the prospective invasion battlefield (map 40). This was essential, because the Allies for a long time could not hope to land as many divisions on the Continent as the Germans had in France.

The Normandy landings. After lengthy study of coastal defenses and disposition of German units, the beaches of Normandy east of the Cherbourg Peninsula were chosen as the area for the assault. Since major ports would be lacking in Normandy in the early stages of the invasion, two artificial harbors were to be towed from Britain and emplaced off the invasion beaches.

Despite a weather forecast of high winds and a rough sea, General Eisenhower made the fateful decision to go ahead with the invasion on 6 June. At 0200 that morning one British and two U. S. airborne divisions were dropped behind the beaches in order to secure routes of egress for the seaborne forces. Next came preliminary aerial and naval bombardments. At 0630, not long after sunrise, the first waves of assault infantry and tanks touched shore. The assault went well on

Gen. Dwight D. Eisenhower talking with paratroopers scheduled to be dropped behind the beaches of Normandy.

the British beaches and at UTAH, westernmost of the U. S. beaches. The going was tougher at OMAHA, the other of the U. S. beaches, where no airborne troops had been dropped. German defense was facilitated by the chance presence of an infantry division, which had been staging practice maneuvers nearby. Many a moment of anxiety still would be felt about the Normandy landings, but as night fell on D-day the fact was that large contingents of two British, one Canadian, and three American infantry divisions, plus three Allied airborne divisions, had made their way ashore on the fortress coast of Europe.

The principles of surprise, simplicity, and economy of force had been governing factors in the first stage of the invasion. Now the emphasis would fall on the principles of security, offensive, and maneuver as the Allies sought to seize at least one major port and accumulate sufficient resources to ward off counterattacks and break out of the limited beachhead. One way the Allies had planned to contribute to security and surprise was by means of an elaborate deception program begun long before the invasion. By creating fictitious headquarters, generating false radio traffic, and by other means, the Allies hoped to deceive the Germans as to the location and extent of the Allied landings and to give the impression of greater strength left behind in England available for a second and stronger invasion farther north along the Pas de Calais.

Cherbourg and the hedgerows. The port of Cherbourg fell three weeks after the invasion at the conclusion of a bitter struggle. Meanwhile, other Allied forces had been deepening the beachhead between Caen and the road center of St. Lo, so that by the end of June the most forward positions were 20 miles from the beaches. An encouraging feature was the lack of a large-scale counterattack, obviously attributable to the efforts of Allied aircraft and French saboteurs to cripple the enemy's communications system and to the deception program. Yet each minor advance still was a back-breaking struggle against stubborn resistance augmented by the peculiar nature of the countryside. This was "hedgerow country" where each field was turned into a separate little fortress by a high bank of earth which nature had reinforced with the roots of shrubs and trees.

Buildup. For all the slow advance and lack of ports, the Allied buildup was swift. By the first of July almost a million men, some 586,000 tons of supplies, and 177,000 vehicles had been landed. General Bradley's U. S. First Army comprised 4 corps with 11 infantry and 2 armored divisions. British strength was about the same.

Breakout. As the battle of the hedgerows continued, the British attempted to break into more open country near Caen, only to be thwarted by German armored units. Thereupon, the Americans sought to push forward on the right end of the line near St. Lo. On the heels of an intensive aerial bombardment, utilizing both tactical aircraft and heavy bombers, the U. S. First Army on 25 July began an attack that achieved a distinct penetration. The U. S. Third Army under General Patton, which had been assembling behind the lines, then entered the campaign. Armored columns poured through the breach in the direction of Brittany, which was deemed vital in Allied reckoning because of its deep port facilities. Already the Canadian First Army had joined the British at the left end of the line.

Eisenhower's plan. General Eisenhower's strategic plan, once his troops were ashore and access to the Breton ports was assured, was to secure a lodgment area as far east as the Seine River, providing ample room for supply and air bases. He then intended to advance into Germany on a broad front, concentrating greatest resources north of the Ardennes region of Belgium under Montgomery's British 21st Army Group but providing a subsidiary thrust south of the Ardennes by the U. S. First and Third Armies operating under the newly activated U. S. 12th Army Group, commanded by General Bradley. The northern route was deemed more important because it led most directly to the Ruhr, the industrial area in the Rhine Valley near Cologne which provided Germany the sinews of war.

Falaise-Argentan pocket. But the situation developed too fast for this plan to be followed all the way. Soon after the penetration near St. Lo, the Germans launched a strong counterattack in hope of cutting off those U. S. troops that were attacking toward Brittany. In

Troops wading ashore from an LCVP at Omaha Beach, D-Day morning.

so doing the Germans unwittingly set the stage for their sound defeat in Normandy, for the Allies seized immediately upon the opportunity to exploit the principle of maneuver to the fullest. While troops of Montgomery's British 21st Army Group headed for Falaise, General Bradley directed mobile columns of both the U. S. First and Third Armies to begin a wide encircling maneuver in the direction of Argentan, near Falaise, roughly one third the way between St. Lo and Paris. The enemy's counterattacking force was caught in a giant pocket. Though a 15-mile gap between Falaise and Argentan was not closed before many of the Germans escaped, more than 70,000 were killed or captured in the pocket, and the Germans lost great masses of materiel. The gap was permanently sealed on 20 August.

Crossing the Seine. While the U. S. First Army was finishing the business of the Falaise-Argentan pocket, Patton's U. S. Third Army drove eastward to the Seine River. Patton had two objectives: to cross the Seine, thereby eliminating it as a likely new German defensive line; and to make a second, wider encirclement to trap those Germans that had escaped from the first pocket. Both he accomplished. In the two pockets the enemy lost almost all of two field armies.

Liberation of Paris. As Patton's troops crossed the Seine, French patriots began to battle the Germans in the streets of the French capital. Though General Eisenhower had intended to bypass Paris, hoping to spare the city heavy fighting and to postpone the necessity for feeding the civilian population, he had to lend support to the uprising lest it be defeated. A column including both U. S. and French troops entered the city on 25 August.

Change in strategic plan. Since the Germans in France had been so soundly beaten, General Eisenhower abandoned the original plan of holding along the Seine River while putting the Brittany ports into operation and establishing a sound logistical structure. Since the Brittany ports were now not close enough to the front, it became more desirable to gain control of Channel ports, including the best in Europe, the Belgian port of Antwerp. To exploit the new situation, General Eisenhower decided to cross the Seine in strength; he reinforced the British 21st Army Group north of the Ardennes by sending the U. S. First Army close alongside the British toward Aachen. The immediate goal of the northern force was Antwerp. Only the U. S. Third Army was to continue on the subsidiary axis south of the Ardennes.

Invasion of Southern France. The Germans in northern France were already faltering when the Allies launched the invasion of southern France (Operation DRAGOON). On 15 August three U. S. divisions, plus an airborne task force and French commandos, operating under Lt. Gen. Alexander M. Patch's U. S. Seventh Army, came ashore on the Mediterranean coast of France southwest of Cannes. Resistance was spotty. In a matter of a few days the U. S. divisions had fanned out from the beaches, and a followup French force was en route to the ports of Toulon and Marseille (map 39).

The basic objectives of the Southern France invasion were—(1) to provide the Allies a supplementary line of communications through the Mediterranean ports and (2) to prevent the Germans in the south from moving north to oppose the operations in Normandy. The success of the operation was spectacular. Allied columns in the south soon were matching the sweeping advances in northern France. On 11 September patrols from the southern force met patrols of the northern force near Dijon. Four days later, on 15 September, the U. S. 6th Army Group under the command of Lt. Gen. Jacob L. Devers became operational. The 6th Army Group with the French First Army and the U. S. Seventh Army on the same day passed from the control of Allied Force Headquarters to the control of SHAEF. The forces from the south were thereafter to continue toward Germany alongside the U. S. Third Army.

The port situation. The port problem of the main OVERLORD forces still was acute. Hitler had made it more difficult by designating the ports as fortresses, to be defended to the last even when bypassed or encircled. On 1 September Cherbourg still was the only major port supplying the forces in the north. In hope of securing Brest, even though it was far behind the front, the U. S. Ninth Army, under the command of Lt. Gen. William H. Simpson, became operational on the Brittany Peninsula on 5 September. When Brest fell two weeks later, the port was a shambles. In the meantime the British 21st Army Group had taken Le Havre and several lesser Channel ports and on 4 September captured Antwerp, its wharves and docks intact. Antwerp still could not be used, for the Germans clung to the banks of the Schelde Estuary, denying access to the port from the sea.

The logistical crisis. The port situation was symptomatic of multitudinous problems that had begun to beset the entire Allied logistical organization. The armies were going so far so fast that the supply services simply could not keep up. Though enough supplies were available on the Continent, it was impossible to get them to the forward positions, which sometimes were more than 500 miles beyond the depots. Extraordinary measures in the field of transportation were adopted, including establishment of a one-way truck route called the Red Ball Express. But enough supplies for continued offensives by a force of the size the Allies now possessed (50 divisions) could not be moved on the spur of the moment.

Terrain and the West Wall. As if the logistical crisis were not enough, the armies soon faced several other obstacles of major proportions. A period of bad weather as winter drew near was inevitable. Also, at the German border the corridors of advance grew more narrow, severely restricting maneuver. Terrain provided another problem in a number of natural and manmade obstacles, like the Moselle, Maas, and Rhine Rivers, the Vosges Mountains, the Huertgen Forest near Aachen, the old French forts about Metz and in the Maginot Line, and the dense fortifications along the German border, called the Siegfried Line or the West Wall. By mid-September the U. S. First Army, now commanded by Lt. Gen. Courtney H. Hodges, had penetrated the West Wall at several points but lacked the means to exploit the breaks.

Operation MARKET-GARDEN. Acutely conscious of the logistical crisis, General Eisenhower assigned first priority to clearing the seaward approaches to Antwerp. On the other hand, he saw an opportunity to make one last bold stroke to exploit German disorganization before logistics should force a halt. He authorized employment of the First Allied Airborne Army (Lt. Gen. Lewis H. Brereton) in support of the British Second Army in an attempt to get across three major water obstacles in the Netherlands (the Maas, Waal, and Lower Rhine), to outflank the West Wall, and to put the British in position for a subsequent drive into Germany along the relatively open north German plain. The airborne attack was called Operation MARKET; the corollary ground attack, Operation GARDEN.

Employing one British and two U. S. airborne divisions, the First Allied Airborne Army launched Operation MARKET on 17 September. On the first day alone approximately 20,000 paratroops and glider troops landed in the largest airborne operation of the war. Though the drops were spectacularly successful and achieved complete surprise, the chance presence of two panzer divisions near the drop zones made swift German reaction possible. Resistance to the ground attack also was greater than expected. The combined operations achieved a salient some 50 miles deep into German territory but fell short of their ambitious objectives, including a workable bridgehead across the Rhine.

The autumn campaigns. Upon the conclusion of the airborne operation, the British 21st Army Group concentrated on opening Antwerp to Allied shipping, but not until 28 November did the first ship drop anchor in the port. The logistical situation nevertheless had been gradually improving as a result of a cutback in offensive operations and the extraordinary efforts of the supply services. In early November resources were sufficient to enable the U. S. armies to launch a big offensive aimed at reaching the Rhine. It turned out to be a slow, arduous fight through the natural and artificial obstacles along the German border. Severe rain and cold added to the difficulties. The largest air attack in direct support of ground troops to be made during the war (Operation QUEEN) failed to make possible an easy advance. By mid-December the U. S. First and Ninth Armies had reached the Roer River east of Aachen, some 23 miles inside Germany, and the U. S. Third and Seventh Armies had contacted the West Wall along the Saar River northeast of Metz. But the Rhine was still a long distance away. The Germans obviously had effected a remarkable recovery from the debacle in France.

German plans. In attempting to assemble sufficient forces for the autumn offensives, Eisenhower had thinned the line in the rugged Ardennes region. This fitted in perfectly with German plans, for as early as July Hitler had begun to think of a counteroffensive on the western front designed to regain the initiative and compel the Allies to settle for a negotiated peace. Over the protests of his generals, who thought the plan too ambitious, Hitler directed an attack by some 30 divisions, carefully conserved and secretly assembled for the operation, through the Ardennes, thence northwestward to Antwerp. During the operation he hoped to cut off and annihilate the British 21st Army Group and the U. S. First and Ninth Armies north of the Ardennes.

The German counteroffensive. Under cover of inclement weather, Hitler concentrated his forces in the forests of the Eifel region, opposite the Ardennes. Before daylight on 16 December the Germans attacked, taking the U. S. VIII Corps by surprise. In most places German gains were rapid, for the American divisions were either inexperienced or seriously depleted from earlier fighting and all were stretched thin.   Yet troubles developed for the Germans from the first. Cut off and surrounded, small U. S. units continued to fight with disturbing efficiency.   At the northern shoulder of the penetration, the troops of the U. S. V Corps refused to budge from the vicinity of Monschau, thereby denying critical roads and limiting the width of the penetration.   At St. Vith American troops held out for eight days to deny a critical road center.   To Bastogne to the southwest, where an armored detachment served as a blocking force, General Eisenhower rushed an airborne division which never relinquished that communications center.   The Germans, denied vital roads and hampered by air attacks as the weather cleared, fell a few miles short of even their first objective, the Meuse River.   The result, after more than a month of hard fighting that cost the Americans some 75,000 casualties and the Germans some 80,000 to 100,000, was nothing but a big bulge in the lines.   The counteroffensive had given the Allied command some anxious moments, but the gallant stands by isolated units had provided time for the U. S. First and Ninth Armies to shift troops against the northern flank of the penetration and for Patton's Third Army to hit the penetration from the south.   The U. S. Third Army's shift and change in direction of attack was one of the more noteworthy instances during the war of successful employment of the principle of maneuver.   By the end of January, U. S. units had retaken all ground they had lost.   A smaller German attack against the U. S. 6th Army Group also had been defeated.   The end of the war in Europe was in sight.

The Russian Campaigns.   A great deal of the hope for an early end to the war in Europe rested with the tremendous successes of the Russian armies in the east.   Having stopped the invading Germans at the gates of Moscow in late 1941 and at Stalingrad in late 1942, the Russians had made great offensive strides westward in both 1943 and 1944.   Only a few days after D-day in Normandy the Red Army had launched a massive offensive which by mid-September had reached East Prussia and the gates of the Polish capital of Warsaw.   In January 1945, as U. S. troops eliminated the German bulge in the Ardennes, the Red Army started a new drive that was to carry almost to the eastern gates of Berlin.

Far greater masses of troops were employed in the east than in the west.   The Germans had to commit more than two million men on the Eastern Front as compared with approximately 700,000 in the West. This was a scale of fighting the western Allies could not have hoped to attain for a long time.   They nevertheless made major contributions in materiel to the Russians.   In the slightly more than two and one-half years from October 1941 to June 1944 the Allies supplied the Russians with nearly 11,000 aircraft, more than 4,900 tanks, and 263,000 vehicles.   The tanks they furnished up to 30 June 1944 would have been enough to outfit more than 18 U. S. armored divisions. The Allied bombing campaign against Germany also aided the Rus-

Ludendorff Railroad Bridge across the Rhine which later became known as the Remagen Bridge.

sians materially, as did the fact that the Germans were blockaded and restricted to the European mainland by Allied naval and air action.

The Final Offensive. *Drive to the Rhine.* Soon after the opening of the Russians' January offensive, the Allies in the West began a new drive to reach and cross the Rhine River, the last major barrier to the industrial heart of Germany. The Germans, exhausted by the over-ambitious effort in the Ardennes, and forced to shift divisions to the east to oppose the Russians, had little chance of holding west of the Rhine. Though they made a stiff fight of it at the Roer River and at points along the border where earlier penetrations of the West Wall had not been made, the Allies in the early days of March were nearing the Rhine on a broad front.

The Remagen Bridge. Though the Germans had made careful plans to destroy all bridges as they retreated across the Rhine, something went amiss at the Ludendorff railroad bridge in the sector of the U. S. First Army at Remagen. On 7 March elements of the U. S. 9th Armored Division found the bridge damaged but passable and immediately seized the opportunity to cross to the east bank. It was a feat of tremendous courage and initiative on the part of the leading platoon leader and his men. Higher commanders acted promptly to exploit it.

Multiple crossings. To the south, troops of the U. S. Third Army on 22 March matched the accomplishment by making a surprise crossing of the Rhine in assault boats. On 23 and 24 March the British 21st Army Group and the U. S. Ninth Army on the north flank of the Allied line staged a full-dress crossing of the river, complete with an airborne attack rivaling in its dimensions the MARKET-GARDEN drop. During the last week of March both the U. S. Seventh and First French Armies of the U. S. 6th Army Group also crossed the river. The final rout of the Germans was under way.

Capitulation. As the month of April opened, the Allied armies fanned out from the Rhine with massive columns of armor and motor-borne infantry. Though resistance was staunch at some points, the general pattern was the same as in the pursuit through northern France and Belgium. The U. S. Ninth and First Armies encircled the Ruhr and, with the help of the new U. S. Fifteenth Army, took 325,000 prisoners. By mid-April the Allied armies in the north and center were building up along the Elbe and Mulde Rivers, where they awaited contact with the Russians. First contact came on 25 April at Torgau. Meanwhile, in the south, U. S. armies had penetrated into Czechoslovakia and Austria. Wholesale surrenders began to take place in almost every sector of the front and in Italy.

With Berlin in Russian hands, Hitler a suicide, and almost all of Germany overrun, emissaries of the German government surrendered to the Allies on 7 May at Reims, France. The next day, 8 May, was designated as V–E Day, the official date of the end of the war in Europe.

Analysis. *The situation on V–E Day.* On 8 May 1945, V–E Day, the U. S. Army had 61 combat divisions (42 infantry, 15 armored, 4 airborne) in Europe, exclusive of Italy. It was an impressive, experienced force, the most powerful the United States ever had assembled in a single theater of operations. Behind the lines thousands of units of varying size and description were performing the invaluable services necessary to sustain this fighting machine. But the cost of victory had been high. Total U. S. casualties in Europe, exclusive of Italy, amounted to 586,628. The enemy, on the other hand, was a completely shattered force. His armies had lost, in the period between D-day landings and the Ardennes counteroffensive alone, almost as many men as the U. S. Army had lost during the entire campaign.

New developments. The battlefields of the Mediterranean area and Europe were proving grounds for American technological and tactical developments. As in earlier wars, each side constantly attempted to outdo the other in improving weapons and other equipment. For example, each side sought to achieve greater armor protection and more powerful tank weapons. This race the Germans won with the Panther, Tiger, and King Tiger tanks, though at the expense of maneuverability, a price the American Army was unwilling to pay. Each side developed more powerful antitank weapons such as the

German multipurpose 88-mm gun and the U. S. 90-mm gun. During the German counteroffensive in the Ardennes, the Americans introduced the proximity fuse on artillery projectiles, a fuse that was also used extensively by antiaircraft artillery. The Germans developed and used the flying bomb or pilotless aircraft and later the supersonic missile, both forerunners of the guided missile that U. S. technicians began to develop soon after the war. These new German developments, and jet aircraft as well, came late in the war and had no decisive effect on the outcome.

Type of warfare. U. S. Army operations in the North African and European campaigns illustrate with classic clarity the principle of the offensive. On occasion, weather, constricted terrain, and enemy concentration combined to form a seemingly insurmountable obstacle to the offensive—in Italy during the winters of 1943–44 and 1944–45, again in Normandy, and along the German West Wall. But American leadership was consistently able to achieve the mass, mobility, and fire power to avoid a stalemate, resume the offensive, and exploit the principle of maneuver to the fullest in wider, more open sectors. A prominent factor in American ability to avoid stalemate was the highly developed infantry-artillery-tank team, the most efficient combination of arms to emerge in the war. Once this team had achieved a breakthrough, the pattern of the pursuit was keyed more to the machine—particularly armor—but even in the pursuit infantry and artillery rolled alongside the tank, helping to maintain the essential momentum.

Principles of war. If U. S. commanders displayed more devotion to some of the time-tested principles of war than to others, it was to the principles of the objective and the offensive. Despite enemy pressure, they never relinquished them except in two instances, in central Tunisia and in the Ardennes. In each case U. S. and British commanders quickly thwarted the enemy's intentions. In both cases it was the violation of the principle of security, through faulty evaluation of intelligence information, which led to the difficulties. In the other campaigns, U. S. commanders displayed full appreciation of the principle of security. In Normandy both surprise and security were achieved primarily through the elaborate deception program begun before the invasion. U. S. achievement of mass through fire power was one of the spectacular accomplishments of the war. Maneuver was applied with success on many occasions—in Sicily by Patton's Seventh Army, in Northern France by the First and Third Armies, and in eliminating the bulge resulting from the Ardennes counteroffensive. Economy of force was particularly evident in Italy. Simplicity was nowhere better demonstrated than in the Normandy landings, despite the complexity inherent in the size and diversity of the invasion forces. From the first, unity of command was present in every campaign.

Causes of German and Italian defeat. Many factors entered into the downfall of the European Axis. One of the most important was the steadfast refusal of the British and Russian peoples during the early stages of the war, when Axis power seemed overwhelming, to accept what appeared to be inevitable defeat. Thereafter the ability of the Allies to bring their manpower and resources to bear on Germany and Italy in a coordinated effort was a most important factor. Certainly the devastating and unprecedented Allied heavy bomber offensive against the German nation contributed much to victory, though the proportion of credit due the strategic air effort still is debated. On the other hand, some of the factors contributing to defeat of the Axis were inherent in its conduct of the war, particularly the inability of the European and Asiatic Axis Powers to coordinate their efforts. Other factors were—(1) the impetuous, piecemeal strategy of the German High Command, which resulted in failure to invade England and in overextension in Russia; (2) the basic ineptitude of Mussolini and the Italians, who sought to expand their empire behind the cloak of German military success and at the expense of German overextension in the Balkans and North Africa; and (3) Axis determination—exemplified particularly by Hitler—to hold onto every parcel of ground previously gained even in the face of obvious overextension.

Certain errors or miscalculations may be attributed to the enemy in the campaigns in which U. S. forces were engaged. In North Africa, for example, Germany and Italy were unaware of Allied intentions until too late. In Normandy, the Germans misjudged Allied intentions. Also in Normandy, Hitler forbade any large-scale withdrawal until after the jaws of the Argentan-Falaise pocket were disastrously near to closing. In the Ardennes, the German objective was too ambitious and resulted in dissipation of Hitler's only strategic reserve at a time when it was vitally needed to oppose a new Russian offensive.

Retrospect. The successful conclusion of the campaigns in Europe and in North Africa reflect remarkable achievements by the United States and Great Britain. Pooling their resources and integrating their war effort in the West, the two nations effected a coalition far more effective than that of the Axis Powers. The USSR, with material support from the western Allies, had waged its own war, but the campaigns were concerted with those of the Allies and were waged with devastating effect. The ground combat forces of the U. S. Army advanced under a mighty shield of air power, and from 1943 on a strategic combined bomber offensive was directed at the vitals of the enemy's economic system. The ground forces had rapidly improved in leadership and combat effectiveness under the guidance of sound military doctrine as laid down in U. S. training literature. The forces of the Allies, in the air and on the ground, were armed and supported with telling effect by the technology and enormous productivity of the American economic system. For the second time in one generation the Germans had been defeated by a powerful Allied coalition in which the United States provided the balance of power. Even before full attention could be turned to the Pacific, a remarkable buildup to support the war against the Japanese had been achieved despite the priority of the European Theater, and the resources made available in the Pacific had been used with such aggressiveness and skill that Japan was already on the verge of prostration and defeat before redeployment of forces from Europe began.

QUESTIONS

1. Discuss the application of the principles of war in the North African campaign.

2. In what way was the breakout in Normandy similar to the breakout in Sicily? What principle of war do both illustrate?

3. Why did the Allies launch the Italian campaign?

4. (a) What were the German objectives in the Ardennes counter-offensive? (b) What principle of war was violated by the Allied forces in the Ardennes, and why?

5. List examples of how logistical capabilities and limitations affected the campaigns in North Africa and Europe.

6. At what point, in your opinion, did the German struggle become hopeless, and why?

Reading List

ARMY AIR FORCES IN WORLD WAR II:
   Craven, Wesley F. and James J. Cate, eds. *Europe: Torch to Pointblank*. Chicago, 1949.
   _____ *Europe: Argument to V-E Day*. Chicago, 1951.
Bradley, Omar N. *A Soldier's Story*. New York, 1951.
Clark, Mark W. *Calculated Risk*. New York, 1950.
Eisenhower, Dwight D. *Crusade in Europe*. Garden City, N. Y., 1948.
Morison, S. E. *Sicily-Salerno-Anzio* and *The Atlantic Battle Won* in HISTORY OF UNITED STATES NAVAL OPERATIONS IN WORLD WAR II. Boston, 1954 and 1955.
Patton, George S. *War as I Knew It*. Boston, 1947.

U. S. ARMY IN WORLD WAR II:

Cole, Hugh M. *The Lorraine Campaign.* Washington, 1950.

Harrison, Gordon A. *Cross-Channel Attack.* Washington, 1951.

MacDonald, Charles B., and Sidney T. Mathews. *Three Battles: Arnaville, Altuzzo, and Schmidt.* Washington, 1952.

Pictorial Record: The War Against Germany and Italy: Mediterranean and Adjacent Areas and *Pictorial Record: The War Against Germany: Europe and Adjacent Areas.* Washington, 1951.

Pogue, Forest C. *The Supreme Command.* Washington, 1954.

Ruppenthal, Roland G. *Logistical Support of the Armies,* vol. I. Washington, 1953.

Wilmot, Chester. *The Struggle for Europe.* New York, 1952.

CHAPTER 23

WORLD WAR II—THE WAR AGAINST JAPAN

Japanese Strategy. Japan entered World War II with limited aims and with the intention of fighting a limited war. Its principal objectives were to secure the resources of Southeast Asia and much of China, and to establish a "Greater East Asia Co-Prosperity Sphere" under Japanese hegemony. In 1895 and 1905 Japan had gained important objectives without completely defeating either China or Russia. Similarly in 1941 Japan did not seriously consider conducting an all-out war against the Allies, and the problem was to prevent a limited war from becoming a total war.

The operational strategy the Japanese adopted to start war doomed their hopes to limit the conflict. Japan believed it necessary to destroy or neutralize American striking power in the Pacific—the U. S. Pacific Fleet at Pearl Harbor and the Far East Air Force in the Philippines—before moving southward and eastward to occupy Malaya, the Netherlands East Indies, the Philippines, Wake Island, Guam, the Gilbert Islands, Thailand, and Burma. Once in control of these areas, the Japanese intended to establish a defensive perimeter stretching from the Kurile Islands south through Wake, the Marianas, the Carolines, and the Marshalls and Gilberts to Rabaul on New Britain. From Rabaul the perimeter would extend westward to northwestern New Guinea and would encompass the Indies, Malaya, Thailand, and Burma. Japan thought that the Allies would wear themselves out in fruitless frontal assaults against the perimeter and would ultimately settle for a negotiated peace that would leave Japan in possession of most of its conquests.

Japanese Expansion. The Japanese were remarkably successful in the execution of their offensive plan, and by early 1942 had reached their intended perimeter. They had used relatively small forces and had dispersed them over a vast area, but they had exploited the advantages of surprise and interior lines, and they had moved into areas where Allied forces were weak. The Japanese gave a striking demonstration of the advantages of the offensive and thorough preparation; they showed how the forces of an aggressive, militaristic state could gain initial advantages over unprepared democracies.

But the Japanese had miscalculated the effect of their surprise attacks at Pearl Harbor and in the Philippines, which brought into the war an aroused United States and lost for Japan all chances of conducting the war on Japanese terms. Though defeated everywhere, the Allies did not seek a negotiated peace, but continued to resist and started striking back. In February and March 1942 small carrier task forces of the Pacific Fleet hit the Marshalls, Wake, and Marcus; bombers from Australia began to harass the Japanese base at Rabaul; Army bombers, flying off a Pacific Fleet carrier, delivered a hit-and-run raid against Tokyo during April. Meanwhile, the United States began to develop and fortify a line of communications across the southern Pacific to Australia, where the Allies began building bases from which to launch major counteroffensives. Build up was also underway in Hawaii and Alaska. Once the Allies became strong enough to threaten the Japanese defensive perimeter from several directions, the Japanese would lose the advantage of interior lines, for Japan did not have and could not produce the means to defend and hold at all points.

Perceiving the danger, the Japanese decided to sever the Allied line of communications to Australia and simultaneously expand the existing perimeter. In the spring of 1942 they pushed southeast from Rabaul to Guadalcanal and Tulagi, moved into western New Britain and southeastern New Guinea, and seized Attu and Kiska in the Aleutians. Discarding as beyond their capabilities plans to invade Australia, the Japanese attempted to reach out in the center to Midway Island, northwest of Hawaii. Defeats the Japanese suffered during this second phase expansion outweighed the strategic importance of their gains. In the naval Battle of the Coral Sea in May and off Midway in June the Japanese lost the bulk of their best naval pilots and planes, as well as some carriers. These losses helped redress the naval balance of power in the Pacific and seriously curtailed the mobility of Japan's carrier striking forces.

The Battle of Midway can be considered the turning point of the Pacific war. After that defeat the Japanese decided that they lacked the naval resources to push on and realized they were dangerously over-extending themselves. They abandoned plans to cut the Allies' South Pacific line of communications and turned their energies to strengthening their perimeter. They had lost the strategic initiative, but they still intended to wage a protracted war of attrition in the hope of yet obtaining a negotiated peace.

Allied Plans. To mid-1942 the Allies were able to take only stop-gap measures to halt the Japanese, while the losses during the opening months of the war made it impossible for the United States to execute prewar plans for action in the Pacific. Moreover, the Allied decision to defeat Germany first prevented deployment of all available resources to the Pacific. The long lines of communication from the United States to Pacific bases, a general shortage of shipping, and the necessity for extensive base development throughout the Pacific further delayed offensive preparations. Nevertheless, by early sum-

Map 41. The Pacific

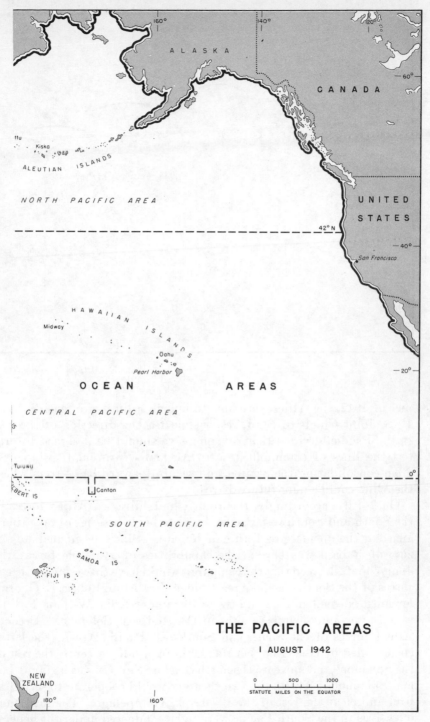

ALASKA

160° 140° 120°

CANADA

Ittu
Kiska
ALEUTIAN ISLANDS

60°

NORTH PACIFIC AREA

UNITED STATES

42° N

San Francisco

40°

HAWAIIAN ISLANDS

Midway

Oahu
Pearl Harbor

20°

OCEAN AREAS

CENTRAL PACIFIC AREA

Tuiuwu

0°

BERT IS

Canton

SOUTH PACIFIC AREA

SAMOA IS

FIJI IS

THE PACIFIC AREAS

I AUGUST 1942

NEW ZEALAND

180° 160°

0 500 1000
STATUTE MILES ON THE EQUATOR

Areas, 1 August 1942

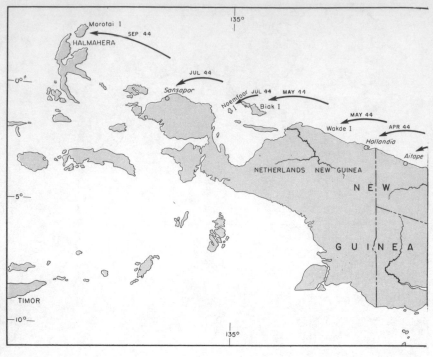

Map 42. The New

mer of 1942, the Allies were able to launch a limited offensive. The U. S. Joint Chiefs of Staff, responsible for the direction of the war in the Pacific, decided that this offensive should be designed to protect the lines of communication to Australia, prevent the Japanese from consolidating their gains, and secure forward bases from which the Allies could mount future drives.

On 2 July, accordingly, the Joint Chiefs directed Allied forces in the South and Southwest Pacific Areas to begin a series of operations aimed at the ultimate recapture of Rabaul. Since the immediate seizure of Rabaul was beyond the capabilities of available forces, the Joint Chiefs decreed that the campaign would have three stages. First, forces of the South Pacific Area (under Vice Adm. Robert L. Ghormley until November 1942 and thereafter under Adm. William F. Halsey, Jr.) would seize base sites in the southern Solomons. Second, Allied forces of the South and Southwest Pacific Areas (the latter commanded by Gen. Douglas MacArthur) would reoccupy the rest of the Solomons and move up the north coast of New Guinea as far as Lae and Salamaua. Third, the two theaters would cooperate to seize Rabaul and clear the rest of the Bismarck Archipelago. The first stage offensives in the South Pacific were to be conducted under the general supervision of Adm. Chester W. Nimitz, whose vast Pacific Ocean Areas command included the North, Central, and South Pacific Areas

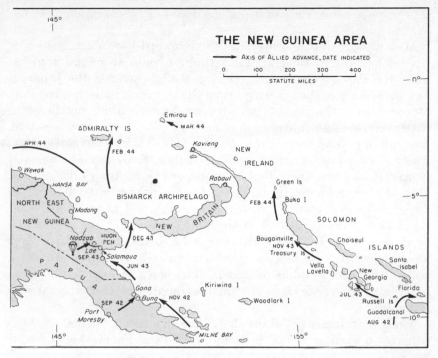

THE NEW GUINEA AREA

→ Axis of Allied advance, date indicated

0   100   200   300   400
STATUTE MILES

Guinea Area.

as subtheaters. Second and third stage operations, including those in the South Pacific Area, would be executed under the strategic direction of General MacArthur. The Joint Chiefs of Staff, reserving to themselves final control of the assignment of tasks, allocation of resources, and timing of operations, would provide, in effect, unified command over Nimitz and MacArthur.

The Campaign Against Rabaul. The offensive began on 7 August 1942 when a Marine division landed on Guadalcanal and nearby islands. The Japanese reacted vigorously, and six times from August to the end of November challenged American naval superiority in the South Pacific in a series of sharp surface engagements. Air battles were almost daily occurrences for a month or more after the landings, and the Japanese sent in strong ground reinforcements, gambling and ultimately losing substantial air and naval resources to hold Guadalcanal, for the Allies proved willing to sacrifice the planes, ships, and men necessary to assure the success of the amphibious assault. Ashore the issue was in doubt for months, and before the island was finally won the South Pacific Area had thrown in two Marine divisions, two Army divisions, and an Army regiment, to mention only the major ground combat elements. The last act came in February 1943, when an Army division moved into the Russell Islands, 35 miles northwest of Guadalcanal. In the Russells and on Guadalcanal, American forces constructed major air and logistical bases in preparation for subsequent advances.

Meanwhile, a Japanese overland drive toward Port Moresby in New Guinea had forced General MacArthur to begin an offensive of his own—the Papuan Campaign. During the late summer the Japanese had pushed across the towering Owen Stanley Mountains toward Port Moresby from the Buna-Gona area on New Guinea's northeastern coast, and by mid-September were only 20 miles from their objective. Australian ground forces drove the Japanese back to the north coast, where the Japanese strongly entrenched themselves around Buna and Gona. It took two Australian divisions, one U. S. Army division, and another U. S. Army regiment almost four months of bitter fighting to dislodge the Japanese. Casualties were high, but as at Guadalcanal the Allied forces learned much about jungle fighting, the importance of air power, and the need for thorough logistical preparation. They also learned that the Japanese soldier, though a skillful, stubborn, and fanatic foe, could be defeated. The myth of Japanese invincibility was forever laid to rest in the jungles of Guadalcanal and Papua.

The Encirclement of Rabaul. After Papua and Guadalcanal the tempo of operations in the South and Southwest Pacific Areas slowed while General MacArthur and Admiral Halsey gathered resources and prepared bases for the next phase. The Japanese, in turn, undertook to reinforce their remaining bases in New Guinea and the Solomons. In March 1943 they attempted to send a large convoy to Lae in New Guinea, but in the Battle of the Bismarck Sea, lost some 3,500 troops and much valuable shipping, principally to Army land-based aircraft. During the following months Rabaul-based planes, reinforced by carrier planes flown in from the Carolines, sought unsuccessfully to knock out American air power in the Solomons.

The Allied advance resumed in late June when U. S. Army troops under MacArthur landed on Woodlark and Kiriwina Islands off eastern New Guinea and at Nassau Bay on the New Guinea coast northwest of Buna. About the same time U. S. Army units of the South Pacific Area went ashore on the New Georgia group in the central Solomons. Both sets of operations were designed to secure additional air bases. The Japanese did not leave the efforts unchallenged, and tried to reinforce New Georgia, losing combat ships they could not spare in an attempt to reduce American naval superiority in the Solomons. Army forces secured New Georgia and its Munda airfield by early August, but the campaign was not over until October, when United States and New Zealand Army troops had occupied Vella Lavella, between New Georgia and Bougainville.

At the end of October New Zealanders and U. S. Marines landed on Treasury and Choiseul Islands to secure bases for a move to

Bougainville. On 1 November Marines landed on Bougainville, a U. S. Army division soon following. Again the Japanese unsuccessfully challenged Allied air and naval powers in the Solomons, and launched strong ground counterattacks against the Bougainville beachhead. By late November 1943, the American beachhead was secure, and with the development of a major air base there the South Pacific's share in second phase advances toward Rabaul virtually ended. The advance had the support of land-based aircraft, and each forward move had been limited to the range of such planes. Japanese air and naval losses during the second phase crippled the Japanese fleet and immoblized it as a striking force for months to come.

Meanwhile, MacArthur's Southwest Pacific Area forces had continued their offensives, with Australian troops carrying most of the burden in New Guinea. In early September a U. S. Army parachute regiment, the first airborne operation of the Pacific War, seized an airfield at Nadzab, inland from Lae and Salamaua. Australian troops cleared Lae and Salamaua by mid-September and, flown into Nadzab, moved on to the Huon Peninsula. A U. S. Army division landed at the western end of the peninsula in January 1944 in an attempt to trap a large Japanese force, but by the time Australian and American units had sealed the western exits to the peninsula in February, most of the Japanese had escaped northwest to Hansa Bay and Wewak.

In the meantime, MacArthur and Halsey had assembled the forces to launch a final offensive toward Rabaul, but the Joint Chiefs had decided that the actual seizure of that objective would be too costly in terms of men, means, and time. They preferred to encircle Rabaul, neutralize it by air bombardment, and push on to seize an offensive base further west, in the Admiralty Islands. A new series of operations to these ends started on 15 December 1943 when U. S. Army units landed on the south coast of western New Britain, and on the 26th a Marine division under MacArthur's control landed on the north coast. In mid-February 1944 New Zealand troops of the South Pacific Area secured an air base site on Green Island, north of Rabaul, and on the last day of the month MacArthur began landing a U. S. Army division on the Admiralties, closing the western and northwestern approaches to Rabaul. Marines under Halsey seized a final air base site on Emirau, north of Rabaul, on 20 March, while Marine and Army units under MacArthur secured additional positions in western and central New Britain from March to May 1944. The major Japanese base at Rabaul, with its 100,000-man garrison, was as effectively out of the war as if destroyed. In the process of encircling Rabaul, the Allies had also left to wither on the vine another important Japanese base at Kavieng on New Ireland, north of Rabaul.

In the last phase of the campaign against Rabaul, a pattern developed that came to characterize much of the war in the Pacific. The

Map 43. The Philippine Area.

Allies would mount no frontal attacks against strongly entrenched Japanese forces if they could avoid such action; they would not advance island-by-island across a vast ocean studded with myriad atolls and island groups. Rather, they would advance in great bounds, limited only by the range of land-based air cover or the availability of carrier-based air support. The Allies would deceive and surprise the Japanese; they would bypass major strongpoints and leave them reduced to strategic and tactical impotence.

The Aleutians. While the Allied offensives against Rabaul had been under way, the Allies had also pushed back the Japanese perimeter in the far reaches of the North Pacific. In May 1943 an Army division went ashore on Attu and after three weeks of costly fighting through Arctic muck and over wind swept ridges, in a cold, almost constant fog, destroyed the Japanese garrison. In August a combined United States-Canadian expedition landed on neighboring Kiska, only to find that the Japanese had evacuated three weeks earlier. With these advances the Japanese perimeter was back to the Kuriles, and the United States was ultimately able to effect a substantial reduction of its garrison in Alaska. The Allies had also opened another strategically important potential axis of advance toward Japan. However, commitments to other theaters, problems incident to operations in the northern regions, and a desire to avoid any chance of compromising Russia's existing neutrality *vis-a-vis* Japan, prevented exploitation of the approach. Further operations in the northern Pacific were limited to nuisance air raids against the Kuriles.

The Drive to the Philippines—Allied Strategy. The campaigns against Rabaul and the Aleutians had been designed to halt the Japaneses and secure bases from which to launch subsequent offensives. Allied strategy for these later offensives took into consideration the probability that an invasion of the Japanese home islands might prove necessary. To insure the success of invasion, the Allies would first have to subject Japan to intensive aerial bombardment; sever Japan's line of communications to the Indies and Southeast Asia by air, surface, and submarine operations; and establish staging bases in the western Pacific to support the final assault. Planners decided that preinvasion bombardment could best be undertaken from fields in eastern China. To develop air bases there, the Allies would have to secure a port on the south China coast, the overland routes from India being inadequate or too insecure for the purpose of moving the requisite men and materiel into China. To seize the needed port, and simultaneously cut Japan's lines of communication to the south, the Allies would have to gain control over the South China Sea. This in turn would require the establishment of major air, naval, and logistical bases in the strategic triangle formed by the south China coast, Formosa, and Luzon.

Unloading supplies at a beach on Leyte, 21 October 1944. Note armored Buffalo on beach.

Strategic planners decided that the best way to reach the triangle would be across the Pacific rather than from the Aleutians, southeast Asia, or China. Long as they were, the lines of communication across the Pacific were shorter and safer than supply lines from starting points other than the west coast of the United States. Moreover, only in campaigns across the Pacific could the Allies employ to best advantage the growing strength of the U. S. Pacific Fleet and its decisive offensive weapon, the fast carrier task force.

Within this strategic framework, the intermediate objective in the western Pacific would be the central or southern Philippines. Here American forces would establish airbases from which to neutralize Japanese air power on Luzon before advancing into the strategic triangle. The Allies could follow two routes to the Philippines—one across the Central Pacific Area via the Gilberts, Marshalls, Marianas, Carolines, and Palaus; the other in the Southwest Pacific Area via the north coast of New Guinea and islands between northwestern New Guinea and Mindanao in the southern Philippines. The Central Pacific route promised to force a naval showdown with the Japanese and, once the Marianas were secured, to provide bases from which the Army Air Forces' new B–29 bomber could strike the Japanese home islands. The Southwest Pacific route was shorter, considering existing bases, and offered more opportunity to employ land-based air power to full advantage. Concurrent operations along both routes would serve to keep the Japanese off balance and offer the Allies many opportunities for surprise.

Here was the key to Pacific strategy after the campaign against Rabaul. The Allies would mount coordinated, mutually supporting drives toward the Philippines. Along both routes commanders would exploit every chance for surprise and acceleration, would bypass Japanese strongpoints whenever possible, and would concentrate air, naval, and ground strength at the decisive points and moments. American forces in the Pacific did not yet have the means to do everything at once, but with the nation's industry in full production the prospects for the successful execution of the strategy grew daily brighter.

The Central Pacific Campaign Begins. The Central Pacific offensive under the new plan had actually started on 20 November 1943, when Admiral Nimitz sent Army and Marine divisions to the Gilbert Islands to seize airbases from which to support subsequent jumps into the Marshalls. Troops and supplies for the Gilberts loaded at Hawaii on newly developed assault shipping and sailed over 2,000 miles to be set ashore by specially designed landing craft and amphibian vehicles. Makin, the Army objective, fell after four days of hard fighting. Tarawa, where the Marines went ashore, proved a bloody affair that provided a stiff test for American amphibious doctrine, techniques, and equipment. Naval gunfire vessels and carrier-based aircraft provided support during and after the assault.

The advance to the Gilberts disclosed that U. S. forces had not entirely mastered certain aspects of amphibious warfare, especially naval gunfire support, coordination of air support, and ship-to-shore communications. But valuable lessons were learned that, added to the earlier experiences of the South and Southwest Pacific Areas, established a pattern of island warfare which represented one of the major tactical developments of the war. First, air and naval forces isolated an objective and softened its defenses. Simultaneously, joint forces would attack or feint toward other islands to deceive the Japanese. The approach of convoys carrying the ground assault forces to the main objective signaled the opening of final, intensive air and naval bombardment of the landing beaches. Whenever practicable, small forces occupied neighboring islands as sites for land-based artillery. Under cover of all these supporting fires, the landing forces moved from ship to shore in echelons, or waves, rocket-firing landing craft in the lead and amphibian tanks and tractors following to carry the assault troops directly onto the beaches and inland. Finally came landing craft with more infantry and with tanks, artillery, and supporting troops. Supplies followed rapidly as the assault forces secured and expanded the beachhead. Amphibious techniques were refined and modified to some extent after the Gilberts, but the lessons learned there made it unnecessary to effect any radical changes in amphibious doctrine throughout the rest of the war.

Accelerating the Pace. The Japanese did not react strongly to the loss of the Gilberts and at the end of January Nimitz' Army and Marine forces moved into the eastern and central Marshalls to seize

Majuro and Kwajalein. The strength employed in this operation proved so preponderant and Japanese defenses so weak that Nimitz was able to accelerate his next advance by two and a half months, and on 17 February 1944 landed Marine and Army units on Eniwetok Atoll in the western Marshalls. Concurrently, he conducted a long-awaited carrier strike against Truk in the central Carolines, considered Japan's key bastion in the Central Pacific. The raid revealed that the Japanese had virtually abandoned Truk as a naval base and the capture of the atoll, set for June, no longer appeared necessary. Nimitz now drew up plans to invade the Marianas in mid-June and move on to the western Carolines and Palaus in mid-September, again accelerating the pace of the advance.

Meanwhile, General MacArthur had also pushed forward the Southwest Pacific Area's timetable. Having landed in the Admiralties a month ahead of his original schedule, he decided to cancel operations against Hansa Bay and Wewak on the northeast coast of New Guinea in favor of a jump to Hollandia and Aitape, on the north-central coast, in April, two months earlier than previously planned. He would then continue northwestward along the coast in a campaign entailing the steady extension of land-based air cover by the seizure of successive airbase sites.

On 22 April 1944 Army forces under MacArthur, supported by a Pacific Fleet carrier task force, landed at Hollandia and Aitape. At neither locale was the issue ever in doubt, although during July the Japanese bypassed at Wewak launched an abortive counterattack against Aitape. Protected by land-based air from Hollandia, MacArthur's Army units next jumped 125 miles northwest on 17 May to seize another airbase site at Wakde Island, landing first on the New Guinea mainland opposite the main objective. A ground campaign about a month and a half long ensued against a Japanese division on the mainland, but without waiting for the outcome of that fight other Army troops, on 27 May, carried the advance northwestward another 180 miles to Biak Island.

The Mutually Supporting Drives. Now the wisdom of conducting twin drives toward the Philippines emerged. The Japanese Navy was preparing for a showdown battle in the Pacific, a battle it expected to fight off the Marianas in June. MacArthur's move to Biak put land-based planes in position to keep under surveillance and to harry the Japanese fleet, which was assembling in Philippines waters before moving into the Central Pacific. Reckoning an American-controlled Biak an unacceptable thorn in their flank, the Japanese risked major elements of their fleet to send strong reinforcements there in an attempt to drive MacArthur's forces off the island. They also deployed to bases within range of Biak about half their land-based air strength from the Marianas, Carolines, and Palaus—planes upon which their fleet depended for support during the forthcoming battle off the Marianas.

Having undertaken two partially successful attempts to reinforce Biak, the Japanese assembled for a third try enough naval strength to overwhelm local American naval units, but just as the formidable force was moving toward Biak, the Japanese learned the U. S. Pacific Fleet was off the Marianas. The Japanese hastily assembled their naval forces and sailed northwestward for the engagement known as the Battle of the Philippine Sea. Having lost their chance to surprise the U. S. Navy, handicapped by belated deployment, and deprived of anticipated land-based air support, the Japanese suffered another shattering naval defeat. This defeat, which assured the success of the invasions of Biak and the Marianas, provided an illustration of the interdependence of operations in MacArthur's and Nimitz' areas, and again demonstrated that the U. S. Pacific Fleet's carrier task forces were a decisive element in the Pacific war.

Army and Marine divisions under Nimitz landed on Saipan in the Marianas on 15 June 1944 to begin a bloody three-week battle for control of the island. Next, on 21 July, Army and Marine units invaded Guam, 100 miles south of Saipan, and three days later Marines moved on to Tinian Island. An important turning point of the Pacific war, the American seizure of Marianas brought the Japanese home islands within reach of the Army Air Forces B–29 bombers, which in late November began to fly missions against Japan from Mariana fields.

At Biak Japanese resistance delayed capture of the best airfield sites until late June. On 2 July, MacArthur's Army forces moved on to Noemfoor Island, 90 miles to the west, in a combined parachute and amphibious operation designed to broaden the base of the Southwest Pacific's air deployment. On 30 July, an Army division continued on to the northwestern tip of New Guinea to secure another air base, and on 15 September MacArthur landed a reinforced Army division on Morotai Island, between New Guinea and Mindanao in the Philippines. On the same day Nimitz sent a Marine division ashore on Peleliu in the southern Palaus, and on the 17th an Army division from Nimitz' command landed on Angaur, just south of Peleliu. An Army regiment secured Ulithi Atoll, midway between Peleliu and the Marianas, on 23 September.

With these landings the approach to the Philippines was virtually completed. The occupation of Morotai proved easy and the island provided airfields for the support of advances into the Philippines and Indies. The Pacific Fleet employed Ulithi, which fell against no opposition, as a forward anchorage. Hard fighting dragged on in the Palaus through November and, as the result of another acceleration in the pace of Pacific operations, these islands never played the role originally planned for them.

In twin drives, illustrative of the principles of maneuver, objective, economy of force, surprise, and concentration of mass at vital points, the Allied forces of the Pacific had arrived in mid-September 1944 at the threshold of their strategic objective, the Luzon-Formosa-China coast triangle. In seven months MacArthur's forces had moved forward nearly 1,500 miles from the Admiralties to Morotai; in ten months Nimitz' forces had advanced over 4,500 miles from Hawaii to the Palaus. The stage was now set for the reconquest of the Philippines.

The Philippine Campaign—Acceleration. At the time of the Morotai and Palau landings, plans for the invasion of the Philippines called for a preliminary assault in southern Mindanao on 15 November to secure airbases for the support of a larger attack at Leyte, in the east-central Philippines, on 20 December. In mid-September, providing strategic support for the Morotai and Palau operations, carrier task forces under Halsey had struck the central and southern Philippines, where American planes found Japanese air strength unexpectedly weak and uncovered few signs of significant ground or naval activity. On the basis of Halsey's reports, MacArthur and Nimitz proposed to the Joint Chiefs of Staff a move directly to Leyte in October, bypassing Mindanao. The Joint Chiefs quickly approved the acceleration, and also ordered Nimitz to cancel an operation to seize Yap, between the Palaus and Ulithi. Nimitz would lend to MacArthur a three-division Army corps that had prepared for Yap, and carrier task forces of the Pacific Fleet would provide general support for Leyte. The decision, illustrating the flexibility of planning in the Pacific, again demonstrated the interdependence of MacArthur's and Nimitz' campaigns.

Leyte. The main assault at Leyte took place on 20 October 1944 with four Army divisions landing abreast in the largest amphibious operation yet conducted in the Pacific. Vice Adm. Thomas C. Kinkaid, MacArthur's naval commander, controlled the amphibious phases, including naval gunfire support and close air support by planes based on escort carriers. Ground forces were under Lt. Gen. Walter Krueger, commanding the U. S. Sixth Army; land-based air forces of the Southwest Pacific Areas, in general support, were commanded by Lt. Gen. George C. Kenney. MacArthur himself exercised unified command over the air, ground, and naval commanders. The fast carrier task forces of the Pacific Fleet, providing strategic support, operated under the control of Admiral Halsey, who reported to Nimitz, not MacArthur. There was no provision for unified naval command, and Halsey's orders were such that he could make his principal mission the destruction of the Japanese fleet rather than the support of MacArthur's entry into the Philippines.

The Japanese had originally planned to make their stand in the Philippines on Luzon, but the invasion of Leyte forced them to recon-

Gen. Douglas MacArthur and members of his staff wading ashore, Leyte.

sider, and they decided that the entire Philippine Archipelago would be strategically lost if the U. S. Army secured a foothold in the central islands. Therefore, they started sending ground reinforcements to Leyte; they increased their land-based air strength in the Philippines in the hope of destroying Allied shipping in Leyte Gulf and maintaining local air superiority; and they dispatched their remaining naval strength to Leyte Gulf to destroy Kinkaid's invasion fleet and to block Allied access to the Philippines. The ensuing air-naval Battle of Leyte Gulf was the most critical moment of the campaign, and proved one of the most decisive actions of the Pacific war.

Admiral Halsey, without consulting MacArthur or Kinkaid, pulled the bulk of his carrier forces northward to intercept part of the Japanese fleet, leaving Leyte Gulf open to other Japanese fleet units. Gallant, desperate action by Kinkaid's old battleships and escort-carrier planes turned back the Japanese in the gulf, assuring the safety of the landing forces. It had been a close thing, and an event clearly demonstrating the dangers of divided command. In the end, however, the combined operations of Kinkaid's and Halsey's forces virtually eliminated the Japanese Navy as a factor in the Pacific war.

With the Leyte beaches secure, U. S. Army units proceeded with the destruction of the Japanese ground forces. Miserable weather bogged down the pace of operations, made supply difficult, delayed airfield construction, curtailed air support, and permitted the Japanese to continue to ship reinforcements to the island. The reinforcement program came to a sudden halt early in December when an Army division executed an amphibious envelopment to Leyte's west coast, and by late December the Sixth Army had secured the most important sections of the island, those required for air and logistical bases. Japanese troops in the mountains of northwestern Leyte continued organized resistance well into the spring of 1945, occupying the energies of large portions of Lt. Gen. Robert L. Eichelberger's newly formed Eighth Army.

Strategy—Luzon, Formosa, Okinawa, and Iwo Jima. The choice of targets next after Leyte lay between Luzon and Formosa, and for months before the decision to go to Leyte the Joint Chiefs had debated the matter. Cogent arguments supported the seizure of either island, but military realities ultimately ruled in favor of Luzon. For one thing the Japanese, in the late summer and early fall of 1944, had overrun airbase sites in eastern China from which the Allies had planned to bomb Japan prior to invasion. Since the Allies did not have the means to engage in extensive land campaigns in China to retake the airfields, the China coast had been eliminated from consideration as an objective, thereby reducing the importance of Formosa as a steppingstone to China. Moreover, the Marianas already provided B–29 bases closer to Tokyo than Formosa. The Formosa operation also promised to be logistically more inexpensive than Luzon, and, finally, MacArthur could move to Luzon three months earlier than Nimitz' forces could reach Formosa.

The Joint Chiefs decided that MacArthur would jump from Leyte to Luzon in December 1944. The forces that Nimitz was assembling for Formosa would be employed to seize Okinawa and other islands in the Ryukyus, 700 miles southwest of Japan, in March 1945. This operation would provide airbases close to Japan and would give the Allies land areas on which they could develop major air and logistical bases for the support of the invasion of Japan. The Allies would also construct air and logistical bases on Luzon, while air and naval forces from Luzon, later aided by units from the Ryukyus, would sever the Japanese lines of communication to southeast Asia and the Indies.

The cancellation of Formosa and the scheduling of Okinawa for March left Nimitz' forces facing a lull in operations during the opening months of 1945, a lull inconsistent with the accepted principle of maintaining constant and unremitting pressure against the Japanese. The Joint Chiefs therefore directed Nimitz to secure Iwo Jima, 750 miles south of Tokyo, in January. The Army Air Forces were also vitally interested in Iwo, because the island could provide an emergency and staging base for B–29's making the long flight from the Marianas, as well as airfields from which fighter planes could escort the big bombers to and from Japan.

The Luzon Campaign. The first step of the Luzon Campaign was the seizure of an airbase in southwestern Mindoro, 150 miles south of Manila, on 15 December 1944, two Army regiments accomplishing the task with ease. The invasion of Luzon started on 9 January 1945, when four Army divisions landed along the shores of Lingayen Gulf. Command arrangements were similar to those at Leyte, and again fast carrier task forces under Halsey operated in general support and not under MacArthur's control. Within three days five Army divisions, a separate regimental combat team, two artillery groups, an armored group, and supporting service units were ashore and had begun a drive down the Central Plains of Luzon toward Manila. The Japanese were incapable of naval intervention at Lingayen Gulf, and their most significant reaction was to throw a number of *kamikaze* (suicide planes) attacks against Kinkaid's naval forces for four days.

Gen. Tomoyuki Yamashita, commanding Japanese forces in the Philippines, did not intend to defend the Central Plains-Manila Bay region, the strategic prize of Luzon. Knowing he would receive no reinforcements and believing the issue in the Philippines had been decided at Leyte, he sought only to pin down major elements of Mac-Arthur's forces in the hope of delaying Allied progress toward Japan. For this purpose he moved the bulk of his troops into mountain strongholds, where they could conduct a protracted, bloody defensive campaign. But Japanese naval forces on Luzon, only nominally under Yamashita, decided to ignore this concept in favor of defending Manila and Manila Bay. Thus, when U. S. Army units reached Manila on 3 February, it took them a month of bitter building-to-building fighting to root out the Japanese. Meanwhile, operations to clear Manila Bay had begun with a minor amphibious landing at the southern tip of Bataan on 15 February. The next day a combined parachute—amphibious assault, involving two Army regiments, initiated a battle to clear Corregidor Island. Other forces cleared additional islands in Manila Bay and occured the south shore. By mid-March the Bay was open for Allied shipping, but an immense salvage and repair job was necessary before the Allies could fully exploit Manila's excellent port facilities.

In the meantime a reinforced Army division had landed near Subic Bay and had cut across the base of Bataan Peninsula to prevent the Japanese from holing up on Bataan as had MacArthur's forces three years earlier. An airborne division undertook both amphibious and parachute landings in southern Luzon to start clearing that region, and an Army regimental combat team made an amphibious assault in southeastern Luzon to secure the Bicol Peninsula. Turning against the Japanese mountain strongholds, MacArthur continued to pour reinforcements onto Luzon, and the land campaign there ultimately evolved into the largest of the Pacific war. MacArthur committed to Luzon ten divisions, two regiments of another division, and three separate regimental combat teams, to mention only the major ground combat forces. Guerillas also played a large role. One guerilla unit came to substitute for a regularly constituted division, and other

Parachute Troops Landing on Corregidor.

guerilla forces of battalion and regimental size supplemented the efforts of the Army units. Moreover, the loyal and willing Filipino population immeasurably eased the problems of supply, construction, and civil administration.

Except for a strong pocket in the mountains of north-central Luzon, organized Japanese resistance ended by late June 1945. The rugged terrain in the north, coupled with rainy weather, prevented Krueger's Sixth Army from applying its full strength to the reduction of this pocket. Eichelberger's Eighth Army took over responsibility for operations on Luzon at the end of June, and continued the pressure against Yamashita's last stand area, which held out until the end of the war.

The Southern Philippines and Borneo. While Sixth Army was destroying Japanese forces on Luzon, Eighth Army ultimately employed five divisions, portions of a sixth division, a separate regimental combat team, and strong guerilla units in its campaign, which began when an Army regimental combat team landed on Palawan Island on 28 February 1945. Here engineers built an airbase from which to help cut Japan's line of communications to the south and to support later advances in the southern Philippines and the Indies. On 10 March, a regimental combat team, later reinforced, landed near Zamboanga in southwestern Mindanao, and soon thereafter Army units began moving southwest toward Borneo along the Sulu Archipelago. In rapid succession Eighth Army then landed on Panay, Cebu, northwestern Negros, Bohol, central Mindanao, southeastern Negros, northern Mindanao, and finally at Sarangani Bay in southern Mindanao, once intended as the first point of re-entry into the Philippines. At some locales bitter fighting raged for a time, but the issue was never in doubt in the southern Philippines and organized Japanese resistance there had largely collapsed by the end of May. Mopping up continued to the end of the war, with reorganized and re-equipped guerilla forces bearing much of the burden.

The last offensives in the Southwest Pacific Area started on 1 May when an Australian brigade went ashore on Tarakan Island, Borneo. Carried to the beaches by landing craft manned by U. S. Army engineers, the Australians had air support from fields on Morotai and in the southern Philippines. On 10 June an Australian division landed at Brunei Bay, Borneo, and another Australian division went ashore at Balikpapan on 1 July in what proved to be the final amphibious assault of the war.

Iwo Jima and Okinawa. Since slow base development at Leyte had forced MacArthur to delay the Luzon invasion from December to January, Nimitz in turn had to postpone his target dates for the Iwo Jima and Okinawa operations, again illustrating the interdependence of the Southwest and Central Pacific Areas. Nimitz had to change his dates primarily because the bulk of the naval resources in the Pacific—fast carrier task forces, escort carrier groups, assault shipping, naval gunfire support vessels, and amphibious assault craft—had to be shifted between the two theaters for major operations.

The Iwo Jima assault finally took place on 19 February 1945, with two Marine divisions, supported by minor Army elements, making the landings. A third Marine division reinforced, while an Army regiment ultimately took over as island garrison. The Marines had to overrun fanatic resistance from firmly entrenched Japanese who held what was probably the strongest defensive system American forces encountered during the Pacific war, and it took a month of bloody fighting to secure the island. In early March a few crippled B-29's made emergency landings on Iwo; by the end of the month an airfield was fully operational for fighter planes. Later, engineers constructed a heavy bomber field and another fighter base on the island.

The invasion of the Ryukyus began on 26 March when an Army division under Nimitz landed on the Kerama Islands, 15 miles west of Okinawa, to secure a forward naval base, a task traditionally assigned to Marines. On 1 April two Army and two Marine divisions executed the assault on the main objective, Okinawa. Two more Army divisions and a Marine infantry regiment later reinforced. Another amphibious assault took place on 16 April, when an Army division seized Ie Island, 4 miles west of Okinawa, and the final landing in the Ryukyus came on 26 June, when a small force of Marines went ashore on Kume Island, 50 miles west of Okinawa. Ground forces at Okinawa were under the U. S. Tenth Army, Lt. Gen. Simon B. Buckner commanding, at first. When General Buckner was killed on 18 June, Marine

Lt. Gen. Roy S. Geiger took over until Lt. Gen. Joseph W. Stilwell assumed command on the 23d.

The Japanese made no attempt to defend the Okinawa beaches, but instead fell back to prepared cave and tunnel defenses on inland hills. Bitterly defending every inch of ground, the Japanese continued organized resistance until late June. Meanwhile, Japanese suicide planes had inflicted extensive damage on Nimitz' naval forces, sinking about 25 ships and damaging nearly 165 more in an unsuccessful attempt to drive Allied naval power from the western Pacific. Ashore on Okinawa, small unit tactics, combined with great concentrations of naval, air, and artillery bombardments, turned the tide of the ground battle. Especially noteworthy was the close support that naval gunfire support vessels provided the ground forces, and the close air support Army, Navy, and Marine aircraft delivered.

The capture of Okinawa and other positions in the Ryukyus gave the Allies both air and naval bases within easy striking distance of Japan. By early May fighter planes from Okinawa had started flights over Japan, and as rapidly as fields became available bombers including units from the Southwest Pacific Area, came forward to mount attacks in preparation for the invasion of the home islands. The forward anchorages in the Ryukyus permitted the Pacific Fleet to keep in almost continuous action against Japanese targets. The Ryukyus campaign had brought Allied forces in the Pacific to Japan's doorstep.

Initial Efforts in the China-Burma-India Area. Except for some minor ground actions in Burma, U. S. Army combat activity in China, Burma, and India during World War II was largely limited to air operations against Japanese forces in China and Burma, and antishipping strikes over the South China Sea. But these combat operations amounted to only a small part of the U. S. Army's activities in these areas. The United States policy of keeping China in the war and increasing the potential of Generalissimo Chiang Kai-shek's ground forces required the Army to undertake a huge logistical effort in the CBI, an effort also aimed at supporting Army Air Forces operations in China.

Early in 1942 the Army sent Lt. Gen. Joseph W. Stilwell to China with the missions of maintaining an overland supply line to China through Burma and coordinating American efforts to train, equip, and supply Chinese ground units. Stilwell also became Chiang's chief of staff in the latter's capacity as Allied commander of the China theater, which nominally included not only China but also French Indo-China and Thailand. Burma, Malaya, the island of Sumatra in the Indies, Ceylon, and the waters of the Indian Ocean formed a separate Allied theater, the Southeast Asia Command, established in August 1943 under Adm. Lord Louis Mountbatten. British Army forces in India remained under Gen. Sir Claude J. E. Auchinleck. Stilwell, in addition to his other duties, commanded all U. S. Army forces in China, Burma, and India.

In May 1942 the Japanese drove British and Chinese forces (the latter operating under Stilwell) out of Burma and cut the overland route to China. For the next 18 months no significant ground activity occurred in the area, and American forces concentrated on the development of an aerial supply route to China and on training Chinese troops. From small beginnings the aerial supply operations grew until by the end of the war the Army Air Force was employing nearly 630 cargo planes to fly supplies into China over the dangerous "hump" in a continuous effort to support the Chinese Army and the Army Air Forces' own operations.

CBI Developments in 1944 and 1945. The aerial supply route could not support all needs—a land route was required to aid the Chinese, to build up means for planned campaigns against the Japanese, and to help develop the air bases in eastern China from which the United States intended to undertake bombardment of Japan in preparation for invasion of the home islands. Moreover, the air effort was expensive in transport aircraft, which, from the global point of view, were scarce. Work accordingly began in 1943 on the southwestern section of a new road (the Ledo Road) from India across northern Burma to China.

In October 1943 Chinese troops under Stilwell had started to clear northern Burma, and in the spring of 1944, a U. S. Army regiment, Merrill's Marauders, and parts of another Army regiment, spearheaded new offensives to secure the route for the overland road. Through most of 1944 operations in northern Burma were indecisive, although enough terrain was secured for engineers to push road construction and to start laying a pipeline 1,800 miles from India to China. Meanwhile, within China, U. S. Army Air Forces units under Maj. Gen. Claire L. Chennault stepped up the pace of their operations, and B–29 bombers, based in India, began using a few fields in China to stage strikes against targets in Manchuria, Korea, and Japan.

The Japanese reacted strongly to the increased air effort and beginning in April 1944 launched ground offensives that overran most of the existing fields and proposed air base sites in eastern China. By late summer the Japanese controlled most of the area from which bombers had been expected to fly against Japan. As already noted, this Japanese success had much to do with eliminating the China coast as a factor in the strategic plan for projecting Allied strength into the Luzon-Formosa-China coast triangle, and helped prompt the decision to move to Luzon rather than Formosa.

With the Chinese unable to halt the Japanese, the aim of Allied strategy in China became limited to keeping alive some semblance of

Chinese resistance.   Relations between Stilwell and Chiang became strained, and in October 1944 Maj. Gen. Albert C. Wedemeyer replaced Stilwell as Chiang's chief of staff and commander of U. S. Army forces in China.   Army units in Burma and India passed to the command of Maj. Gen. Dan I. Sultan as Commanding General, India-Burma Theater, an Army administrative and logistical organization.   Sultan's missions were to push construction of the Ledo Road and the laying of the pipeline across northern Burma, to help the Army Air Forces step up the flow of supplies into China, and, in general, to support the China Theater and Chennault's air operations.

U. S. Army ground combat operations in both China and Burma now ceased, and the Army turned its attention to training Chinese forces, providing advisors for Chinese divisions in the field, and planning a drive to the China coast that never transpired.   The Chinese ultimately cleared part of northern Burma.   British forces, whose offenses in central and southern Burma began to show results in late 1944, carried the rest of the combat load in Burma.   By the end of the war Japanese resistance had collapsed in most of Burma and the Japanese had begun withdrawing their forces from southern and eastern China to Manchuria and the homeland.   From hopeful beginnings, the CBI had sunk to the status of a sideshow in Allied strategy for the defeat of Japan.

The End of the Pacific War.   Since they could make no effort to restore the situation in China, Allied forces in the Pacific, during the summer of 1945, stepped up the pace of air and naval attacks against Japan.   In June and July carrier-based planes of the U. S. Pacific Fleet and Army Air Forces planes from the Marianas, Iwo Jima, and Okinawa struck the Japanese home islands continuously.   During July Pacific Fleet surface units bombarded Japan's east coast, and in the same month a British carrier task force joined in attacking on Japan.   Meanwhile, Army planes from the Philippines hit Japanese shipping in the South China Sea, and extended their strikes as far as Formosa and targets along the South China coast.   At the same time American submarines redoubled their efforts to sweep Japanese shipping from the sea and sever the shipping lanes from Japan to the Indies and southeast Asia.   Throughout the war submarines had preyed on Japanese merchant and combat vessels, playing a major role in isolating Japan from its conquests and thereby drastically reducing Japan's ability to wage war.

After Germany's surrender in May the United States had embarked upon a huge logistical effort to redeploy more than a million troops from Europe, the United States, and other inactive theaters to the Pacific.   The aim was to complete the redeployment in time to launch an invasion of Japan on 1 November, and the task had to be undertaken in the face of competing shipping demands for demobilization of long-service troops, British redeployment, and civil relief in Europe. By the time the war ended, some 150,000 men had moved directly from Europe to the Pacific, but a larger transfer from the United States across the Pacific had scarcely begun. In the Pacific, MacArthur and Nimitz had been sparing no efforts to expand ports and ready bases to receive the expected influx and to mount invasion forces. The two commanders were also completing plans for the invasion of Japan, while the Joint Chiefs of Staff had appointed MacArthur to the command of all U. S. Army forces in the Pacific, simultaneously giving Nimitz control of all U. S. Navy elements.

By mid-summer of 1945 most responsible leaders in Japan realized that the end was near. In June, those favoring peace began to come out in the open, and Japan sent out peace feelers through the Soviet Union, which they feared might also be about to enter the war. As early as the Yalta Conference of February 1945 Churchill, Roosevelt, and Stalin had discussed Russian participation in the war against Japan, and throughout 1945 American planners understood that Russia would come into the war three months after the defeat of Germany. At the Potsdam Conference in July 1945, Russia reaffirmed its decision to declare war on Japan. At this conference the United States and Britain, with China joining in, issued the famed Potsdam Declaration calling upon Japan to surrender promptly, and about the same time President Truman decided to employ the newly tested atomic bomb against Japan in the event of continued Japanese resistance.

Despite the changing climate of opinion in Japan, the Japanese did not immediately accept the terms of the Potsdam Declaration. Accordingly, on 6 August a lone American B-29 from the Marianas dropped an atomic bomb on Hiroshima. On the 9th the Soviet Union came into the war and attacked Japanese forces in Manchuria; on the same day another B-29 dropped a second atomic bomb on Nagasaki. The next day Japan sued for peace, and with the signing of surrender terms aboard the U. S. S. *Missouri* in Tokyo Bay on 2 September the bitter global war had come to an end.

Summary and Analysis. In winning the Pacific war the Allies had found it unnecessary to press home their attacks and destroy the Japanese military forces except for the Japanese fleet. By the end of the war Japan's navy had virtually ceased to exist; Japanese industry had been so hammered by air bombardment that Japan's ability to wage war had been seriously reduced; and submarine and air actions had cut off sources of raw material. At the time of the surrender Japan still had 2,000,000 men under arms in the homeland and was capable of conducting a tenacious ground defense. About 3,000 Japanese aircraft were also operational. Nevertheless, the Japanese could not have continued the war for more than a few months. On the other hand, the fact that an invasion had not been necessary certainly spared many American lives.

Atomic Bombing of Nagasaki, 9 August 1945.

The great arbiter of the Pacific war had been American industrial power, which produced a mighty war machine. Out of this production had come the Pacific Fleet, a potent force that could overcome the vast reaches of the Pacific upon which the Japanese had depended so heavily as a defensive advantage. The decisive combat element of the fleet was the fast carrier task force, which carried the war deep into Japanese territory and supported advances far beyond the range of land-based aircraft. Land-based air power also played a decisive part in the war. When carriers were not available to support offensives, it was land-based aviation that measured the distance of each forward move. Land-based aviation also proved important in providing close support for ground operations, while aerial supply operations and troop movements contributed greatly to the success of the Allied campaigns.

Both naval and air forces were dependent upon shore bases, and the war in the Pacific demonstrated that even in a predominantly naval-air theater, ground combat forces are an essential part of the offensive team. The Japanese had also been dependent upon far-flung bases, and much of the Allied effort during the war had gone into the seizure or neutralization of Japan's bases. Thus, the Pacific war was in large measure a war for bases. On the other hand the U. S. Pacific Fleet, in one of the greatest logistical developments of the war, went far in the direction of carrying its bases with it by organizing fleet trains of support vessels that were capable of maintaining the fleet at sea over extended periods.

The development and employment of amphibious assault techniques was another important facet of the Pacific war, and one that repeatedly demonstrated the need for joint, unified command. Air, ground, and naval teamwork supremely important in the Pacific war, occasionally broke down, but the success of the Allied campaigns illustrates that all three elements achieved the necessary teamwork to a large degree. Strategic air bombardment in the Pacific, designed to cripple Japan's industrial capacity, did not get underway until 1945 was well along. The damage inflicted on Japanese cities was enormous, but the net effect, as in the case of the bomber offensive against Germany, remains unsettled. The submarine, on the other hand, certainly played a vital role in reducing Japan's capabilities by taking a huge toll of Japanese shipping and by helping to cut Japan off from the resources of southeast Asia.

In the final analysis Japan lost because the country did not have the means to fight a total war against the combination of industrial, air, naval, and human resources represented by the United States, the United Kingdom, and the British Commonwealth of Nations. Admiral Isoroku Yamamoto, commander of Japanese Fleet at the outbreak of war, put his finger on the fatal weakness of the Japanese concept of war when he stated: "It is not enough that we should take

Guam and the Philippines, or even Hawaii and San Francisco. We should have to march into Washington and sign the treaty in the White House." This the Japanese could never do, and because they could not they had to lose the war.

QUESTIONS

1. What was the major weakness of the Japanese strategy at the outset of the war? What were the reasons for the initial success of the Japanese plan?

2. What strategy did the Allies adopt against Rabaul? Why did they finally decide not to capture it?

3. Describe the two routes by which the Allies advanced toward the Philippines. Give an example of mutual support between the forces along these two routes.

4. In what ways was unity of command illustrated in the war against Japan?

5. Describe the tactics of amphibious assault. How did carrier-based aircraft increase the distance of Allied advance?

6. Analyze the principles of war as applied in the invasion of Iwo Jima.

7. Why does amphibious warfare require teamwork among the three services?

8. What became the ultimate mission of the China-Burma-India Theater during World War II?

9. Summarize the major reasons for Allied victory over Japan in World War II.

Reading List

THE U. S. ARMY IN WORLD WAR II:

Appleman, Roy E., *et al. Okinawa: The Last Battle.* Washington, 1948.

Cannon M. Hamlin. *Leyte: The Return to the Philippines.* Washington, 1954.

Crowl, Philip A., and Edmund G. Love. *Seizure of the Gilberts and Marshalls.* Washington, 1955.

Miller, John, jr. *Guadalcanal: The First Offensive.* Washington, 1949.

----------. *CARTWHEEL: The Reduction of Rabaul.* Washington, 1959.

Milner, Samuel. *Victory in Papua.* Washington, 1957.

Morton, Louis. *The Fall of the Philippines.* Washington, 1953.

Office of the Chief of Military History. *Pictorial Record: The War Against Japan.* Washington, 1951.

Romanus, Charles F., and Riley Sunderland. *Stilwell's Mission to China*. Washington, 1953.

———. *Stilwell's Command Problems*. Washington, 1956.

———. *Time Runs Out in CBI*. Washington, 1959.

Smith, Robert Ross. *The Approach to the Philippines*. Washington, 1953.

Stauffer, Alvin P. *The Quartermaster Corps: Operations in the War Against Japan*. Washington, 1956.

THE ARMY AIR FORCES IN WORLD WAR II:

Craven, Wesley F., and James L. Cate (Eds.). I. *Plans and Early Operations*. Chicago, 1948.

———. IV. *The Pacific: Guadalcanal to Saipan*. Chicago, 1950.

———. V. *The Pacific: MATTERHORN to Nagasaki*. Chicago, 1953.

HISTORY OF UNITED STATES NAVAL OPERATIONS IN WORLD WAR II:

Morison, Samuel E. III. *The Rising Sun in the Pacific*. Boston, 1948.

———. IV. *Coral Sea, Midway, and Submarine Actions*. Boston, 1950.

———. V. *The Struggle for Guadalcanal*. Boston, 1951.

———. VI. *Breaking the Bismarcks Barrier*. Boston, 1950.

———. VII. *Aleutians, Gilberts and Marshalls*. Boston, 1951.

———. VIII. *New Guinea and the Marianas*. Boston, 1953.

———. XII. *Leyte. June 1944—January 1945*. Boston, 1958.

Eichelberger, Robert L. *Our Jungle Road to Tokyo*. New York, 1950.

Krueger, Walter. *From Down Under to Nippon*. Washington, 1953.

Volckmann, Russell W. *We Remained*. New York, 1954.

CHAPTER 24

1945–1950

The United Nations. By the end of World War II a radical change had taken place in America's position in world affairs. After two major wars in a single generation, the political leaders of the United States believed that only through participation in a collective security organization could the Nation remain free. This radical shift in American policy had a profound effect on all phases of national policy but chiefly on military and foreign affairs.

In searching for the means to preserve peace the United States and its allies agreed that something more than words would be needed. The Atlantic Charter of 1941 marked the first step in this quest for a positive instrument of world peace. In this declaration President Roosevelt and England's Prime Minister, Winston Churchill, not only restated the principles of international collaboration but also looked forward to "the establishment of a wider and more permanent system of general security." Following this, in 1943 at Moscow, the United States, Great Britain, Russia, and China signed a declaration that called for, among other things, an international organization with some form of effective force to maintain international peace and security. Further conferences at Dumbarton Oaks in 1944 and at Yalta in 1945 continued to stress such an organization. Finally, the leading nations of the world meeting at San Francisco in 1945, established the United Nations Organization.

The charter of the United Nations incorporated the ideas and principles enunciated in the wartime conferences and recognized the measures that were necessary to maintain peace; "effective collective measures" were to be taken "for the prevention and removal of threats to the peace and for the suppression of acts of aggression", and authority was granted for the use of armed force if peaceful means failed to resolve the threat. The Security Council was to have sole authority and responsibility to determine when the peace was threatened and what action or actions might be taken to restore amity, including the use of armed force. The charter also gave the Security Council the authority to call on member states to furnish armed forces when the council decided such action was necessary.

Demobilization. One of the chief reactions to the end of the war was the American desire to return immediately to normal life. This meant changing over American industry from the production of armaments to civilian goods, drastically cutting armament expenditures, and sharply reducing military strength. The demobilization of the wartime army became the Army's most immediate and pressing problem.

Demobilization planning. Planning for demobilization of the Army began in 1943, over two years before the end of the war. As a basis for planning, officials of the War Department assumed that (1) the United States would emerge as the world's foremost military power and would be prepared for action in many parts of the world; (2) the war in Europe would terminate before the Japanese surrender; (3) the United States would furnish an important share of large-scale occupation troops; and (4) public opinion would demand a rapid demobilization. The initial planning was based on the amount of shipping that would become available for transferring the troops, and the number of troops to be deployed to the Pacific to speed up the offensive against the Japanese. For planning purposes it was estimated that the war against Japan would last at least a year after the surrender of Germany. During this interim, the first demobilization period, the flaws that developed in the demobilization system could be eliminated and the system would undergo considerable revision before being used after final victory. The second period of demobilization would be that following the defeat of Japan but prior to the attainment of normal peacetime conditions; and the third period that in which the Army would be composed of permanent military personnel.

Although the unit system of demobilization had been the type most often used in the past by the United States Army and had many advantages, still the troops in World War II had been mobilized on an individual basis and, therefore, the proponents for the individual system argued, should be discharged individually. The natural outgrowth of this method was the Adjusted Service Rating or "point system." This method gave each individual a number of points for length of service, combat participation and awards, time spent overseas, and parenthood. By these impartial means those men who had been in the service the longest and participated in combat would be released from the service first.

The actual demobilization plan, including the basic policies and the execution, was set forth in draft form in August 1944 although the specific points were not finally decided on until 23 April 1945. Immediately on the surrender of Germany, 8 May, it was announced that redeployment would begin on 12 May. Planning was immediately started on the second period demobilization, based on the assumption that V–J Day would not take place for 18 months. But the surrender of Japan in August 1945 left the War Department with incomplete plans. Consequently the current plan was modified and emergency provisions quickly drawn up.

Drastic Reduction of the Army. Large-scale demobilization went into effect immediately after Japan surrendered. At that time the Army's strength stood at 8,020,000 men. At the end of the fiscal year 1946 the total 1,889,690 represented a decrease of 6,133,614 in the 9-month period that followed V–J Day. From then on the decline became more gradual. The reasons behind this rapid demobilization were varied. They included: public pressure on the Army to speed up the return of personnel to civil life; the lack of men under voluntary enlistment; a decreasing budget; the nonworkable selective service extension of 1946; and the terminal leave act of the same year.

The War Department, meanwhile, had instituted an intensive recruiting campaign that brought in over one million volunteers by October 1946, and brought the Army to its authorized strength. Because of this the War Department decided not to induct any more men under the Selective Service Act and the act was allowed to expire. The Army then completed its demobilization program by 30 June 1947 when the last nonvolunteers were discharged.

The effects of demobilization. The breakdown in planned demobilization under public pressure and fiscal restrictions sharply reduced the combat effectiveness of practically every unit. Indiscriminate release of men from the service left units without the necessary trained personnel to operate and maintain arms and equipment. This lack of trained maintenance personnel caused vast amounts of complex equipment to deteriorate. Near the end of 1945 Generals Eisenhower and MacArthur estimated that their ground troops could operate in an emergency for a limited period at about 50 percent of wartime efficiency. Although in November 1945, Mr. Patterson stated that the cut in planned strength for 1946 would not have an adverse effect on United States national policy, it was publicly admitted by other War Department officials that there was no relation whatsoever between the rate of demobilization and any future plans for the Army. And at the same time American diplomats abroad protested this weakening of United States military strength and stated that it made their efforts in combating Russian intransigency less effective. Their pleas were largely ignored, and by June 1947 the United States Army had been reduced to a shadow of its wartime strength.

Military Reorganization. Postwar changes in the Armed Forces were designed to attain effective military strength at minimum cost to the economy and to provide the means of implementing national policy by coordinating military planning with that of other departments and agencies of the Government. Congress enacted the necessary legislation to effect these changes with the passage of the National Security Act in 1947. This legislation, as the act states, was intended "to provide for the establishment of integrated policies and procedures for the departments, agencies and functions of the Government relating to national security . . . to provide for the effective strategic direction of the armed forces and for their operation under unified control and for their integration into an efficient team of land, naval and air forces." The principal features of the act were creation of the National Security Council, organization of the National Military Establishment headed by a Secretary of Defense, and establishment of the Air Force as a separate arm.

The National Security Council. Under the act of 1947 the National Security Council consisted of the President, the Secretaries of State and Defense, the Service Secretaries, and the Chairman of the National Security Resources Board. (This latter body also was authorized by the act.) The National Security Council advised the President on matters of coordinating military, foreign, and domestic policies as they pertained to national defense. Specifically, the Council made recommendations to the President on national policies with relationship to the Nation's military strength. The Council also advised the Chief Executive on policies pertaining to national security as they affected the several departments of Government. Finally, the Council carried out duties directed by the President to coordinate the policies of the several departments that related to national security.

The National Military Establishment. Prior to World War II, proposals designed to bring the Armed Forces under unified command had few positive results. The World War II arrangements for joint strategic direction and for unity of command in the theaters were applied with outstanding success, but did not carry with them any corresponding unity in the administrative establishments of the War and Navy Departments. And the wartime arrangements were temporary ones that gave way to separatist tendencies at war's end, particularly in the Pacific.

During the war a number of studies were made, and plans drawn up by the War Department, the Joint Chiefs of Staff, and individual legislators, for uniting the Army and Navy under a single head. After the war the Army continued its efforts at unification but met strong opposition from the Navy. On the other hand, the Army Air Forces supported unification, with the additional objective of attaining status as a separate and equal service.

The efforts dating back to 1912 to bring the military services under unified control culminated in the passage of the National Security Act of 1947 providing for the organization of a National Military Establishment under a Secretary of Defense. The unification provisions of the Act were essentially a compromise between the Army's desire for strong centralized control vested in a single Secretary and the Navy's desire for separate and autonomous departments. The National Military Establishment, as provided by the Act, consisted of the Departments of the Army, Navy, and Air Force, and the Office of the Secretary of Defense. Included within the latter were the Joint Chiefs of Staff, the Munitions Board, and the Research and Development Board. The Secretary of Defense was made a member of the President's Cabinet and became responsible for formulating general policy in the Establishment, exercising general direction and control over the armed forces and supervision of the Department's budgets. He was also charged with coordinating the logistics systems of the various services to eliminate waste and duplication. In his efforts he was to have the assistance of the Munitions Board, charged with planning for the military aspects of industrial mobilization and coordination of military production, procurement and distribution plans, and of the Research and Development Board, charged with responsibility for formulation of the military research and development program. Each service retained most of its autonomy since all three were to be "separately administered" as executive departments under the Secretary of Defense and each had direct access to the President and representation on the National Security Council through its civilian secretary. The act implicitly recognized the role claimed for air power by its proponents by making the Air Force a separate and independent service. Finally, the National Security Act made the Joint Chiefs of Staff a statutory body and charged them with the function of acting as "principal military advisers to the President, the National Security Council, and the Secretary of Defense." Under the direction and authority of the President and the Secretary of Defense, the Joint Chiefs were to be responsible for formulation of strategic plans, joint logistic plans, joint training policies, and policies for coordinating military education, for review of major materiel and personnel requirements of all armed services in the light of strategic plans, establishment of unified commands in strategic areas, and "strategic direction of the Military Forces."

Service Roles and Missions. The National Security Act did not spell out the particular roles and missions of the three services nor their relationship to the Joint Chiefs and the unified commands they were to establish. On these points broad interservice agreements were reached at Key West and Newport in 1948. By these agreements, the JCS were to have general direction of all combat operations but would not exercise this authority directly as a corporate body. Instead they would designate "one of their members as their executive agent" for each of the unified commands. In the division of service responsibilities, the Army was given the primary functions of organizing, equipping and training forces for operations on land, providing Army forces for air defense of the United States and occupation of territories abroad. The Navy and Air Forces were assigned similar functions of preparing forces for sea and land-based operations respectively. The Navy retained control of sea-based aviation and of the Marine Corps with the tactical aviation that supported it. Otherwise, Air Force jurisdiction over everything that flew was virtually complete including strategic air warfare, air transport, and combat air support of the Army. No mention at all was made of the relatively new field of guided missiles.

Tactical Reorganization. Within the Army a number of changes took place in the tactical organization of field units as a result of both experience gained in World War II and the development of new weapons. Most of these changes reflected the great emphasis on fire power and mobility. For instance, the emergence of the tank-infantry-artillery team as a dominant factor in the tactical employment of ground troops led to the inclusion of a tank battalion in the organization of the infantry division and a tank company in the infantry regiment. At the same time the cannon and antitank companies were dropped from the regiment, but the loss of these weapons was made up by adding a 4.2″ mortar company and recoilless rifles to the regiment. Division fire power was increased by adding an antiaircraft battalion and by upping the number of howitzers in each artillery battery from four to six. Research for better clothing, rations, engineer, transportation, signal, and other equipment resulted in vast improvement of these items. The success of airborne operations in the war and the necessity for rapid deployment of troops in combat led to further refinements in this form of troop employment. In the field of nuclear fission and jet and rocket propulsion the Ordnance Corps launched a long-range program to explore the use of these new forces. The Corps' research centered around development of atomic artillery projectiles and guided ground-to-ground and ground-to-air missiles as a further addition to the fire power of field armies. At the same time the Ordnance Corps continued research to improve the standard weapons. One new type of weapon, the recoilless rifles, emerged from this research shortly after the end of the war. Light enough to be hand-carried, these rifles fired 57-mm and 75-mm high explosive shells without any recoil, thereby greatly increasing the fire power of the infantry. During World War II the Navy and Air Force took over the mission of seacoast defense while the Coast Artillery Corps, which had been charged principally with harbor defense, devoted its efforts almost exclusively to antiaircraft artillery, which frequently performed a dual role by delivering fire on ground targets. Consequently, in the interest of flexibility and economy of force the antiaircraft artillery was merged with the field artillery and the Coast Artillery Corps was abolished. Similarly the mechanization of the Army made the horse cavalry obsolete. Before the end of World War II the horse cavalry had either been mechanized or fought as infantry. In the reorganization armor was made a continuation of the cavalry with all the traditions and honors of the earlier arm.

The Army School System. The Army school system came in for its share of reorganization and refinement after World War II. The scope of instruction was broadened to keep abreast of the development of new weapons and new strategical and tactical concepts. The interdependence of foreign and military policies and of the armed services, as illustrated in the war, placed greater emphasis on the joint aspects of all military operations while the technical advances made during and after the conflict called for highly specialized training of officers and enlisted men. Besides expanding the instruction given in its schools the Army took steps to enlarge the school system itself. The Army War College, closed during the war, was reopened to prepare selected Army officers for duty as commanders and as General Staff officers at the highest United States Army levels. On the recommendation of the Army, the Joint Chiefs of Staff organized three schools to train senior officers of the armed forces and selected civilians in planning and executing joint strategy and mobilization of the Nation's resources during war. The first, the Armed Forces Staff College, was established to train selected officers of the Army, Navy, and Air Force in planning and executing joint military operations, such as occurred in World War II. The second, the Industrial College of the Armed Forces, was established to train senior officers of the three armed services in the many aspects of mobilizing the Nation's resources for war. The third, the National War College, was established to train selected officers of the armed forces and of the civilian governmental departments for duties connected with the execution of national policy.

The Reserve Components. The requirements of a strong postwar force for national security called for changes in the status and organization of the Country's Reserve components. As inheritors of the Militia system that dated back to colonial times, the National Guard and the Organized Reserve Corps, who made up the Reserve components, played a major part in America's participation in both world wars. Now, the speed with which modern war can be initiated and the advances in the technology of warfare placed the emphasis on actual rather than potential strength. But, since it was not economically feasible to maintain a large and permanent ground force, the Army, shortly after the end of the war, began reorganization of the Reserve components in order to make them an integral part of the Army of the United States and to bring them to a state of readiness for combat. The goal of this reorganization was a National Guard capable of immediate mobilization with fully trained and equipped units ready to fight anywhere in the world in defense of the United States and an Organized Reserve Corps trained and organized for rapid mobilization and expansion to supplement the Regular Army and National Guard. Both components began working toward accomplishment of their respective missions. With an authorized strength of 350,000 men (its actual strength was about 75,000 less) the National Guard organized infantry and armored divisions, regimental combat teams, artillery battalions, and supporting units. The Reserve Corps, with 750,000 men on its rolls, organized along similar lines. Both components established training programs under active Army guidance. The enactment, in 1948, of Selective Service and legislation that authorized inactive duty training pay and retirement benefits added impetus to this program. As a result of these efforts the National Guard and Organized Reserve Corps contributed hundreds of thousands of trained men during the Korean conflict.

Morale. Since combat effectiveness is a dependent upon morale as it is upon training and weapons the Army took steps to improve the welfare of its troops. In late 1945 the War Department appointed a board of officers, headed by Lt. Gen. James Doolittle, to explore methods whereby the personal welfare of the individual soldier could be improved. The board put forward many recommendations that were adopted in one form or another. For instance the board restated the well-known principle that *esprit de corps* depended on leadership, and that leadership could be improved by better selection of officers and noncommissioned officers. The board recommended that these leaders be given more effective training. The Department of Defense adopted the "Uniform Code of Military Justice" to apply to all the services. As another step, the troop information and education program, established during the war, became a permanent function of command. The chief objectives of this program were to impart to the individual soldier a cooperative spirit in accomplishing any mission, pride in his unit and himself, and appreciation of world-wide happenings in order that he might understand the necessity for his service. The program also continued the opportunity for the individual soldier to improve and increase his education so that he might better perform his current assignment and prepare himself for positions of increasing responsibility.

Occupation. The U. S. Army overseas during this period was deployed over a large part of the world carrying out a number of various missions. The larger part of this force was concentrated in Germany and Japan to carry out United States occupation policies.

American occupation policy in Europe stemmed from the agreements made between Prime Minister Churchill, President Roosevelt, and Premier Joseph Stalin at Yalta in February 1945 and elaborated upon at the Potsdam Conference in July 1945. In brief, these agreements called for the complete disarmament and demilitarization of Germany, elimination of all vestiges of the Nazi Party, and reconstruction of political life on democratic principles. In the economic field Germany was forbidden to manufacture armaments, and the production of consumer goods and agricultural products was stressed. Also

Germany was divided into four zones of occupation—British, French, Soviet, and U. S.—for purposes of administering the occupation, but economically it was to be treated as a single unit. The city of Berlin, deep within the Soviet Zone, was similarly divided, thus creating further fragmentation within a divided country and complicating the problems of occupation. Reparations were to be paid by the removal of stipulated industries and by the appropriation of external German assets. Each zone commander governed his own zone. Matters concerning Germany as a whole were dealt with by the Allied Control Council, which consisted of the four zone commanders.

The Army carried out its occupation responsibilities, delineated in a directive from the Joint Chiefs of Staff, chiefly through the Office of Military Government for Germany. This office took measures to disband the German military forces in the American Zone. More than eight million German soldiers, sailors, and airmen were returned to civil life after careful screening. German military installations in the zone were disposed of or destroyed along with factories employed to manufacture arms. Military Government also prevented a resurgence of armament manufacture by keeping close surveillance of the remaining German industries and setting a level of production that restricted industries readily convertible to the making of arms.

Destruction of the Nazi Party proceeded rapidly. Military and civilian personnel accused or suspected of war crimes and all members of the party who were more than nominal participants were apprehended. German courts of "denazification," closely supervised by Army personnel, tried over 800,000 German men and women on various charges. Meanwhile an international tribunal tried the major leaders of the Nazi Party for crimes against humanity. Of these, 10 were eventually executed. Removal of Nazis from all public offices, from the courts, and from the police organization; abolition of party propaganda; and the institution of free elections completed the destruction of Hitler's organization. Meanwhile, in the absence of a German government, the Office of Military Government for Germany governed the zone. The edicts of Military Government for control of the population and for the general security of the United States Zone were enforced through the U. S. Constabulary. This special, highly mobile force operated throughout the whole zone as a police force to maintain order and discipline among the people and to detect and prevent uprisings.

In contrast to the procedures adopted for the German occupation, the Big Three Powers did not lay down any general policy for governing Japan. Instead, the United States, acting for the United Nations, assumed exclusive control of the defeated nation and established the occupation policy to be followed. This policy, drawn up jointly by the War, Navy, and State Departments and approved by President Truman, stripped Japan of all her empire and limited her sovereignty to the Japanese home islands, disarmed and demilitarized the nation, encouraged the development of a democratic government, and permitted development of an economy to meet the peacetime requirements of the Japanese people. Finally, the policy called for military occupation under a Supreme Commander, Allied Powers, to enforce the surrender and control of Japan but charged the Supreme Commander to work through the Japanese Government, including the emperor, whenever possible.

General of the Army Douglas MacArthur became Supreme Commander for the occupation of Japan and immediately began implementing the program. In September 1945 General MacArthur directed the Japanese Government to demobilize and dissolve the country's armed forces. The Government accomplished the actual tasks without incident under the supervision of the occupation army. By December 1945 all elements of the military forces of Japan in the home islands were disbanded. At the same time high officials of the Army and Navy and of the Government were arrested and tried for war crimes. An international tribunal, similar to the one in Germany, sat in judgment on 25 of these officials. Seven were given the death penalty and subsequently executed. Lesser officials were tried and sentenced by United States military commissions in Japan.

Removal of the militarists from power enabled the more democratic elements to transform the Japanese Government into a constitutional democracy. Under supervision of the Supreme Commander extensive political and governmental reorganization took place. By 1948 the legislation necessary to implement the new constitution, adopted the previous year, had been enacted and the Diet emerged as the representative body of the people.

The Cold War. Before World War II had been long ended, the Soviet Union gave every appearance of having abandoned the nominal cooperation that had existed during the war. Violating his wartime pledges, Stalin brought Poland, Czechoslovakia, and all the Balkan nations except Greece under Soviet domination. Greece, meanwhile, was in the throes of civil war, with the rebels receiving aid and comfort from Communist Bulgaria and Yugoslavia. Efforts to solve occupation problems ran into Soviet-created road blocks and Germany remained a vexing problem. In the Middle East, Soviet troops remained in Iran after the agreed upon deadline for their removal had passed. Turkey felt strong Soviet pressure for exclusive rights in connection with the Dardenelles. In the Far East, a Soviet-sponsored, Communist government fastened itself on Korea north of the 38th Parallel. Communists fanned the sparks of rebellion in Malaya, the Philippines, and Indo-China. Chinese Communist armies were fighting a full-scale war against the Nationalist Government of Chiang Kai-shek. The tension thus aroused was heightened by the existence of a huge Soviet army, by intensified Soviet propaganda and subversive activities, and by the development of nuclear weapons.

Economic Assistance. Since the end of the war the United States had been assisting Europe to get back on her feet economically. Nearly three billion dollars had been allotted the Army for relief in the occupied areas of Europe and the Far East. Additional billions had been given to support the United Nations Relief and Rehabilitation Agency. But more than interim aid was needed. With large areas devastated by the fighting, industries destroyed, and millions homeless and on the verge of starvation it was obvious that Europe could not rebuild its economy without outside help. In addition, the Soviet Union aggravated the situation by sealing off eastern Europe with its highly productive agriculture from the rest of the Continent. Efforts to resolve the differences between the Russians and the Western Powers failed at the Moscow Conference of March-April 1947. As the economic crisis deepened and relations with the Soviet Union deteriorated further, the United States moved to bring order out of the economic chaos and materially strengthen the nations of Europe.

In March 1947 President Truman went before the Congress and asked for $400,000,000 to provide economic and military assistance for Greece and Turkey. After some debate, the Congress, in May 1947, granted President Truman's request. A few weeks later, General Marshall, then Secretary of State, in June of the same year proposed that the United States, in cooperation with the nations of Europe, including the Soviet Union and its satellites, launch a program of economic assistance that would lead to rehabilitation of the European economy. The general felt that economic stability in Europe was a prerequisite to world peace and that America must do every thing possible to foster this stability. President Truman called a special session of Congress in October 1947 to act on General Marshall's proposals, which became known as the "Marshall Plan." Meanwhile a meeting of the "Big Four" Foreign Ministers in London in November failed to accomplish anything. Finally, in April 1948, the Congress enacted the necessary legislation authorizing the European Recovery Program, or Marshall Plan. It authorized the Government to contribute more than 12 billion dollars over a period of four years to assist European economic recovery.

The Berlin Blockade. Soviet counteraction to American efforts to rebuild the European economy came swiftly. Besides rejecting participation in the program the Russians, in October 1947, announced the organization of a permanent committee for coordinating the activities of the Communist parties in Europe. Then, as the United States

Congress enacted the Marshall Plan, Soviet military authorities in Berlin began cutting off the city from the rest of western Europe. In Berlin each occupying power administered its own sector and matters pertaining to the city as a whole were supposed to be settled in an Allied Control Council by unanimous agreement. But from the time of its creation disagreement marked the deliberations of this body and led to the division of the city into an east and west Berlin. By June 1948 the Russians had cut off all land and water traffic with Berlin and the only means of entry was by air. Gen. Lucius D. Clay, the American Military Governor of Germany, then called on the Air Force to supply the city with food and other necessities by air. From June 1948 to May 1949 the Air Force and the Army, working together, kept the city supplied. Hundreds of American aircraft (there were also some British planes operating in this airlift) daily flew thousands of tons of food, clothing, coal, and other vital goods into the western sectors of Berlin. By the spring of 1949 a daily average of 8,000 tons of supplies reached the capital by air.

In addition to calling for the airlift General Clay immediately halted all shipments of goods from West Germany into the Soviet Zone of Germany. The British commander imposed a similar restriction, and by the spring of 1948 East Germany felt the shortage of industrial goods and materiel that she normally received from the West. The successful efforts of the Air Force and the Army to keep the city supplied and the Anglo-American counterblockade brought realization to the Communists that their efforts to drive the Western Powers out of Berlin had failed, and the blockade of the city was lifted 12 May 1949.

The North Atlantic Treaty. Although the failure of the Berlin blockade demonstrated American ability to counter Soviet moves, the events of 1948 and earlier clearly indicated that stronger measures were needed to block any further extension of Communist power.

A beginning toward collective security in Europe was made in early 1948 when the Low Countries, England, and France signed a treaty of mutual economic and military assistance. This was followed by Senate authorization to enter into defensive alliances and give military assistance to countries joining with the United States in preserving peace. This action cleared the way for the United States to join with Canada and the powers of Western Europe in a defensive alliance. This pact, called the North Atlantic Treaty, united Great Britain, the United States, and 10 western European nations in a common security system. Approved by the Senate in April 1949, the treaty provided for mutual assistance, including the use of armed force in the event of attack upon one or more of the signatory powers. To make the treaty an effective instrument rather than a paper agreement, the member nations established a supreme military headquarters in Europe under the command of General Eisenhower to organize and plan the defense of western Europe and its approaches. Each country earmarked forces to be placed under this command, which received the title of Supreme Headquarters, Allied Powers Europe.

Mutual Defense Assistance. While negotiations leading to the North Atlantic Treaty were under way in 1948, the National Security Council had been considering the matter of military aid to non-Communist nations. Under a number of different programs, some of them a continuation of World War II aid, the United States had made military equipment and training assistance available to Greece, Turkey, Iran, China, Korea, the Philippines and the Latin American republics. The National Security Council now recommended that such aid be extended to the North Atlantic Treaty members and that all the separate aid programs be combined into one. Following President Truman's approval of the recommendation, appropriate legislation was drafted and submitted to Congress immediately after ratification of the North Atlantic Treaty. In October 1949 Congress passed the bill providing for a Mutual Defense Assistance Program. Appropriations for military aid in Fiscal Year 1950 amounted to slightly more than $1,314,000,000. To implement the program the Department of the Army, as the executive agency, sent each recipient country a military assistance advisory group. Composed of Army, Navy, and Air Force sections, each group advised and assisted the government to which it was sent in determining the amount and type of aid needed. In addition these advisory groups trained the armed forces of each country in the use and tactical employment of the materiel and equipment it received from the United States.

The Department of Defense. During this period the United States was looking to its own defense organization. The National Security Act of 1947 had brought the Nation's armed forces under unified control. But a major weakness was revealed when unified control began operating.

\As pointed out by Mr. Kenneth C. Royall, Army Secretary, this weakness lay in the fact that each Department still maintained its self-sufficiency within the framework of the National Military Establishment and decisions thus had to be reached by mutual cooperation. He felt that military organizations could not operate on the voluntary cooperation theory and that unification should be strengthened by giving the Secretary of Defense stronger control over the three Departments. The first Secretary of Defense, Mr. James V. Forrestal, confronted with many problems of his office that were almost impossible to meet under the provisions of the act, brought the proposals of the Secretary of the Army to the attention of the President, who asked the Congress for legislation to amend the Act of 1947. In 1949 the Congress enacted legislation changing the name of the National

Military Establishment to the Department of Defense, and altering the membership of the National Security Council to include the Vice President. This legislation also increased the powers of the Secretary of Defense, and provided a Chairman of the Joint Chiefs of Staff. The Departments of the Army, Navy, and Air Force lost their status as executive departments and became separate military establishments under the control of the Department of Defense.

The Army Reorganization Act of 1950. Following the unification of the armed forces the Congress passed the Army Reorganization Act in 1950. The chief objectives of this legislation, as stated by Gen. J. Lawton Collins, then Army Chief of Staff, were to achieve simplicity and flexibility in the Army's statutory organization. The Act of 1950 eliminated or revised previous legislation pertaining to Army organization, some of which dated as far back as the War of 1812. It made the Secretary of the Army directly responsible for conducting all the affairs of the Army. At the same time it gave him the broad powers necessary to carry out this responsibility. It placed the Army staff under his direct control by permitting him the right to establish the duties and powers of the staff. In addition the act permitted the Secretary of the Army to assign some of his duties to the Under Secretary and Assistant Secretary of the Army, although responsibility still rested with the Secretary of the Army. The Army Chief of Staff became responsible for carrying out the approved plans and policies of the Department of the Army. He had supervision of all personnel and units of the Army and was responsible to the Secretary of the Army for the Army's efficiency, combat readiness, and plans for operational employment. The act combined previous legislation to provide a full Army staff and made provisions for enlarging this staff as the need arose. Tactical organization of the Army was left to the Secretary of the Army, who could create such commands and forces as he deemed best. Field training came under the supervision of the chief of the Army Field Forces. His function was to supervise the Army's training, develop tactical doctrine, control the Army's school system, and keep the Chief of Staff informed on the status of the field units' combat readiness. The act also placed both the Transportation and Military Police Corps, organized on a temporary basis during the war, on a permanent footing within the structure of the Army. Finally, all the technical services, except the Medical Department, received the designation "Corps." The Medical Department became the Army Medical Service and embraced all phases of the Army's medical activities.

Additional Tension in the Cold War. Two significant events that occurred in the closing days of 1949 greatly increased the existing world-wide tension. First, in the late summer the Soviet Union succeeded in setting off a nuclear explosion, thereby eliminating the

Western World's strategic advantages as the sole possessor of nuclear weapons. The second event followed in November when the Chinese Communists forcing the evacuation of Chiang Kai-shek's government and remaining Nationalist Chinese forces to the island of Formosa, gained control of all of the Chinese mainland, thus threatening the United States position in the Far East.

Conversely, during this period of increasing tension America's need of strong armed forces conflicted with the desire to attain economy in the Government. As a result, when the recommended budget for the fiscal year 1951 went to Congress it contained only enough funds to maintain an army of 10 divisions, a 48-group Air Force, and a Navy with 238 major combat ships. But unlooked-for events in Asia suddenly changed all of this.

Background of the Korean Conflict. In September 1945, the United States and the Soviet Union had arbitrarily selected the 38th parallel as a convenient boundary to accept the surrender of Japanese troops stationed in Korea. The Americans took the surrender below the parallel, the Soviets above it. By agreement, a joint commission from the two occupying powers was to develop a four-power trusteeship through which the United States, the Soviet Union, the United Kingdom, and China would guide a provisional Korean Government until the Koreans were able to govern themselves. This would meet provisions of World War II's Cairo Conference and the Potsdam Declaration of Self-Determination to which the Soviet Union had subscribed. But the commission made little progress toward formation of a trusteeship, principally because Soviet members obstructed settlement by deliberately presenting demands that were unacceptable to the Americans. Meanwhile, the Soviets sponsored and abetted a Communist regime in northern Korea.

In November 1947, the United States referred the problem of Korea to the United Nations. Two months later, in January 1948, a United Nations commission entered Korea to supervise free elections throughout the peninsula. But Soviet authorities refused to let the Commission enter North Korea, and the North Korean people did not take part in the elections. The United Nations, therefore, sponsored an elected government that became the Republic of Korea in the southern half of the peninsula. After this action both the United States and the Soviet Union withdrew their forces from Korea and the nation was left divided.

From its inception as a republic, South Korea was a target of North Korean propaganda and terrorism. Border raids, guerilla warfare, bribery, strikes, sabotage, economic strangulation, and intensive anti-republican propaganda were weapons with which the North Koreans attempted to destroy the South Korean Government. The North Koreans played on nationalism, always a strong feeling among the inherently proud Koreans, and began campaigning on 3 June 1950 for new elections that would unify the divided country. But, quite clearly, the North Korean plan would have made Korea a communistic state, and South Korea rejected the proposal. North Korea authorities then decided on full-scale hostilities to bring South Korea into the Soviet sphere.

Summary. In the years immediately following World War II, the United States adopted a new approach to the problem of national security. Rejecting the traditional policy of temporary alliances to meet emergencies, the United States sought to preserve peace through collective action within the United Nations Organization. But Soviet expansionism and the advent of the cold war divided the nations into two contesting camps with conflicting policies. Failing to reach a compromise and determined to preserve the peace, the United States offered economic and military aid to the non–Communist world, while the nations of western Europe, Canada and the United States joined in pledging their mutual support through the North Atlantic Treaty.

Meanwhile the United States also sought to strengthen its own military establishment. Public demand and budgetary reductions had brought about a rapid demobilization of the wartime Army to such a point as to create doubt that the Army's postwar responsibilities could be met. Since national security rested on the combined efforts of several departments of the government, it was clear that these efforts had to be closely coordinated. The National Security Act of 1947 provided the means to effect such coordination by establishing the National Security Council. At the same time the needs of national security and the lessons of the late war led to the creation of the National Military Establishment, which brought the Nation's military forces under one head. In addition, national security and the advent of new and radical weapons wrought considerable changes in the structural and tactical organization of the Army. These changes reflected the growing importance of fire power and mobility and of keeping abreast of technical improvements in weapons and equipment. In 1949 the National Security Act was amended to bolster the authority of the Secretary of Defense and improve the working structure of his Department. The Army sought and obtained a simplification and modernization of its top command organization in the interests of flexibility and economy.

The measures adopted by the United States to strengthen the free world were no sooner under way than the mounting world tension gave way to war in Asia. The uneasy peace in Korea, controlled in the north by a Communist regime and in the south by a democratic government, collapsed under the division. Peaceful attempts to unite Korea failed, and the Communist north adopted aggression as the means of uniting the divided nation.

QUESTIONS

1. How did United States postwar policy affect the Nation's armed forces?

2. What major revisions were made in America's postwar defense organization?

3. What reorganization measures did the Army adopt to meet the requirements of national defense?

4. What was the Army's role in implementing United States policy abroad?

5. Discuss the measures taken by the United States to strengthen the free world.

6. What were some of the causes of the Korean Conflict?

Reading List

Clay, Lucius D. *Decision in Germany.* New York, 1950.

Price, Harry B. *The Marshall Plan and Its Meaning.* New York, 1955.

Sapin, Burton M., and Richard C. Snyder. *The Role of the Military in American Foreign Policy.* (Doubleday Short Studies in Political Science.) New York, 1954.

United States Army:

 Korea—1950. Washington, 1952.

 Sparrow, John C. *History of Personnel Demobilization in the United States Army.* Washington, 1952. (DA Pam 20–210.)

Warren, James, D. *N.A.T.O. and Its Prospects.* New York, 1954.

CHAPTER 25

KOREA

Outbreak of Hostilities. On 25 June 1950, a North Korean force equivalent to 10 divisions invaded South Korea. In its narrowest sense, the invasion marked the beginning of a civil war between peoples of a divided country. In a larger sense, it represented an eruption of tensions between the two great power blocs that had emerged from World War II.

The North Korean People's Army. There is some evidence that the North Koreans were confident they could capture all of South Korea before any outside power could intervene effectively. Their confidence was based largely on the strength of the North Korean People's Army, formed around a hard core of veterans who had fought with Soviet and Chinese forces during World War II, and afterward, as a part of Chinese Communist armies, against Nationalist China. Equipped and carefully trained by the Soviet Union during and after the occupation of Korea, the North Korean Army was, except in air and naval support, an efficient fighting force; and the infantry and armored units that crossed the parallel in the initial attack constituted some of its best forces.

The South Korean Army. By contrast, the South Korean Army of 95,000 ill-equipped and poorly trained men was a highly ineffective force. Actually it represented more a constabulary than an army. During and after the American occupation of southern Korea, an American military staff assisted the South Koreans in organizing, equipping, and training a small army. But limited equipment, restricted command authority, and a policy that allowed the South Korean Military Establishment to become no more than an internal security force made it impossible for the Americans to create an army capable of meeting a well-armed and well-trained foe.

Seoul Falls. The very first engagement of the conflict, when the North Koreans crushed South Korean defenses at the 38th parallel, demonstrated the superiority of the North Korean Army. On 28 June, three days after the opening attack, a tank-infantry force leading the main North Korean thrust entered Seoul, the South Korean capital located near the west coast 35 miles below the parallel (map 44). Secondary North Korean spearheads in central and eastern Korea kept pace with the main drive. In the face of the onslaught, the South Korean Army retreated in disorder, leaving most of its equipment behind. Whatever effectiveness it may have possessed was already

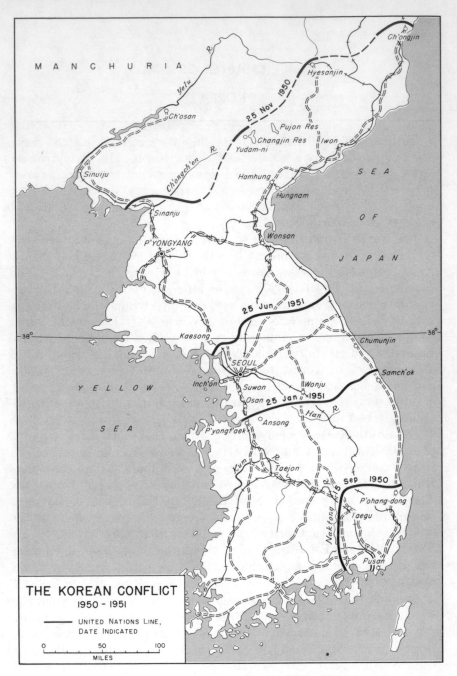

THE KOREAN CONFLICT
1950 - 1951

UNITED NATIONS LINE,
DATE INDICATED

0   50   100
MILES

Map 44. The Korean conflict, 1950–1951.

lost. The North Korean Army halted, and then only briefly, to regroup before crossing the Han River below Seoul.

Stunned by this planned Communist aggression, the free world turned to the United Nations. For the first time since its founding this world body faced a full-scale war. The existence of the United Nations now depended on how well it met the challenge.

The United Nations Reacts. The United Nations Organization swiftly denounced the North Korean armed aggression. On 25 June the U. N. Security Council demanded immediate cessation of hostilities and withdrawal of North Korean forces to the 38th parallel. When that failed, the Security Council, on 27 June, urged United Nations members to furnish military assistance to the South Korean republic.

U. S. Forces Enter the Conflict. Anticipating the Council's call, President Truman, on 26 June, authorized U. S. air and naval forces to attack North Korean troops and installations located in South Korea. Then on 29 June he broadened the range of U. S. air and naval attack to targets in North Korea and authorized the use of U. S. Army troops to protect Pusan, Korea's major port at the southeastern tip of the peninsula. Meanwhile, General of the Army Douglas MacArthur, top military commander in the Far East, flew from his headquarters in Japan to Korea to reconnoiter the battle scene. After watching South Korean troops flounder in attempts to organize defenses south of the Han River, MacArthur recommended to Washington that a U. S. Army regiment be committed in the Seoul area at once and that this commitment be built up to two divisions. In response, President Truman, on 30 June, authorized MacArthur to use all forces available to him.

U. S. military strength in the Far East. MacArthur had at hand the 1st Cavalry, 7th, 24th, and 25th Infantry Divisions, all under the U. S. Eighth Army in Japan, and the 29th Regimental Combat Team on Okinawa. None of these was prepared for battle. Each division lacked a third of its organic infantry and artillery units and almost all of its armor, and its existing units were far understrength. The regiment on Okinawa was proportionately short. Weapons and equipment were war-worn remnants of World War II. Some weapons, medium tanks in particular, could scarcely be found in the Far East, and ammunition reserves amounted to a 45-day supply. Since intensive combat training had been largely neglected for occupation duty, the undermanned Far East forces fell far below full combat efficiency.

Initial engagement. The speed of the North Korean drive coupled with American unpreparedness dictated initial strategy and tactics. American forces, compelled by their general unreadiness to disregard the principle of mass, entered Korea piecemeal to trade space for

*Medium Tank M4A3 on a street of a South Korean village near Yech'on,
24 July 1950.*

time. On 2 July two rifle companies and a few supporting units of
the 24th Division flew from Japan to Pusan and from there moved
by train and truck to defensive positions near Osan, 30 miles below
Seoul. The mission of this small group was to fight a delaying action
to gain time for the movement of more troops from Japan. In the
meantime, the North Koreans renewed their southward advance, and
on 5 July a North Korean division supported by 30 tanks collided
with the small American force. The Americans held their positions
subbornly for nearly five hours, then were outflanked and shoved
back with heavy casualties and the loss of all equipment save small
arms.

Reinforcements arrive. By that time the remainder of the 24th
Division had reached Korea and had taken blocking positions along
the Kum river north of Taejon, 60 miles southeast of Osan. Strung
out to the east, remnants of the South Korean Army held positions
50 miles above Taegu. The 25th Division landed in Korea on 14
July and occupied defenses east of the 24th; the 1st Cavalry Division
arrived four days later.

The 24th Division lost Taejon on 20 July, after North Korean forces
established bridgeheads over the Kum River and encircled the town.
Despite the arrival of the 29th RCT on 26 July, American and South
Korean troops all along the line fell back steadily to the southeast
under constant North Korean pressure; by early August the North
Koreans had cornered them in a small portion of southeastern Korea.

The United Nations Command. Actual and probable commitment of military forces from the U. N. membership, meanwhile, posed a problem as new as the U. N. organization in one respect but as old as the unity of command principle in another. For greatest efficiency the various national contingents entering the conflict had to be unified under a single command. By resolution on 7 July the U. N. Security Council asked the United States to form a unified command and to appoint a commander. The United States complied by establishing the United Nations Command, the first of its kind, in late July, and President Truman appointed General MacArthur to lead it. Thereafter, all military forces from contributing nations joined the U. N. Command as they reached the theater of operations.

The U. S. Eighth Army. General MacArthur assigned command of ground troops in Korea to the U. S. Eighth Army under Lt. Gen. Walton H. Walker. On 13 July General Walker established an advanced headquarters at Taegu, assuming command of all American ground troops on the peninsula and, at the request of the South Korean President, Syngman Rhee, of the South Korean Army. As ground forces from other U. N. member countries reached Korea, they, too, passed to Walker's command.

The Pusan Perimeter. Alarmed by the rapid shrinkage of U. N. held territory, General Walker early in August declared the strategy of trading space for time at an end and ordered a final stand along a 140-mile perimeter around Pusan. Although a long line and few troops left numerous and wide gaps in Walker's "Pusan Perimeter," he now held an important advantage over his adversary—shorter interior lines of communications. Pusan had become a well-stocked Eighth Army supply base, and was the hub of a fair rail line and road net leading to the battlefront. At the same time, the enemy's over land supply lines to North Korea had become longer, and less and less tenable under constant U. N. air attack. Moreover, British and American warships had wiped out North Korean naval opposition and had clamped a tight blockade on the Korean coast.

Thirteen North Korean infantry divisions and one armored division hammered at the Pusan Perimeter for a month and a half. Failing to recognize the value of concentrating forces for decisive penetration at one point, the North Koreans dissipated their strength in piecemeal attacks at various points along Eighth Army's line. Necessarily, Eighth Army's defense hinged on a rapid shuttling of troops to block a gap or reinforce a position where the threat appeared greatest at a given moment. But by rushing his scant reserves from one critical area to another, General Walker launched short and quick counterattacks that inflicted heavy casualties on the North Koreans and prevented serious penetrations.

While the North Koreans lost heavily during repeated attempts to crack Eighth Army's defense, Eighth Army's combat power grew.

By mid-August the 2d Division (Army), the 1st Marine Brigade, and four battalions of medium tanks arrived from the United States, and the 5th Regimental Combat Team from Hawaii. Before the month was out Great Britain committed its 27th Brigade from Hong Kong, and American military advisers restored a semblance of order among five South Korean divisions. Thus, as the North Koreans lost irreplaceable men and equipment, U. N. forces acquired an offensive capability.

Envelopment and Breakout. Almost from the start of the conflict General MacArthur worked on plans for a decisive blow that would turn the tide of battle. His plan was based in large part on an evaluation of Korea's terrain. Korea is a peninsula of mountains. Main ranges run the length of the east coast and spur ranges spread southwesterly across most of the peninsula. Myriad peaks and ridges forming these ranges, although not notably high, are unusually steep. Their number and precipitousness, as Walker's forces already had discovered, markedly curtailed the mobility of the highly motorized and mechanized U. S. forces. By and large motor movement was restricted to Korea's roads, which were few in number and indeed primitive. The main roads, and the rail lines, followed paths of least resistance through scant lowlands. Since the lowlands lay principally along the west coast, Korea's primary communications system was centered in the west. Most of the main roads and rail lines converged on Seoul from the south and southeast and wound through the western lowlands to the north.

Therefore, MacArthur planned an amphibious landing at Inch'on, a port on the Yellow Sea 25 miles west of Seoul, to be followed by an advance on the capital city to cut the main routes of communications over which most North Korean troops and supplies traveled south. In concert with this move, Eighth Army was to make a general northward advance. Enemy troops who survived Eighth Army's attack and withdrew over the main road net would walk into the guns of the amphibious force that had come in behind them. In the east, enemy forces could make only a slow and difficult escape through the precipitous, almost trackless mountains.

MacArthur's plan appeared dangerous to his superiors and to the Navy. Since MacArthur would be committing his last reserves to the landing, the U. S. Joint Chiefs of Staff anticipated serious consequences if Inch'on were strongly defended. Naval authorities considered the extreme Yellow Sea tides and narrow channel approaches to Inch'on as big risks to the shipping that would carry and support the amphibious force. MacArthur, nonetheless, held to his plan: he built up supplies and pieced together a landing force from the 7th Division, the greater part of the 1st Marine Division, which was sent from the United States, and the 1st Marine Brigade, which he pulled out of the line in Korea to fill out the Marine division. He

INFANTRYMEN KEEP A SHARP LOOKOUT for movement in the Communist-held area in Korea, as U. N. artillery drops white phosphorus on the area.

assigned command of the landing to the newly activated U. S. X Corps, which would operate independently of Eighth Army under the leadership of Maj. Gen. Edward M. Almond.

The Inch'on landing. General Almond's corps swept into Inch'on on 15 September. Against light resistance, a Marine regiment covered by strong air strikes and naval gunfire quickly captured the port city proper, and, after the full division had landed, the Marines pressed toward Seoul. The 7th Division came ashore in the wake of the Marine advance. One regiment struck southeastward for Suwon, south of Seoul, while the remainder of the division joined the Marines in the fight for the capital city. On 29 September Almond's forces were in Seoul, and in a dramatic ceremony General MacArthur turned the city back to President Rhee.

Eighth Army attacks. General Walker launched Eighth Army's offensive on 16 September, the day following the landing at Inch'on. His command, now consisting of the U. S. I, ROK I and ROK II Corps and within a week the U. S. IX Corps as well, made little progress at first. But when the portent of Almond's envelopment and Walker's frontal attack became clear to the North Koreans, they fled to the north and Eighth Army rolled forward and made contact with the U. S. X Corps on 26 September. Large numbers of enemy troops

Inch'on.   Men and equipment being unloaded on the beach during the invasion.

escaped to North Korea through the eastern mountains, but enemy casualties were high, and by 30 September Eighth Army's prisoner of war cages held over 100,000 captives.   Remnants of six North Korean divisions hid in the mountains of South Korea to fight as guerillas, posing a large enough threat for Walker to commit his U. S. IX Corps against them.   The North Korean Army, nevertheless, had ceased to exist as an organized force below the 38th parallel by the end of September.   This was a spectacular success, and illustrates an application of the principles of the offensive objective, maneuver, and surprise.

U. S. Forces Enter North Korea.   After driving the North Korean Army above the 38th parallel, U. N. forces awaited a decision whether to cross the parallel in pursuit.   In making the decision American authorities, acting in behalf of participating U. N. nations, constantly kept in mind that crossing the parallel might, by sparking Chinese and Soviet entry into the conflict, bring on another world war.   On the other hand, these authorities realized that failure to erase communism in Korea would leave the South Korean people in no better position than that of 24 June 1950.   Choosing to risk Chinese and Soviet participation, President Truman on 27 September authorized U. N. forces to enter North Korea.   On 3 October Communist China's Foreign Minister, Chou En-lai, warned that Chinese troops would enter the conflict if other than South Korean forces crossed the 38th parallel. This did not prevent the United Nations General Assembly from voting on 7 October for the restoration of peace and security throughout Korea, thereby giving tacit approval to entry into North Korea by U. N. military forces.

Eighth Army renews attack. In the east, Walker's ROK I Corps crossed the 38th parallel on 1 October and advanced up the east coast to capture Wonsan, North Korea's major seaport, on 10 October. His ROK II Corps, meanwhile, crossed the parallel and advanced through central Korea. In the west, Walker's remaining forces relieved Almond's corps in the Seoul area and on 9 October crossed the parallel to move on P'yongyang, the North Korean capital. Meeting but slight resistance, these forces covered the 90 miles to P'yongyang in 10 days. Three days later, Walker's troops were in Sinanju, 40 miles above P'yongyang. Within another week, Walker's westernmost division crossed the Ch'ongch'on River at Sinanju and reached a point only 18 air miles from the Manchurian border. Troops from a division farther to the east went even deeper: a South Korean regiment dashed northward and entered the town of Ch'osan on 26 October, to become the first contingent of U. N. troops to reach the Yalu River.

U. S. X Corps lands at Wonsan. Almond's U. S. X Corps, meanwhile, prepared a second amphibious landing, this time on the east coast of North Korea. After being delayed until mines could be cleared from Wonsan harbor, Almond's 1st Marine Division landed at Wonsan on 26 October; 3 days later, his 7th Division came ashore at Iwon, 80 miles farther to the north. Neither division met opposition since both landing areas already had fallen to the ROK I Corps.

Adding the ROK I Corps to his command upon landing, General Almond set out to capture the iron and steel mills, communications network, port installations, and power and irrigation plants of northeastern Korea. ROK I Corps followed the coastline toward the ironworks at Ch'ongjin, 120 miles above Iwon. The Marines moved 50 miles north of Wonsan to industrial Hamhung and its port, Hungnam, then struck inland for the Changjin Reservoir, 45 miles to the northwest. From Iwon, the 7th Division attacked northwestward toward the Pujon Reservoir and the Yalu River.

A new threat appears and fades. The outlook for U. N. forces in the last week of October was distinctly optimistic. For all practical purposes the North Korean Army appeared to exist only as a "rabble at arms," and on 24 October MacArthur issued orders for attacks by U. S. Eighth Army and U. S. X Corps that he hoped would carry his forces to the Manchurian border and restore peace to Korea before the onset of winter. But brief clashes with Chinese troops between 25 and 28 October in both Walker's and Almond's sectors posed a new threat. Chinese prisoners taken during these engagements gave de-

Hyesanjin, near the Manchurian Border, 21 November 1950. Infantrymen and a medium tank M4A3 in a rubble-strewn street of the town.

ceptive identities to their military organizations; hence, it was not clear whether a few makeshift units of Chinese volunteers had reinforced the North Koreans or whether the presence of Chinese troops represented full intervention by Communist China.

Battles with Chinese troops, costly to both sides, continued through the first week of November. In the face of the new opposition, Walker decided that he must advance on a broader front, and that he must build up his supplies before he could mount a large effort. He therefore withdrew his extended forces to the lower bank of the Ch'ongch'on River but kept a bridgehead over the Ch'ongch'on above Sinanju. Walker believed that three Chinese divisions, about 30,000 troops, opposed his army. Estimates placed one, possibly two, divisions ahead of Almond's forces in the east. Then, on 8 November the larger Chinese units abruptly broke contact with the U. N. forces and withdrew, obscuring their purpose and intentions in Korea.

The fact of Chinese participation in the conflict was a good reason for MacArthur to reconsider his plans for all-out attack to the Yalu River, but not reason enough to abandon them. He still planned to send Walker's forces northward through western and central Korea, starting on 24 November, while Almond's troops cut enemy supply lines in an enveloping movement to the northwest, beginning on 27 November. Between 8 and 23 November Eighth Army and U. S. X Corps advanced cautiously against moderate resistance to gain favorable positions from which to launch their all-out offensive. Then on 24 November Walker attacked, with the Eighth Army and the ROK II Corps in line. His forces aimed for intermediate terrain objectives that would give him access to good routes for the final march to the border. His army was spread across as broad a front as its size would permit, not concentrated for a major advance along any single axis, thus not deployed in strict accordance with the principle of mass. For 24 hours his troops encountered only moderate resistance. But on 25 November Chinese forces stopped Walker's attack cold with a sudden and furious attack of their own. The attack took the Eighth Army completely by surprise indicating quite clearly that Walker had not applied the principle of security in his advance.

The Chinese Intervene. The weight of the Chinese assault struck ROK II Corps on Eighth Army's right flank and the South Koreans fell away under the impact. Walker called out his reserves to restore the flank, but Chinese forces beat back the reserves and threatened to envelop the remainder of Eighth Army after four more Chinese armies joined the attack on 27 November.

On the same day, two Chinese armies hit Almond's forces in the east, attacking along both sides of the Changjin Reservoir. After encircling two battalions of the 7th Division on the east side of the reservoir and the 1st Marine Division at Yudam-ni on the west, the Chinese cut the Americans' supply line and withdrawal route by blocking the road between the reservoir and Hamhung.

Eighth Army withdraws. In Eighth Army's sector, wave after wave of attacking Chinese struck the weakening U. N. line until defenders involuntarily fell back under the weight of the enemy's numbers. Walker countered by leaving one division to fight a delaying action while he pulled the bulk of his troops back to new defensive positions near P'yongyang. On 5 December, after Chinese forces again threatened his right flank, Walker withdrew his army from P'yongyang to positions along the Imjin River near the 38th parallel. During the withdrawal Walker evacuated his wounded and most of his supplies by water, rail, and air. Other supplies were burned. Thousands of fleeing Korean civilians clogged Eighth Army's route of withdrawal, slowing trucks carrying U. N. troops to their new positions; but the Chinese had little motor transport to use in the pursuit, and Eighth Army managed to break contact without serious interference.

U. S. X Corps withdraws. Almond's forces also withdrew, retiring toward the east coast. His right flank units reached the coast with little difficulty, but the Marines and the 7th Division's two battalions encircled at the Changjin Reservoir had to fight their way out. Supplied by air drops, the Marine-Army force of about 14,000 men fought through successive Chinese roadblocks as it moved southeastward through steep, snow-covered mountains toward the port of Hungnam.

At the same time, the U. S. 3d Division, newly arrived from the United States, the ROK I Corps, and the rest of the 7th Division formed a perimeter around Hungnam. This consolidation was part of a plan by General MacArthur to evacuate U. S. X Corps by water. Since he could perceive no tactical advantage in holding a beachhead on the eastern coast of North Korea, MacArthur had decided to move U. S. X Corps to South Korea to reinforce Eighth Army.

While U. N. ships gathered in the waters off Hungnam to take his forces out of North Korea, Almond sent a relief column inland to help hold the route of withdrawal for his men fighting their way to the coast. After the relief column met the retiring troops, the two groups made their way to the coast by 11 December. On the same day, Almond started his evacuation. While enemy troops continually attacked the Hungnam defenses, the perimeter gradually contracted and tightened about the port as Almond loaded his troops and supplies aboard ships in the harbor. On 24 December he pulled his rear guard off the Hungnam beaches, successfully completing the difficult operation of withdrawal from a hostile shore, and sailed for the Pusan area to join Eighth Army.

Eighth Army, 31 December. In the west, Eighth Army had fought no large-scale battle with the Chinese since the first week of December. After breaking contact with the Chinese, who were forced to wait at the 38th parallel for supplies and replacements, Eighth Army organized a 140-mile, coast-to-coast defense line just below the parallel by the end of December. Along this line were five corps: the U. S. I and IX west and north of Seoul, the South Korean III, II, and I to the east, in that order. U. S. X Corps went into Army reserve.

As Eighth Army developed its defenses, there was an important change of command. On 23 December General Walker was killed in a motor vehicle accident, and, at General MacArthur's request, Lt. Gen. Matthew B. Ridgway was named Eighth Army's commander. Ridgway's instructions from MacArthur were to defend his positions—if necessary, to fall back to successive positions to the south—but to keep his army intact at all costs.

The Enemy's New Year's Offensive. On the other side of the 38th parallel, the enemy concentrated his ground strength above Seoul and pushed large quantities of supplies into his forward areas. Here was clear indication that he was about to resume the attack and that Seoul would be his next objective.

At daybreak on 1 January 1951 enemy troops attacked along Eighth Army's entire front. As expected, the major effort was directed against Seoul. Although Eighth Army presented a stronger front than it had in November, the enemy offensive quickly gained momen-

Gen. Matthew B. Ridgway with one of the division commanders at an airstrip in Korea, October 1951.

tum. Rather than risk destruction by defending in place, General Ridgway established a bridgehead around Seoul to delay the enemy and deny him the use of the Han River bridges, and pulled back the rest of his army to a line running along the south bank of the Han below Seoul then eastward to the coast through the villages of Yangp'yong, Hongch'on, and Chumunjin. By rolling with the punch, Ridgway believed he could conserve his strength until the enemy attack bogged down for lack of supplies and replacements, then could strike back.

When enemy forces quickly followed up their initial success and crossed the frozen Han River to the east and west of Seoul, Ridgway ordered another withdrawal. Beginning on 3 January, he moved his forces to a line running from positions on the west coast 40 miles below Seoul eastward through the towns of P'yongt'aek, Ansong, Wonju, and Samch'ok. Enemy forces followed closely. In the west, the last Eighth Army troops pulled out of Seoul on 4 January, and engineers blew the remaining Han River bridges as enemy columns entered the city from the north.

Once Seoul fell, only light Chinese forces pushed south of the city and enemy attacks in the west diminished. In central and eastern Korea, heavy fighting continued as U. N. troops in those regions withdrew to their new sectors, but by mid-January enemy pressure subsided along the entire front. Again, enemy ranks were depleted and supplies low. As U. N. troops restored and developed positions along the P'yongt'aek-Samch'ok line, Ridgway's reconnaissance forces discovered that the enemy had set out light screening forces to maintain contact and had withdrawn the bulk of his troops to regroup and reequip.

Eighth Army's Spoiling Attacks. General Ridgway gave his troops their objective for the next four months when he declared that he was no longer interested in land gains. "We are interested only in inflicting maximum casualties to the enemy with minimum casualties to ourselves. To do this we must wage a war of maneuver—slashing at the enemy when he withdraws and fighting delaying actions when he attacks."

To attain this objective, Eighth Army began a cautious, probing advance on 25 January. Moving on a wide front through a succession of phase lines, Ridgway's troops attacked slowly and methodically, ridge by ridge, phase line by phase line, wiping out each pocket of resistance before making the next advance. Although enemy screening forces fought back vigorously and launched occasional counterattacks, Eighth Army moved steadily and, by 1 March, regained the lower bank of the Han River.

By then the spring thaw had come to South Korea, swelling streams and turning the countryside into mud. Under those conditions Eighth

Army's advance was a test of endurance for both men and equipment. Ridgway's forces, nevertheless, succeeded in recapturing Seoul by mid-March, and by 19 March held a line that crossed Korea just below the 38th parallel.

Meanwhile, behind his screening positions a few miles above the 38th parallel, the enemy assembled troops and equipment for an offensive. Even though reentry into North Korea seemed a formidable undertaking in light of events of late 1950, Ridgway could not permit the enemy to prepare an attack unmolested. Therefore, on 5 April, he unleashed his troops in an attack toward an objective line designated Kansas, roughly 10 miles above the parallel, whose capture would carry Eighth Army through important enemy supply and troop concentration areas. On reaching this line at mid-April, Ridgway sent part of his force toward Line Wyoming, which looped above the western portion of Kansas through another important enemy supply area.

As Ridgway's forces advanced above Line Kansas, more evidence of the enemy's build-up appeared. As a precaution, Ridgway published on 12 April a plan for orderly delaying actions to be fought when and if the enemy attacked. This was one of his last acts as commander of Eighth Army. The day before, 11 April, President Truman had relieved General MacArthur of command in the Far East in one of the most controversial episodes of the conflict and at the same time had named Ridgway as MacArthur's successor. On 14 April Ridgway turned over the Eighth Army to Lt. Gen. James A. Van Fleet.

The Enemy's Spring Offensive. *The April attack.* The threatened offensive came on the night of 22 April, when enemy forces launched strong attacks in western Korea and lighter attacks in the east. After the enemy's attack in the west carried him below the 38th parallel, he concentrated his effort against Seoul. In the east, his attack also carried below the parallel but not in such depth as in the west.

According to previously laid plans, General Van Fleet withdrew through a series of delaying positions, finally establishing defenses along a line running northeastward across the peninsula from positions a few miles north of Seoul. Along this line Eighth Army halted the enemy's attack by the end of April. When enemy forces withdrew to recoup their losses, Van Fleet used the lull in battle to improve his defense line. Meanwhile, he planned an offensive designed to carry Eighth Army back to Line Kansas, but signs of another enemy attack led him to postpone it.

The May attack. Van Fleet had interpreted the signs correctly. After darkness on 15 May the enemy resumed his spring offensive. Expecting the next enemy assault against Seoul, Van Fleet had strengthened his defenses in the west, but this time the enemy drove a salient into Eighth Army's east-central position. Adjusting forces to place more troops in the path of the enemy's attack and laying down tremendous amounts of artillery fire, Van Fleet exacted heavy enemy casualties and contained the enemy attack after it had penetrated 30 miles through Eighth Army lines. Determined to prevent the enemy from regathering strength for another attack, Van Fleet immediately ordered his forces forward in counterattack. Disorganized after their own attack, enemy forces resisted stubbornly only where their supply installations were threatened. Elsewhere, Eighth Army advanced with almost surprising ease, and by 31 May was just short of Line Kansas. Van Fleet then prepared to advance part of his force back to Line Wyoming.

The U. N. War Policy Changes. To this point, the conflict had been one of movement. Like a free-swinging pendulum, hinged above the center of Korea, it had changed direction several times, arcing first below and then above the 38th parallel. But each swing had been smaller as the pendulum lost momentum. For Eighth Army, at least, there was little prospect of substantial reinforcement. As a result—in fact, as a gradual development since the time of Chinese intervention— U. N., and especially U. S., objectives in the conflict shifted from military victory to political settlement.

The United Nations' hope for a negotiated peace carried with it a restriction on military operations. After 1 June ground forces could not, without approval from Washington, make a general advance north of an east-west line generally along the 38th parallel. The only tactical operations permitted were those necessary to protect Eighth Army, to maintain contact, and to harass the enemy. Here was the basic pattern of U. N. military operations through the rest of the conflict.

Lines Kansas and Wyoming. On 1 June, as part of his army advanced toward Line Wyoming and the remainder drove forward to consolidate on Line Kansas, Van Fleet ordered his troops to build a strong defense line once they gained their objectives. Van Fleet had no other choice since present objectives marked generally his limit of advance.

Eighth Army reached Lines Kansas and Wyoming in mid-June. Recapture of these lines meant that all of South Korea except for a small area in the west was clear of enemy troops. To compensate for the enemy's hold south of the 38th parallel, Eighth Army held territory north of the line in central and eastern Korea. Upon halting, Van Fleet's forces began to fortify their positions and, aside from patrolling and clashing locally with enemy screening forces, spent the remainder of June developing their defenses. Enemy forces used the respite to reorganize after losing heavily. Indeed, as the first year of the conflict ended, the fighting took the appearance of a stalemate.

510

The Armistice Conference.   On 23 June 1951, Jacob Malik, the Soviet Union's delegate to the United Nations, made a public statement that implied Chinese and North Korean willingness to discuss terms of an armistice.   Communist China's government followed Malik's lead with an announcement that indicated its own desire for a truce, and President Truman authorized General Ridgway to arrange an armistice conference with his enemy counterpart.   Through an exchange of radio messages, both sides agreed to conduct negotiations beginning on 10 July at Kaesong, in what was then no-man's land in the west but would become a neutral area.

The Static War.   At the first armistice conference the two delegations agreed that hostilities would continue until an armistice agreement was signed.   Yet it seemed unlikely that either side would open any large-scale offensive as long as peace talks were in session. Indeed, with defense for tempo and a negotiated peace for keynote, action along the front, except for brief, violent episodes, never regained the momentum of the first year.

By 26 July the two armistice delegations had fixed the points to be settled in order to bring about an armistice.   But immediately thereafter enemy delegates seemed more concerned with gaining concessions than compromising differences.   To U. N. delegates it appeared that the enemy sought to delay negotiations so as to gain time to strengthen his forces, and thus strengthen his position at the bargaining table and on the field of battle.

This last possibility did not escape General Van Fleet.   While enemy delegates continued to delay and finally broke off negotiations on 22 August, after charging that U. N. aircraft had attacked neutral Kaesong, Van Fleet launched a series of limited-objective attacks to improve Eighth Army's defensive position.   His U. S. X and ROK I Corps in east-central Korea fought for terrain objectives five to seven miles above Line Kansas, among them Bloody and Heartbreak Ridges, to drive enemy forces from positions that favored an attack on Line Kansas.   These objectives were won by the last week of October.   In the west, U. S. I Corps struck northeastward on a 40-mile front to secure a new line 3 to 4 miles beyond the Wyoming line in order to protect important supply routes that lay only a short distance behind the existing western front.   U. S. I Corps met less resistance than its sister corps to the east and captured the new positions by 12 October.

Negotiations resume.   Successful advances in August, September, and October gave Eighth Army possession of commanding ground along the entire front, and may have had an influence on the enemy, who now agreed to return to the armistice conference.   Negotiations resumed on 25 October, this time at Panmunjom, a tiny settlement seven miles southeast of Kaesong.

Since the armistice conference was back in session, the possibility of peace loomed larger, and, since Eighth Army now controlled excellent defensive positions, the cost of further assaults would be more than results could justify. For these reasons General Ridgway on 12 November ordered Van Fleet to defend his present front, limiting attacks to those necessary to strengthen the main line of resistance and to establish an outpost line. Hope for an early armistice grew when, on 27 November, the two delegations agreed that a line of demarcation during an armistice would be the present line of contact, provided an armistice agreement was reached within 30 days. Thus while both sides awaited the outcome of negotiations, fighting tapered off to patrol clashes, raids, and small battles for possession of outposts in no-man's land.

Stalemate. Discord over several issues, including the exchange of prisoners of war, prevented an armistice agreement in the 30 days between 27 November and 27 December. The prisoner of war quarrel heightened in January 1952 after U. N. delegates proposed to give captives a choice in repatriation proceedings. By the Geneva Conventions of 1949, which govern present-day warfare, prisoners are to be "set at liberty" at the end of a war. Accordingly, the United Nations maintained that those prisoners who did not wish to return to Communist control could be repatriated elsewhere. The enemy's representatives protested vigorously, insisting that all captives held by Eighth Army be returned to their side. Thus, as 1952 opened, there appeared to be no easy path to an armistice.

While argument continued, both sides tacitly extended the 27 November provisions for a line of demarcation. This had the effect of holding battle action in 1952 to the pattern of the 30-day waiting period. Both sides fought artillery duels, dispatched patrols, set up ambushes, launched raids, and fought bitter contests for outpost positions. The tempo of battle followed the seasons, quickening during spring and summer, diminishing as winter approached. The men who fought small-scale but furious battles on oddly shaped land masses in no-man's land such as Sniper Ridge, the Hook, the T-Bone, and Old Baldy, experienced all-out warfare, but the lines remained substantially unchanged as the year ended. In the meantime, the armistice conference recessed once again without coming to agreement. Indeed, peace prospects at the end of 1952 seemed as remote as at the year's beginning.

The End of the Conflict. Operations early in 1953 resembled those of the previous year (map 45). Through February, a month in which Lt. Gen. Maxwell D. Taylor replaced General Van Fleet as Eighth Army commander, and through March and April the front remained generally quiet. The pace of battle quickened in May when Chinese forces launched regimental-sized attacks against five outposts guarding approaches to Eighth Army's western positions. A larger battle flared in central Korea on 10 June, when three Chinese divisions struck down both sides of the Pukhan River against ROK II Corps' main defenses. Brushing aside South Korean counterattacks, the Chinese drove the right of ROK II Corps two miles to the south before South Korean troops could contain the attack.

Armistice developments. Armistice negotiations had resumed in April. The prisoner exchange problem finally was settled by providing each side an opportunity to persuade those captives refusing repatriation to their homeland to change their minds. With this obstacle removed, the delegates quickly negotiated remaining matters so that by 18 June terms of an armistice were all but complete. But on that date South Korean President Syngman Rhee, who from the beginning had objected to any armistice that left Korea divided, ordered the release of those North Korean prisoners who had refused repatriation. Within a few days most of the North Korean prisoners broke out of prison camp and disappeared among the cooperative South Korean people. Since these captives had been guarded by South Korean troops, United Nations Command officials disclaimed responsibility for the break, but the enemy's armistice delegates denounced the action as a serious breach of faith. It took more than a month to repair the damage done by President Rhee's order.

The last battle. Enemy forces used this delay to wrest as much ground as possible from U. N. control. Again they attempted to penetrate Eighth Army's line in central Korea. On the night of 13 July, three Chinese divisions opened the last battle with an attack down the U. S. IX Corps-ROK II Corps boundary, and in a short time the bulk of five Chinese armies reinforced the offensive. Under the heavy blow ROK II Corps and the right flank division of U. S. IX Corps fell back eight miles to positions below the Kumsong River. To counter the enemy's offensive, General Taylor committed American divisions at the shoulders of the enemy penetration and sent the ROK II Corps in a counterattack toward the south bank of the Kumsong River. There, by Taylor's order, the South Koreans established a new main line of resistance on 20 July.

Armistice. Taylor made no move to restore the original ROK II Corps line, for by 20 July negotiators at Panmunjom had reached agreement on all armistice terms. At 1000, 27 July, the chief of each armistice delegation signed the agreement. A few hours later Gen. Mark W. Clark, who had replaced General Ridgway as head of the United Nations Command, and the enemy commanders signed the papers. By prior agreement fighting was to stop 12 hours after the first signatures had been placed on the armistice documents. Thus, at 2200, 27 July 1953, hostilities ended.

By the terms of the Armistice, the existing front line remained the boundary between North and South Korea. Troops on each side withdrew two kilometers, establishing a demilitarized boundary zone

Self-propelled 155-mm guns firing on enemy targets, November 1951.

across which military trespassing was prohibited. The introduction
of additional troops or of new weapons by either side was banned,
though replacement in kind was permitted. Both a Military Armistice Commission, composed of U. N. and Communist officers, and a
Neutral Nations Supervisory Commission with representatives from
Sweden, Switzerland, Czechoslovakia and Poland, were established to
oversee the enforcement of these terms. Similarly, a Neutral Nations
Repatriation Commission, with India added as umpire and custodian
of prisoners, was set up to handle the voluntary repatriation of
prisoners. Finally, the Armistice terms recommended the holding of
a political conference for final settlement of the whole Korean
question.

Summary and Analysis. *U. N. forces.* In the Korean conflict, the
United Nations Organization (Soviet bloc excepted) for the first time
committed military forces to enforce its resolution against armed
aggression. Under American leadership, the U. N. Command developed into an international group of ground, air, and naval forces
representing the Republic of Korea, 20 U. N. member countries, and
one other non-U. N. nation.

Of U. N. contributors, the United States, Great Britain, Australia,
New Zealand, Canada, Turkey, Greece, France, Belgium, Luxem-
bourg, the Netherlands, Thailand, the Philippines, Colombia, and
Ethiopia furnished ground combat troops. India, Sweden, and Nor-

way supplied ground medical facilities, and Denmark sent the hospital ship *Jutlandia*. Air forces came from the United States, Australia, Canada, and the Union of South Africa. Naval forces arrived from the United States, Great Britain, Australia, Canada, and New Zealand. Italy, a non-U. N. country, sent a hospital unit late in 1951.

The basic task of American leaders charged with creating an effective fighting force from the troops of a number of nations included in the Eighth Army was the development of standard organization and equipment. As a practical measure, since command and bulk of equipment were American, operations had to be conducted according to American methods. Although the problems were as diverse as the origins of the troops, a general cooperative attitude among the varied units allowed American leaders to build a cohesive war machine.

Among American units, themselves, the biggest problems were those of insufficient numbers, inadequate training, and equipment shortages. An expeditious flow of enlisted and officer replacements, accelerated training programs, and emergency equipment renovation and procurement procedures substantially reduced these handicaps. Noteworthy among steps taken to meet personnel needs was the calling to active

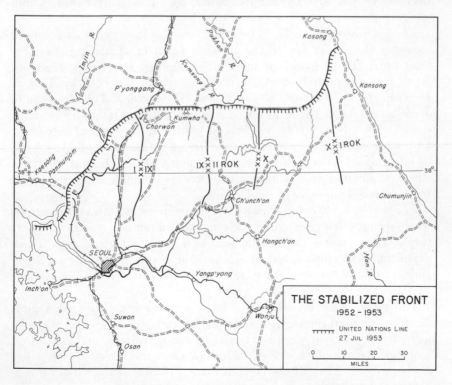

Map 45.   The Stabilized Front, 1952–1953.

duty of a large percentage of ROTC graduates. For example, of 26,751 Army lieutenants called to duty between September 1951 and June 1953, 18,649, or 70 percent, were graduates of the ROTC program.

Enemy forces. Bringing another innovation to the conflict, the Soviet Union for the first time employed military forces solely from its satellite bloc in Asia against a major power. Whereas not many years ago military forces in Asia, aside from those of Japan, were held in low regard by the western powers, events in Korea proved these forces capable. Although the Chinese and North Koreans used a hodge-podge of Japanese, Chinese, and Russian weapons and had fewer heavy guns and less ammunition than U. N. troops, they made up their lack of fire power with manpower and with what occidental forces would call reckless tactics. Indeed, the enemy expended troops as readily as U. N. forces spent ammunition. From that fact stem stories of screaming hordes rushing pell-mell toward U. N. positions. But what appeared as disorganized "human sea" attacks amounted to costly but effective constant-pressure tactics based on the simple principle that, if enough men hit a position enough times, they will eventually take it. The enemy's basic weakness was his inability to sustain an attack. He was most vulnerable to countermoves when he withdrew after his attacks bogged down for a lack of supplies and replacements.

The U. N. strategy. U. N. military strategy in the conflict followed a clear outline. At first it amounted to a matter of trading space for time until troops could be marshalled against the North Koreans. Next came a period of maneuver marked by the bold landing at Inch'on and a breakout at the Pusan Perimeter. The decision to drive to the Yalu River followed. When Chinese intervention frustrated this effort, strategy dictated cautious, methodical advances, with emphasis on destroying enemy troops rather than making territorial gains. Then after armistice negotiations began, political strategy dictated still different military methods, and an active defense replaced offensive ground action.

The pattern of ground combat. Even in mountainous localities where ranges are gentle and well defined, mountain warfare, by its very nature, creates difficult tactical and logistical problems. These problems were emphasized in Korea, where the mountains are steep and have little system, and were further complicated by the extreme variations in Korea's climate.

The rough terrain severely restricted the capabilities of armor. Tanks were used during the first year of fighting as a maneuver element but even then were restricted to roads, valleys, and the lower, more gentle mountain slopes. Most of the time tanks played a fire support role. Thus of the combat arms, infantry and artillery dominated the battlefield. U. N. artillery is credited with having been the greatest enemy killer. But the infantry had the arduous and vital

516

task of dislodging enemy forces from positions atop steep ridges. Climbs made by infantrymen under fire, even under ideal conditions, would be discouraging. All troops who supported the combat arms deserve a share of credit for successes enjoyed by U. N. forces. It is perhaps possible to single out the engineers for extra laurels since by their efforts the roads and bridges along supply lines were kept usable, and, on occasion, they dropped their tools and fought as infantrymen.

The cost. In 37 months of fighting, U. N. forces lost almost 74,000 men killed and 250,000 wounded. Of those killed, 44,000 were South Koreans, 27,000 were Americans, and 3,000 were from other U. N. countries. The effect of U. N. fire power and the enemy's costly tactics is reflected in an estimate of 1,350,000 dead and wounded suffered by the Chinese and North Koreans. Thus the casualty ratio was four to one in favor of U. N. forces. In terms of territorial gain the enemy was the loser, winning 850 square miles of territory previously controlled by South Korea but giving up 2,350 square miles of North Korea.

QUESTIONS

1. What was the United Nation's initial strategy? How was it implemented?

2. Discuss the decision to land at Inch'on and the effect of the landing.

3. Discuss the decision to advance to the Yalu River. Was it tactically sound?

4. Did the separate existence of U. S. X Corps between September and December 1950 represent a breach of the principle of unity of command? Discuss.

5. What influences shaped Eighth Army's cautious, methodical advances between January and April 1951?

6. What events and factors led to a virtual stalemate on the battlefield during the last two years of the conflict?

7. Discuss the influence of terrain on the conduct of combat operations.

8. Since there was no military victory for either side, what is the significance of the Korean conflict?

Reading List

Clark, Mark W. *From the Danube to the Yalu.* New York, 1954.
Geer, Andrew. *The New Breed.* New York, 1952.
Karig, Walter. *Battle Report: The Korean War.* New York, 1952.
Marshall, S. L. A. *The River and the Gauntlet.* New York, 1953.

Montross, Lynn and Nicholas A. Canzona. *The Pusan Perimeter*. Washington, 1954.

————. *The Inchon-Seoul Operation*. Washington, 1955.

————. *The Chosin Reservoir Campaign*. Washington, 1954.

Poats, Rutherford M. *Decision in Korea*. New York, 1954.

U. S. Army. Office Chief of Military History:

Gugeler, Russell A. *Combat Actions in Korea*. Washington, 1954.

Pictorial Volume: Korea: 1950. Washington, 1952.

Pictorial Volume: Korea: 1951–1953. Washington, 1956.

Westover, John G. *Combat Support in Korea*. Washington, 1955.

CHAPTER 26

SINCE KOREA

The armistice in Korea in July 1953 brought no real peace to a troubled world. In the Soviet Union new leaders emerged to replace the old dictator, Joseph Stalin, who died on 6 March 1953, but the new leadership brought few real changes in Soviet policy. Despite some gestures toward a philosophy of "competitive coexistence," the new Communist dynasty seemed dedicated to the same old goal of expansion. In Asia Red China had emerged as a new and dangerous giant towering above its weak neighbors. The dual menace of the two great Communist powers forced the United States, fully and finally wakened by the Korean War to the world-wide nature of the Communist challenge, to assume new commitments as the leader of the Free World and to take on an unaccustomed burden of permanent military preparedness.

The shape this military preparedness had to take was determined in no small part by the amazingly swift development of new weapons of great destructive power and the means of delivering them over long distances. The cold war came to center as much in the scientific laboratories and on the testing grounds as in the traditional political arena. In this atmosphere of widening commitments and feverish scientific progress the military problems of the United States took on a new and awesome complexity. Meeting these complex problems required an increasing degree of joint effort on the part of all three of the armed services. This history of the U. S. Army since 1953 must therefore be treated within the framework of the whole national defense establishment and the problems it had to face.

The Rearmament Effort. When the Korean War came to a close the United States was at the peak of a general rearmament effort to which the war had given the impulse. Military appropriations for fiscal years 1951–53 totalled 155.6 billion dollars, almost five times what they had been during the previous three years. The Army's share came to slightly over one-third of this sum, approximately 54 billion. Rearmament involved a partial mobilization of both manpower and industry, and its aim was not simply to provide the sinews for the hot war in Korea, but to enable the United States to cope with the Communist threat on a world-wide basis. The goal was to provide a reasonable defensive strength in terms of balanced air, ground, and naval forces to serve as a deterrent to Communist aggression and to establish a mobilization base that could be rapidly expanded in case the deterrent failed. For strategic reasons preparations were geared to a "year of greatest danger," a year when it was assumed Soviet military strength would reach its peak and the threat of general war would be greatest. There was, however, no lack of appreciation that these preparations might have to be carried on into the indefinite future.

The manpower goals of the rearmament program were generally reached by mid-1952. Total personnel in the Army, Navy, and Air Force increased from 1,460,000 to 3,636,000 in two years. The Army expanded from a skeleton force of less than 600,000 men to almost 1,600,000, enough to provide twenty divisions and supporting troops. This Army expansion took place in three stages. In the first over 310,000 Reservists and National Guardsmen were called to active duty, both as individuals and in units, as trainers and for immediate defense missions. The next stage was the absorption of volunteers and selective service inductees, and the third the release of most of the reserves and their replacement by the men they had trained. Whereas 15 percent of Army strength in July 1951 was composed of National Guardsmen and Reservists, by July 1953 this proportion had fallen to 1.5 percent and the proportion of selectees had risen from 40 to 57.5 percent.

Progress in training the new units organized, and in equipping the expanded Army with modern military equipment, was necessarily slower than the recruiting of manpower. Training was vastly complicated by the tremendous turnover in personnel, almost 50 percent during the last year of the Korean War. Equipping of units was slowed by the long lead time involved in the production of major military items. Not until mid-1952 were the products of the partial mobilization begun in 1950 forthcoming in any significant volume. This serves to explain why the war in Korea had to be fought for the most part with materials on hand or on order at the time the war began.

NATO. American rearmament was closely tied in with the effort of the other nations joined with the United States in the North Atlantic Treaty Organization (NATO) to create a balanced force to protect the critical area in Western Europe. The initial American contribution to NATO consisted of six Army divisions and impressive air and naval forces. Moreover, American equipment furnished under the Mutual Defense Assistance Program (MDAP) and American economic assistance to NATO nations were both vital factors in enabling the alliance to maintain forces in the field. By mid-1953 NATO had approximately 50 divisions, together with about 4,000 tactical aircraft and 1,600 naval vessels. The NATO Council in early 1953 decided that this was about as much as the economies of the constituent countries could stand and that future efforts should be devoted to what was known as infrastructure—the building of an adequate network of airfields and perfection of logistical arrangements and communications. The accession of Greece and Turkey to the alliance in 1952 provided important flank protection and added about 25 additional divisions to NATO strength. There was reason to hope that in case of a Soviet move the national Communist forces of Yugoslavia would also oppose the USSR. While there was still great disparity between the massive forces of the USSR and its satellites and those of the western alliance, there was good reason to believe that NATO forces backed by American air-atomic power would act as a sufficient deterrent to Soviet aggression in Europe.

The Hydrogen Bomb. Though the major emphasis during the 1950–53 period was toward making up previous deficiencies in conventional armament, the period also saw revolutionary developments in the field of atomic weapons. On 1 November 1952 the United States exploded its first fusion or thermonuclear device at its atomic testing grounds in the Pacific. The USSR was less than a year behind setting off its own thermonuclear detonation in August 1953. The world soon learned that it would have to live with power great enough to destroy the largest cities at one blow. The original fission bomb had necessitated the invention of a new measurement—the kiloton, equivalent to one thousand tons of TNT. By this measure, the bombs dropped in 1945 generated about 20 kilotons of power, roughly a thousand times that of the largest blockbusters of World War II. By 1953, President Eisenhower announced, the United States was capable of producing fission bombs with 25 times this force or 500 kilotons. By contrast the force of the hyrogen bomb had to be measured in megatons, or millions of tons of TNT equivalent. Over and above its blast effect, the mushrooming clouds of the H-bomb contained poisonous radioactive matter that, carried by prevailing winds, could contaminate an area for miles around. While for some time after 1953 the United States would retain a lead in the means of delivery of thermonuclear weapons, from August 1953 onward it was clear that the day would come when the USSR would attain practical thermonuclear parity. The shadow of the H-bomb had come to stay as perhaps the most important single factor in shaping the future course of the cold war.

Other Atomic Weapons. The H-bomb was the most fearsome product of an advancing atomic technology, but not the only one. The uses to which atomic energy could be put, both destructive and constructive, seemed limitless. The Navy developed an atomic-powered submarine that promised to revolutionize sea warfare in the future. More important for the Army, atomic science produced a wide variety of warheads of variant power ranging from a fraction of a kiloton to megaton-range weapons. At the atomic tests in the

Pacific in 1955 a so-called "clean" bomb was exploded, one from which radioactive fallout was drastically reduced. These devolpments gave impetus to the search for practicable methods of using atomic explosives in ground warfare. By 1953 the Army had a 280-mm cannon in operation capable of firing an atomic shell, but it was too immobile and unwieldy to be entirely satisfactory. Hopes for the future use of atomic warheads in land battle soon came to rest primarily on new developments in the field of ballistic missiles.

Guided Missiles. In truth, missile delivery systems promised to have almost as revolutionary an effect as atomic explosives themselves. In the United States, from 1945 until 1950, missile research went forward at a snail's pace; but by the end of the Korean War all three services were actively developing missiles, each seeking delivery systems best suited to its particular mission. In the USSR work on missile weapons apparently went forward full speed from 1945 onward. Both countries sought missiles within a wide field of ranges and purposes. At one end stood the Intercontinental Ballistic Missile (ICBM), which, combined with the H-bomb, many regarded as the ultimate weapon against which no defense was possible. At the other end were tactical missiles of short range primarily suited for land battle. In between lay a broad field of intermediate range (IRBM), ground-to-air, air-to-air, and air-to-ground missiles that could serve a multiplicity of military purposes.

The New Look. Immediately on assuming office in 1953, the Eisenhower Administration began a review and re-evaluation of the military posture of the United States in the light of both the world-wide nature of the Communist threat and the new weapons developments. The upshot of this re-evaluation was a military program popularly identified as the New Look. The underlying philosophy of the New Look was that military preparations must not be geared to any one critical year but should be continued indefinitely into the future, and that these preparations must be carried out without placing an inordinate burden on the American economy. This new policy of long-range preparations at maximum economy clearly pointed to a greater emphasis on air-atomic power. As Secretary of State John Foster Dulles put it, the basic decision was to "rely primarily upon a great capacity to retaliate, instantly and at places of our own choosing." The doctrine of massive retaliation clearly meant that the United States would not in the future necessarily limit its effort to local defense as it had in Korea but would apply its air-atomic power in whatever degree and in whatever area it would be most advantageously employed. To achieve "more security at less cost" the stress would be on atomic weapons of all types as substitutes for conventional ones and the masses of manpower required to use them, and on concentrated mobile power rather than forces expensively dispersed around the world.

522

Impact on the Army. The New Look philosophy, taken in conjunction with the end of hostilities in Korea, produced a gradual reduction in Army strength in the years following. It is worth noting, however, that the Korean War was not followed by an immediate and drastic demobilization as all other American wars had been. The 1,534,000-man ground army in existence at the end of the Korean War was cut step by step to a level of around 900,000 men by June 1958. While an intensive effort was made to make as many cuts as possible in the service establishment, the number of active divisions also had to be reduced from 20 to 15, in large part by withdrawing divisions from the Far East. The seven Army divisions in Korea at the time of the signing of the Armistice was reduced to two in step with the training and equipping of Republic of Korea troops. The last Army division was withdrawn from Japan in 1957.

Continental Air Defense. In view of the rapid strides the USSR was making in developing atomic bombs and building a strategic air force to deliver them, the United States had to look to the modernization of its air defenses. By 1957 a virtually complete radar warning net had been installed in cooperation with the Canadian Government. The distant early warning (DEW) line was constructed across northern Canada and Alaska, and was supplemented by other lines across middle and southern Canada, by extensions in the Aleutians chain, by radar towers off shore, and by naval picket ships and airborne early warning craft. Operational responsibility for air defense was entrusted to the Continental Air Defense Command (CONAD) for which the Air Force was executive agent, but all three services shared in the effort. The Army's main contribution lay in the field of ground antiaircraft defense. In this field the Army developed the first operational antiaircraft missile, the NIKE AJAX, a weapon with far greater range, altitude, and accuracy than any existing antiaircraft gun. By mid-1956, NIKE AJAX units were on site in 22 vital defense areas, and a new version had been developed, NIKE HERCULES, of even greater range and altitude. With an atomic warhead, a single NIKE HERCULES promised to make possible destruction of whole fleets of enemy bombers. By 1958 it was replacing the AJAX at selected sites. Meanwhile, work went forward on the HAWK, a missile designed to meet the threat of low-flying aircraft. While the ability to deliver a retaliatory blow remained the principal deterrent against atomic attack, improved air defenses heightened the value of the deterrent and promised to exact a high cost in any attack by manned enemy bombers.

The Place of the Reserves. It was becoming increasingly clear by 1953 that wars in the future would depend more on forces in being when the war started than on war potential, and that this country would never again have time to train its great reserves of manpower behind a shield provided by allies abroad. An essential feature of the New Look was therefore an effort to provide reserve forces that could be mobilized rapidly to fulfill a wartime role without extensive additional training.

By legislation passed during the Korean War Congress placed a theoretical "military obligation" on all physically and mentally qualified males between the ages of 18½ and 26 for a total of eight years of combined active and reserve military duty. The reserve was divided into two categories, the Ready Reserve, which could be ordered to duty on declaration of an emergency by the President, in numbers authorized by Congress, and the Standby Reserves, which could only be ordered to duty in war or emergency declared by Congress. To fulfill his military obligation, a young eligible male had several alternatives. By spending five years of his eight-year obligation on active duty or in a combination of active duty and membership in the Ready Reserve, he could transfer to the Standby Reserve for his last three years. Or he might join the National Guard at eighteen and by rendering satisfactory service there for ten years avoid active duty unless his Guard unit were called into federal service. For college students there was also the alternative of enrolling in an ROTC course and, on its successful completion, spending two or three years on active duty and the remainder of the eight years as a reserve officer.

This system had many weaknesses. There was really no compulsory military obligation beyond existing selective service arrangements, and draft quotas dwindled rapidly after the conclusion of the Korean War. Similarly, the armed services found it impossible to accommodate all ROTC graduates for their required active duty. The obligation to remain in the reserve carried with it no compulsion either to enlist in a reserve unit or to participate in continued training. Since enlistees in the National Guard required no prior training, Guard units had to spend most of their time drilling recruits. Thus the reserve, while strong enough numerically, fulfilled none of the requisites for rapid mobilization in case of need, and there was no assurance that it would be kept up to strength by a steady input of young reservists.

Reserve Forces Act of 1955. To remedy these weaknesses Congress, at the urging of the President, passed new reserve legislation in 1955. While this act reduced the term of obligatory service from eight to six years, it imposed a requirement for active participation in reserve training on those passing out of the armed services with an unexpired obligation. It also authorized voluntary enlistment of young men between the ages of 17 and 18½ in the reserve up to a total of 250,000 per year. These youths would receive six months of basic training after which they would pass into the Ready Reserve for 7½ years additional service. As long as they participated satisfactorily they would be exempt from indiction under selective service. All ROTC graduates were to receive reserve commissions, but those in excess of current needs would serve six months on active duty followed by 7½ years in the reserve instead of a two or three year tour within a six year military obligation. The President was authorized, without further Congressional action, to call a million Ready Reservists to duty in an emergency proclaimed by him. He could also recall selected members of the Standby Reserve, and continuously screen the Ready Reserve to eliminate nonparticipants.

Congress refused to enact certain clauses desired by the administration. Provisions for inducting youths 17 to 19 years of age to supplement voluntary enlistments, for obligatory six months active duty training of National Guard enlistees who had not had prior service, and for transferring obligated reservists to the National Guard if its manpower requirements were not met by voluntary enlistment, were all rejected. Moreover, the law was to apply only to discharged members of the armed forces who entered after its passage, thus referring full implementation for at least two years. These omissions made it doubtful that the legislation would in fact insure a sufficiently large input of young reservists, and threatened to keep National Guard units in a semitrained state. To overcome this last defect, the Department of Defense late in 1956 issued an order requiring six months' active training of Guard enlistees who lacked prior service. After a Congressional hearing this order, with important modifications, was allowed to stand.

For all its defects, the Reserve Forces Act of 1955 was a major forward step toward the goal of organizing an effective reserve that could be mobilized rapidly in war or emergency. Its full effects were just beginning to be felt in 1957 and 1958. On the Army side, a mobilization schedule was set up for the various units in both the Army National Guard and the Army Reserve. The tendency, as in the Active Army, was toward reducing overall numerical strength while concentrating on training those units that could be mobilized and deployed in the early stages of any conflict. While the irregularity of voluntary enlistments and restricted funds kept many of these units below their authorized strength, the efficiency of the reserve forces as a whole rapidly improved from 1955 onward.

Widening Commitments. The world-wide nature of the Communist threat forced the United States to accept an ever-widening defense perimeter. By the end of the war in Korea, this country already had defensive alliances of varying nature with fourteen NATO nations, twenty Latin American nations, Australia, New Zealand, and Japan. Recurrent crises in the years following produced new commitments.

The Far East. The armistice in Korea left in its wake a difficult problem of establishing a comprehensive defense structure in the Far

East in the face of the growing power of Red China. In Korea itself the armistice terms were violated by the Communists almost from the beginning and a buildup of forces north of the armistice line proceeded apace. The United States in 1954 signed a Mutual Defense Treaty with South Korea, pledging its aid in case of renewed Communist attack, and it undertook to arm and support a total of twenty South Korean divisions. Even though the bulk of United States forces were withdrawn, it was not until 1957 that the United States moved to modernize the equipment of its remaining two divisions and the South Korean forces it was supporting.

The Korean situation was, nevertheless, generally stabilized. After the armistice, Communist pressure shifted to Southeast Asia and the Chinese Nationalist stronghold on Taiwan. Late in 1954, the United States signed a Mutual Defense Treaty with the Chinese Nationalists pledging assistance in defending Taiwan against Communist attack, and the determination to fulfill this treaty was made even more positive, in the face of an open threat of Communist invasion, by a Congressional Resolution in January 1955 empowering President Eisenhower to employ the armed forces of the United States to defend Taiwan and the Pescadores.

The most difficult problem of all was in Southeast Asia. The end of the war in Korea enabled the Chinese Reds to step up their aid to the Communist rebels in Indo-China. Despite extensive American material aid, the French and loyal native forces in the area were unable to hold. Serious proposals of active intervention by American air and naval forces were made but finally rejected. In the end a settlement was reached in a conference at Geneva in 1954 providing for partition of Viet Nam much as Korea had been partitioned and for the withdrawal of the French from the area. The settlement left the whole of Southeast Asia dangerously exposed to further Chinese Communist aggression. To bolster defenses in the area, the United States extended military and economic aid to the remaining free Indo-Chinese states—South Viet Nam, Laos, and Cambodia—and entered into the Southeast Asia Collective Defense Treaty to provide the framework of an allied defense structure. This regional defense pact was signed on 8 September 1954 by the United States, France, Britain, New Zealand, the Philippine Republic, Thailand, and Pakistan. The contracting parties recognized that aggression in Southeast Asia should be regarded as a common danger and that each party would act to meet it "in accordance with its constitutional processes."

The Middle East. By 1955 a tenuous stability seemed to have been established in the Far East. Meanwhile, tension mounted in the Middle East and North Africa, where the entire Arab world was in a state of unrest intent on throwing off the last vestiges of control by European powers, and implacably hostile to the new state of Israel. In an area where intense internal conflicts seemed virtually insoluble, the principal American interest lay in the creation of a solid defense front against aggression by the USSR and the protection of access of the west to the vital oil fields lying around the head of the Persian Gulf. Thus this country was a principal supporter, though not a signatory, of the Baghdad Pact of 1955 by which Turkey, Iran, Iraq, Pakistan, and the United Kingdom pledged to cooperate for their mutual security and defense. The establishment of this defensive alliance along the northern tier of states in the Middle East was designed to fill the gap in the defense line between NATO and Southeast Asia.

In 1954 Gamal Abdel Nasser emerged as virtual dictator of Egypt with ambitions to unite the Arab world under his banner. Nasser scorned the Baghdad Pact and even after the British agreed to evacuate their military bases in the Suez Canal Zone he remained hostile toward them and toward the Israeli. Failing in his efforts to secure arms from the United States, in the fall of 1955 he concluded a deal with the Communists whereby arms ostensibly from Czechoslovakia were to be furnished in exchange for Egyptian cotton. Following the consummation of the deal, Egypt entered into a military alliance with Syria and Saudi Arabia, and Syria also negotiated an arms deal with the Czechs.

Then in July 1956, Nasser nationalized the Suez Canal, an extremely serious blow to the British and French. Failing to secure satisfactory settlement in protracted negotiations, these two NATO nations decided on military action. When the Israeli invaded the Sinai Peninsula on 29 October 1956, the British and French announced their intention of moving into the Suez Canal Zone unless hostilities between Egypt and Israel were stopped immediately. While this invasion was under way, the matter was taken to the United Nations where the British and French were practically without support. The United States and the USSR joined in demanding a cease fire. The upshot was that the British, French, and Israeli agreed to withdraw their forces and a United Nations (UN) military force, consisting of troops from neutral nations, was formed to enforce the peace and oversee the rehabilitation of the Suez Canal.

After the Suez Crisis, in an effort to block the USSR in its effort to further increase its influence in the Middle East, the United States early in 1957 adopted the Eisenhower Doctrine. This doctrine, embodied in a Congressional Resolution similar to that on Taiwan, pledged American military assistance to nations in the Middle East endangered by Communist aggression and empowered the President to use the armed forces of the United States for this purpose. It was in consequence of this pledge that the United States sent military forces into Lebanon in the summer of 1958.

Mutual Security and the MAAG's. These far-flung commitments were not, except in the NATO area and Korea, supported by major overseas deployments of U. S. Army forces. The Army's role in supporting them lay rather in the maintenance of a mobile reserve force and in its contributions to the equipping and training of foreign armies. By the end of 1956, the United States was furnishing military assistance to 38 different nations; the Army was represented in Military Assistance Advisory Groups (MAAG's) in 25 countries and Army missions were performing MAAG functions in ten others. It was calculated that altogether the United States was assisting in training and equipping the equivalent of 200 ground divisions in other nations of the Free World.

The New Face of the Cold War. By 1955 the USSR was rapidly closing the gap and moving toward thermonuclear parity with the United States. Both countries had mastered the technique of dropping an H-bomb from a plane and, following in the wake of the Americans, the Soviet Union had developed an intercontinental jet bomber. The intercontinental ballistic missile appeared to be only a few years away. In this atmosphere of an emergent balance in thermonuclear capabilities, the heads of state of the United States, the USSR, Britain, and France met at Geneva in July 1955. While the conference produced no agreement on concrete issues, it did result in some relaxation of tension, a seeming tacit recognition on both sides that full-scale atomic war was now too suicidal to be undertaken. But the relaxation carried with it no diminution of the effort on both sides to forge ahead in the race for development of superior weapons of destruction. And while this race for weapons supremacy went on at one level, at another the USSR intensified its efforts to extend its influence into such areas as the Middle East and Africa, as the Suez Crisis soon bore witness. During that crisis, the USSR did not satisfy itself with action within the United Nations, but also threatened to send "volunteers" to Egypt and to bombard London and Paris with intermediate range missiles. At the same time, by brutal repression of a revolt in Hungary and defiance of the protests of the UN General Assembly, the USSR gave additional evidence of its intent to rely on its growing military might.

The New Look in NATO. In the changed situation, there was a considerable slackening of the effort of NATO nations to create an effective ground defense. While the infrastructure program showed great progress, the number of available army divisions shrank. NATO nations, faced with serious internal economic problems, found it difficult to maintain their contributions to the common defense. Great Britain, pursuing a New Look program of its own, announced its intention of cutting conventional forces to the bone and undertaking the development of thermonuclear bombs and a strategic air force to deliver them. France had to divert a considerable proportion of its NATO troops to the suppression of rebellion in Algeria. The new

West German Army of 12 divisions, agreed on in 1954, took shape but slowly. Increasingly, NATO plans came to rest on the assumption that atomic weapons would be used in ground defense.

The Military Dilemma. The shadow of the H-bomb thus created a military dilemma of considerable proportions. War, throughout the long history of mankind, had been the ultimate arbiter of disputes between nations. It was easy to say that the H-bomb had made war obsolete, but not so easy to find a practical substitute for force as an instrument of national policy, particularly in a situation where there was no community of interest between the two major powers except that perhaps inherent in a common desire to avoid a war in which the whole structure of civilization itself might be destroyed.

The theory of limited war. This dilemma gave rise to a theory, widely voiced by students of national security policy, that wars in the future would be limited wars in which neither side would apply the full power at its command. Proponents of this theory argued that wars were fought for specific political ends and that total war in the thermonuclear age could result only in mutual destruction without any political end being gained by either side. They pointed out that the USSR since the end of World War II had been engaged in nibbling at the periphery of the Free World and that the dangers of this continued nibbling seemed greater than those of all-out attack. To meet these nibbling tactics, the limited war school insisted that war could still be used as an instrument of national policy but only if it was limited, as the war in Korea had been, as to political objectives, geographical area, or the nature of weapons used and targets chosen for attack.

There was a difference of opinion among the proponents of limited war as to whether the United States should be prepared to use small atomic weapons in such conflicts or whether primary reliance should be on conventional weapons. The majority held that the use of tactical nuclear weapons would best enable the West to profit from its superior technological positions. This conclusion was in keeping with the philosophy of the New Look, both in the United States and NATO.

The problem that had emerged then was basically a question of what kind of a war to prepare for. The ability to deliver a certain and sure return blow should an enemy attempt an atomic attack on the United States clearly was the first prerequisite of national survival, but meeting this first prerequisite would not necessarily prevent the Communist powers from attempting gradual penetrations of Free World positions using Soviet retaliatory power as a shield. The answer seemed to lie in maintenance of forces ready to fight limited as well as all-out war, all part of strength in being designed to prevent the outbreak of either type. The difficulty lay in doing so without placing an impossible strain on the American economy.

The Army in the Atomic Age. It was with the conviction that limited war was indeed a likely contingency in the future and that even in a general atomic war land action would be required before any victory could be decisive that the Army's leaders undertook the challenging task of revamping the Army's structure and doctrine to enable it to fufill its mission in the atomic age. Within the limits of resources allotted to it, the Army in the years following Korea pushed ahead with the development of new concepts, new weapons, and new tactical formations. The basic premise behind these new concepts was that the Army must be versatile, maintaining a capability to fight with either atomic or conventional weapons. The emphasis was on mobility both strategic and tactical, and on a high ratio of fire power to manpower with either type weapons.

The atomic battlefield. The Army visualized the atomic battlefield of the future as having much greater breadth and depth than battlefields of the past. The key to battle success would lie in mobility, dispersion, superior intelligence, and communications. There would be no fixed lines but a checkerboard disposition of units with wide gaps between them. Units would concentrate to take objectives and disperse rapidly afterward so as not to provide a profitable target. The problem would be to find the enemy, determine his disposition, and then to destroy him by using atomic weapons.

New weapons and equipment. For operations on such a battlefield troops would need radically improved types of equipment—conventional weapons with greater fire power, artillery or missiles capable of delivering either atomic or conventional warheads, and improved means of battlefield movement, communications, and reconnaissance. In view of the need for rapid mobility, the goal was to make all this equipment air transportable. Rapid strides were made in meeting these requirements. Improvements were registered in conventional weapons all along the line and new short range missiles were developed as the main reliance for an atomic capability. By 1958, the CORPORAL and HONEST JOHN, with ranges up to 75 miles, and the REDSTONE, with a range of 200 miles were in operational units. New and lighter versions were under development. The LACROSSE, a shorter range missile for close support of infantry, was emerging from the development stage. For battlefield mobility, the main reliance was on armored troop carriers that would not be roadbound, and helicopters and other short-range low performance aircraft.

Tactical organization. A new concept of tactical organization was introduced in 1956, centering around the pentomic division and the missile commands. As opposed to the triangular infantry division of World War II with its three regimental combat teams, the pentomic infantry and airborne divisions were composed of five battle groups, each a self-contained force capable of independent operations.

The armored division underwent less drastic change because it was already better adapted to the requisite pattern of mobility and dispersion. While the pentomic division had its own organic artillery and missiles with an atomic capability, the heavier and longer range missiles were concentrated in supporting missile commands.

Logistics. Reorganization of the Army for nuclear warfare called for a concurrent streamlining of the logistics system. In the atomic age, the Army could no longer count on supplying its troops on the lavish scale of World War II or Korea, or, at least in general war, on any sustained production of munitions once war began. Use of ports, large central depots, and rail lines might well be impossible. The new logistics system stressed reduction of requirements to absolute essentials, prestocking of depots in the United States and key overseas areas, lightning processing of requisitions by electronic machines, delivery of essential items by air transport or fast naval vessels, reliance on delivery over beaches by roll-on, rolloff vessels and aerial tramways rather than on fixed port installations, and use of supply carriers capable of cross-country movement. The working out of a new logistics system based on these principles was one of the most difficult of the many problems of preparing the Army to fight in the atomic age.

Progress by 1958. By mid-year 1958 all of the fifteen remaining Regular Army divisions had been reorganized along pentomic lines. The next step envisaged was to reorganize the National Guard and Army Reserve divisions to conform to the Regular establishment. Although the basic lines of development had been laid down, the Army was still experimenting in an effort to perfect its concepts, develop the best types of equipment, and solve a myriad of problems relating to manpower, logistics, and intelligence. Much of the new equipment needed was still in the research and development stage or existed only in prototype. Even where placed under production, most of it was in short supply. The target date for realization of most goals was 1962.

Army deployment plans. The Army in 1958 was deployed in keeping with the New Look concept of a highly mobile central reserve as a substitute for scattered ground garrisons. In Europe five divisions remained as part of the NATO forces, two were posted in Korea, and one in Hawaii. The other seven were concentrated as a strategic reserve in the United States. Out of this reserve was created a Strategic Army Corps (STRAC) of four divisions, two airborne and two infantry, as a fire brigade constantly on the alert for movement. The other divisions in the strategic reserve were earmarked to serve as a STRAC reinforcement and as a training base for the expansion of Active Army forces in a prolonged emergency or war. It was contemplated that in this case divisions from the Ready Reserve would be brought into the active establishment and readied for deployment.

The Sputnik Challenge. The question of preparations for limited war was at least temporarily shoved into the background when on 4 October 1957 the USSR launched the first successful earth satellite. This development came in the wake of other indications that the Russians were moving into the lead in the ballistic missile field. The USSR was known to have operational intermediate range missiles and on 26 August 1957 Moscow radio announced the successful launching of an intercontinental ballistic missile. The launching of Sputnik I, weighing 184 pounds, indicated that the USSR had developed the rocket thrust to launch an ICBM, and the launching on 3 November 1957 of Sputnik II, reported to weigh 1,118 pounds and carrying a live dog, made it little less than certain. The United States had been planning to launch an earth satellite early in 1958 as a part of the International Geophysical Year, but it was to be nothing like the size of the Soviet Sputniks. This alarming revelation of Soviet scientific progress raised fears that the USSR would have a battery of ICBM's ready while the United States was still depending on manned bombers to deliver its retaliatory blow. Even more alarming was the general knowledge that the USSR was moving ahead so rapidly in the application of science to weapons technology. Many saw in the Sputniks the beginning of a race for the control of space for military purposes, a race in which the United States was already behind.

The U. S. reaction. The American reaction to Sputnik was a strong one. The effort to put an American satellite into space was expedited and the Army's JUPITER–C was used for the first successful launching on 31 January 1958. Before the end of the year four other American satellites had been placed into orbit, two more by JUPITER–C, a third by the Navy's VANGUARD, and the fourth and largest by the Air Force's ATLAS. None, however, gave evidence of a powerful rocket thrust as the USSR demonstrated with its Sputniks. The development of American intermediate and long range missiles was expedited. Late in November 1958 the Air Force announced the successful test firing of its ATLAS ICBM over a range of more than 6,000 miles. Meanwhile agreements were reached with some of the NATO nations in the Council meeting in December 1957 for placing intermediate range missiles on their territory and the first THOR was sent to England late in 1958. New legislation permitting sharing of atomic secrets with its allies enabled the United States to make a start in equipping NATO contingents with tactical atomic weapons. Work on an antimissile missile and on a radar warning net that would detect missiles as well as manned aircraft also went forward. The development of the antimissile missile was an Army task and a third member of the NIKE family, the NIKE ZEUS, was projected for this role.

Reorganization of the Department of Defense. The Sputnik crisis also brought to a head long smoldering dissatisfaction with the existing organization of the Department of Defense. The President had in the very early part of his administration carried through a reorganization, but by 1958 it was clear that it had been entirely too modest to provide the degree of unification and rapid decision-making that the United States now required. In the earlier plan, the Munitions Board and the Research and Development Board had been abolished, the number of Assistant Secretaries of Defense increased from three to nine, and the powers of the Chairman of the Joint Chiefs of Staff increased. The three service secretaries had been given the power, previously exercised by the military service chiefs, to act as executive agents for unified commands. While the system enhanced the power of both the civilian Secretary of Defense and the civilian service secretaries, it did little either to promote service unity or to facilitate decision-making.

On 3 April 1958 the President asked Congress for new legislation granting greater powers to the Secretary of Defense over the three services, strengthening the organization of the JCS, and establishing a single chain of command running from the President through the Secretary of Defense to various operational commands. Though the President's plan encountered serious opposition in Congress and was considerably modified by Congressional action, its basic features remained intact in the Defense Reorganization Act of 6 August 1958. Henceforth all military operations were to be under unified command emanating from the President to the Secretary of Defense, with the JCS as principal planners and advisers in directing operations. The system of using service secretaries as executive agents was to be eliminated. The three service departments were to be "separately organized" but not "separately administered," as the National Security Act of 1947 and its amendments in 1949 had stipulated. The Secretary of Defense was granted greater freedom in shifting functions among the services subject to the veto power of Congress in certain instances. A Director of Research and Development was to be appointed in the Department of Defense, replacing two of the assistant secretaries, to exercise supervision over the research and development programs of all services. The position of the Joint Chiefs as a corporate body was strengthened, and to free the individual Chiefs of Staff from routine duties and enable them to devote more time to JCS work, their Vice Chiefs were to be granted additional power to handle service matters. The Joint Staff serving the JCS was enlarged though under the restrictions that it was not to "operate" nor be organized as "an overall Armed Forces General Staff." The Chairman of the Joint Chiefs, in consultation with members of the JCS and the Secretary of Defense, was to select and manage the enlarged Joint Staff and its Director.

Under this act the service departments were to remain in control of raising, training, equipping and organizing the forces to be furnished unified commands and developing the weapons and equipment they would use operating under the general supervision of the Secretary of Defense. Service chiefs would remain in control of all those parts of their services not assigned unified commands, and service components of these commands would still receive their support through channels of their own services.

The necessary steps to put this new measure of unification into effect were underway at the end of 1958. A new unified Joint Staff took shape, replacing the old joint committees. One by one, beginning with the U. S. Forces in Europe, various operational commands were removed from the executive agent system and placed under direct Department of Defense control.

Prospects for the Future. Despite all the furor it generated, the Sputnik crisis led to no basic change in the general direction of American defense policies. And while it tended to shift the emphasis back to the laboratories and testing grounds and produced predictions that the struggle for control of space would determine the future destiny of mankind, it nowise diminished the old struggle for local advantage between the Communist powers and the Free World in the terrestrial sphere. The last half of 1958 brought new crises in the Middle and Far East and in the old arena at Berlin to which no simple solution seemed possible. What the future held in store, no prophet could foretell. But it seemed a safe estimate that the cold war would continue for an indefinite period in both the race for supremacy in scientific achievement and its applicaton to weapons of war and in local conflicts of great complexity. There seemed in 1958 a greater need than ever before for versatile military forces capable of meeting challenges of varying intensity in almost every area in the world. There could be no doubt that in meeting these challenges the United States Army would continue to play a vital and indispensable role, though necessarily in the future as a member of a tri-service team rather than as an independent operating agency.

Summary and Conclusion. In facing the challenges of the atomic age, the Army could look back with pride on the contributions it had made to the development of the United States as a nation and world power. In a very general way, the history of the United States Army may be broken down into three periods: colonial, continental expansion, and overseas operations. During the colonial period (1607–1775) the militia of the various colonies defended the settlers while they were establishing themselves in America, and helped England eliminate the French from North America. During the period of continental expansion (1775–1898) the militia and volunteers of the various states and the Continental Army and its successor, the

Regular Army, played a vital role in bringing the United States into being, in winning important extensions of national territory, in saving the nation from internal destruction, and in exploring, policing, and governing vast regions of the west. In the wars of these first two periods, the Army's activities were concentrated on problems vital to the establishment, maintenance, and expansion of a great nation based on new concepts of individual freedom and representative government. In the third period, beginning with the Spanish-American War and continuing through the present, the Army has carried the flag to the four corners of the earth, its role that of a principal instrument for promoting American policies and American interests overseas and protecting the nation against the menace of tyrannical power. In the two great world wars of the Twentieth Century and in Korea it has fought alongside a multitude of allies and in the increasing complexity of modern war its operations have become inseparably intertwined with those of its sister services, the Navy and the Air Force. With the emergence of the United States as leader of the Free World in a struggle with militant Communism, it seems likely that within the foreseeable future the Army's principal task will continue to be the support of national objectives overseas as part of both an American and Allied military combination.

The Army as an instrument of force. It is as an instrument of force—the primary mission of an army—that the United States Army has played its major role in American history. As an instrument of force the Army has made it possible for the United States to achieve its independence and to protect the national interest against skillful enemies in operations ranging from desperate hand-to-hand engagements with savages, equipped with bows and arrows and tomahawks or spears and bolos, to vast battles with modern motorized and armored forces. More than 450,000 Army men have sacrificed their lives on the battlefield and more than 1,300,000 have been wounded in the nation's wars. It involves no disparagement of the role of the other services to say that historically the Army has played the predominant role in most of America's wars to date. With the advent of the H-bomb and the intercontinental ballistic missile, it would be unrealistic to expect that this will necessarily be true in the future. Army doctrine today is tri-service doctrine emphasizing the necessity for combined operations under unified command. Yet even in this present age it is well to keep in mind that, as General Ridgway, former Army Chief of Staff, has said, ". . . wars are won by the achievement of domination over human beings, and the territory they inhabit, and . . . only land forces can achieve and maintain such domination." The Army of today is an integral part of the American deterrent to Communist aggression and a flexible instrument for the application of force if and when national policy requires it.

Other contributions. In addition to its primary role as an instrument of force, the Army has also made contributions to the development of the United States in such fields as education, exploration, conservation, flood control, emergency relief, engineering, sanitation, medicine, transportation, communications, aviation, conduct of diplomacy, and preservation of domestic order. Great ports and navigable rivers, flood control and power dams, the Washington Monument, and the Panama Canal are tangible evidences of the Army's vast peacetime contribution to the nation.

Civilian control and the citizen Army. In the last analysis the U. S. Army has always been and remains a product of the society from which its men are drawn. Its leaders have consistently adhered to the principle that the Army is merely an instrument of civilian authority. This principle was firmly established in practice by General Washington during the Revolutionary War, and embodied in the Constitution of the United States as a fundamental safeguard of republican institutions. At least until recently also, American military policy has been based on the maintenance of very small Regular forces and reliance on citizen-soldiers in case of national emergency. In the thirteen colonies every able-bodied man was a member of the Militia and could be called out in case of need, and this system continued at least theoretically in force during the first century of national existence. It was usually, nonetheless, the citizen volunteer who swelled the Army's ranks in earlier wars. Both the militia and the volunteer principle gave way, in the wars of the Twentieth Century, to the idea of universal obligation for military duty under selective service in time of national emergency. It was this principle that made possible the great national armies of World War I and II and the limited expansion that took place during the Korean War.

Selective service in wartime provides no means of obtaining a trained force ready for immediate action at any time, something the Militia was at least supposed to be. In an age where forces in being may very well determine the outcome of a war, the principle of reliance on masses of citizen soldiers seems necessarily to be giving way to the concept of large professional forces supported by a selected body of trained reserves. The increasing complications of modern warfare, the great rapidity with which attacks can be launched with modern weapons, and the extensive overseas commitments of the United States have negated the traditional American concept and practice of preparing for wars after they have begun. Yet even if the Army is to be increasingly professional or semiprofessional, it must continue to be representative of the people and subject to their control through the institutions of representative government.

Honored tradition. The vast majority of officers and men who have fought under the colors and standards of the United States Army, now decorated with many streamers in recognition of sacrifices on far-flung battlefields, have performed in the highest traditions of the service established in the War of the American Revolution. On the whole, the Army has been made up of capable and well-disciplined troops and has been commanded by skillful and dedicated leaders. The Reserve Officers' Training Corps units and their predecessors, back to the first to be established at Norwich in 1819, have furnished a great many of these leaders—some of the very highest in distinction and rank. The records established by the military men of the past are a challenge to those who serve today. The environment has changed mightily since the Army and the nation were born in the year 1775. For the flintlock muskets of the Continentals have been substituted death dealing missiles capable of destroying cities half a world away. But it will still be the spirit, courage, and endurance of men, individually and in mass, that will determine the destiny of the United States in its struggle for survival in our own time.

QUESTIONS

1. During the period of the Korean War, what preparations were made to meet the threat of Communist aggression in Europe?

2. Discuss the effect of the development of the hydrogen bomb and of guided missiles on the problem of American national security.

3. What steps did the Army take to adapt its organization and tactics to the requirements of the atomic age?

4. Distinguish between limited and total war. Considering the commitments of the United States, give examples of areas in which the United States Army might be used in limited war.

5. In the New Look, what was the place of the reserves in the national defense system? In what way did this differ from the traditional American concept?

6. What were the most significant features of the Department of Defense reorganization of 1958? In what ways did it affect the position of the Department of the Army?

Reading List

Finletter, Thomas K., *Foreign Policy: The Next Phase.* New York, 1958.

Furniss, Edgar S., ed., *American Military Policy: Strategic Aspects of World Political Geography.* New York, 1957.

Gavin, James M., *War and Peace in the Space Age.* New York, 1958.

Kaufmann, William W., ed., *Military Policy and National Security.* Princeton, N. J., 1956.

Kissinger, Henry A., *Nuclear Weapons and Foreign Policy.* New York, 1957.

Millis, Walter, *Arms and Men.* New York, 1956.

Osgood, Robert E., *Limited War, the Challenge to American Strategy.* Chicago, 1957.

Ridgway, Matthew B., *Soldier: The Memoirs of Matthew B. Ridgway.* New York, 1956.

Stanley, Timothy W., *American Defense and National Security.* Washington, 1956.

PUBLICATIONS
OF
OFFICE, CHIEF OF MILITARY HISTORY

Since the Office of the Chief of Military History was charged with carrying out the Army's history program, this Special Staff Agency has published more than forty volumes in its comprehensive series UNITED STATES ARMY IN WORLD WAR II. Ten additional volumes are in the hands of the printer and will be available by mid-1960. This Office has produced as well a rich variety of special historical publications and Department of the Army pamphlets valuable to both soldier and civilian. All OCMH publications are available to ROTC units through local PMS&T's by normal requisition (AR 310–2) or through the medium of interlibrary loan.

The level and type of assignment and responsibility attained by an officer or student will determine his reading program. Among the OCMH publications listed below are books appropriate to all grades of officer from student to senior commander. All officers and military students who seek advancement in their professional careers will find in these books a wealth of historical experience applicable to current military problems. These books form the means for rounding out and completing a military education.

Any questions on the Army's historical program in general or OCMH publications in particular should be addressed to the Office, Chief of Military History, Department of the Army, Washington 25, D.C.

Personal copies of volumes listed below with price may be ordered from the Superintendent of Documents, Government Printing Office, Washington 25, D.C. Enclose the correct amount in cash, check, or money order (made out to Superintendent of Documents) with your order. Estimated publication dates for volumes in or nearing the printing stage are shown in parentheses. All other volumes unless otherwise noted are in the research and writing stage.

WORLD WAR II

The series UNITED STATES ARMY IN WORLD WAR II will consist of some 80 volumes covering virtually every aspect of that conflict.

The War Department

Army Ground Forces

Army Service Forces

The Western Hemisphere

The War in the Pacific

The Mediterranean Theater of Operations

The Ordnance Department: Overseas_____ Unpublished

The Quartermaster Corps: Organization, Supply, and $3.75
Services, Volume I.

The Quartermaster Corps: Organization, Supply, and $4.00
Services, Volume II.

The Quartermaster Corps: Operations in the War $4.00
Against Japan.

The Quartermaster Corps: Operations in the War Unpublished
Against Germany.

The Signal Corps: The Emergency (To December $3.50
1941).

The Signal Corps: The Test (December 1941 to July $4.50
1943).

The Signal Corps: The Outcome (Through 1945)____ (1961)

The Transportation Corps: Responsibilities, Organi- $3.75
zation, and Operations.

The Transportation Corps: Movements, Training, and $4.25
Supply.

The Transportation Corps: Operations Overseas_____ $6.50

Special Studies

Chronology: 1941–1945_____ (1960)
Civil Affairs: Soldiers Become Governors_____ (1961)
The Employment of Negro Troops_____ Unpublished
Master Index: Reader's Guide I_____ $0.50
Master Index: Reader's Guide II_____ (1960)
Military Relations Between the United States and (1959)
Canada.
Rearming the French_____ $4.25
Statistics _____ Unpublished
Three Battles: Arnaville, Altuzzo, and Schmidt_____ $4.50
The Women's Army Corps_____ $6.25

Pictorial Record

The War Against Japan_____ $4.00
The War Against Germany and Italy: Mediterranean $4.00
and Adjacent Areas.
The War Against Germany: Europe and Adjacent $3.75
Areas.

COLD WAR AND KOREA

The Origins of the Cold War, 1945–1947_____ Unpublished
The Problems of the Cold War, 1947–1950_____ Unpublished
Defense of Western Europe, 1950–1954_____ Unpublished

The Army and the Military Assistance Program_____ Unpublished
Theater Logistics in the Korean Conflict_____ Unpublished
Combat in Korea, 25 June 1950–24 November 1950____ (1961)
Combat in Korea, 24 November 1950–June 1951_____ Unpublished
Combat in Korea, July 1951–July 1953_____ Unpublished
Korea—1950 _____ $1. 50
Korea 1951–53_____ $2. 50

SPECIAL PUBLICATIONS

The Army Lineage Book: Infantry_____ $2. 00
Command Decisions_____ (1960)

SPECIAL MILITARY STUDIES
(Department of Army Pamphlets)

DA Pam

20–200   The Writing of American Military His- $1. 50
          tory—A Guide.
20–210   History of Personnel Demobilization in the $1. 00
          United States Army.
20–211   The Personnel Replacement System in the $2. 50
          United States Army.
20–212   History of Military Mobilization in the $3. 75
          United States Army, 1775–1945.
20–213   History of Prisoner of War Utilization by $2. 00
          the United States Army, 1776–1945.

The two subseries listed below are part of the series "Axis Operations in World War II." Publications in the German Reports Subseries are not for sale to the general public. They are available at post libraries, the Library of Congress, certain depository libraries, and may be secured through interlibrary loan. Other pamphlets are available to ROTC units through local PMS&T's.

German Operations Subseries

DA Pam

20–243   Antiguerrilla Operations in the Balkans   (Out of stock)
          1941–44).
20–244   The Soviet Partisan Movement (1941–44)_ $2. 25
20–255   The German Campaign in Poland 1939__ $2. 00
20–260   The German Campaigns in the Balkans   (Out of stock)
          (Spring 1941).
20–261a   German Campaign in Russia (1941–42), $1. 25
          Planning and Operations, Part I.
20–261b   German Campaign in Russia (1943–45),   Unpublished
          Operations, Part II.

German Reports Subseries

All correspondence concerning unpublished documents should be addressed to the Office, Chief of Military History, Department of the Army, Washington 25, D.C.

INDEX

By Order of *Wilber M. Brucker*, Secretary of the Army:

L. L. LEMNITZER,
General, United States Army,
Chief of Staff.

Official:
R. V. LEE,
Major General, United States Army,
The Adjutant General.

Distribution:
Active Army:

DCSOPS (2)	ZI Armies (5)
ACRSC (2)	Svc College (2)
CMH (5)	Br Svc Sch (2) except
CUSARROTC (2)	USAIS (5)
USARCARIB (5)	Mil Dist (2)
USARHAW/25th Inf Div (5)	Sector Comd (Res) (2)
USARAL (5)	USA Corps (Res) (2)

NG: None.
USAR: None.

For explanation of abbreviations used, see AR 320–50.

U.S. GOVERNMENT PRINTING OFFICE : 1959 O—504978